THE GUINN
WHO'S WHO

General Editor: Colin Larkin

GUINNESS PUBLISHING

Dedicated to James Hamilton

FIRST PUBLISHED IN 1994 BY
GUINNESS PUBLISHING LTD
33 LONDON ROAD, ENFIELD, MIDDLESEX EN2 6DJ, ENGLAND
ALL EDITORIAL CORRESPONDENCE TO SQUARE ONE BOOKS

GUINNESS IS A REGISTERED TRADEMARK OF GUINNESS PUBLISHING LTD

BRITISH LIBRARY CATALOGUING-IN-PUBLICATION DATA
A CATALOGUE RECORD FOR THIS BOOK IS AVAILABLE FROM THE BRITISH LIBRARY

ISBN 0-85112-788-6

CONCEIVED, DESIGNED, EDITED AND PRODUCED BY
SQUARE ONE BOOKS LTD
IRON BRIDGE HOUSE, 3 BRIDGE APPROACH, CHALK FARM, LONDON NW1 8BD

EDITOR AND DESIGNER: COLIN LARKIN
ASSISTANT EDITOR: ALEX OGG
EDITORIAL AND PRODUCTION: SUSAN PIPE AND JOHN MARTLAND
SPECIAL THANKS: DIANA NECHANICKY, TONY GALE, MARK COHEN,
SIMON DUNCAN, DAVID ROBERTS, SARAH SILVÉ AND GUY BIRCHALL OF L & S

IMAGE SET BY L & S COMMUNICATIONS LTD

PRINTED AND BOUND IN GREAT BRITAIN BY THE BATH PRESS

EDITORS NOTE

The Guinness Who's Who Of Rap, Dance & Techno forms a part of the multi-volume Guinness Encyclopedia Of Popular Music. There are now 14 titles available in the series, with further volumes and new editions now planned.

Already available:
The Guinness Who's Who Of Indie And New Wave Music.
The Guinness Who's Who Of Heavy Metal.
The Guinness Who's Who Of Fifties Music.
The Guinness Who's Who Of Sixties Music.
The Guinness Who's Who Of Seventies Music.
The Guinness Who's Who Of Jazz.
The Guinness Who's Who Of Country Music.
The Guinness Who's Who Of Blues.
The Guinness Who's Who Of Soul.
The Guinness Who's Who Of Folk Music.
The Guinness Who's Who Of Stage Musicals.
The Guinness Who's Who Of Film Musicals & Musical Films
The Guinness Who's Who Of Reggae

Pictorial Press supplied the photographs featured on pages 6, 65, 75, 77, 121 132. The rest were supplied by press agents and record companies (with particular thanks to Jive, Ichiban, Warp, Rising High and Network.

This book documents the rise of rap and dance in the 80s and early 90s.
Rap began in the streets of the Bronx, New York, where first Kool Herc, then Afrika Bambaataa and Grandmaster Flash held sway. The trajectory is traced through the development of electro in the early 80s until the arrival of LL Cool J and Run DMC and the B-Boy period.
Public Enemy and NWA were the next wave, as rap became a deeply politicized voice for dispossessed black youth. The legacy of the former, in particular, transcends music, and takes on a deep sociological and cultural significance.
In the 90s with the arrival of the two Ices, opinions on the rap art form vary enormously. Too often criticisms directed at the music are inaccurate, while some are entirely justified. Taking in the new wave of stars like Snoop Doggy Dogg, Dr Dre and Wu Tang Clan, this book attempts to set these in their proper context.
Considering its primacy in the current UK music scene dance music's profile has not been enhanced by commensurate documentation. To rectify this situation in one (half) book is impossible. The further research carried us into dance music the more we understood the depth of the subject and the myriad of artists and styles involved. In the end the five hundred or so entries that have been included merely scratch the surface. They do, however, provide a good guide to the music's mainstays.
The approach has been to first identify the key participants in Chicago House and Detroit Techno, whose ideas haves continued to inform commercial and underground dance music well into the mid-90s.
Bearing in mind the anonymity associated with many working in these waters (though there are several exceptions, from Farley Jackmaster Funk and Kevin Saunderson through to the Aphex Twin and Andy Weatherall), it has often proved more useful to document important releases by looking at particular labels etc.
Often it has not been possible to cover every angle that we would have liked to have done because of lack of space or the difficulty in obtaining information. While many, many

people have helped by supplying this to us, other record companies have been deeply suspicious of our intentions. This is a regrettable but understandable situation considering the music's competitive and *ad hoc* nature. It is something which we intend to put right in the next volume.

We would welcome any updates, corrections and suggestions as to future inclusion that readers might suggest (which, naturally, also applies to the rap section).

The vast amount of writing and research was undertaken (voluntarily) by the assistant editor Alex Ogg. He immersed himself in the subject for many months and presented a complete text which is formidable and extraordinarily detailed. He deserves a huge pat on the back and a long lie down. We would like to thank the following for their help in enabling Alex Ogg to write and compile this volume of the series:

Dawn Wrench for some final proof-reading. Nick Horn – proprietor of Unicorn Records in Cambridge, a dance music expert whose guidance in selection of artists and background information was crucial to that part of the book. Much of the writing was informed by not only the records and magazines he leant, but also his personal recall of events in the development of dance music.

Justin Onyeka and Paul Ryan – of Power Moves. Justin and his colleagues were responsible for playing the advisory role on the rap section. We many not always have seen eye to eye on the selection/relative merits of certain artists, but the debate this engendered, and their considerable knowledge and insight into the music, played a crucial role

Several record labels/press people have been helpful with information. However, the following deserve a special mention for going above and beyond: Sharon and Kieran at Jive, Nick at Network and Amy at Rising High.

Sean Barrett helped with some last minute computer hitches, as did The Apple Centre in Cambridge and Andy and Chris at Macawmac. Susan Pipe as always co-ordinated everything with quiet calm.

Colin Larkin, August 1994

RAP

A

Above The Law

Gangsta rappers from Pomona whose ultra-violent lyrics betray a keen nose for breezy rhythm tracks, largely constructed/sampled from 70s soul. They also utilise live keyboards, bass and guitar to back the rhymes of the self-styled 'hustlers', - Cold 187um (b. Gregory Hutchinson), K.M.G. The Illustrator (b. Kevin Dulley), Total K-oss (b. Anthony Stewart) and Go Mack (b. Arthur Goodman). Their debut album consisted of two quite separate themes on the Mega and Ranchin' sides. The first dealt with graphic, unpleasant street violence narratives, while the second observed leering sexual scenarios. It was an unappetising mix, despite the presence of label boss Eazy-E on 'The Last Song' (both he and Dr Dre chaired production while they were still on speaking terms), and some otherwise attractive instrumental work. The follow-up mini-album, *Vocally Pimpin'*, at least boasted improved studio technique, but their second long playing set bombed. Cold 187 (as he is now known) would go on to production duties for Kokane's *Funk Upon A Rhyme* debut album for Ruthless/Relativity.
Albums: *Livin' Like Hustlers* (Ruthless 1990), *Vocally Pimpin'* (Ruthless 1991, mini-album), *Black Mafia Life* (Ruthless 1993), *Uncle Sam's Curse* (Ruthless 1994).

AD

Brooklyn, New York-based rock/rap crossover artists, highly politicised and polished. They take their name from lead rapper Anthony DeMores' (b. 1969, Brooklyn, New York, USA) high school adventures, as MC AD. He met guitarist David Tarcia at Bard College, a liberal arts school in New York State. Despite the lofty luxury of their education (DeMore was a theatre student with one play behind him), he was brought up in the Bronx and Brooklyn, the son of a lorry driver father. 'Bard made me more political. I saw people who didn't have the slightest understanding of my culture, and saw how they reacted to me and the other blacks and Latinos who were in that white middle-class world'. Joined by bassist Aaron Keane and drummer Mervin Clarke, DeMore has taken this specific indignation into the recording world with their debut LP on Rage Records. Not to be confused with the group of the same name who recorded for Kerygama in the late 80s.
Album: *AD* (Rage 1993).

Afrika Bambaataa

b. Afrika Bambaataa Aasim, 4 October 1960, New York, USA. His name taken from that of a 19th Century Zulu chief, translating as 'Chief Affection', Bambaataa was the founding father of New York's Zulu Nation. The name was inspired by the film *Zulu*, starring Michael Caine, and the code of honour and bravery of its black participants. A loose community of mainly black street kids, Zulu Nation and its head, more than any other element, helped transform the gangs of the late 70s into the hip hop crews of the early 80s. Bambaataa himself had been a member of the notorious Black Spades, among other sects, and from 1977 to 1985 he had a social importance to match his towering MC and DJ profiles, organising break-dance competitions and musical events promoting the ethos of peace and racial tolerance. By 1980 he was the pre-eminent hip hop DJ in New York, commanding massive followings and eclipsing even Grandmaster Flash in popularity. He made his recording debut the same year, producing two versions of 'Zulu Nation Throwdown' for two rap groups associated with the Zulu Nation - Cosmic Force and Soul Sonic Force. Signing to the independent label Tommy Boy, he made his first own-name release in 1982, as Afrika Bambaataa & The Jazzy Five, with 'Jazzy Sensation' (based on Gwen Guthrie's 'Funky Sensation'). It was followed by his seminal 'Planet Rock', a wholly synthesized record, this time based on Kraftwerk's

'Trans-Europe Express'. In one leap it took hip hop music far beyond its existing street rhyme and percussion break format. The contribution of Arthur Baker and John Robie in programming its beats is also highly significant, for in turn they gave birth to the 'electro' rap movement which dominated the mid-80s. 'Planet Rock' also gave its name to the record label Bambaataa established in the Bronx. 'Looking For The Perfect Beat' continued the marriage of raw lyrics and synthesized electro-boogie, and was another major milestone for the genre. The follow-up album, *Beware (The Funk Is Everywhere)* even included a take on the MC5's 'Kick Out The Jams' (produced by Bill Laswell). Bambaataa also recorded an album as part of Shango, backed by Material members Laswell and Michael Beinhorn, in a party dance vein which accommodated a cover of Sly Stone's 'Thank You'. Never one to stay in one place for long, he went on to record two vastly different and unexpected singles - 'World Destruction' with ex-Sex Pistols' vocalist John Lydon, and 'Unity' with the funk godfather, James Brown. He fell out of the limelight in the latter half of the 80s, as new generations of disc jockeys and rappers stepped forward with their own innovations and fresh beats. However, *The Light* included an enterprising cast (UB40, Nona Hendryx, Boy George, Bootsy Collins, Yellowman and George Clinton - the latter a huge early musical and visual influence on Bambaataa). *The Decade Of Darkness (1990-2000)* also went some way towards redressing the balance, including an update of James Brown's 'Say It Loud (I'm Black, I'm Proud)'. Bambaataa's influence on rap's development is pivotal, and is felt in many more subtle ways than, say, the direct sampling of his work on 90s crossover hits like 95 South's 'Whoot, There It Is' or Duice's 'Dazey Duks'.
Albums: *Planet Rock - The Album* (Tommy Boy 1986), *Beware (The Funk Is Everywhere)* (Tommy Boy 1987), *The Light* (Capitol 1988), *The Decade Of Darkness (1990-2000)* (1991), *Hip Hop Funk Dance 2* (1992). With Zulu Nation: *Zulu Nation* (1983). With Shango: *Funk Theology* (Celluloid 1984).

Afro-Planes

Four Atlanta, Georgia, USA-based young rappers, mixing Jimi Hendrix with Funkadelic samples, shot through with an Afrocentric consciousness and a taste for the comic. Their debut album convincingly berated Ice Cube for endorsing sales of malt liquor, among some effective skits and parodies about the rap arena and their place within it.
Album: *Afro-Planes* (BMG 1994).

Afros

Taking as their theme crazy 70s fashions in general, and blaxploitation movies in particular, the Afros were led by the clean-shaven Hurricane and Koot Tee, while DJ Kippy-O arrived adorned in the much reviled 70s haircut from which they took their name. Hurricane was formerly a DJ for the Beastie Boys, recording for their Grandy Royal imprint. Sight gags aside, their raps took in political viewpoints alongside wry looks at black culture. The repartee was old school, with call and response rhymes over a churning, funky backbeat.
Album: *Kickin' Afrolistics* (CBS 1990).

Ahmad

b. c.1975. From South Central Los Angeles, Ahmad utilised the half-sung, half-rapped approach invoked by Snoop Doggy Dogg and Domino. He was signed to Giant after rapping freestyle in front of president Cassandra Mills, who signed him on the spot. The rhythm tracks on his debut were built with the help of his high school pal Kendal Gordy, son of Motown's Berry Gordy. Old soul loops and R&B dominated, and he often revealed the lyrical incisiveness to match. Carefully avoiding the excesses of gangsta rap clichés, Ahmad proffered instead a highly articulate narrative: 'There's millions of ordinary, average, real people there (the South Central ghetto), who are trying to do the right thing and get out of the situation. But a lot of rappers don't touch on that - they just talk about the gangbanging, like it's so great and hunky-dory and glamorous. It's not at all, because I've been to many funerals and I realise that the time has come to stop all this bullshit'. His first single, 'Back In The Day', emphasised this view,

Afrika Bambaataa

with an excellent discussion on the merits of old school hip hop culture.

Album: *Ahmad* (Giant 1994).

Akinyele

b. c.1970, Queens, New York, USA, to Panamanian parents, like so many others Akinyele (whose name translates as 'honour comes into the family') first started rhyming after hearing 'Rapper's Delight' for the first time. He went to the same high school as Nas, Kool G Rap and Large Professor, working together as part of a team and also individually. Together with Nas he would rap on Main Source's 'Live At The BBQ' cut from *Breaking Atoms*. And when Akinyele signed to Interscope, Large Professor was the only producer he wanted. The first single from the set was 'Ak Ha Ha! Ak Hoo Hoo?', which introduced his trademark blend of sprightly braggadocio, often punctuated by a 'drop', wherein his voice lowers in pitch to emphasise a key word. The title of his debut album may have raised eyebrows, but he is in fact a no-drink, no-drugs rapper. 'The name of the album is *Vagina Diner*, only because I'm a cunning linguist, not a cunnilinguist'.

Album: *Vagina Diner* (Interscope 1993).

Ali Dee

Rap production star, who formerly worked alongside the Bomb Squad, learning much of his craft from them. He operates his own Manhattan recording studio and business, Gabrielle Productions, while his credits include work on 7669's debut album, and the Collision/Warner Bros. rapper, L-Boogie. So far he has released one, largely unsuccessful, solo set.

Album: *Bring It On* (EMI 1993).

Alkaholics, Tha

Rapping outfit specialising in fun, funky tunes, propelled by the tri-axled rapping partnership of J-Ro (b. James Robinson, c.1970, Los Angeles, California, USA), Tash (b. Rico Smith, Ohio, USA) and DJ E-Swift (b. Eric Brooks, Ohio, USA). Despite raised eyebrows over their name and gaudy stage performances, Tha Alkaholics have become popular proponents of 'party rap'. J-Ro

had intended to become a rapper since the age of 13, spending countless hours in his bedroom attempting to make tape recordings when he should have been at school, or later, work. He eventually got together with his two accomplices, who had already formed a partnership for house parties, with E-Swift switching to turntable duties. They came in to King Tee's sphere just as he was searching for a back-up band, and they joined him in time for his *Tha Triflin' Album*, and its attendant single, 'I Got It Bad Y'All'. It was the latter which kickstarted Tha Alcoholics' career, having adopted their name from a suggestion made by King Tee. From there it was on to support slots with Ice Cube, KRS-1 and Too Short, allowing them the opportunity to hone their skills in front of a live audience. On their return a major label contract was awaiting them, the first results of which were the high-profile singles 'Make Room' and 'Likwit'.

Album: *21 And Over* (RCA/Loud 1993).

Allen, Tito

One of the first Latin rappers, with 'Salsa Rap' on Allegre, a self-appointed reflection on the role of Hispanics within the hip hop community. Afterwards the mantle would be taken up by other artists, but Allen's was an important first footprint.

ALT

b. Al Trivette, Rosemonte, California, USA. His initials standing for 'Another Latin Timebomb', ALT is also short for his real name. Having been raised in Rosemonte, just four miles east of Los Angeles, he witnessed at first hand the problems that drugs and violence had caused in the Latin community. He was quickly picked up by a major label, keen to capitalise on hardcore street rap, but unwilling to allow it free reign. His debut album was hampered by strictures not to use foul language, and a parting of the ways followed soon after. Linking instead with the Inner City independent, he previewed his second set with a characteristic single, 'Riding' High', a diary of a day in the Latin 'hood.

Albums: *ALT* (East West/Atlantic 1991), *Stone Cold World* (Inner City/Par 1993).

AMG

b. Jason Lewis, 29 September 1970, Brooklyn, New York, USA. Male US rapper, and purveyor of unappetising fare in the over-familiar style of ghetto misogyny. Typical titles on his debut album, which unaccountably made number 63 in the Billboard charts, included the ominous title-track, 'Lick 'Em Low Lover', and 'Mai Sista Izza Bitch'. His justification: 'OK, so my record's nasty. But come on. I'm surrounded by negativity. If I go make a positive record, it might flop. So here's what I do: I use me something negative to make enough money to do something positive'. This is, remember, a man who was turned down for a job at McDonalds.
Album: *Bitch Betta Have My Money* (Select 1991).

Anotha Level

Freestyling old school-fixated newcomers from Los Angeles, California, Anotha Level boasts a four man MC crew - Ced Twice, Stenge, Imani and Bambino. They are protégés of producer Laylaw, ex-manager of Above The Law, who had previously produced cuts for Ice Cube (who executive-produced the album) and Yo Yo. Preoccupations on their debut album included girls and Super Nintendo, while the omnipresent Cube guested with them on one cut, 'Level-N-Service', and the Pharcyde joined the party for 'Phat-T'. Subtle sexism permeated through on tracks like 'Don't Stimulate', but it stopped short of obnoxiousness. Arguably the best cut was 'Let Me Tell Ya', the opening track, which featured dancehall DJ Don Jagwarr.
Album: *On Anotha Level* (Priority 1994).

Antoinette

b. Queens, New York, USA. Antoinette first joined issue with the record buying public when Hurby 'Lovebug' Azor introduced her via his compilation album, *Hurby's Machine*. Heralded as a tough-talking rap mama, there quickly proved more to Antoinette than the clichés that suggested. Though fresh and natural, her debut was largely straightforward gangster-talk. But the follow-up established her as a much more flexible talent, as her raps moved through sexually implicit narratives to defiant snatches of feminist tract, over waves of music which encompassed funk, go-go and house.
Albums: *Who's The Boss* (Next Plateau 1989), *Burnin' At 20 Below* (Next Plateau 1990).

Arabian Prince

One of NWA's founding fathers, though he seems to have been somewhat omitted from that group's history, the Arabian Prince's solo career has failed to ignite. Based in Compton, California, his talents were spread thin over an album's length, though *Brother Arab* did include the memorable 'She's Got A Big Posse' cut. A more subdued delivery than expected did little to maximise the workaday party and sex posturing.
Album: *Brother Arab* (Orpheus 1989).

Arrested Development

Atlanta, Georgia rap/soul collective headed by Speech (b. Todd Thomas, 1968, Milwaukee, Wisconsin, USA; lead vocals), whose parents published the Milwaukee Community Journal. He originally met DJ Headliner (b. Timothy Barnwell, 1967) while they were studying at the Art Institute Of Atlanta. Speech, when known as DJ Peech, had already formed Disciples Of Lyrical Rebellion, a proto-gangsta outfit, which evolved into Secret Society. They soon switched musical tack to a more community-conscious act, changing the name to Arrested Development and gradually picking up new members. These included Aerle Taree (b. Taree Jones, 1972; vocals, clothes design), Montsho Eshe (b. Temelca Garther, 1974; dancer), and Rasa Don (b. Donald Jones, 1968; drums). They developed an Afrocentric outlook/philosophy, moving into the same house while maintaining their individual day-time jobs. Afterwards veteran spritualist Baba Oje (b. 1933), who Speech had known as a child, was added as the group's symbolic head man. Influenced heavily by Sly & The Family Stone, when Arrested Development arrived on 1992's music scene they brought an intriguing blend of rural charisma and wisdom. While most modern rap uses urban dystopia as its platform, this band drew on a black country narrative as well as more universal themes such as 'Revolution'. They were no illiterate bumpkins, either; Speech writes a regular column for the *20th Century African* newspaper and takes his views on race issues on lecture tours. Cited by many critics as the most significant breakthrough of 1992, singles 'People Everyday' and 'Mr Wendal' confirmed their commercial status by enjoying lengthy stays in the UK Top 10. Their debut album (titled after the length of time it took them to gain a record contract after formation) also embraced a number of issue-based narratives, 'Mama's Always On The Stage' a nagging pro-feminism treatise, and 'Children Play With Earth', an exhortation for kids to get back in touch with the natural world which surrounds them. They released the live album, *Unplugged*, early in 1993, taken from their set at New York's Ed Sullivan Theatre the previous December, featuring an expanded 17-piece line-up. 1993 would also bring two Grammy Awards, Best New Artist and Best Rap Duo Or Group. Though their career is still in its infancy, Arrested Development have already taken the rap/soul format in to previously uncharted and genuinely exciting waters. Speech's first production project, with fellow Southern funk-rappers Gumbo, would also meet with critical approval. A second album proper, *Zingalamaduni*, Swahili for 'beehive of culture', emerged in 1994, once again extending their audience beyond the hip hop congnoscenti. As well as introducing new vocalist Nadirah, plus DJ Kwesi Asuo and dancer Ajile, it saw the departure of Taree who had gone back to college. More splendid lyrics ('The revolution will be fought by those of like minds, not just those of the same race' - from 'United Minds') proliferated.

Albums: *Three Years, Five Months, And Two Days In The Life Of...* (Chrysalis 1992), *Unplugged* (Chrysalis 1993), *Zingalamaduni* (Chrysalis 1994).

A Tribe Called Quest

A three-piece US male rap group consisting of Q-Tip (Johnathan Davis), Ali Shaheed Muhammed, and Phife (Malik Taylor, all b. c.1970, in Queens or Brooklyn, New York). They formed at school in Manhattan where they started out as part of the Native Tongues collective, with contemporaries such as Queen Latifah and the Jungle Brothers, and

were given their name by Afrika Baby Bam from the latter. Following their August 1989 debut, 'Description Of A Fool', they would hit with 'Bonita Applebum' a year later, based apparently on a true figure from their school. Their biggest success came the following year with the laid back 'Can I Kick It?', typical of their refined/jazz hip hop cross-match. It would later be used extensively in television advertisements. Q-Tip also appeared on Deee-Lite's 1990 hit, 'Groove Is In The Heart'. As members of the Native Tongues Posse they were promoters of the Africentricity movement which set out to make US Africans aware of their heritage, a theme emphasised in their music, and that of like-minds including De La Soul (Q-Tip guested on 'Me, Myself And I'). While their debut was more eclectic, even self-consciously jokey, *Low End Theory* saw them return to their roots with a more bracing, harder funk sound. They were helped in no small part by jazz bassist Ron Carter (Miles Davis and John Coltrane), whose contribution rather dominated proceedings. Tracks like 'The Infamous Date Rape' stoked controversy, while samples from Lou Reed, Stevie Wonder and Earth Wind And Fire were employed in a frugal and intelligent manner. By *Midnight Marauders* there were allusions to the rise of gangsta rap, although they maintained the ethos of positivity heavily themed on their debut. Q-Tip has appeared in the 1992 film *Poetic Justice* opposite Janet Jackson, and lent his production know-how to projects with Tony! Toni! Tone! (whose Raphael Wiggins made an appearance on *Midnight Marauders*), Nas, Tiger Apache and labelmate Shaquille O'Neal. They were rewarded with the Group Of The Year category at the inaugural *Source Magazine* Hip Hop Award Show in 1994, before being pulled off stage by the arrival of 2Pac and his Thug Life crew, attempting to steal some publicity.

Albums: *People's Instinctive Travels And The Paths Of Rhythm* (Jive 1990), *Low End Theory* (Jive 1991), *Revised Quest For The Seasoned Traveller* (Jive 1992), *Midnight Marauders* (Jive 1993).

Audio Two

The sons of First Priority label boss Nat Robinson, and brothers of MC Lyte, Mike and DJ Gizmo

A Tribe Called Quest

Dee certainly began their careers with a pedigree. Though occasionally they have fallen foul of the PC lobby, there is much to like outside of their sexist/homophobic aberrations. Their narratives offer unflinching vignettes of Brooklyn inner-city life, with a good eye for detail, particularly on breakthrough singles 'Top Billing' and 'Hickeys On My Neck'. Their second album contained a career high and low, the elegiac, distressing 'Get Your Mother Off The Crack', soured by the openly anti-gay 'Whatcha Lookin' At'.

Albums: *What More Can I Say* (First Priority/Atlantic 1988), *I Don't Care - The Album* (First Priority/Atlantic 1990).

B

B., Derek

b. Derek Bowland, 1966, Bow, East London, England. Derek grew up a fan of the Who as well as the more conventional black sounds of Aretha Franklin, Al Green and Bob Marley. He started out as a DJ when he was 15 as part of a mobile unit touring London clubs. He then moved into radio, working for pirate stations such as KISS FM and LWR before beginning his own WBLS station. In 1987 he became bored with the DJ role and took a job at the Music Of Life label as the nearest thing to an A&R man. Alongside Simon Harris (world yo-yo champion, it has been alleged) he signed several of the most notable early UK hip hop groups, including Overlord X, MC Duke, Hijack, the She Rockers and Demon Boyz. He subsequently started to record his own material for the label. Whilst in New York (visiting his family who had moved there), Derek met the DJ Mr Magic, who played his record to the Profile label, granting him a licensing deal in the US. His debut single, 'Rock The Beat', and its follow up, 'Get Down' (which featured the rapping of EZQ - Derek B under another pseudonym) both made an

early impact. His hip hop sounded a little hamfisted in comparison to New York's more natural feel, which made the self-congratulatory raps sound increasingly hysterical: 'We kept on goin' for hours and hours, Straight after to the bathroom for a shower, Just before leaving she held me close and said, I think you're the greatest thing in bed' ('Get Down'). He hit the UK charts in 1988 with 'Goodgroove' and suddenly became a media cause celebre, even appearing as the only rapper on the Free Mandella bill at Wembley Stadium. Further minor hits came with 'Bad Young Brother' and 'We've Got The Juice', after he set up his own Tuff Audio label, through Phonogram. However, that relationship declined when he attempted to push for a harder sound. Further one-off deals with a variety of labels failed to offer anything of significance, though while at SBK he did ghost-write tracks for Vanilla Ice. He is currently a member of PoW.

Album: *Bullet From A Gun* (Tuff Audio 1988).

B., Stevie

Miami, Florida-based Latin hip hop artist whose records are bedecked with vocals for which the term crooning isn't too strong. As well as dance numbers and rap excursions he is equally adept at balladeering. In fact the latter style gave him his first crossover hit, 'Because I Love You (The Postman Song)'. However, long before he entered the mainstream Stevie B was selling huge quantities of his product, going platinum and gold on several records in ethnic and secular markets. As his career progressed, the mood swung from rap to slick dance or swingbeat. Whatever, it was all carried off with a lack of subtlety and pre-teen image-focus which was not altogether appealing.

Albums: *Party Your Body* (LMR 1988), *In My Eyes* (LMR 1989), *Love & Emotion* (LMR 1991).

B-Boy Records

B-Boy was formed in 1987 in the Bronx's East 132nd Street, by Jack Allen and Bill Kamarra. The label, one of the first specialist independent rap concerns, came to prominence with the advent of Boogie Down Productions' *Criminal Minded*. It would go on to release no less than three related items following the death of Scott La Rock - *Man And His Music, Hot Club Version* and then the 'remix' selection, *A Memory Of A Man And His Music*. The label's most notable other signings were the Cold Crush Brothers and J.V.C.F.O.R.C.E., alongside lesser lights like KG The All, Michael G, Levi 167, Spyder D, Sparkey D, etc. However, just as it was gaining a foothold in rap circles Bill Kamarra was imprisoned and the momentum was lost.

Selected albums: Boogie Down Productions: *Criminal Minded* (B-Boy 1987). Various: *B-Boy Sampler* (B-Boy 1988).

Baker, Arthur

Baker began in music as a club DJ in Boston, Massachussets, laying down soul and R&B for the club-goers. He moved into production for Emergency Records shortly thereafter, including work on Northend and Michelle Wallace's 'Happy Days' (his first record, only released in Canada, was Hearts Of Stone's 'Losing You'). This pre-empted a move to New York where he became intrigued by the rap scene of 1979. He entered the studios once more, this time in tandem with Joe Bataan, to record a pseudo rap record, 'Rap-O-Clap-O', but the projected record company, London, went under before its release. The proceeds of the session did emerge later, though Baker went uncredited, after he returned to Boston. His next project was 'Can You Guess What Groove This Is?', by Glory, a medley affair which hoped to find a novelty market. From there, back in New York, he hooked up with Tom Silverman's Tommy Boy operation to record 'Jazzy Sensation' with Afrika Bambaataa and Shep Pettibone. Afterwards he would partner Bambaataa in the devastating 'Planet Rock' release, before starting Streetwise Records. Though interwoven with the development of hip hop, Baker's later releases were inspired by the club scene (Wally Jump Jnr's 'Tighten Up', Jack E Makossa's 'The Opera House' and Criminal Orchestra Element's 'Put The Needle On The Record'). He would go on to become an internationally renowned producer, working with legends like Bob Dylan and Bruce Sprinsteen. In 1989 he collaborated with the Force MD's, ABC and OMD among others on a showcase album which saw Baker working through various dance styles under his own auspices. A year was spent working on a biography of Quincy Jones' life before returning in 1991 with rapper and former MTV security guard Wendell Williams for club-orientated material like 'Everybody'.

Album: With the Backbeat Disciples: *Merge* (A&M 1989).

Basehead

aka dcBasehead, from Maryland, Washington, USA. Offering a melting pot spiced with chunks of rap, R&B, reggae and funk, Basehead is one Michael Ivey (vocals, guitar, writer, producer), backed by his DJ, Paul 'Unique' Howard, guitarist Keith Lofton and bass player Bill Conway. The mainstream media has seen fit to label them alternative dance, intelligent rap, or sundry other ill-fitting garb, but possibly the most accurate description was that of 'first rap slackers'. A debut album was recorded, intially for small independent concern Emigre, in 1991, on a tiny budget, 'There are hip hop elements in there, but if a hardcore hip hop fan bought it, they might be disappointed' was his frank response to *Spin* magazine in 1992.

Albums: *Play With Toys* (Emigre/Imago 1991), *Not In Kansas Anymore* (Imago 1993).

Beastie Boys

Former hardcore trio who would go on to find international fame as the first crossover white rap act of the 80s. After forming at New York University original members John Berry and Kate Shellenbach would depart after the release of 'Pollywog Stew', leaving Adam 'MCA' Yauch (b. 15 August 1967, Brooklyn, New York, USA), Mike 'D' Diamond (b. 20 November 1965, New York, USA) and the recently recruited guitarist Adam 'Ad Rock' Horovitz (b. 31 October 1966, Manhattan, New York, USA) to hold the banner. The group was originally convened to play at MCA's 15th birthday party, adding Horovitz to their ranks from The Young And The Useless (one single, 'Real Men Don't Use Floss'). Horovitz, it transpired, was the son of dramatist Israel Horwitz, indicating that far from being the spawn of inner-city dystopia, the Beasties all came from privileged middle class backgrounds. They continued in similar vein to their debut with the *Cookie Puss* EP, which offerred the first evidence of them picking up on the underground rap phenomenon. The record, later sampled for a British Airways commercial, would earn them $40,000 in royalties. Friend and sometime band member Rick Rubin quickly signed them to his fledgling Def Jam label. They would not prove hard to market. Their debut album revealed a collision of bad attitudes, spearheaded by the raucous single, 'Fight For Your Right To Party', and samples of everything from Led Zeppelin to the theme to *Mister Ed*. There was nothing self-conscious or sophisticated about the lyrics, Mike D and MCA reeling off complaints about their parents confiscating their pornography or telling them to turn the stereo down. Somehow, however, it became an anthem for pseudo rebellious youth everywhere, scoring a number 11 hit in the UK. In the wake of its success *Licensed To Ill* became the first rap album to top the US charts. By the time follow-up singles 'No Sleep Till Brooklyn' and 'She's On It' charted, the band had become a media *cause celebre*. Their stage shows regularly featured caged, half-naked females, while their Volkswagen pendants resulted in a crime wave with fans stealing said items from vehicles throughout the UK. A reflective Horovitz recalled how that never happened in the US, where they merely stole the car itself. More disturbing, it was alleged that the band derided terminally ill children on a foreign jaunt. This false accusation was roundly denied, but other stories of excess leaked out of the Beastie Boys camp with grim regularity. There was also friction between the group and Def Jam, the former accusing the latter of withholding royalties, the latter accusing the former of withholding a follow-up album. By the time the band re-assembled after a number of solo projects in 1989, the public, for the most part, had forgotten about them. Rap's ante had been significantly raised by the arrival of Public Enemy and NWA, yet *Paul's Boutique* remains one of the genre's most overlooked pieces, a complex reflection of pop culture which is infinitely subtler than their debut. Leaving their adolescent fixations

behind, the rhymes plundered cult fiction (*Clockwork Orange*) through to *The Old Testament*. It was co-produced by the Dust Brothers, who would subsequently become a hot production item. Moving to California, *Check Your Head* saw them returning, partially, to their thrash roots, reverting to a guitar, bass and drums format. In the meantime the Beasties had invested wisely, setting up their own magazine, studio and label, Grandy Royal. This has boasted releases by Luscious Jackson, plus The Young And The Useless (Adam Horwitz's first band) and DFL (his hardcore punk project). Other signings included DJ Hurricane (also of the Afros), Noise Addict and Moistboyz. There has been a downside too. Horovitz pleaded guility to a charge of battery on a television cameraman during a memorial service for River Phoenix in 1993. He was put on two years probation, ordered to undertake 200 hours community service and pay restitution costs. His connections with the Phoenix family came through his actress wife Ione Sky. He himself had undertaken film roles in *The Santa Anna Project*, *Roadside Prophets* and *Lost Angels*, also appearing in a television cameo for *The Equalizer*. By this time both he and Diamond had become Californian citizens, while Yauch had become a Buddhist, speaking out in the press against US trade links with China, because of that country's annexation of Tibet. *Ill Communication* was another succesful voyage into inspired Beastie thuggism, featuring A Tribe Called Quest's Q Tip, and a second appearance from Biz Markie, following his debut on *Check Your Head*.

Albums: *Licensed To Ill* (Def Jam 1986), *Paul's Boutique* (Capitol 1989), *Check Your Head* (Capitol 1992), *Ill Communication* (Capitol 1994). Compilation: *Some Old Bullshit* (Capitol 1994).

Beatnuts

The Beatnuts principally established their name with remix credits for Prime Minister Pete Nice, Naughty By Nature, Da Lench Mob and Cypress Hill, also producing for Chi Ali, Da Youngstas and Fat Joe. The trio comprises Psycho Les, Ju Ju and Fashion. Their own material, which kicked off with the *Intoxicated Demons* EP, features a light touch and plenty of humour. This should not mask the level of innovation and insight they bring to their recordings however, with samples drawn from their direct environment (ie children talking) rather than movie themes and old funk records. Lyrically, too, they were a fresh proposition: 'I possess more chicks than PMS' being one killer, forgiveably sexist, line. The release of that debut EP had been delayed when Fashion was arrested on a drug-related charge and imprisoned for six months. He had previously recorded 'Let The Horns Blow' with members of De La Soul and Chi-Ali in 1991.

Album: *The Beatnuts* (Violator/Relativity 1994).

BG The Prince Of Rap

b. Washington DC, Maryland, USA. One of rap's woefully inadequate types, BG, the self-proclaimed Prince Of Rap, specialises in empty rhetoric. He is an ex-GI, now based in Germany, who one reviewer unkindly renamed the 'Prince Of Wack'. On the other hand Columbia introduced him as the 'most exciting dance/rap act to emerge from Germany since Snap!', which gave some indication of his style, and the record company's marketing gambit. BG was happily involved in Washington's go-go movement until he was introduced, via an army colleague, into the world of hip hop. When his regiment moved to Germany he took part in local rapping competitions there, until he came to the attention of producer Jam El Mar, of Jam And Spoon fame. The resulting 'Rap To The World' 45 was a major hit in German clubs, and its follow-up, 'This Beat Is Hot', made it into that country's national Top 20.

Album: *The Power Of Rhythm* (Columbia 1992).

Big Daddy Kane

b. Antonio M. Hardy, 10 September 1969, Brooklyn, New York, USA. Self-styled 'black gentleman vampire' whose KANE moniker is an acronym for King Asiatic Nobody's Equal. Kane followed his cousin in to hip hop by rapping in front of a beatbox for his first shows on Long Island, New York. Aided by his DJ Mr Cee, he has released several albums of laconic, fully realised songs pitched halfway between soul and rap. His tough but sensual work is best sampled on the hit singles 'Ain't No Stoppin' Us Now' and 'Smooth Operator'. The production skills of Marley Marl and the deep groove worked up by Mr Cee play no small part in the refined ambience of his better work. Despite being an obvious ladies' man, his appeal is enhanced by his ability to also handle tough street raps, of the nature of the debut album's 'Raw', his contribution to Public Enemy's 'Burn Hollywood Burn', or his own Afrocentric, Muslim tracts. He also joined with Ice-T on a speaking tour of black high schools in Detroit in the late 80s. A huge fan of soul, obvious similarities to Barry White are given further credence by the duet he shares with that artist on *Taste Of Chocolate*. On the same set he also produced a comedic duet with Rudy Ray Moore. He can, however, be guilty of the rap genre's unfortunate ability to insult women, the fantasy world of songs like 'Pimpin' Ain't Easy' springing easily to mind. He has straddled the rap and mainstream R&B markets with his more recent, decidedly mellow albums, and also worked widely as a freelance lyricist for Cold Chillin', writing with Roxanne Shante and Biz Markie among others.

Albums: *Long Live The Kane* (Cold Chillin' 1988), *It's A Big Daddy Thing* (Cold Chillin' 1989), *Taste Of Chocolate* (Cold Chillin' 1990), *Prince Of Darkness* (Cold Chillin' 1991), *Daddy's Home* (Cold Chillin' 1994).

Biz Markie

b. Marcel Hall, 8 April 1964, Harlem, New York, USA. Playful member of Marley Marl's posse, whose appeal could be defined as rap's most polar-opposite to adult orientated rock. Delivering his tales of bogey-picking, bad breath and other niceties in a jerky manner which comes close to self-parody, Markie has found himself a niche market in adolescent circles. His progress was aided by an unlikely hit single, 'Just A Friend', in 1989. Resolutely old school, his 1993 album features 'Let Me Turn You On' over a sample of 'Ain't No Stoppin' Us Now', on which he actually sings. The set's title, *All Samples Cleared!*, is more than an unjustified whinge at copyright laws. Each and every sample was cleared by the relevant artist's representatives, after Markie had previously come under threat of imprisonment. This stemmed from his sampling of Gilbert O'Sullivan's 1972 ballad 'Alone Again' on his *I Need A Haircut* album. Judge Kevin Thomas Duff awarded punitive damages ruling that 'sampling is theft under criminal law', giving rap's practitioners the world over sleepless nights in the process. Which, in retrospect, made Markie's choice of title for his 1989 set, *The Biz Never Sleeps*, ominously prophetic.

Albums: *Goin' Off* (Cold Chillin' 1988), *The Biz Never Sleeps* (Cold Chillin' 1989), *I Need A Haircut* (Cold Chillin' 1991), *All Samples Cleared!* (Cold Chillin' 1993).

Black Moon

Brooklyn based rappers whose entrance on the New York scene was rewarded with sales of over 200,000 of their debut cut, 'Who Gots The Props'. Black Moon, who comprise 5ft Excelerator, DJ Evil Dee and Buckshot (later joined by T.R.E.V.), signed with Nervous Records' offshoot, Wreck, despite stern competition, in 1991. There were certainly offers on the table from major companies: 'It seems to me that whenever anyone signs with a major company here in the US, and I'm specifically talking about rappers, they begin to lose control of their careers, their destiny'. Black Moon (signifying Brothers Lyrically Acting Combining Kickin' Music Out On Nations) have also revealed similar enlightenment in the way they handle their own affairs. They have set up their own production and management companies, Beat Minerz (Evil Dee and his brother Mr. Walt) and Duck Down (Buckshot and Big Dru Ha). The latter also looks after the affairs of Wreck's second signing, Smif and Wessun. They were also involved in the signing of a third addition, Helter Skelter. Musically, Black Moon are a throwback to rap's old school - bleak bass and beatbox underpinning their considered raps for minimalist impact. Their debut album was afforded strong critical reaction, no less than KRS-1 himself noting it to be: '...the phattest shit I've heard in a long time'. It included their second single, 'How Many MC's (Must Get Dissed)', before they embarked on a national tour with Das EFX. Buckshot also worked with Special Ed and Master Ace, as the Crooklyn Dodgers, on the title-track to Spike Lee's film, *Crooklyn*.

Album: *Enta Da Stage* (Wreck 1993).

Black Radical Mk II

b. Felix Joseph, South London, England. Joseph grew up listening to Jamaican reggae from Peter Tosh and Bob Marley, as well as the indigenous version propelled by Steel Pulse. However, when he picked up on Public Enemy and Boogie Down Productions for the first time he was an instant convert to the rap phenomenon. Although his convictions and ideas were clear, he sometimes lacked the dexterity to express them, as the *This Is War* EP's 'Hard Timez' revealed: 'They fuck us up just like we're vaginas, They even fucked up the miners, They gave them a disease that was called Heseltinisis'. Cuts like 'Sumarli' were more impressive, demonstrating his commitment to women's rights. An economics graduate, Joseph spent much of 1993 on an all-black film project, *Welcome To The Terrordome*.

Album: *The Undiluted Truth* (Mango/Island 1991).

Black Sheep

Rap duo who comprise Andre 'Dres' Titus (b. c.1967, Sanford, North Carolina, USA) and William 'Mista Lawnge' McLean (b. 11 December 1970, Sanford, North Carolina, USA), who are based in the Bronx, New York, though they actually met in North Carolina in 1983. Titus' father, an army officer, was stationed there, while McLean's mother had relocated to the state while he was in school. He was sharing the bill with Sparkie Dee at a gig when her DJ, Red Alert, advised him that if he ever moved back to the capital to give him a call. He did just that in 1985, linking up with the Jungle Brothers and A Tribe Called Quest, before phoning Titus to invite him to join a band. Finally together they arrived from a similar angle to the Native Tongues Posse, of which they were members, but doused their Afrocentricity in humour. Their self-produced debut album made the Billboard Top 30, mainly on the back of the excellent single, 'The Choice Is Yours', the video to which brought the band an MTV award. The album which housed it was filled with spoken interludes, heightened accents and ramschackle comedy. By the advent of their second long playing set the duo had toughened up slightly, but kept their musical stance sprightly. The album was prefaced by a single, 'No Way, No How'. They had also set up their own label operation, One Love Records, the first signing to which was a crew entitled Legion.

Album: *A Wolf In Sheep's Clothing* (Mercury 1991), *Non Fiction* (Mercury 1994).

Blade

b. Armenia, but settled in New Cross, London. One of the most forceful presences in UK rap, Blade is widely regarded for his ability to tear up audiences live (though indie Carter USM fans bottled him offstage when he acted as the latter's support). More impressive still is his commitment to his art. After starting rapping at age 12, he financed his career by literally hand-selling his records as they emerged, slowly building up a network of fans. His debut album on his own label included contributions from Sista Nubia, MC Mell 'O' and Afriqsoul on 'As Salaamo'. Blade's ferocious, Chuck D-styled delivery has marked him out as practically the only UK rapper to carry off a hardcore stance with conviction. However, he was still fiercely independent. He opened a subsription service to raise £25,000 for the recording of his second album, and received it from his enthusiastic fan base. The resultant set celebrated Blade's victory over the music industry. It included an answaphone message from someone in the business who had originally turned Blade down, and was now pleading to be in on the action.

Albums: *Survival Of The Hardest Workin'* (691 Influential 1992), *The Lion Goes From Strength To Strength* (691 Influential 1993, double album).

Bloods And Crips

Not so much a rap group as a recorded example of inter-gang co-operation in Los Angeles following the beating of Rodney King. The Bloods and the Crips are that area's most notorious tribes, but they got together to push their version of the ghetto story, on two sides of an LP, rather than fighting it out hand to hand, gun to gun. The result was an impressive social document and a historical nicety, but hardly an essential listening proposition. Album: *Bangin' On Wax* (Dangerous 1993).

Blood Of Abraham

Media-worthy Los Angeles rap outfit comprising Jewish MCs Benyad and Mazik, plus DJs JJ and Lott Loose, The group's origins can be traced to high school when they first started writing poetry, which evolved into rap. Their early shows saw them discovered by NWA's Eazy-E. Newsworthy not least because of Eazy-E's former employer's on-record comments about the nation of Israel. Accordingly, Blood Of Abraham were a mite suspicious of his motives, not wishing to be perceived as 'gangsta rappers'. They did, however, sign to Ruthless via his endorsement. A debut album was soon forthcoming, which musically utilised comic spoken word samples and looping bass-heavy rhythmic structures. However, their efforts to cakewalk racial territory, notably on cuts like 'Niggaz And Jewz (Some Say Kikes)', was clumsy. Their response was most effective when tackling black racism towards Jews: 'Pull out the butt and let the smoke get deep, Cuz the Jews are the brothers that the niggas shouldn't fuck with'. The set, which ended with a sample from Travis Bickle, *Taxi Driver*'s notorious psychonaut, was produced by Bret 'Epic' Mazur, who had introduced them to Easy-E, alongside Lott Loose. A single, 'Stabbed By The Steeple', attacking organised religion, was also released from the album, but failed to achieve anything more than the gimmick coverage the band have become so irritated by.

Album: *Future Profits* (Ruthless/Relativity 1993).

Blow, Kurtis

b. Kurt Walker, 9 August 1959, Harlem, New York, USA. A producer and rap pioneer who had one of the genre's earliest hits with 'Christmas Rappin' in 1979, written for him by J.B. Ford and *Billboard* journalist Robert Ford Jr. Blow had previously studied vocal performance at the High School Of Music and Art at the City College of New York. Afterwards he began working as a DJ in Harlem where he added his first tentative raps to liven up proceedings. By which time he had made the acquaintance of fellow City College student Russel Simmons (see Run DMC), who convinced him to change his name from Kool DJ Kurt to Kurtis Blow. Playing in small clubs alongside other early innovators like Grandmaster Flash, he signed to Mercury records just as the Sugarhill Gang scored the first rap chart success with 'Rapper's Delight'. Blow in turn became the first rap artist to cut albums for a major label. His 1979 hit, 'The Breaks', for which his partner Davy D (b. David Reeves Jnr, originally titled Davey DMX, and best known for recording 'One For The Table (Fresh)') provided the first of his backing tracks, was a massive influence on the whole hip hop movement. The early 80s were quiet in terms of chart success, before he re-emerged in 1983 with the *Party Time* EP and an appearance in the movie, *Krush Groove*. *Ego Trip* was an impressive selection bolstered by the presence of Run DMC on the minor hit '8 Million Stories'. He also rapped on Rene and Angela's hit 'Save Your Love (For Number One)', doubtless an experience he would not wish to be reminded of. He has also produced for the Fearless Four, Dr Jeckyll And Mr Hyde among others. His yearly album cycle continued with the patriotic *America*, whose earnest, sensitive moments (particularly 'If I Ruled The World', which appeared on the soundtack to *Krush Groove* and as a single) were rather undermined by the presence of 'Super Sperm'. The following year he organised the all-star King Dream Chorus and Holiday Crew who recorded the Martin Luther King tribute, 'King Holiday', which argued for MLK's birthday to be enshrined as a national holiday. *Kingdom Blow* featured guest appearances from the likes of Bob Dylan, and George Clinton on an amazing interpretation of 'Zip-A-Dee-Doo-Dah'. However, Blow has been largely overtaken by the young guns of the genre (notably Run DMC, ironically) he helped to create, a fact underlined by the miserable reception offered the misnomered *Back By Popular Demand*, and he hasn't scored a chart hit since 'I'm Chillin' in 1986.

Albums: *Kurtis Blow* (Mercury 1980), *Deuce* (Mercury 1981), *Tough* (Mercury 1982), *Ego Trip* (Mercury 1984), *America* (Mercury 1985), *Kingdom Blow* (Mercury 1986), *Back By Popular Demand* (Mercury 1988). Compilation: *Best Of* (Mercury 1994).

Body Count

Ice-T's spin-off metal/hardcore band who rose to alarming fame via the inclusion of the track 'Cop Killer' on their debut Warner Brothers album. Other songs included titles like 'KKK Bitch' and 'Bowels Of Hell', but it was 'Cop Killer' which effectively ended Ice-T's tenure with his record company, and brought him the status of public enemy number one within the American establishment. Body Count made their debut during the inaugural Lollapalooza US festival tour in 1991, preceding the release of the album. The line-up was completed by Ernie-C (guitar), D-Roc (guitar), Mooseman (bass) and Beatmaster V (drums), whom Ice-T knew from Crenshaw High School in South Central. Although occasionally suffering from the misogynistic street language common to much US west coast rap, their material contained forceful anti-drug and anti-racism themes, particularly 'Momma's Gotta Die Tonight', which addressed the issue of institutionalised bigotry being passed down through successive generations. The band continued touring, and were fortunate enough to be given the opening slot on the Guns'N' Roses/Metallica North American trek, exposing them to a more mainstream audience. In the meantime the LA Police Department were taking extreme exception to 'Cop Killer', a song which they viewed as dangerous and inflammatory ('I got my twelve guage sawed off, I got my headlights turned off, I'm 'bout to bust some shots off, I'm 'bout to dust some cops off'). The fury aimed at Ice-T, now officially number 2 in the FBI National Threat list, came thick and fast; Charlton Heston read out the lyrics to 'KKK Bitch' to astonished shareholders at Time Warner's AGM. 'Cop Killer' also appeared in the Warner's block-buster *Batman Returns*; which consequently faced calls for boycotts. Among the other opponents were Oliver North, president George Bush, and the Texas police force, who called for a nationwide boycott of Time Warner, including their Disneyland complex. The possibility of millions being wiped off Warners' share value had seen a U-turn. The pivotal moment came when death threats were received by record company employees, and the track was eventually replaced with a spoken word message from former Dead Kennedys' frontman and noted anti-censorship lobbyist, Jello Biafra. Undettered, Ice-T has resolved to continue in authority-tackling mode, and Body Count persist as an ongoing musical concern.

Album: *Body Count* (Sire 1992).

Bomb Squad

Public Enemy's production arm, made up of four cornerstones: Chuck D (b. Carl Ridenhour), Eric 'Vietnam' Sadler, Hank Schocklee and Keith Schocklee. As well as spearheading Public Enemy's dense, embittered records they were soon in demand for work on all manner of projects. Arguably the most successful was Ice Cube's *Amerikkka's Most Wanted* opus, but other clients included Ali Dee, Doug E. Fresh, Run DMC, Leaders Of The New School, Son Of Bazerk and many more. They also clued in outsiders to their technique by allowing younger producers like Gary G-Wiz to work alongside them. In 1990 Hank Schocklee launched the SOUL (Sound Of Urban Listeners) label with former Def Jam Promotion Vice President Bill Stephney. The first signings were Young Black Teenagers. By the advent of Public Enemy's fifth album proper, *Muse Sick N Our Mess Age*, in 1994, the Bomb Squad had been enlarged to include the aforementioned G-Wiz, Kerwin 'Sleek' Young (who played a large role in shaping Professor Griff's *Pawns In The Game*), EZ Moe Bee (featured on Big Daddy Kane's *Looks Like A Job For...*) and Larry 'Panic' Watford.

Boogie Down Productions

This Bronx, New York-based rap duo comprised DJ Scott La Rock (b. Scott Sterling, c.1962, d. 27 August 1987) and rapper KRS-1 (b. Lawrence 'Kris' Parker, 1966, USA). KRS-1 (aka K.R.S.-One) is an acronym for Knowledge Reigns Sumpreme Over Nearly Everyone, and 'edutainment' remained a central theme in the work of Boogie Down Productions. Similar to most New York rap crews, their lyrics highlighted the problems of blacks living in a modern urban environment, compounded by the increasing drug problems, gang wars and usage of weaponry on the streets. Indeed, La Rock and KRS-1, who had formerly worked with 'joke' rap act 12:41 ('Success Is The Word') met at a homeless people's shelter in the Bronx, where La Rock was a counsellor and KRS-1 a client. Following their first release, 'Crack Attack', their debut album, *Criminal Minded*, was produced in conjunction with fellow Bronx crew, the Ultramagnetic MC's. It was a set which actively suggested that young blacks were entitled to use 'any means necessary' in order to overcome years of prejudice and discrimination. It shifted over 500,000 copies and was instrumental in kick-starting the gangsta rap movement. After Scott La Rock became the victim of an unknown assassin while sitting in a parked car in the South Bronx, KRS-1's lyrics enforced an even stronger need for a change in attitude, demanding an end to violence and the need for blacks to educate themselves. *Criminal Minded* had, of course, depicted the duo wielding guns on its sleeve. The follow-up sets, *By All Means Necessary* and *Ghetto Music: The Blueprint Of Hip-Hop*, are arguably just as convincing; tracks like 'The Style You Haven't Done Yet' taking pot shots at KRS-1's would-be successors. There was certainly much to admire in KRS-1's style, his method becoming the most frequently copied in aspiring new rappers. He was also setting out on lecture tours of American universities, even writing columns for the *New York Times*. Like contemporaries Public Enemy, KRS-1/Boogie Down Productions retained the hardcore edge necessary to put over their message, and in doing so, brought a more politically aware and mature conscience to the rap scene. However, 1990's *Edutainment* possibly took the 'message' angle too far, featuring only lacklustre musical accompaniment to buoy KRS-1's momentous tracts. The live set which followed it was not the first such hip hop album (2 Live Crew beating KRS-1 to the punch), but it was certainly the best so far, with a virulent, tangible energy. Since the release of *Sex & Violence*, KRS-1 has elected to release new material under his own name and abandoned the Boogie Down Productions moniker.

Albums: *Criminal Minded* (Sugarhill/B-boy 1987), *By All Means Necessary* (Jive 1988), *Ghetto Music: The Blueprint Of Hip Hop* (Jive 1989), *Edutainment* (Jive 1990), *Live Hardcore Worldwide: Paris, London & NYC* (Jive 1991), *Sex And Violence* (Jive 1992).

Boo-Yaa T.R.I.B.E.

Of Samoan descent, Boo-Yaa T.R.I.B.E. were born and bred in the Los Angeles neighbourhood of Carson, where their father was a Baptist minister. Life was tough, evidence of which exists in their choice of name (slang for a shotgun being discharged). Running with the Bloods gang, every member of the clan had endured a stretch in prison, and one of their brothers, Robert 'Youngman' Devoux, was shot dead before the family turned musical. The brothers freely admit to having had involvement with drug production and brokering, as well as gun running. Ultimately the group took the death of their kin as a sign from God, and headed for Japan to escape the gang warfare, staying with their Sumo wrestler cousin. There they subsisted by working as a rap/dance outfit in Tokyo, which convinced them their success could be imported back to LA. Island were the first to see a potential market for a sound which fused gangster imagery with hardcore hip hop, and obtained their signatures. They appeared in Michael Jackson's Disney film *Captain EO* as breakdancers, as well as television shows *Fame* and *The A-Team*. The line-up boasts lead rapper Ganxsta Ridd (aka Paul Devoux), EKA, Rosco, Ganxsta OMB, The Godfather (aka Ted Devoux), and Don-L. Some members of the Los Angeles Police Department still harbour suspicions that the Tribe is merely a front for their continued illicit activities, but powerful singles like 'Psyko Funk' represented a genuine, bullying rap presence. They returned in 1994 with a second album, featuring further gangland narratives like 'Kreepin' Through Your Hood' and 'Gangstas Of The Industry' - a putdown of fake posturing for profit.

Album: *New Funky Nation* (4th & Broadway 1990), *Bullet Proof* (1994).

Born Jamericans

Washington DC-based dancehall reggae/rap duo, comprising Edley Shine (b. Horace Wayne, Washington, USA), the group's DJ (in the reggae sense) or toaster, and Natch (b. Norman Hewell, USA), a singer. Both were born in America in the mid-70s but traced parentage and musical lineage to Jamaica. Edley, in fact, developed his skills by rapping over his parents' reggae collection, and Natch too grew up on a steady diet of vocalists like Pinchers and Pliers. They met when Natch was visiting a local record shop and heard Edley rehearsing in an adjacent room. Delcicious Vinyl received a tape and promptly invited them to relocate to Los Angeles. 1994 saw a debut single, 'Boom Shak-A-Tack', and an album. Though they have supported Shabba Ranks on tour, they are being marketed primarily in rap terms.

Album: *Kids From Foreign* (Delicious Vinyl 1994).

Boss

b. Detroit, Michigan, USA. A self-avowed 'Born Gangsta' pushing hardcore rap feminism into new territories, Boss announced her intentions with the inviting debut 45, 'I Don't Give A Fuck', a phrase regularly repeated on her debut album. Originally operating alongside partner MC Dee, the album detailed their experiences on the streets of South Central, Los Angeles, and New York. The overriding factor was to encourage women to take control of their own lives, rather than expecting the benevolence of a male figure to help them out. In turn she has set up her own production company, Boss Productions, to help other aspiring hip hop stars in Detroit. She also completed soundtrack work, recording 'Run, Catch, And Kill' for the *Mi Vida Loca* movie.

Album: *Born Gangstaz* (DJ West 1993).

Brand Nubian

From the Bronx, New York, and led by Grand Puba Maxwell (b. Maxwell Dixon; ex-Masters Of Ceremony), Brand Nubian's work is as cool, classy and unaffected as hip hop comes. Joined by Lord Jamar (b. Lorenzo Dechelaus, 17 September 1968, New Rochelle, New York, USA), Sadat X (b. Derrick Murphy, 29 December 1968, New

Rochelle, New York, USA) and DJ Alamo (the latter two cousins), Puba kicked out reams of Muslim-influenced thinking, backed by steals from some of soul music's greatest moments. Wry humour, including namechecks for characters as diverse as Englebert Humperdink, were frequent. So too were accounts of the Five Percent Nation's Islamic beliefs. Samples of James Brown and Roy Ayers ensured the backing was never less than interesting. In 1991 Grand Puba split to go solo, taking DJ Alamo with him, but Brand Nubian elected to continue as a three piece unit with the addition of DJ Sincere. Their first album following his defection was *In God We Trust*, focused more on their intensely held beliefs with tracks such as 'The Meaning Of The 5%', 'Allah And Justice' and 'Ain't No Mystery'. The album title referred to a significant element of Five Percent doctrine. 'We represent ourselves as god', said Lord Jamar, 'and we're not trusting any mystery in the sky to help us with what we have to do. When a religion teaches you to depend on something else instead of being self-sufficient, then that becomes the downfall of people'.
Album: *All For One* (Elektra 1990), *In God We Trust* (Elektra 1993), *Word Is Bond* (Elektra 1994).

Brother D

From the Bronx, New York, and one of the earliest 'reality' rappers, Brother D. (b. Daryl Aamaa Nubyahn) was the maths teacher who recorded the mighty 'How We Gonna Make The Black Nation Rise', on Clappers (a label set up by expatriate Jamaican Lister Hewan Lowe). Based on the popular Cheryl Lynn 'Got To Be Real' break, it acted as a soundtrack to the political organisation National Black Science.

Brotherhood

London-based hardcore hip hop trio comprising Spice, Dexter and Shylock, which actually began in the mid-80s. At that time it was a 15-piece collaboration between mixed-race DJs, breakdancers, graffiti artists and rappers. Eventually the line-up was trimmed to its present number, who originally recorded under an eye-catching moniker, the Jewish Public Enemy. They released

a solitary 1991 single, 'Descendants Of The Holocaust', before two of the group left, leaving Shylock as the only original member. He added Spice and Dexter, refining their formula to 'hip hop with punk attitude and energy'. Their hard edged sound was unveiled on a single, 'Wayz Of The Wize', and the *XXIII* EP. They also contributed 'Crashin' The System', which sampled Phil Collins' 'In The Air Tonight', to a compilation album. Presumably with sample clearance, as it was released on Collins' label, Virgin.

Bushwick Bill

A founder member of the notorious Geto Boys, Bushwick Bill (b. Richard Shaw, Jamaica, West Indies) struck out solo in 1992 with a comparatively successful solo album. Despite losing his right eye in a shooting in May 1991, the myopia of his debut recording was in a much longer-established tradition.
Album: *Little Big Man* (Rap-A-Lot 1992).

C

Campbell, Luther

The 'godfather' of Miami rap, Campbell grew up with four brothers in an area of the town known as Liberty City. At 15 he joined the Ghetto Style DJ's - seven teenagers who hung around at radio station WEDR and African Square Park. He graduated from Miami beach High in 1978, going on to promote concerts by visiting rap groups like Run DMC and Whodini. With the money generated he and the Ghetto Style DJ's purchased the Pac Jam disco in the summer of 1985. While promoting a California group, 2 Live Crew, he suggested they sign to his new label. They assembled a single together, 'Throwing The D', based on a new dance move, and recorded in front of Campbell's mother's house. However, when distribution caused further problems this too was sorted in-house. In the wake of the record's success Luke Skywalker records was inaugurated on a more permanent footing. Later the title would be shortened to simply Luke when George Lucas filed suit over copyright of the film character's name. His career with 2 Live Crew continued through the late 80s and 90s in a blaze of publicity, until by 1993 he was recording solo, with or without the band's backing. In 1994 Campbell announced plans to launch his own girlie magazine, in an effort to redress the balance of this 'pro-white artistic genre'. Entitled *Scandalous*, the idea was that it should be along the lines of *Penthouse*, but using Afro-American 'models'. Luther himself purchased a yacht to house the magazine's offices. It is sad that such efforts to redress the evils of racism should be at the expense of another oppressed section of society. But that is the logic of 2 Live Crew/Campbell to a tee. As well as rapping exiles like Professor Griff, Luke records is also home to R&B outfits like H-Town. For all his bad press it should be remembered that Luke Campbell is the official sponsor of the Miami Easter Egg Hunt in Liberty City.

Albums: As Luther Campbell Featuring The 2 Live Crew: *Banned In The USA* (Luke 1990). Luther Campbell solo: *Luke In The Nude* (Luke 1993).

Candyman

b. 25 June 1968, Los Angeles, California, USA. Formerly a member of Tone Loc's backing posse of rappers and dancers, Candyman emerged in 1990 with a Top 40 Billboard album success, *Ain't No Shame In My Game*. It was full of Loc's familiar party vibes, with the odd more distasteful cut like 'Melt In Your Mouth 69'.

Album: *Ain't No Shame In My Game* (Epic 1990).

Captain Rapp

Rapp is an old school rapper, famed for 'Badd Times (I Can't Stand It)', a Los Angeles answer to 'The Message' (complete with Chic stylings). He grew up with LA's Uncle Jam's Army, where he fought to earn a slice of the microphone action. He was transported over to New York to little effect, and subsequent record deals never happened.

However, 'Badd Times' (released on Saturn in 1983) remains a keynote in the development of West Coast rap.

Cash Crew (UK)

Attempting to come across like west London's very own Public Enemy, Cash Crew enjoyed a brief flirtation with the hip hop public in the late 80s/early 90s. Comprising a trio of DJ Loose, Trim and Champion, they earned their only real notoriety with a vicious putdown of Betty Boo (then part of the Outlaw Posse) on 'Bouquet Of Barbed Wire'. It soon became apparent that the Ladbroke Grove team had neither the attack nor the subtlety to carry off the gangsta act. They did, at least, set some new benchmarks for UK rap, being the first to appear at London's Marquee Club in 1989, and the first to release an 'ecology rap', 'Green Grass', two years later. After a restorative period they released a new 4-track EP in 1994, *Anything Can Happen*, which saw them reduced to a duo. DJ Loose had moved to Brooklyn, New York, and Champion had rechristened himself Jamal. They additonally set up their own Streetministry label, and began to work with different rappers and producers, including Phreaks Of Nature and the Laylow Posse, on new collaborative projects. Their regular meetings at Hyde Park's Speaker's Corner on Sunday afternoons also helped to spark a debate about UK hip hop and black issues. Not to be confused with the Sugarhill, US recording artists of the same name.

Album: *Will It Make My Brown Eyes Blue* (FWTAS 1991).

Cash Crew (US)

Entirely different to the similarly titled UK group, this Cash Crew arrived far earlier in hip hop's development. They recorded a solitary single for Sugarhill, 'Breaking Bells (Take Me To The Mardi Gras)', in 1982. This was a heavily restructured (basically utilising the break only) version of Bob James' cover of Paul Simon's 'Take Me To The Mardi Gras' original.

Cash Money And Marvellous

Among the earliest Philadelphia-based rap crews, Cash Money's Joe 'The Butcher' Nicolo-produced 1988 set was widely, and unjustly, ignored. With a strong funk undertow the raps embraced the juvenile humour of Kid N Play in a wholly engaging manner. Money had previously won the 1988 DMC Mixing Championships. They disappeared from the rap scene before they were able to consolidate on their debut set.

Album: *Where's The Party At?* (Sleeping Bag 1988).

Casual

b. c.1974. East Oakland, California-based rapper who specialises in old school lyrical battles, and the dissing of 'sucker MCs'. Hardly an engaging prospect, but the jazz flourishes (the result of his father's record collection) and light production offered a stylistic diversion to most of his neighbourhood's fare. Casual was the latest outpouring of Del Tha Funkee Homosapien's Hieroglyphics enclave, alongside Souls Of Mischief etc. He retained that spirit of combative rhyming which Hieroglphyics have done much to reinstate: 'I think that MCing should be a competitive thing, almost like a sport. The only way an MC can keep polishing and sharpening his skills is to test them against the competition and the up and coming youngbloods.' Likewise there was plenty of old school braggadocio, tempered by an occasional foray into more serious matters ('Chained Minds' and 'Loose In The End' being good examples from his debut set). The musical backing was the province of jazz-funk breaks from Roy Ayers and others.

Album: *Fear Itself* (Jive 1994).

Caveman

Wycombe, England-based rap crew whose earnest tales of 'Streetlife' were deemed dubious by some critics, who didn't feel that their geographical location merited such machismo sentiments. However, image aside, Caveman was an adept and engaging outfit of more skill than most UK-based hip hip crews. Comprising MCM, Diamond J and the Principle, songs like 'Fry You Like Fish' (their second single) were justifiably lauded. Willing to look outside of staple rap sources (choosing to sample Jimi Hendrix rather than James Brown), signing to US label Profile, many were disappointed when the group dissolved early in 1993. However, their second album had been significantly weakened by the defection of the Principle. MCM would go on to a solo career, stating: 'Basically, among other things, I felt Caveman had done its time in the rap community'. In truth splitting was also the only way out of their contracts with Profile records, following disagreements within the band. The Principle's first post-Caveman project would be *The Principle Presents 499*, again for Profile, which arrived in 1994.

Albums: *Positive Reaction* (Profile 1991), *The Whole Nine Yards... And Then Some* (Profile 1992).

Chi-Ali

b. c.1976, New York, USA. At just 15 years of age, Chi-Ali (his real name) recorded his first single. Suitably entitled 'Age Ain't Nothin' But A Number', it announced his arrival as the youngest member of the Native Tongues Posse. Afrika Bambaataa, Black Sheep, the Jungle Brothers and Brand Nubians were all on hand to appear in the video. The song itself was, ironically, a little juvenile, recounting his ability to enter clubs and chat up women even though he was too young for either. Elsewhere on his debut album things became less credible still, lines like 'Are you going to be allowed to stay up and watch the Superbowl this weekend' notwithstanding.

Album: *The Fabulous Chi-Ali* (Violator 1992).

Chill EB

An articulate, highly politicised rapper linked with Jello Biafra's Alternative Tentacles label, the original home to pre-Disposable Heroes Of Hiphoprisy outfit the Beatnigs. Together with his DJing partner RD, Chill EB's harsh rhymes are tempered by sweet female vocal interludes, in an arresting combination. Chill grew up in Oakland, California, and at 6' 5' was a leading basketball player (a high school colleague was Michael Jordan). Via 45s like 'Menace To Society' his profile was stamped large across American television screens, and he also won an award for his work with Los Angeles' homeless. 'Menace To Society', which revolved around the true story of a 13 year old boy dealing in drugs to help feed his sister and brother ('I only rob the rich to feed my family, And now they call me a menace to society'), inspired a film of the same name (though the cut was not included on its soundtrack), and was also dubbed on to two television films. Less nobly Chilly also found time to appear in adverts for Sega games.

Album: *Born Suspicious* (Alternative Tentacles 1994).

Chill, Rob G.

b. Rob Frazier, Queens, New York, USA. Rob Chill remains best known for having his 'Let The Words Flow' hijacked by German house act Snap. This was taken by producers Benito Benites and John Garrett Virgo III and revitalised with Penny Ford's distinctive vocals, bringing them a huge worldwide hit. Chill got little of the credit (although he was namechecked in the titles) and has so far proved unable to follow up this success.

Album: *Ride The Rhythm* (Wild Pitch 1990).

Chubb Rock

b. Richard Simpson, 28 May 1968, Jamaica, West Indies. The cousin of Hitman Howie Tee, Simpson moved to New York at an early age. A rap colossus, his ample frame has seen him compared with Barry White, with whom he duetted on his second album. Chubb Rock started his own band in New York, but after dropping out of college elected to set out on a solo career. The first results of this were a debut album which sank without trace. However, the promotional single for his second album, 'Caught Up', caught the public's interest. This introduced them to his most consistent effort so far, on which humour and reflections on urban violence sat side by side. By the dawn of the 90s and his third album, interest in Chubb had escalated to the point at which it spawned no less than three Billboard number 1 hits. He has also appeared on film, in the movie, *Private Times*.

Albums: *Featuring Hitman Howie Tee* (Select 1988), *And The Winner Is...* (Select 1989), *Treat 'Em Right* (Select 1991, mini-album), *The One* (Select 1991), *I Gotta Get Mine Yo! - Book Of Rhymes* (Select 1992).

Cold Chillin'

Record label distributed through Warner Bros and overseen by that company's A&R man Ben Medina with Fly-T's Tyrone Williams, the label manager, and producer Marley Marl. Cold Chillin' has grown quickly since it was first mooted as a possibility by Williams and Marl, signing with Warners in 1987. As well as recording, Marl has gone on to produce most of the label's output. The title translates as 'really kickin'', and the label quickly struck strong sales with material from Biz Markie, MC Shan and Big Daddy Kane.

Selected albums: Biz Markie: *Goin' Off* (Cold Chillin' 1988). MC Shan: *Down By Law* (Cold Chillin' 1988). Marley Marl: *In Control Volume 1* (Cold Chillin' 1988). Big Daddy Kane: *It's A Big Daddy Thing* (Cold Chillin' 1989).

Cold Crush Brothers

The Cold Crush Brothers traced their origins to the Bronx freestyle ethos of the late 70s, when the line-up was fronted by Kay Gee The All, EZ AD and Grandmaster Caz. The latter, who had been rumoured to be one of the lyricists behind the early Sugarhill releases, and also led the Mighty Force Emcees, opted out in the early 80s, at which point DJ Tony Crush climbed behind the decks. He provided the group with their distinctive brass and reed riffs, drawn from old Stax and soul classics. The Cold Crush Brothers were responsible for the 'Punk Rock Rap' single/novelty, on Aaron Fuchs' Tuff City label. They had formerly recorded for Elite and Smokin', but by the end of the 80s they had moved on to B-Boy, as a duo comprising simply Kay Gee and DJ Tony Crush. The double a-side 12-inch, 'Feel The Horns'/'We Can Do This', gave them a minor hit, but it proved to be a fleeting success.

Album: *Troopers* (B-Boy Records 1988).

Compton's Most Wanted

Gangsta traditionalists of black and white origins whose reinstatement of NWA and Ice Cube's Compton agenda was initially fierce but tiresome. Their naked aggression was only tempered by deft production, but elsewhere they have brought nothing new to the gangsta palate. *It's A Compton Thing* contained enough obscenities to ensure that it was also made available in a censored version, but at least by *Music To Driveby*, whose cliched title did not bode well, they had honed their punishing, forceful formula. Lead rapper MC Eiht's pseudonym, incidentally, stands for 'Experienced In Hardcore Thumpin''. The other pivotal member is DJ Slip, who has produced for other acts like DFC, with whom Eiht has duetted.

Albums: *It's A Compton Thang* (Orpheus 1990), *Straight Checkn'Em* (Orpheus 1991), *Music To Driveby* (Orpheus 1992), *We Come Strapped* (Epic 1994).

Conscious Daughters

Oakland, California sistas whose radical street women manifesto has proved among the most convincing of its type. CMG and the Special One both possess a powerful arsenal of vocal effects and characters, a combination that was ably backed on their debut by the production skills of Paris, for whose Scarface emporium they record. The Conscious Daughters had come across Paris in familiar fashion, thrusting a demo cassette into his hand, in the vein hope of him supporting their cause. Paris eventually came through with his promise to do something with the duo, albeit a long time after their initial meeting in 1991. When they did record, references to the treatment of women by gangsta rappers abounded, especially on tracks like 'Wife Of A Gangsta' and 'What's A Girl To Do', which saw them namecheck the Fu-Schnickens, with whom they toured. The attitude appears to be a direct response to gangsta mythology and misogyny, particular the brand traded on by local rapper Too Short: 'The bitch ho shit sells, but if that's all a man can talk about then we can do the same back.'

Album: *Ear 2 Tha Street* (Scarface 1993).

Consolidated

Highly political rap/rock trio comprising Adam Sherbourne (vocals, guitar; the son of an American Two Star General), Mark Pistel (sampler/technician) and Philip Steir (drums). Their approach to rock music reflects the anti-establishment, left field approach of Crass or Minor Threat; their 'mission' is to agitate, to provide more than a passive spectacle for an audience to consume. At the end of gigs the microphone is turned open to the audience, a format which has annoyed as well as intrigued paying customers (witness 'Play More Music', on which they are berated by audience members for not doing just that). As a background to their generally impressive arrangements, projected visuals comprise various images of totalitarianism, linking such themes as animal abuse to men's treatment of women. Acknowledging themselves as 'Typical Men' despite their political stance, they also co-operate with the polemic of female cohorts the Yeastie Girls. The latter achieved recognition for their frank exposition of the importance of cunilingus to a good relationship. While Consolidated continue to tread a path on the right side of dogma, their status as artists of conscience serves as a reminder of the potential of music to inform and improve. Sherbourne has also recorded solo as Childman.

Albums: *Consolidated* (Antler 1989), *The Myth Of Rock* (Nettwerk 1991), Business Of Punishment (London 1994). Adam Sherbourne as Childman: *Childman* (Childman Nettwerk 1993).

Cookie Crew

Clapham, South London rap duo comprising MC Remedee (Debbie Pryce, a former chef for the Ministry Of Defence) and Susie Q. (Susie Banfield, sister of the Pasadenas' Andrew Banfield), both b. c.1967. They put the act together in 1983, originally as a 13 piece collective entitled Warm Milk and the Cookie Crew, after which they were picked up by the Rhythm King label. The breakthrough followed when they recorded 'Rok Da House' with their producers, the Beatmasters. Originally to have been used as an advert for soft drink Ribena, it became a UK hit in December 1987, and is often credited with being the first 'hip-house' record. Signing to ffrr, they went on to work with producers such as Stetasonic, Gang Starr, Black Sheep, Davey DMX, Daddy 'O' and Dancin' Danny D, and later added Dutch singer MC Peggy Lee as a 'human beatbox'. Their DJs also include DJ Maxine and DJ Dazzle, who were among a succession of collaborators. 1989 proved their watershed year, with the hits 'Born This Way', 'Got To Keep On' and 'Come And Get Some'. They were also prominent as part of the Black Rhyme Organisation To Help Equal Rights (B.R.O.T.H.E.R.) along with Overlord X, Demon Boyz, She Rockers, and many other black rap acts in the UK. On their second album they teamed up with jazz fusion artist Roy Ayers for a new version of his 'Love Will Bring Us Back Together'. However, all was not well between the Cookie Crew and London. The latter wished to reflate the duo's chart profile via more commercial material. The Cookie Crew, for their part, wanted to concentrate on more hardcore hip hop. A bizarre compromise was reached in the summer of 1992 when two singles, 'Like Brother Like Sister' and 'Crew's Gone Mad' were released side by side. The former was a hip house pop tune, the latter a biting rap track, in an experiment to decide the direction of their future career. In the event, the group had run its course anyway, and Remedee would go on to form the New Wave Sisters with Trouble & Bass (another female rap duo) and Dee II, also setting up a concert and club agency - 786 Promotions.

Albums: *Born This Way!* (London 1989), *Fade To Black* (London 1991).

Coolio

Distinguished by his visual apparition, which includes braids stood on end in vaguely mohican bravado, Coolio is a Compton-born rapper with a chequered past. Boasting of a long, though infrequently recorded, history in hip hop, Coolio can claim to have appeared alongside other West Coast luminaries such as Dr Dre when he was still with the World Class Wreckin' Crew. He even signed to Ruthless records for a brief, and once again unproductive spell. His debut release was 'Whatcha Gonna Do', one of the very first Los Angeles rap records. The next chapter of his career was little more than a relationship with freebase cocaine. After attending rehab classes Coolio managed to pull together some semblance of normality by working as a fire-fighter, and embarked on a more disciplined attitude to his musical career. First came an alliance with WC and DJ Alladin as part of WC & The MADD Circle, in turn becoming part of the 40 Theivz, a hip hop community made up of producers, rappers and dancers. Coolio eventually turned once again to his own career, supported by a friend entitled Wino. Together they signed to Tommy Boy records. The first results were the 45, 'County Line', which recalled his negative experiences on Welfare, and an impressive debut album which forced many critics to wonder at what hip hop had passed up on in earlier years.

Album: *Home Alone* (Tommy Boy 1994).

Cosmic Force

Alongside Soul Sonic Force, Cosmic Force were the second arm of Afrika Bambaataa's Zulu Nation network. They joined with the latter for his debut release on Winley Records (see Paul Winley) 'Zulu Nation Throwdown', featuring the talents of female rapper Lisa Lee, herself an ex-member of Soul Sonic Force.

Credit To The Nation

Among the most commercially viable of new UK hip hop groups, Credit To The Nation comprise Matty Hanson (b. 1971, Wednesbury, West Midlands, England, aka MC Fusion), with his dancers, Tyrone and Kelvin (aka T-Swing and Mista-G). Credit To The Nation broke through in 1993 after several months of sponsorship by agit-prop anarchists Chumbawamba, with whom they recorded their first, joint single. They also shared a lyrical platform which attacked racism, sexism and homophobia. Hanson took time out to point out the flaws in the gangsta philosophies of Ice-T, Onyx and the like, but received short shrift from hardcore hip hop fans. Credit To The Nation broke through with 'Call It What You Want', which cheekily sampled the guitar motif used by Nirvana on 'Smells Like Teen Spirit'. This helped

Coolio

them find an audience in hip indie kids outside of the hardcore rap fraternity. There was a backlash to be observed: after threats to his life he was eventually forced to move out of his home in Wednesbury, West Midlands. The band continued with the release of the singles 'Teenage Sensation', which went Top 30, and 'Hear No Bullshit, See No Bullshit, Say No Bullshit' - often dedicated to the likes of East 17 and Kriss Kross on stage. Cuts on their debut album included pro-female tracks like 'The Lady Needs Respect', the anthemic 'Pump Your Fist', on which Tyrone enjoys a rare chance to rap, and 'Rising Tide', influenced by the election of BNP councillor Derek Beacon. Among the samples were Benjamin Britten, Glenn Miller, the Sex Pistols and even the Coldstream Guards. Album: *Take Dis* (One Little Indian 1993).

Cypress Hill

Another of the new rap breed to extoll the creative use of marijuana/hemp, Los Angeles-based Cypress Hill, with songs such as 'I Wanna Get High', 'Legalise It' and 'Insane In The Brain' all advocating marijuana as a cultural replacement for alcohol, are champions of NORML (National Organisation For The Reform Of Marijuana Laws). However, the reason for their widespread success lies instead with their blend of full and funky R&B, tales of dope and guns adding the final sheen to the rhythm. The band comprise DJ Muggs (b. Lawrence Muggerud, c.1969, of Italian descent) on the decks, and vocalists B-Real (b. Louis Freeze, c.1970, of Mexican/Cuban descent) and Sen Dog (b. Sen Reyes, c. 1965, Cuba), a former running back for Los Angeles' Centennial High. An additional member is Eric Bobo - their sometime percussionist. Sen Dog had come to Los Angeles from his native Cuba at the age of 14. With his younger brother Mellow Man Ace, he had formed the prototype rap outfit, DVX, and claims to have invented the Spanglish 'lingo' style. After his brother left he hooked up with former 7A3 members DJ Muggs and B-Real, who was one of the same breakdancing crew as Mellow. Their debut set was only available in the UK on import for some time, though in the US it created a lot of interest almost immediately. Spanning two

years songwriting, it eventually went platinum. Longstanding B-boys, touring for free and opening for Naughty By Nature in 1991, Cypress Hill represented rap's new wave. After the militancy and radicalism of Public Enemy and NWA, Cypress Hill were advocating escapism via pot, and making it sound very attractive indeed. The second album, rather than pursuing a more commercial bent, was informed by the dark events in their home city ala Rodney King. *Black Sunday* debuted at Number 1 in the US R&B and Pop charts, while the gun-touting 'Cock The Hammer' turned up on the soundtrack to Schwarzenegger's mega-flop, *Last Action Hero*. Their reputation for violent lyrics (a method they justified as: 'not promoting, more explaining what goes on') was underscored when they appeared on the soundtrack for another film, *Mad Dog And Glory*, in a scene which accompanies a drug killing. Their breakthrough in the UK came when they supported House Of Pain on dates through 1993. The latter group, and several others, benefited from the services of DJ Muggs in-demand production skills (Ice Cube, Beastie Boys etc). Their most recent soundtrack appearance occurred when they recorded a track with Pearl Jam, 'The Real Thing', for the film *Judgement Night*.

Albums: *Cypress Hill* (Ruffhouse 1991), *Black Sunday* (Columbia 1993).

D

D., Donald

The first artist to feature via Ice-T's deal between the Rhyme Syndicate and Epic Records, Donald D's influence in the 90s proved to be marginal. His anti-drugs stance was hammered home on his debut release, 'FBI (Free Base Institute)'. However, such vision was not evident elsewhere, his debut album containing the crude and thoroughly nasty 'Just Suck', which gloried in the Rhyme Syndicate's gangbanging activities: 'I can listen to the radio and hear George Michael sing 'I Want Your Sex' - but 'Just Suck' is to do with sex. So if they can play that song, why can't they play my song?'. Such a stupefying poverty of logic hardly helps to justify Donald D's case. Although he has since moved to the West Coast, Donald D's roots were in the Bronx, where he was a sporty, athletic youth, from a good family, until he caught the hip hop bug. He met Ice-T in 1985 when he was visiting California with *Notorious'* eventual co-producer, Afrika Islam.
Album: *Notorious* (Epic 1990).

Da Lench Mob

Hardcore gangsta rappers and protégés of Ice Cube, signed to his Street Knowledge label. Da Lench Mob were originally employed as backing musicians on their benefactors' first three solo recordings, before eventually seeing their own debut on *Guerillas In The Mist*. The title, an obvious pun on the film of similar name, was picked up by the band from a police report issued after attending a Los Angeles domestic incident. Although Da Lench Mob share many lyrical concerns with Ice Cube, there is a distinct moral tone stressed in their distrust of drugs and dealers. Front person J-Dee numbers amongst the more articulate of rap's inner city spokesmen. He was joined by the backing duo of T-Bone and Jerome Washington (aka Shorty). However, after his arrest for attempted murder and subsequent imprisonment, J-Dee was dropped from the band at the end of 1993. This was caused, according to press statements, because of contractual obligations Da Lench Mob were enforced to comply with. His replacement was Maulkley, ex-rap duo Yomo and Maulkley. Ironically, it was always Da Lench Mob's intention to recruit Maulkley, but contractual problems, once again, prevented this at the commencement of their career. His vocals were dubbed over their previously completed set, *Planet Of The Apes*. However, T-Bone too would subsequently be charged with murder, and East West dropped the band in 1994.
Album: *Guerillas In The Mist* (Street Knowledge 1992), *Planet Of The Apes* (Street Knowledge 1994).

Da Youngstas

A trio of young rappers from Philadelphia who are visually distinguished by their closely shaved heads, but the appearance is deceptive. Far from the Onyx school of macho hardcore rap, Qu'ran, Taji and Tarik arrived with a much more scholarly view of things, from a profoundly Muslim perspective. Sadly, many of their lyrics were ghost-written for them, which in the world of rap, where self-expression is everything, led many to view them as contrived.
Albums: *Da Youngstas* (East West 1991), *The Aftermath* (East West 1993).

Daddy-O

b. c.1961, Brooklyn, New York, USA. A founder member of Stetsasonic, and for some time one of hip hop's most influential figures, Daddy-O is remembered fondly as the 'Quincy Jones' of rap. While still a member of the band he worked in communities furthering the A.F.R.I.C.A. programme - an anti-apartheid album and study guide. He has also spoken at several college seminars. When Stetsasonic broke up in 1990, Daddy-O was called in to provide remixes for swingbeat classics like Mary J. Blige's 'Real Love' and Shanté Moore's 'Love's Taken Over'. Before long everyone from Jeffrey Osbourne, Third World and They Might Be Giants to the Red Hot Chilli Peppers were on his casebook, as well as more conventional hip hop concerns such as K9, Queen Latifah and Audio Two. Elsewhere he kept busy by producing jingles for Casio Electronics, Alka Seltzer and Pepsi, amongst others. His debut solo album, and promotional single 'Brooklyn Bounce', saw a welcome return to the freewheeling old school trickery which had been conspicuous by its absence in hip hop. However, this was a 90s version, though a more politically directed album had been recorded but scrapped in deference to the one which eventually saw the light of day.

Album: *You Can Be A Daddy But Never Daddy-O* (Brooktown/Island 1993).

Dane, Dana

A graduate of New York's High School Of Music And Art, notable for being the first hip hop star to offer his name to a fashion range or shop, which most major artists subsequently imitated, Dana Dane's reputation was also built on a solid musical platform (generally provided by DJ Clark Kent) of hard East Coast rhythms and smooth production. His quasi-British accent customised unusual, pop-orientated songs like 'Cinderella', which became a huge crossover success.

Albums: *Dana Dane With Fame* (Profile 1987), *Dana Dane 4 Ever* (Profile 1990).

Darkman

b. Brian Mitchell, c.1970. Rapper of West Indian heritage who grew up in Finsbury Park and Shepherds Bush, London, but also spent three years in the Caribbean. The reggae tradition in west London was very strong at the time and it was with the sound systems that he first learnt his craft as an entertainer, setting up his own system, Platinum. There he would alternate between Jamaican patois 'chatting' and a more conventional rap style, also learning production and helping out local groups Outlaw Posse and Cash Crew. He set up his own label, Powercut, in 1987. One of its earliest releases, One Love Sound featuring Joe 90's 'This Is How It Should Be Done', was widely appraised as the first to combine reggae and hip hop. In its wake Powercut was signed to Warners subsidiary Slam Jam, via dance producer Danny D. The deal

never worked, with only one song from sixty demos submitted, the Powercut Crew's 'Firin'', seeing the light of day. It left Mitchell embittered, an anger expressed in his first release as Darkman, 'Whats Not Yours', included on the *Jus The Way* compilation. This largely featured acts housed on Darkman's new Vinyl Lab record label. Through this Beechwood collection Steve Jarvier, Darkman's partner in his north London record shop, was headhunted by Polydor. He was placed in charge of that label's ailing Wild Card subsidiary, to which he brought Darkman. His breakthrough disc, 'Yabba Dabba Doo', was another track to be inspired by anger, this time his impotent rage at watching a documentary on the killing of Stephen Lawrence. With its *Flintstone* rallying call (Mitchell is a big cartoon fan) it brought him overground approval, and sponsorship deals with Magnum Hi-Tech clothing and Vicious Circle. All this while he was still pursuing his performance arts and animation courses. The follow-up single, 'She Used To Call Me', maintained his commitment to the rap/reggae interface: 'Everyone should just dig into themselves and then it would just come. A lotta people don't look back, they forget where they come from, just live for today...' Despite his protestations to the effect that UK hip hop needs its own identity, there was some criticism of his gun-fixation as being irrelevant to indigenous audiences, but this was a minor carp.

Album: *Worldwide* (Wild Card 1994).

Das-EFX

Drayz (b. Andre Weston, 9 September 1970, New Jersey, USA) and Skoob (b. Willie Hines, 27 November 1970, Brooklyn, New York, USA; Skoob is 'books' spelled backwards) are two easy-natured rappers whose success story is of the genuine rags to riches variety. As college friends who had met during English classes, they entered a rap contest at a small Richmond, Virginia nightclub. Luckily for them Erick Sermon and Parrish Smith of EPMD were in attendance, and, despite not winning, they walked off with an instant record contract. The judgement shown by EPMD proved impeccable when Das-EFX's debut release, *Dead Serious*, charted strongly. Soon they were touring together, despite the fact that neither Drayz nor Skoob were old enough to legally enter the premises on some of the dates. As rap aficionados began to look once more to the old school and its freestyle vocals, Das-EFX were the perfect modern proponents, with their jagged, cutting rhymes and sweet wordplay. They developed a wonderful habit of making words up if they could not find something appropriate in the dictionary to shore up their rhymes: 'We're not too worried about really putting heavy messages in our records - we just try and make sure all the lyrics are super dope'. It was a style that was to be, in typical hip hop fashion, quickly adopted and mimicked by a hundred other artists, and by the time of their follow-up some of its impact had been lost. Their debut self-production, 'Freak It', followed in 1993, and was the first release to see them drop their familiar tongue-flipping style, which detractors accused them of copying from UK rappers like the Demon Boyz.

Albums: *Dead Serious* (East West 1992), *Straight Up Sewaside* (East West 1993).

Davey D

b. David Reeves, Queens, New York, USA. Formerly titled Davey DMX, due to his patronage of the Oberheim DMX machine, Reeves started in a group, Rhythm And Creation, when he was just 16. He subsequently picked up on the DJ's art, importing the new 'scratch' style from the Bronx and becoming the first Queens DJ to incorporate the cut and mix template. He honed his technique playing neighbourhood parties, generally because he was too young to gain entrance to proper clubs. He formed a team called Solar Sound, but this broke up when he was given the opportunity to work with Kurtis Blow, an association which would last several years. At the same time he played guitar in Orange Crush, alongside Larry Smith and Trevor Gale, providing production for Run DMC. He has also recorded solo, debuting with 'One For The Table (Fresh)' on Tuff City, before moving over to Def Jam.

Album: *Davy's Ride* (Def Jam 1987).

De La Soul

Garlanded with the dreadful label of 'Daisy Age Soul' (Da Inner Sound, Y'All), Long Island New Yorkers Posdnous (b. Kelvin Mercer, 17 August 1969), Trugoy the Dove (b. David Jude Joliceur, 21 September 1958), and Pasemaster Mace (b. Vincent Lamont Mason Jnr, 24 March 1970) were contemporaries of Queen Latifah, Monie Love and A Tribe Called Quest. With the aforementioned groups they formed the Native Tongues Posse, who were at the forefront of the black renaissance of the early 90s. Less harsh than many of their fellow rappers, De La Soul's pleasantly lilting rhythms helped them chart their debut LP - one of the first such acts to cross into the album market. Produced by Stetsasonic's Prince Paul, it revealed an altogether delightful array of funky rhythms and comic touches. As well as hit singles like 'Me Myself And I', and 'The Magic Number', they also charted in conjunction with Queen Latifah on 'Mama Gave Birth To The Soul Children' and guested on the Jungle Brothers' 'Doing Our Own Dang'. Some of De La Soul's more esoteric samples ranged from Curiosity Killed The Cat to Steely Dan, though their mellow approach belied difficult subject matter. *De La Soul Is Dead*, however, saw them return to tougher rhythms and a less whimsical melodic approach. Evidently they had grown tired of the 'Hippies of hip hop' tag dreamt up by their press officer. With over 100 artists sampled, they sidestepped injunctions by gaining clearance from all concerned artists (previously they had been sued by the Turtles), though it delayed the album for over a year. When it did emerge it was roundly denounced by critics, who were not taken by De La Soul's drastic gear change. However, infectious songs like 'Ring Ring Ring (Ha Ha Hey)' kept their profile high in the singles chart. *Buhloone Mindstate* saw them move back towards the stylings of their debut, and received better press.

Albums: *3 Feet High And Rising* (Tommy Boy 1989), *De La Soul Is Dead* (Tommy Boy 1991), *Buhloone Mindstate* (Tommy Boy 1993).

Death Row

Record company set up by Dr Dre after he

complained bitterly about restraint of trade and monies owed by his previous employers, for whom he produced several million-sellers. Not content with cursing Ruthless General Manager Jerry Heller, and begin sued by Eazy-E, he finally managed to find a deal with Jimmy Iovine at Interscope. Iovine agreed to finance Dre's own label, Death Row. Marlon 'Suge' Knight also contributed. Unfortunately, Knight revealed a similar propensity for trouble that has marred Dre's career. He was charged with assault with a deadly weapon in late 1993. Knight allegedly attacked two rappers, Lynwood and George Stanley, with a gun in July 1992, at Dr Dre's recording studio. The attack was witnessed by both Dre and Snoop Doggy Dogg, and concerned the use of, of all things, an office telephone. The money Knight invested in Death Row was drawn from the publishing rights he partly owned for Vanilla Ice's hit album - a huge irony in the wake of the war of words between Vanilla and the West Coast gangsta rappers a few years previously. Several months later Dr Dre's *The Chronic* justified his decision to back the rapper by becoming a huge crossover success. The label also released the big-selling soundtrack to basketball film *Above The Rim*, ensuring that Death Row's first three albums all went multi-platinum. But is was Snoop Doggy Dogg's huge debut that really capped the label's multi-million status. Other artists signed to the label include Dat Nigga Daz, Kurrupt, Lady Of Rage and Jewell.

Selected albums: Dr Dre: *The Chronic* (Death Row 1993). Snoop Doggy Dogg: *Doggy Style* (Death Row 1993). Various: *Above The Rim* (Death Row 1994).

Definition Of Sound

South East London duo who pair commercial raps with a fully fledged pop song format, aided by soul choruses and touches of psychedelia and reggae. Samples are sprayed liberally amongst rock hooks, with a lyrical focus that spans anti-drug messages and new age mysticism. The group comprise Kevwon (b. Kevin Anthony Clark, 1971) and The Don (Desmond Raymond Weekes, 1969). Kevwon is a former graffiti artist who guested on Krush's pioneering UK house hit 'House Arrest' in

1987. He joined ex-body-popper The Don in 1988 to form Top Billin', a precursor to Definition Of Sound. Their two generic hip hop singles ('Straight From The Soul' and 'Naturally') sampled the staple James Brown records then in vogue. As part of the Soul Underground tour of 1989 they became the last 'Western' group to play East Berlin before the wall came down. However their career was scuttled when their label, Dance-Yard, collapsed. Under their new banner they have proved a much more decisive and durable act, with samples now worked in to arrangements with a greater degree of insight and ingenuity. Occasional outings with Coldcut, PP Arnold and X Posse have increased their profile, and they are also one of the few hip hop/rap crews of their generation who tackle playing live with any fluidity. Their debut album featured the singles 'Now Is Tomorrow' and 'Wear Your Love Like Heaven'. The former not only featured the soulful vocals of Elaine Vassell, but also boasted a notable b-side cut, 'Moira Jane's Cafe'. Whereas most rap/dance acts have found a remix or edit to be sufficient for the flip, the song, with its coded drug references and use of Them's 'Gloria' riff, is among their finest moments. In the wake of the subsequent failure of 'Dream Girl', it achieved a-side status in its own right.

Album: *Love And Life; A Journey With The Chameleons* (Circa 1991), *The Lick* (Circa 1992).

Def Jam

Russell Simmons (b. c.1956) and Rick Rubin's (b. c.1961) noted street rap label, who brought the world the skewed genius of the Beastie Boys and the militancy of Public Enemy. The label made its debut with T La Rock and Jazzy Jay's 'It's Yours', a record released in conjunction with Partytime/Streetwise. Managing director Simmons (brother of Run DMC's Joe Simmons) was described as 'The mogul of rap' by *The Wall Street Journal* as early as 1984, following his early managerial coups. A year later Def Jam had netted a landmark distribution deal with Columbia, the first results of which were the LL Cool J smash, 'I Can't Live Without My Radio'. Simmons also concurrently managed the affairs of Whodini, Kurtis Blow, Dr Jeckyll And Mr Hyde and Run

De La Soul

DMC, co-producing the latter's first two albums alongside Larry Smith. Rubin's credits included the label debut by T La Rock and Jazzy J. Together they helmed Run DMC's platinum set *Tougher Than Leather*, before Rubin's productions of LL Cool J and the Beastie Boys' enormously successful debut sets. The biggest signing, however, would be Public Enemy, though Simmons was at first unconvinced of their potential. The Rubin/Simmons partnership dissolved in acrimony in 1987. Simmons would go on to head several other business ventures, including Rush Management, the Phat Farm clothing line and HBO's Def Comedy Jam, continuing to manage the careers of R&B artists like Alyson Williams, Oran' Juice' Jones, Tashan, the Black Flames etc. Rubin, meanwhile, left his post at Def Jam to set up Def American in 1988. There he continued to enjoy success with a variety of artists, including several thrash metal outfits like Slayer. He earned himself a series of rebukes in hip hip circles when he released a record by the latter with lyrics which gloried in allusions to an Aryan race war. He maintained his links with rap, though, via similarly outrageous concerns like the Geto Boys. On August 27 1993 Rubin officially dropped the 'Def' from the Def American imprint, reasoning that now the word Def had been incorporated into the latest edition of a major US dictionary, it no longer had the street suss value it once enjoyed. He 'buried' it via an elaborate New Orleans style funeral, complete with Dixieland band. Def Jam continued in its own right, though it left its original deal with Columbia and is presently distributed through Polygram. In 1992 it had opened a West Coast subsidiary, DJ West, to pick up on some of the action there, signing Boss and MC Sugs.

Selected albums: Beastie Boys: *Licensed To Ill* (Def Jam 1986). Public Enemy: *Yo! Bum Rush The Show* (Def Jam 1987), *It Takes A Nation Of Millions To Hold Us Back* (Def Jam 1988), *Fear Of A Black Planet* (Def Jam 1990). LL Cool J: *Bigger And Deffer* (Def Jam 1987). EPMD: *Business As Usual* (Def Jam 1991).

Def Jef

Californian rapper who made a big impression with his 1989 debut set, but has largely disappeared from view in the interim. Decidedly on the Afrocentric trip, Def Jef's minimalist hip hop beats propelled his consciousness messages with excellent clarity. He also appeared in the films *Deep Cover* and *Def By Temptation* and worked on Shaquille O'Neal's debut album.

Album: *Just A Poet With Soul* (Delicious Vinyl 1989), *Soul Food* (Delicious Vinyl 1990).

Del Tha Funky Homosapien

Formerly a part of his cousin, Ice Cube's backing band, Da Lench Mob, Del (b. Teren Delvon Jones, 12 August 1972, Oakland, California, USA) earned his first, glowing reviews for his debut solo set in 1992. Far from the hardcore streak of his more celebrated relation (though there are definite similarities in musical inclination), Del offered a more detached viewpoint, laced with humour. Like many of his West Coast rap colleagues, there was a scarcely disguised debt to the rhythms of P-Funk and George Clinton in his work, acknowledged in its title. However, this approach was abandoned for the follow-up, a much more dour, self-consciously worthy affair (this time without Cube on production) that completely lost the magic of his debut, and placed him at a definite crossroads in his career. However, if Del has faltered, then the achievements of his Hieroglyphics crew (Casual, Souls Of Mischief etc.) have gone some way to compensating.

Albums: *I Wish My Brother George Was Here* (1992), *No Need For Alarm* (Elektra 1993).

Delicious Vinyl

This highly prominent label was co-founded by Mick Ross and Matt Dike in 1987, both DJs and promoters who were bored and frustrated by the dearth of good hip hop records. Despite Delicious Vinyl being hailed by the media as the harbinger of the 'new West Coast sound', each partner originally hailed from New York. With Eric B and Rakim's laidback sampling/breakbeat technique in vogue, they set about finding artists who could provide them with similar, great cuts for their club

Detroit's Most Wanted

nights. The label's offices were established next to a Thai restaurant in Melrose Avenue, Los Angeles. The first major artist they hooked up with was Young MC, who released the label's debut record ('Know How'). His career took off almost immediately, as did that of Tone Loc, whose hilarious narratives of sexual gratification made a nice bookend to Young MC's adolescent tales (even though Young MC was the writer behind both). *Wild Thing*, in particular, set up the label for the foreseeable future, going triple platinum. From there the ride was an easier, though still eventful one. The label's major success of the 90s has been the Pharcyde and Master Ace, though they also benefited from the US success of Brit-musicians Brand New Heavies. In 1994 the label signed a distribution deal with East West to make their product more readily available worldwide, marking the association with the release of a compilation album, *Natural Selections*. This introduced several of their new signings, including the Wascals, Born Jamericans (a dancehall/rap cross) and Angel. The latter was the first to sign to their new subsidiary, Brass Records. Ross is stoical about the label's evolution and success, suggesting its secret lies in the fact that 'all of the artists on the label that are creating music have good taste'. Dike is also known for his work with the Dust Brothers (alongside radio DJ's John Simpson and John King) - having produced/remixed for the Beastie Boys and Mellow Man Ace in addition to the aforementioned Young MC and Tone Loc.

Selected album: *Natural Selections* (Delicious Vinyl 1994).

Demon Boyz

The Demon Boyz comprise Mike J. and Darren (nicknamed Demon due to his 'Spock-like ears'). An English underground phenomenon, the Demon Boyz rap owes a stylistic debt to reggae, notably on tracks like 'Sweet Jamaica'. This was housed on the belated follow-up to their 1989 debut album, which saw them switching to the Rebel MC's Tribal Bass empire. This completed the circle for the duo, who had made their debut performing on the mic at the Rebel's Broadwater

Farm sound system parties. They showed they were in touch with the club scene too by incorporating raps like the breakbeat-feast, 'Dett', and genre-defining single, 'Jungle-Ist'. Many have acknowledged the manner in which US artists like Das EFX have incorporated their 'wiggedy diggedy' delivery.

Albums: *Recognition* (Music Of Life 1989), *Original Guidance - The 2nd Chapter* (Tribal Bass 1993).

Detroit's Most Wanted

Self-styled motor city gangstas, Detroit's Most Wanted arrived on the hardcore hip hop scene in 1991 with a strong-selling debut album propelled by singles like 'City Of Boom'. The album was nominated for album of the year in the Soul Train awards. The follow-up brought further singles chart success with 'The Money Is Made' and 'Pop The Trunk'. The third album in the series was previewed by a tribute single, 'Keep Holding On', which was dedicated to Motsi's nephew, Ja-Vanti Abrams, whose life ended after four months. The group is built around rapper Motsi Ski (b. Reginald Adams, c.1970, Detroit, Michigan, USA), who is actually the grandson of soul legend Jackie Wilson, who brought out the young Motsi to perform with him on occasion.

Albums: *Tricks Of The Trade* (Bryant/Ichiban 1991), *Tricks Of The Trade II - The Money Is Made* (Bryant/Ichiban 1992), *Many Faces Of Death, Vol. III* (Bryant/Ichiban 1993).

DFC

DFC originally stood for the Dope Flint Connection when members Al Breed and T-Trouble E toured in 1991 with their partner, MC Breed. Afterwards they took time out to perfect a formula which was finally unveiled with the Top 5 success of their debut album, *Things In Tha Hood*. Reduced to a duo, the group subsequently advised interested parties that DFC now conferred the status 'Da Funk Clan'. Four of the songs on the debut were recorded in Los Angeles with Warren G., while the other tracks were culled from sessions in Atlanta, the remainder drawn from work with DJ Slip and MC Eiht (of Compton's Most Wanted), again in LA. MC

Breed, Al's cousin, also returned to help out with advice and suggestions. 'Caps Get Peeled', a duet with MC Eiht, would give the group a major hit single.

Album: *Things In Tha Hood* (Assault/Big Beat 1994).

Diamond D

One of rap music's top flight production experts, who, although he really broke through in the 90s, started out as DJ way back in 1979, going on to join Jazzy Jay's team in the early 80s. He followed that with engagements for Master Rob (who also appeared in the *Wild Style* film as one of the Romantic Fantastic Five) as a component of the Ultimate Force. They released one single on Strong City Records, 'I'm Not Playing', but it was not considered lyrically tough enough by prevailing hip hop standards. Diamond D pressed on, teaching himself rhyming to add to his deck skills, making a debut appearance on A Tribe Called Quest's 'Show Business'. Together with his Psychotic Neurotics posse Diamond D made his 'solo' debut with 'Best Kept Secret' on Chemistry/Mercury Records. It was an attempt to reinstate the principals of the old school Bronx pioneers in lyrical showdowns and couplets. The album which followed saw co-production assistance from DJ Mark the 45 King and Large Professor (Main Source). However, it is as a producer Diamond D remains best known, and his client list is growing. These include Showbiz & AG (often working in tandem with the former), Lord Finesse, Apache, the Geto Girlz, Chill Rob G, Run DMC and Brand Nubian. Diamond D is, incidentally, not the white artist of the same name, who arrived on the scene much later but had coprighted the name.

Album: *Stunts, Blunts & Hip Hop* (Chemistry/Mercury (1992).

Digable Planets

Psychedelic jazz rappers who, alongside Gang Starr, have been hailed as the instigators of the whole genre/phenomenon. Contextually they are more accurately the legacy of De La Soul/PM Dawn's Daisy-age rap, as might be detected from their colourful pseudonyms; Doodle Bug, Butterfly and Ladybug. This conveyed their kooky, spaced-out philosophy, their names derived from an admiration for the community structures of ants and insects. Musically it was a delicious combination of wordplay and dreamy jazz backing, the group admitting that 'We use a lot of the colloquialisms that came out of jazz'. However, there was an underlying political bent, as expressed on debut album cuts like 'La Femme Fetal', an attack on the Pro-Life lobby who firebomb abortion clinics.

Albums: *Reachin' (A New Refutation Of Time And Space)* (WEA 1993).

Digital Underground

Among rap's most faithful P-Funk advocates, Digital Underground, whose line-up perms up to seven members, were formed in the mid-80s in Oakland, California by Shock-G (b, Gregory E. Jacobs; keyboards, vocals) and Chopmaster J (samples, percussion). Other key members included DJ Fuze (b. David Elliot, 8 October 1970, Syracuse, New York, USA). Shock-G subsequently introduced his alter-ego, Eddie 'Humpty Hump' Humphrey, and Money B. According to Digital legends, back in 1987 Humphrey sustained severe burns in a freak kitchen accident. He was forced to continue his rapping career with the addition of a false nose, worn to cover the grisly remains of his existing olfactory avenue. Instead of hiding the event surreptitiously, however, Humphrey chose a joke nose, leading to much merriment and a series of records paying tribute to his new, improved hooter. Among these were 'The 'Humpty Dance' routine, wherein the protagonist extols his ability to still, despite such deformity, get his snout into the object of his desire's pants. Typically, there is a good natured verve to the recording which militates against any possible offence. Their staple diet of P-Funk and Funkadelic samples is evident on most of their recordings, including a concept debut album. The subtext was the ruse of a mad scientist marketing a drug which caused the recipients to have wet dreams. Shock-G/Humpty Hump adopted the characters of two dealers, and

Digital Underground

despite the threadbare plot it actually managed to exceed its comic potential. Alongside the samples it also introduced live piano and musicians, which were also in evidence on the follow-up, *This Is An EP*. The latter included two tracks from the dreadful *Nothing But Trouble* film in which Digital Underground appeared. However, *The Body Hat Syndrome,* its name alluding to prophylactics, paid simply too many compliments to the P-Funk coalition, ending up sounding highly derivative. Tupac Shakur, formerly a full-time member, joined for a few verses on 'Wussup Wit The Luv', complaining about drug dealers selling to children, a rare outbreak of moral responsibility. There were three newcomers for *Body Hat*: DJ Jay Z, Clee and Saafir (aka the Saucy Nomad). The album also came with an invitation to vote in the Humpty Dance Awards, run by their fan club. In the grim world of hardcore rap Digital Underground offered a welcome release from corpses and curses.

Albums:: *Sex Packets* (Tommy Boy 1990), *Sons Of The P* (Tommy Boy 1991), *The Body-Hat Syndrome* (Tommy Boy 1993).

Dirt Nation

New York rap trio comprising JB (b. Brooklyn, New York, USA), KD (b. Jamaica, West Indies) and E Depp (b. New Jersey, USA). Specialising in smooth, easily palatable (at least musically) goods, Dirt Nation's debut 45, 'Khadijah', became a summer 1993 hit throughout urban America. Quoting Curtis Mayfield, Jimmy McGriff and Marvin Gaye, and alluding to the golden age of soul in its mellow rhythms too, 'Khadijah' was a tribute to the womenfolk often degraded as 'bitches' and 'ho's' in gangsta rhymes. The group met at school in Maryland, relocating to Manhattan in search of a record deal. There they recorded their debut single, plus a track with rapper Biggy Smalls (Mary J. Blige). Their debut album's title was lifted from the movie of the same name, while a collaboration with Guru of Gang Starr has also been mooted.

Album: *Three The Hard Way* (1994).

Disco Four

The Disco Four, who included in their number the son of Enjoy Records' president Bobby Robinson, were arguably most famous for their 'Country Rock Rap' cut for that label. Produced by early hip hop innovator Pumpkin, it used cow horns and hoe-down instrumentation to arrive at a sound that inspired Malcolm McLaren's 'Buffalo Gals' novelty. The Disco Four, whose origins were in the Bronx sound system days (Troy B was in an early incarnation of the Fearless Four), didn't last much longer, though they did switch to Profile for a hit and miss mini-career.

Disposable Heroes Of Hiphoprisy

A hugely innovative contemporary hip hop band who comprised Rono Tse (percussion) and Michael Franti (vocals). Both residents of the Bay area of San Francisco, the duo worked together for several years, most notably in *avant-garde* industrial jazz band the Beatnigs. Following their inception as the Disposable Heroes they won significant allies amongst press and peers; support slots to Billy Bragg, U2, Public Enemy, Arrested Development and Nirvana demonstrating the range of their appeal. Their sound recalled some of the experimental edge of their former incarnation, while Franti's raps were arguably the most articulate and challenging of his generation. Typically he broke down his subject matter beyond the black/white rhetoric of much urban rap, and was willing to place his own inadequacies as a person at the forefront of his manifesto. When he called himself a 'Jerk' in the intensely personal 'Music And Politics', Franti took rap into a whole new dimension. Examples of his skilled deployment of words litter the band's debut album; 'Imagination is sucked out of children by a cathode-ray nipple, Television is the only wet-nurse, that would create a cripple' (from 'Television The Drug Of The Nation', which also bemoans the amount of violence visited upon an average American child through his television set). 'Language Of Violence' took to task rap's penchant for homophobia, forging a link between a wider circle of prejudice. Franti was more effective still when dealing with subjects on a personal level; 'I was adopted by parents who loved me; they were the same colour as the kids who called me nigger on the way home from school' (from 'Socio-Genetic Experiment'). One unfortunate consequence of Franti's eloquence was that the Disposable Heroes became the token rap band that it was 'safe for white liberals to like'. Otherwise there was precious little to fault in them. In 1993 they recorded an album with *Naked Lunch* author, William Burroughs. However, as the year closed they informed the press that the Disposable Heroes were no longer a going concern, with both parties going on to solo careers. The first result of which was Franti's album, as Spearhead, with producer Joe 'The Butcher' Nicolo. There were also liaisons with the Disposables' live guitarist Charlie Hunter, and a projected dub album with Adrian Sherwood. Rono, meanwhile, has worked with Oakland rappers Mystic Journeymen.

Albums: *Hiphoprisy Is The Greatest Luxury* (4th & Broadway 1992). With William Burroughs: *Spare Ass Annie & Other Tales* (4th & Broadway 1993).

DJ Biznizz

b. Billy Ntimih. Alongside the Underdog DJ Biznizz is the UK's leading rap producer, with most of the important UK artists (Cookie Crew, London Posse, Caveman, Monie Love, MC Mell 'O' and Cash Crew) having sought his favours. He has also remixed for the Cookie Crew ('Love Will Bring Us Back Together') and House Of Pain ('Jump Around') and established his PD3 and Points Proven collectives. The floating personnel involved in these two rallying groups are fascinating in themselves. Byron the Greek is co-owner of the Hitt Recording Studio and had previously worked as a rock guitarist. Cutch is a session drummer, and Dego has worked with DJ Silk Worm of Digable Planets and is now part of the production team. Female vocalist Face has providing backing to Don-E and Gabrielle as well as rap groups Son Of Noise, MC Mell 'O' and London Posse. Fly was previously in rap group Rap Conscious, while Niles Hailstnoes had previously worked with reggae artists like Misty In Roots, Mad Professor and Delroy Wilson. Ola The Soul Controller is an ex-patriate Canadian rapper. Together with DJ Biznizz this assorted personnel has been responsible for a number of releases with

the stated intention to 'smash the stigma attached to British rap'.

Album: *Does Anybody Really Know What Time It Is?* (Syncopated Productions 1993).

DJ Hollywood

Just like DJ Flowers and Kool Herc, Hollywood was one of the earliest DJ/MC artists, yet one whose legacy does not confer his true status because his performances predated rap recordings (the posthumous 'Um Tang Tum Tang' aside). His background was as a compere at the Apollo Theatre in Harlem, where he chatted over disco records between performers. Grandmaster Flash remembers him as 'one of the greatest solo rappers that ever there was', for his later performances at venues like Club 371.

DJ Jazzy Jeff And The Fresh Prince

The Fresh Prince (b. Will Smith, 25 September 1968, Philadelphia, Pennsylvania, USA) is just as famous for being the star of television series *The Fresh Prince of Bel Air*, wherein he plays a streetwise tough (or homeboy, to use the requisite parlance) who suffers culture shock when transplanted into an affluent Beverley Hills' household. However, this is very much a second career for Smith. Together with DJ Jazzy Jeff (b. Jeffrey Townes, 22 January 1965, Philadelphia, Pennsylvania, USA), this young duo had already cut a highly successful debut album. Smith actually got the show because of the airing of his raps on MTV. Musically the duo operate in familiar territory, working a variety of inoffensive, borrowed styles to quite good effect. Jazzy Jeff started DJing in the mid-70s when he was a mere 10 years old, (though he is not to be confused with the similarly-titled Jazzy Jeff who cut an album, also for Jive, in 1985). He was frequently referred to in those early days as the 'bathroom' DJ, because, hanging out with better-known elders, he would only be allowed to spin the decks when they took a toilet break. He met the Fresh Prince at a party, the two securing a recording deal after entering the 1986 New Music Seminar, where Jeff won the coveted Battle Of The Deejays. Embarking on a recording career, the obligatory

Disposable Heroes Of Hiphoprisy

James Brown lifts were placed next to steals from cartoon characters like Buggs Bunny, which gave some indication of their debut album's scope. In the late 80s they cemented their reputation with million-selling teen anthems like 'Girls Ain't Nothing But Trouble', which sampled the *I Dream Of Jeannie* theme, and was released three weeks before Smith graduated from high school. They became the first rap act to receive a Grammy Award for their second long player's 'Parents Just Don't Understand', even though the ceremony was boycotted by most of the prominent hip hop crews because it wasn't slated to be 'screened' as part of the television transmission. In its wake the duo launched the world's first pop star 900 number (the pay-phone equivalent of the UK's 0898 system). By January 1989 3 million calls had been logged. *He's The DJ, I'm The Rapper* contained more accessible pop fare, the sample of *Nightmare On Elm Street* being the closest they come to street-level hip hop. The raps were made interesting, however, by the Prince's appropriation of a variety

of personas. This is doubtless what encouraged the television bosses to make him an offer he couldn't refuse, and *The Fresh Prince Of Bel Air*'s enormous success has certainly augmented his profile (he also moved on to dramatic film roles, beginning with *Six Degrees Of Separation*). Jeff, meanwhile, has formed A Touch Of Jazz Inc, a stable of producers working on rap/R&B projects. The duo picked up a second Grammy for 'Summertime' in 1991, before scoring a shock UK number 1 in 1993 with 'Boom! Shake The Room', the first rap record (Vanilla Ice and MC Hammer aside) to top the British singles chart.

Albums: *Rock The House* (Word Up 1987), *He's The DJ, I'm The Rapper* (Jive 1988), *And In This Corner* (Jive 1990), *Homebase* (Jive 1991), *Code Red* (Jive 1993).

DJ Magic Mike

b. Michael Hampton, Orlando, Florida, USA. Arguably critically and commercially ignored due to his south east location, Magic Mike is a talented rap producer and executive vice-president of Cheetah Records. His most memorable moments arrived on his 1991 album, *Ain't No Doubt About It*, which featured highly commercial party raps like 'Suckers Frontin'' and 'Just Crusin''. Other cuts like 'Class Is In Session' were reprised for his collaboration with MC Madness a year later. All were flavoured with Hampton's distinctive use of house textures and Miami bass.

Albums: *Bass Is The Name Of The Game* (Cheetah 1990, double album), *Ain't No Doubt About It* (Cheetah 1991). As Vicious Base featuring Magic Mike: *Back To Haunt You!* (Cheetah 1991). With MC Madness: *Twenty Degrees Below Zero* (Cheetah 1992).

DJ Mark The 45 King

DJ Mark broke through with his production of Lakim Shabazz's debut set, *Pure Righteousness*, though Latee's 'This Cut's Got Flava' 12-inch had earned him his first production credit. He has gone on to become a hip hop backroom guru ranking alongside Marley Marl and Hank Shocklee (Bomb Squad). As a young man he was the record boy for the Funky Four Plus One More, at which time he learnt the art of beatbox and turntable craft. He would also record solo, releasing an album for Aaron Fuchs' Tuff City label entitled *45 Kingdom*, which saluted the achievements of rappers on the smaller disc. The cut 'The 900 Number' was another tribute, in this case to the Akai 900 sampler. He has also produced numerous breakbeat albums, the most recent being *The Lost Breakbeats Vols. 1&2* (45 King Records)>

Albums: *Rhythmical Madness* (Tuff City 1989), *45 Kingdom* (Tuff City 1990), *45 King Introduces The Flavour Unit* (Tuff City 1991).

DJ Pete Jones

One of the earliest hip hop DJs, enjoying a residency at the 371 club and taking Grandmaster Flash under his wing, he also introduced Afrika Bambaataa by allowing him to play on his system. The latter adapted his 'switch' mechanism for changing channels on the decks to great account, effectively inventing 'scratch' DJing in the process.

DJ Jazzy Jeff & The Fresh Prince

DJ Pogo

One of hip hop's prime spinners, Pogo made his name through the World DJ Championships. From there he took on remix and production work for UK rap troupes like London Posse, Demon Boyz, MC Mell 'O', and Monie Love, as well as US imports like House Of Pain and Cypress Hill and even the Fine Young Cannibals. This in addition to his regular stints on London's Kiss FM Radio Station. He was also the prime mover behind PLZ (Party A La Mazon), together with Brooklyn born and bred duo Regi and Fredi, who had been operating out of London since 1987. Regi is a former dancer while Fredi is a business student turned rapper. They met Pogo in 1990, releasing their first record as PLZ two years later ('If It Ain't PLZ...'/'Bad Person' on Go For The Juggler Records). Producing positive industry reaction, it was followed by the *Build A Wall Around Your Dreams* EP and a debut long playing set.
Album: As PLZ: *Parables And Linguistic Zlang, Volume One* (Go For The Juggler 1993).

DJ Premier

The musical foundation of Gang Starr, DJ Premier (b. Chris Martin, Brooklyn, New York, USA) has also become one of hip hop's most respected producers and remixers in his own right. As a child his interest in music was demonstrated by the fact that he collected records from the age of four. Unlike many of the original producers, Premier learned his craft through technology and experimentation rather than the manual dexterity ethos of scratching ('I believe that sampling is an art form if you don't abuse it'). He recorded his first demos with Boston rapper MC Topski, and after Gang Starr's success there was no stopping him. Those artists who have benefited from the Premier production tradition include Jeru The Damaja, Nas, KRS-1, Branford Marsalis, Da Youngstas, Neneh Cherry, Heavy D, Subsonic 2, Cookie Crew, K-Solo and Lady Of Rage. His remix roster includes Shyheim, Boss, Loose Ends, MC Solaar, Fat Joe and MOP.

DJ Quik

b. David Blake, 18 January 1970, Compton, California, USA. Artist whose deification of his hometown, where he had grown up the youngest of ten children, pervaded both his first two albums ('Born And Raised In Compton' on his debut, and minor hit single 'Jus Lyke Compton' on the follow-up set). At the age of 12 he began to learn the art of DJing, but it wasn't until NWA exploded on the West Coast that he actually considered these skills might provide a career. He began recording cassettes, one of which found its way into the hands of Profile A&R man Dave Moss, head of their newly opened Los Angeles office. His debut set saw comparisons to Prince, though in mode of operation rather than musical terms: Quik writing, rapping, producing and arranging the set in its entirety. Rather than repeating the gangsta stance of his near-neighbours NWA (though he claimed to be a former member of the Bloods gang), Quik confirmed that 'There's a fun side to Compton, too', reflecting this in songs about sex (the rather too obvious 'Sweet Black Pussy' - I'm like Noah's Ark, My bitches come in pairs'), alcohol ('8 Ball') and marijuana ('Tha Bombudd'). His biggest hit, however, came with the Top 50-breaking 'Tonite'. He has also produced widely for Compton groups like 2nd II None and Penthouse.
Albums: *Quik Is The Name* (Profile 1991), *Way 2 Funky* (Profile 1992).

D-Nice

b. Derrick Jones, 19 June 1970, Bronx, New York, USA. An important member of the Boogie Down Productions crew since its inception, Jones became the group's DJ and beatbox having befriended Scott La Rock. D-Nice finally stepped out into the solo spotlight with 1990's *Call Me D-Nice*. KRS-1 kept tabs on his old partner by adding his vocals to cuts like 'The TR-808 Is Coming', which boasted of his familiar 808-derived sound. However, D-Nice also struck out on his own groove, straying into more commercial musical territory, and sticking to the self-aggrandisement themes of old school rappers rather than KRS-1's more conscious-related themes. There were only two exceptions. 'Glory', which measured the role of the black man in the American Civil War, a theme touched on in the film of the same name. Or 'A

Few Dollars More', which painted a sympathetic portrait of the means justifying the ends in terms of inner city poverty. The album gave him two number 1 US rap singles with 'Crumbs On The Table' and the title-track, 'Call Me D-Nice'. For his second album he invited Too Short, KRS-1, Naughty By Nature and funk guitarist Jean-Paul Bourelly along for the party. Though he was branching out musically, 'Rhyming Skills' continued the path laid by 'The Tr-808 Is Coming', with its bass-heavy, stomping arrangement. There were also cuts like 'Get In Touch With Me' which, admirably, espoused the cause of women, though this contrasted with the 'bitch and ho baitin' 'Check Yourself'. Though he has found significant commercial reward after stepping out from behind the turntable, the more pleasing aspects of his solo work remain his funk-based deck skills.

Albums; *Call Me D-Nice* (Jive 1990), *To Tha Resuce* (Jive 1991).

D.O.C.

b. Tray Curry, c.1970, Texas, USA. D.O.C. was one of the world's most promising rappers, before his career was cut short by a freak automobile accident that crushed his throat and left him unable to rap. Nowadays he hangs with Dr Dre's Dogg Pound posse and contributed to the *Chronic* set. On his debut album future Dre protégé Michelle'le was heard for the first time, alongside former NWA personnel Eazy-E, Ice Cube and MC Ren. There was a fluidity of rhythmic expression apparent on the disc which could have predicted the runaway success of subsequent Dre protégé, Snoop Doggy Dogg. It also included D.O.C.'s killer rap, 'Portrait Of A Masterpiece', which would grace any collection of Rap's greatest hits. Recent reports suggest that D.O.C. may be able to take the mic again with the aid of vocal surgery.

Album: *No One Can Do It Better* (Ruthless 1988).

Doctor Ice

b. c.1965, USA. Rapper thus named because he wanted to belong to the medical profession while at school, eventually declining such a career because 'it meant too many more years to go

through'. Ice was formerly a member of U.T.F.O., with whom he remained for five years, and before that Whodini, as a live dancer (one of the first such occurences). Striking out solo he enlisted the aid of Full Force member Brain 'B-Fine' Lou to write new material. The record was completed within one month. Ice toured to support it, appearing in white coat and with a medical team as part of the 'theme'. His two dancers were presented as 'patients', and his DJ 'the surgeon'. Other songs traced different 'concepts' but were similarly narrative: in the single excerpt, 'Sue Me', Ice is depicted in the accompanying video driving a white Porsche until his alter ego, Doctor Dread, crashes into him in a taxi, with riotous court scenes and accusation and counter-accusation following. 'Love Jones' featured contributions from Full Force and Cheryl 'Pepsi' Riley (Pepsi & Shirley), while the album closed with 'True Confessions', which featured a cameo from Lisa Lisa and Blair Underwood of *L.A. Law* fame, on a song concerning an unhappy married couple and their interceding lawyer. Renaming himself simply Doc Ice, he switched to *Ichiban* to set up his own Selph Records, which housed his *Rely On Selph* set. In the intervening years, rather than hanging up his stethascope as many had assumed, he had developed a career in acting and choreography, working on several high profile commercials and the feature film, *Don't Let Your Meat Loaf*.

Album: *The Mic Stalker* (Jive 1989), *Rely On Selph* (Selph/Ichiban 1993).

Dodge City Productions

London based duo who filter jazz and rap into a cohesive music, usually fronted by the voice of Ghida De Palma. Principal members Dodge (b. Roger Drakes) and I.G. also employ guest musicians such as the Young Disciples and jazzmen Ronnie Jordan and Steve Williamson, as and when the need arises, alongside rappers like MC Bello (Of Brothers Like Outlaw/KLF fame) and MCM. Dodge and I.G. have also remixed for Gang Starr, Digital Underground and Naughty By Nature. Singles like 'Unleash Your Love' have led to them being viewed as the new Soul II Soul in some corners, particularly in the way in which they

Doctor Ice

operate as a collective, with live shows usually featuring no less than eight people on stage at any given time.

Album: *Steppin' Up And Down* (4th & Broadway 1993).

Dog, Tim

b. Timothy Blair, 1 January 1967, Bronx, New York, USA. A dropout from St John's University in Queens, Dog's 'Fuck Compton' shot was one of the most notorious releases in rap's chequered history. Yet this anti-NWA tirade (at one point he sings 'Shut up bitch, You can't sing' while having intercourse with Eazy-E's 'girlfriend') was an undeniably forceful epithet, for all its wanton tribalism (legend has it that it inspired death threats from the West Coast). Dog was also a guest member of Ultramagnetic MCs for a period, appearing on their 'Chorus Line' anthem. In 1994 Dog made a surprise signing to Phonogram's Talkin' Loud label, home of the likes of Incognito and Galliano. He has since recorded a song, 'Bitch Wid A Perm', dedicated to Snoop Doggy Dogg, which is as yet unreleased.

Album: *Penicillin On Wax* (Ruffhouse 1991), *Do Or Die* (Ruffhouse/Columbia 1993).

Domino

b. c.1972, St. Louis, Misouri, USA. From the new school of rappers hailing from Long Beach, California, Domino typifies the area's preoccupation with cool, languid, almost sexual delivery. His hybrid accent is accounted for by the fact that he spent his first seven years in St. Louis. He had begun singing professionally in night clubs like Marla Gibbs' Crossroads and Sir Alex in Compton before he embarked on a rap style. Just as contemporaries like Snoop Doggy Dogg spice their rhymes with outbursts of actual singing, Domino repeats the feat, with slightly less contentious lyrics, to an arguably greater degree of success. In fact Domino had been Snoop's 'homie' at Junior High. After a childhood spent listening to soul and funk standards from the Stylistics and Funkadelic, he caught the rap bug and began writing words for himself and Snoop. According to Domino, Snoop couldn't resist the temptation to

'go gangsta' when it was offered to him on a plate by Dr Dre, and the duo split. Domino's perseverence with a more cognitive style was eventually rewarded. After several years of trying to get the major labels to listen, he signed with the small independent, Outburst. 'Getto Jam' underlined his appeal: these were still tough talking rap words, but sauntered through in an easy, inviting fashion. The buzz created by the track saw him and Outburst signed up for distribution by Def Jam. Samples from Kool And The Gang sat side by side with lines like: 'Everybody loves them dead presidents' on his debut album. This was combined with a more realistic overview of Domino's place in the scheme of things, with rhymes discussing his desire for sexual gratification ('Ass For Days') contrasting with morally tinged attitudes to safe sex ('Raincoat'), from which he even launched a condom range of the same name. Similarly, rather than the glorification of the drive-by shooting so evident in the work of others, there is a matter of fact discourse instead on the hassles of getting paid ('Money Is Everything'). Such platitudes saw him discussed in one magazine as 'a soft spoken businessman who will make an excellent bank manager when he gets sick of making records'. His own view: 'There's so much going on in the 'hood apart from guns and murder'. However, he did face criticism on his first British outing when misguided punters paid £10 to hear him perform three songs at a PA, when they had expected a full gig. Not to be confused with the production specialist Domino of Del Tha Funkee Homosapien's Hieroglyphics crew fame.

Album: *Domino* (Outburst 1994).

Doug E. Fresh

b. Douglas E. Davis, St Thomas, Virgin Islands, though he grew up in the Bronx and Harlem districts of New York. Self-proclaimed as 'The Original Human Beatbox', ie being able to imitate the sound of a rhythm machine, Fresh broke through in 1985 with the release of one of rap's classic cuts, 'The Show'. Joined by partner MC Ricky D (aka Slick Rick), the single matched rhymes with a bizarre array of human sound effects, courtesy of Fresh. It marked a notable

departure in rap's development, and was so distinctive it began a small flurry of similarly inclined rappers, as well as Salt 'n' Pepa's answer record, 'Showstopper'. Despite its impact, it was a song that was hardly representative of Fresh fare: far too much of his recorded material is workmanlike and soundalike. A debut album included live contributions from Bernard Wright (synthesiser) and Jimmy Owens (trumpet), as well as a dubious anti-abortion cut. The follow-up saw him allied to Public Enemy's Bomb Squad production team. To give him his due Fresh was very nearly rap's first superstar, but rather than capitalise on 'The Show', he would end up in court trying to sue Reality Records for non-payment of royalties on the song. He was also the first genuine rapper to appear at Jamaica's Reggae Sunsplash festival, stopping in the West Indies long enough to record alongside Papa San and Cocoa Tea. He made something of a comeback at the end of 1993 with the release of party record 'I-Right (Alright)', which saw him reunited with Slick Rick (recently returned from a period of incarceration), signing to Gee Street Records. Fresh has also enjoyed the distinction of seeing a 'Doug E. Fresh' switch added to the Oberheim Emulator, in order to provide samples of his human beat box talents.
Albums: *Oh, My God!* (Reality 1985), *The World's Greatest Entertainer* (Reality 1988).

Down South

Richmond, Virginia-based rappers Shawn J-Period and Soda Pop (ably assisted by DJ Myorr) combined a winning mix of jazz, funk, reggae, bluegrass and salsa on their debut recordings for Atlantic. The smooth, lolling rhythms proved intriguing but too insubstantial in their own right to convey the mix of reality/party themes, despite production expertise from the Beatnuts, T-Ray and others. However, the promotional single, 'Southern Comfort', with a guest vocal by label mates Jomanda, was strong. Rather than being dedicated to the alcoholic drink, it was addressed to their former locale, the trio having shipped over to New York. Down South had formed in 1990 when Pop and J-Period, who are first cousins, met Myorr at high school. Myorr had formerly worked

in a lowly position at Def Jam, and it was his connections that led to them signing with Atlantic. Album: *Lost In New York* (Big Beat/Atlantic 1994).

Dr Dre

b. Andre Young, South Central, Los Angeles, USA. Widely regarded, by *Rolling Stone* at least, as the chief architect of West Coast gangsta rap, Dre's musical career began as a DJ at Los Angeles dance club, Eve After Dark. There he would splice up a mix of new records with soul classics like Martha And The Vandellas. The club had a back room with a small four-track studio where he, together with future-NWA member Yella and Lonzo WIlliams, would record demos. The first of these was 'Surgery', a basic electro track with a chorus of 'Calling Dr Dre to surgery'. These sessions, and nights at Eve After Dark, taught him the turntable techniques he would later bring to NWA, after forming the World Class Wreckin' Cru at the age of 17. Although other former members such as Ice Cube had laid the ground for rap's immersion into the mainstream, the success of Dre's debut solo effort, *The Chronic*, confirmed its commercial breakthrough. It also signalled a change in tack by modern gangsta rappers. The music now took its cue from the funk of George Clinton and Funkadelic. Dre freely admits to the influence Clinton played on his life: 'Back in the 70s that's all people were doing: getting high, wearing Afros, bell-bottoms and listening to Parliament-Funkadelic. That's why I called my album *The Chronic* and based my music and the concepts like I did: because his shit was a big influence on my music. Very big'. To this end he created a studio band for the sessions, which included the R&B talents of Tony Green (bass) and Ricky Rouse (guitar). While Dre's lyrics were just as forceful as those that had graced NWA, there was also a shift in subject matter. *The Chronic* referred heavily to the recreational use of marijuana, taking its name from a particularly virulent, and popular, brand. Together with the efforts of Cypress Hill, cannabis was now the drug of choice for the gangsta rapper, with crack cocaine much discussed but rarely endorsed. *The Chronic* would go on to spend eight months in the Billboard Top 10. At least as important was Dre's growing reputation as a producer. His work with Eazy E, D.O.C., Above The Law and, most importantly, Snoop Doggy Dogg, broke new ground. Snoop had already rapped with Dre on the hit singles, 'Deep Cover' and 'Nuthin' But A 'G' Thang'. However, the *Doggy Style* opus would break box office records, bringing gangsta rap to the top of the album charts. Many sustained the belief that Dre was the driving force behind its success, the producer himself acknowledging: 'I can take a three year old and make a hit record with him'. At the same time he was dismissive of his own, pioneering efforts for NWA, particularly the epoch-making *Straight Outta Compton*: 'To this day I can't stand that album, I threw that thing together in six weeks so we could have something to sell out of the trunk'. During his involvement with the NWA posse he became the house producer for Eazy-E's Ruthless Records. Seven out of eight albums he produced for the label between 1983 and 1991 went platinum, but he broke from Ruthless over what he alleged was under-payment. Dre's on-record sneers at Eazy-E began shortly afterwards, including *The Chronic*'s 'Dre Day', a putdown which Eazy-E would countermand for his reply, 'Muthaphukkin' Gs'. Like many of rap's leading lights, Dre never strayed far from controversy, even after he bought into the comfort of a luxury home in San Fernando Valley. As if to reinstate himself as a 'true gangsta', Dre waged a war of attrition with authority. TV host Dee Barnes filed a multi-million dollar lawsuit against him for allegedly throwing her against the wall of a Hollywood nightclub in 1991. He was also convicted of breaking the jaw of a record producer (he was sentenced to house arrest and was fitted with a tracking device), and was detained by mounted police after a fracas in a New Orleans hotel lobby. Eazy-E sued him, while Dre complained bitterly about restraint of trade and monies owed, cursed Ruthless General Manager Jerry Heller, and finally managed to find a deal with Jimmy Iovine at Interscope, who let him set up his own label, Death Row. Dre has also produced an album for one of his many girlfriends, Michel'le, while in 1993 his younger half-brother, Warren G., signed a solo deal with Def Jam. His hot production skills clearly outshine his limited rapping ability, which he himself has little confidence in.

Album: *The Chronic* (Death Row 1993).

Dr Jeckyll And Mr Hyde

Consisting of Bronx duo Andre Harrell (Jeckyll; b. c.1959) and Alonzo Brown (Hyde), alongside DJ Scratch On Galaxy (b. George Llado), Dr Jeckyll and Mr Hyde enjoyed a steady stream of success in the early 80s. Their best remembered song, 'Genius Rap', constructed over the Tom Tom Club's 'Genius Of Love', sold over 150,000 records for Profile in 1981. Previously Brown had recorded the label's second release, and first rap record, as Lonnie Love ('Young Ladies'). 'AM:PM', backed by the Kurtis Blow-produced 'Fast Life', also earned the duo healthy chart placings. However, when their debut album bombed both elected to concentrate on non-performing careers. Harrell established Uptown, scoring huge success with Heavy D as well as the New Jack Swing prime movers, notably Teddy Riley's creations. Brown would work in executive posts at Cold Chillin' and Warner Brothers before heading up A&R for A&M. The duo still remain good friends and suggest a reuinion from time to time, though nothing more tangible than their joint sponsorship of the Groove B. Chill act has yet to surface.

Album: *The Champagne Of Rap* (Profile 1986).

Dream Warriors

A key part of the surprisingly active Canadian rap scene, West Indian duo King Lou (b. Louis Robinson, Jamaica, West Indies) and Capital Q (b. Frank Lennon Alert, 10 August c.1969, Port Of Spain, Trinidad, West Indies - so named because his father was a John Lennon fan) had to come to the UK to get a record deal with 4th & Broadway. Previously they had released a single, 'Let Your Backbone Slide', on a New York independent. Their blend of hip hop superstructure with jazz tempo arrived via arch lyrics, overflowing with obscure mystic imagery, from the pen of King Lou. The sound was big and loose, often punctuated by samples from television themes and psychedelic and

African chants. They scored almost immediately with 'Wash Your Face In My Sink', and the success continued with 'My Definition Of A Boombastic Jazz Style', derived from a Quincy Jones television theme tune. They also charted when moving in to reggae with 'Ludi' in 1991 (Ludi is a West Indian board game), and worked with Jazz legend Slim Gaillard shortly before his death the same year.

Albums: *And Now The Legacy Begins* (4th & Broadway 1991), *Subliminal Simulation* (EMI 1994).

DRS

Their initials an acronym for 'Dirty Rotten Scoundrels' (in itself not a million miles away from the moniker adopted by thrash band DRI - Dirty Rotten Imbeciles), DRS are, predictably, a gangsta rap quintet. However, when Pic, Blunt, Endo, Deuce Deuce and Jail Bait finish with the hardnosed rhymes they offer a surprising, and by no means unwelcome, line in close harmony a capella. Their early inroads into the R&B charts were credited largely to this; it was something of a novelty to hear such down-and-dirty reality tales sung rather than spat out. Based in Los Angeles, their debut album took its title from the preferred burial mode of their local gangster homeboys. The production company associated with the album, Roll Wit It Entertainment, boasted Hammer as a silent partner.

Album: *Gangsta Lean* (Capitol 1993).

Duke Bootee

b. Edward Fletcher. Bootee was formerly a New Jersey schoolteacher in Newark until the East Coast rap bug hit. As part of the Sugarhill house band/retinue, he wrote the chorus and several sections of 'The Message'. He also contributed to 'Message II', 'New York, New York' and sundry other label hits. His debut solo album comprised a rap side and a song side, with the former seeing further assistance from old Sugarhill friends. Though the song side was disappointing, he proved himself a talented rapper and maintained his reputation as an accomplished lyricist on the rest of the album.

Album: *Bust Me Out* (Mercury 1984).

Dust Brothers

Rap remix/production crew, who comprise Matt Dike of Delicious Vinyl fame, alongside radio DJs John Simpson and John King. In addition to fostering the career of Delicious Vinyl's big acts (Tone Loc, Young MC etc.), they have also afforded Mellow Man Ace and the Beastie Boys their skills and expertise. Not to be confused with the UK remix team of the same name (who, confusingly enough, are big fans of the Beastie Boys).

E

Eazy E

b. Eric Wright, 7 September 1973, Compton, California, USA. There are those critics who do not take well to Eazy-E's 'whine', but his debut kept up NWA's momentum by managing to offend just about every imaginable faction, right or left. Attending a fund-raising dinner for the Republican party and having lunch with police officer Tim Coon, one of the LAPD's finest charged with the beating of Rodney King, hardly helped re-establish his hardcore credentials. His work as part of NWA, and as head of Ruthless Records, had already made him a household name. However, solo his raps lacked penetration, even if the musical backdrop was just as intense as that which distinguished NWA. His debut solo album contained a clean and dirty side. The first was accomplished with very little merit, cuts like 'We Want Eazy' being utterly pointless. The 'street' side, however, offered something much nastier. Lyrics like 'I might be a woman-beater, But I'm not a pussy eater' set the tone, a lame rewrite of Yellowman's 'Nobody Move' failing to pull his head above water. His ongoing rivalry against former NWA member Dr Dre has provided much of his lyrical subject matter, including his 1994 single, 'Real Muhaphukkin' G's', which was essentially a re-write of Dre's 'Dre Day'. Eazy-E has subsequently moved on to production for artists like Tairrie B and Blood Of Abraham, which is just as well if his debut offering is any true indication of his rapping talents.

Album: *Eazy-Duz-It* (Ruthless/Priority 1988), *It's On (Dr. Dre 187UM) Killa* (Ruthless/Relativity 1994).

Ed.Og & Da Bulldogs

Boston, Massachusetts-based hip hop crew who debuted with the singles 'Be A Father To Your Child' and 'I Got To Have It'. The latter, with its engaging horn lick, was quickly pilfered as a sample by many other artists, becoming the number 1 hit in Billboard's Hot Rap chart. 'Be A Father To Your Child' was also widely revered for its strong moral sentiments. DJ Cruz and Ed. Og (b. Edward Anderson, Roxbury, Massachusetts, USA) are the main cogs in Da Bulldogs, who followed up the singles by cutting a widely regarded debut album. Samples from the set have been repeatedly recycled by other hip hop artists, notably Heavy D. Anderson's lyrics span tales of the 'hood and takes on his own sexual chemistry, as advertised on the promotional singles for their second long playing set, 'Skinny Dip (Got It Goin' On)' and 'Love Comes And Goes'. The latter was dedicated to those lost in street violence, who include Anderson's father. With production expertise thrown in by Joe 'Rhythm Nigga' Mansfield, Diamond D and the Awesome 2 (Special K and Teddy Tedd), it proved a certain East Coast hit. The Ed.Og acronym stands for Everyday Day, Other Girls, while the Bulldogs suffix represents Black United Leaders Living Directly On Groovin' Sounds.

Albums: *Life Of A Kid In The Ghetto* (Chemistry/Mercury 1991), *Roxbury 02119* (Chemistry/Mercury 1994).

Electro

Kickstarted by Afrika Bambaataa's 'Planet Rock', electro music harnassed the video game craze and attendant appetite for electronica and tied it to a computerised beat. For some time it became *the* sound of hip hop. In the wake of 'Planet Rock', rap's journeymen, new and old alike, hitched themselves to the bandwagon, as releases like 'Magic Wand' (Whodini), 'Play At Your Own Risk' (Planet Patrol) and 'Hip Hop Be Bop (Don't Stop)' (Man Parrish) testify. More conventional dance music, too, was heavily influenced by these new techniques, notably the Peach Boys and D-Train. It took Bambaataa, however, to equal 'Planet Rock', when he unveiled 'Looking For The Perfect Beat'. Although electro held sway on the rap scene for a surprising length of time (old school rap having run its course was unable to mount an effective challenge), it would be blown away quickly and irrovocably with the arrival of Run DMC and their more minimalist, robust approach.

Enjoy Records

One of the earliest labels to promote hip hop, Enjoy Records was owned by Bobby Robinson, whose background in R&B stretched back to 1946, when he ran the Happy House Records' store. He elected to pursue a career in musical production when he realised that all the A&R men were coming to him for advice on what was marketable, and that he could cut out the middle man. Enjoy was actually inaugurated in 1963 with King Curtis' 'Soul Twist'. When rap arrived his Harlem based operation was the first to record (though the second to approach) Grandmaster Flash And The Furious Five. They released the solitary 'Superrappin' before their contract was bought out by Joe Robinson (not a relation, though an old sparring partner from R&B days) of Sugarhill Records. Somewhat ironic, given that Bobby had decided to cash in on the latter's success, launching the label with the Funky Four Plus One More's 'Rappin' And Rocking The House'. As Flash recalled: 'Bobby didn't really have the push to get us out there. We got kinda angry with him and we went to the 'Hill'. Other notable Enjoy releases included the Treacherous 3/Spoonie Gee's agenda-setting 'The New Rap Language'.

'Bodyrock' and 'Heartbeat' followed in 1981, before the Treacherous 3 also elected to join Sugarhill. An epithet which might have been recorded in posterity on the Enjoy headstone. Robinson's son was a member of the Disco Three, who also recorded on the label.

EPMD

Erick 'E' Sermon (b. 25 November 1968, Brentwood, Long Island, New York, USA) and Parrish 'P' Smith (b. 13 May 1968, Brentwood, Long Island, New York, USA) are two rappers who did much to revitalise a flagging rap scene with an early outburst of controlled creative energy, *Unfinished Business*. Taking samples from rock sources such as Steve Miller, as well as underground dance music, they worked up a healthy, funk fuelled groove. Particularly effective among their early recordings was the rap manifesto on 45, 'So Whatcha Sayin'. Their early struggles to attract record company interest are best observed in the 1989 single, 'Please Listen To My Demo', which documents their malaise. By then, however, they had recorded their first two albums. *Strictly Business* was distinguished by an amusing idea for a new dance entitled 'The Steve Martin', while the goofball fun continued on *Unfinished Business*, which in many ways sounded just like that. Unrestrained anarchy in the studio appeared to be the order of the day, with improvised lines, interruptions and jokey singing forming the basis of proceedings. It included contributions from K-Solo (Kevin Madison), who had previously worked in a pre-EPMD band with Smith, and would go on to record a solo album under his tutelage They moved to Def Jam in time for their third album, a much more accomplished affair (at least musically) with tighter production and harder beats. Despite the prevailing ethos, they never felt the need to provide a direct political agenda like many rap groups, seeing music as a source of personal self-advancement. This is openly demonstrated by the titles of their LPs, and the fact that their initials stand for Erick And Parrish Making Dollars. However, the manner in which EPMD tried to accommodate new lyrical concerns was less than satisfactory. Their raps continued to chastise their peers as 'sucker MC's', which was by now little more than cliche, while tracks like 'Gold-Digger' lashed out at the type of women who don't sign pre-nuptial agreements just so they can walk away with a poor man's loot. Ironically, one of the better cuts on *Business As Usual* was 'Rampage', a collaboration with LL Cool J, whose artistic fortunes had witnessed a similar decline in recent years. *Business Never Personal* simply continued in remorseless EPMD style. The duo split in 1993, Sermon being the first to embark on a solo career with 'Stay Real' and the *No Pressure* album. The latter's title reflected, wryly, on the fact that most considered Smith to be the 'talent' of the band. Yet *No Pressure* was an excellent collection which did much to lay that myth to rest.

Albums: *Strictly Business* (Fresh/Priority 1988), *Unfinished Business* (Fresh/Priority 1989), *Business As Usual* (Def Jam 1991), *Business Never Personal* (Def Jam 1992). Solo: Erick Sermon: *No Pressure* (RAL 1993). Parrish Smith: *Shade Business* (PMD/RCA 1994).

Eric B and Rakim

A Queens, New York rap duo consisting of Eric Barrier (b. Elmhurst, New York, USA) and William 'Rakim' Griffin (b. William Griffin Jr, Long Island, New York, USA) who use additional musicians such as Sefton the Terminator and Chad Jackson as required; Rakim is the lyricist, Eric B the DJ. Or, as Rakim himself put it in 'I Ain't No Joke': 'I hold the microphone like a grudge, Eric B hold the record so the needle don't budge'. They met in 1985 when Eric was working for the New York radio station WBLS and was looking for NY's top MC. They started working together before emerging with the demo, 'Eric B Is President'. Released as a 45 on an obscure Harlem independent Zakia Records in the summer of 1986, it eventually led to a deal with 4th and Broadway. Their long playing debut was preceded by a standout single of the same name, 'Paid In Full', which inspired over 30 remixes. When the album arrived it caused immediate waves. Representatives of James Brown and Bobby Byrd took legal action over the sampling of those artists' works. Conversely, they helped to galvanise

Brown's career as a legion of rap imitators cut in on his back catalogue in search of samples. They also originated the similarly coveted 'Pump Up The Volume' sample. As well as Eric B. putting the funk back into rap music, Rakim was responsible for introducing a more relaxed, intuitive delivery which was distinctly separate from the machismo of Run DMC and LL Cool J. That influence can still be detected in present day records by big name West Coast stars. The duo hit the UK charts in 1987 with 'Paid In Full (The Coldcut Remix)', though the duo themselves hated the version. Later hits included 'Move The Crowd', 'I Know You Got Soul', 'Follow The Leader' and 'The Microphone'. A succession of label moves (Chrysalis to Island to MCA) seem to have diminished their probable impact, though the band themselves have never gone out of their way to cross over into the mainstream. Instead, each of their albums to date have offered a significant musical development on the last, Rakim's raps growing in maturity without sacrificing impact. The split came in the early 90s, with Rakim staying with MCA to deliver solo material like 'Heat It Up', produced by new co-conspirator Madness 4 Real, included on the soundtrack to Mario van Peebles vehicle, *Gunmen*.

Albums: *Paid In Full* (4th & Broadway 1987), *Follow The Leader* (MCA-Uni 1988), *Let The Rhythm Hit 'Em* (MCA 1990), *Don't Sweat The Technique* (MCA 1992).

Everlast

b. Eric Schrody, USA. A former graffiti artist and protégé of Ice-T, Everlast was one of the few white members in the Rhyme Syndicate posse. Otherwise everything on his debut album was as it might have been expected to be: hardcore visions of violence, extensive use of expletives, and puerile, anatomical descriptions of women. There was, at least, room for an anti-PMRC rap, and samples drawn from the diverse tangents of Sly And Robbie, Sly Stone and even Bannanarama and the Knack. Hampered by his sometime description as 'the Caucasian Sensation', Everlast was introduced to hip hop while at summer camp, a friend there teaching him both graffiti and

elementary street rap. Everlast laid down a couple of tracks with the help of his friend's DJ partner, Bahal, and Ice-T liked what he heard. He released his first single as far back as 1988. Everlast toured the UK supporting Ice-T, but seems to have abandoned his solo career since joining House Of Pain.

Albums: *Forever Everlasting* (Warners 1990).

Express

b. Simon Francis, c.1967, England. A bright new hip-hop talent from Northampton, Express has been rapping since 1981. However, his musical path took a different slant when he joined a local industrial dance unit. Eventually, following a major label debacle, he and his partner Stuart left London to regroup. Together they elected to keep their music independent, setting up their own imprint, Expressive Records, to this end. In October 1993 Express' first record, the *Hit The Hook Heavy* EP, arrived. It quickly attained cult popularity, not least for its references to TV fare like *Inspector Morse* and the absence of Chris Waddle from the England World Cup football squad. Even Ian Paisley got a namecheck, as the *New Musical Express* pronounced its verdict with a Single Of The Week award. Other songs also contained references to black Newcastle footballing sensation Andy Cole. However, if anyone had marked Express as a novelty act he brought about a quick rethink with 1994's follow-up, 'Gone To The Dogs'. This, as the title suggested, was a young black man's reflection on the election of a British National Party politician to the Isle Of Dogs (London) council.

F

F9s

London duo, named after the highest function button available to them on their computer keyboard. The F9s are technocrats with samplers, as might be suggested by the name, but Uncle B. Nice is also a confident rapper, who won the DMC UK rap championships in 1989. His messages are backed by DJ Mr Islam, aka Rizla. They began their career with a three-track EP in May 1991, after which they earned a reputation as powerful advocates of forward thinking Christianity. This led them into conflict with some of the advocates of the Nation Of Islam, notably Professor Griff. They were similarly vocal about British hip hop crews who didn't use their platform to put forward a positive message, criticising many of their peers: 'They're not gathering any white fans. They talk about racism, but they only talk to black people. Why do you need to be taught racism if you are already black'.
Album: *The F-9's Are A Hip Hop Band* (Kold Sweat 1992).

Fab 5 Freddy

b. Frederick Braithwaite, Brooklyn, New York, USA. Freddy grew up with lawyer parents, his father managing jazz musicians like Max Roach and Clifford Brown. Nowadays best known for his hosting of *Yo! MTV Raps*, Freddy began life as a rap promoter and grafitti artist, abandoning his college courses in 'logic' for the pleasures of decorating I.R.T. trains in pastiches of Andy Warhol's Campbell's soup fetish. He was responsible for the establishment of the Roxy, a former roller-skate rink turned hip hop venue, alongside English-born Cool Lady Blue (he got Afrika Bambaataa his first gig there). After being namechecked by Blondie's 1981 hit 'Rapture', he was invited to make a rap record for the French Celluloid imprint, who had commissioned Bill Laswell and Michael Beinhorn to provide them

with five 'rap' singles. 'Une Sale Histoire' duly emerged, while female rapper Beside, from California, but also rapping in French, took b-side duties. Freddy also appeared on the 'New York City Rap Tour In Europe' line-up. This consisted of breakdancers, artists and rappers, a club of which Freddy has never really counted himself a member: 'I thought it was a cool fuckin' scam. The paintings wasn't moving to fast. It wasn't like I was fighting to launch a career as a rapper. I was just tyrin' to get the rent paid'. Freddy has gone on to a successful career as video director to KRS-1, Snoop Doggy Dog etc.

Fat Boys

From the Bronx, New York, the Fat Boys were originally known as the Disco 3, before deciding to trade in the appellation in exchange for something more gimmicky. The bulk of their material dealt with just that, emphasising their size, and did little to avert the widely held perception of them as a novelty act. The trio consisted of Darren 'The Human Beatbox/Buff Love' Robinson, Mark 'Prince Markie Dee' Morales, and Damon 'Kool Rockski' Wimbley. They were discovered by Charlie Stetler (later manager of MTV's Dr Dre and Ed Lover), whose interest was aroused by Robinson's amazing talent for rhythmic improvisation, effectively using his face as an instrument. It was Stetler that suggested they take the name-change, after winning a nationwide talent contest at Radio City Music Hall in 1983. Legend has it that this was prompted during an early tour European tour when Stetler was presented with a bill of $350 for 'extra breakfasts'. Their initial run of records were produced by Kurtis Blow, and largely discussed the size of the group's appetites. All their LPs for Sutra offered a consistent diet (a phrase not otherwise within the Fat Boy lexicon) of rock, reggae and hip hop textures, with able if uninspiring raps. Their fortunes improved significantly once they signed up with Polydor, however. *Crushin'* is probably their best album, crammed with party anecdotes that stand up to repeated listening better than most of their material. It yielded a major hit with the Beach Boys on 'Wipe Out' in 1987. One year and

one album later they scored with another collaboration, this time with Chubby Checker on 'The Twist (Yo' Twist)'. It peaked at number 2 in the UK chart, the highest position at the time for a rap record. In truth the Fat Boys had become more pop than hip hop, though the process of revamping rock 'n' roll chestnuts had begun as far back as 1984 with 'Jailhouse Rock'. Also contained on *Coming Back Hard Again* was a strange version of 'Louie Louie' and 'Are You Ready For Freddy', used as the theme song for one of the *Nightmare On Elm Street* films. They also starred in another movie, *Disorderlies*, after appearing with Checker as part of Nelson Mandela's 70th Birthday Party at Wembley Stadium in June 1988 (they had previously been the only rap participants at Live Aid). The decade closed with the release of *On And On*. It proved a hugely disappointing set, overshadowed by its 'concept' of being a 'rappera', and offering a lukewarm adaptation of gangsta concerns. News broke in the 90s of a $6 million law suit filed against their former record company, while Robinson was put on trial in Pennsylvania for 'sexual abuse of a minor'. Prince Markie Dee went on to a solo career, recording an album as Prince Markie Dee & The Soul Convention. He also produced and wrote for Mary J. Bilge, Christopher Williams, Father, El DeBarge, Trey Lorenz and others. The Fat Boys true legacy remains firmly in the era of rap party records, Swatch television ads and cameo appearances on *Miami Vice*.
Albums: *Fat Boys* (Sutra 1984), *The Fat Boys Are Back!* (Sutra 1985), *Big & Beautiful* (Sutra 1986), *Cruisin'* (Tin Pan Apple/Polydor 1987), *Coming Back Hard Again* (Tin Pan Apple/Polydor 1988), *On And On* (Tin Pan Apple/Mercury 1989). Compilations: *The Best Part Of The Fat Boys* (Sutra 1987), *Krush On You* (Blatant 1988). Prince Markie Dee solo: *Free* (Columbia 1992).

Fatback Band

There are many, including genuine authorities such as Afrika Bambaataa, who state that 'King Tim III (Personality Jock)' by Fatback, released on Spring Records in 1979, is the first true hip hop record. 'King Tim' was actually the b-side to 'You're My Candy Sweet', before radio programmers and listeners made it the more popular selection. The rap was delivered by the band's master of ceremonies/warm up act, the eponymous King Tim III. After appearing solo on 'Charley Says! (Roller Boogie Baby)', backed by the Fatback Band, he would disappear into the mists of hip hop mythology. Archivists may like to note that 'King Tim III' is included on the *Fatback XII* album. Elsewhere, Fatback remained a predominantly R&B-based funk band. They were originally formed by Johnny King (guitar), Earl Shelton (saxophone), George Williams (trumpet), George Adam (flute), Johnny Flippin (bass) and Bill Curtis (drums). Later members included Saunders McCrae (keyboards) and Richard Cromwell (trombone).
Albums: As Fatback Band: *Raising Hell* (Event 1976), *Night Fever* (Spring 1976). As Fatback: *Fired Up 'N' Kickin'* (Spring 1978), *Fatback XII* (Spring 1979), *Hot Box* (Spring 1980), *14 Karat* (Spring 1980), *Tasty Jam* (Spring 1981), *Gigolo* (Spring 1982).

Father

b. Timothy Brown, New York, USA. Father's debut album included the Top 20 US hit, 'I'll Do 4 U', and a powerful scene-setter between Father and Lady Kazan. On his return in 1994 for a belated third album, *Sex Is Law*, he dropped the MC suffix he had previously employed. It tied in with a switch in image too, from lovers rock hip hop to down and dirty gangsta pimp. Gimmicky raps like '69' were the order of the day, as Father perved his way through a succession of saucy rhymes. There was a nod to the New Jack Swing movement with cuts produced by Teddy Riley and Pete Rock, who added an En Vogue sample to 'R&B Swinger'. Other samples included the Jackson Five's 'I Want You Back'. The sexual lyrics were given a brief respite on his duet with Little Shawn, 'For The Brothers Who Ain't Here', a touching commemoration of loss in the ghetto.
Albums: As Father MC: *Father's Day* (Uptown 1989), *Close To You* (Uptown 1992). As Father: *Sex Is Law* (Uptown 1994).

Fearless Four

One of the earliest and more satorially-challenged of rap's formations, the Fearless Four numbered MC's the Great Peso (b. Mitchell Grant, 5 December 1959), the Devastating Tito (b. Tito Dones, 27 May 1964), Mighty Mike C (b. Michael Kevin Clee, 10 March 1963) and DLB the Microphone Wizard (b. 25 April 1965), aided by a complement of two DJs; Master O.C. (b. Oscar Rodriguez Jr, 22 September 1962, Manhattan, New York, USA) and Krazy Eddie (b. Eddie Thompson, 25 July 1960). The band was originally started by Tito and Master O.C., when they were known as the Houserockers Crew, selling their tapes across Manhattan and the Bronx. They gradually picked up members, first Mike Ski, then the Great Peso and Troy B, who arrived fresh from the Disco Four. He was subsequently replaced by DLB, before Mike Ski also departed for marriage and a 9 to 5 job. The line-up was completed by Mighty Mike C and Krazy Eddie, a second DJ who took his name from a local record store renowned for its zany commercials. They first struck for the Enjoy label in 1981 with 'Rockin' It' which, hot on the trail of Afrika Bambaataa's 'Planet Rock' success, used Kraftwerk's 'The Mean Machine' as well as excerpts from Spielberg film *The Poltergeist*. The follow-up was 'It's Magic', based on a Cat Stevens' song, before moving to Elektra. Their career there began with 'Just Rock', built on Gary Numan's 'Cars', and remixed by Larry Levan. The band claimed it to be the first 'punk rap', but that failed to deny it flop status. 1983's 'Problems Of The World Today', produced by Kurtis Blow, was an improvement. Master O.C., meanwhile, would produce the Fantasy Three's 'Biters In The City'. The Fearless Four continued to plough a furrow into the mid-80s, but the hits had long since dried up.

Fesu

His Fesu moniker a corruption of his real name Yusef, this Greenspoint, Texas-based rapper kicked off his career with a singles on his own label, Air-Run-Boy, 'Salt N Da Game'. The follow-up, 'Streets Of Greenspoint' picked up a lot of local radio coverage, but it was with the lauded 'Blind, Cripple And Crazy' 45 that he really made headway. *The Source* magazine were particularly impressed, promoting him as a major new talent. Although born a Muslim, it was not until he encountered the teachings of Louis Farakhan that Fesu found a spiritual direction and became a member of the Nation Of Islam, a process recounted in the single. He would go on to record a 1994 duet with Bobby Womack entitled 'Going Round N' Circles'.

Flavor Flav

b. William Drayton, 16 March 1959, Roosevelt, Long Island, New York, USA. Flav needed no introduction to the public on the commencement of his solo career. The sharp banter of Public Enemy had been both heightened and lightened via his interjections as stool pigeon to Chuck D. However, his personal life had won him some degree of infamy too. In February 1991 he was arrested at his Long Island home, and charged with assault on his girlfriend and mother of his three children, Karen Ross. After pleading guilty to third degree assault he was sentenced to 30 days imprisonment and served with an exclusion order. Just as his debut solo album was announced in the press, he again caught the headlines when he was arrested in the Bronx after allegedly trying to shoot another man in a dispute over a woman. That album has yet to see a release.

Force MD's

Often neglected next to the adventures of Afrika Bambaataa or Grandmaster Flash, Staten Island's Force MD's were nevertheless a vital component in rap's development. They were originally titled the LDs, working as a street-corner act in the manner of the Jackson 5, with TCD, Stevie D and Trisco and Mercury holding the reigns. Alongside Planet Patrol, they were the first to instigate doo wop hip hop, before changing tack to largely soul-based harmonies. They employed formation steps alongside breakdance routines as visual inducement, adding impersonations of television theme tunes and popular stars of the day, often performing on the Staten Island ferry. They became Dr. Rock and the MCs when they were joined by a DJ of that title, introducing scratching into their nascent act (in his absence a DJ Shock would deputise). Their later career is best aired on their hit single, 'Tender Love', a US number 10-peaking Jimmy Jam/Terry Lewis ballad, but elsewhere there is little to suggest historical reassessment is overdue. The MD component of the name is short for Musical Diversity.

Albums: *Love Letters* (Tommy Boy 1984), *Chillin'* (Tommy Boy 1986), *Touch And Go* (Tommy Boy 1987), *Step To Me* (1990), *For Lovers And Others* (1992).

Freddie Foxxx

MC whose career has seen more highs and lows than most. By the age of 13 he had built his reputation in his local Westbury, Long Island area, as a talented freestyler. He recorded a debut album in 1989, produced by Eric B, which promptly sank without trace. He was left to lick his wounds as the hip hop populace forgot his name. However, a resurgence in his fortunes was kickstarted by collaborations with KRS-1 ('Ruff Ruff'), then Naughty By Nature ('Hot Potato'), before he was signed to Queen Latifah's Epic subsidiary Flavor Unit. It was his third record deal. His first release for his new home was 'So Tough'. This boasted his sharply observed lyrics about the ghetto, 'We went from African kings, to Martin Luther King, now they wanna make us all Rodney Kings'. He also produced videos which reminded would-be gangstas about the realities of prison life, and helped found Dream House, a Brooklyn charity which helps local youths out of the negative downward spiral of poverty and homelessness.

Albums: *Freddie Foxx Is Here* (1989), *Crazy Like A Foxx* (Flavor Unit/Epic 1994).

Freestyle Fellowship

From South Central Los Angeles, but definitely not of the gangsta rap persuasion. Freestyle Fellowship are named after their undoubtedly superior rhyming abilities and dextrous word play. Comparisons to De La Soul and the Dream Warriors frustrated them, but the impressive thing about the group, as revealed on singles like 'Hot Potato', with its samples from Dizzy Gillespie and Kool And The Gang, was the dizzy speed of their delivery and appetite for innovation. The group comprise Mikah Nine, Mtulazaji (Peace), Self Jupiter, Aceyalone and DJ Kiilu, who grew from the Los Angeles Good Life Cafe collective. Mikah Nine had formerly recorded with Carmet Carter and the Wailers. However, the most important music in the Freestyle Fellowship cocktail is undoubtedly jazz, whose experimental edge is reflected in their lyricism (which follows a distinctly non-linear formula).

Albums: *To Whom It May Concern* (Sun Music 1991), *Inner City Griots* (Island 1993).

Fugees

New York crew whose name is shortened from Refugees, due to two of the three rappers being expatriate Haitians. Their style is that of dry, cushioning beats, matched by the clever wordplay of rappers Wyclef 'Jef' Jean (b. Haiti), Lauryn Hill (b. USA) and Prakazrel 'Pras' Michel (b. Haiti). The sound is not exactly unfamiliar; and the title of their debut album, *Blunted On Reality*, seemed to suggest they were coming from a similar direction to Cypress Hill/Digable Planets. However, the group are all non-users, the title signifying instead their belief that they do not need to smoke the weed to induce a state of heightened perception and relaxation. Similarly, their lyrical concerns are somewhat different, as might be expected of a group where the majority of members also attended university courses. Some of their targets included America's perception of Haitians as 'Boat People' (Prakazrel intends to return to his native Haiti, using profits from his music to held build schools and decent roads on the island).and their own, mixed gender status. 'Our music is a paradoxical thing. We blend soft and hardcore elements into it'. Musically this includes rapping over acoustic guitars, as well as more upbeat numbers, both modes in which Fugees excell.

Album: *Blunted On Reality* (Ruffhouse/Sony 1994).

Full Force

Six-piece rap/R&B ensemble from Brooklyn, New York, comprising the three George brothers,

Brian 'B-Fine', Paul Anthony and 'Bowlegged' Lou, plus cousins 'Baby' Gerry Charles, Junior 'Shy Shy' Clark and Curt 'TT' Bedeau. In addition to their three hit albums (all placed in the lower reaches of the Billboard Top 200), the sextet also provided production for protégés Lisa Lisa & Cult Jam, as well as U.T.F.O., Cheryl 'Pepsi' Riley and even James Brown. Full-Force's debut album saw their anthropology rewarded with friends like Lisa Lisa, U.T.F.O., Howie Tee and the Real Roxanne dropping in. B-Fine would also help ex-U.T.F.O. man Doctor Ice write songs for his debut album. They also found time to appear in *Krush Groove*, *House Party 1 and 2*, and form their own independent label, Homegrown Records. The first signing to their new empire was rap group Scream. A more dubious honour was also being the only rap/hip hop group to ever be lent vocal assistance by Samantha Fox (on *Smoove*).

Albums: *Full Force* (Columbia 1985), *Full Force Get Busy 1 Time!* (Columbia 1986), *Guess Who's Comin' To The Crib?* (Columbia 1987), *Smoove* (Columbia 1989), *Don't Sleep* (Columbia 1994).

Funkdoobiest

One of the hardest working crews in hip hop, Funkdoobiest comprise Son Doobie, DJ Ralph M the Mexican and Tomahawk Funk (aka T-Bone). Hailing from Los Angeles, they are managed by Happy Walters, who also looks after Cypress Hill and House Of Pain, with whom they have frequently played live. Prior to their establishment as a band Ralph M had worked on the now defunct Los Angeles radio station KDAY, at only 13 years of age, going on to DJ for Kid Frost. Funkdoobiest's debut single was the incessant 'Bow Wow Wow', which instantly launched them into the hearts of a nation of B-boys. Typically, their debut album was a reinstatement of old school principles, as Son Doobie eulogised in interviews: 'I'm an old skool supremacist. I'm a hip hop inspector, I'm a fundamentalist, to me hip hop is a religion. You know it can't be trivialised'. The title-track of their second album was released as a single, and as well as a Little Richard sample featured a guest first verse from Cypress Hill's B-Real. Unfortunately it proved to be the best

segment on the single, which was in turn the best track on the album. Ralph M has gone on to produce tracks for both House Of Pain and Mellow Man Ace. Funkdoobiest are certainly not the most politically correct rappers. Many of their lyrics are vividly pro-pornography, Son Doobie's alter ego being the 'Porno King'. At least their commitment to rap's history is as staunch as their fondness for exposed flesh.

Album: *Which Doobie U B* (Immortal 1993), *Wopbabuloop* (Immortal 1993).

Funkmaster Flex

aka Stretch Armstrong. One of New York's most prominent modern hip hop DJs (with Hot 97), Funkmaster Flex has also turned his skills to production and remix work for other artists, as well as making his own recordings. He started out in rap as DJ for the band Deuces Wild, before picking up his first radio gigs for Chuck Chillout at Kiss FM in 1987. He went on to play the Manhattan club circuit until the end of the decade, having already served his apprenticeship on block parties in the early 80s. Together with his 'Flip Squad', which started as a partnership with Big Kap but expanded to include DJ Enuff, DJ Boodakhan, DJ Riz, Frankie Cutlass and Biz Markie, he has gone on to become a prominent remixer. His own recording career kicked off with 'Dope On Plastic', for Bobby Konders' label Massive B. It was followed by 'Six Million Ways To Die' and 'C'Mon Baby' for Nervous subsidiary Wreck Records.

Funky Four (Plus One More)

The Funky Four's background is an interesting one, with Lil' Rodney Cee having been part of the street-jivers the Magnificent Seven between 1977 and 1978. The Funky Four were founded when KK Rockwell and DJ Breakout, adding first Keith Keith and then female MC Sha Rock. Rahiem joined, then departed to take up an engagement with Grandmaster Flash. Keith Keith also left. With the addition of Lil' Rodney Cee, then Jazzy Jeff, the group became the Funky Four. None of the group were older than 17 when they signed with the Enjoy label, opening that imprint's account (in rap terms) with 'Rappin' And Rocking The House'. This utilised the Cheryl Lynn break, 'Gotta To Be Real', over which a 16-minute rap commentary was placed. The drums were programmed by Pumpkin, arguably rap's first production hero, and it was an impressive overall introduction. Shortly afterwards they switched to Sugarhill, adding the Plus or + One More suffix. In addition to this cast DJ Mark The 45 King would act as Breakout's 'record boy', locating and passing records up to the decks as his DJ requested them. They made their debut for Sugarhill with 'That's The Joint', a song arranged by jazz-funk organist Clifton 'Jiggs' Chase. Their performances at Bronx house parties included full-blown dance routines, a rare precursor to the vibrant live hip hop of Stetsasonic. After a clash album with the Cash Crew, their career petered out somewhat, though Jazzy Jeff would go on to a brief solo career with Jive. Lil' Rodney Cee and KK Rockwell would go on to be partners in fellow under-achievers, Double Trouble. At which time Cee would marry Angela 'Angie B' Brown of Sequence fame.

Funky Poets

Presenting one of the more positive images of young black men in the ghetto, the Funky Poets are a four-piece whose intelligent lyrical trickery is defiantly old school, yet whose outlook has been unquestionably informed by the Afrocentricity noises of the Jungle Brothers and De La Soul. The group is made up of brothers Paul and Ray Frazier and their cousins Christian Jordon and Gene Johnson. Together they broke through on the hit single, 'Born In The Ghetto', on which they recounted the urban tale of a young sister learning that she is pregnant at the age of 14. The narrative was turned round, making the situation a positive, with the central character emerging renewed, defiant and proud. 'We're just telling young black people that there is hope, despite the negative things they face everyday living in neighbourhoods that resemble war zones'. Their lyrics are sharply focused to this end, notably on the self-explanatory 'Message To A Funky Poet' poem, which contains couplets relaying the black inner-city experience in its many shades, from crack-dealing to bar-b-queues and fountains gushing from fire hydrants.
Album: *True To Life* (Epic 1993).

Fu-Schnickens

Brooklyn, New York rap trio who comprise Poc Fu (Prophet Overseeing Creativity), Chip Fu (Creative Harmony:Intertwine Perfection) and Moc (Manifest Culture) Fu. Not content with wearing ludicrous Oriental costumes, the band also claim to have descended on the world of rap via a mythical fireball. The Fu part of their names and the band's moniker indicates 'For Unity', while 'Schnickens' is a wholly invented term signifying 'coalition'. Raised in East Flatbush in Brooklyn, the trio were discovered at the Carwash club, a specialist showcase event. Soon after Phil Pabon took over their affairs as manager, and began to set up dates for the group all over New York. They finally earned their break with an appearance in Feburary 1991 at the 1st Annual Rap Conference, at Howard's University in Washington DC. An A&R representative from Jive saw and liked their performance, and asked them to submit a tape. They received a contract in return. Famed for their onstage humour and high-speed delivery (including perfectly executed backward raps), they opened their account for their new employers with the dancehall-flavoured 'Ring The Alarm!', the warmth and humour of which typified the contents of their well-received debut album.
Album: *Don't Take It Personal* (Jive 1992).

G

G., Warren

b. Warren Griffin III, c.1971, Long Beach, California, USA. Half-brother to Dr Dre, this sibling began to make his own presence felt in the rap scene of the mid-90s. He had already helped form Dre's Dogg Pound collective (with Nate Dogg and best friend Snoop Doggy Dogg). Having produced a track for MC Breed ('Gotta Get Mine'), and appeared on both *The Chronic* and *Doggystyle*, he also wrote, produced and guested on Mista Grimm's 'Indo Smoke' and 2Pac's 'Definition Of A Thug'. The latter appeared on the film *Poetic Justice*, the former on the US R&B number 1 soundtrack album, *Above The Rim*. Griffin's own cut, 'Regulate', was the keynote to that set. It also became his debut single, the first on Chris Lighty's new Violator imprint, built around a prominent sample of Michael McDonald's 'I Keep Forgettin''. Despite his musical pedigree and hardcore delivery, he continues to deflect descriptions of himself as a gangsta rapper.
Album: *Regulate... G Funk Era* (Violator/RAL 1994).

Gang Starr

Arguably hip hop's most literate, challenging act on both musical and lyrical fronts, comprising Guru Keith E (b. Keith Allam, Roxbury, Massachussets, USA; vocals and lyrics) and DJ Premier (b. Chris Martin, Brooklyn, New York, USA; music). Guru was born the son of a Boston municipal and superior court judge, but moved to Brooklyn following graduation with a degree in business administration from Atlanta's Morehouse College. He had previously worked as a counsellor in a maximum detention home in Boston, an experience which would inform many of his lyrics. Gang Starr was in existence before DJ Premier joined, originally also consisting of fellow rapper Damo D-Ski and DJ Wanna Be Down. Their early labours are recalled on cuts like 'The Lesson' and '

Bust A Move', both of which were produced by DJ Mark The 45 King. However, they were at that time still Boston based, and in the end opted to pursue more geographically convenient projects. Premier, meanwhile, had relocated to Texas to attend college, but left demos of his work with various labels before his departure. In Texas he put together the Inner City Posse, who finally saw their demo get some attention. Premier was offered a deal with Wild Pitch, but only on the condition he lost his original rapper. The label put him in touch with Guru instead, who had chanced upon one of Premier's demo tapes in their offices, and a marriage made in hip hop heaven was born. However, Premier had to return to college in Texas, and so the duo's liaison took place largely over the phone, and by sending each other tapes. The fruits of their labour were unveiled on a debut album, *No More Mr Nice Guy*, completed in ten days while Premier was on vacation. 'Manifest', taken from the album, picked up airplay on *Yo! MTV Raps*, and caught the attention of film director Spike Lee. In the process of completing his new film, *Mo Better Blues*, Lee was greatly impressed by album track 'Jazz Thing', and asked his musical director, Branford Marsalis, to track Gang Starr down. Marsalis urged the duo to cut a recording of Lotis Eli's poem about the history of jazz to a hip hop rhythm, for inclusion on the film's soundtrack. The song they eventually came up with would see release as 'Jazz Thing'. Not only one of rap's most crucial moments, 'Jazz Thing' also gave Gang Starr a manifesto for their subsequent career. Credited with popularising jazz-rap, they took the form to its logical conclusion with *Step In The Arena*, before retreating to hardcore pastures for *Daily Operation*. Both Guru and Premier have strived to be seen as individuals outside of the Gang Starr hallmark. A joint collaboration with the Dream Warriors on 'I've Lost My Ignorance' aside, each has increased their profile with solo projects. Premier has produced widely for KRS-One, Fu-Schnickens, Big Daddy Kane and Heavy D among many others, while Guru set up the winning Jazzamatazz situation. The latter comprised his distinctive rap style with the best of modern freeform jazz. An interesting departure considering that Premier has always used samples rather than live instruments, though since *Daily Operation* he has been forced to credit and clear them. Though such forays encouraged speculation that Gang Starr were about to split, the duo belied the critics with a storming return on *Hard To Earn*. Back to his freestyle, flowing best, it was the second outing for the posse of rappers that Guru had formed into the Gang Starr Foundation: Jeru The Damaja, Big Shug (who was a collaborator with Guru in his early days in Boston), Little Dap and Felachi The Nutcracker. Over four albums Gang Starr have proved themselves to be rap's most consistent, dynamic team.

Albums: *No More Mr Nice Guy* (Wild Pitch 1990), *Step In The Arena* (Chrysalis 1991), *Daily Operation* (Chrysalis 1992), *Hard To Earn* (Chrysalis 1994).

Gangsta Pat

b. Patrick Hall, Memphis, Tennessee, USA. Gangsta Pat is the son of Willie Hall, who had played with R&B greats like Isaac Hayes, and continues his family's musical traditions by playing all the instruments on his releases. He is also responsible for their writing, composition and production. He quickly rose to prominence with his debut album and single (the introductory 'I Am The Gangsta'). Both became hot items in the south west of America, while a second set spawned hit singles in 'Gangsta Boogie' and 'Stay Away From Cali'. The video for the former was particularly well received, capitalised on the then vogueish hip hop dance craze of the same name. Transferring to Wrap/Ichiban, Pat has continued to hone his skills and, despite the critical backlash against gangsta rap, maintains that his music is about 'talent, cool rhymes and doin' things on your own'.

Album: *#1 Suspect* (Atlantic 1990), *All About Comin' Up* (Wrap/Ichiban 1993), *Sex, Money And Murder* (Wrap/Ichiban 1994).

Gerardo

b. Gerardo Mejia III, 16 April 1965, Guayaquil, Ecuador. Latin rapper based in Los Angeles (he moved to Glendale, California at the age of 12), whose rhymes jump athletically between Spanish and English. In 1985 Gerardo won two separate

televised street-dance competitions, leading to him landing roles in the films *Colors*, playing a gang leader, and *Can't Buy Me Love*. He would go on to enjoy crossover success with 'Rico Suave' making US number 7 in April 1990, his debut album boasting an appearance by rap grandfather George Clinton. The title of the collection translates as 'more rhythm'. Though his rapping style is well-heeled, his appeal seems to have more to do with the MTV/video generation than any innovative subject matter or technique. Among other things he is notorious for taking the stage bare-chested and with his zip undone to tantalise his female followers.

Album: *Mo' Ritmo* (Interscope 1991).

Get Set VOP

Rap duo comprising real life brothers Infinite Kundalini and Kwabena The Triumphant, or Mark and Scott Batson as their mother knew them. Raised in the Bushwick sector of Brooklyn, New York, the brothers were driven by their desire to shatter stereotypes about people who hail from the projects, as they do: 'It's the voice that's been dying to be heard; the voice of civilised people standing up and saying, "Hey, we're not all killers and murderers"'. The group were first spotted while playing support for Maverick recording artist Me'Shell during the Washington Area Music Association's 1990 convention. Leotis Clyburn of Polydor was in attendance, but lost touch until two years later when he saw their name under the live listings. The first result of a long-term deal was the single, 'Pretty Brown Babies (Pro Seed)', and live dates with Jazzamatazz, with whom they have frequently been compared thanks to their mellow, jazzy groove.

Album: *Voice Of The Projects* (Polydor 1993).

Geto Boys

Houston, Texas-based gangsta rappers, led by the notorious Bushwick Bill (b. Richard Shaw, Jamaica, West Indies), Brad 'Scarface' Jordan and Willie 'D' Dennis, alongside DJ Ready Red (b. Collins Lyaseth). The latter had left the band by early 1991. In fact the Geto Boys had originally started with a completely different line up in 1988;

featuring Jukebox, Ready Red and Johnny C, with Bushwick a dancer. When Johnny C and Jukebox quit (Jukebox was subsequently jailed for murder) former Rap-A-Lot solo artists Scarface and Willie D were added by the record company. It was this line-up which made the headlines. In 1990 the David Geffen company refused to distribute *Grip It! On That Other Level*, following the controversy over some of its lyrics (which included allusions to necrophilia). The group returned to Rap-A-Lot, but shortly afterwards Bushwick Bill forced his girlfriend to shoot him after threatening their baby (he lost an eye). Their next album was bedecked with a picture of him being pushed through a hospital by his two pals after the incident. A fair introduction into the world of the Geto Boys, characterised by thoroughly nasty, sensationalist tales, which made their work difficult to evaluate objectively. Some of the most vile sequences of words ever used in popular music appear on their debut album, glorying in rape, mutilation and violence. Though at first appearance a cocktail of pure hatred, hidden beneath their more self-serving statements were tiny vignettes filled with persuasive detail - 'Life In The Fast Lane' on their debut, and 'Mind Playing Tricks On Me' on the follow-up being the best examples. Not that this is nearly enough to forgive them their otherwise dangerously stupid attitudes. Certainly though, the defence of 'reporting from the front-line' would seem to be more honourable in their case than many others, bearing in mind Bushwick Bill's aforementioned partial blinding, and the alarmingly high gun profile of the deep south. The group have gone on to concentrate more on their solo careers, following internal friction (Bushwick and Willie D at several points refusing to appear on stage at the same time)..

Albums: As the Ghetto Boys: *Grip It! On That Other Level* (Rap-A-Lot 1990). As the Geto Boys: *The Geto Boys* (Def American 1990), *We Can't Be Stopped* (Rap-A-Lot 1991), *Best Uncut Dope* (Rap-A-Lot 1992), *Till Death Us Do Part* (Rap-A-Lot 1993).

Ghetto Mafia

An Atlanta, Georgia-based crew. The Ghetto Mafia are, as their name implies, a hardcore outfit, relentlessly exploring the life cycle of the young, alienated black man. The group is fronted by the twin rapping talents of Nino and Wicked. The lead-off single for their debut album, 'Everday Thang In The Hood', introduced guest vocals by MC Breed, who would also helm the production of the album. These were nothing if not controversial songs - 'Mr President' talking about not only assasinating the President, but wiping out his whole family for good measure.
Album: *Draw The Line* (Funktown 1994).

Goats

Philadelphia rap trio, whose number includes Oatie Kato, Madd and Swayzack. From early in their career they made a conscious decision to play live (without DAT, often rapping freestyle) whenever possible, and earned immediate notoriety by playing at a celebration of Columbus' discovery of America - educating their audience about the degradation native Americans consequently suffered. They were snapped up by Sony/Columbia subsidiary Ruffhouse on the basis of their first, four-track demo. Their debut album was a joy, with alter-egos Chickenlittle and his kid brother Hangerhead acting as tour guides through the strange world of 90s America. Their political targets included Dan Quayle ('A Quayle is a bird, and bird's have bird brains'), while 'Drive By Bumper Cars' parodied hardcore rap. Their puns were incisive, often touchingly comic: ('Hey Mr Columbus! You took all my money/No I didn't kid, I discovered it'). Singles like 'Do The Digs Dug?' again returned to the rights of the oppressed, singling out Leonard Peltier, a community leader in South Dakota in 1973, as 'Our Mandella'. After all, they reasoned, Peltier was still in prison. However, their UK appearances in 1993 without founder member Oatie fuelled rumours of a split, which were confirmed on the advent of a second album which saw Swayzack taking the lead on a less-politicised set. As he commented on the founder member's departure: 'There's a lot of personal stuff that nobody knew. None of us got along with him'.
Albums: *Tricks Of The Shade* (Ruffhouse/Columbia

1993), *No Goats, No Glory* (Ruffhouse/Columbia 1994).

Grand Puba

b. Maxwell Dixon, New Rochelle, New York, USA. A founder member of Brand Nubian, and before that Masters Of Ceremony, Puba kicked off his solo career with a track, 'Fat Rat', on the *Strictly Business* soundtrack. When his debut album was unveiled, the smooth reggae backing was subjugated by Puba's by now familiar lyrical subject matter. Born the son of a Five Percent Nation Islamic father, Puba's raps reinstated that doctrine just as forcefully as he had done with Brand Nubian, but it was generally a more playful set. It included a guest appearance from Mary J. Blige. Puba himself would guest on Fat Joe's *Represent* album, on 'Watch The Sound'.
Album: *Reel To Reel* (Elektra 1992).

Grandmaster Flash

b. Joseph Saddler, 1 January 1958, Barbados, West Indies, but raised in the Bronx, New York. This pivotal force in early rap music grew up in the South Bronx, studying at Samuel Gompers Vocational Technical High School, spending his leisure time attending DJ parties thrown by early movers such as Grandmaster/DJ Flowers, MaBoya and Peter 'DJ' Jones. The latter took him under his wing, and Flash intended to combine Jones' timing on the decks with the sort of records that Kool Herc was spinning. Hence in the early 70s Saddler set about discovering the way to 'segue' records (commonly pronounced segway) smoothly together without missing a beat, highlighting the 'break' - the point in a record where the drum rhythm is isolated or accentuated - and repeating it. With admirable fortitude, Saddler spent upwards of a year in his apartment on 167th Street experimenting. The basis of his technique was to adapt Herc's approach, using two turntables each spinning the same record. He would then interrupt the flow of the disc offering the basic rhythm by overlaying the 'break', repeating the process by switching channels on the mixer, as necessary. The complexity and speed of the operation (the second desk would have to be rotated backwards to the beginning of the 'break' section) earned him the nickname Flash when he brought the style to his public, owing to the rapid hand movements. However, attention grabbing though this was, the style had not yet quite gelled into what Flash required. He decided, instead, to invite a vocalist to share the stage with him. He worked in this respect with first Lovebug Starski, then Keith Wiggins. Wiggins would eventually come to be known as Cowboy within Grandmaster Flash's Furious Five, in the process becoming one of the first 'MCs', delivering rhymes to accompany Flash's turntable wizardry. Flash continued in the block/park party vein for a considerable time, often illegally by hooking up his sound system to an intercepted mains cable until the police arrived. One person, at least, saw some commercial potential in his abilities, however. Ray Chandler stepped up and invited Flash to allow him to promote him, and charge an entrance fee (previous hip hop events had always been free). Initially incredulous at the thought that anyone would actually pay to see them, Flash nevertheless accepted.

Flash put together a strong line-up of local talent to support him: Grandmaster Melle Mel (b. Melvin Glover) and his brother Kid Creole (b. Nathaniel Glover) joining Cowboy, this line-up initially titled Grandmaster Flash And The 3 MCs. Two further rappers, Duke Bootee (b. Ed Fletcher) and Kurtis Blow subsequently joined, but were eventually replaced by Rahiem (b. Guy Todd Williams, ex-Funky Four) and Scorpio (b. Eddie Morris, aka Mr Ness). The Zulu Tribe was also inaugurated, with the express purpose of acting as security at live events: with Flash popularising the rap format, rival MCs sprang up to take their mentor and each other on. These head to heads often had the result of garnering the participants equipment as prizemoney. A crew who were not popular could expect to see their turntables and sound system rehabilitated for their troubles. Just as Jamaican sound system owners like Duke Reid and Coxsone Dodd had done in the 60s, Flash, Kook Herc and Afrika Bambaataa would hide their records from prying eyes to stop their 'sound' being pirated.

Grandmaster Flash

Similarly, record labels were removed to avoid identifying marks. The Furious Five, meanwhile, made their debut proper on September 2nd, 1976. Shortly afterwards they released their first record, 'Super Rappin'', for Enjoy. Although hugely popular within the hip hop fraternity, it failed to make commercial inroads, and Flash tried again with 'We Rap Mellow' (as the Younger Generation on Brass) and 'Flash To The Beat' (as Flash And The Five for Bozo Meko). However, it would be Joe Robinson Jr. of Sugarhill Records who finally bought out their Enjoy contract. He had seen the Grandmaster in action at Disco Fever, 'hip hop's first home', which had opened in the Bronx in 1978. His wife, Sylvia, wrote and produced their subsequent record, a relationship which kicked off with 'Freedom'. On the back of a major tour, certainly the first in rap's embryonic history, the single sold well, earning a gold disc. The follow-up 'Birthday Party' was totally eclipsed by 'Grandmaster Flash On The Wheels Of Steel', the first rap record to use samples, and a musical *tour de force,* dramatically showcasing the Flash quickmixing and scratching skills. Memorable enough, it too was overshadowed when Sugarhill brought the band in to record one of Robinson's most memorable compositions (written in tandem with Bootee): 'The Message'. The single, with its daunting, apocalyptic rumblings, significantly expanded not just rap but black music's boundaries, though the Furious Five had been less convinced of its worth when it was first offered to them in demo form. In just over a month the record went platinum. In the wake of the record's success Flash enquired of his Sugarhill bosses why no moneys were forthcoming. When he did not receive satisfactory explanation, he elected to split, taking Kid Creole and Rahiem with him, signing to Elektra Records. The others, headed by Melle Mel, would continue as Melle Mel and the Furious Five, scoring nearly instantly with 'White Lines (Don't Do It)'. Bearing in mind the subject matter of Mel's flush of success, it was deeply ironic that Flash was now a freebase cocaine addict. In the 80s Flash's name largely retreated into the mists of rap folklore until he was reunited with his Furious Five in 1987 for a Paul Simon hosted charity concert in

New York, and talk of a reunion in 1994 eventually led to the real thing. Back with the Furious Five he hosted New York's WQHT Hot 97 show, 'Mic Checka', spinning discs while prospective rappers rang up to try to pitch their freestyle rhymes down the telephone. Unfortunately the reunion would not include Cowboy, who died on 8 September 1989 after a slow descent into crack addiction. Flash also helped out on Terminator X's *Super Bad* set, which brought together many of the old school legends.

Albums: As Grandmaster Flash And The Furious Five: *The Message* (Sugarhill 1982), *Greatest Messages* (Sugarhill 1984), *On The Strength* (Elektra 1988). As Grandmaster Flash: *They Said It Couldn't Be Done* (Elektra 1985), *The Source* (Elektra 1986), *Ba-Dop-Boom-Bang* (Elektra 1987). Compilations: Grandmaster Flash And The Furious Five/Grandmaster Melle Mel: *Greatest Hits* (Sugarhill 1988).

Grandaddy IU

Cool, ascerbic hip hop artist, who only lets himself down by indulging in cheap sexual innuendo, often followed by graphic descriptions of his conquests. Which detracts enormously from the spare, jazzy tones which carry his best rhymes with a feathery touch.

Albums: *Grandaddy IU* (Cold Chillin' 1990), *Lead Pipe* (Cold Chillin' 1994).

Grandmaster Slice

b. c.1967, South Boston, Virginia, USA. Slice began to flex his rapping skills at the age of 11, going on to DJ and dance for a group titled Ebony Express by the advent of his teenage years. He subsequently formed his own combo, playing at parties in and outside of his hometown, taking his talents seriously enough to record his first demo tapes. It was while attending Halifax County Senior High School that Slice hooked up with Scratchmaster Chuck T. (b. Charles Fulp), who became his road manager and DJ. They had known of each other's rapping interests, having previously gone head to head in an after-school talent show. Together they released a debut album on independent distributor Selecto Hits Records, which was subsequently picked up by Jive. They had been suitably impressed by one of the album cuts, 'Thinking Of You', a slow-climbing hit throughout the US.

Album: *The Electric Slice (Shall We Dance)* (Selecto Hits/Jive 1991).

Grandmixer DST

b. Derek Howells, 23 August 1960, New York, USA. Born and raised in the South Bronx - the tough spawning ground of many of the finest first-generation hip hop artists - scratch DJ DST was a member of Afrika Bambaataa's street gang/sound system crew the Zulu Nation, before quitting to carve out a solo career in 1982 with the single 'Grandmixer Cuts It Up' on French label Celluloid, backed by the Infinity Rappers (KC Roc and Shahiem). With a formidable underground reputation behind him, he achieved international breakthrough in 1983 as the scratcher on Herbie Hancock's 'Rockit', and was also prominently featured on other tracks from Hancock's album *Future Shock* the same year. It was the first collaboration between jazz and hip hop, until then seen as mutually exclusive forms. In 1984 he enjoyed an international dancefloor hit with his own single, 'Crazy Cuts'. He raised his profile further with a series of collaborations with avant-funk/jazz producer Bill Laswell, producer of *Future Shock* and 'Rockit', appearing on a wide range of Laswell-produced tracks by Deadline, Manu Dibango, Foday Musa Suso and Material. A supremely talented, musical scratcher, DST's star faded in the late 80s as new generations of DJs replaced him in hip hop's notoriously short-shelf-life marketplace. (DST derived his tag from the New York garment district's Delancey Street, where the young DJ was often to be found in the late 70s adding to his collection of fashion wear).

Albums: *Crazy Cuts* (Celluloid 1984). With Herbie Hancock: *Future Shock* (CBS 1983). With Deadline: *Down By Law* (Celluloid 1984).

Gravediggaz

A rap 'supergroup' of sorts, featuring ex-Stetsasonic personnel Prince Paul (b. Paul Huston) and Fruitkwan, rechristened the Undertaker and the Gatekeeper respectively, plus Poetic the Grym Reaper and RZA the Ressurector. Poetic was formerly of Two Poetic, and RZA the Ressurector also sits behind the decks for the Wu Tang Clan. Prince Paul started the group after his Doo Dew label collapsed, needing a new venture to express his frustration. He had originally contacted his fellow band members with the intention of putting together a compilation album. Early singles included 'Diary Of A Madman', in the gothic/horror style the group had evolved, which utilised loops donated by RNS (famed for his production of Shyheim's debut set). The band toured in the US with the Wu Tang Clan, while Prince Paul considered further offers to produce for Soul II Soul (having already made the groundbreaking *3 Feet High And Rising* with them) and Living Colour.

Album: *Niggamortis* (Gee Street 1994).

Gumbo

In the wake of Arrested Development's huge crossover success, it seemed inevitable that Speech's first venture as a producer would create considerable media interest. Gumbo share more than Speech's input with Arrested Development, notably the affable but politicised Afrocentric vision, and the lolling, unhurried pace. Gumbo comprise three principals; mother figure Deanna Dawn (raps, vocals), percussionist and dancer Gichii Gamba and lead rapper Faluke Kele Fulani (b. c.1976), the latter writing the group's lyrics, .Although the comparisons to Arrested Development and PM Dawn will not be easy to shed, they have been greeted with enthusiasm by an audience already worked up on the idea of black cultural rap which does not romanticise an urban base. Signed to Cooltempo in the UK, their debut album was soaked in funk and Afro-Cuban rhythms, with jazz samples culled from John Coltrane to Charlie Mingus.

Album: *Droppin' Soulful H20 On The Fiber* (Chrysalis 1993).

Gunshot

East London rapping trio comprising MC Mercury, Alkaline and DJ White-Child Rix. Brought up in Leytonstone and Newham, and raised on a diet of reggae, 2-Tone and the Jam, the school friends came together in early 1990. Although their breakthrough did not come until *Patriot Games* in 1993, which saw them heralded as one of the UK's few legitimate answers to US hip hop, they had released a steady stream of quality singles; 'Battle Creek Brawl', 'Crime Story' and 'Clear From Present Danger'. 'Mind Of A Razor' in late 1993 also featured some metal guitar riffs courtesy of Napalm Death's Shane, while 'Killing Season' boasted a sample of Bob Hoskins dialogue in *The Long Good Friday*. The title of their album is a reference to their own view that UK rap has a lot more to offer than hanging on to the coat-tails of its cousins across the Atlantic. It also chose to tackle domestic issues rather than glamorise the life of the rapper, celebrate the size of his phallus or chuck insults at lady friends. The band continued their associations with alternative guitar bands by

remixing for S.M.A.S.H. in 1994.
Album: *Patriot Games* (1993).

G-Wiz, Gary

b. North Carolina, USA. A white hip hop producer, who moved to Freeport, New York, at the age of six. Musically-inclined parents, who owned a nightclub and booked acts like the Coasters and Drifters, were an early influence. Teaching himself first drums then computer programming, he sat in on the decks behind two rappers as part of New York rap group 516. In 1985 he met Chuck D of Public Enemy for the first time, and the two struck up a friendship, as G-Wiz was invited to work alongside Eric Sadler and Keith Schocklee as part of the Bomb Squad. When Schocklee formed his S.O.U.L. label, G-Wiz brought him their first act, Young Black Teenagers, who he would go on to produce and manage. His own production credits had begun with Public Enemy's *Apocalypse '91: The Enemy Strikes Black* album, and 'Can't Truss It' single. He would subsequently work with Run DMC ('Oooh Watcha Gonna Do', '3 In The Head'). Further work with Public Enemy followed on *Greatest Misses*, while Aaron Hall's 'Don't Be Afraid', for

Gumbo

the *Juice* film soundtrack, gave him a hit record. His remix client base has branched out beyond the hip hop frontier, including work for Janet Jackson, Bel Biv Devoe, Rakim, Peter Gabriel, Lisa Stansfield, Anthrax, Helmut and Sinead O'Connor.

H

Hammer

b. Stanley Kirk Burrell, 30 March 1962, Oakland, California, USA. Immensely popular rap artist, originally working under the MC Hammer prefix, who synthesized the street sounds of black cultural alienation, or his interpretation thereof, to great commercial gain. After failing in professional baseball and attending a college course in communications, Hammer (named after his likeness to Oakland A's big hitter Henry 'Hammerin' Hank' Aaron) joined the US Navy for three years. Indeed, his first forays into music were financed by baseball players Mike Davis and Dwayne Murphy, allowing him to form Bustin' records and release the solo single, 'Ring 'Em'. He had previously been part of religious rap group The Holy Ghost Boys. Together with a backing band consisting of two DJs and singers Tabatha King, Djuana Johnican and Phyllis Charles, he cut a 1987 debut set, *Feel My Power*. A minor hit, it did enough to bring Hammer to the attention of Capitol Records. After contracts were completed, including a reported advance of $750,000 (unheard of for a rap artist), the album was reissued under the title *Let's Get It Started*. Such success was overshadowed, however, by that of the follow-up, *Please Hammer Don't Hurt 'Em*. Following massive exposure due to sponsorship deals with British Knights footwear and Pepsi Cola, the album began a residency at the top of the US charts for a record-breaking 21 week run. The single, 'U Can't Touch This', embodied his appeal, with near constant rotation on pop channel MTV, and dance routines

which were the equal of Michael Jackson. The single sampled Rick James' 'Super Freak', creating a precedent for follow-ups 'Have You Seen Her' (the Chi-Lites) and 'Pray' (Prince; 'When Doves Cry'). Whilst an on-going duel with white rapper Vanilla Ice raged, critics pointed out the plagiarism which underpinned both artist's most successful work. Unperturbed, Hammer was being praised as a suitable role model for black youth (not least by himself), and was honoured by 'MC Hammer Days' in Los Angeles and Fremont. His first single to be free of sampling, 'Here Comes The Hammer', became an unexpected failure by stalling at number 51 in the US charts, despite its appearance on the soundtrack to *Rocky V*. A multitude of awards, including Grammys, Bammys and International Album Of The Year at the Juno awards in Canada, reflected the global success of the album. Its long awaited successor, *Too Legit To Quit*, featured a direct challenge this time: 'I'm taking on Michael Jackson from a spirit of competition...It's an opportunity to put on the world's greatest musical event...You've had Ali and Frazier...so why not Hammer versus Jackson?'. The sleevenotes to the album expanded on his desire for black youth to rid themselves of drugs and resurrect their Christian morality through self education. His exposure to US audiences already included the TV adventures of cartoon hero 'Hammerman', and a Mattel Hammer doll and attached ghetto blaster. However, his ability to sustain a challenge to the Jackson crown would inevitably be limited by his own admission that: 'I'm not a singer. I'm a rapper'. Despite a soundtrack hit with 'The Addams Family', heavily promoted in the film of the same title, Hammer's fortunes declined. In 1992 *The San Francisco Examiner* reported that Hammer faced financial ruin after poor attendances for his *Too Legit To Quit* tour, promoting an album that had seen him tracing a more R&B-based groove. Though Hammer denied there was any truth in such stories, it was obvious a re-think was needed. 1994 brought a huge image switch, from harem pants and leather catsuits to dark glasses and a goatee beard. The resultant album pulled in producers G-Bomb from Grand Jury Records, the Hines brothers from Detroit, Teddy Riley and members of the Dogg Pound, and specifically went after the Oakland G-Funk sound of artists like Too Short. Hammer as a gangsta rapper? As Simon Price of the *Melody Maker* bluntly pointed out: 'Please Hammer, don't hurt me. My sides are killing me'.

Albums: As MC Hammer: *Feel My Power* (Bustin' 1987), *Let's Get It Started* (Capitol 1988), *Please Hammer Don't Hurt 'Em* (Capitol 1990). As Hammer: *Too Legit To Quit* (Capitol 1991), *The Funky Headhunter* (RCA 1994).

Hard 2 Obtain

H20, as they perfer to be abbreviated, hail from Long Island, New York, with a sound that combines the local influences of Public Enemy, EPMD and De La Soul. The three man crew is made up of Taste, DL and DJ Six Seven, the latter's title derived from his vertical height. Their debut album revealed them to be competent freestylers, with a mature, reflective edge on titles like 'Shit We Do'. Production help was offered by the Stimulated Dummies, previously behind Grand Puba. The jazzy samples and laid-back groove placed the record as a direct descendent of the former's work, minus the Islamic references.

Album: *Ism And Blues* (1994).

Heavy D And The Boyz

Self-proclaimed 'overweight lover of rap from money earnin' Mount Vernon', Heavy D (b. Dwight Myers, 24 May 1967, Jamaica, West Indies) fronted a mainstream rap outfit which has been considered the genre's equivalent of Luther Vandross. Though the vast majority of his material represents rap's familiar call to procreation, Heavy D's rhymes are imbued with warmth rather than breast-beating machismo. Similarly, though he makes much of his muchness (titles like 'Mr. Big Stuff' are frequent), there is more to Heavy D than novelty. His debut album, helmed by Teddy Riley, comprised funk alongside hints of the New Jack Swing sound the producer was in the process of creating. Riley was also in tow for the follow-up, though this time he was in the company of fellow rap production legend Marley Marl, among others. Q-Tip (A Tribe Called Quest), Big Daddy Kane

and Pete Rock and CL Smooth all featured on 'Don't Curse', a posse cut from *Peaceful Journey*. The album also included a tribute to former band member T-Roy (b. Troy Dixon, c. 1968, d. 15 July 1990). One of his trio of backing vocalists (the Boyz), the singer was killed in an accident on their 1991 tour. The other 'Boyz' are G. Whiz (b. Glen Parrish) and DJ Eddie F (b. Edward Ferrell). Success continued unabated when 'Now That We've Found Love' became a UK number 2 in July 1991, profiling a fresh, Jamaican DJ influenced style. He also made a high profile guest appearance on Michael Jackson's 'Jam' single and sister Janet's 'Alright With Me'. Strangely, despite this success MCA did not see fit to offer *Blue Funk*, which saw Heavy return to hardcore territory with guest production from Pete Rock and DJ Premier (Gang Starr), an immediate UK release. His 1994 set *Nuttin' But Love* saw him reunite with rap's top rank of producers, including old hands Marl, Riley and Rock, alongside Erick Sermon, Trickmasterz and Troy Williams. It was another superb package. He shares the same management company as Hammer and has become one of rap's heavyweights in more than the literal sense.

Albums: *Living Large* (MCA 1987), *Big Tyme* (Uptown 1989), *Peaceful Journey* (Uptown 1991), *Blue Funk* (Uptown 1992), *Nuttin' But Love* (Uptown 1994).

Hi-C

From Compton, California, (though born in Louisiana) Hi-C is some way short of the in-yer-face gangsta rap made famous by that area: 'I'm into music first, messages later. I'm not hardcore and I don't constantly say "black this" or "black that"'. Hi-C introduced his pleasant, personable fare to a national audience in 1990 when singles like 'I'm Not Your Puppet' rose high in the Billboard charts. He also took high profile roles in movies, including *Encino Man*, *CB4* and *South Central*. In *CB4* it was Hi-C who provided the voice and lyrics for the Chris Rock character's on-screen raps. He is backed on record by DJ Tony A from Wilmington, California.

Albums: *Skanless* (Skanless 1991), *Swing'n* (Skanless 1993).

Hijack

British hip hop crew who garnered much attention via their debut 45, 'Style Wars', on Simon Harris' Music Of Life label, going on to record for Ice-T's Rhyme Syndicate. Ice-T had been doing a interview for Capitol Radio when the band's 'Hold No Hostage' was played to him. Reactions to the voice of Kamanchi Sly, a powerful MC, have often been positive, and their stage show is very effective. They also earned themselves a little celebrity via their 'Don't Go With Strangers' warning to young children. DJ Supreme from the band (who also include DJ Undercover, Agent Clueso, Agent Fritz and Ulysees) also released superior breakbeat albums like 1992's *Stolen Beats And Ripped Off Samples*.

Album: *The Horns Of Jericho* (Rhyme Syndicate 1993).

Hoez With Attitude (HWA)

Whilst taking gangsta rap's misogynist attitudes to task may be a positive move, adopting the latter's agenda to do so seems less well-advised. All in all HWA ('Baby Girl' Kim Kenner, Goldie and Jazz) are a tragic concept stretched ever thinner over scuttling Miami-bass rhythms. Emigrating from Chicago to Los Angeles in the late 80s, within a year they had unveiled an album that would sell nearly 400,000 copies. A group destined to earn their notoriety off skimpy stage wear rather than anything constructive they might have to offer, musically or lyrically.

Albums: *Livin' In A Hoe House* (Ruthless 1990), *As Much Ass Azz U Want* (Ruthless 1994, mini-album).

Honky

Honky were formed from the ashes of Club St Louis, a small time rap duo who attracted some music biz attention in the early 90s. That outfit signed to East West, releasing a solitary single. When they lost their deal in 1992 they returned home to Doncaster, disillusioned. Matt, responsible for the group's music, soldiered on as a studio engineer, before teaming up once more with his old rapping partner, Kyle, the line-up completed by Stu, Joloise and Rosa. Together they wrote the song which would become the debut Honky release. 'KKK (Koffee Koloured Kids)' emerged on ZTT in 1993. It concerned Kyle's alienation at being the son of a white mother and black father, and his exclusion from both societies. A follow-up, 'The Whistler', proved similarly thoughtful. Again it concerned Kyle's parentage, this time discussing his father's temper, which could always be detected by his whistling before an impending act of violence.

Album: *The Ego Has Landed* (ZTT 1994).

House Of Pain

Hardcore Irish American hip-hoppers whose origins can be traced to Taft High School in Los Angeles (former students of which include Ice Cube). The band comprise lead rapper Everlast (b. Eric Schrody, USA), his co-lyricist Danny Boy (b. Daniel O'Connor, USA), and DJ Lethal (b. Leor DiMant, c.1974, Latvia). Everlast was originally signed to Warner Brothers, and was often to be seen 'hanging' with Ice-T and his Rhythm Syndicate at that time. With House Of Pain he scored a debut Top 10 hit with the impressive 'Jump Around', a good example of the street poetry hybrid which they branded 'Fine malt lyricism'. 'Jump Around' seemed to offer the pinnacle in House Of Pain's career, however. Their debut album gloried in self-styled Gaelic dressing. 'Shamrocks And Shenanigans', an ode to their spurious links with the Emerald Isle, contained a novelty sample of David Bowie's 'Fame'. Elsewhere the album's grooves were populated with familiar, dumb macho lines, delivered with a quite singular lack of dexterity: 'I feel blessed, I'm casually dressed, I wear a gun, But I don't wear a vest'. No strangers to controversy, House Of Pain were involved in two near riot on their 1993 tour with Rage Against The Machine; once in Baltimore when they refused to take the stage, and again when a member of the band's road crew was assaulted by security staff at a Manchester Academy gig. This was only a matter of days after the rapper had been arrested at JFK Airport in New York for illegal possession of a handgun. Such incidents led to his being subject to a tracking device and house arrest for three months in 1994.

House Of Pain

The press were also starting to ask awkward questions about Sinn Fein tattoos. Everlast has ventured in to the world of films, appearing in both the US rap movie, *Who's The Man* (alongside Public Enemy, Heavy D etc), and the Dennis Leary flick, *Judgement Day*, where, unsurprisingly, he played a gangster. House Of Pain also opened a pizza restaurant, in partnership with Mickey Rourke (House Of Pizza). *Same As It Ever Was*, despite the title, proved to be a much more impressive outing, with Everlast unleashing his frustration with his 'imprisonment' and the media in tracks like 'Back From The Dead'
Album: *House Of Pain* (Tommy Boy 1992), *Same As It Ever Was* (Tommy Boy 1994).

Hustlers HC

Three young Sikhs from west London, fronted by Hustler MC, who confront those factors relevant to their ethnic and geographical societies via a hip hop beta beat. Touted as part of the new 'Asian Cool' alongside Trans-global Express and Fun-Da-Mental, their debut single, 'Big Trouble In Little Asia', came out at the same time as Gurinder Chadha's groundbreaking film, *Bhaji On The Beach*. It was a similarly themed address to the cross-cultural problems facing the Asian community. They also run the Bombay Jungle nightclub, a mixed bhangra/hip hop venue, in London. They are managed by Simon Underwood (ex-Pop Group and Pigbag).

Hype-A-Delics

Rap crew, based in the Templehof region of Berlin, though only DJ Derezon (b. Berlin) is a native German. The two MC's, Rodski (b. New York, USA) and BMG the Funky Funktioneer (b. Flint, Michigan, USA) are both relics of America's armed presence in West Germany, where their fathers were in the services. Both, however, are now married and settled in their adopted country. Derezon and Rodski had worked together under different names for several years, signing to Ariole as the Hype-A-Delics in 1991. After one single they departed and added BMG - who had formerly worked with his own crew back in Flint (Rodski had also been a friend of Doctor Ice in his Brooklyn days). They have subsequently inaugurated their own Juiceful Records, now home to several German hip hop crews including Cheeba Garden and Islamic Force. This imprint released their debut album in 1994, which reflected their concerns over the rise of the right wing in Europe, as well as dissing the police and praising the herb.

Album: *More Funk For You Ass* (Juiceful 1994).

Ice Cube

b. Oshea Jackson, June 1969, Crenshaw, South Central Los Angeles, California, USA. Controversial hardcore rapper who formerly worked with the equally inflammatory NWA. Following a relatively stable background, both his mother and father working at UCLA, Cube entered the homeboy lifestyle. 'One day I was sitting in class with a friend called Kiddo and we had some time on our hands, so he said let's write a rap'. At the age of 16 he penned his first important rap; 'Boyz 'N The Hood', which was later recorded by Eazy-E. He subsequently spent time with CIA, an embryonic rap outfit produced by Dr Dre. As guest lyricist, he brought NWA '8 Ball' and 'Dopeman', which would comprise the opening salvo from the band. After studying architectural draughtsmanship in Phoenix, Arizona, he returned to the NWA fold in time for the ground-breaking *Straight Outta Compton*. He would leave the group at the tail-end of 1989, amid thinly veiled attacks on NWA's Jewish manager Jerry Heller. His debut album, recorded with Public Enemy producers the Bomb Squad, drew immediate mainstream attention with its controversial lyrical platform. As well as homophobia and the glamorisation of violence, his work was attacked primarily for its overt sexism; raps about kicking a pregnant girlfriend ('You Can't Fade Me') notwithstanding. Conversely, Ice Cube overlooks a production empire (Street Knowledge) run for him by a woman, and he also fostered the career of female rapper Yo Yo (who appears alongside him defending her gender on *AmeriKKKa's Most Wanted*'s 'It's A Man's World'). The politicisation of his solo work should also be noted; in his NWA days he had once written 'Life ain't nothing but bitches and money', but his words since then have incorporated numerous references to black ideology which add up to something approaching a manifesto. His defence against critical discomfort with his rhymes, 'I put a mirror to black America', has been hijacked by many other, less worthy cases. To Ice Cube's credit, he went on to produce two excellent sets, *The Predator* and *Lethal Injection*. The former in particular boasted a much more discursive approach to the problems of the ghetto, including reflections on the Los Angeles riots and the Rodney King beating. Perhaps it was marred by the blunt sexism of tracks like 'Cave Bitch', but it was certainly an advance. Musically it was typified by a stirring 'One Nation Under A Groove', with a lead vocal by the song's writer, George Clinton. In 1993 he also teamed up with fellow rapper Ice-T, with whom he shares more than a similarity in name, to launch a fashion range incorporating a gun logo. No stranger to controversy, Ice Cube looks like becoming better acquainted with commerce too. His 1992 film *Trespass*, re-titled after the LA Riots deemed original moniker *Looters* unsavoury, saw him team up with Ice-T once more. He had already starred in John Singleton's 1991 hit film, titled after his first rap, *Boyz 'N The Hood*, and later appeared in the same director's *Higher Learning*. Having completed four million-selling albums, Ice Cube's career has attracted the attention of those outside the hip hop fraternity. 'It Was A Good Day' gave him a massive profile via MTV. Like Ice-T, Cube was targeted on right wing assassination lists discovered by the police in 1993. However, his career has continued unabated. Street Knowledge has provided Da Lench Mob and Kam with successful albums on which Cube has acted as executive producer, and he has set up a second subsidiary, titled after his posse, Lench Mob, and written several screenplays.

Albums: *AmeriKKKa's Most Wanted* (Priority 1990), *Death Certificate* (Priority 1991), *The Predator* (Priority 1992), *Lethal Injection* (Priority 1993).

Ice-T

One of the most outspoken rappers on the West Coast, Ice-T (b. Tracy Marrow, c.1958, Newark, New Jersey, USA) boasts (sometimes literally) a violent past in which he was shot twice - once whilst involved in an armed robbery. His name, fittingly, is taken from black exploitation author Iceberg Slim, and he is backed on record by Afrika Islam and DJ Aladdin's hardcore hip hop. His first record was actually 'The Coldest Rapper' in 1983, which was improvised over a Jimmy Jam and Terry Lewis rhythm, and made him the first Los Angeles hip hop artist. Unfortunately, he was subsequently held under contract by mogul Willie Strong for several years. Disillusioned, he made his money from petty and not so petty crime, and also appeared in the breakdance film *Breakin'*, which included his 'Reckless' cut on the soundtrack. He followed it with the faddish 'Killers' 45, wherein he dressed himself up as a full blown medieval warrior. The breakthrough, however, came with 'Ya Don't Know', which was widely credited with being the first West Coast hip hop artefact (although the honour was undoubtedly Ice-T's, the real beneficiary should have been the obscure 'The Coldest Rapper' cut). Four LPs in just three years created something of a stir in the US, based as they were largely on his experiences as a gang member in Los Angeles. In 1989 he reached the lower end of the UK charts with 'High Rollers', but did better the following year teaming up with Curtis Mayfield on a remake of 'Superfly'. He is married to Darlene who normally appears semi-clad on his record sleeves, and owns a pit pull terrier affectionately titled Felony. For a time, too, he delighted in inviting journalists to his luxury Beverley Hills home to show them his personal armoury of semi-automatic weapons. Success has also enabled him to start his own record company, Rhythm Syndicate. His vision of the black man as

sophisticated and articulate (being hard as nails is, of course, *de rigeur*) ranks him among the most potent forces in contemporary black culture. His refusal to engage in a white liberal agenda (he was the first rap artist to have warning stickers placed on his album sleeves) has irritated many, but helped establish him as an authentic spokesperson for dispossessed black youth. Debut album *Rhyme Pays*, with an Uzi emblazoned on the cover, served as a mission statement: hardcore raps on street violence and survival being the order of the day. By the time of its follow-up, there was demonstrably greater imagination displayed in terms of backing music. Like many of his West Coast bretherin, Ice-T had rediscovered funk. Notable tracks included 'Girls L.G.B.N.A.F., which the PMRC later discovered stood for 'Let's Get Butt Naked And Fuck'. Their reaction to this (arguably among the least offensive statements on Ice-T's records) was so overheated that the debate heavily informed his follow-up set. However, his crowning glory so far was *OG* (an acronym for Original Gangster which has passed into rap's lexicon) which ranks alongside the best work of Ice Cube, Public Enemy or NWA in terms of sustained intensity, yet managed to maintain a little more finesse than his previous work. In 1991, with appealing irony, he starred as a cop in the movie *New Jack City*. He had earlier contributed the title-track to the LA gangster movie, *Colors*, rapping the title song. He also appeared with former NWA and solo artist Ice Cube in the Walter Hill film *Looters*. (re-named *Trespassers* due to its release at the same time as the LA riots), as well as *Surviving The Game* and the cult comic hero movie, *Tank Girl*. His other soundtrack credits include *Dick Tracy*. Ice-T's hobbies include his own thrash metal outfit, Body Count, who released an album in 1992 and stirred up immeasurable controversy via one of its cuts, 'Cop Killer' (detailed under Body Count entry). Little wonder that he was targeted on right wing assassination lists discovered by the police in 1993. His album from that year, *Home Invasion*, saw him take on the mantle of agent provocateur in the young white male's home, a theme reinforced in its cover and title - Ice-T was a threat in your neighbourhood, with another manifesto of spiteful

Ice Cube

intent ('I'm takin' your kids' brains, You ain't getting them back, I'm gonna fill 'em with hard drugs, big guns, bitches, hoes and death'). Then he went and spoiled all the good work by writing a book, the *Ice-T Opinion*, which was so full of dumb ideas that it pretty-much discredited such achievements. On March 22nd 1994 he introduced Channel 4's *Without Walls*, a documentary on the rise of the blaxploitation movies. His own life would make an excellent documentary subject. He continues to fascinate those on both sides of the rap lobby, and, as he notes in *Home Invasion*'s 'Ice Muthafuckin' T': 'Every fucking thing I write, Is going to be analysed by somebody white'.

Albums: *Rhyme Pays* (Sire 1987), *Power* (Sire 1988), *Freedom Of Speech...Just Watch What You Say* (Sire 1989), *OG: Original Gangster* (Syndicate/Sire 1991), *Home Invasion* (Priority 1993), *Born Dead* (Priority 1994).

Further reading: *The Ice-T Opinion* (Pan 1994).

Ichiban

Ichiban is a Georgia corporation which was founded in Atlanta in 1985 by John E. Abbey (London-born former proprietor of *Blues & Soul* magazine) and his wife, Nina K. Easton, who took the company title from the Japanese for number one. Their goal, to provide an outlet for black music, be it blues, gospel, jazz, R&B or rap has remained constant. Since its inception Ichiban has grown to become the distributor of some 20 to 30 labels. The company first came into contact with rap music when approached to distribute Vanilla Ice's *To The Extreme* album in 1990 (later picked up by SBK). As Abbey admitted, 'We literally stumbled into rap'. Their next project was MC Breed's 'Ain't No Future In Yo' Frontin', via Swamp Dogg's SDEG label. Bouyed by these initial successes, Ichiban launched its primary rap stable, Wrap Records. Product included a second MC Breed album, plus music from Success-N-Effect, Kilo and Gangsta Pat. Other releases filtered through on subsidiary rap imprints like380 Recordings, Easylee and Mo' Money, and for a time the Nastymix operation was also distributed through Ichiban's offices. The company's catalogue has extended to a point at which over 60% of its releases are in the rap/hip hop field, and they possess one of the most talented rosters of new artists in the US. Apart from the aforementioned artists, some of these include Detroit's Most Wanted, Kid Sensation, Kwamé, Menace To Society, 95 South, Treacherous 3, Snoman and MC Shy D.

Ignorance

A London hip hop duo comprising Mark Martin and Trevor who formerly found fame and fortune as dancers for the Pet Shop Boys. They kicked off their own career at Polydor with the 'Phat Girls' 45, a politically correct attempt to redress hip hop's attitudes to women. They also took a non conventional approach to their music, choosing a ska mix over the more preferred funk/jazz stylings of their American neighbours. This was done primarily to reinstate the Black British experience, reflecting the sounds of reggae and calypso which were so evident where they grew up. And there was no cussing of bitches and ho's to be found on their debut album, either: 'I mean, when we went to school we never had rucksacks with Uzis in 'em! To me, all that infatuation with being a hard superhuman with a gun by your side is bollocks. It's just a weak excuse for people that are insecure.'

Album: *The Epitome Of Ignorants* (Polydor 1994).

Ill (Featuring Al Skratch)

aka Big Ill The Mack, who first came to prominence in his home town of Brooklyn by appearing on a freestyle tape that was circulated after a performance at a Big Daddy Kane birthday party (where he successfully 'dissed' both the birthday boy and other 'sucker MCs'). He made an impressive vinyl debut, backed by DJ Al Skratch, with the anthemic 'Where My Homiez?' 12-inch for Mercury. The track was produced by LG, brother of Easy Mo Bee (Rappin' Is Fundamental).

Album: *Creep Wit' Me* (Mercury 1994).

Illegal

Illegal are diminutive youngsters Lil' Malik Edwards and Jamal Phillips. Far from the cutesy Kriss Kross school of teen-rappers, Illegal won a degree of notoriety when curtailing an interview

Ice T

with a US rap magazine and offering to 'smoke' the interviewer. Their debut album boasted production from heavyweights like Erick Sermon, Diamond D, Lord Finesse, Biz Markie and others. Having subsequently split, Malik featured as part of Snoopy Doggy Dogg's Dog Pound, appearing on albums by the latter and Warren G.
Album: *The Untold Truth* (Rowdy 1993).

Intelligent Hoodlum

b. Percy Chapman, c.1968, Rikers Island, USA. The Hoodlum grew up on the same street as Marley Marl, whom he pestered every day to try and get a record out, after having picked up the rap bug from his cousin Kadiya. Finally Marl acquiesced, and Hoodlum had his first record released, 'Coke Is It'. It was later re-titled 'Tragedy', after the Hoodlum's own sorry tale. He was only 14, but instead of further releases he sought a life of crime to support his crack habit. Inevitably he found himself in prison, Rikers Island no less, on a one to three year sentence. However, the prison term gave him the chance to cool off, and he spent his time reading avidly. Having got through black conscious standards by Malcolm X and Elijah Muhammed, he was paroled just as Public Enemy arrived on the scene. He played *It Takes A Nation Of Millions To Hold Us Back* nearly constantly, Chuck D's bleak messages striking a chord with Hoodlum, one which connected back to his incarcerated reading. Although he returned to the drug trade to support himself, he also took himself off to college to learn more about his new heroes, Marcus Garvey and Malcolm X. Eventually he met up with Marley Marl again, by now a major hip hop talent, who invited him to perform some more raps. The eventual results were the improvised 'Party Pack' and 'Vitally Tragic'. The latter explained the origins of his names: Tragic refers to his past, as a man who hurt himself and could not see outside his own existence of crime and drugs. The Intelligent Hoodlum moniker indicated a path for the future, renouncing his illegal moves but acknowledging the necessary part his criminal past had played in his development. The intelligent prefix inferred his desire to learn, and use his new-found wisdom for the benefit of

himself and others. As was clearly demonstrated on his debut album by the ferocious protest of 'Black And Proud' or 'Arrest The President'. Now a practising Muslim, and affiliated to the Nation of Islam, Hoodlum also set up his own organisation, MAAPS - Movement Against the American Power Structure.
Album: *Tragedy* (A&M 1990), *Saga Of A Hoodlum* (A&M 1993).

J

J-Blast And The 100% Proof

One-off spoof merchants notable for their articulate 'dissing' of De La Soul. 'Break Ya Dawn' was a specific attack on Prince Be and his cohorts, released, tellingly enough, on the Geek St label, in 1992. It was introduced by a sample of Bruno Brookes using entirely forced language such as 'peace' and 'respect', before the outfit waylay Prince Be and a host of other 'pseuds'. Though of UK origins, the protagonists identities remained hidden, until J Blast went on to join the Scientists Of Sound.

Jamal-Ski

b. Jamal Mitchell, New York, USA. By the time he released his debut solo album, Jamal-Ski's name had already cropped up on several high profile releases. Most notable among these were Boogie Down Production's *Edutainment* and the Brand New Heavies' *Heavy Rhyme Experience Vol. 1*. Jamal-Ski grew up in Manhattan, and was a product of the hip hop cultural experience, from rapping through to sound system parties, graffiti and breakdancing. He originally hung around with the Rocksteady Crew and Afrika Bambaataa's Zulu Nation. His chosen path mixes traditional, old school rap with the rhythms of reggae. His musical heritage is certainly impressive, his father a jazz drummer who appeared alongside Stan Getz and

Chet Baker, which allowed him to meet luminaries such as Thelonious Monk, ensuring that music remained in his blood through adolescence. He attended New York university for a year before moving to Oregon to play with reggae and ska bands, eventually returning east to take up the hip hop cudgels.

Album: *Rough Reality* (Columbia 1993).

Jazzamatazz

A collaboration between seasoned jazz exponents and Guru (b. Keith Allam, Roxbury, Massachussets, USA), of Gang Starr. Some of the names involved included N'Dea Davenport (Brand New Heavies), Carleen Anderson, Courtney Pine, Branford Marsalis, Roy Ayers, Donald Byrd, Lonnie Liston Smith and French rapper MC Solaar. An inventive combination, highlighted by a single, 'No Time To Play', featuring the vocals of Paul Weller's missus D.C. Lee, which in turn helped relaunch the latter's career. The Jazzamatazz project's roots were undoubtedly laid in Gang Starr's 'Jazz Thing', a collaboration with Marsalis which Spike Lee has used to theme his film, *Mo' Better Blues*.

Album: *Jazzamatazz* (Chrysalis 1993).

Jazzy Jay

Bronx studio-based DJ (b. c.1963, Bronx, New York, USA) who was one of the early movers in Afrika Bambaataa's Zulu Nation movement, travelling with his mentor from early park and block parties to the stadia of the Roxy and the *Planet Rock* tour. In a less-publicised role he was also Rick Rubin's original partner in Def Jam, and co-produced the label's first single, T La Rock's 'It's Yours' (with lyrics written by his brother, Special-K). His own label (with Rocky Bucano), Strong City, would unveil records by Busy Bee, Ultimate Force, Ice Cream Tee, Don Baron and Grand Puba's first outfit, Masters Of Ceremony. Regular visitors and pupils of his Bronx studio have included Diamond D, Fat Joe Da Gangster, Showbiz and AG and Skeff Anslem. Jazzy Jay grew up in the Bronx River region, and started DJing in his early teens. Kid Cassidy and Sundance were his first two MC recruits, playing together in the park

by Soundview Houses, distributing tapes of the shows to other early hip hop fans. After working with the Chuck City Crew from Bronxdale he received the call from Bambaataa, and debuted with them in 1977. He was promoted to the head of the Jazzy 5 enclave, and was partially behind the 'Jazzy Sensation' cut. He had already hooked up with Rubin whom he had met at the Club Negril, before 'Planet Rock' took off. Though neither the liaison with Rubin nor his Strong City venture actually afforded him great finanical reward, Jay has gone on to maintain the respect afforded him by the hip hop community with a series of productions which have never been less than competent, and often much more.

Jazzy Jeff

A former member of the Funky Four, Jazzy Jeff should not be confused, as frequently and quite naturally happens, with DJ Jazzy Jeff. The latter, alongside The Fresh Prince, shares not only his name, but also his label and producer. Though the original Jazzy Jeff has largely been eclipsed by the duo, he is a rapper of some historical note. His able, clear rhymes decorated a likeable album for Jive in the mid-80s, aided by Bryan 'Chuck' New and Phil Nicholas of the Willesden Dodgers. Eschewing the macho delivery and breast-beating more familiar at the time, *On Fire* included the vulnerable tribute 'My Mother (Yes I Love Her)' alongside material that frowned upon the ghetto's drug problems. 'King Heroin (Don't Mess With Heroin')' is actually one of rap's few lyrics about that drug in a subculture obsessed with cannabis, crack and cocaine.

Album: *On Fire* (Jive 1985).

JC001

b. 16 June 1966. Alongside Daddy Freddy, rapper JC001 boasts one of the world's most fearsome, animated rap deliveries (coming second to the latter in the *Guinness Book Of Records* contest). His maniacal rants adorn a mixed hip hop/ragga backing, with samples lifted from classic Jamaican fare (Dave And Ansell Collins' 'Double Barrel' on the 'Cupid' 45, etc). Born of part Indian/Catholic parentage, he first listened to ragga rhymes on

David Rodigan's *Roots Rockers* programme, but he bought into rap with the advent of electro and 'Planet Rock'. After performing at blues parties and carnivals he joined the pirate radio stations. His first record emerged in 1987, 'I Diss Therefore I Am', built on the Ethiopians' 'Train To Skaville', before collaborating with others for 'Bad Place To Get Hit'. Though his press image is one of devilish intensity and spite, his lyrics trace strong anti-racism sentiments. He collaborated with the Beatmasters on their 1991 comeback single, 'Boulevard of Broken Dreams'.

Album: *Ride To The Break* (Anxious/East West 1993).

Jeru The Damaja

His stage name in full reading Jeru The Damaja: D Original Dirty Rotten Scoundrel, Jeru (b. Kendrick Jeru Davis, c.1971) is a native New Yorker, whose name refers to the 'first god', son of Egyptian deities Osiris and Isis (his father was a Rastafarian). Having at one time earned a living changing tyres for Greyhound buses, he made his first demos with his homeboy/DJ PF Cuttin', before meeting up with Guru of Gang Starr at their 'Manifest' video shoot. His hardcore, Brooklyn style was thus premiered on Gang Starr's *Daily Operation* album (on 'I'm The Man'). Jeru also worked freestyle on their live shows. In turn DJ Premier would produce Jeru's debut cut, 'Come Clean'. This had been originally issued as a promo single entitled 'Gang Starr Doundation Sampler', on Gang Starr's own label, Illkid Records. His approach was resolutely old school: 'A long time ago rhyming was about having some skills, and what I tried to do is say let's bring it back to the skills and forget about the guns, take it to the skills level and then we'll see who the real men are'. His debut album was widely venerated in both the specialist and general music press, not least due to one of Premier's most effective productions and Jeru's clear, heavily enunciated style.

Album: *Ths Sun Rises In The East* (Payday/Double Vinyl 1994).

Jive Records

A subsidiary of the Zomba group, founded by chairman Clive Calder, Jive was established in the UK in 1981. In response to the growing base of its US rap roster, Jive Records US was inaugurated three years later, where it has gained a significant market-share. The first rap single to emerge on the label (which also covered sundry other musical styles, including dance and pop) was Whodini's 'Magic Wand'. Whodini also presided over the imprint's first rap album, a self-titled set from 1983. Although steady success continued with artists like Kool Moe Dee, Boogie Down Productions, Wee Girl Papa Rappers, A Tribe Called Quest and others, the label's real commercial breakthrough act would be Jazzy Jeff And The Fresh Prince. Although already several albums into their career (including a debut set, *He's The Rapper And I'm The DJ*, which would be Jive's biggest seller), 'Boom! Shake The Room' gave the duo a surprise UK number 1. The group had formerly won the first ever Grammy for rap with 'Parent's Just Don't Understand' in 1988.

Selected albums: Whodini: *Whodini* (Jive 1983). DJ Jazzy Jeff And The Fresh Prince: *He's The DJ And I'm The Rapper* (Jive 1988). Boogie Down Productions: *By All Means Necessary* (Jive 1988), *Ghetto Music: The Blueprint Of Hip Hop* (Jive 1989). A Tribe Called Quest: *People's Instinctive Travels And The Paths Of Rhythm* (Jive 1990).

JJ Fad

B-Boy period Los Angeles female rap trio, comprising M.C.J.B. (b. Juana Burns), Baby D (b. Dania Birks) and Sassy C (b. Michelle Franklin). Their collective name stands for 'Just Jammin' Fresh And Def'. Boosted by an eponymous Top 30-peaking single, their debut album made a small dent in the album charts, after which little was heard from the group.

Album: *Supersonic - The Album* (Ruthless 1988).

Jungle Brothers

Rap innovators and precursors to the sound later fine-tuned by De La Soul, PM Dawn *et al*. Following on from Afrika Bambaataa, the Jungle Brothers: Mike G (b. Michael Small, c.1969, Harlem, New York, USA), DJ Sammy B (b. Sammy Burwell, c.1068, Harlem, New York,

USA) and Afrika Baby Bambaataa (b. Nathaniel Hall, c.1971, Brooklyn, New York, USA) were unafraid of cross-genre experimentation. The most famous demonstration being their version of Marvin Gaye's 'What's Going On', though their incorporation of House music on 'I'll House You' is another good example. They made their debut for Warlock/Idlers Records in October 1987, before signing to Gee Street. As part of the Native Tongues coalition with Queen Latifah, A Tribe Called Quest and others, they sought to enhance the living experiences of black men and women by educating them about their role in history and African culture. In many ways traditionalists, the Jungle Brothers carefully traced the lines between R&B and rap, their admiration of James Brown going beyond merely sampling his rhythms (including the basis of their name - which shares the godfather of soul's initials). A second album was slightly less funky and more soul-based, particularly effective on cuts like 'Beyond This World'. It has been argued that the Jungle Brothers' failure to break through commercially had something to do with the fact that they were initially signed to a New York dance label, Idlers. More likely is the assertion that audiences for macho skulduggery greatly outnumbered those for which intelligent, discursive hip hop was a worthwhile phenomenon in the late 80s.

Album: *Straight Out The Jungle* (Idlers/Warlock 1988), *Done By The Forces Of Nature* (Warners 1989), *J Beez Wit The Remedy* (1993).

Just Ice

b. Joseph Williams Jr, Ft. Greene, Brooklyn, New York, USA. Just Ice (aka Justice) was thrust to prominence in 1987 when his name was to be found attached to the headline 'Murder, Drugs and the Rap Star'. The caption was emblazoned on the cover of the Washington Post. The text revealed that the rapper had been held and questioned in connection with the murder of a drug dealer (at no time were charges laid against him). Members of the Washington black community were so outraged by the implied racism and lack of factual reporting in the story that they picketed the newspaper's offices for several months. This has

somewhat overshadowed the artist's recording career.

Albums: *Kool & Deadly* (Fresh 1987), *The Desolate One* (Sleeping Bag 1989).

K

K-Solo

b. Kevin Maddison, Central Islip, New York, USA. K-Solo is a part of the Hit Squad, the EPMD clique whose other members include Das EFX and Redman. Maddison had, in fact, been involved in a pre-EPMD band with Parrish Smith, before making vocal contributions to the group's *Unfinished Business*. Parrish would be on hand to provide production tutelage for K-Solo's debut album, a perfunctory demonstration of his story-telling skills highlighted by the stylish 'Tales From The Crack Side'. K-Solo is an acronym for Kevin Self Organisation Left Others.

Album: *Tell The World My Name* (Atlantic 1990), *Spellbound* (Atlantic 1991), *Times Up* (Atlantic 1992).

Kaliphz

Manchester, England-based hip hop crew, managed by former 808 State member Martin Price, and combining five youths from Rochdale, four of Asian descent, one of Polish. The group, whose name translates as 'King' or 'Messenger' in an Arabic tongue, were pulled together after 2Phaaan (pronounced Du-farn, b. c.1967) and Jabba Da Hype (aka The Alien) saw the Rock Steady Crew performing at the Runcorn Ideal Homes Exhibition in 1982 and became embroiled in the breakdancing and graffiti movements in their neighbourhood, forming breakdance crew Dizzy Footwork the same year. They were soon joined by Hogweed, and the trio began hanging out together, before finally adding Chokadoodle and

SniffaDawg (b. c.1974) to complete the line-up. Initially they performed a capella, before being signed by London records after Radio 1 DJ Pete Tong picked up on them. Legend has it that Martin Price was forced to fight each member, breaking his nose in the process, before they would allow him to become their manager. The group are backed by a production team entitled Funk Regulators, a junior back-up rap squad the Underhogs, an all-female troupe the Berserkers, a mixed race group Freaks Of Nature, and a freestyle solo rapper, Paraphinalia. They were initially reluctant to be tagged 'Asian rap', because 'We can hold our own, we don't have to advertise the fact that some of our members happen to be Asian'. They created a big impact at the 1992 In The City Music Seminar, following it with the release of a keenly anticipated debut EP, *Vibe Da Joint*. Fuelled by explosive lines like 'Here comes a Paki with a *bona fide* line', the Kaliphz declared their intent to subvert the power of the Paki-putdown by reclaiming it, just as blacks had done with 'nigga'.

Kam

b. Craig Miller, c.1971, Watts, California, USA, before settling in Compton with his mother and brother. With his lyrical worldview drawn from the inter-gang arena of Los Angeles, Kam chose to call for unity rather than glorify the bloodletting of the Crips and Blood brotherhoods. Unfortunately, though his rhymes were deftly weighted tracts against the dissolution of the ghetto, generally arguing for his Muslim beliefs ('So it's hard to keep calm, When I'm accused of being racist, For Loving my people first....'), Kam's delivery lacked the heavyweight impact of Messrs Ice-T and Cube. The latter was the major influence in his career, picking him up as the first artist on his Street Knowledge empire. He made his debut with 'Every Single Weekend' on the *Boyz N The Hood* soundtrack, before guesting on 'Colorblind', a cut from Cube's *Death Certificate* set. He has also written for Yo Yo.
Album: *Neva Again* (East West 1992).

Katch 22

British *avant garde* rap troupe headed up by MC

Huntkillbury Finn (b. Andrew Ward) and producer Mad Marga (b. Steven Andre), whose additional personnel include DJ Killerman Twice (b. Nicholas Swaby), Cavey (b. Ian Williams; producer), Malika B Poetess (b. Malika Booker) and singer Ann Gray. Their imaginative utilisation of beats and rhythms appropriated from a variety of sources like jazz, dub and ska, place them squarely in the Black British underground tradition. They have also operated in an admirably collective manner, handing the mic over to a number of contributors (including a healthy female ratio) and collaborating with other groups like Cookie Crew, Hijack and Son Of Noise. The mainstays have also given production assistance to several other Kold Sweat outfits, including Rude Boy Business, Superb C and Ambassadors Of Swing.
Albums: *Diary Of A Black Man Living In The Land Of The Lost* (1991), *Dark Tales From Two Cities* (Kold Sweat 1993, double album).

Kid Frost

b. Arturo Molina Jr, 31 May 1964, Los Angeles, California, USA. Mexican-descended rapper who was raised on military bases in Guam and Germany, but did most of his growing up in East Los Angeles, where he began delivering rhymes in 1982. He was inducted into the ranks of Uncle Jam's Army, as the West Coast began to accomodate the innovations of the Bronx. A major force in the establishment of Latin hip-hop, Frost brought together several other Hispanic rappers for the Latin Alliance project in 1991. Before then he had made strides with his 1990 solo set, another important signpost in the sub-genre's development. His blend of Chicano social observation and pulsing rap breakbeats provided him with a considerable audience outside of his own socio-genetic bracket. Now signed to Virgin, Kid Frost deploys the intelligence to sample not only from funk's back-catalogue, but also that of the salsa tradition of his own people.
Album: *Hispanic Causing Panic* (Virgin 1990), *East Side Story* (Virgin 1992).

Kid 'N Play

Among rap's most innocuous outfits, Kid 'N Play

Kid Sensation

came to light in 1988 through an album that to date represents their best work; and typified their happy go lucky, cartoon style. So much so that the group were offered their own cartoon series, following their appearance in *House Party* (*Kid 'N Play's Funhouse* is a spin-off from the film, including actual dialogue). Kid (b. Christopher Reid) and Play (b. Christopher Martin) concentrate heartily on a youthful style of braggadocio, typified on their debut album by the two-timing morality sequence, 'Undercover' (which featured guest vocals by the Real Roxanne), or the self-explanatory 'Rollin' With Kid 'N Play'. Their music is underpinned by the production of mentor Hurby Luv Bug, while their wholesome messages like 'Don't do drugs' and 'Stay in school' are unlikely to offend middle-class American sentiments.

Albums: *2 Hype* (Select 1988), *Kid 'N Play's Funhouse* (Select 1990), *Face The Nation* (Select 1991).

Kid Sensation

b. Steven Spence, Seattle, Washington, USA. Rapper who first came to fame as Sir Mix-A-Lot's DJ and keyboardist, before scoring a minor success with his own debut album. After graduating in 1988, he became part of the Sir Mix-A-Lot posse behind 1988's platinum-selling *Swass* set. It encouraged him to embark on his own career, which was soon rewarded when his debut album provided three hit singles, 'Back To Boom', 'Seatown Ballers' and 'Prisoner Of Ignorance'. His self-aggrandising title was reflected in the cool braggadocio of much of the material on offer, but by the advent of a follow-up album there was a message behind the rhymes. 'I'm trying to show I'm a down to earth guy, it's more of what I'm all about'. The b-side of the album's promotional single, 'Ride The Rhythm', was 'The Way I Swing'. This was a duet with the Seattle Mariner's all-star centerfielder, and Sensation's sporting idol, Ken Friggy Jr.

Album: *Rollin' With Number One* (Nastymix 1990), *The Power Of Rhyme* (Nastymix 1992).

Kilo

b. c.1972. Prolific young artist who was raised by his grandparents in the north west projects of Atlanta, known as Bowen Homes. Turned on to hip hop, he recorded his first demos at the age of 15 with the help of his DJ Red Money. These recordings eventually crystallised into a debut set that was released on the local Arvis imprint. The album would sell over 40,000 copies in the South East region, its sales profile buoyed by the attendant hit single, 'Cocaine'. *A-Town Rush* was similarly successful, again almost entirely on the back of local sales. Kilo went on to win Atlanta's Coca Cola Music Awards for the best Rap Artist in March 1992, prompting a bidding war within the rap label community. Wrap/Ichiban won out, and promptly re-released and re-promoted the artist's first and second albums. The duo returned to the studio in 1993 with a slightly less commercial approach, which made the resultant album less airplay-friendly, but it was again highly regarded by the critics (and spawned the hit single 'Tick Tock'). Kilo's second album from the same year was granted the production expertise of Carl Cooley, 'C' Dorsey and Craze, and was another ample demonstration of his resonant, high-pitched delivery and lyrical skill.

Albums: *America Has A Problem...Cocaine* (Arvis Records 1991), *A-Town Rush* (Arvis Records 1992), *Bluntly Speaking* (Wrap/Ichiban 1993), *Git Wit Da Program* (Wrap/Ichiban 1993). Compilation: *The Best And The Bass* (Wrap/Ichiban 1994).

King Just

b. c.1974. Another of the new crop of Staten Island (aka Shaolin) rappers, whose appropriation of the 'Shaolin' martial arts ethos saw him compared to neighbours the Wu Tang Clan. He made his debut with the 'Warrior's Drum' 12-inch, which became a huge underground hit in 1994. Backed by his crew/gang, Blackfist (also the title of his label, operated through Select), it was competent hardcore but seemed somewhat unoriginal in the context.

Kilo

King Sun

Mediocre artist whose records contain the over-familiar self-deifying advocacy of a rash of other rappers, alongside Afrocentric/Islamic concerns. Matters began more promisingly in 1987 when he teamed up with D Moe for the 'Hey Love' minor hit, which borrowed liberally from 'Moments In Love' by the Art Of Noise. Nothing in his more recent work has proved other than dispensable, however, and he remains best known for his bravery in dissing Ice Cube while the latter was peforming.

Albums: *XI* (Profile 1989), *Righteous But Ruthless* (Profile 1990), *King Sun With The Sword* (Profile 1991).

King Tee

b. Los Angeles, California, USA. Based in Compton, King Tee made his first entrance into music as a mixer for Houston's KTSU and KYOK radio stations. Through his radio connections he recorded his first record, 'Payback's A Mother', for Greg Mack's Mackdaddy Records. A contract with Capitol brought two albums together with producer DJ Pooh, but negligible success. However, he did have his moments. The first album was distinguished by jokey cuts like 'I Got A Cold', on which he delivered a remarkable impression of a vexed sinus. The follow-up was harder, tracks like 'Skanless' extolling the joys of bedding his friend's wife. 'Time To Get Out' was a rare flash of insight, and by far the best track on show. Tee did at least introduce the world to the potentially far more interesting Tha Alkaholics.

Albums: *Act A Fool* (Capitol 1989), *At Your Own Risk* (Capitol 1990).

KMD

Long Beach, Long Island, New York-based rap outfit who have allied their breakbeats to a strong moral and political stance. This was made evident by their commitment to be a 'positive Kause (sic) in a Much Damaged Society', on their 'Rap The Vote' college tour of the US, an attempt to encourage young people to vote. They were a key element in 3rd Bass's RIF production roster, whose MC Serch (who discovered them) and Pete Nice handled executive production duties on *Mr Hood*. The fluid sound of the latter featured twisted riffs and hip hop holding together a barrage of samples. However, the following years would not prove easy ones for the band. Their DJ, Subroc, brother to lead rapper Zevlove X, was killed in a car accident in 1993. The band were just readying themselves for the release of a promotional single ('What A Niggy Know'), when they were called into a meeting with label bosses on April 8 1994, where chairman Bob Krasnow informed them that they were not happy with the artwork for *Black Bastards*. This featured a 'Sambo' character being hung by the noose. The thinking, on KMD's part, was to 'execute the stereotype'. However, R&B Billboard columnist Terri Rossi had already taken issue with the image, without really understanding the statement. It was a classic case of Time Warner paranoia in the wake of the 'Cop Killer' issue, dropping the band even though they were prepared to discuss changes, and hardly the tonic a recovering Zevlove needed. Ironically, the music on the second long playing venutre was a more sober affair, in a more reflective mode ala A Tribe Called Quest. It was lyrically informed by Last Poet Gylan Kain's spoken jazz (notably the *Blue Geurilla* set).

Album: *Mr Hood* (Elektra 1991), *Black Bastards* (Elektra 1994; withdrawn).

K-9 Posse

K-9 Posse were the unhappy result of Arista attempting to gatecrash the hip hop party in the late 80s. The group were formed at Fairleigh Dickinson University in Teaneck, New Jersey, by Wardell Mahone and Vernon Lynch. The two rappers were in need of a DJ and up to the decks stepped Terrence Sheppard in 1988. Conscious rhymes about 'Someone's Brother' were present on their debut album, but no hit singles were forthcoming and the band soon disappeared from the face of the rap world.

Album: *K-9 Posse* (Arista 1989).

Kokane

Kokane was previously premiered as the dancehall DJ featured on NWA's *Efil4Zaggin'*. He moved over to more traditional rapping for his solo debut, which featured guest appearances from Above The Law's Cold 187um (who also produced, and was responsible for giving Kokane his nickname), Tha Alkaholics (on 'All Bark And No Bite'), while 'Don't Bite The Phunk' continued Ruthless' 'house policy' of lambasting Dr Dre. Like much of the rest of the album's tired G-funk formula, it was a somewhat misplaced and unoriginal move.

Album: *Funk Upon A Rhyme* (Ruthless 1994).

Kold Sweat

Innovative and highly regarded UK hip hop operation, who initially made their name by staking over £6,000 of studio time in the embryonic Katch 22, allowing them to spend a month recording their *Diary Of A Blackman*. Their other artists include the F9s, SL Trooper's (who began the catalogue with 'Knowledge...Put Your Brain in Gear'), Rude Boy Business, Unanimous Decision, Korperayshun, Black Prophets and Son Of Noise.

Selected album: Various: *Raw Flavours Volume 1* (Kold Sweat 1994).

Kool G Rap And DJ Polo

New York-based protégés of the omnipresent Marley Marl, Kool G (b. Nathaniel Wilson, 20 July 1968, Elmhurst, Queens, New York), so called to infer 'Kool Genius Of Rap', has yet to build a commensurate profile following three rich, undervalued albums. This despite hardcore benchmarks like 'Streets Of New York', and a marvellous debut single, 'It's A Demo'. 'Streets Of New York' was housed on a second album produced by Eric B and Large Professor and featuring guest appearances from Big Daddy Kane and Biz Markie. Their third album was passed over by Warners when they saw the sleeve - which merrily depicted the duo in baraclavas feeding steak to a pair of rotweilers, while in the background stand two white males on chairs with nooses around their necks. As if to send the censorship lobby into further frenzy there was a guest appearance for Ice Cube, one of their oldest enemies, on the enclosed record. The best of their admittedly patchy first three albums were pieced

together for *Killer Kuts*.

Albums: *Road To The Riches* (Cold Chillin' 1989), *Wanted: Dead Or Alive* (Cold Chillin' 1990), *Live And Let Die* (Cold Chillin' 1992). Compilation: *Killer Kuts* (Cold Chillin' 1994).

Kool Herc

b. Clive Campbell, 1955, Kingston, Jamaica, West Indies, moving to New York in 1967. Kool Herc (aka Kool DJ Herc) owns the rights to the accolade 'first hip hop DJ', though his talent was never captured on record. Illustrating the connections between reggae and rap which have largely been buried by successive hip hop generations, Herc brought his sound system to block parties in the Bronx from 1969 onwards. By 1975 he was playing the brief rhythmic sections of records which would come to be termed 'breaks', at venues like the Hevalo in the Bronx. His influence was pivotal, with Grandmaster Flash building on his innovations to customise the modern hip hop DJ approach. Herc's methods also pre-dated, and partially introduced, sampling. By adapting pieces of funk, soul, jazz and other musics into the melting pot, he would be able to keep a party buzzing. With his sound system the Herculords, he would tailor his sets to the participants, most of whom he knew by name. He would call these out over improvised sets: 'As I scan the place, I see the very familiar face...Of my mellow: Wallace Dee in the house! Wallace Dee! Freak For Me!'. Grandmaster Flash himself admits he would often be so embarassed when Herc picked him out of the crowd and offered him elementary lessons in the art of DJing that he would have to leave. Nevertheless, the pack eventually caught up and his influence was dying down when his career was effectively aborted by a knife fight. He was an innocent bystander when three youths attempted to push past his house security and he was stabbed three times, twice in the side and once across his hands. After that his club burned down and, as he himself recalls: 'Papa couldn't find no good ranch, so his herd scattered'. As one of hip hop's founding fathers, Kool Herc's reputation and influence has outlasted the vaguaries of musical fashion. A status no doubt boosted by the fact that he has not

Kool Moe Dee

attempted to launch a spurious recording career on the back of it. A shame though, that he has never seen the commercial rewards of his innovations, though he was the subject of celebration at the Rapmania Festival in 1990.

Kool Moe Dee

Once of original rap pioneers Treacherous 3, Kool Moe Dee (b. Mohandas DeWese, Harlem, New York, USA) has carved a solo career bracing his old school style against the more urbane concerns of the new wave. He originally started rapping in his native Harlem by grabbing the mic at house parties, soon hooking up with his Treacherous colleagues L.A. Sunshine and Special K. However, with intrest failing in the group following the arrival of Run DMC *et al*, he elected to leave the group: 'Rap is repetitous. It gets to the pont where you wana hear hard beats, then it goes back to where you wanna hear melodies. You just gotta be on the right vibe at the right time'. He would go on to graduate from SUNY at Old Westbury, before his solo CV started in earnest when he joined up with Teddy Riley for the crossover hit, 'Go See The Doctor', a cautionary account of the dangers of AIDS. Released on Rooftop Records, it won him a fresh contract with Jive. Much of his notoriety as the 80s progressed involved a long-running duel on record with LL Cool J, the first flowering of which was the title-track to his second, platinum-selling album. A succession of minor hit singles has ensued, including 'Wild, Wild West', 'They Want Money' and 'Rise And Shine', the latter featuring Chuck D (Public Enemy) and KRS-1 on complementary vocals. He also became the first rap artist to perform at the Grammy Awards (following the success of *Knowledge Is King*), and continued to fight back against gangsta rap's mysognist vocabluary: 'When you get funke funke wisdom, then you'll understand, The woman is the driving force for any powerful man, From birth to earth to earth to rebirth, it ain't a curse, Put your thoughts in reverse'. This from a man who has already written over half a dozen screenplays, several of which were close to deals in 1994.

Albums: *Kool Moe Dee* (Jive 1986), *How Ya Like Me Now* (Jive 1987), *Knowledge Is King* (Jive 1989), *Funke, Funke Wisdom* (Jive 1991). Compilation: *Greatest Hits* (Jive 1993).

Kool Rock Jay

b. Leo Dupree Ramsey Jr, Oakland, California, USA. A rapper whose depictions of urban reality were addressed with a detached, almost resigned air. He began to freestyle at the age of 10, when his radio first picked up rap on the Californian airwaves. He adopted the style, and wrote his own words to the beats he heard, competing with the neighbourhood boys to perfect his delivery. His principle influneces were the political heavyweights Public Enemy and KRS-1. He hooked up with his DJ, Slice (b. Michael Brown, though he was known in Oakland circles as the 'Beat Fixer'), at a party in Fresno, adding Nate The Great (b. Jonathon Matthews) and Chuck Nice (b. Charles Johnson). As they built a strong local reputation the final jigsaw piece arrived in the shape of producer Lionel 'The Super Duper Dope Hook Man' Bea. Through him the group won a contract with Jive Records. Their debut album was premiered by their best-known cut, 'It's A Black Thing', released as a single. Decidedly on the Afrocentricity theme, it was critically well-received but afterwards their camp remained comparitively quiet.

Album: *Tales From The Dope Side* (Jive 1990).

Krispy 3

Chorley, Lancashire, England-trio comprising Mr Wiz, Sonic G and Microphone Don, who made their reputation with two strong 1991 cuts, 'Destroy All The Stereotypes' and 'Don't Be Misled', both of which showcased their jazz/rap leanings. Their debut album, however, only included three tracks not released on their initial brace of 12-inches, which lessened its impact. Much more representative was a subsequent set for Kold Sweat, which included an attack on music business nepotism in 'Who Ya Know' while the title-track argued against the virtual ending of the vinyl format (ironic given that their debut set was issued on CD only).

Albums: *Krispy 3* (Gumh 1992, CD-only), *Can't*

Melt The Wax (Kold Sweat 1993), *Head Out Da Gate* (Kold Sweat 1993, mini-album).

Kriss Kross

Two black youths from Atlanta, Georgia, USA, who topped the Billboard charts with 'Jump', a song anchored by the bass line to the Jackson 5's 'I Want You Back'. Chris 'Mack Daddy' Kelly (b. 1978) and Chris 'Daddy Mack' Smith (b. 10 January 1979) were both just 13 years old when they scored with 'Jump', the fastest selling single the US had seen for 15 years. In the process they instigated a batch of 'kiddie rap' clones. They were discovered in 1991 by writer/producer Jermaine Dupree, himself only 19, when he was shopping for shoes in Atlanta. Influenced by the likes of Run DMC and Eric B And Rakim, their visual character was enhanced by their determination to wear all their clothes backwards. Strangely enough, considering their natural teen appeal, they were signed up to the genuinely hardcore New York label Ruffhouse, home of Tim Dog and others. *Totally Krossed Out* sold over four million copies and spawned another hit, 'Warm It Up'.
Album: *Totally Krossed Out* (Ruffhouse 1992), *Da Bomb* (Ruffhouse 1993).

KRS-1

b. Lawrence Krisna Parker, 20 August 1965, New York, USA. The kingpin of Boogie Down Productions and a genuine hip-hop pioneer, KRS-1's standing is reflected not only in terms of his music, but also his lecture tours of the US, appearing at Yale, Harvard, and countless other institutions to the dismay of some members of those establishments. His list of achievements is hardly limited to this, however. He has been given the keys to Kansas City, Philadelphia and Compton, California. He was nominated for the NACA 1992 Harry Chapman Humanitarian Award, and holds the Reebok Humanitarian Award, and three Ampex Golden Reel Awards. He inaugurated the Stop The Violence Movement, and recorded 'Self-Destruction', which raised over $600,000 for the National Urban League, and the

human awareness single, 'Heal Yourself'. He has collaborated with REM (rapping on 'Radio Song', Michael Stipe returning the favour by assisting on the HEAL project), Sly And Robbie, Shelley Thunder, Shabba Ranks, Ziggy Marley, Billy Bragg, the Neville Brothers, Kool Moe Dee, Chuck D of Public Enemy and Tim Dog, among many others, and taken part in several important benefit shows for Nelson Mandella, Earth Day etc., as well as attending rallies with Jesse Jackson. Following the death of his erstwhile partner, Scott La Rock (whose violent exit played a significant role in KRS-1's anti-violence tracts), he has been joined on recent recordings by Gang Starr's DJ Premier and Kid Capri. His post-BDP work combines hints of ragga with strong, bass driven funk and beatbox samples. He remains one of the philosophically more enlightened rappers: in particular fighting against the use of the terms 'ho' and 'bitch' when discussing women. His first album to be released outside of the Boggie Down Productions banner was *Return Of Da Boom Bap*, though many references to his past remained. 'KRS-One Attacks', for instance, looped part of the *Criminal Minded* title-track, and 'P Is Still Free' updated his 1986 anti-crack opus, 'P Is Free'. KRS-1 remained as arrogant as they come: 'I'm not a rapper. I am rap. I am the embodiment of what a lot of MCs are trying to be and do. I'm not doing hip-hop, I am hip-hop'. The early 90s also saw some words and actions that would seem to contradict earlier statements, notably his physical attack on Prince B of PM Dawn. 'The way I stop the violence is with a baseball bat and beat the shit out of you...If negativity comes with a .22, positivity comes with a .45. If negativity comes with .45, positivity comes with an Uzi: The light has got to be stronger than darkness'. An adequate rebuttal, but apparently all PM Dawn had done to diss KRS-1 was to suggest in a copy of *Details* magazine that: 'KRS-1 wants to be a teacher, but a teacher of what?'. In retaliation KRS-1 and his posse invaded the stage during the following night's PM Dawn gig at the Sound Factory Club in New York, throwing Prince Be offstage and commandeering the microphone for his own set. The whole event was filmed live by *Yo! MTV*

Raps. Though he later apologised publicly, in private KRS-1 was telling the world that he was tired of MCs and hip hop crews disrespecting him. That he feels it necessary to so piously protect it is the only real blemish on his reputation.

Albums: *Return Of Da Boom Bap* (Jive 1993). Various: *HEAL: Civilization Versus Technology* (Elektra 1991).

K7

Manhattan-based, Latin-flavoured hip hop crew who saw chart success in 1993 with the addictive and anthemic 'Come Baby Come'. The quintet combine energetic R&B arrangements with clean raps, a style which has been unkindly referred to as 'The Hispanic Take That'. Led by K7, who gives the group their name, they also feature DJ Non-Stop, Prophet, Tre Duece and LOS. K7's attitude to labelling is unequivocal: 'My music is male bonding on a hip hop level. It's not rap music'. The party-jam spirit of their debut single was present alongside more of the same on their debut album, which included the bilingual 'Zunga Zeng' cut, as well as a rather embarrassing attempt at 'A Little Help From My Friends'.

Album: *Swing Batta Swing* (Tommy Boy 1994).

Kurious

b. c.1969. Of Puerto Rican descent, Kurious (Jorge Antonio Alvarez) broke big in late 1992 with the underground smash, 'Walk Like A Duck'. Based in uptown Manhattan (as described in the single, 'Uptown Shit'), Jorge and his Constipated Monkey crew won their reputation as talented freestylers, Jorge himself earning the title 'Freestyle King'. Despite the kudos his name inspired in the early 90s, by 1994 he was making a staunch bid to crossover with the radio-friendly 'I'm Kurious', originally written as long ago as 1991. His debut album, too, was three years in the making, eventually emerging as the debut platter on Prime Minister Pete Nice's Hoppoh Records. It was titled *Constipated Monkey* because of protracted negotiations between Hoppoh and Def Jam, who he had originally signed a contract with. He had worked as a messenger for Def Jam Records in

KRS-1

1988, before Russell Simmons offerred him a contract. However, after he rose to prominence because of his open mic dexterity, he decided to honour a verbal arrangment with Nice instead. His debut album was produced in conjunction with the Stimulated Dummies and the Beatnuts. It featured excellent, thoughtful rhymes of the ilk of 'Spell It With J (Yes, Yes Jorge): 'Malt liquor got me trapped so my rap is controversial, Might drink the brew but I won't do the commercial'. It revealed the depth of the education his single parent mother had encouraged him to pursue at Farleigh Dickinson University.

Album: *A Constipated Monkey* (Hoppoh 1994).

Kwamé

b. Kwamé Holland, East Elmhurst, Queens, New York, USA. Mild-mannered rapper whose relatively sunny disposition enshrines his recording profile. Something of a welcome change to the OG's and their attendant posturing, he is supported on stage and record by his backing band A New Beginning, variously credited in the titles of his first three releases. Growing up in and around the New York jazz set, he mingled happily with musicians of the order of Stevie Wonder and Lionel Hampton, the latter giving Kwamé his first set of drums. His debut album was produced by Hurby Luv Bug Azor, while the second was something of a 'concept' affair. This and his third set, *Nastee*, brought a string of hit singles in 'Only You', 'The Rhythm', 'The Man We All Know And Love', 'One Of The Big Boys', 'Nastee' and 'Sweet Thing'. He moved to Wrap in 1994 for *Incognito*, recorded alongside partners DJ Tat Money and A-Sharp in Atlanta, Georgia. 'This record is growth', he eulogised, 'It's my reincarnation, and I return Incognito'.

Albums: *The Boy Genius* (Atlantic 1989), *A Day In The Life - A Pokadelic Adventure* (Atlantic 1990), *Nastee* (Atlantic 1991), *Incognito* (Wrap/Ichiban 1993).

L

Lady B

Lady B's debut single was originally released on the Tec label, based in Philadelphia. Afterwards it was picked up by Sugarhill, who re-packaged it in a slightly re-recorded version. Entitled 'To The Beat Y'All', it told of Jill (from the nursery rhyme scenario of Jack and Jill fame) falling pregnant, rather than just down the hill, and advising her of her stupidity in not using contraception. Fellow Sugarhill act Sequence would come back at her with the answer record 'Simon Says', extending the onus of responsibility to the man.

Lady Of Rage

Coming to prominence via her engaging support/crowd-warmer spot on tours with Snoop Doggy Dogg and mentor Dr Dre, the Lady Of Rage also part-times as hairdresser to the stars of the Dogg Pound. She was living in New York when Dre called her at her job at Chung King Studios, where she was the receptionist. He had heard her guesting on the LA Posse album, having also performed with Chubb Rock and Branford Marsalis. She did not believe it was Dre until he sent her an air ticket in the post, but Rage has remained in Los Angeles since she arrived there in 1990. Part of the Dogg Pound alongside luminaries like Snoop Doggy Dogg, and signed to Dre's Death Row Records, her debut release was the ruffhouse 'Afro Puffs' cut, also featured on the basketball movie, *Above The Rim*.

Laquan

b. c.1975, Los Angeles, California, USA. Rapper whose debut set was surprisingly mature, especially in its grasp of social issues, considering he was barely 16 when he recorded it. Though the harmonies were gentle, Lacquan's words were not, accusing President Bush of 'Living large while others starve', among other charges. His debut album featured a live band and backing singers, orchestrated by Bel Biv Devoe studio crew

Leaders Of The New School

Richard Wolf and Bret Mazur, adding a soulful sheen to proceedings.

Album: *Notes Of A Native Son* (4th & Broadway 1990).

Last Poets

Coming out of the poverty-stricken ghetto of Harlem, New York in the mid-60s, there are many who claim the Last Poets to be the first hip hop group proper. Comprising Suliaman El Hadi, Alafia Pudim, Nilijah, Umar Bin Hassan (aka Omar Ben Hassan - as with other personnel name alterations occurred frequently) and Abio Dun Oyewole, the Last Poets formed on May 19th 1968 (Malcom X's birthday). Hassan wasn't actually an original member, joining the band after seeing them perform on campus and insisting on membership. Together the Last Poets cut powerful protest gems like 'Niggas Are Scared Of Revolution' and 'White Man's Got A God Complex'. Their legacy, that of the innovative use of rap/talk over musical backing, has born obvious fruit in subsequent generations of hip hop acts. Oyewole would leave after their debut album. They reformed in 1984, with two 12-inch singles, 'Super Horror Show' and 'Long Enough', although the group was still split into two separate camps. More recently Hassan released a solo LP featuring Bootsy Collins, Buddy Miles and others, after a period of seclusion, and drug and family problems. He has been keeping company with rap stars like Arrested Development and Flavor Flav, and also starred in John Singleton's *Poetic Justice* film. Whilst not bitter about failing to reap the financial rewards which subsequent rappers have done, Hassan remains philosophical: 'As far as I'm concerned we made a market, for those young boys to have their careers...I understand that some brothers are still trying to find their manhood. But it ain't about drive-by shootings. That's madness. Self-destruction. Real gangsters don't go around shooting everybody'. Another former Last Poet, Jalal Nuridin, who released an album alongside Kool And The Gang and Eric Gale under the title Lightnin' Rod (*Hustlers Convention*), went on to become mentor to the UK's acid jazz fusion team, Galliano. Incidentally, this is a different Last Poets

to the one comprising David Nelson, Felipe, Luciano and Gylan Kain who titled themselves the Original Last Poets and recorded an album for Juggernaut in 1971.

Albums: *The Last Poets* (Douglas 1970), *This Is Madness* (Douglas 1971), *Oh My People* (Celluloid 1985), *Freedom Express* (Acid Jazz 1989). Compilation: *Right On!* (Collectables 1986). Umar Bin Hassan solo: *Be Bop Or Be Dead* (Axiom 1993). Jalal Nuridin solo: As Lightnin' Rod: *Hustlers Convention* (Douglas 1973).

Latin Alliance

A consortium of Latin and Hispanic hip hop artists formed by Kid Frost in October 1989, which included other luminaries such as Mellow Man Ace and A.L.T. Topics such as slavery in Puerto Rico and other ethno-centric concerns such as exploitation and alienation dominated. The most effective track was 'Latinos Unidos', which celebrated the cultural and social identity of the race. It produced one Top 60 single, 'Low Rider (On The Boulevard)'.

Album: *The Latin Alliance* (Virgin 1991).

Lazy, Doug

More widely known for his production work, Lazy's own recorded output betrays not only a love of hip hop energy, but also an eye for house music's pulsing rhythms. As a producer he is one of the more credible exponents of the hip house movement, while his solo hits include 'Let It Roll' and 'Let The Rhythm Pump', the latter based on Funkadelic's 'One Nation Under A Groove'. He also appeared on Raze's 1991 single, 'Bass Power'.

Album: *Doug Lazy Gettin' Crazy* (Atlantic 1990).

Leaders Of The New School

Highly touted Uniondale, New York-based hip hop troupe, combining aggressive vocals with loping bass beats, and like many of the newer rap artists deploying lyrics which extol the joys of marijuana. However, they retain an experimental edge - particularly in their complex rhythmic structures and 'mysticism'. They are fronted by the giant Busta Rhymes (b. c.1972), an impressive rapper who served a long apprenticeship freestyling

LeShaun

before cutting his first record. Backed by Charlie 'The Freestyle Wizard' Brown, Dinco 'The Rhyme Scientist' D and Milo In De Dance (aka The Cut Monitor), the Leaders concern themselves not only with the current problems facing black culture in general and hip hop in particular, but also its immediate past: 'Leaders Of The New School learnt from the old school and groups like the Cold Crush Brothers. We then developed our own unique style which a lot of people have started to copy'. It was certainly true that the band had etched a real impression with their debut, with three tracks produced by Eric Sadler of the Bomb Squad. The temptation to make their second set a facsimile of the winning formula was avoided, subtitling the album 'The Inner Mind's Eye - The Endless Dispute With Reality'. This was unified by the central concept of: 'Good and bad is internal in everyone and nobody but you can touch that. When you understand your mind, you understand your self and you'll be able to choose what direction you move in'.

Albums: *A Future Without A Past* (Elektra 1991), *T.I.M.E.* (Elektra 1993).

LeBlanc, Keith

LeBlanc was previoulsy an anonymous drummer/keyboard player as part of the Sugarhill Gang's house band in New Jersey, but cut himself a slice of the action in 1983 when he recorded the before-its-time Malcolm X anthem, 'No Sell Out', for Tommy Boy Records. This fused sections of the black leader's speeches with a cut-up dance groove. It led to disputes between Tommy Boy and Sugarhill over ownership of the speeches (LeBlanc had defected when he learned that Sugarhill were not going to pay any royalties to the Malcolm X estate), while LeBlanc was also questioned on his part in the process - he was, after all, white. However, the record was sanctioned by Betty Shabazz, Malcolm X's widow, and the song played no small part in pushing the name of the black leader back into the political firmament. It was also released a year later, intended as a tribute to the UK's striking miners. By 1986 LeBlanc had assembled an album, *Major Malfunction*, which included contributions from his old and future sparring partners Doug Wimbush and Skip McDonald. They too had been part of Sugarhill's house band, and would go on to join LeBlanc as Tackhead took shape. They were also present for LeBlanc's second 'solo' album *Stranger Than Fiction*, which again spanned boundless experimentation and styles, but maintained a strong political edge. By 1991 Leblanc had joined with Tim Simenon (Bomb The Bass) in a new project, entitled Interference (singles included 'Global Game').

Albums: *Major Malfunction* (World 1986), *Stranger Than Fiction* (Nettwerk/Enigma 1989), *Time Traveller* (Blanc 1992).

LeShaun

b. c.1973. Female rapper whose debut album was an acclaimed, thoughtful variant on the gangsta rap trip. LeShaun had become a single mother at the age of 18, experiences recalled in tracks like 'Young Girlz', and brought maternal widom to bear on a number of her better cuts. The influence of Queen Latifah, her stated idol, was undeniably strong. She also collaborated on the Lords Of The Underground cut, 'Flow On'.

Album: *Ain't No Shame In My Game* (Tommy Boy 1993).

Liberty Grooves

Notable UK record label/shop run in Tooting, South London by Johnny F, a long time collector and fan of hip hop music, which opened in May 1992. Liberty Grooves began by releasing breakbeat albums and material from UK artists like the Gutter Snypes and Sniper, and also signed a licensing deal with American label Dolo. The first fruits of this marriage have been two acclaimed albums, *Freestyle Frenzy 1&2*, which showcased artists like Nas, Large Professor, Q-Tip (A Tribe Called Quest), Wu Tang Clan and more, freestyling on DJ Stretch Armstrong's New York radio show.

Selected albums: *Freestyle Frenzy 1&2* (Liberty Grooves/Dolo 1993/1994).

Lifers Group

A rap troupe culled from the bowels of the US

criminal underworld, namely Rahway State Pennitentiary in East Jersey. Put together by the thinking of inmate 660604 (Maxwell Melvins), this was an intriguing project that gathered together the incarcerated 'lifers' to discourage those who still had their freedom from living the gangsta rap lifestyle to the full. The nightmare vision of prison life was revealed in intimate, gory detail on tracks like 'The Real Deal', while the cover rammed home the message with pictures of the criminals and the cells they were forced to occupy. The set was recorded in three months after the Disney-funded Hollywood Basic Records, ever sensitive to a good cause, had heard of the scheme.
Album: *Belly Of The Beast* (Hollywood Basic 1991).

Lin Que

Previously known as Isis, Lin Que is a tough-talking New York rapper who rose to fame as part of Blackwatch, the militant consciousness movement which also spawned X-Clan. She was joined on several tracks of her debut album by Professor X of the former outfit, who offered priceless interjections of a religious/moral nature. However, not everyone found the production values to be up to scratch, and she become vulnerable to the 'Blackwatch hype' backlash which has also affected the career of X-Clan. She has since joined MC Lyte's Duke The Moon management where she works in an A&R capacity.
Albums: *Rebel Soul* (Island 1990).

LL Cool J

Long-running star of the rap scene, LL Cool J (b. James Todd Smith, 16 August 1969, St. Albans, Queens, New York, USA) found fame at the age of 16, his pseudonym standing for 'Ladies Love Cool James'. As might be inferred by this, LL is a self-professed ladykiller in the vein of Luther Vandross or Barry White, yet he retains a superior rapping agility. Smith started rapping at the age of 9, after his grandfather bought him his first DJ equipment. From the age of 13 he was processing his first demos. The first to respond to his mail-outs was Rick Rubin of Def Jam, then a senior at New York University, who signed him to his fledgling label. The first sighting of LL Cool J came in 1984 on a 12-inch, 'I Need A Beat', which was the label's first such release. However, it was 'I Just Can't Live Without My Radio', which established his gold-chained, bare-chested B-boy persona. The song was featured in the *Krush Groove* film, on which the rapper also performed. In its wake he embarked on a 50 city US tour alongside the Fat Boys, Whodini, Grandmaster Flash and Run DMC. The latter were crucial to LL Cool J's development: his *modus operandi* was to combine their beatbox cruise control with streetwise B-boy raps, instantly making him a hero to a new generation of black youth. As well as continuing to tour with the trio, he would also contribute a song, 'Can You Rock It Like This', to Run DMC's *King Of Rock*. His debut album too, would see Rubin dose the grooves with heavy metal guitar breaks first introduced by Run DMC. LL Cool J's other early singles included 'I'm Bad', 'Go Cut Creator Go', 'Jack The Ripper' and 'I Need Love' (the first ballad rap, recorded with the Los Angeles Posse), which brought him a UK Top 10 score. Subsequent releases offered a fine array of machismo funk-rap, textured with personable charm and humour. Like many of his bretherin, LL Cool J's career has not been without incident. Live appearances in particular have been beset by many problems. Three people were shot at a date in Baltimore in December 1985, followed by an accusation of 'public lewdness' after a 1987 show in Columbus, Ohio. While playing rap's first concert in Cote d'Ivoire, Africa, fights broke out and the stage was stormed. Most serious, however, was an incident in 1989 when singer David Parker, bodyguard Christopher Tsipouras and technician Gary Saunders were accused of raping a 15-year old girl who attended a backstage party after winning a radio competition in Minneapolis. Though LL Cool J's personal involvement in all these cases was incidental, they undoubtedly have tarnished his reputation. He has done much to make amends, including appearances at benefits including Farm Aid, recording with the Peace Choir, and launching his *Cool School Video Program*, in an attempt to encourage children to stay at school. Even Nancy Reagan invited him to

Monie Love

headline a 'Just Say No' concert at Radio City Music Hall. Musically, Cool is probably best sampled on his 1990 set, *Mama Said Knock You Out*, produced by the omnipresent Marley Marl, which as well as the familiar sexual braggadocio included LL's thoughts on the state of rap past, present and future. The album went triple platinum, though the follow-up, *14 Shots To The Dome*, was a less effective attempt to recycle the formula. Some tracks stood out: 'A Little Something', anchored by a sample of King Floyd's soul standard 'Groove Me', being a good example. Like many of rap's senior players, he has also sustained an acting career, with film appearances in *The Hard Way* and *Toys*, playing a cop in the former and a military man in the latter.

Albums: *Radio* (Columbia 1985), *Bigger And Deffer* (Def Jam 1987), *Walking With A Panther* (Def Jam 1989), *Mama Said Knock You Out* (Def Jam 1990), *14 Shots To The Dome* (Def Jam 1993).

London Posse

One of Britain's first credible rap acts, utilising rhymes built over expertly executed ragamuffin breaks, with cockney accents thrown in for good measure. Unfortunately, London Posse were not free of the misogyny made more explicit by the gangsta rappers (tracks like 'Sexy Gal' and 'Living' imply that the entire female gender is out *en masse* to rob them of their money). London Posse at least possess wit and a nose for rhythm to dilute their urban warnings. Stylistically it could be dated by its Eric B And Rakim-styled delivery. The band comprise Rodney and Bionic (who is titled thus due to the artificial limb he wields).

Album: *Gangster Chronicles* (Mango/Island 1990).

Lords Of The Underground

Based in Newark, New Jersey, Lords Of The Underground came to prominence via tours with Cypress Hill and Funkdoobiest, with whom their music shares more than a passing acquaintance. The group first met at college where all the band were majoring in radio communication. The frontmen are Doitall and Mr Funke (aka Mr Funky). The former also has acting interests, taking his first role in the film *The School Game*. They are backed by their DJ, Lord Jazz. Doitall and Mr Funke were originally solo artists, collaborating for the first time on a cut called 'Psycho'. 'Flow On' was eventually issued as a single, remixed by Pete Rock, while the debut collection was produced by Marley Marl. They have also been responsible for fostering the career of Rated R.

Album: *Here Come The Lords* (Pendulum/Elektra 1993).

Love, Monie

b. Simone Johnson, 2 July 1970, Battersea, London, England. Monie Love is a black, female rapper who has lived in New York since 1989. Her first recordings were with childhood friend MC Mell 'O', Sparki and DJ Pogo, under the banner Jus Bad Productions, who formed in 1987. They released a solitary single 'Freestyle'. Love started recording solo with DJ Pogo in 1988, releasing 12-inch singles on obscure underground labels which were eventually spotted by DJ Tim Westwood, who asked them to do a single for his Justice label. There were several delays in releasing it, so instead they approached Cooltempo with 'I Can Do This', which became a hit in early 1989. Love has since worked with many other rap groups including the Jungle Brothers, who she met at a London gig in September 1988. They subsequently introduced her to the Native Tongues Posse, while Afrika Baby Bambaataa would produce her debut album. There have also been collaborations with Andy Cox and David Steele of the Fine Young Cannibals on the summer 1990 single 'Monie In The Middle', and with the band True Image, who are best known for performing the theme to the *Cosby Show*. They featured on Monie's Christmas 1990 single, 'Down To Earth'. Previous hits included 'I Can Do This', 'Grandpa's Party' (a tribute to the original Afrika Bambaataa), and her biggest hit, the Spinners' cover - 'It's A Shame (My Sister)'. In 1991 she teamed up with Adeva, as well as working with Queen Latifah and Almond Joy on the Bold Soul Sisters feminist project. Tracks on her debut album like 'RU Single' were intelligent attacks on the expectations and stereotypes of black women. Despite maturity beyond her years, she recognised that this phase of her career was still an apprenticeship; 'To me, rap is a school. The heads are split between Public Enemy and KRS One's Boogie Down Productions. The students are me, Jungle Brothers, De La Soul... but the best thing about it is that the classroom is open to all'. She would go on to appear in Forest Whittaker's Harlem film, *Strapped*.

Album: *Down To Earth* (Warners 1990), *In A Word Or 2* (Cooltempo 1993).

Lovebug Starski

b. Kevin Smith, 13 July 1961, New York, USA. One of the pioneering forefathers of hip hop culture, Starski has seen commerce move rap away from what he originally envisioned. Still remembering the days in the Black Spades when 'we used to push refrigerator-size speakers through the blocks', his role in the developmental parties was pivotal. At the age of 13 he began spinning records on the playground of the Forrest Housing Project (at which time he also adopted his stage name, from the popular television show *Starsky & Hutch*). The *modus operandi* would be to set up two turntables in the South Bronx parks, or mix live at parties. He was among the first to begin 'rapping' over the records he played. Although technically too young, Starski would sneak into a West Bronx club, 371, where his friends DJ Hollywood and Peter 'DJ' Jones worked, initially under the guise of roadie. From there his reputation brought him prestige placements at upmarket venues like Dancetaria and Stardust Ballroom, before eventually being offered a residency at Disco Fever - rap's first proper home. In 1981, he released his first single, 'Positive Life', quickly followed by 'Funky Pledge', a typical Lovebug message rap preaching the virtues of education, responsibility and self-respect. By 1983, with hip-hop showing signs of moving overground, Starksi cut his first proper record deal with Fever Records, owned by Sal Abatiello, the manager of Disco Fever. 'You Gotta Believe', on which he collaborated with producer Larry Smith (Whodini etc) would go on to sell nearly a million copies. It also became the theme for WABC-television's *Big Break Dance Contest*. It was followed by the masterful 'Do The Right Thing' (produced by Kurtis Blow) and the title theme for the movie, *Rappin'*. In 1986 he enjoyed crossover hits with 'House Rocker' and 'Amityville'. For a period in the mid-80s it looked as though Starski would truly break through. He was to be seen in the same company as Luther Vandross, Sade and Michael Jackson, and found a one-off album deal with Epic. Unfortunately, the resulting record sunk without trace, and Starski became another hip hop pioneer to fall by the wayside. His slide into cocaine dependency was complete, and he returned to the streets until he was busted for possession in 1987. He was finally released in December 1991. He returned, fittingly, to his old haunt, Disco Fever.

Albums: *House Rocker* (Epic 1986), *Lovebug* (Epic 1987).

L'Trimm

Cutesy rappers whose 'Grab It!' was a literal answer to Salt-N-Pepa's 'Push It'. As the pun might suggest, their records are dominated by a locker-room approach to sexuality, and anatomical revelry of the old school. The duo are Tigra (b. 1970, New York, USA) and Bunny D. (b. Chicago, Illinois, USA).

Albums: *Grab It!* (Time X/Atlantic 1988), *Drop That Bottom* (Atlantic 1989), *Groovy* (Atlantic 1991).

Lucas

b. c.1970, Copenhagen, Denmark. His mother an artist and his father a writer, Lucas moved around the world from an early age, finding his most permanent port of call in New York. There he immersed himself in the prevailing hip hop culture on the Lower East Side, rubbing shoulders with old school crews like Kid Crush as he became first a breakdancer, secondly a DJ, and finally a rapper. By 1990 he was signed to Uptown Records as part of Key West, billed as the label's 'first white artist'. When that band fell from favour Lucas worked briefly with Chubb Rock and Kool Keith (Ultramagnetic MCs), DJing for The Lifers Project, before leaving New York for England. His debut single for WEA, 'Wau Wau Wau'/'Work In

Progress', revealed the experience he had gained. While the a-side was an easily likeable jazz-tinged affair, distinguished by a sample left on his answaphone by a drunken kid, the b-side cut, featuring the vocals of Fay Simpson (Nu Colours) and Junior Dangerous, spanned rap, soul and ragga. Lucas also became prominent in UK hip hop circles for his production skills (Nu Colours, Shara Nelson).

Album: *Living In A Sillicone Dream* (WEA 1994).

M

Maestro Fresh Wes

Until the release of his self-proclaiming 1994 album, Fresh Wes had been one of the Canadian hip hop fraternity's most closely guarded secrets. With production aid from DJ Showbiz (of Showbiz and AG fame), the MC's rhymes were delivered in old school New York style, emphasising a punning ability and freestyle approach, which was competent though hardly innovative. The introduction of jazzy overtones too, was not exactly revolutionary by this stage, though the single 'Fine Tune Da Mic' was well-received.

Album: *Nah! Dis Kid Can't Be From Canada* (LMR 1994).

Main Source

There has been much swapping and shifting in the constantly evolving line-ups of Main Source, formed in Toronto, Canada, but based in New York. The original MCs were K-Cut and Sir Scratch, though Large Professor (b. Paul Mitchell) excused himself after their first album, which included choice cuts like 'Just A Friendly Game Of Baseball. Professor would go on to work with A Tribe Called Quest, Nas, who had debuted on the debut album's 'Live At The BBQ' cut, and others.

He was replaced by Mikey D, who was installed in time to become chief rapper on their second set, the invitingly titled *Fuck What You Think*, on which they were also joined by Shaheem, a female MC recruited straight from high school (on the title-track and 'Set It Off'). Their fresh, jazzy platform was well served by the indignant, often complex lyrical matter they pursued. In the light of delays over the release of their *Fuck What You Think* set they parted company with label Wild Pitch, and Mikey D also broke ranks - claiming he did not get along with K-Cut and Scratch, looking for a solo deal instead.

Albums: *Breaking Atoms* (Wild Pitch 1990), *Fuck What You Think* (Wild Pitch 1994).

Major Force

Highly regarded Japanese hip hop crew, who would eventually have to move to London, save lead rapper Kan Takagi, to gain significant exposure. Sponsored by James Lavelle (of the Mo' Jazz label), Major Force appeared on compilations such as *The Jazz Hip Jap Project*. Takagi, meanwhile, was joined by Q Tip (A Tribe Called Quest), Jamal-Ski and the Jungle Brothers on his debut solo album.

Mantronix

DJ Curtis Mantronik (b. Kurtis Kahleel, 4 September 1965, Jamaica, West Indies, moving to Canada at age seven, then New York as a teenager) is the creative force behind these New York-based hip hop innovators, a multi-instrumental talent whose knowledge of electronics is instrumental to the band's sound. That sound, electro rap in its purest form, as suggested by the band's name, was highly popular in the mid-80s. Kahleel's use of samplers and drum machines proved.pivotal to the genre's development, not least on tracks like 'Music Madness', which used a snatch of 'Stone Fox Chase' by Area Code 615 (better known in the UK as the theme to *The Old Grey Whistle Test*). Indeed, the raps of MC Tee (b. Tooure Embden) often seemed incidental to the formula. The duo met at Manhattan's Downtown Record Store in 1985, where Mantronik was mixing records behind the turntables and introducing customers to new releases. A few weeks later, they made a demo tape and started looking for a label. Soon afterwards, William Socolov, the astute founder of independent label Sleeping Bag, was in the store and was sufficiently impressed with the demo tape Mantronik played him to offer a deal. The group's first single, 1985's 'Fresh Is The Word', was a huge street and dancefloor hit, as was their production of Tricky Tee's 'Johnny The Fox'. In late 1985 they released their first album, the adventurous *Mantronix*, which included the hit singles 'Bassline' and 'Ladies', and took the marriage of street rhyme and electronic studio wizardry to new heights. Mantronix further built their reputation with their production of Joyce Sims' 'All And All' and 12.41's 'Success Is The Word', before going on to record their second album, the competent but relatively disappointing *Music Madness*. The duo were one of the most popular acts at the historic UK Fresh hip hop festival at London's Wembley Arena in the summer of 1986, but were dropped by Sleeping Bag a year later. Mantronix appeared to have run out of fresh ideas and had been overtaken by a new generation of rappers/studio maestros. In the late 80s Tee signed up to the USAF, to be replaced by two stand-in rappers, Bryce Luvah (b. c.1970; cousin of LL Cool J) and DJ Dee (b. c.1969, Mantronik's cousin). They did hit the UK charts with *This Should Move Ya*'s promotional single, 'Got To Have Your Love'. The latter featured the vocal sheen of Wondress, while the attendant album featured a cover of Ian Dury And The Blockhead's 'Sex And Drugs And Rock 'n' Roll'. The distinctive Mantronix bass lines were still in place, though by now Kahleel was branching out into soul and R&B horizons. Possibly their best material in this format is 1991's *The Incredible Sound Machine*, which saw the introduction of singer Jade Trini. Kahleel continues to produce for others, notably English vocalist Mica Paris. In the modern age he composes all his music on an Apple Macintosh computer, a trait he shares with many of techno's leading lights..

Albums: *Mantronix* (Sleeping Bag 1985), *Music Madness* (Sleeping Bag 1986), *In Full Effect* (Capitol 1988), *This Should Move Ya* (Capitol 1990), *The Incredible Sound Machine* (Capitol 1991).

Compilation: *The Best Of (1986-1988)* (1990).

Marley Marl

b. Marlon Williams, 30 September 1962, Queens, New York, USA. Widely revered for his considerable production skills, notably for his cousin MC Shan, Big Daddy Kane, Master Ace, Roxanne Shante and Biz Markie, Marl's work is inhabited by a spirit of accessible, old school gusto. He has been widely congratulated for his innovative sampling techniques, using the SP1200 on hip hop landmarks like *Eric B For President*. He also acts as host on the weekly *Rap Attack* radio programme on the WBLS-FM station in New York. The selected albums listed below sample some of this work, including contributions from Shante and Kane, plus Kool G. Rap, Chuck D, LL Cool J, King Tee and Chubb Rock.

Selected albums: *In Control Volume 1* (Cold Chillin' 1988), *In Control Volume II* (Cold Chillin' 1991).

Marxman

Marxist rap crew whose political stance, in the final analysis, won them more fans than their music did. Yet for a period in late 1992/early 1993, they mounted an effective bid as supercharged champions of ultra left hip hop. Fronted by rappers MC Hollis and Phrase, plus musician Oisin, if Marxman's political motives weren't already guaranteed to stoke controversy, then the subject of their debut single, 'Sad Affair', was. Discussing Northern Ireland, with the explicit statement that English troops should be withdrawn, it was naturally banned by the BBC (David Tong attempted to play it but had it edited from his show - objections were made to the fact that the lyrics contained the IRA slogan 'tiocfaidh ar la' - 'Our Time Will Come'). Both sides of the debut used traditional Irish instruments (three quarters of the band are Irish-born), and the follow-up, 'Ship Ahoy', featured Sinead O'Connor. Other guest contributions have included the tin whistle of traditional Irish musician Davey Spillane. Contrastingly, both 45s emerged on Giles Peterson's laid-back Talkin' Loud empire. A third, 'All About Eve', actually made the UK Top 30, before 'Ship Ahoy' was re-released. The sleeve of

MC Breed

their debut LP confirmed their allegiances: 'Marx, Engels, Lenin, Rosa Luxemburg, Bobby Sands... and all those who have devoted themselves to the overthrow of the bourgeoisie'. Though they were allied to a major (Polygram), Marxman still set their sights on the death of capitalism. In the final analysis, however, there was simply too much analysis.

Album: *33 Revolutions Per Minute* (Talkin' Loud 1992).

Master Ace

Raised in Brooklyn, Master Ace (aka Masta Ace) became a hip hop DJ in the 70s before adjusting to MC status by 1983. He won a rapping competition two years later which earned him studio time with producer Marley Marl, before a collegiate interlude followed. He contributed to the *In Control Volume 1* set by Marl, and the latter's label, Cold Chillin', offered him a deal. His debut album, *Take A Look Around*, was fuelled by Marley Marl's funk throb and included a duet with Biz Markie. Songs like 'Brooklyn Battles' attempted to look through the blood and rage circus of urban decadent rap. He had earlier contributed to the Brand New Heavies' *Heavy Rhyme Experience* set. His second album was better yet, the title-track, 'Slaughtahouse', a clever parody on the absurd machismo of gangsta rap: '99 rappers wanna kill to sound ill, You couldn't find their brains with a drill'. However, the graphic presentation of the video failed to impress MTV who banned it. He enjoyed more success with the Crooklyn Dodgers project (alongside Special Ed and Buckshot of Black Moon), scoring with the Spike Lee soundtrack single, 'Crooklyn'. He describes himself as a hip-hop purist, and certainly his wordy, considered narratives owe a debt to Gil Scott-Heron.

Albums: *Take A Look Around* (Warners 1990), *Slaughtahouse* (Delicious Vinyl 1993).

Masters Of Ceremony

Nowadays chiefly remembered for the exploits of lead rapper Grand Puba (b. Maxwell Dixon), who would go on to front Brand Nubian before selecting a solo career. Masters Of Ceremony's singular album release was a pedestrian affair, divorced of the religious dogma, or indeed the musical precision, which characterised the work of Brand Nubian. Without which their attempts to fascimile a Public Enemy sneer wore fatally thin. However, it did include a major hit in 'Sexy'

Album: *Dynamite* (4th & Broadway 1988).

MC Breed

MC Eric Breed (b. c.1972, Flint, Michigan, USA) was originally supported by his cousin Al Breed (of DFC fame) in the early 90s, before that artist would go solo with the aid of T-Trouble E. Both Breeds would, however, remain firm friends, Eric going on to a support/advisory capacity on the latter's debut album. Under the title MC Breed And DFC, he had scored a crossover hit single (US number 66) with the debut album's 'Ain't No Future In Yo' Frontin'', a typical slice of hardnosed gangsta vanity (a theme revisited on the second set's 'Ain't To Be Fucked With', retitled 'Ain't To Be Flexed With' for single consumption). 'Ain't No Future In Yo' Frontin'' continues to enjoy a healthy half-life and has been much sampled by other rap artists. The album which bore it was produced with the aid of Bernard Terry, of Ready For The World fame. The follow-up set again saw him working with Terry and his DJ/Producer Flash Technology, its chart profile buoyed by a further three successful singles. After sessions for a third set were completed, he was invited to join George Clinton for his 'Paint The White House Black' ensemble single. When *The New Breed* emerged it brought a harder-edged sound, as might have been anticipated by its title. It featured guest apearances from 2Pac ('Gotta Get Mine'), Clinton (on the video to 'Tight') and D.O.C. Production was assisted by Warren G and Colin Wolfe. Long-term friend D.O.C. would also contribute a song to Breed's fourth set, entitled 'B.R. Double E. D'. Other guests included DFC and Jamal of Illegal fame on an album whose high watermark was set by the 'Teach My Kids' cut.

Albums: *MC Breed & DFC* (S.D.E.G. 1991), *20 Below* (Wrap/Ichiban 1992), *The New Breed* (Wrap/Ichiban 1993), *Funkafied* (Wrap/Ichiban).

MC Buzz B

b. Shorn Braithwaite. Eco-conscious UK rapper who allies his intelligent, highly wordy raps to a jazz/soul-funk melange which is characterised beyond anything else by its cool, restrained vibe. He debuted for Manchester independent Play Hard with the 12-inch only 'Slaphead' in May 1988, following it with 'How Sleep The Brave' and 'The Sequel' the following year. It was enough to procure a contract from Polydor Records, who released his ironically-titled debut album in 1991. However, a series of singles, 'The Last Tree', 'Never Change' (delayed due to problems in obtaining clearance on a sample from Bruce Hornsby's 'That's Just The Way It Is') and 'Don't Have The Time' during that period failed to break him, as he became yet another UK hip hop under-achiever. He made a comeback in 1993 by providing the vocal to Lionrock's 'Pocket Of Peace'.
Album: *Words Escape Me* (Polydor 1991).

MC Duke

Together with his DJ Leader One, this British MC released 'The Final Conflict' in 1990, which left substantial imprints in the relatively virgin soil of UK hip hop. Raised in east London, MC Duke made his recorded debut on Music Of Life's compilation, *Hard As Hell*. Later he would make his home there, releasing two relatively succesful solo albums. He picked up *Hip Hop Connection* magazine's 1990 award for Best British Recording Artist, and even broke the Top 75 of the UK charts with 'I'm Riffin''/'English Rasta', before the recession cut in. Despite two solid singles for the Shut Up And Dance label, his fortunes declined. Duke has gone on to produce the 90s compilation series *The Royal Family*, to showcase new British rap talent. In turn he set up his own label, Bluntly Speaking Vinyl, formed in conjunction with Dan Donnely (Suburban Base Records). The initial releases included a 12-inch by Phat Skillz (essentially MC Duke) and material from a new group, IQ Procedure.
Album: *Organised Rhyme* (Music Of Life 1989), *Return Of The Dread-I* (Music Of Life 1991).

MC Eric

b. Eric Martin, 19 August 1970, Cardiff, Wales. MC Eric, aka Me One, is of Jamaican descent, though he grew up in Wales as the youngest of twelve brothers and sisters. It was via his stint in Technotronic (notably the 'This Is Technotronic' refrain, appearing in said video with his notorious 'skyscraper' hairstyle) that he first graced television screens and stereos. He had been introduced to the band via his girlfriend, Ya Kid K. 'I was 18 and Ya Kid K was 17 when we came into Technotronic and we knew that the money wasn't good'. He has also contributed to material from artists as diverse as Madonna and Jazzy Jeff. His debut solo album, promoted by a single, 'Jealous', was an artistic success, with deceptively subtle shades to its musical spine, bouyed by piano motifs and lolloping bass. Following its release, however, he seems to have became another of rap's many yesterday men. In the meantime he had a child with Ya Kid K, one Eric Jnr.
Album: *I Beg Uno Ceasefire* (Polydor 1991).

MC Lyte

b. Lana Moorer, 11 October 1970, Queens, New York, USA, but raised in Brooklyn. The daughter of First Priority boss Nat Robinson, and sister to the Audio Two brothers, Lyte began her career in fine style with the 45 'I Cram To Understand U (Sam)', released when she was still a teenager. The story told of personal deceit in a relationship, the narrator unable to compete for her boyfriend's attentions with his new mistress - crack. It was delivered with such force that it still has few peers in terms of adult, hardcore female rap. Lyte has gone on to underscore her patent scouring wit, often referring to the out of control egos of her male counterparts, with synthesizer and funk beats coalescing beneath. Her debut album additionally sampled Ray Charles, Helen Reddy and the Four Seasons. Her songs are populated by fully realised characters, though its an unfortunate truism that they often wind up dead (via AIDS, lung cancer, violence or drugs). Despite the contributions of Grand Puba on her second album, which was musically solid, there was a lack of lyrical progression which limited its appeal. At which time she has also found time to appear in the video to Sinead O'Connor's 'I Want Your Hands (Show Me)'. *Ain't No Other* included attacks on fellow rappers Roxanne Shanté ('Steady F. King') and an answer record to Apache's 'Gangsta Bitch' ('Ruffneck', which would go gold when released on single). Rap forerunner KRS-1 introduced the tracks in a pseudo ragga style. Like Queen Latifah and others before her, she has founded her own management company, Dupe The Moon Productions, which also handles Isis and Brooklyn rappers Born In Hell. She was also, again like Latifah, bitten by the acting bug.

Albums: *Lyte As A Rock* (First Priority 1988), *Eyes On This* (First Priority 1989), *Act Like You Know* (First Priorty 1991), *Ain't No Other* (First Priority 1993).

MC Mell 'O'

b. Battersea, London, England. One of the earliest members of the UK's indigenous rap clan, Mell 'O' began his career in the best traditions of hip hop by breakdancing and body-popping in the streets of Covent Garden during the early 80s. He modelled himself on Grandmaster Melle Mel, calling himself Grandmaster Mellow in tribute, eventually abbreviating it to MC Mell 'O'. These activities would be followed by improvised jam sets at the Charing Cross Centre youth project. He also cruised with sound systems like First Class and Young Lion, and reggae remains a strong component in his Cockney-delivered rhymes (he was among the first British rappers to reject the process of imitating East or West Coast American accents). Together with fellow pupils Monie Love, DJ Pogo and Sparkie D, he formed the DETT (Determination, Endeavour and Total Triumph) collective, based on the New York Native Tongues principle. Together they released a solitary record, 'Freestyle', in 1987. This underground jamming scene lasted for several years, and it was not until 1989 that he released his first records. After a well-received debut album for Republic, he swiched to Jazzie B (Soul II Soul)'s Funki Dred label. However, he fell victim to record company politicking (when Motown pulled their finanical backing for Funki Dred). A completed album, due for release in 1992, was scrapped. Worse, Jazzie B held on to his contract meaning he wasn't released until December 1993. In the meantime his only sighting was as part of Island Records' *The Rebirth of Cool* set, with 'Open Up Your Mind'. Freed from Funki Dred at last, he signed to the Stereo MC's' Natural Response label in 1994. He had at least spent some of the intervening period working - notably on projects with Izit and the Young Disciples. His debut release for his new home was *The First Chronicles Of DETT*, in the summer of 1994. The first track on the record was 'I Hear Voices', which tackled the problem of mental illness in immigrant black generations, and was another intelligent, illuminating epistle from one of the genuine talents of the British hip hop scene.

Album: *Thoughts Released* (Republic 1989).

MC 900ft Jesus

aka Dallas, Texas-based Mark Griffin, one of the more credible examples of white hip hop. Alongside his musical cohort DJ Zero, Griffin explores a wide variety of styles including jazz and industrial dance. The lyrics, especially on his second album, track a more personal, introspective path than many of his peers. He made his debut in 1989 with the self-titled *MC 900ft Jesus With DJ Zero* EP, which highlighted his distinctive vocal style, which could hardly be described as rap in conventional terms, and reflected more the spoken word narratives of the beat poets. However, he had certainly been listening to the rise of hip hop on the East Coast, as his liberal steals from Public Enemy testify. His debut album centred around club rather than studio directed material. Later, he scored a degree of infamy when his single, 'The City Sleeps Tonight', caused an outcry in Baltimore, where its inflammatory lyrics coincided with an outbreak of arson. Griffin moved to Rick Rubin's Def American label in time for a projected third album.

Albums: *Hell With The Lid Off* (Nettwerk/CIR 1990), *Welcome To My Dream* (CIR 1991).

MC Pooh

b. Lawrence Thomas, USA. Rapper who emerged

in the 90s with lyrical preoccupations including sex, money and murder (his debut album even housed one cut of that title). Other songs included the socio-political 'The Projects', but elsewhere the tasteless sexual jibes continued on 'I Eat Pussy' and 'Your Dick'.

Album: *Funky As I Wanna Be* (Jive 1992).

MC Ren

b. Lorenzo Patterson, Compton, Los Angeles, USA. Another of NWA's personnel to launch a solo career, Ren has thus far failed to share the high profile of many of his former colleagues. He opened his slate with the *Kizz My Black Azz* EP, the title of which was a thinly veiled reference to the actions of Vanilla Ice. For his debut album Ren hooked up with a slew of producers, including Rhythm D, the Whole Click (which featured Ren's brother Juvenile) and Denmark-based crew Solid Productions. A deal with the latter was first mooted when Ren met them while they were working on the soundtrack to the *CB4* film, on which they encouraged Ren to participate. However, Ren has proved unable to replicate the lyrical incisiveness of Ice Cube nor the satisfying musical stance of Dr Dre. Allusions to the wisdom of the Nation Of Islam have revealed little in the way of insight or character.

Albums: *Kizz My Black Azz* (Ruthless 1992, mini-album), *Shock Of The Hour* (Ruthless 1993).

MC Serch

b. Michael Berrin, Queens, New York, USA. After splitting from white rap trio 3rd Bass, Serch remained with Def Jam for the launch of his solo career in 1992. Shortly afterwards he would take up a position as A&R Vice President for Wild Pitch Records. His sole solo hit thus far proved to be 'Love Will Show Us'.

Album: *Return Of The Product* (Def Jam 1992).

MC Shan

b. Shawn Moltke, 8 September 1965, Queens, New York, USA. Moltke enjoyed an unusual start to his hip hop career. Rather than the drudgery of demo cassettes and auditions, he was first spotted by his future Cold Chillin' boss as he attempted to steal his car. Nevertheless, with the early guiding hand of cousin Marley Marl, Shan has gone on to provide an inconsistent but occasionally interesting legacy. His debut album was the archetypal B-boy artefact, replete with Marl's stripped down production and conscious and party rhymes (the best example of the former being the anti-drugs track 'Jane, Stop This Crazy Thing!', the worst instance of the latter 'Project 'Ho'). The follow-up was more musically varied, but Shan's voice lacked the agility to compete with some exquisite samples. He dispensed with Marl in time for *Play It Again, Shan*, which, as the title might suggest, saw a bid for more mainstream territory. Apart from the instructional 'It Ain't A Hip Hop Record', there was little to distinguish this collection and its lacklustre Heavy D-styled performance.

Albums: *Down By Law* (Cold Chillin' 1987), *Born To Be Wild* (Cold Chillin' 1988), *Play It Again, Shan* (Cold Chillin' 1990).

MC Shy D

b. Peter Jones, Bronx, New York, USA. Shy D is the cousin of Afrika Bambaataa, and grew up with the sounds and philosophy of the Zulu Nation. Moving to Atlanta in 1978, he made his name via his debut single 'Rapp Will Never Die' in 1985, before joining Luke Skywalker (now Luke) Records for 'I've Gotta Be Tough' and 'Shake It'. These releases, some of the first on the label, featured the prominent 'Miami bass' sound. After two well-received albums he set up his own Benz Records imprint in 1990, but his fortunes declined thereafter, 1991 being spent in the Georgia State Penal System. More fruitful was his liaison with Wrap/Ichiban Records, which saw the release of a quality single ('True To The Game') and album which re-acquainted him with the hip hop public.

Album: *Gotta Be Tough* (Luke Skywalker 1987), *Comin' Correct* (Luke 1988), *Don't Sweat Me* (Benz Records 1990), *The Comeback* (Wrap/Ichiban 1993).

MC Solaar

b. Dakar, Senegal, but raised in Cairo and Paris, MC Solaar is the most prominent of the new breed of French rappers. His debut album (translating as

Who Sows The Wind Will Reap The Beat) gave him four Top 10 French singles, the album itself moving over 200,000 copies. It brought him to the attention of the UK's Talkin' Loud imprint. They, like many others, were impressed by his free-flowing, relaxed style, and its easy musical backdrop, formulated by his DJ/producer Jimmy Jay. Gang Starr were so taken with the album that after a single hearing they asked if they could remix the title-track. Solaar also took part in many collaborative projects for the Talkin' Loud stable (United Future Organization, Urban Species) and the Guru of Gang Starr-orchestrated Jazzamatazz project. His own material most often concerns sad stories about malcontents in the stream of French life. The wordplay and nuances do not translate easily, but the musicality of the French language does. As well as rappers like Big Daddy Kane, Solaar draws his inspiration from the French literary tradition of Baudelaire and Jaques Prevert.

Album: *Qui Seme Le Vent Recolte Le Tempo* (Talkin' Loud 1993).

MC Trouble

b. Latasha Rogers, c.1972. MC Trouble became Motown's first female rapper when she appeared in 1990 with a debut album and attendant singles ('High Roller' etc) at the tender age of 18. Backed by the soul undertow more familiar with the label, her rhymes were contrastingly harsh and cutting. Trouble's talents were obvious to many. Above and beyond being a talented contemporary rapper, she was also responsible for writing, arranging and producing her debut set. Her conscious raps included the likes of 'Black Line', which parodied black talk shows, while in a romantic mode cuts like 'Make You Mine' were offered a smooth, soulful sheen. A guest appearance by Full Force was pleasing but incidental. She passed away in the early 90s.

Album: *Gotta Get A Grip* (Motown 1990).

Mean Machine

Though somewhat unfairly consigned to the wastebasket of history, Mean Machine deserve their place in the hip hop hall of fame by dint of

MC Shy D

being the first crew to rap in Spanish, in 1979. As such they would serve as a signpost to subsequent generations of Latino rappers, from Kid Frost to Mellow Man Ace, to Cypress Hill and K7.

Melle Mel and the Furious 5

Melle Mel (b. Melvin Glover, New York City, New York, USA) was a typical black 'ghetto child' whose interest in music originally stemmed from the Beatles. He soon embraced the earliest sounds of Hip Hop in the mid 70s, becoming a breakdancer with the D-Squad. As a DJ with his brother Kid Creole he was influenced by others in the profession like Klark Kent and Timmy Tim who used to talk rhymes whilst playing music. The pair started their own brand of rapping and around 1977 set up with another DJ, Grandmaster Flash - who gave Melle Mel his new name. Flash already had one MC - Cowboy - with him, and so the new team became Grandmaster Flash and the 3MCs. Over the next couple of years they were joined by Scorpio and then Rahiem. Spurred by the success Of 'Rapper's Delight' by the Sugarhill Gang, Flash's team recorded 'We Rap More Mellow' under the name The Young Generation. Both it and a second single ('Sugar Rappin') flopped but then they signed to Sugarhill Records as Grandmaster Flash and the Furious Five. Together they recorded one of rap's greatest standards, 'The Message'. A hugely significant record which took hip hop away from braggadocio into social commentary, the featured vocalist was Melle Mel. Subsequent releases over the next few years came out under a wide variety of names and the battle for best billing plus squabbles with management and record company eventually led to the group splitting in two in 1984. A deep rift between Flash and Mel came about because, according to the latter: 'We'd known that Sugarhill was crooks when we first signed with 'em, so the plan had always been to build it up to a certain point where... they couldn't keep on taking the money that they was taking! That's what I'd been banking on, but those that left didn't seem to see it the same way'. Mel retained Cowboy and Scorpio and recruited another of his brothers King Louie III plus Tommy Gunn, Kami Kaze, and Clayton

Savage. Flash had inaugurated a $5 million court action against Sylvia Robinson's Sugarhill label to attain full rights to the Grandmaster Flash name, which he lost. The group's new operating title was thus Grandmaster Melle Mel & The Furious Five. The name was forced on the band by Sugarhill, though it infuriated Flash and Mel himself was unhappy with it. Singles like 'Beat Street Breakdown Part 1', and 'We Don't Work For Free' would fail to break the upper echelons of the charts, though Mel did appear on the intro to Chaka Khan's worldwide smash 'I Feel For You'. There was also a UK Top 10 hit with 'Step Off', after which his popularity cooled. By 1987 the mutual lack of success encouraged the separated parties to reunite as Grandmaster Flash, Melle Mel & The Furious Five for a Paul Simon hosted charity concert in New York. The intervening years between then and Mel's appearance on Quincy Jones' 'Back On The Block' were lost to drug addiction. Painfully ironic, considering that Mel's best known record remains 'White Lines (Don't Do It)', an anti-drug blockbuster which was credited to Grandmaster Flash and Melle Mel. It first hit the charts in 1983 and re-entered on several occasions. Originally targeted specifically at cocaine, it was revamped in 1989 by Sylvia Johnson because of the crack boom. Its pro-abstinence stance was not physically shared by the protagonists. When Mel was in the studio in 1982, laying down the vocal track, he admits that the 'only thing I was thinking about in that studio was listening to the record, joking and getting high'. In 1994 news broke that Mel was back and fighting fit (taking the trouble to perform press-ups for interviewers to prove the point), and working on a new album with former Ice-T collaborator Afrika Islam. He also linked with Flash for his 'Mic Checka' radio show.

Albums: *Work Party* (Sugarhill 1984), *Stepping Off* (Sugarhill 1985).

Mello K

Rapper Mello K boasts an intriguing marketing strategy: 'My rhymes are basically about females because they take to the music and they encourage guys to buy it'. Of West Indian descent, Mello K was brought up a native of New York, and first emerged as a serious artist in 1990. It was then that he was given the opportunity to work with Keith Sweat and Charlie Wilson from the Gap Band, subsequently forming his own posse, 40 Deep, hooking up with producer Monti Blues and reggae DJ Shawnie Ranks. Through Ranks Mello K debuted on his L.A. Boy Records. He also guested on the single 'Do Me', a slow-burning narrative reminiscent of lovers rock. It is this sort of material which gives Mello K his name, but he is equally capable of gruff, hard-nosed raps.

Album: *Hard & Mello* (L.A. Boy 1993).

Mellow Man Ace

b. Ulpiano Sergio Reyes, 12 April 1967, Havana, Cuba, though he moved to the US at the age of four. Ace was brought up in Los Angeles, where he made his entrance in 1990 with a debut rap LP on Capitol that swtiched between his native Spanish and English. With production offered by the Dust Brothers and Def Jef (among others), the most successful exposition was a bilingual rap over Santana's 'Evil Ways', entitled 'Mentirosa'. This was released as a single (US number 14), and he was among the key participants in the Latin Alliance project, but younger, more capable brothers have largely taken up the mantle of hispanic rap these days. These include his own blood brother, 'Sen Dog', of Cypress Hill.

Album: *Escape From Havana* (Capitol 1990), *Brother With 2 Tongues* (Capitol 1992).

Melodie MC

b. Kent Lövgren, Sweden. Dance/rap artist who began his career as a breakdancer at the age of 12 - proving good enough to be entered in major championship events throughout his native Sweden. He maintained his allegiance to the hip hop cause, releasing two moderately successful singles, 'Feel Your Body Movin' and 'Take Me Away', in 1992. His breakthrough came the following year with 'Dum Da Dum', whose dance stylings proved popular throughout Europe,

Menace To Society

especially in Germany where it sold some 200,000 copies. The follow-up, 'I Wanna Dance', was less strong, but repeated the chart success, and acted as a prelude to a debut album for the Sidelake Virgin label.
Album: *Northern Wonderland* (Sidelake Virgin 1993).

Menace To Society

Not related to the film of the same name, Menace To Society offer reality or slice of life raps about their immediate surroundings in Inkster, a suburb of Detroit, Michigan. The group's lead rapper is AGQ (b. Kevin Riley; AGQ being an acronym for American Genuine Quality) alongside Rhythm Layer Riccola (b. Andre Brintley) and Frank Nitty (b. Franchot Hayes). Their debut single, 'Streets Of Hell', set out their agenda: 'Although some of our lyrics appear to be harsh, they come to you with the reality of today's street life'.
Album: *Life Of A Real One* (Cush/Ichiban 1993).

Mercedes Ladies

A very early hip hop group, the first all-female such aggregation, which featured Zena Z, Debbie D, Eva Deff, Sherry Sheryl, alongside DJs RC and Baby D. Their origins in the Bronx, they were often to be found supporting the Funky Four at house parties and jams. Baby D, whose sassy 'frontin'' earned her lessons at the hands of Grandmaster Flash himself, would go on to a contract for East West, then Polydor, recording the LPs *Dream About You* and *ESP*.

Merlin

b. London, England. Hardly the 'new rap messiah' that his second album proclaimed him to be, Merlin nevertheless cut an intriguing figure in the British rap scene of the 90s. He was still a teenager when the record was released, but he had already chalked up a fair reputation for his late 80s releases on Rhythm King (including being arrested for stealing cheques from Mute Records just before he made an appearance on *Top Of The Pops*. One of the most notable examples of his craft was the single, 'Born Free', with its prototype UK hip hop lyrics.

Albums: *Merlin* (Rhythm King 1989), *The New Rap Messiah* (MCA 1991).

Michel'le

b. Michele'le (pronounced Me-Shell-Lay) Toussaint, c.1972, Los Angeles, California, USA. One time girlfriend and protoge of Dre Dre, Michel'le's career exploded and then disappeared with equal velocity, after she retired to have a baby. She first came to prominence as a backing vocalist for Dre's World Class Wreckin' Cru, before guesting on the D.O.C.'s remarkable debut album. Her own 1990 set brought immediate platinum status, preceded as it was by the US Top 10 single, 'No More Lies'. She also appeared on the pro-awareness single 'We're All In The Same Gang' alongside other members of the NWA posse with Hammer, Tone Loc, Digital Underground and Young MC.
Album: *Michel'le* (Ruthless 1990).

M.O.P.

Their name standing for Mash Out Posse, Lil' Fame and Billy Danzenie were the faces behind one of Select Records' freshest hardcore arrivals of 1994. They came to prominence when 'How About Some Hardcore', included on the *House Party 3* soundtrack, took off. Fame had already made his debut with three cuts on 4th & Broadway's 1992 compilation set, *The Hill That's Real*. After a projected solo deal with the label fell through, he hooked up with old friend Danzenie, then fresh out from a prison stretch. When 'Hardcore' succeeded they elected to make the partnership a permanent one. Both had grown up in Brownsville, Brooklyn, New York, and brought a sense of justice to their summaries of urban life. M.O.P. was the title of the gang they ran with, who in turn descended from the Tomahawks. M.O.P. thus started life as an 11-piece', but, according to legend, four of that number were cut down in gang fights, and five more are in jail. The sole remainder numbered Fame and Danzenie, alongside producer/manager Lazy Laz. Their debut album, produced by Darryl D, included the predictable put-downs of 'F.A.G.''s (fake-ass gangstas), while 'Blue Steel' confirmed that

'Nowadays shit is for real - so I'm packin' blue steel'.
Album: *To The Death* (Select 1994).

Movement Ex

A Los Angeles, California-based duo combining Lord Mustafa Hasan Ma'd and DJ King Born Khaaliq, whose Afrocentric/Muslim opinions (they support the Five Percent Nation Islamic creed) are frankly and sharply put. The production of their debut, recorded when they were still teenagers, was dense and tightly-wrought, engaging the listener with its austere atmosphere. Subjects included drugs, gun-running, ecology, history and sexually transmitted diseases.
Album: *Movement Ex* (CBS 1990).

Ms Melodie

b. Ramona Parker, Flatbush, Brooklyn, New York, USA. Gruff female rapper whose self-written rhymes and couplets were aided and abetted by the production skills of her (now ex-) husband KRS-1, on her debut album. The conscious lyrics were occasionally insightful, with 'Remember When' added a fitting testimony to the growth of the hip hop movement: 'The street is the root of the tree that branches out to R&B'. Melodie had formerly served time on Boogie Down Production's roster of artists. She came from a musical family; her father played saxophone and clarinet, while her mother and sisters were regulars in the local church choirs. Though her first love was soul, Melodie was immediately drawn into the emerging hip hop world when it hit her native Brooklyn streets. In additon to her work with BDP, she had also made a film appearance in the blaxploitation movie parody, *I'm Gonna Git You, Sucka*, in 1987. Her abilities also extended to fashion design which incorporated her 'sophiticated B-girl' look. The 90s have not been kind to Melodie who has been swept aside by the tide of new rap stars.
Album: *Diva* (Jive 1989).

Nas

b. Nasir Jones, c.1974, Long Island, New York, USA. From the tough Queensbridge housing projects which brought the world Marley Marl, MC Shan and Intelligent Hoodlum, Nas is a highly skilled hip hop artist whose music is crafted with a degree of subtlety and forethought often absent from the genre. He was heavily influenced by his jazz-playing father, and started rapping at the age of nine, graduating to a crew entitled the Devastatin' Seven in the mid-80s. He met Main Source producer Large Professor in 1989, in the course of recording his first demo tape. The producer introduced him to the group itself, and he would see his debut on Main Source's 1990 album *Breaking Atoms*, guesting on the cut 'Live At The BBQ', where he was part of a skilled chorus line, alongside Large Professor and Akinyele. However, though he was widely applauded for his contribution he failed to build on the impact, drifting through life and becoming disillusioned by the death of his best friend Will, and the shooting of his brother. He may well have stayed on the outside of the hip hop game had not MC Serch (Nas had guested on his 'Back To The Grill') searched him out, to provide a solo track for the *Zebra Head* film. 'Half Time', again recorded with the Large Professor, was the result. A debut album followed, with contributions from the cream of New York's producers: Premier (Gang Starr), Pete Rock and Q-Tip (A Tribe Called Quest). A hefty unit which Columbia were happy to pay the bill for, judging Nas to be their priority rap act for 1994. Nas, who had by now dropped his 'Nasty' prefix, honed a rapping style that was at once flamboyant, but with a lyrical armoury that far surpassed the expected humdrum 'bitches and ho's' routines. Serch, now A&R head of Wild Pitch, once declared Nas: 'Pound for pound, note for note, word for word, the best MC I ever heard in my life'. There was now evidence to suggest he may have been correct.

Album: *Illmatic* (Columbia 1994).

Native Tongues Posse

An informal gathering of artists based in New York, USA, which set about to confirm and celebrate the history of black women and men. Intrinsic to the rise of 'Afrocentricity' in rap music, the coalition included the Jungle Brothers, De La Soul, A Tribe Called Quest, Queen Latifah and Monie Love. A critical lashback ensued in due course, with some of the proponents, or at least some of their adherents, criticised for their obsession with 'Afrocentric trinkets'. However, the movement as a whole was one imbued with positivity and intelligence, and the Native Tongues Posse played no small part in shifting rap's agenda from the self to the social.

Naughty By Nature

From New Jersey, the trio of Treach (b. Anthony Criss, 2 December 1970, East Orange, New Jersey, USA), Vinnie (b. Vincent Brown, 17 September 1970, East Orange, New Jersey, USA) and DJ Kay Gee (b. Keir Gist, 15 September 1969, East Orange, New Jersey, USA) are a rap troupe utilising the funkier rather than darker aspects of gangsta hip hop. Heavily influenced by the patronage of Queen Latifah, the language was blue but not always in the overtly sexual sense. 'Ghetto Bastard', for example, was a master stroke, pickled in the atmosphere of the street and exact in its execution of ghetto vernacular. Unlike many other hardcore outfits, Naughty By Nature were not afraid of injecting a touch of soul into the mix (once more, ala Queen Latifah), which makes the best of their work all the more endearing. They gave Tommy Boy their biggest ever hit with the 12-inch 'OPP', the largest-grossing authentic rap single in the US in 1990, selling over a million copies ('OPP' stands for 'Other People's Pussy', incidentally, though that did not prevent several generations enthusiastically singing along to 'I'm down with OPP', making the record an American equivalent to the Shamen's 'Ebeneezer Goode'). A second album upped the sleaze factor with some lyrics, but still maintained the group's best

traditions elswhere. The single lifted from *19 Naughty III*, 'Hip Hip Hooray', became another monster hit, helped in no small part by a Spike Lee-filmed video. Treach himself was to be found in Houston acting in the film *Jason's Lyric*, though he had appeared previously in the widely-ridiculed *Meteor Man*. He has written his own film treatments, inbetween bungie jumping sessions in Daytona with close friend Pepa (Salt N Pepa). He also launched the Naughty Gear clothing line. Kay Gee, meanwhile, earned a production deal with Motown, intial fruit from which was characterised by Zhane's debut album and hit single, 'Hey Mr. Deejay'.

Albums: *Naughty By Nature* (Tommy Boy 1991), *19 Naughty III* (Tommy Boy 1993).

Nefertiti

b. c.1973, Chicago, Illinois, USA, but raised in Los Angeles. Hardcore Islamic rapper, who as a baby was held in the arms of none other than Elijah Muhammed himself. Both her grandparents were employed by the founder of the Nation Of Islam, and their views have found a new conduit in Nefertiti. She began rapping at the age of 14, but this is just one of the means of expression and communication employed by her. She also works alongside Californian activist Jim Brown on the Amer-I-Can programme, to stabilise inter-gang violence and maintain truces in Los Angeles. She also lectures widely on self-awareness and improvement. Her first recorded messages came as guest appearances on records by Professor Griff and King Tee, and from an early age she was warming up crowds before Public Enemy and Louis Farrakhan shows. Although she signed to a major label, she insisted on a far-sighted contract stipulation: that Mercury pay to put her through college. The first results of this was the *LIFE* set, standing for Living In Fear Of Extinction. This included controversial calls for repatriation to Africa, never mind an Islamic State. She was joined on the record by MC Lyte, with whom comparisons have most frequently been made. She is also not to be confused with the UK rapper of similar name.

Album: *LIFE* (Mercury 1994).

Naughty By Nature

Nemesis

Dallas trio comprising The Snake, Big Al and MC Azim. Their first single, 'Oak Cliff', appeared in 1987, but it would be four years down the line before their debut long player, *To Hell And Back*. It was promoted by the single, 'I Want Your Sex'. As their spokesman Azim was happy to point out, 'To be young gifted and black is a blessing that has been treated as a sin'. Undoubtedly this has played a part in holding back their career, as too has prejudice against Texan rappers generally.

Albums: *To Hell And Back* (Profile 1990), *Munchies For Your Bass* (Profile 1991).

New Kingdom

Hardcore hip hop duo from Brooklyn, New York, comprising rapper Nosaj (his real name Jason, backwards) and DJ Sebastian. Their debut single was 'Good Times', a rock hip hop crossover effort on Gee Street which used a sample of Joe Walsh (of James Gang)'s guitar playing and looped it. Their major influence is Curtis Mayfield, and their output reflects a good deal of his social vision. 'Good Times', for example, was written about their desire not to lose their appetite for life as they grow older. They take a full band on tour with them and have live skateboarding at their events, much in the mode of hardcore punk bands. There is certainly a 'cartoon' element to the band, their lyrics generally being abstract, non-linear collages. Their beats, however, are more restrained, as pointed out in the self-explanatory lyric: 'Pouring no lies, no suits, no ties, No need to rush, we love to fuck time'. A genuine return to the old school aural values, their debut album was produced by the band in conjunction with Scott Harding of the Lumberjacks.

Album: *Heavy Load* (Gee Street 1993).

Nice & Smooth

Based in New York City, Gregg Nice (b. Greg Mays) and Smooth Bee (b. Daryl Barnes) emerged in the late 80s with an album for independent concern Fresh Records, a matter of weeks before the label closed its doors. Their self-titled album did emerge, however, as did the two singles it yielded, 'More & More Hits' and 'Funky For You'. They switched to Def Jam for an album and hit single, 'Sometimes I Rhyme Slow', which made US number 44. Album tracks like 'Hip Hop Junkies' suggested they were authentic converts to the history of the movement, and indeed they spanned several of its styles and lyrical concerns. For their second collection they enlisted the help of some of rap and dance music's biggest heavyweights: Bobby Brown ('Return Of The Hip Hop Freaks'), Slick Rick ('Let's All Get Down'), Everlast ('Save The Children') and Jo Jo Hailey of Jodeci ('Cheri'). The duo had been trying to arrange a collaboration with Brown for some time, Barnes having previously written lyrics for his *King Of Stage* album, singing back-up vocals on tours by the latter and New Edition. Despite the supporting cast it was a set that maintained Nice And Smooth's traditions of deep funk and lyrical pyrotechnics.

Album: *Nice & Smooth* (Fresh 1989), *Ain't A Damn Thing Changed* (Def Jam 1991), *The Jewel Of The Nile* (Def Jam 1994).

95 South

From the Chill Deal Boys (who recorded albums for Quality Records) stable, and part of Toy Productions, 95 South were credited with starting a mini-revival in electro hip hop with their huge 1993 hit, 'Whoot! There It Is'. Sampling Afrika Bambaataa's epic 'Planet Rock', the single returned to good-time, basic beat-box tunes, with lyrics concentrating on the party angle, underpinned by the mighty Florida/Miami Bass sound. It was released in ompetition with Tag Team's similarly themed record. and was followed by an album which, good as it was in its own right, offered more of exactly the same. The group comprises Bootyman, Church's, Black and DJ Marcus. Together they created a monster in 'Whoot!' that refused to die; after high profile appearances on programmes like *The Arsenio Hall Show* it was adopted by both the New Orleans' Saints and Philadelphia Fillies as their theme tune. All of which was lapped up by the protagonists: 'We are a group with a simple message. We are positive, not political or controversial. We make fun music that anyone can get into'.

95 South

Album: *Quad City Knock* (Wrap 1993).

N2-Deep

A white rap trio based in Vallejo, Calfornia, USA. They were formed by their DJ and producer, Johnny 'Z' Zunino, who introduced MCs Jay 'Tee' Trujillo and TL Lyon. The title-track of their debut gave them a substantial crossover hit (reaching US number 14), though their legitimacy as an act within the hardcore Profile fraternity was confirmed with cuts like 'What The Fuck Is Going On?'.

Album: *Back To The Hotel* (Profile 1992).

NWA

The initials stand for 'Niggers With Attitude' which was the perfect embodiment of this Los Angleles group's outlook. They comprised Dr Dre (b. Andre Young), DJ Yella (b. Antoine Carraby), MC Ren (b. Lorenzo Patterson) and Eazy-E (b. Eric Wright, 7 September 1973, Compton, California, USA). Founder member Ice Cube (b. Oshea Jackson, c.1970, South Central, Los Angeles, California, USA), arguably the most inspiring of the rapping crew, departed for a solo career after financial differences with the band's manager (which would later be recorded in a highly provocative song which attacked him for, amongst other things, being Jewish). However, all the band's members had long CV's: Dr Dre had DJ'd for World Class Wreckin' Crew, and had produced Ice Cube's first band, CIA. Both Eazy E and DJ Yella had recorded and produced several rap discs under their own names, the former funding his Ruthless label, allegedly, through illegal activities. Other early members of the posse included Arabian Prince and D.O.C. NWA's first single was 'Boyz N' The Hood', marking out their lyrical territory as guns, violence and 'bitches'. Though *N.W.A. And The Posse* was their debut album, they only performed four of the raps on it, and to all intents and purposes *Straight Outta Compton* counts as their first major release. For those attracted to the gangsta rappers first time round, this was more of the same only sharper and more succinct. A landmark release, in its aftermath

NWA

rap became polarised into two distinct factions; traditional liberal (reflecting the ideas of Martin Luther King) and a black militancy redolent of Malcolm X, albeit much less focussed and reasoned. In 1989 the FBI investigated *Straight Outta Compton*'s infamous 'Fuck Tha Police', after which Cube left the group. It set a precedent for numerous actions against NWA, including the first time anyone in the music industry had received a threatening letter from the FBI. *Efil4zaggin* (Niggaz4life spelt backwards) which made US number 1, also topped the outrage factor of its predecessor by addressing gang rape and paedophilia, in addition to the established agenda of oral sex, cop killing and prostitution. Musically it contained furious blasts of raggamuffin and 70s funk, but that was somehow secondary. It did reveal some humour in the band; ie on 'Don't Drink That Wine' (which jokingly encourages drug abuse instead), or lines like; 'Why do I call meself a nigger, you ask me? Because my mouth is so muthafuckin' nasty, Bitch this bitch that nigger this nigger that, In the meanwhile my pockets are getting fat.' However, such wit was stretched paper thin over a clutch of expletives and obscenities. The UK government used the Obscene Publications Act to seize copies but were forced to return them following legal action. Ultimately the BPI withdrew their support from Island Marketing's successful action. Counsel for the defence was Geoffrey Robertson QC, who had played a similar role in the infamous *Oz* trial of 1971. Expert testimony from Wendy K of Talkin' Loud Records, rap author David Toop and psychologist Guy Cumberbatch of Aston University swung the case. This prompted a variety of statements from British MPs outlining their intention to toughen up the law. However, even the anti-censorship lobby must concede that NWA's by turns ludicrous ('Find 'Em Fuck 'Em And Flee') and dangerous ('To Kill A Hooker') songs have blurred the generally positive influence of the rap movement. As the decade progressed it became obvious that the remaining members of NWA were spending more time on their solo projects, Dr Dre in particular enjoying huge success both as an artist and producer. His

acrimonious parting from Eazy-E over monies owed through Ruthless Records was celebrated in records by both artists. Yella has been quiet, co-production credits on Ruthlesss aside, while Ren released a disappointing solo ablum and EP.

Albums: *NWA And The Posse* (Ruthless 1987), *Straight Outta Compton* (Ruthless 1989), *Efil4zaggin'* (Ruthless 1991).

Oaktown's 3-5-7

Half-hearted female rap troupe whose strings were pulled by an indulgent Hammer. Following the latter's defection from Capitol the group appear to have been washed up in the blood-letting. The group comprised local Oakland, Calfornia-rappers Sweet LD (b. Djuana Johnican), Terrible T (b. Tabatha King), Vicious C and Sweat P. The latter was formerly a cheerleader with the Oakland Raiders. By 1991 only Johnican and King remained.

Albums: *Wild And Loose* (Capitol 1989), *Fully Loaded* (Capitol 1991).

O'Neal, Shaquille

b. c.1971, Newark, New Jersey, USA. O'Neal is the star of the previously obscure Orlando Magic basketball team ('Rookie Of The Year' in 1992). After the media picked up on his demonstrative play, notably his cult slam-dunk action, he emerged as a major multi-media star of the early 90s. So much so that a record contract was around the corner, and the format was hip hop. His generally sport-related raps like '(I Know I Got) Skillz' and 'Shoot Pass Slam' kept the cash-tills rattling, the latter song being the soundtrack to the Reebok commercials he was the high profile star of. He did possess some history in the hip hop idiom, having previously been a breakdancer in Newark until his size made the activity impossible/ludicrous. Later he moved to Germany

Shaquille O'Neal

where his father, Sgt Phillip Harrison, took a post. He relocated to San Francisco to attend high school, playing for 68-1, who won the state championship. From there he was picked up by Louisiana State University coach Dale Brown, from where he joined Orlando. Basketball and music are by no means his only interests. In February 1994 he appeared in his first film, *Blue Chips*, with Nick Nolte. Incredibly, he had already penned his own autobiography, at the age of 21. His recording career was recovering from critical reaction to his long playing debut, which featured over-familiar Gap Band breakbeats funnelled through maestros like Erick Sermon (EPMD), Def Jef, Ali Shaheed (A Tribe Called Quest) and Fu-Schnickens. The final set was delivered for the approval of no lesser men than Scarface, Big Daddy Kane and Ice Cube. At least it gelled a great deal better than Paul Gascoigne or Waddle/Hoddle's ill-advised attempts to crossover from sporting to musical superstardom.
Albums: *Shaq Diesel* (Jive 1993).

Onyx

Hardcore gangsta rappers from Queens, New York, fronted by Sticky Fingaz (b. Kirk Jones), Pedro, Big DS and Suave, whose intense, gun-fixated, hard as nails image has become a popular recepticle for ill-conceived teenage fantasies in both the US and UK. They originally recorded a solitary single for Profile, 'Ahh, And We Do It Like This' before switching to Columbia. Boasting titles like 'Blac Vagina Finda', bald heads, and bad attitudes, their debut album was co-produced by Jam Master Jay (Run DMC). Nevertheless, it sold by the truckload, arguably because the music itself, on cuts like 'Throw Ya Gunz', was undeniably exciting. Almost as if to live up to his image, Fingaz found himself in trouble for allegedly asaulting a passenger on a United Airlines flight to New York from Chicago O'Hare airport. The fracas was caused by Jones' refusal to remove his Walkman in line with flight dictates. Fingaz faced a misdemeanour charge in Chicago as a result. Group member Fedro apeared in Forest Whitaker's film *Strapped* in 1993.
Albums: *Bacdafucup* (Columbia 1993).

Organized Konfusion

Duo comprising Pharoahe Monch and Prince Poetry, whose music is distinguished by both a rare knack for samples/rhythm tracks and a smooth lyrical flow. Hailing from Jamaica and New York respectively, the band's members absorbed everything from jazz and reggae to gospel in their youth. They met at high school in 1986, signing to a small independent after honing their skills. No vinyl emerged from the deal, and they switched instead to Disney-funded Hollywood Basic, scoring immediate success with the number 1 rap hit, 'Walk Into The Sun', and a well-received debut long player (which also included a second hit single in 'Open Your Eyes'). The title-track from their second album set out their stall with an attack on racist taxi drivers, and music industry incompetents. Joined by Q-Tip (A Tribe Called Quest) on 'Let's Funk', these were just two of the best tracks on an excellent album, with Po the '...exec with the intellectual concepts that elevate you like steps' ('Let's Organize').
Albums: *Organized Konfusion* (Hollywood Basic 1991), *Stress: The Extinction Agenda* (Hollywood Basic 1994).

Original Concept

Long Island four-piece who made an early impression on hip hop's underground scene with their 1986 single, 'Knowledge Me'/'Can You Feel It', following it with the mighty 'Pump That Bass'. The former was mainly notable for being the first of several rap tracks to sample the Art Of Noise's 'Close To The Edit'. On album Original Concept concentrated squarely on entertainment, using comedic raps over dance-orientated grooves. Mainman Dr Dre (not the Dre of NWA/solo fame) went on to DJ for the Beastie Boys and co-host *Yo! MTV Raps* with Ed Lover.
Album: *Straight From The Basement Of Kooley High* (Def Jam 1988).

Osby, Greg

b. 1961, St Louis, Misouri, USA. New York-based saxophonist who has attached jazz's cool to a militant hip hop beat. Following his work with the M-Base project (including Steve Coleman and

Cassandra Wilson), Osby decided he wanted to record a more free-ranging, one-off hip hop record: 'The purpose for this record was to function as an 'either/or', meaning that it could rest solely as a hardcore hip hop record without any jazz or musicians at all, and that it also would be a strong musical statement wthout breakbeats or anything. I wanted it to bridge the gap'. Alongside jazz men like Geri Allen and Darrell Grant, he enlisted the aid of hip hop producers Ali Shaheed Muhammed (A Tribe Called Quest) and Street Element, and a variety of rappers. Osby had actually begun life as an R&B musician, only discovering jazz when he attended college in 1978. Though setting up M-Base as a street-sussed jazz/hip hop enclave, he had little time for the work of Gang Starr or Digable Planets, who sample from jazz but do not, generally, work with live musicians. That did not stop him from being bracketed alongside those artists however.
Album: *3-D Lifestyles* (Blue Note 1993).

Out Cold Cops

This gang of law enforcement toughs caused the Detroit Police Department to launch an internal enquiry when it was discovered that the crew was made up of their officers. After peforming on television's the *Jerry Springer Show*, they released an album, *Diary Of A Killer*, which recounted the joys of brutalising prisoners and criminals, thereby presenting their employers with a PR nightmare.
Album: *Diary Of A Killer* (1994).

Outkast

Atlanta duo comprising Andre 'Dre' Benjamin and Antoine 'Big Boi' Patton, who broke big with 'Player's Ball' - produced by TLC backroom gang Organized Noise. It comprised tales of the streets of their local East Point and Decateur neighbourhoods. Sadly songs like 'Get Up And Get Out' introduced wholly regrettable lines like 'I learned the difference between a bitch and a lady, but I treated them all like ho's'. They are signed to LA & Babyface's LaFace imprint.
Album: *Southerplayalisticadillacmuzik* (LaFace 1994).

Outlaw Posse

Duo comprising DJ K Gee and rapper Bello, originally titled Brothers Like Outlaw, who saw the potential of their debut album neutered by a long-delayed release schedule. Disillusioned, it was some small time before the release of their next record, the 'Party Time' 45, which included a sample of the Cookie Crew's 'Born This Way'. Here they worked with a singer (Alison Evelyn) and live percussion. Although some accused them of jumping the jazz-rap bandwagon, they had actually prefaced their interest in such things as long ago as their 1989 debut single, 'Original Dope', which sampled Donald Byrd. Bello rapped memorably on the KLF's 'What Time Is Love', and also produced tracks for Upfront, while Karl has remixed for numerous artists inlcuding Queen Latifah, Mica Paris, Young Disciples and Omar. The group enlisted a live crew entitled Push, and gigged widely through Europe and Scandanavia during the 90s, eventually shortening their name to simply Outlaw. The group split shortly thereafter, Bello going on to record solo as Mister Bello. He also inaugurated his own label, Krazy Fly, to which he signed Upfront Ruddies, a crew he also manages.
Album: *My Afro's On Fire* (Gee St 1990).

Overlord X

b. c.1968. Hackney, London, England. Overlord X is a Brit-rapper who first arrived on Music Of Life's *Hard As Hell* compilation. However, he made his name with the verve of two excellent albums for Island Records, which were particularly successful in Europe. Indeed *X Versus The World* went platinum in France, making it the most popular hardcore hip hop album in that territory. Although not immediately recognisable as hardcore in the musical sense, there remained a lyrical exactitude which defied compromise. The influence of Public Enemy and Chuck D in particular has always been self-evident, notably on cuts like 'Prologue 1990', which featured a sample of the former's 'Bring The Noise'. However, Overlord had little time for NWA's ghetto-romanticism: 'Trying to say we're niggers, who the fuck are you? Coming from this brother with an attitude' ('You Can't Do It In London'). An alliance with ragga stars Midrange and Kandy on *X Versus The World* proved his diversity. He also produced their recordings as part of the X-Posse, and began work on his own film and a documentary about Hackney. Perhaps Overlord X's influence in the medium of television has had the greatest impact, however. Terry Jarvis, a well-known BBC producer, directed the promo clip, '14 Days In May', through which Janet Street-Porter commissioned him to provide continuity links between sections of *Def II*. He subsequently became producer for that show for 18 months, before providing the title-song and music for sit-com *The Real McKoy*. However, a 1992 record deal with Jarvis was less successful. His imprint, Down To Jam, was financed by Motown, but its life span was truncated by financial considerations. Overlord X, no longer employing that name, regrouped in 1994 as part of Benz.

Albums: *Weapon Is My Lyric* (Mango Street 1988), *X Versus The World* (Mango Street 1990).

P

Papa Chuk

b. Charles Roberts, c.1969, Austin, Texas, USA. Hardcore hip hop artist from Houston, Texas, where he moved in 1991 from his native Austin. As a child Papa Chuk, 'The Desolate One', practised rapping along to b-side instrumentals purchased for him by his mother, and was obviously strongly influenced by Naughty By Nature's Treach in his delivery. His debut album saw him also introduce a Jamaican patois/dancehall style, notably on cuts like 'Make Way For The Rudeboy', though other tracks like 'Desert Dog' and 'Down And Dirty' needed more to distinguish them.

Album: *Badlands* (Pendulum 1994).

Paris

b. c.1968, San Francisco, California, USA. Paris is a hardcore black Muslim rapper, widely shunned by the mainstream for his militant views. Based in San Francisco, Paris recorded his first single, 'Scarface Groove', in 1989. However, his breakthrough came with 'Break The Grip Of Shame', a typically informed and effective rant against the degradation of black communities and the need for change. It was a sublime piece of West Coast hardcore, the first fruits of his deal with Tommy Boy, which saw him hailed on MTV. The video was a provocative cocktail of footage containing uniformed revolutionaries in Africa, and images of Malcolm X and the Black Panthers. This was a fitting introduction to Paris' craft, a self-made man who remains responsible for his own production and management, backed only by DJ Mad Mike. He graduated from the University of California in 1990 with an economics degree, and is a supporter of Louis Farakhan and the Nation Of Islam. Public Enemy took him on tour and they could have found fewer more suitable warm-up acts. Despite being accused in some quarters of being dour and worthy, Paris nevertheless injected a focused, reasoning intelligence where discussions of evil reached beyond the lure of the bedroom or the villainy of the local law enforcement agency. However, tracks like 'Bush Killer' were openly inflammatory, even if they were also fun - a good example of his willingness to bookend cerebral discussion with revenge fantasies. He runs his own record label, Scarface, set up in 1987, which at one point looked likely to sign up Ice-T following his split with Warners. He did, however, produce several acts from the Bay Area, and also cut an album with the critically-acclaimed Conscious Daughters, though his excellent *Sleeping With The Enemy* set would not see a UK release. He was accused of assaulting Chris Joyce, an executive for the company which originally distributed Scarface Records, in 1994.

Albums: *The Devil Made Me Do It* (Scarface/Tommy Boy 1990), *Sleeping With The Enemy* (Scarface/Tommy Boy 1992).

Party Posse

Afflicted with poverty at their inception, this band of Harlem, New York-rappers originally practiced in the most un-party-like space of their local graveyard. The trio of DJ Alphonse Constant and rappers Randall Barber and Tedd Lewis were undeterred, believing that if they could 'party there, (they) could party anywhere'. In actual fact that piece of hallowed ground has achieved something approaching notoriety since, being used for a Doug E. Fresh video. They formed in Harlem in the late 80s, passing by unobserved until Kool Moe Dee visited their school. Inspired by him, they eventually won themselves a contract through his manager, who organised an audition for Moe Dee's home label, Jive. Moe Dee would also make an appearance on their debut album ('Just Look At Us'), which was characterised by old school positivity ('Strivin'') and locker room humour ('Steppin' In Doo Doo')

Album: *It's Party Time* (Jive 1989).

Pharcyde

Spaced-out rhymers who first hit big with 'Ya Mama', a series of ridiculous and escalating insults (also referred to as 'Snaps' or 'Playing The Dozens') traded between the vocalists, on the Delicious Vinyl label. It was typical fare from this free-flowing West Coast crew, though somewhat derivative of A Tribe Called Quest and Dream Warriors. However, their observations remained genuinely funny, housed in swinging, almost harmonised rap couplets, jazz breaks and quirky narratives: 'We're all jigaboos – might as well take the money' was a half-stinging, half self-mocking assertion. The single, 'Passing Me By', even contained a definition of old school stylings. They contributed one of the most effective cuts on the Brand New Heavies' *Heavy Rhyme Experience* collection, and returned the favour by remixing the latter's 'Soul Flower'. Based in Los Angeles, their goofy, fast talking style defied the early 90s rash of gangsta vinyl from that area with a dogma–deflating blend of cool, loopy rhythms and cultural lyrics. The group comprise Romye, Tre, Imani, Fat Lip, DJ Mark Luv and J-Swift.

Albums: *Bizarre Ride II The Pharcyde* (Delicious Vinyl 1992).

PM Dawn

One of the few rap acts who also sing in a more conventional fashion, PM Dawn consist of brothers Prince Be (Attrell Cordes) and DJ Minute Mix (Jarrett Cordes). They are from New Jersey where their step-father was a member of Kool And The Gang. Their backgrounds were shrouded in tragedy; their real father having died of pneumonia when they were children, and their brother Duncan drowning when he was two years old. They came from a highly musical family – 10 of their aunts and uncles were rappers and DJs in the genre's early days in the 70s, when Prince Be started rapping as a youngster at family parties. They were equally influenced by 60s pop and duly incorporated harmonies in their work – hence the later tag, Daisy Age Soul. They cut demos in 1989, including their first song, 'Check The Logic', at a Long Island studio. After signing to the Gee St label, they took the name PM Dawn, indicating 'the transition from dark to light'. A debut single, 'Ode To A Forgetful Mind', was released in January 1991. Its follow-up, 'A Watcher's Point Of View', broke the UK charts, introducing their melodic hip hop to a larger audience. Their debut album saw them turned away by representatives of the Beatles in their attempts to sample 'Let It Be'. They had been more successful in negotiations with Spandau Ballet, who allowed them to build the song 'Set Adrift On Memory's Bliss' out of 'True'. PM Dawn went as far as to promote the release with an old 'new romantic' picture of Hadley and co, confirming their mischievous humour. It hit number 3 in the UK charts. When the album emerged in September 1991, it saw them grow out of the De La Soul comparisons that had previously plagued them, as one of the most concise, creative forces in rap/dance. All seemed to be running smoothly for PM Dawn in 1991, until an unfortunate experience at the end of the year. While Prince Be took part in the live filming of a gig at New York's The Sound Factory, Boogie Down Productions main man KRS-1 became angered at what he considered disrespectful remarks made by Prince Be during a *Details* magazine interview, and forcefully evicted him from the stage, smashing a record on Minute Mix's turntable in the process. 1992 saw two minor UK hits, 'Reality Used To Be A Friend Of Mine' and 'I'd Die Without You', which featured on the soundtrack to Eddie Murphy's *Boomerang* film. With Prince Be also appearing in a Nike trainers' commercial, the latter 45 climbed to US number 3. Following the release of 'Looking Through Patient Eyes', which heavily sampled George Michael's 'Father Figure', PM Dawn released a long-awaited second album in April 1993. While writing tracks for *The Bliss* album, Prince Be had Boy George in mind, and the former Culture Club singer duetted on 'More Than Likely', which also became a single. 'Fly Me To The Moon', meanwhile, sampled U2's 'The Fly'. However, critics still considered it to be a lesser album than their stunning debut. Minute Mix, meanwhile, had changed his name to J.C. The Eternal, and Prince Be had become The Nocturnal. PM Dawn also contributed to the AIDS benefit *Red Hot And Dance*, as well as remixing for Simply Red, and several benefit shows (Earth Day, LIFEbeat's CounterAid, etc).

Albums: *Of The Heart, Of The Soul, Of The Cross, The Utopean Experience* (Gee St 1991), *The Bliss Album...? (Vibrations Of Love & Anger & The Ponderance Of Life & Existence)* (Island 1993).

Poor Righteous Teachers

Trenton, New Jersey-based trio comprising the gregariously named Wise Intelligent, Culture Freedom and Father Shaheed, all advocates of the Five Percent Islam creed. Their debut album inlcuded the hot 'Rock Dis Funky Joint' 45, and sold over 400,000 copies, crossing over into the pop market. Their second album included the groundbreaking pro-women single cut, 'Shakiyla (JHR)', but failed to match the sales of its predecessor. *Black Business* was a celebration of the progress made by their black brothers and sisters in commerce and business, and was produced by Shaheed with the aid of Tony D. It included the single 'Nobody Move', which was inspired by albino reggae toaster, Yellowman. Indeed, PRT's most distinctive attribute is Wise Intelligent's highly effective blending of the reggae DJ's intonation with his partners hip hop skills.

Album: *Holy Intellect* (Profile 1990), *Pure Poverty* (Profile 1991), *Black Business* (Profile 1993).

Pop Art

Hip hop record label, based in Philadelphia, controlled by Lawrence Goodman, the cousin of Steady B. The latter issued an impressive answer record to LL Cool J's big hit, 'I Can't Live Without My Radio', which established the imprint. Its other high profile releases included another artist well versed in the tradition of answer records, Roxanne Shante. Goodman is now the manager of Da Youngsters.

Positive-K

From Queens, New York, Positive-K (b. c.1967, Bronx, New York, USA) is yet another of rap's mouthpieces to augment his B-boy/breakbeat hip hop with messages from the Nation Of Islam. After being inspired by his view of a Grandmaster Flash show in Echo Park from his grandmother's window, he immersed himself in hip hop culture as a child. He was 18 years old when he made his first appearance on vinyl with the *Fast Money* compilation, subsequently hooking up with First Priority. A second various artists' credit came with the label's 1988 compilation *Basement Flavor*. His releases for the label would include 'Quarter Gram Pam', 'Step Up Front' and 'I'm Not Havin' It', at the same time as he duetted with Grand Puba on Brand Nubian's debut set. He moved over to his own Creative Control Records for the release of 'Night Shift', which was subsequently picked up by Island/4th & Broadway. It was produced by Big Daddy Kane, who also guest rapped. Positive had met him some years previously when enjoying a bus ride rap battle between New York and Philadelphia. More successful still, however, was 'I Got A Man', which established him both in his native country and the US. Somewhat less cerebral than previous efforts, it was still great fun, with lines boasting that 'I'm a big daddy longstroke, your man's Pee Wee Herman'. In the afterglow of its success his Creative Control empire flourished, signing artists like Raggedyman.

Album: *Da Skills Dat Pay Da Bills* (Island 1992).

Professor Griff

POV

New Jersey four-piece comprising Marc Sherman (b. c.1974, aka The Rapper Extraordinaire), Ewarner 'E' Mills (b. c.1974), Hakim 'HB' Bell (b. c.1975) and Lincoln 'Link' DeVulgt (b. Virgin Islands) whose sound encompasses reggae and R&B, with the uniting structure of hip hop rhythms. Their initials stand for Point Of View. Within their line-up stands not only a conventional rapper, but also one (Link) who takes a reggae/dancehall DJ approach. They made their debut with 'Anutha Luv', under the tutelage of Hakim Abdulsamad (the Boys etc.). But it was Michael Bennet who decided to take the group to Jamaica, recording the sweet 'Summer Nights' single at his Kingston studio. They boast of distinguished parentage too; bandleader Hakim 'HB' Bell is the son of Robert 'Kool' Bell, of Kool And The Gang fame, who served as co-executive producer on their debut album. This comprised two quite distinct sides. The first, the 'Beat U Up' side, was formulated by uptempo dance and swing material, while the second, 'Beat U Down', offered Link's dancehall chants and Sherman's hip hop verses set to the impressive soulful harmonising of the whole group. It included their duet with Jade, 'All Thru The Nite'. Their backgrounds (Sherman's father is an import/export director) have disabused them of any naivety about the music business, and each member owns their own separate publishing company. Hakim is also responsible for HB Productions, which handled (in tandem with Robert Bell) backroom duties on the band's debut album.
Album: *Handing' Out Beatdowns* (Giant/RCA 1993).

P.O.W.E.R.

Their initials standing for People Oppressed by the World's Empire Ruling elite, it wouldn't take genre commentators long to predict a similarity in style and presentation to Consolidated. POWER too deal in doses of polemic rap spliced with heavy rhythmic surges and undulations. The group comprises Krys Kills and Che 'Minister Of Defence' - a rapper and DJ respectively who met while studying law at college in Portland, Oregon.

Their debut single 'Racemixer' emerged on Nettwerk/Play It Again Sam Records, as did a follow-up album crammed with message-lyrics like 'Geurilla Warfare' and 'Modern Day Slavery'.
Album: *Dedicated To World Revolution* (Nettwerk 1994).

Prime Minister Pete Nice and Daddy Rich

After the split of 3rd Bass, of the three former members MC Serch was the first to release a solo album, *Return of The Product*. The remaining two, DJ Daddy Rich and Pete Nice (b. Peter Nash) spent a year cutting their debut set. 3rd Bass were always going to be a tough act to follow, and the fact that Nice was still self-consciously rapping about being white in a black market did not help. However, there was much to like in the sustained intelligence of his rhymes, and Rich's convuluted rhythmic strutures. Nice also set up his own record label, Hoppoh, signing talented Latino newcomer Kurious.
Album: *Dust To Dust* (1993).

Prince Paul

b. Paul E. Huston, 2 April 1967, Amityville, Long Island, New York, USA. Alongside Daddy-O, Prince Paul is the second of Stetsasonic's founding members to enjoy notable extra-curricular activities. Similarly his production credits take pride of place in his list of achievements. Probably his proudest moment came in helming De La Soul's *3 Feet High And Rising*, though other credits included the Fine Young Cannibals. His other notable productions included the anti-crack 'You Still Smoking That Shit?', and 'Don't Let Your Mouth Write A Check That Your Ass Can't Cash'. He set up his own Doo Dew label in the 90s, with signings including Resident Alien. However, by 1994 the deal with the label's sponsors had turned sour and he embarked instead on a collaboration with old-Stetsasonic hand Fruitkwan as part of the rap super group Gravediggaz.

Priority Records

A record company which was stablished in 1985, originally to piece together compilation records,

Priority has established itself in the intervening period as one of America's most pre-eminent rap stable. Former Captiol employee Bryan Turner (b. Canada), the label's president, acknowledges the hit-and-miss nature of their business plan: We didn't sit down and decide to have a rap label, it just sort of happened. Rap was exciting - it was music that kids really wanted'. However, the label has never been strictly a one-genre affair. They still package compilations, and alongside their high-profile hip hop acts, who have included NWA, Ice-T (following his departure from Warners) and Ice Cube, their most recent signings include Carole King. However, they would lose their deal with Eazy-E's Ruthless nest when their contract expired in 1993, allowing the latter to move to Relativity Records.

Selected albums: NWA: *Straight Outta Compton* (Ruthless/Priority 1988). Ice Cube: *Amerikkka's Most Wanted* (Priority 1989).

Professor Griff

Brought up in Long Island New York along with 13 brothers and sisters, Griff (b. Richard Griffin, Long Island, New York, USA) formed The Universal Revolutionary Freedom Fighters Society (TUFFS) in his youth, providing study groups and martial arts training for young people. It was while he was offering a security service that he first met Chuck D of Public Enemy. Griff's CV subsequently included a residency as part of Public Enemy's 'Security Of The First World' team, before, in the best traditions of hip hop, he managed to stoke huge controversy before he ever performed his first rap. As Public Enemy's 'Minister Of Information', Griff went on record to state that the Jewish people were responsible for the majority of the world's wickedness, including the selling of his own race into slavery. The quote's explosive value had little to do with the fact that Griff's historical vision so obviously lacked substance, but it served instead to bring rap right into the mainstream of racial debate, highlighting the danger of allowing a platform to those neither gifted nor educated enough to use it (it is worth noting, however, that Griff inists he was misquoted). His role as Public Enemy's diplomat ended when he was unceremoniously ejected, but Griff persevered with a solo career that has produced music of some note. Fuelled by what many commentators have ascribed as paranoia theory, his second album, after signing with Luther Campbell's record label, revealed tight, harsh funk backing to his incendiary polemic, backed by his own band, the Asiastic Disciples.

Albums: *Pawns In The Game* (Skywalker 1990), *Kao's II Wiz *7* Dome* (Luke 1991), *Disturb N Tha Peace* (Luke 1992).

Profile Records

One of the earliest of hip hop labels, formed in 1981 in New York by Steve Plotnicki and Cory Robbins with a loan from their parents of $70,000. The catalogue began with a single by Grace Kennedy, before their second release, and first rap record, 'Young Ladies' by Lonnie Love. They were down to the last $2,000 of their parents' investment when they scored their first hit, with 'Genius Rap' by Dr. Jeckyll and Mr. Hyde (namely Andre Harrell, now president of Uptown Enterpises, and Alonzo Brown, who was also 'Lonnie Love', respectively). Another significant benchmark was Run DMC's 'Sucker MCs' 1983 cut, a ruffhouse hit which helped to establish the 'new school' tradition, as well as enlarging rap's vocabulary. Run DMC continued to provide the label with their greatest successes throughout the decade. In January 1994 Plotnicki bought out Robbins to take sole ownership of the label.

Selected albums: Run DMC: *Raising Hell* (Profile 1986). Special Ed: *Youngest In Charge* (Profile 1989). Poor Righteous Teachers: *Holy Intellect* (Profile 1990). Various: *Diggin' In The Crates Volume One* (Profile 1994).

Public Enemy

Hugely influential and controversial New York rap act, frequently referred to as 'The Black Sex Pistols'. Public Enemy were initially viewed either as a radical and positive avenging force, or a disturbing manifestation of the guns 'n' violence-obsessed, homophobic, misogynist, anti-Semitic attitudes of a section of the black American ghetto underclass. The group's origins can be traced to

1982 and the Adelphi University, Long Island, New York. There college radio DJ Chuck D (b. Carlton Douglas Ridenhour, 1 August 1960, Roosevelt, Long Island, New York City, USA) and Hank Shocklee were given the chance to mix tracks for the college station, WBAU, by Bill Stephney. Together they produced a collection of aggressive rap/hip hop cuts under the title *Super Special Mix Show* in January 1983. They were eventually joined by Flavor Flav (b. William Drayton, 16 March 1959, Roosevelt, Long Island, New York City, USA), who had previously worked alongside Chuck D and his father in their V-Haul company in Long Island, and rang the station incessantly until he too became a host of their show. 1984 saw Shocklee and Chuck D mixing their own basement hip hop tapes, primarily for broadcast on WBAU, which included 'Public Enemy Number 1', from which they took their name. By 1987 they had signed to Rick Rubin's Def Jam label (he had first approached them two years earlier) and increased the line-up of the group for musical and visual purposes - Professor Griff 'Minister Of Information' (b. Richard Griffin), DJ Terminator X (b. Norman Rogers) and a four-piece words/dance/martial arts back-up section (Security Of The First World). Shocklee and Chuck D were also to be found running a mobile DJ service, and managed Long Island's first rap venue, the Entourage. The sound of Public Enemy's debut, *Yo! Bum Rush The Show*, was characteristically hard and knuckle bare, its title-track a revision of the original 'Public Enemy Number 1' cut. With funk samples splicing Terminator X's turntable sequences, a guitar solo by Living Color's Vernon Reid (on 'Sophisticated Bitch'), and potent raps from Chuck D assisted by Flav's grim, comic asides, it was a breathtaking arrival. That Public Enemy were not only able to follow-up, but also improve on that debut set with *It Takes A Nation Of Millions To Hold Us Back*, signified a clear division between them and the gangsta rappers. Their nearest competitors, NWA, peaked with *Straight Outta Compton*, their idea of progress seemingly to become more simplisticly hateful with each subsequent release. Public Enemy, on the other hand, were beginning to ask

questions. And if America's white mainstream audience chose to fear rap, the invective expressed within 'Black Steel In The House Of Chaos', 'Prophets Of Rage' and 'Bring The Noise' gave them excellent cause. That anxiety is cleverly exploited in the title of the band's third set, *Fear Of A Black Planet*. Despite their perceived antagonistic stance, they proved responsive to some criticism, evident in the necessary ousting of Professor Griff in 1989 for an outrageous anti-Semitic statement made in the US press. He would subsequently be replaced by James Norman, then part-time member Sister Souljah. *Fear Of A Black Planet*, their first record without Griff's services, nevertheless makes use of samples of the news conferences and controversy surrounding his statements, enhancing the bunker mentality atmosphere which pervades the project. The 45, '911 Is A Joke', an attack on emergency service response times in ghetto areas, became the subject of a barely credible Duran Duran cover version, strangely confirming Public Enemy's mainstream standing. *Apocalypse 91* was almost as effective, the band hardly missing a beat musically or lyrically with black pride cuts like 'I Don't Wanna Be Called Yo Nigga' and 'Bring The Noise', performed with thrash metal outfit Anthrax. In September 1990 it was revealed that they actually appeared in an FBI report to Congress examining 'Rap Music And Its Effects On National Security'. Despite their popularity and influence, or perhaps because of it, there remains a large reservoir of antipathy directed towards the band within sections of the music industry (though more thoughtful enclaves welcomed them; Chuck D would guest on Sonic Youth's 1990 album, *Goo*, one of several collaborative projects). Either way, their productions in the late 80s and early 90s have been hugely exciting - both for the torrents of words and the fury of the rhythm tracks, and in the process they have helped to write rap's lexicon. 1988's 'Don't Believe The Hype' has become as powerful a slogan in the late 80s/early 90s as 'Power To The People' was almost 20 years earlier. Similarly, the use of 'Fight The Power' in Spike Lee's 1989 film *Do The Right Thing* perfectly expressed supressed anger at the Eurocentric nature of American culture and history. In recent times several members of the band have embarked on solo careers, while Hank Shocklee and his brother Keith established Shocklee Entertainment in 1993, a production firm and record label. They released their first album in three years in 1994 with *Muse Sick N Hour Message* (Music And Our Message), though touring arrangments were delayed when Terminator X broke both his legs in a motorcycle accident. The album was released on July 4th - American Independence Day. Again it proved practically peerless, with cuts like 'So Watcha Gone Do Now' putting the new breed of gangsta rappers firmly in their place. Public Enemy's legacy extends beyond rap, and has attained a massive cultural significance within black communities. The effect on the consciousness (and consciences) of white people is almost as considerable.

Albums: *Yo! Bum Rush The Show* (Def Jam 1987), *It Takes A Nation Of Millions To Hold Us Back* (Def Jam 1988), *Fear Of A Black Planet* (Def Jam 1990), *Apocalypse '91 The Enemy Strikes Black* (Def Jam 1991), *Muse Sick N Hour Mess Age* (Def Jam 1994). Compilations: *Greatest Misses* (Def Jam 1992, features six 'new' tracks), *Twelve Inch Mixes* (Def Jam 1993).

Pudgee The Phat Bastard

Having already written part of MC Fatal's verse on the Main Source track 'Live At The BBQ', and providing material for both Roxanne Shanté and the Ghetto Girls, Pudgee came to his solo career with something of a reputation. Insisting on a formulaic blend of sexual boasting, the predictability of his rhymes, though occasionally amusing, were tempered effectively by the funky backing of Trackmasterz. His debut album boasted a head to head clash with Kool G Rap, with whom Pudgee's voice has often been compared.

Album: *Give 'Em The Finger* (Giant 1993).

Public Enemy

Q

QDIII

b. Quincy Jones III. British-born, Los Angeles, California, USA-based hip hop producer. The son of Quincy Jones, QD got the rap bug as a breakdancer for Nike, before attending jams and street parties. There he was introduced to the work of the new rap kings, which built on his abiding love of soul legends like Stevie Wonder. However, it was the production work of Mantronik (Mantronix) which really caught his attention, especially a track entitled 'Cold Getting Dumb' by Just Ice. Among his earliest commissions as a producer/remixer was a cut for T La Rock, 'Nitro', while he was still living in New York. He next approached Warner Brothers, who suggested he put together a compilation album to showcase new talent. The resultant Soundlab eventually led to Justin Warfield being signed - whose expansive debut album was helmed by QDIII. It also spurred QD on to further production work, most notably with LL Cool J and Ice Cube. These two heavyweights anchored his reputation via the highly successful 14 Shots To The Dome (three tracks) and Lethal Injection (four tracks) respectively. He has gone on to produce and remix for a myriad of other talents, including Tairrie B, Naughty By Nature, Da Lench Mob, Yo Yo (both the latter two out of Ice Cube's stable), En Vogue, Special K, Queen Latifah and the Whooliganz. He continues to run his own company, Soundlab productions, titled after the compilation album that made his reputation.

Queen Latifah

Rap's first lady, Queen Latifah (b. Dana Owens, March 18 1970, East Orange, New Jersey, USA) broke through in the late 80s with a style which picked selectively from jazz and soul traditions. The former Burger King employee has maintained her early commitment to answer the misognyist armoury of her male counterparts, and at the same time impart musical good times to all genders.

After working as the human beatbox alongside famale rapping crew Ladies Fresh, she was just 18 years old when she released her debut single, 'Wrath Of My Madness', in 1988. A year later her debut long player enjoyed fevered reviews: an old, wise head was evident on the top of her young shoulders. Production expertise from Daddy-O, KRS-1, DJ Mark the 45 King and members of De La Soul doubtlessly helped as well. By the time of her third album she had moved from Tommy Boy to a new home, Motown, and revealed a shift from the soul and ragga tones of Nature Of A Sista to sophisticated, sassy hip hop. She has subsequently embarked on a career as an actor, notably in the hit streetwise black comedy, Living Single, where she plays magazine boss Khadijah James. He film credits already include Juice, Jungle Fever and House Party 2. As if that wasn't enough, she additionally set up her own Flavor Unit record label and management company in 1993, as an outlet for new rap acts as well as her own recordings. The first release on it, 'Roll Wit Tha Flava', featured an all-star cast including Naughty By Nature's Treach, Fu-Schnickens' Chip-Fu, Black Sheep's Dres and D-Nice. She also guested on the Shabba Ranks' single, 'Watcha Gonna Do'. Previous collaborations had included those with De La Soul ('Mama Gave Birth To The Soul Children', in that band's infancy) and Monie Love (the agenda-setting 'Ladies First'). Queen Latifah represents an intelligent cross-section of hip hop influences. Though she is a forthright advocate of her race's struggle, she is also the daughter of and brother to policemen. Black Reign, in fact, is dedicated to the death of that same brother: 'I see both sides. I've seen the abuse and I've been the victim of police who abuse their authority. On the other side you've got cops getting shot all the time, you got people who don't respect them at all'. Whilst a little too strident to live up to the Arabic meaning of her name (Latifah equates to delicate and sensitive), Queen Latifah is one of the most positive role models for young black women (and men) in hip hop culture: 'Aspire to be a doctor or a lawyer, but not a gangster'. As one of the singles lifted from Black Reign advocates: 'UNITY (Who You Calling A Bitch?)'.

Albums: *All Hail The Queen* (Tommy Boy 1989), *Nature Of A Sista* (Tommy Boy 1991), *Black Reign* (Motown 1993).

Raheem

From the Geto Boys' Houston, Texas stable, Raheem embraces that group's familiar offensiveness, but has no little musical dexterity to offer. His debut album spanned reggae ('Punks Give Me Respect') and rock ('Shotgun'), but some of the words on the follow-up were so nasty that he was elevated to the level of 'the new Scarface'. A dubious honour but one which Raheem would doubtless relish.

Album: *The Vigilante* (Rap-A-Lot 1988), *The Invincible* (Rap-A-Lot 1992).

Rap-A-Lot Records

Houston, Texas-based rap label run by James Smith (b. c.1964), who has seen considerable financial reward for his efforts in promoting ultra-hardcore rappers like the Geto Boys and sundry spin-off projects. One of several items of real estate to his name is a 30 acre ranch where he hosted *Source Magazine*'s debate about gangsta rap. His opinion: 'This rap shit is the biggest challenge to this government in a long-ass time. It's bigger than Martin Luther King and all them'. His empire has expanded to include new talent like 5th Ward Boys and Raheem, though they hardly provide stylistic diversity.

Selected albums: Geto Boys: *We Can't Be Stopped* (Rap-A-Lot 1991). Scarface: *The World Is Yours* (Rap-A-Lot 1993).

Rappin' Is Fundamental

Among the forerunners of one of rap's many clashes with different genres, in this case doo-wop. The trio consists of Easy Mo Bee (b. Osten Harvey, brother of producer 'LG' Harvey), JR and AB Money, all Brooklyn neighbours, raised under the paternal wing of their local church. JR (b. Darron Strand) decided to put on hold his career in Wall Street for the music business in 1987. There is little to dislike about Rappin' Is Fundamental and their mix of funky beats with breezy a cappella breaks and doo wop harmonies, with the possible exception of their rather laborious name. Influenced by vocal harmony groups like the Flamingos, they were certainly among the more sophisticated members of New York's hip hop culture. They were keen to differentiate themselves from anything so one-dimensional: 'We don't want to be looked on as just rappers. We're born singers, we're *bona fide* dancers and natural rappers. We're all round entertainers.' However, they were dropped by A&M, after their debut album stiffed, but were still active in 1994, independently releasing 'Helluva Guy'.

Album: *The Doo Hop Legacy* (A&M 1991).

Raw Breed

Alongside Onyx, with whom Raw Breed are all too frequently compared, this Bronx, New York troupe encapsulate the 'Nastee nigga' term which has been coined to address their sound. After a brief sojourn with Jam Master Jay of Run DMC, Raw Breed hooked up with Ice-T's Rhyme Syndicate to launch their career. The band comprise Mark Rippin (cousin of Ultramagentic MC's Kook Keith) and four others, and kicked off their career with the 'Rabbit Stew' 45, which dissed 'all the wack MCs, and wack groups that came out in '93'.

Album: *Loon Tunz* (1993).

Raw Fusion

Comprising Digital Underground members DJ Fuze and Money B, who opened their account with 'Throw Your Hands In The Air'. Instead of following the P-Funk fixation of their erstwhile employers, as Raw Fusion the duo concentrated instead on a more mellow, reggae tinged delivery. Despite the presence on their debut of old sparring partners Shock G. and Shmoovy Shomoov, along with Tupac Shakur, the resulting album was no classic. A second set introduced filthy rhymes from Money B, dubbed up by Fuze, on 'Freaky Note', but again failed to capture the magic of Digital Underground at their best.

Album: *Live From The Styletron* (Hollywood Basic 1992), *Hoochiefied Funk* (Hollywood Basic 1994).

Real Roxanne

b. Adelaida Martinez. One of a strange flurry of rapping namesakes to emerge in the late 80s, after the release of U.T.F.O.'s 'Roxanne Roxanne'. This Puerto Rican female MC, based in New York, was arguably the most talented, releasing a powerful debut album aided by the production genius of Jam Master Jay (Run DMC), Howie Tee and Full Force, who were behind U.T.F.O.'s original 'Roxanne Roxanne', and discovered Martinez when she was waitressing in Brooklyn. Sadly, when the 'Roxanne' fracas finally died down, she was left without a bandwagon to hitch her career to.

Album: *The Real Roxanne* (Select 1988), *Go Down (But Don't Bite It)* (Select 1992).

Rebel MC

After leaving his Double Trouble partners (Michael Menson and Leigh Guest), famed for the bubblegum ska hit 'Street Tuff', London based former electronics student Rebel MC (b. Michael Alec Anthony West, 27 August 1965, Tottenham, London, England) has earned greater plaudits as a solo artist. Double Trouble would go on to score minor hits with 'Love Don't Live Here Anymore' and 'Rub-A-Dub', without their former leader. Originally considered the UK's Hammer, the Rebel's more recent work is characterised by ragga beats, fast rhymes and roots harmonics. It was heartfelt music with a solid Rastafarian message. It was learned, no doubt, from his earlier stints on the live reggae circuit, having set up the Beat Freak sound system with jungle innovator DJ Ron. The single 'Rich An' Getting Richer' was an excellent social commentary rant with dub synchronized, orchestral mixes. On *Black Meaning Good* he was joined by Tenor Fly, Barrington Levy, PP Arnold, and Dennis Brown, the more political agenda emphasized by its sleeve dedication to: 'scapegoats of the British judicial system'. 'Rebel Music', meanwhile, was remixed by Pasemaster Mase of De La Soul. The son of a semi-pro cricketer, West helped start the 'People Against Poverty And Oppression Movement', and joined with 'Musicians Against The War' in the days of the Gulf conflict. More lastingly, he helped establish his own Tribal Bass label, working with homegrown UK rap talent like the Demon Boyz and others.

Album: *Black Meaning Good* (Desire 1991), *Word, Sound And Prayer* (Desire 1992). With Double Trouble: *21 Mixes* (Desire 1990).

Red Fox

b. c.1970, St. Catherine, Jamaica, West Indies. An artist who un-self-consciously mixes hip hop and reggae, Red Fox was initially compared to Yellowman when he appeared at sound systems in his native country, due to his light complexion. However, it wasn't until he moved to New York (still at the tender age of 16) that his musical career found its feet. Following stage shows alongside dancehall stars like Shabba Ranks and Buju Banton, he hooked up with producer Peter McKenzie to record 'Come Boogie Down' on FM Records. It quickly became a cult item both in his adopted home of Brooklyn and back in Jamaica. In 1992 he teamed with Brand Nubian to duet on the memorable 'Black Star Liner' cut. That outfit returned the compliment to Red Fox on 'Hey Mr. Rude Boy', from his debut album, *As A Matter Of Fox*. It was preceded by the roughneck 'Dem A Murderer' 45, which, like the album, entwined dancehall and rap into a presentable cocktail. Further singles 'Born Again Black Man', a straight reggae song, and 'Ghetto Gospel', sandwiched an appearance at Jamaica's annual Sting festival.

Album: *As A Matter Of Fox* (Elektra 1993).

Redhead Kingpin And FBI

b. David Guppy, c.1970, Englewood, New Jersey, New York State, USA, and nicknamed after his bright red hair. Guppy is a polite, dignified humourist whose raps mingle coy allusion without lapses into vulgar detail. After all, his mother is a serving member of the police force, and he refused

Red Fox

to swear on his albums in case she heard the cussing. His career began when he hooked up with Gene Griffin's Sutra Records, via an introduction from his former camp counsellor. He determindedly set out his stall against B-boy culture, insisting instead on moral rectitide in all matters. If that seeemed a little boring, then the message was rescued by his excellent breakthrough single, 'Do The Right Thing'. Although he has gone on to score several minor hits with songs like '3-2-1 Pump', he has yet to equal that moment of artistic and chart success. His backing band, the FBI (For Black Intelligence), consisted of DJ Wildstyle, Bo Roc, Lt. Squeak, Buzz and Poochie. The group later changed its name to Private Investigations.

Album: *A Shade Of Red* (Virgin 1989), *The Album With No Name* (Virgin 1991), *React Like You Know* (Virgin 1993).

Redman

New Jersey-based rapper whose debut album broke the Top 50 of the US Billboard album charts, failing to get a UK release until much later in the year, after it had moved over 300,000 copies on home turf. Enshrining the new ethos of cannabis as the drug of choice ('How To Roll A Blunt'), there was also room for the traditional braggadacio ('Day Of Sooperman Lover', 'I'm A Bad'). As superb an album as it was, from the cover shot of the artist up to his elbows in blood onwards, many critics also noted it was a little close to EPMD. Not surprising considering that he was a member of .their Hit Squad, alongside K-Solo and Das EFX, and that Erick Sermon had produced it. Infact Redman had spent two years living with the latter when both his parents chucked him out of their respective homes because he was 'selling drugs and shit'.

Album: *Whut? Thee Album* (RAL 1992).

Relativity Records

New York-based label which originally preached the word of rock guitar ala Joe Satriani and Steve Vai, initially as part of Important Record Distributors in 1979. Come the 80s and the label was licensing 'alternative' UK rock like the Cocteau Twins and Gene Loves Jezebel, while Sony purchased a 50% stake in the company in 1990. However, in 1991 the musical climate was changing, and president Barry Kobrin and his staff noted the commercial progress of rap and hip hop records. Their first tentative signing was 2 Black 2 Strong, which never worked out. A&R chief Peter Kang was subsequently given a wider brief, and the company brought rap label Violator under their wing. The first successful release was Chi Ali's debut album in March 1992, which inspired confidence throughout the label with its 70,000 sales (in half the time it would have taken an established rock outfit to move that many copies). Together with its distribution company, Relativity Entertainment Distribution, the company then signed a deal in 1993 with Ruthless Records, and also established the new Lifestyle imprint. Which effectively meant that under one company HQ there existed no less than three powerful hip hop camps: Ruthless (Eazy-E, Hoez With Attitude, Kokane, Blood Of Abraham, MC Ren), Violator (Fat Joe, Beatnuts, Chi Ali) and Lifestyle (Black Caesar). In addition Relativity signed its first 'own brand' artist, Common Sense. Their biggest initial success came with Fat Joe's 'Flow Joe' single, a Billboard Rap number 1 hit, while Alan Grumblatt, vice president of marketing, wished aloud in 1994 that Relativity would become 'the number 1 rap label in the country' by the end of the millenium.

Represent Records

Collective rap troupe/record label, based in Nottingham, England. The group numbers four DJs and five rappers, who include label head and general spokesperson Parks. However, it was one of his fellow rapping crew, Mr 45, who first brought the label to the wider public's attention via his 'Radford (You Get Me)' cut on the *Ruffneck* EP. Also part of the operation is a soul band and a reggae artist, D-Link. The collective was set up on the back of an enterprise allowance grant, which allowed them to build their own DIY studio having previously recorded demo tapes on more primitive equipment. There is no connection between Represent and the well-thought of UK hip hop fanzine of similar name.

Rob Base And DJ E-Z Rock

Light-hearted, New York-based rap unit distinctive through its exploration of musical genres, and an aversion to speech-only raps. Samples and lifts from Motown, James Brown (pariculary on the latter's production of Lyn Collins' 'Think (About It)', which gave them a breakthrough hit in 1988 with 'It Takes Two') and others set the tone for the duo, while Base's lyrics, although tending to highlight his romantic prowess, do so in a way which doesn't reach the listener as egotistical. He got into trouble for sampling Maze's 'Joy And Pain', however, when he neglected to credit its source. Base (b. Robert Ginyard, Harlem, New York) jettisoned DJ E-Z Rock (b. Rodney Bryce, Harlem, New York) in time for his second album, which this time round hoisted choruses from Marvin Gaye, Edwin Starr and even native American rock band, Redbone. The most effective slice of the action was a reworking of Starr's classic 'War' cut.
Albums: *It Takes Two* (Profile 1988). As Rob Base: *The Incredible Base* (Profile 1989).

Rock, Pete

One of rap's most respected producers, only Marley Marl is ahead of him on the quality/quantity thresholds. It was the latter that introduced Pete Rock to the world via his WBLS *Marley Marl In Control Show* in 1989. Rock has gone on to work with everyone from forerunners Heavy D (his cousin), Slick Rick, EPMD and Run DMC (including their first single, 'Down With The King') to new talents in the shape of Lords Of The Underground (actually offering vocals on their 'Flow On') Nas and K-Solo. Other projects include his soundtrack work on *Who's The Man* and *Menace II Society*. His remix roster is almost as impressive, with engagements with Brand Nubian, Public Enemy, House Of Pain, Das EFX, Father and non-rap artists like Shabba Ranks and Johnny Gill. Based in Mount Vernon, New York, he went on to join with C.L. Smooth for a release under his own name. The album housed the hit single (US 48) 'They Reminisce Over You (T.R.O.Y.)'. He

also put together the Untouchables producer network/umbrella organisation for the activities of himself and co-conspirators Eddie F, Dave Hall and Nevelle Hodge.
Albums: With C.L. Smooth: *Mecca & The Soul Brother* (Elektra 1992). *The Main Ingredients* (Elektra 1994).

Rocksteady Crew

Breakdance/hip hop pioneers led by the celebrated Crazy Legs (b. Richie Colon) - one of the earliest examples of Latin influence in the hip hop genre - and Frosty Freeze (b. Wayne Frost). When B-boys first embraced 'The Freak' craze (inspired by Chic's song of the same title), the Rocksteady Crew stayed true to their origins and became the most successful and widely respected of the breakdancers. They dealt firmly in old school hip hop culture which included grafitti, breakdancing, and tongue-twisting, call and response rhymes. They were as much acrobats as dancers, displaying their wares in Central Park alongside competing crews like the Incredible Breakers, Magnificent Force and U.T.F.O. As breakdancing evolved they threw new shapes, enlisting the developing cultures of dance, including moonwalking, bodypopping and robotics. Displaying a combination of the latter they were committed to celluloid history via a scene in the 1983 dance movie, *Flashdance*. They were also a huge influence on other crews, the Kaliphz being just one of the hip hop groups formed after seeing them perform (in this case on a rare UK excursion).
Album: *Ready For Battle* (Charisma 1984).

Rodney O And Joe Cooley

Street-orientated duo who, having lacked adequate repayment on their first three albums (each of which sold 200,000 copies), elected to go it alone on the fourth, *Fuck New York*. They had to sell their cars and possessions to get it done, but they were confident of a return having taken control of the means of production. On that album's provocative title, Rodney elaborates: 'The crux of the LP is about the people who are ripping off New York rap fans. It speaks about the reluctance of some New York people to break a West Coast artist because they feel that rap started in New York'. It was hardly the most diplomatic way to introduce themselves to East Coast hip hop fans, however.

Selected album: *Fuck New York* (Psychotic Records 1993).

Ron C

b. Ronald Pierre Carey, Oakland, California, USA. Rapper Carey moved to Dallas at the age of 17. However, by the spring of 1990 he anticipated gangsta's rap's flirtation with unlawfulness by being convicted of 'Possession of a controlled dangerous substance with intent', ensuring an unseemly hiatus in his recording career.

Album: *'C' Ya* (Profile 1990), *Back On The Street* (Profile 1992).

Roots

Philadephia-based rap crew comprising rapper Tariq Trotter (aka Black Thought), rapper Malik B, bass player Hob and drummer Ahmir Thompson. Specialising in old school freestyling, many comparisons to Digable Planets or Gang Starr's jazz-flavoured hip hop followed the release of their debut mini-album. However, the Roots are more of a self-contained musical unit, relying on their own talents rather than samples or session musicians. The band was started in 1987 when Trotter and Ahmir were students at Philadelphia High School For The Performing Arts. They learned to earn a crust on the busking circuit, until their manager arranged a European tour for them. They were spotted by Geffen while playing in Germany, who signed the group (for the US, Talkin' Loud taking responsibility for the UK). A second long playing set, *Do You Want More*, featured top jazz guests plus the Roots' own rap protégés, the Foreign Objects.

Albums: *From The Ground Up* (Geffen 1994, mini-album), *Do You Want More* (Geffen 1994).

Roxanne Shanté

b. Lolita Shanté Gooden, 9 November 1969, Queens, New York, USA. Shanté came to prominence at the tender age of 14 via her belated answer record to U.T.F.O.'s 1984 rap hit, 'Roxanne, Roxanne'. Gooden was walking outside a New York housing project when she overheard three men discussing U.T.F.O.'s cancellation of a show they were promoting. In turn Gooden offered them a reply record. The onlookers, DJ Mister Magic, Tyrone Williams and Marley Marl, took her up on the offer. Her version, 'Roxanne's Revenge', mixed sassy, indignant raps with a funky backbeat. It was a massive hit, which sold over a quarter of a million copies in the New York area alone, and spawned a flood of answerback records (well over a hundred at the final count), as rappers queued to take up the challenge. U.T.F.O. replied by suing her for using their b-side as the rhythm track. Shanté was still only fourteen years old, and forced to stay away from school because of all the attention. Her arrival was cemented by further singles 'Have A Nice Day' and 'Go On Girl', produced by Marly Marl, with lyrics penned by Big Daddy Kane. Her debut album saw the conscious rhymes of songs like 'Independent Woman' (though it was written for her by a man) spliced by saucy narratives like 'Feelin' Kinda Horny'. By 1986, Shanté was being edged from the centre of the female rap stage by The Real Roxanne (Adelaida Martinez) and her turntable wizard Hitman Howie Tee. Perhaps her most infamous post-'Roxanne' moment came with the release of 'Big Mama', which would see her take out her frustrations by dissing other female rappers Queen Latifah, MC Lyte, Yo Yo and Monie Love.

Albums: *Roxanne's Revenge* (Pop Art 1987), *Bad Sister* (Cold Chillin' 1989), *The Bitch Is Back* (Livin' Large 1992).

Run DMC

New York rappers Joe Simmons (b. 24 November 1966, New York, USA; the brother of Russell Simmons, their Rush Management boss), Darryl 'DMC' McDaniels (b. 31 May 1964, New York, USA) and DJ 'Jam Master Jay' (b. Jason Mizell, 1965, New York, USA) originally came together as Orange Crush in the early 80s, becoming Run DMC in 1982 after graduating from St. Pascal's Catholic School. They had known each other as children in Hollis, New York, Mizell and

McDaniels even attending the same kindergarten. After circulating demos the group signed to Profile Records for an advance of $2,500, immediately scoring a US underground hit with 'It's Like That'. However, it was the single's b-side, 'Sucker MCs', which created the stir. It single-handedly gave birth to one of rap's most prevalent terms, and almost became a genre in its own right. Many critics signpost the single as the birth of modern hip hop, with its stripped down sound (no instruments apart from a drum machine and scratching from a turntable, plus the fashion image of the B-boy: street clothing, chiefly sportswear, and street language). In the wake of the single's success their debut album went gold in 1984, the first time the honour had been bestowed upon a rap act. They cemented their position as hip hop's men of the moment with furious touring, and appearances on the *Krush Groove* film, a fictionalised account of the life of Russell Simmons, who was now joint-head of Def Jam with Rick Rubin. They also took a hand at the prestigious King Holliday (a Martin Luther King tribute) and Sun City (Artists Against Apartheid) events. They broke further into the mainstream on both sides of the Atlantic in 1986 when, via Rubin's auspices, they released the heavy metal/rap collision 'Walk This Way' (featuring Steve Tyler and Joe Perry of Aerosmith). Its disinctive video caught the imagination of audiences on both sides of the Atlantic. The partnership had been predicted by earlier singles, 'Rock Box' and 'King Of Rock', both of which fused rap with rock. By 1987 *Raisin' Hell* had sold three million copies in the US, becoming the first rap album to hit the R&B number 1 mark, the first to enter the US Top 10, and the first to go platinum. It would not be their only such achievement. Run DMC also became the first rap group to have a video screened by MTV, the first to feature on the cover of *Rolling Stone*, and the first non-athletes to endorse Adidas products (a sponsorship deal which followed rather than preceded their 'My Adidas' track). Sadly, a projected collaboration with Michael Jackson never took place, though they did duet with Joan Rivers on her television show, and held street seminars to discuss inter-gang violence. Subsequent efforts have

been disappointing, although both *Tougher Than Leather* and *Back From Hell* contained a few tough-like-the-old-times tracks ('Beats To The Ryhme', 'Pause' etc.) among the fillers. The former album was tied to a disastrous film project of similar title. In the 90s Daniels and Simmons experienced religious conversion, after the former succumbed to alcoholism and the the latter was falsely accused of rape in Cleveland. Singles continued to emerge sporadically, notably 'What's It All About', which even sampled the Stone Roses. Despite an obvious effort to make *Down With The King* their major comeback album, with production assistance offered by Pete Rock, EPMD, the Bomb Squad, Naughty By Nature, A Tribe Called Quest, even Rage Against The Machine, and guest appearances from KRS-1 and Neneh Cherry, it is hard to shake the view of Run DMC as a once potent, now spent force. Unsurprisingly, this is not their own outlook, and as Simmons is keen to point out: 'The Run DMC story is an exciting story. It's a true legend, its the sort of life you want to read about'.

Albums: *Run DMC* (Profile 1984), *King Of Rock* (Profile 1985), *Raising Hell* (Profile 1986), *Tougher Than Leather* (Profile 1988), *Back From Hell* (Profile 1990), *Down With The King* (Profile 1993). Compilation: *Together Forever: Greatest Hits 1983-1991* (Profile 1991).

Ruthless Rap Assassins

Manchester, England-based, and self-styled 'North Hulme' soundsculptors comprising Dangerous 'C' Carsonova (vocals, turntables), MC Kermit Le Freak (vocals) and Paul Roberts (guitar). Ruthless Rap Assassins formed in that district in the mid-80s, earning their reputation via local gigs. They were signed by EMI in 1987 after they had heard their debut single, 'We Don't Care'. Placed on the Syncopate subsidiary, the first result was the *Killer Album*, whose 'Go Wild' effectively sampled Steppenwolf's 'Born To Be Wild'. Even better was 'The Dream', which utilised the funked up groove of Cynade's 'The Message' to underpin this tale of West Indians moving to England in the 50s, and the subsequent dashing of their hopes and spirits. The militant aesthetics of *Killer Album* came as

something of a shock to those who still considered such daunting music the preserve of inner-city Americans. The follow-up selection, however, cut much deeper. Tracks like 'Down And Dirty' proved an effective parody of rap's pre-occupation with matters sexual, while 'No Tale, No Twist' observed some clever jazz touches. The group remained inventive and militant, the single 'Justice (Just Us)', proving a particularly defiant swipe at the majority white populace. Though they split afterwards due to record label and public indifference, the Ruthless Rap Assassins' legacy as the first worthwhile UK hip hop band remains.
Albums: *Killer Album* (Syncopate 1990), *Think - It Ain't Illegal Yet* (Murdertone 1991).

Ruthless Records

Eazy-E's record label, by legend founded on his illegal activities, which for several years offered the rap world incisive, definitive gangsta hip hop documents. The only real hitch in the plan came when house producer Dr Dre, so central to much of the label's success (which at the time included nine gold albums), left in bitter acrimony in the early 90s. The public slanging match he engendered with Eazy-E and General Manager Jerry Holler did not abate until Dre persuaded Jimmy Iovine at Interscope to let him set up his own label, Death Row. In 1993 Relativity Records stepped in to bring Ruthless, whose stable now boasted Hoez With Attitude, Kokane, Blood Of Abraham and MC Ren, under their wing after the original deal with Priority expired. Yet, post-Dre, the label's fortunes have continued to flag.

S

Salt 'n' Pepa

Cheryl 'Salt' James (b. Brooklyn, New York, USA) and Sandra 'Pepa' Denton (b. 9 November 1969, Jamaica) grew up in the Queens district of New York City. They became telephone sales girls and envisioned a career in nursing until fellow workmate and part time producer Hurby 'Luv Bug' Azor stepped in. He got them to rap for his group the Super Lovers (credited on record as Supernature) on his answer record to Doug E. Fresh's 'The Show'. They started recording as Salt 'n' Pepa (adapted from Super Nature recording 'Showstopper') under Azor's guidance and released singles such as 'I'll Take Your Man', 'It's My Beat', and 'Tramp', the latter a clever revision of the old Otis Redding/Carla Thomas duet. They also used the female DJ Spinderella (aka Dee Dee Roper), backing singers and male erotic dancers to complete their act. Their big break came in 1988 when a re-issue of an earlier single - 'Push It' - reached the UK number 2 spot and was also a hit on the US R&B chart. Later that year a remake of the Isley Brothers' 'Twist And Shout' also went into the Top 10. In between those two they released 'Shake Your Thang' (once again a take on an Isley Brothers' track, 'It's Your Thing') which featured the instrumental group EU. Nominated for the first ever Rap Grammy in 1989, they refused to attend the ceremony when it was discovered that the presentation of that particular bauble would not be televised - withdrawing to show solidarity with hip hop's growing status. Their most confrontational release was the 1991 'Let's Talk About Sex' manifesto, something of a change of tack after the overtly erotic 'Push It'. 'Do You Want Me' was similarly successful, encouraging the record company to put out *A Blitz Of Salt 'N' Pepa Hits*, a collection of remixes, in their absence. Both Salt and Pepa were otherwise engaged having babies (Pepa in 1990, Salt in 1991. DJ Spinderella would make it a hat-trick of single mothers in the group a short time later). In the interim they could content themselves with being the most commercially successful female rap troupe of all time, and the first to go gold. They subsequently enjoyed an invitation to appear at President Clinton's inauguration party. They returned to the charts in 1994 with their highly successful collaboration with En Vogue, 'Whatta Man'. It was a return to their naughty/nice personas, typically suggestive and salacious. After all, the charts would indeed be a boring place without Salt 'n' Pepa.

Albums: *Hot Cool & Vicious* (Next Plateau 1987), *A Salt With A Deadly Pepa* (Next Plateau 1988), *Black's Magic* (Next Plateau 1990), *Very Necessary* (London 1993). Compilations: *A Blitz Of Salt 'N' Pepa Hits* (London 1991), *The Greatest Hits* (London 1991).

Sampling

The art of sampling was first introduced to an international audience in 1979 when the Sugarhill Gang used a reconstructed Chic track, 'Good Times', as backing for their 'Rapper's Delight' success. Others followed, notably Grandmaster Flash' 'Adventures Of Grandmaster Flash On The Wheels Of Steel', which featured cut and paste segments from Chic, Queen, Blondie and other rap artists including Spoonie Gee and the Sugarhill Gang. Similarly Afrika Bambaataa's 'Planet Rock', which many cite as the first real hip hop record, utilised the work of others, in this case Kraftwerk's 'Trans-Europe-Express'. While hip hop and rap remained underground there was little interest taken by anyone in the format. However, as soon as corporations sniffed out profits half a dozen law suits were brought against those who had indulged in 'copyright violation'. Among the most notable sufferers were England's Shut Up And Dance. Long considered an act of plagiarism at best, it is only in recent years that sampling the work of older artists has been seen to be beneficial to both parties. Many artists, from James Brown to Spandau Ballet, have seen their work reassessed and reappraised in the wake of major hip hop aritsts sampling their work. By allowing Us3 to ransack the Blue Note vaults the same label experienced a

doubling in their US sales when *Hand On The Torch* broke big. In many ways it has become the stamp of approval to an artists' longevity: certainly all the major rock acts from the Beatles (2 Live Crew and others) to Jimi Hendrix (the Pharcyde) have experienced their wares being rehabilitated. Among the most-sampled catalogues are the works of James Brown (hugely influential in the initial development of rap) and George Clinton and P-Funk/Parliament (specifically in the West Coast traditions of Ice Cube and Too Short). Also popular have been more conventional rock sources like Grand Funk Railroad (KRS-1 and De La Soul) and Aerosmith (Run DMC), reggae (Bob Marley in particular) and jazz. Like everything else, sampling cuts both ways: in September 1991 Chuck D of Public Enemy sued the marketing company promoting St. Ides Malt licquor for using his voice without permission. Public Enemy also took legal action against Madonna for using their rhythm to underscore her 'Justify My Love' single.

Scarface

b. Brad Jordan, USA. Formerly a member of Houston's nastiest, the Geto Boys, Scarface's 'official' solo debut (an album of sorts had prefigured *Mr Scarface Is Back*) was a familiar roll-call of sex and street violence, with the titles reading like a litany of horror movies ('Body Snatchers', 'Born Killer', Diary Of A Madman'). The follow-up repeated the formula to an ever greater degree of success, eventually going platinum. Though there was much skullduggery and blatant misogyny apparent again, there was at least light to lift the shade. The hardcore rapper was not too hardcore to include tracks like 'Now I Feel Ya', which spoke openly of his relationship with his son and parents. In real life he suffers from depression, which was also documented on bloodcurdling tracks like 'The Wall'. His suicide attempt, triggered by his girlfriend announcing she was leaving him, had been depicted on the sleeve of a previous Geto Boys album. The first single from a projected fourth album was 'Hand Of The Dead Body', a duet with Ice Cube which defended rap against various charges laid at its door in the 90s. The key to Scarface's craft can be located in the fact that he boasts of first seeing the film *The Warriors* at age eight. Sadly, he never quite grew out of it.

Album: *Mr. Scarface Is Back* (Rap-A-Lot 1991), *The World Is Yours* (Rap-A-Lot 1993).

Schoolly D

b. Jesse B. Weaver Jr., Baltimore, Philadelphia, USA. Posturing street rapper who, together with his DJ Code Money (b. Lance Allen, USA), was an early pioneer in 'gun rap', a format which featured an abundance of violence and vendettas, and the glorification of the MC's personal armoury. Allied to the usual sexual declamation, it was a limited worldview but a partially effective one. Following 1984 singles 'Maniac' and 'Gangster Boogie', Schoolly D released an independent, eponymous album that was notable for the track 'PSK - What Does It Mean'. PSK transpired to be an acronym for Park Side Killers, a gang of Schoolly's aquaintence in Philadelphia. Though this breakthrough album will ensure Schoolly D's name remains hallowed in the annals of gangsta rap, he has done little since that would otherwise justify his inclusion. Still rapping over the basic, unadventourous scratching of Money, Schoolly D has not been seen to move on; whereas greater intellects have explored gang violence as a means of illustrating the big picture, Schoolly D has proved happy merely to indulge in, admittedly horrific, reportage. Song titles like 'Mr Big Dick' and 'Where's My Bitches' speak volumes about the lyrical insight displayed on the vast majority of his output. The first light at the end of the tunnel came with *Am I Black Enough For You?*, which at least incorporated a few more socio-political concerns, with cuts like 'Black Jesus' opening up new, potentially much more interesting, avenues of provocation. The title-track, too, was more insightful than previous fare had led us to expect: 'All I need is my blackness, Some others seem to lack this..'. By the time of his 'comeback' album of 1994, Schooly had progressed further still. Renouncing the basic samples that had underscored most of his career, he now employed a full live band, including Urge Overkill's Chuck Treece, Joe 'The Butcher' Nicolo and co-producer Mike Tyler.

Albums: *Schoolly D* (Schoolly-D 1986), *Saturday Night - The Album* (Schoolly-D 1987), *The Adventures Of Schoolly D* (combining both *Schooly D* and *Saturday Night - The Album*) (Rykodisc 1987), *Smoke Some Kill* (Jive 1988), *Am I Black Enough For You?* (Jive 1989), *How A Black Man Feels* (Capitol 1991), *Welcome To America* (Ruffhouse/Columbia 1994).

Scientists Of Sound

Boasting four different birth locations (Nigeria, Maruitius, St Lucia, Jamaica), the Scientists Of Sound are based in England, and comprise J-Blast 'The Weak Rhyme Wrecker' (ex-J-Blast And The 100% Proof), DJ Aybee 'The Underground Nigga', Kool Sett and Cherokee 'Mr Mibian'. A colourful press release claimed they were originally one person, travelling through the universe, when they were split into four component parts and spread around the globe. After adapting the personas of indigenous creatures, they reunited in England as a result of influencing their parents to travel to the UK. This unwieldy ethos was continued in their live shows (a choerographed approach often compared to Leaders Of The New School) and embraced in the way each member as regarded as a different anatomical appendage of the central being: J-Blast the mouthpiece, Kool Sett the heart, etc. Signed to the Underdog's Bite It! label after debuting with a 1992 EP, their first release for their new employer was 1994's 'Bad Boy Swing'.

Scott-Heron, Gil

b. 1 April 1949, Chicago, Illinois, USA. Raised in Jackson, Tennessee, by his grandmother, Scott-Heron moved to New York at the age of 13 and had published two novels (*The Vulture* and *The Nigger Factory*) plus a book of poems by the time he was 12. He met musician Brian Jackson when both were students at Lincoln University, Pennsylvania, and in 1972 they formed the Midnight Band to play their original blend of jazz, soul and prototype rap music. *Small Talk At 125th And Lenox* was mostly an album of poems (from his book of the same name), but later albums showed Scott-Heron developing into a skilled songwriter whose work

was soon covered by other artists: for example, Labelle recorded his 'The Revolution Will Not Be Televised' and Esther Phillips made a gripping version of 'Home Is Where The Hatred Is'. In 1973 he had a minor hit with 'The Bottle'. *Winter In America* and *The First Minute Of A New Day*, for new label Arista, were both heavily jazz-influenced, but later sets saw Scott-Heron exploring more pop-oriented formats, and in 1976 he scored a hit with the disco-based protest single, 'Johannesburg'. One of his best records of the 80s, *Reflections*, featured a fine version of Marvin Gaye's 'Inner City Blues'; but his strongest songs were generally his own barbed political diatribes, in which he confronted issues such as nuclear power, apartheid and poverty and made a series of scathing attacks on American politicians. Richard Nixon, Gerald Ford, Barry Goldwater and Jimmy Carter were all targets of his trenchant satire and his anti-Reagan rap, 'B-Movie', gave him another small hit in 1982. An important precursor of today's rap artists, Scott-Heron once described Jackson (who left the band in 1980) and himself as 'interpreters of the black experience'. However, by the 90s his view of the development of rap had become more jaundiced: 'They need to study music. I played in several bands before I began my career as a poet. There's a big difference between putting words over some music, and blending those same words into the music. There's not a lot of humour. They use a lot of slang and colloquialisms, and you don't really see inside the person. Instead, you just get a lot of posturing'. In 1994 he released his first album for ten years, *Spirits*, which began with 'Message To The Messenger', an adress to today's rap artists: '...Young rappers, one more suggestion before I get out of your way, But I appreciate the respect you give me and what you got to say, I'm sayin' protect your community and spread that respect around, Tell brothers and sisters they got to calm that bullshit down, 'Cause we're terrorizin' our old folks and we brought fear into our homes'.
Albums: *Small Talk At 125th And Lenox* (Flying Dutchman 1972), *Free Will* (Flying Dutchman 1972), *Pieces Of A Man* (Flying Dutchman 1973), *Winter In America* (Strata East 1974), *The First Minute Of A New Day* (Arista 1975), *From South Africa To South Carolina* (Arista 1975), *It's Your World* (Arista 1976), *Bridges* (Arista 1977), *Secrets* (Arista 1978), *1980* (Arista 1980), *Real Eyes* (Arista 1980), *Reflections* (Arista 1981), *Moving Target* (Arista 1982), *Spirits* (TVT Records 1994). Compilations: *The Revolution Will Not Be Televised* (Flying Dutchman 1974), *The Mind Of Gil Scott-Heron* (1979), *The Best Of Gil Scott-Heron* (Arista 1984). *Tales Of Gil* (Essential 1990; double album), *Glory: The Gil Scott-Heron Collection* (Arista 1990). Video: *Tales Of Gil* (1990).

2nd II None

Tha D and KK, who once attended high school with DJ Quik, comprise this Compton, California-based hip hop duo. Their debut album including two minor hit singles, 'If You Want It' (US number 64) and the more thought-provoking 'Be True To Yourself' (number 78).
Album: *2nd II None* (Profile 1991).

Sequence

The original female rap trio, comprising Gwen 'Blondie' Chisholm, Angela 'Angie B' Brown and Cheryl 'Cheryl The Pearl' Cook. They began their recording career with the unenviable task of following up the Sugarhill Gang's runaway success with 'Rapper's Delight' for the same label. The three members had performed together in their native South Carolina at dances and club dates. They first came to the attention of their future employers when the Sugarhill Gang played a date in that state, performing a version of 'Funk You Up' in the dressing room by way of audition. That track would become the second Sugarhill release, and another rap standard. Follow-up releases included 'Simon Says', a response record to labelmate Lady B's 'To The Beat Y'All'. Using lines drawn from the Shirley Ellis cut, 'The Clapping Song', it firmly stated how responsibility for 'Jill's' pregnancy was not hers alone. Angie Brown would later marry Lil' Rodney Cee of the Funky Four Plus One (at that time part of Double Trouble).
Album: *Sequence* (Sugarhill 1987).

Gil Scott-Heron

Shabazz, Lakim

At the forefront of the Nation Of Islam movement, Shabazz entered the stage with *Pure Righteousness*, an early production by DJ Mark the 45 King, which submitted a powerful blow for the Afrocentricity movement. Shabazz began his rapping whilst still at school, his interest initially awakened through an appetite for poetry. He took part in a succession of low-key, competitive MC clashes, until meeting the 45 King, who had recently relocated from New Jersey to New York. After losing contact for a while, he heard Mark mentioned on the radio, and called him up. Together they put together a handful of tracks, and Shabazz was subsequently signed to Tuff City via label boss, Aaron Fuchs. The second of his albums for the latter featured a more oppressively pro-Muslim stance, especially the unequivocal 'When You See A Devil Smash Him'.
Albums: *Pure Righteousness* (Tuff City 1988), *The Lost Tribe Of Shabazz* (Tuff City 1990).

Shadz Of Lingo

Hailing from Atlanta, Georgia, rappers Lingo and Kolorado alongside DJ Rocco have won plaudits for their furious mix of hip hop, dancehall reggae and jazz styles, only occasionally lapsing into the cool groove of geographical neighbours like Arrested Development. Their background as jingle writers partially explains this eclecticism. Having met at high school in Virginia, the trio decided to make a career in music, after several abortive attempts at rapping, by forming their own production company in 1988. When they launched Shadz Of Lingo they hit on an effective old school style, inviting producers of note such as Erick Sermon (EPMD), Diamond D. and Solid Productions in to help them. Live, the band are noted for their freestyle approach, with Kolorado claiming never to write lyrics down, tailoring them instead for each individual occason.
Album: *A View To A Kill* (ERG 1993).

She

Female MC who debuted with 'Miss DJ (Rap It Up!)', on the Clappers Record label, produced by Dennis Weedon. However, she would go on to record under sundry other titles, including Ms DJ and her own name, Sheila Spencer. Before her break in the music world she had sung in Brooklyn choirs from the age of five, and trained as an actress. Her resumé is undoubtedly a varied one. She would later become a national figure via her role as Thomasina in NBC's soap, *Another World*. She also previously sung backing vocals for Kurtis Blow's debut album, and was Muhammed Ali's cheerleader.

She Rockers

Comprising school mates Donna McConnell and Antonia Jolly, who formerly worked with Alison Clarkson (later Betty Boo) before that artist broke solo. Originally intending to become a news journalist and tennis pro respectively, their discovery of rap, particularly the work of Run DMC, LL Cool J and other B-boys, turned them onto the hip hop bug. They decided to form the band with Clarkson after seeing Salt 'n' Pepa play live at London's Astoria venue. They took their name from an extension of McConnell's stage name (She-Rock), and saw their debut recording, 'First Impressions', housed on the compilation *Known To Be Down*. Unlikely though they viewed it to be at the time, the track came to the attention of none other than Chuck D of Public Enemy. The result was a collaboration with Professor Griff called 'Give It A Rest', which also featured DJ Streets Ahead. However, on returning to England from the US, Clarkson chose the solo route leaving her former partners as a duo. Two singles, 'Jam It Jam' and 'Do Dat Dance', marked out their new territory - cultured hip-house. The latter was produced by no less than Technotronic. Their roots in pop, dance and rap were given equal billing on the attendant album, which brought a blend of mellow, often humourous raps, with an undertow of house music and the disco strains of Chic. There were conscious raps among allusions to their love life, 'How Sweet It Is' pointing out how violence at hip hop shows was overexposed compared to much greater outbreaks elsewhere. The set was neutered, they claimed, by pressure from their record company. They had wanted it to be a hardcore hip hip set. A public disclaimer about the album being only half good, and not having had any say on the track listing, did not help its sales profile.

Albums: *Rockers From London* (Jive 1990).

Shinehead

b. Edmund Carl Aitken, Kent, England. Although born in the UK, Aitken's family moved to Jamaica when he was two years old, then emigrated to New York in 1976 where he settled permanently. Counting among his influences a diverse array of artists including the Jackson 5 and Otis Redding, together with numerous reggae performers, Shinehead began singing at the age of 19, mixing the Jamaican toasting style with the more urbanized hip-hop which was developing in New York. After studying electrical and computer engineering his first musical activity came with Downbeat International in 1981, with Brigadier Jerry becoming a formative influence. He quickly developed a reputation for an astonishing range of dancehall skills; mimicking, singing, DJing, selecting, rapping and even whistling to great effect over Downbeat's stock-in-trade Studio One dub plates. It was there he gained his name: by virtue of his distinctive, closely cropped hairstyle. In late 1983 he joined forces with Claude Evans, who ran the African Love sound system-cum-label in Brooklyn. Evans managed to procure a rhythm track the Wailers had reputedly played for Bob Marley, who had died before using it. In 1984 Shinehead voiced 'Billie Jean'/'Mama Used To Say' over two sides of the rhythm and scored a massive hit for African Love. The debut album, *Rough And Rugged,* which followed in 1986 showcased his remarkably varied talents with a blend of dancehall, ballads, rap and reggae that yielded further hits in the shape of 'Know How Fi Chat', 'Hello Y'All' and 'Who The Cap Fits'. That same year he guested on Sly And Robbie's popular 'Boops' and was signed to Elektra in 1987. Their alliance has proved to be a disappointing one. The second album, *Unity,* was merely the first set re-arranged (some by Run DMC's Jam Master Jay), and contained many of the same tracks, some of which were by then four years old. Increasingly new material was aimed at the US crossover market, and despite the success of 'Strive' with his fading roots audience in 1990, his fortunes have taken a distinctly downward turn. *Sidewalk University* again assembled the services of assorted pop/rap/dance personnel in a bid for commercial reward, with the single 'Jamaican In New York' selling reasonably well. It is a long way removed from the dazzling attributes shown on his earlier work, although he continues to make combative appearances on sound systems both in the US and Jamaica.

Selected albums: *Rough And Rugged* (African Love Music 1986), *Unity* (African Love/Elektra 1988), *The Real Rock* (African Love/Elektra 1990), *Sidewalk University* (African Love/Elektra 1993), *Troddin'* (Elektra 1994).

Showbiz & AG

Bronx-based compatriots of Diamond D, Showbiz & AG were forced to make their mark in hip hop by establishing their own independent label, Showbiz Records, to house their debut EP, *Soul Clap*. This emerged in late 1991, and immediately created a buzz, leading them into a deal with London Records. AG had previously worked freestyle battles with Lord Finesse in high school, who introduced him to Showbiz. The partnership formed, they hustled through New York in a failed bid to get a contract. However, when their debut EP landed, particularly through the sucess of the 'Diggin' In The Crates' cut, they were hot news on the scene. Their profile was galvanised by Showbiz's highly successful remix of Arrested Development's 'Tenessee'. He has gone on to foster the careers of Big L and Deshawn.

Album: *Represent* (London 1992).

Shyheim

b. Shyheim Franklin, c.1979, Statten Island, New York, USA. Child prodigy who does not take kindly to comparisons to Kriss Kross *et al*, whose debut album emerged when he was only 14. He had first come to hip hop via the sounds of LL Cool J and Run DMC, and as a child learnt to rap along with them before graduating to verses of his own. His break came when producer RNS heard him rapping on the street in front of his block in Stapleton Projects, a dwelling he also shared with the young Shyheim. Together they worked on demos in RNS' studio, before attracting the interest of Virgin Records. More talented than most, Shyheim's depiction of inner ghetto violence did strike a chord, and was not related in the tedious 'my gun's bigger than your gun' mantra of too many artists. His 'On And On' single, for example, contained the somehow touching line: 'Ain't never had a good Christmas, So who's Santa Claus?'. Compared by many to a young Rakim (Eric B and Rakim), Shyheim's posse of homeboys (Do Lil's, Rubberbandz, KD, the Down Low Wrecker) were all present on his debut album, as were his 'brother artists', the Wu Tang Clan (Prince Rakeem of that crew being his next-door neighbour).

Album: *Aka The Rugged Child* (Virgin 1994).

Simmons, Russell

b. c.1958, Hollis, Queens, New York, USA. Simmons' artistic and business sense has seen him become the ultimate B-Boy millionaire, bullet-proof Rolls Royce notwithstanding. His entrepreneurial interests began by promoting disco parties while he was studying sociology at City College Of New York. Rush management was formed in 1979, and quickly escalated following the success of Kurtis Blow and Fearless Four. His first writing credit came with Blow's 'Christmas Rap'. However, no one can accuse Simmons of having fortune fall in his lap. He was part of the Rush team who picketed MTV in order to get them to play black videos (Run DMC's 'Rock Box', although Michael Jackson was the first to be played), and has maintained his commitment to black development. Throughout the 80s Def Jam, the label, would be the dominant force in the music, via the work of Run DMC and Public Enemy. Though he would eventually split from Rick Rubin, Simmons' stature in the eyes of the hip hop audience has hardly decreased. In 1993 Rush Management was valued at $34 million, with seven record labels, management, fashion (the Phat line) and broadcasting interests. The president of

the company is Carmen Ashurst-Watson, but Simmons remains responsible for the company ethos: 'My only real purpose is managing and directing. I sacrifice all the time for my artists. It's my job to make sure they have rich black babies'.

Simplé E

Talented female rapper who broke through in 1994 with her debut single 'Play My Funk', a Top 20 US R&B chart success. Taken from the *Sugar Hill* motion picture soundtrack, and produced by Dwayne Wiggins of Tony Toni Tone!, it revealed her to be able to switch from sung passages to gripping raps without missing a beat. Her debut album was aided by the production of Terry T and S.I.D. Reynolds.

Album: *The Colourz Of Sound* (Beacon 1994).

Sindecut

North London rap collective Sindecut spent their early days performing at the Swiss Cottage Community Centre, before releasing an eponymous debut single in 1986. Other members congregated around the nucleus of rapper Crazy Noddy and DJ Fingers, including Lyne Lyn (rapper), DJ Don't Ramp (producer), Mix Man G, Mad P and, later, Spike Tee and Louise Francis. Various members travelled to America in 1987/88 to get a deal with B-Boy Records, but lost out on the chance of a deal when label boss Bill Kamarra was sent to prison. They elected to set up their own label, Jgunglelist, instead (an interesting use of the term before it was hijacked by the 'jungle' club movement). The Sindecut made their name with the infectious rhythms of 'Posse'. It was an imposing stew of ragga vocals and hip hop breaks. Their first club hit, though, was 'Sindecut Kickin' Yeah', on another independent label, Baad . They grew up with the similarly formulated Soul II Soul, merging soul and reggae with rap: 'Its just our influences really. Americans have a lot of influences but they tend to make one type of music. We want to make music that we are influenced by and put it together into a new sound'. Their debut album showcased raps backed by orchestrated strings and frantic live drums - an almost 'new age' hip hop affair.

Shyheim

Album: *Changing The Scenery* (Virgin 1990).

Sir Mix-A-Lot

Seattle based DJ/MC and producer (b. Anthony Ray) who broke with 'Posse On Broadway', a statement of intent released on his own label in 1986, which would go on to sell over a million copies. Further crossover success arrived with rap's second great rock/rap coalition: a cover of Black Sabbath's 'Iron Man', performed in conjunction with Seattle thrash outfit Metal Church. By the time of his second album Sir Mix-A-Lot was sampling Prince's 'Batdance', and maintaining his sharp, political edge - though he is too light-hearted and deft of touch to be considered truly gangsta. His Rhyme Cartel is signed to Def American records, and he can boast a platinum and gold album for *Swass* and *Seminar*, respectively. Sir-Mix-A-Lot's use of unlikely sources, the synthesized pop of Devo and Kraftwerk measured against the conscious lyrics of rappers like Public Enemy, was a unique combination. However, there were some crude sexual japes on tracks like 'Mack Daddy', and he was hardly shown in the best light by the pro-gun swagger of 'No Rods Barred'. He did enjoy another huge hit in 'Baby Got Back', however.
Albums: *Swass* (Nastymix 1988), *Seminar* (Nastymix 1989), *Mack Daddy* (Def American 1992), *Chief Boot Knocka* (American Recordings 1994).

Sister Souljah

b. Lisa Williamson, USA. Rapper who became something of a *cause celebre* when President-elect Bill Clinton verbally attacked her during his campaign. On June 13 1992 he declared that Souljah had made 'racist remarks' and 'advocated violence against whites' in an interview with *Rolling Stone* magazine. As if having such political heavyweights on her case were not enough, she also found herself being sued by former producer Michael Shinn, after she listed him as a 'two-faced backstabber' on the sleevenotes to her 1992 Epic album. The source of their inital disagreement was not disclosed, but she was dropped from the label after its release in any case. The album is still worth

investigating however, notably on cuts like 'State Of Accomodation: Why Aren't You Angry?' and 'Killing Me Softly: Deadly Code Of Silence', which featured guest shots from Chuck D and Ice Cube respectively. She also worked with Public Enemy, joining the band in late 1990 after accompanying them on their US lecture tour. However, her contribution (rapping on 'By The Time I Get To Arizona' from *The Enemy Strikes Black*) was disappointing and her tenure with the band was a brief one. She had already appeared on Terminator X's single, 'Wanna Be Dancin' (Buck Whylin')', and would also guest on his debut solo album.
Album: *360 Degrees Of Power* (Epic 1992).

Skinny Boys

Comprising brothers MC Shockin' Shaun (b. Shaun Harrison, Bridgeport, Connecticut, USA) and DJ Super Jay (b. James Harrison, Bridgeport, Connecticut, USA), plus their cousin Jock Box (b. Jacque Harrison, Bridgeport, Connecticut, USA). After first being drawn to the funk of James Brown and George Clinton, these young men were invigorated by the East Coast rap phenomenon. Super Jay grew particularly enamoured of Grandmaster Flash, and ditched his previous instruments (accordion and organ) to concentrate on DJing with a local partner. He was subsequently joined first by his brother, then cousin Jock Box, whose 'human beatbox' style resembled that of the Fat Boys' Darren Robinson. Indeed, the Skinny Boys moniker was a tongue-in-cheek reference to the latter band. Playing local skating rinks, they eventually came to the attention of Mark and Rhonda Bush. The former would offer the trio production, while the latter managed them and wrote their raps ('based on our ideas', the Skinny Boys claimed). In 1985, their first 12-inch single emerged, 'We're Skinny Boys'/'Awesome', on their manager's Bush label. A second single, 'Feed Us The Beat'/'Jock Box' saw them switch to Warlock, which also released their debut album. On the back of this exposure the trio were eventually signed to the Jive imprint. They would tour with the likes of Jazzy Jeff And The Fresh Prince, Kool Moe Dee, Salt 'n' Pepa and, suitably, the Fat Boys, building a strong local following. Their second album, once again helmed by the Bushes, included 'I Wanna Be Like', which namechecked Prince, Michael Jackson and Bill Cosby as suitable role models. Despite the good intentions and strong start, the title of their final album for Jive in 1988 proved sadly ironic.

Albums: *Weightless* (Warlock 1986), *Skinny & Proud* (Jive 1987), *Skinny, They Can't Get Enough* (Jive 1988).

Sleeping Bag Records

New York City based rap label who first brought the world Mantronix and Todd Terry. The label was inaugurated by Willie Socolov and Arthur Russell when they released the latter's 'Go Bang' as Dinosaur L. The second single was 'Weekend' by Class Action. While that 45 was being plugged by Juggy Gayles, Socolov met with Gayles' son, Ron Resnick. Resnick would become vice-president of the company, as they went on to establish a rap platform which boasted EPMD before they defected to Def American. Other acts included Joyce Sims and Cash Money And Marvellous. Socolov and Russell were no musical purists, and were happy to describe themselves as: 'Two white, middle-class, Jewish hucksters'. Incidentally, Sleeping Bag was named after Socolov's ultimate bachelor behaviour - having a sleeping bag over his mattress to save making the bed. They opened a UK office through Rough Trade in 1990, but afterwards their influence waned.

Selected albums: Mantronix: *Mantronix* (Sleeping Bag 1985). Cash Money And Marvellous: *Where's The Party At* (Sleeping Bag 1988). T La Rock: *On A Warpath* (Sleeping Bag 1990).

Slick Rick

b. Richard Walters, South Wimbledon, London, England. Of Jamaican parentage, Walters moved to the US at the age of 14, going on to attend New York's High School of Music & Art. By the time his solo career started, Slick had already enjoyed his five minutes of rap fame (as MC Ricky D) by backing Doug E. Fresh on his masterpiece, 'The Show'. Not the most enlightened of hip hop's rappers, as 'Treat Her Like A Prostitute' on his debut album confirmed, Slick Rick does, however, live up to his name on his more impressive numbers. These included his standard, 'The Ruler'. It was also impossible to argue with the superb production by Rich himself alongside Jam Master Jay (Run DMC) and Hank Schocklee and Eric Sadler (the Bomb Squad). His second album was recorded in just three weeks while he was out of jail on bail, and facing up to ten years for attempted murder (shooting his cousin and his friend, then undergoing a high speed car chase which ended in both him and his girlfriend breaking legs). It continued the jazzy rhythms of his debut, which would attain platinum status in his adopted US homeland. Rick's confident, efficient half-sung delivery also proved a powerful influence on subsequent rappers, including Snoop Doggy Dogg.

Albums: *The Great Adventures Of Slick Rick* (Def Jam 1988), *The Ruler's Back* (Def Jam 1991).

Smif N Wessun

Brooklyn, New York, USA-based outfit, named after the famous gun-making duo, Smif N Wessun arrived as the second act on Nervous Records' subsidiary, Wreck, in 1993. Rappers Tek and Steele first broke vinyl cover with two tracks, 'Black Smif n Wessun' and 'U da Man', housed on Black Moon's *Enta Da Stage* album. The association with the latter began when they used dancer Tracy Allan, who turned out to be Buckshot's sister, on stage in their early days. They would go on to support their mentors on their national tour with Das EFX. The production team responsible for *Enta Da Stage*, DJ Evid Dee and his brother Mr. Walt (aka Da Beatminerz), were also present for Smif N Wessun's debut single, 'Bucktown'. It would move over 75,000 units in its first three weeks of release.

Album: *The Shining* (Wreck 1994).

Smith, Larry

b. Hollis, Queens, New York, USA. Smith formed Orange Crush (which also featured Davey DMX - or Davey D - and Trevor Gale), in his first foray into hip hop. After which he would go on to become one of rap music's most important producers. His credits included work with Jimmy

Snoman

Spicer and early Kurtis Blow, before he oversaw the first two Run DMC albums. In the process he helped to create the spare, minimalist rhythm tracks and sound which would define the 'new school'. His influence waned as the 80s progressed, though he did helm three albums by Whodini.

Snoman

b. LeBaron Frost, Alexandria, Virginia. An alternative to the rural langour of fellow Atlanta, Georgia-based rappers Arrested Development or Gumbo, Snoman's ruse is to retreat to the East Side old school artistry of the pioneering hip hop artists and B-Boys. He began writing his first poetry at the age of nine, and was subsequently inspired by the imported sounds of Run DMC. Following an appearance on the Conquest Of A Nation compilation he made his personal bow with the single, 'Money'. Backed by DJ Nabs, Snoman created a smooth, flowing blend of hip hop with intelligent, often introspective rhymes: 'It's very important to me that I write good, strong lyrics especially since I found it hard to express myself when I was growing up'.
Album: The Exceptional One (Conquest/Ichiban 1993).

Snoop Doggy Dogg

b. Calvin Broadus, 1971, Long Beach, California, USA. Snoop Doggy Dogg's commercial rise in 1993 was acutely timed, riding a surge in hardcore rap's popularity, and smashing previous records in any genre. Doggy Style was the most eagerly anticipated album in rap history, and the first debut album to enter the Billboard chart at number 1. With advance orders of over one and a half million, media speculators were predicting its importance long before a release date. As is de rigeur for gangsta rappers such as Snoop, his criminal past casts a long, somewhat romanticised shadow over his current achievements. He was busted for drugs after leaving high school in Long Beach, and spent three years in and out of jail. He first appeared in 1990 when helping out Dr Dre on a track called 'Deep Cover', from the film of the same title. Dogg was also ubiquitous on Dr Dre's breakthrough album, The Chronic, particularly on the hit single 'Nuthin' But A 'G' Thang', which he wrote and co-rapped on. After presenting a gong to En Vogue in September 1993 at the MTV video awards, Dogg surrendered himself to police custody after the show, on murder charges. This was over his alleged involvement in a driveby shooting. Inevitably, as news spread of Dogg's involvement interest in his vinyl product accelerated, and this played no small part in the eventual sales of his debut album. Critics noted how closely this was styled on George Clinton's Atomic Dog project. Many also attacked the abusive imagery of women Dogg employed, particularly lurid on 'Ain't No Fun'. His justification: 'I'm not prejudiced in my rap, I just kick the rhymes'. If the US press were hostile to him they were no match for the sensationalism of the English tabloids. During touring commitments to support the album and single, 'Gin And Juice', he made the front page of the Daily Star with the headline: 'Kick This Evil Bastard Out!'. It was vaguely reminiscent of the spleen vented at the Sex Pistols in their heyday, and doubtless a good sign. He was asked to leave his hotel in Milestone, Kensington on arrival, and Terry Dicks, a bastion of Tory godd taste, also objected to his presence in the country. A more serious impediment to Snoop's career is his imminent trial on charges of accessory to the murder of Phillip Woldermarian, shot by his bodyguard McKinley Lee.
Album: Doggy Style (Death Row 1993).

Son Of Bazerk

Flavor Flav protege rapper backed by a six-piece No Self Control troupe whose employment of the Bomb Squad on their long playing debut drew favourable comparisons to the masters, Public Enemy, themselves. Likewise hailing from Long Island, New York, he is best known for the single, 'Change The Style'. Chuck D went so far as to describe him as the 'hardest rapper' he had ever heard. The band's second single was 'Bang (Get Down, Get Down)', housed on Bill Stephney and Hank Schocklee's SOUL label.
Album: Bazerk Bazerk Bazerk (MCA 1991).

Soul Sonic Force

With Cosmic Force, the Soul Sonics were part of Afrika Bambaataa's ever-expanding Zulu Nation enclave. Alongside scratch DJ Jazzy Jay, Pow Wow and G.L.O.B.E., they featured rapper Mr Biggs, who had been working with Bambaataa as far back as 1974. Pow Wow, in turn, had a hand in producing 'Planet Rock', while G.L.O.B.E. was responsible for patenting the 'MC popping' technique, a desription he preferred to rapping, which saw him dropping in and out of rhymes at short notice, producing an effect not unlike a faulty microphone. He was also responsible for may of the group's lyrics. He had met Bambaataa while he was attending Bronx River High School, and was already friends with Pow Wow, who had perfected his rapping skills in nearby parks. Soul Sonic Force began as a nine-piece affair, which MC's gradually dropping out, including Lisa Lee who would remain with Bambaataa as part of Cosmic Force. In tandem with their mentor they would appear on four hugely influential singles, 'Zulu Nation Throwdown Part 2', 'Planet Rock', 'Looking For The Perfect Beat' and 'Renegades Of Funk'. Their impetus was interrupted in 1983 when both Mr Biggs and Pow Wow were convicted for armed robbery. When Bambaataa resurrected the name again in 1991 for *Return To Planet Rock*, it was merely a disguise for the Jungle Brothers.
Album: With Afrika Bambaataa: *Planet Rock: The Album* (Tommy Boy 1986).

Souls Of Mischief

Part of Del Tha Funkee Homosapien's Oakland-based Heiroglyphics enclave, Souls Of Mischief debuted with some panache on their 1993 album. With samples drawn from a selction of artists as diverse as Grover Washington, Curtis Mayfield and Main Source, it demonstrated their ability to blend mellow beats without the jive pimp talk so readily available in their neck of the woods from Too Short. The group comprises Tajal (b. c.1977), A-Plus (b. c.1976), Opio (b. c.1976) and Phesto (b. c.1977). Their recording career began when Del's cousin, Ice Cube, sorted him out with a recording contract, he in turn suggesting the Souls Of Mischief should be next up. They recorded a song with Del entitled 'Burnt' (featured on the b-side to 'Mistadobalina'), from whence they were spotted. Tajal and A-Plus were kickin' lyrics alongside label-mate Spice-I while still in eighth grade, and their vocal dexterity was a standout feature on their debut album, with combatitive rhymes overlaying the production work of A-Plus, Del, and Heiroglyphics production guru, Domino. This group certainly operate well together, hardly suprising since: 'We all went to the same elementary school, junior high, and most of us went into the same high school'.
Album: *'93 Till Infinity* (Jive 1993).

South Central Cartel

Fronted by MC Havoc Da Mouthpiece, whose father was a member of the Chi-Lites, the ranks of South Central Cartel are also inhabited by rappers Prodeje, Havikk Da Rymesman, LV Da Voice (the group's 'singer') and DJ's Kaos #1 and Gripp. Formed in 1986, the group which evolved into SCC had originally titled themselves Mafia Style and New Authority. The group hail from Los Angeles, as made explicit in the choice of their title, and released material on their own GWK (Gangstas With Knowledge) label. Like Compton's Most Wanted before them, they peddled hard street narratives, best displayed on singles like the self-explanatory 'Gang Stories'. They managed to sell over 200,000 copies of their debut album on GWK, before flirting with a contract to the Quality emporium. Eventually Havoc contacted Russel Simmons, whom he had met while at a Black Music convention, which led to the band joining Sony's RAL/Def Jam stable for *'N' Gatz We Trust*. As with previous work this boasted live musician backing, the advantages of which were tempered by the fact that they largely stuck to recreations of generic George Clinton riffs. However, in the wake of South Central Cartel's success Prodoje, who helmed the production, has gone on become a successful mixer and producer, working with Public Enemy, LL Cool J and Spice 1. SCC themselves also scripted and starred in a public service film encouraging young people to use their vote.
Albums: *South Central Messages* (GWK 1992), *'N Gatz We Trust* (RAL/Def Jam 1994).

Souls Of Mischief

Special Ed

b. Edward Archer, c.1973, Brooklyn, New York, USA. Special Ed debuted with a superb, precise album, produced with numbing ferocity by Hitman Howie Tee. Archer had previously practised his lyrics in junior high school, perfecting his rhymes until he hooked up with Tee who agreed to produce some tracks for him. These were promptly delivered to Profile Records who immediately expressed an interest and sanctioned Special Ed's debut album. Though he was only 16 when this was released, the rhymes were mature and supremely confident. Over half a million sales confirmed his arrival. There was a more romantic discourse evident on the follow-up, which while less abrasive, was still an examplory introduction. Still largely with Tee, he produced four of the tracks himself. He also introduced a number of his friends, including his brother Drew Archer and homeboys 40-Love, Little Shawn and DJ Akshan. There was, however, a three year hiatus between *Legal* and his third album, proposed for 1993 release. The time was spent: 'Working with groups and putting together a studio and office in Brooklyn'. He also produced a track for Tupac Shakur's *Strictly For My Niggaz*. He was reported to be working with Gang Starr's DJ Premier, Large Professor and A Tribe Called Quest's Q-Tip on sessions for the new album, while further collaborations placed him alongside Master Ace and Buckshot (Black Moon) in the highly successful Crooklyn Dodgers project ('Crooklyn').
Albums: *Youngest In Charge* (Profile 1989), *Legal* (Profile 1990).

Spice 1

b. Byron, Texas, USA. Part of the new wave of Oakland rappers., Spice 1 was discovered by his neighbourhood's most imposing figure, Too Short. Though he was born in Texas, he was raised in Hayward, before spending the final years of his adolesence in Oakland. A second album, *187 He Wrote*, contained plenty of the funky beats for which that area is renowned. This was gangsta rap in its most primal form, including cuts like 'I'm The Fuckin' Murderer', and the single, 'Dumpin' 'Em In Ditches'. Despite its simplistic formula, the album proved a runaway success. going from number 97 to number 1 in Billboard's R&B chart in one week.
Album: *Spice 1* (Jive 1992), *187 He Wrote* (Jive 1993).

Spoonie Gee

b. Gabe Jackson, Harlem, New York, USA. Spoonie-Gee was so-called because he only ever ate with that utensil when he was a child. As a youngster he proved adept at poetry, and was often to be found hanging out at the Rooftop Club, where early DJs like DJ Hollywood and Brucie B held sway. His recording career began at Enjoy Records, whose owner, Bobby Robinson, was his uncle. His most notable records included 'New Rap Language' with the Treacherous 3, backed by his own standard, 'Love Rap', on the flip. It featured his brother, Pooche Costello, on congos. They had grown up together in the same house as Bobby Robinson, his wife acting as surrogate mother when her sister died when Spoonie was just 12. Later he cut the family ties to join the growing band of deserters housed on the competing Sugarhill imprint. His hits for the label included 'Spoonie's Back' and 'Monster Jam', plus a reissue of his debut for Peter Brown's Sound Of New York USA label, 'Spoonin' Rap'. His career slowed in the mid-80s, and in 1984 he was to be found working in a rehabilitation centre for the mentally disabled. Three years later he once again found success, this time on Aaron Fuch's Tuff City label, with the Marley Marl/Teddy Riley-produced *The Godfather*.
Album: *The Godfather* (Tuff City 1987).

Steady B

b. Warren McGlone, c.1970, Philadelphia, USA. Steady B boasts distinguished lineage, he is the cousin of Lawrence Goodman, owner of the Pop Art label. Perhaps Steady B's lack of headline reviews has more to do with his decision to stay in his native Philadelphia rather than any lack of talent or forbearance. Originally inspired by old school rappers Run DMC and Whodini, his debut release was infact a direct answer record to another big influence, LL Cool J. 'I'll Take Your Radio' being a challenge to the originator of 'I Can't Live Without My Radio'. He was just 15 years old, and a steady stream of hits would follow: 'Fly Shante', 'Just Call Us Def' and 'Do Tha Filla'. On the back of these cult items he won himself a contract with Jive, which has seen the release of five albums in as many years. Although none have brought great commercial reward, each has seen workmanlike performances straddling both the pop-rap and hardcore markets. He has now launched a new group, C.B.E.

Albums: *Bring The Beat Back* (Jive 1987), *What's My Name?* (Jive 1987), *Let The Hustlers Play* (Jive 1988), *Going Steady* (Jive 1990), *Steady B V* (Jive 1991).

Stetsasonic

Among rap's elder statesmen with origins in 1981, Brooklyn's Stetsasonic were hugely influential on a number of fronts. They were one of the few bands of their generation to promote the use of live instruments, and there was simply no hip hop comparison to their onstage power. Via their 'A.F.R.I.C.A.' 45 (1985) they helped usher in a new wave of black consciousness and ethnocentricity/positivity, which both De La Soul and the Jungle Brothers would further streamline. Proceeds from the song were handed over to the Africa Fund for humanitarian relief projects. Alongside Run DMC, Stetsasonic were instrumental in promoting the rock/rap crossover, yet maintained an articulate rap narrative, best sampled on their classic second album, *In Full Gear*. 'This Is A Hip Hop Band' they announced on its cover - it was, but not like any hip hop band had sounded before. They were joined by the Force MD's on an exemplory version of the Floaters' 'Float On', and also tackled the contextual rap history lesson of 'Talkin' All That Jazz', which would pre-date the jazz/rap phenomenon by at least three years. Their third album included direct political point-making exercises like 'Free South Africa'. Fittingly, it was Stetsasonic who were chosen to represent rap at the Nelson Mandela concert in London. DJ Prince Paul (b. Paul Huston) and lead rapper Daddy-O (b. c.1961, Brooklyn, New York, USA) were the lynchpins

behind the group, who also included Delite, Fruitkwan (aka Fuquan) and DBC. The split came in 1990 when Daddy-O decided, not entirely unilaterally, that Statsasonic were beginning to exhaust their possibilities. Both Prince Paul and Daddy-O subsequently become in-demand producers and remixers. The former has produced Fine Young Cannibals, in addition to underscoring De La Soul's *3 Feet High And Rising*, while Boo-Yaa Tribe adopted his hard funk drum effect. Daddy-O, meanwhile, remixed for Mary J. Blige, also working with artists as diverse as Queen Latifah, Big Daddy Kane (notably *It's A Big Daddy Thing*) and the Red Hot Chilli Peppers. DBC recorded a handful of tracks for independent labels. Any bad blood which may have existed at the time of their dissolvement would appear to have been forgotten when the news broke that the original line up recorded together again in 1993, with a view to a release the following year. 1994 also saw Prince Paul collaborating with Fruitkwan as part of the Gravediggaz.

Albums: *On Fire* (Tommy Boy 1986), *In Full Gear* (Tommy Boy 1988), *Blood Sweat And No Tears* (Tommy Boy 1991).

Stop The Violence Movement

Set up by prominent members of the New York hip hop community, the Stop The Violence Movement was just that - a lobby to bring about a ceasefire in the endless gang warfare in the black ghettos. Numbering amongst its contributors Kool Moe Dee, Public Enemy, Stetsasonic, Boogie Down Productions and many others, a single was released on the Jive imprint, 'Self Destruction', in 1989. It would become the movement's anthem.

Subsonic 2

Include Me Out was widely praised as one of the most impressive debuts of 1991, a legitimate compliment to one of UK rap's most inriguing new formations. DJ Docta D and MC Steel provide the hands on the steering wheel, which veers wildly from R&B to funk and Motown, taking in breakbeats and some of the smarter rhymes heard in the parish. The pair met after Steel addressed a demo, recorded on his own portable studio, to Heatwave Radio. This pirate station, helmed by Docta D, took to the tape in a big way, with continued requests urging him to seek out the cassette's creator. Afterwards they spent three years working together on new material, with cuts like 'Dedicated To The City', with its captivating jazz saxophone, boosted by the literacy of English and Russian graduate Steel. While the title recalled many hardcore rappers concerns about authenticating themselves with tales of urban mayhem, 'Dedicated' is merely a delightful nod to the lyricist's direct environment, a celebration of its vibrancy and variety. Or 'Unsung Heroes Of Hip-Hop', which cleverly mocks the sheepish competition between hardcore crews which too often merely produces imitation: 'Well, do you really wanna base a career, On an '84 Run DMC idea?'.

Albums: *Include Me Out* (Columbia 1991).

Sugarhill Gang

Englewood, New Jersey troupe, whose 'Rapper's Delight' was hip hop's breakthrough single. They gave the music an identity and a calling card in the first line of the song: 'A hip-hop, The hi-be, To the hi-be, The hip-hip-hop, You don't stop rockin'. Master Gee (b. Guy O'Brien, 1963), Wonder Mike (b. Michael Wright, 1958) and Big Bank Hank (b. Henry Jackson, 1958) saw massive international success in 1979 with 'Rappers Delight', based on the subsequently widely borrowed rhythm track from Chic's 'Good Times', over which the trio offered a series of sly boasts which were chatted rather than sung. Joe Robinson remembers the song's elevation to commercial status: 'Sylvia brought this to me, a 15 minute record on a 12-inch disc. No 15 minute record has ever got played on the radio, so I said, what am I gonna do with this? But all I had to do with it was get one play anywhere and it broke'. Considered at the time to be something of a novelty item, 'Rapper's Delight' was significantly more than that. Sylvia and Joe Robinson had recruited the three rappers on an *ad hoc* basis. Hank was a former bouncer and pizza waiter, and

brought fresh rhymes from his friend Granmaster Caz (see Cold Crush Brothers). The backing was offered by Positive Force, a group from Pennsylvania who enjoyed their own hit with 'We Got The Funk', but became part of the Sugarhill phenomenon when 'Rapper's Delight' struck. They would go on to tour on the Gang's early live shows, before the Sugarhill house band took over. Smaller hits followed with 'The Love In You' (1979) and 'Kick It Live From 9 To 5' (1982), before the group faded and fell apart in the early 80s. The Sugarhill Gang were already assured of their place in hip hop's history, even if reports that Big Bank Hank was working as a Englewood garbage man in the 90s are correct.

Albums: *Rappers Delight* (Sugarhill 1980), *8th Wonder* (Sugarhill 1982).

Sugarhill Records

Joe Robinson Jr and Sylvia Robinson were behind this label, named after the comparatively affluent locale in Harlem, though they themselves had moved to Englewood in New Jersey. It was not necessarily the first rap label, but by far the biggest and most important. The inspiration came from their teenage children's enthusiasm for the hip hop movement and its celebrity MCs, particularly the 'live jam' tapes. Sylvia already had a music legacy. It is widely recalled that she had scored a Top 20 hit in 1973 with 'Pillow Talk'. However, she had also scored as Little Sylvia for Savoy, and duetted with her guitar tutor Houston 'Mickey' Baker', at which time she also met Joe, on the duet 'Love Is Strange'. Joe's background, conversely, was in real estate, but he gained an introduction to music via his wife. Together they opened a club entitled the Blue Morocco in the Bronx, and by the end of the 60s had started the All Platinum label. This housed soul and funk records by George Kerr, Linda Jones, the Universal Messengers and others. Joe also owned the rights to the Chess back-catalogue. They convinced Morris Levy to assist them in a new venture and, in 1979, Sugarhill's rap agenda was launched with 'Rapper's Delight'. By sampling the huge Chic hit 'Good Times', it effectively gave birth to the debate over artistic authorship which has dominated rap since. It did, however, have precedents, one of which Sylvia Robinson was only too aware of: 'Strange Love' had also been subject to disputes over plagiarism. Their reputation as financially irrascible operators is enshrined in rap legend, though so is their contribution to the development of the music. Employing the Sugarhill house band (Keith LeBlanc, Skip McDonald, Doug Wimbush - who had met as part of Wood Brass & Steel, a funk outfit who had also performed regular duties for the Robinsons' former label All Platinum - later to move to the UK and become Tackhead), a steady stream of rap classics followed. These included Four Plus One's 'That's The Joint', and 'The Message' and 'White Lines' by Grandmaster Flash and Grandmaster Melle Mel respectively. The success was rapid, but led to complications over finance. Specifically, they were accused of not paying their artists' royalties, a charge they defend vehemently. Despite the acrimony over the Grandmaster Flash And The Furious Five in-fighting debacle, Joe Robinson Jr, for one, does not countenance their widely read press statements: 'Who gives a fuck what those fuckin' bums think? Them guys was drug addicts using crack when it first came out. Flash never wrote a song, never did a rap - son of a bitch was never in the studio when a record was made out of here. It's all in the court records'. He was referring to the 1983 case, which, although they won, forced Sugarhill into financial difficulties. They linked up with MCA but to no avail. Sugarhill would eventually go under in the mid-80s following problems with distributors. They had been left behind by new technology - their policy of never hiring outside producers severely damaging them when sequencers and samplers were introduced, as no-one in the company knew how to use them. They eventually sold their ownership of Chess, but the Robinsons remain in the music business, and currently run publishing and licensing companies in New York (Sylvia had made a brief return to recording with 'Good To Be The Queen', an answer record to Mel Brooks' 'Good To Be The King' rap). As for the late lamented Sugarhill, it is nice to see at least one label with as colourful a history as the music it played such a major role in advancing.

Selected compilations: *Rapped Uptight Vol. 1* (Sugarhill 1981), *Rapped Uptight Vol. 2* (Sugarhill 1982), *Old School Rap: The Sugarhill Story* (Sequel 1992), *The Sugarhill 12-inch Mixes* (Castle 1994).

Sweet Tee

b. Toi Jackson, Queens, New York, USA. Female MC, re-discovered by Salt 'N' Pepa's producer Hurby Lovebug, whose breakthrough single was 'I Got Da Feelin''. She had originally recorded for her father, Paul Winley, ('Vicious Rap', 'It's Like That Y'All') and Champion Records ('Its My Beat' with Jazzy Joyce). 'Vicious Rap', produced by her mother, carried a false arrest narrative, and was one of the prototype conscious rap singles. Her father remembers because 'Everytime I look at her she had her head in her notebook'. Rather than concentrating on her homework, however, she was instead busy manufacturing her rhymes. However, there was little to be heard from her following a singular album for Profile in 1989, and two singles, 'On The Smooth Tip' and 'Let's Dance'.
Album: *It's Tee Time* (Profile 1989).

T

T La Rock

b. c.1961, Bronx, New York, USA. Although he did not gain prominence until the 90s, old school rapper T La Rock can boast quite a heritage. His brother, Special K, was signed to the original Sugarhill label. He had also met Rick Rubin of Def Jam, before the latter had got his label underway. Together the duo recorded 'It's Yours' on Party Time records. La Rock fell out with Rubin when he discovered that he was also fostering the career of LL Cool J, who would inherit his king of the B-boys title. He cut one album, produced by himself, DJ Doc and DJ Mark The 45 King in 1987 for Virgin subsidiary Ten.

When he resurfaced in the 90s with *On The Warpath* Todd Terry was in the producer's chair. The original version of the record, which had taken four months to record, was scrapped in favour of a new Terry production. He had initially come to the Sleeping Bag offices to offer La Rock the chance to rap over one of his productions. The resulting album, which was originally to have included on stage banter and was vaunted to the press as *On Tour*, contained a much less hardcore, more commerical slant than expected. As a concession to his long-term supporters it also included 'Its Yours', which had previously been a much sought after and unobtainable old school classic. Alongside this were excursions into swingbeat, and a return to old B-boy stylings in 'Warpath'.

Albums: *Lyrical King* (Ten 1987), *On A Warpath* (Sleeping Bag 1990).

Tairrie B

Tairrie (pronounced Terry) was one of executive producer Eazy-E's less successful protégés. Heralded as the rap Madonna, she failed to achieve sales with her debut album. This despite having two tracks produced by Schooly D and the eloquence of cuts like 'Ruthless Bitch'. Some critics suggested that the delivery, though tidy and competent, lacked power.

Album: *The Power Of A Woman* (Comptown 1990).

Terminator X

b. Norman Rodgers. One of the last of the Public Enemy fold to release a solo record, Terminator X's efforts reflect his work with his principal employers, minus the intrusion of Chuck D or Flavor Flav. Aimed squarely at the dance end of the hip hop market, *Valley Of The Jeep Beets* was primarily a collection of deep, bass-driven hip hop chops, and confirmed him as one of the finest DJs. It saw vocal contributions from Andrew 13 and Sister Souljah, on a combination of hard funk and scratchy raps. As Public Enemy prepared to tour in support of their 1994 album he was involved in a serious motorbike accident, breaking both his legs. However, that did not deter the release of his second solo outing. The highlight of this set was 'G'Damn Datt DJ Made My Day', on which he duelled on the turntable alongside Grandmaster Flash. Other old school legends like the Cold Crush Brothers and Kool Herc popped up elsewhere.

Album: *Terminator X And The Valley Of The Jeep Beets* (CBS/Columbia 1991). With The Godfathers Of Threatt: *Super Bad* (RAL 1994).

3rd Bass

Comprising MC Serch (b. Michael Berrin, 6 May 1967, Queens, New York, USA), Prime Minister Pete Nice (b. Peter Nash, 5 February 1967, Brooklyn, New York, USA) and DJ Richie Rich, 3rd Bass were one of the few white US rap teams to maintain any degree of credibility. Def Jam's second white Jewish act (after the Beastie Boys), they were a million miles apart from their better known precursors. At their best they combined raw intelligence with strong humour and a powerful musical delivery. Their debut album, produced with the help of Prince Paul (Stetsasonic) and Sam Sever (who originally encouraged the then solo Nice and Serch to team up), was bolstered by mighty cuts like 'Steppin' To The AM', with its melange of TV samples and urban paranoia. Nice was a particularly effective mic. man, whose classes in modern poetry at Columbia University clearly shone through. However, the extent to which 3rd Bass seemed to be anxious about their skin colour was reflected by two tracks on *Derelicts Of Dialect* which both pilloried Vanilla Ice (notably 'Pop Goes The Weasel'). Elsewhere they could be assured and effective, 'Product Of The Environment' on their debut being a case in point. Nice would go on to a successful new career alongside Rich, while Serch would become A&R Vice-President of Wild Pitch Records.

Albums: *The Cactus Album* (Def Jam 1989), *The Cactus Revisited: 3rd Bass Remixes* (Def Jam 1990), *Derelicts Of Dialect* (Def Jam 1991).

Toddy Tee

b. c.1965, Compton, Los Angeles, California, USA. One of the Los Angeles old school, Toddy Tee is as signifcant to the development of West

Coast rap as Afrika Bambaataa is to the New York scene, though he rarely receives the credit. This probably has a great deal to do with the lack of musical archive his career has produced. One important such document was the *Batteram* tape, a live outing circulated in similar fashion to the Zulu Nation's 'throwdowns'. It was later revisited in Ice-T's 'Six', and documented the LAPD's new weapon in the war against crack houses, an armoured car that they could drive straight into suspect's houses. The tape was one of a sequence traded between Toddy Tee and fellow rhymer Mixmaster Spade, but proved much more popular than anything which had gone before. In the wake of its success it was eventually released as a single on Evejim in 1986, which would add 'Just Say No' to Tee's discography two years later. However, this provides scant testimony to the man's influence.

Tommy Boy

A record label hugely important to the development of hip hop and rap, Tommy Boy was the tiny entity which brought the world Afrika Bambaataa, Keith LeBlanc ('Malcolm X'), and the songwriting/production genius of Michael Jonzun and Arthur Baker. The label was formed by Tom Silverman in his living room on East 85th Street in New York. He had previously been running a magazine entitled *Dance Music Report*, in the process of which he became captivated by the electro funk movement in Europe. Early Tommy Boy releases included projects by Bambaataa's MCs, recording under the name Cotton Candy. The breakthrough release was 'Jazzy Sensation', built on Gwen McRae's 'Funky Sensation' and concocted by Bambaataa, and producers Baker and Shep Pettibone. It was a precursor to 'Planet Rock', a hugely successful collision between Kraftwerk's 'Trans Europe Express' and Alan Shacklock's Ennio Morricone-inspired 'The Mexican', which lit the 'electro' fuse. Tommy Boy was instrumental in developing the sound, which dominated rap in the mid-80s. Afterwards they explored rap's fallout with quality signings like Queen Latifah and Digital Underground. Their second great innovation arrived with the introduction of De La Soul and 'Daisy Age Soul'.

In its wake the label was signed up to Warners, and Big Life also picked up several of their artists for UK distribution, though there were plans to open a UK office in 1994. Their biggest ever hit, however, came with Naughty By Nature's 'OPP'. Recent worldwide chart successes include K7 and House Of Pain.
Selected albums: Queen Latifah: *All Hail The Queen* (Tommy Boy 1989). De La Soul: *3 Feet High And Rising* (Tommy Boy 1990). Naughty By Nature: *Naughty By Nature* (Tommy Boy 1991). Digital Underground: *Sex Packets* (Tommy Boy 1990).

Tone Loc

Tongue in cheek Los Angeles artist (b. Anthony Smith - his stage name derived from his Spanish nickname, Antonio Loco), Tone Loc's hoarse raps boast of incredible personal sexual allure, allied to a background of smooth jazz, soul and bluebeat. His debut album featured the two worldwide 1990 hits, Wild Thing' and 'Funky Cold Medina', both built on sparse rock samples. The songs were written by Marvin Young, aka Young MC, 'Wild Thing' going on to become America's second biggest-selling single of all time. It also created one of the strangest moral panic scares of its era, when certain pundits suggested it gave rise to the 'Wilding' craze, where young black men prowled the streets in order to rob, rape and kill. This was simple paranoia, and clearly had nothing to do with the career of Smith, whose alarmingly deep, husky vocals, always enabled a sense of humour and self-deprecation to permeate through his recordings. *Loc'ed After Dark* made the US number 1 spot, only the second rap album to do so. 'All Through The Night', the first single from his follow-up LP featured the Brand New Heavies in support. However, its failure to crack the Top 20 indicated a small reversal in his fortunes. He has also contributed dialogue to the animated film, *Bebe's Kids*, and starred in *Posse*
Albums: *Loc'ed After Dark* (Delicious Vinyl 1989), *Cool Hand Loc* (Delicious Vinyl 1991).

Too Short

b. Todd Shaw, 28 April 1966, South Central, Los

Angeles, California, USA. Diminutive rapper from Oakland, California, where he moved at age 14, whose rhymes push his sexual prowess beyond the boundaries of the credible, and then some. His first introductions to rap, not a familiar form on the West Coast at this time, came after hearing the Sugarhill Gang and Melle Mel. 'Me and my partner at the time - Freddy D - started using local slang words and naming streets, neighbourhoods and people in our raps. We'd make 30 minute tapes to sell in the streets'. On the back of three years hustling, Too Short eventually signed to indepedent label 75 Girls. His first two albums, though musically valid, suffered from an over-reliance on hackneyed tales of pimping and gun fights. After three albums he set up his own Dangerous Music company in 1986, co-founded with manager Randy Austin. *Born To Mack* whistled up sales of over 200,000, from the trunk of the artist's car, and Jive records became intrigued by this parochial phenomenon. They re-packaged *Born To Mack* which went on to go gold. Lyrical matters had, however, only improved marginally on the arrival of his first Jive album proper, *Life Is...Too Short*, which went platinum and stayed in the US pop charts for 78 weeks. The artist has never offered much in the way of justification: 'No one can lay any guilt trips on me and tell me that I'm corrupting the youth of America or that I'm disrespecting all females. It's just a money thing'. Despite such myopia, the album was at least a more considered effort than the following collection, *Short Dog's In The House*, where titles like 'Bitch Killa' illustrated the sort of material on offer. Its saving grace was a double take with Ice Cube on his anti-censorship hymn, 'Ain't Nothing But A Word To Me'. The largely unappetising lyrical fare rode roughshod over an otherwise acceptable melange of funk and breakbeats. Musically, Too Short had always based his career on a limited diet of samples drawn from Sly Stone, Graham Central Station, Kool And The Gang etc. Although *Short Dog's In The House* gave him his second platinum album, 90% of those sales were exclusively in Oakland and its neighbouring districts. Something of a departure, especially for an artist as one-dimensional as Too Short, arrived with *Shorty The Pimp*. This exaggerated his hustling image, inspired by *Superfly* and other blaxploitation films, and extolled the adventures of his semi-autobiographical alter-ego Shorty the Pimp. It saw the introduction of permanent collaborators Art Banks and Shorty B. *Get In Where You Fit In*, meanwhile, quickly retraced his steps to earlier material, rapping over crude sexual anecdotes, and sent him straight to number 1 in the US R&B charts. However, there was evidence that by 1994 Too Short was growing a little jaded with his one-track career, and its effect on his private life: 'I'm not in control of my bad boy image anymore. It's grown legs and run away with itself. People believe Too Short the raper's Too Short the man'. His detractors might well summon up the phrase poetic justice.

Albums: *Born To Mack* (Dangerous 1986, Jive 1987), *Life Is...Too Short* (Dangerous 1988), *Short Dog's In The House* (Jive 1990), *Shorty The Pimp* (Jive 1992), *Get In Where You Fit In* (Jive 1993).

Total Devastation

Three-piece rap crew from California, composed of lead rapper Rasta Red Eye (b. Peurto Rica), lyricist Soopa Dupa (b. Cuba) and DJ Tuf Cut Tim The Fat Beat Maker (b. Mexico). Their home turf is nicknamed 'The Mission', a tightly-knit Hispanic community within San Francisco. Although they all grew up in the neighbourhood, it wasn't until a New Year's Eve Party in 1988 that they discovered they shared the same musical tastes. Together they created Hogstatus, a fully-blown production company, in anticipation of their forthcoming career. Eventually PGA Records picked up on their demos, releasing their debut single, 'Many Clouds Of Smoke', in 1993. Selling over 60,000 copies in California alone, its pro-marijuana lyric did not disuade major label Arista from taking an interest.

Album: *Total Devastation* (Arista 1993).

Treacherous 3

One of the forerunning creative forces within rap music, comprising original members Kool Moe Dee, L.A. Sunshine, Special K and DJ Easylee. The group was formed in 1978, releasing their debut

Too Short

single a year later, 'New Rap Language', on Enjoy Records. From its title to its dialogue, it predicted the new age of black rap music. It was followed by hip hop standards 'Body Rock' and 'Feel The Heartbeat', before the group moved to Sugarhill for 'At The Party', 'Action' and 'Yes We Can Can'. In 1986 Kool Moe Dee left to record his debut solo set, *Go See The Doctor*. The other members also pursued their own projects in the interim. However, in March 1994 the original line-up reunited to perform on *Old School Flava*. Recorded in Atlanta and New York, the album featured a roll call of old and new school rap heroes in its credits: Grandmaster Flash, Doug E Fresh, Big Daddy Kane, Chuck D, KRS-1, Melle Mel, Rakim (Eric B And Rakim), Heavy D, Raheem (Furious Five) and Tito (Furious Four). As Easylee commented at the project's announcement: 'The new school of rap seems to be looking for identity and roots. This is the right time for us to reunite, because the new rap family is opening their arms to the old school, paying respect to those who got the ball rolling'.
Album: *Old School Flava* (WRAP 1994).

Tricky

b. c.1964, Knowle West, Bristol, England. Laid-back hip hopper. formerly of Bristol unit Massive Attack, rapping on 'Daydreamin'' and 'Five Man Army' from the latter's *Blue Lines* debut, also writing and producing one track, 'Karma Coma', for its follow-up. In late 1993 he released his first solo single, 'Aftermath', which came after informal sessions with Mark Stewart (ex-Pop Group, Mark Stewart & The Mafia, On-U-Sound System etc.) on a four-track mobile. He employed the services of 18-year old local girl Martina (though the song was recorded when she was only 15) on vocals, releasing it on his own Naive label. Despite its strong critical reception, Tricky was, in the best traditions of Massive Attack, reticent about his abilities: 'I don't really consider myself to be a rapper. I'm more of a lyricist really'. He pondered his future, and mentioned his intention to rechristen himself Moxonqyaye in interviews.

Trouble Funk

At the forefront of Washington's early 80s go-go music scene, Trouble Funk's call and response vocals, and Mack Carey's mighty percussion, predicted the emergence of rap, notably on the single 'Drop The Bomb'. Trouble Funk's first album of similar title was released on the Sugarhill imprint, hip hop's first home. In truth they were more accurately a development of the physical funk tradition (Parliament etc.). Go-go was developed by Chuck Brown from drum breakdowns he would use in clubs to link Top 40 covers. Trouble Funk are still active, and ever popular in their native home of Washington, though their potential to crossover has long since dissipated.
Albums: *Drop The Bomb* (Sugarhill 1982), *In Times Of Trouble* (DETT 1983), *Saturday Night Live From Washington, D.C.* (Island 1985), *Trouble Over Here/Trouble Over There* (Island 1987).

25th Of May

This controversial and short-lived rap act from Liverpool, England, courted trouble with singles like 'Fuck The Right To Vote' and 'It's Alright', which extolled the virtues of shoplifting. Inaugurated at the Sefton Park Trade Union Centre, the band comprised Steve Swindells (vocals), Jimmy Mathias (DJ) and Nigel Cope (bass). They came to prominence at the same time as Merseyside was swaying to the sounds of 60s retro pop acts like Rain and the Real People. This was anathema to Swindells in a period when he judged black hip hop to be 'eclipsing all other forms of music'. They signed to Arista Records just as Mathias and Cope were busted for drug possession in May 1991. Overcoming the contradictions of being a 'white' Public Enemy proved a big stumbling block, however, and their media blitz had cooled by the following year.
Album: *Lenin And McCartney* (Arista 1992).

2 Live Crew

Rap headline-makers from Miami, Florida (via California), who formed in 1985 around central figure Luther Campbell. 2 Live Crew became unlikely figures in a media censorship debate when,

Treacherous 3

in June 1990, *As Nasty As They Wanna Be* was passed sentence on by a judge in Broward County, Florida. In the process it became the first record in America to be deemed legally obscene (a federal appeal court overturned the decision in 1993). Their right to free speech saw them defended by sources as diverse as Sinead O'Connor, Bruce Springsteen and Motley Crue, but the overbearing impression remained that 2 Live Crew were a third-rate rap outfit earning first division kudos by little more than circumstance. Their debut set, recorded before Campbell became an actual member, marked out the band's territory. To this end, 2 Live Crew have several times expressed themselves to be an adult comedy troupe, 'The Eddie Murphys of Rap', in the best traditions of crude party records by Blowfly and others. Hence 'We Want Some Pussy' and other, inconsequential, mildly offensive tracks. Campbell was the founder of the band's record label, Luke Skywalker Records (shortened to Luke Records when film-maker George Lucas, who created the Luke Skywalker character in the film *Star Wars*, filed suit), while Campbell's compatriots in 2 Live Crew numbered rappers Trinidad-born Chris Wong Won, New Yorker Mark Ross and California DJ David Hobbs (under the psuedonyms Brother Marquis and Fresh Kid Ice on the 'clean' version of *Move Somethin'*). Their music was underpinned by the familiar 'Miami Bass' sound, of synthesised, deep backbeats. *As Nasty As We Wanna Be*, replete with 87 references to oral sex *alone*, included the notorious 'Me So Horny', built around a sample from *Full Metal Jacket*. It is an unquestionably offensive lyric, but not any more so than the lyrics of the Geto Boys or others. There are probably worse examples within the 2 Live Crew's own songbook - 'The Fuck Shop', which samples Guns N'Roses guitar lines, or 'Head Booty And Cock' which became almost a battle-cry, notably when repeated, Nuremburg-like, by chanting fans on the Phoenix, Arizona-recorded live album. Advocates of record stickering such as the Parents Music Resource Center (PMRC) and Forida attorney/evangelist Jack Thompson, argued strongly that the group's records should not be available for sale to minors. A retail record store owner arrested for selling a copy of their *Move Somethin'* - albeit to an adult - was later acquitted. The group itself was then arrested for performing music from the *Nasty* album in an adults-only club, sparking charges by anti-censorship groups that the law enforcement officials were becoming over-zealous. There is not much doubt that this was true - Miami has one of the biggest pornography industries in the country, and it was obvious the moguls behind it were not being pursued with equal vigour, if they were being pursued at all. Not that the band were going out of their way to help improve their public image (whilst doubtless realising the commercial advantages of such notoriety). Luther Campbell claimed on CBS network TV show *A Current Affair* during 1992 that he had had oral sex on stage with female fans in Japan. Campbell had been aquitted a year previously for giving an obscene performance in his home state, Florida. In 1993 they became legal ground-breakers again, this time over their 1989 parody of Roy Orbison's 'Pretty Woman'. For the first time, Acuff Rose Music Inc were suing an artist on the grounds that their version tarnishes the image of the original. On top of all the heat Campbell released a solo album, *Banned In The USA*. The scandal abated somewhat, and as 2 Live Crew's otherwise unremarkable career progressed, there was even an AIDS awareness ditty on *Nasty Weekend* - 'Who's Fuckin' Who'. They also promoted safe sex with their own brand of Homeboy Condoms, one of their more acceptable acts of mysoginist titilation.

Albums: *The 2 Live Crew Is What We Are* (Luke Skyywalker 1986), *Move Somethin'* (Luke Skyywalker 1988), *As Nasty As They Wanna Be* (Luke Skyywalker 1989), *As Clean As They Wanna Be* (Luke Skyywalker 1989), *Live In Concert* (Effect 1990), *Sports Weekend (As Nasty As They Wanna Be Part II)* (Luke 1991), *Sports Weekend (As Clean As They Wanna Be Part II)* (Luke 1991). Compilation: *Best Of* (Luke 1992). As Luther Campbell Featuring The 2 Live Crew: *Banned In The USA* (Luke 1990). As The New 2 Live Crew: *Back At Your Ass For The Nine-4* (Luke 1994). Luther Campbell solo: *Luke In The Nude* (Luke 1993).

2 Live Jews

A crude spin-off from the ranks of 2 Live Crew, this was Miami-based MCs 'Moisha' Lambert and Joe 'Easy Irving' Stone's idea of a good joke. The song titles gave the game away very quickly: 'Oui! It's So Humid', 'Accountant Suckers' and 'Beggin' For A Bargain'.

Album: *As Kosher As They Wanna Be* (Kosher 1990).

2Pac

b. Tupac Amaru Shakur, 16 June 1971. A controversy-laced former Digital Underground hip hop star, Tupac has enjoyed a degree of crossover success with 'I Get Around'. The album which housed it, *Strictly 4 My N.I.G.G.A.Z.* offered a rare degree of insight, with glints of wisdom like 'Last Wordz' - 'United we stand, divided we fall, they can shoot one nigga, but they can't shoot us all'. To further his views he ran the Undreground Railroad network for troubled teenagers in his native Oakland. However, such a statement did not mention any of the less strenuous lengths the law might go to in silencing him. He was accused in 1993 of involvement in the shooting of two plain clothes policemen and one count of forceful sodomy. He was already on bail for an outstanding battery charge for allegedly striking a woman who asked for his autograph. He had also been arrested in Los Angeles for carrying a concealed weapon and assaulting a driver. After appearing in director John Singleton's film *Poetic Justice*, alongside Janet Jackson, he was dropped from the same director's *Higher Learning*. Shakur took things into his own hands when he was also removed from the set of Allen Hughes *Menace II Society*, attacking the director, for which charges were also laid. He did however, make it on to the final cut of *Above The Rim*, and had already turned in a memorable performance in *Juice*. Further controversy followed when a tape of *2Pacalypse Now* was found in the possession of a man arrested for murder. All of which added to the resonance of the title of his third album.

Album: *2Pacalypse Now* (Interscope 1992), *Strictly 4 My N.I.G.G.A.Z.* (Interscope 1993), *Me Against The World* (Interscope 1994).

2 Too Many

West Philadelphia act sponsored by local boys made good DJ Jazzy Jeff And The Fresh Prince. 2 Too Many's debut single, 'Where's The Party', was hugely reminiscent of their better-known colleagues' style, with a penchant for fun over gangsta or soicio-political concerns. The duo comprise Jazz (b. Armique Shartez Wyche, c.1972), L'il Troy (b. Troy Carter, c.1973) and Ant Live (b. Anthony Fontenot, c.1974). They had been rapping together since the late 80s, before Jazz and Troy linked up in the 9th Grade, bringing aboard cousin Ant to finalise the band's line-up. They took their name from their high-school poverty; whenever they would attempt to embark on an evening's entertainment or activity, they always found enough to pay for one, and thus became: 2 Too Many. However, fortunes changed when they met Will Smith (aka the Fresh Prince) when he was recording next door to their rehearsal room. They introduced themselves and invited him to see them play. The result was a contract with his own Willjam Productions through Jive Records. He teamed them up with Hula and Fingers, the producton duo behind his huge 1991 success, 'Summertime'. They envisaged long careers on the strength of this, spending many hours researching the music business in libraries to make sure they would not be taken advantage of, and acquainting themselves with management and production disciplines.

Album: *Chillin' Like A Smut Villain* (Jive 1992).

U

U-Krew

First formed, as the Untouchable Krew, as far back as October 1984, the U-Krew are a rap five-piece from Portland, Oregon, USA, led by drum programmer Larry Bell and lead rapper Kevin Morse. They scored quick hits with 'If U Were Mine' (US number 24) and 'Let Me Be Your Lover' (number 68), but faded afterwards.

Album: *The U-Krew* (Enigma 1990).

Ultramagnetic MC's

This Bronx, New York-based four piece rap troupe incorporate the best traditions of jazz and funk in their polished, rhythmic style. Having worked with Boogie Down Productions' KRS-1 among many others, the Ultramagnetic MC's have earned their reputation at the forefront of rap. The band comprises: Maurice Smith (aka PJ Mo Love; DJ), Keith Thornton (aka Kool Keith; lead MC), Trevor Randolph (aka TR Love; rapper and co-producer) and Cedric Miller (aka Ced Gee; MC and co-producer). The group emerged from posses such as The People's Choice Crew and New York City Breakers as Kool Herc and Afrika Bambaataa's work saw hip hop break cover. Their own backgrounds can be traced to underground basement clubs like the Audobon Ballroom, Sparkle and the Back Door. Their first album served as a direct influence on the 'Daisy Age' rap of subsequent acts such as De La Soul and PM Dawn, although those bands have left Ultramagnetic MCs trailing in their commercial wake. Singles such as 'Give The Drummer Some' showed them in their best light: call and response raps demonstrating individual members self-espoused talent in the best traditions of the old school. They were not always so dextrous however. While *Funk Your Head Up* included the excellent single cut, 'Poppa Large', it also housed the appalling 'Porno Star'. On *Four Horsemen*, and its attendant singles, 'Two Brothers With Checks'

and 'Raise It Up', the group unveiled an 'intergalactic hip hop' concept, and a new methodology (notably Kool Keith rhyming in double-speak on 'One Two, One Two'. More down to earth was 'Saga Of Dandy, The Devil & Day', an account of the negro baseball league co-written with historian James Reilly. Ced Gee and TR Love have offered their production skills to several artists including Boogie Down Productions' landmark *Criminal Minded Set*, as well as Tim Dog's infamous 'Fuck Compton'.

Albums: *Critical Beatdown* (1988), *Funk Your Head Up* (London 1992), *Four Horsemen* (Wild Pitch 1993).

UMC's

A popular underground hip hop concern from Staten Island who broke big when 'Blue Cheese' dropped. Hass G and Kool Kim (both b.c.1971) were initially noted for the wild, funk-fuelled rhythm motifs, and freestyle rhymes that dominate their recordings. The group, together with producer RNS, were originally titled the Universal MC's, but when signed to Wild Pitch (via their friends Gang Starr) they decided it sounded too old school. They first met while catching the ferry home from the Statue Of Liberty, where they both had summer jobs. They had actually made their debut in 1989 on tiny New York independent Rough Justice, on a compilation album that included their 'Invaders Of My Fruit Basket' and 'Party Stylin''. 'Blue Cheese' and 'One To Grow', the latter featured on Island's *The Rebirh Of Cool* set, gave them immediate hits with Wild Pitch. However, by the advent of their second album they had 'toughened up'. 'Our new direction comes from what we went through after having two number 1 singles'. After which record company hassles intervened. When they came back with a more hardcore attitude, as demonstrated by the second album's 'Time To Set It Straight' and 'Hit The Track', they still maintained the positivity evident on their earlier recordings. 'I remember a time when if a brother pulled out a gun on somebody he was a punk. Or if you jumped somebody you was a pussy'. Some critics lamented the loss of their more playful personas, but they

were undoubtedly masters of both approaches.
Albums: *Fruits Of Nature* (1992), *Unleashed* (Wild Pitch 1994).

Underdog

aka Trevor Jackson. One of hip hop's most prominent remixers and production experts, Jackson also oversees the succesful Bite It! label and design company. His love of rap was developed during a childhood spent listening to Grandmaster Flash and his old school companions on import, and he even tried to become a self-taught scratcher. Eventually he turned to sampling instead, inspired by the Art Of Noise's cut-up technique. Bite It! was originally formed for the design of record sleeves, notably Stereo MC's *33, 45, 78*, but began releasing hip hop product in the 90s. Among these artists were Scientists Of Sound and the Brotherhood, though his first remix commission was for the-then unheard ragga artist C.J. Lewis. However, Jackson's hip hop remixing abilities were what brought him to the public's attention, notably House Of Pain's 'Top Of The Mornin' To Ya' - which broke the UK Top 10. After a further House Of Pain production, 'Who's The Man', he also undertook remixing duties for the Pharcyde's 'Soul Flower', the Young Black Teenagers' 'Tap The Bottle' and New Kingdom's 'Good Times' - three deeply satisfying and impressively diverse hip hop readings. There was also work for house divas Shara Nelson ('Down That Road', 'One Goodbye In Ten') and Carleen Anderson ('Nervous Breakdown') as well as U2 ('Stay'). More tongue-in-cheek was a remixed version of the Sabres Of Paradise staple, 'Theme', in which Jackson appeared to attack the cult of personality surrounding Andy Weatherall.

Unique 3

Dance and rap chart crossover act, of not-inconsiderable ability, and a wide range of talents. Their debut album kicked off with 'Music Melody', which dented the UK charts, a sharp, witty rap, before continuing with the techno-flavoured 'Gicicality', the Detroit house of 'Theme III' and the ragga tinges of 'Reality'. Sadly, their acquaintance with the charts seems to have been a passing one.
Album: *Jus' Unique* (Ten 1990).

Uptown Records

Uptown was launched in Manhattan, New York, in 1986, as a specialist black label, concentrating primarily on R&B styled rap. The label was set up by Andre Harrell (b. c.1959), formerly part of Dr. Jeckyll And Mr Hyde, who scored a major hit in 1981 with 'Genius Rap'. After leaving the duo he went to college to study communication and business, before joining Russell Simmons at Rush Management. It has been said that Harrell left Def Jam when he failed to persuade Simmons that they could market Heavy D as 'sexy'. Nevertheless, it was via that act that the label was established, and the 'big guy' also introduced Harrell to one of his most significant early signings, the proto-New Jill Swing act Gyrlz (Uptown having already provided the platform for Guy). Other acts on the label would include Jodeci and Mary J. Blige, becoming one of the pre-eminent dance/hip hop labels of its age. Harrell, who also produced the movie *Strictly Business*, himself described his tastes as those of 'a lifestyle entertainment entrepreneur'.
Selected albums: Heavy D And The Boyz: *Big Tyme* (Uptown 1989), *Nuttin' But Love* (Uptown 1994). Father MC: *Father's Day* (Uptown 1989). Guy: *Guy* (Uptown 1989).

Urban Species

Since their formation in Tottenham, London, in the late 80s, Urban Species have been widely tipped as the next potential breakthrough in UK hip hop. They originally comprised lead rapper Mint (b. Peter Akinrinola) and DJ Renegade (b. Winston Small), whose partnership principally involved messing about in their north London bedrooms, since when they have added the services of toaster Slim (b. Rodney Green). The trio started to produce small runs of white labels, distributing them under the names of either Mint or Renegade. This earned them a reputation among both the pirate radio stations and clubs, where they would be invited to appear. Even the hip New York stations Kiss and WBLS picked up on one of their tracks, 'It's My Thing', but the group were hamstrung by finances and unable to capitalise. Their next cut, 'Got To Have It', was the one that brought them to the attention of Talkin' Loud boss Giles Peterson. By 1991 he had their signatures. Their eclectic blend of ragga, dub, and even acoustic folk rumblings has seen them placed in several musical categories; from soul to rap and jazz fusion, and comparisons to Arrested Development continue to flourish. Their second single as Urban Species, 'Listen', shared its title with their first LP, and featured 'fourth' member Lynette Bracewaite, alongside live guest musicians such as Galliano and Incognito. Guest vocalists have also included MC Solaar (a fellow traveller on the Talkin' Loud roster) and Maysa Leak, and Urban Species have built their reputation as much on the back of impressive live appearances as much as their studio touch.

Album: *Listen* (Talkin' Loud 1993).

Us3

One of 1993's most intriguing musical experiments, Us3 comprise Geoff Wilkinson and Mel Simpson. Wilkinson was best known for his Jazz DJ work, and met Simpson at his own Flame studio, where they discovered mutually inclusive tastes. Together they struck upon the idea of sampling some of their favourite old jazz tunes and mixing them in with their own material. The resultant 'And The Band Played Boogie' was released on Coldcut's Ninja Tune imprint, featuring the rapping of Born 2B, and created a critical buzz. By hook or by crook the record came to the attention of executives at jazz label Blue Note, who quickly deduced that most of the samples were lifted directly from their own catalogue. The miscreants were summoned, but then Capitol took the wholly laudable and progressive step of working out a deal whereby the duo could enjoy unlimited access to the Blue Note label archives. The result was an album of richly textured jazz and hip hop, with guests including rappers Tukka Yoot (b. Jamaica), Kobie Powell and Rahsaan (all three of whom would secure deals with Capitol in the wake of the album's success), and jazzmen Gerald Presencer, Dennis Rollins, Tony Remy and Steve Williamson. The album, which was preceded by the singles, 'Cantaloop'

and 'Riddim', proved a worldwide hit, selling particularly strongly in the US. The foresight of the copyright holders at Blue Note has been amply rewarded too: since the release of *Hand On The Torch* interest in Blue Note back-catalogue has escalated and sales have doubled. Even Herbie Hancock, on whose 'Cantalope Island' the single 'Cantaloop' was loosely based, expressed his appreciation for their efforts. It would be used on the soundtrack to the *Super Mario Bros* film, and Barry Levinson's *Jimmy Hollywood*. They were also enlisted for Stephen Spielberg's *Flintstones*. In the wake of their success, especially in the US and Europe, Wilkinson was asked by Toshiba/EMI to A&R a compilation of new London jazz musicians. In 1994 Us3 were piecing together a second album, having already remixed the first selection, and have embarked on collaborative material with the Ragga Twins (famed for their contributions to Shut Up And Dance).

Album: *Hand On The Torch* (Blue Note 1993), *Us3 The Jazz Mixes* (Blue Note 1994).

U.T.F.O.

Their initials standing for UnTouchable Force Organization, East Wimbush, Brooklyn-based U.T.F.O. comprised the talents of Doctor Ice, Kangol Kid (both concurrently breakdancers for Whodini) and The Educated Rapper, later joined by Mix-Master Ice. Their second single, 'Roxanne, Roxanne' set the New York City rap kids alight as they complained of an unobliging female, over a rhythm track built from Billy Squier's 'The Big Beat', and produced by Full Force. It would see an answer record from Roxanne Shanté which outsold their own version, and a whole industry which grew up around the phenomenon (the Real Roxanne, the Original Roxanne, and Sparky D). The trio turned to rock/rap crossover for *Lethal*, before reggae and swingbeat took over on their most recent work. Nothing, however, has managed to replicate the success of their landmark single. *Bag It And Bone It* looked to crude sexual rhymes for sales but even that missed that boat.

Albums: *U.T.F.O.* (Select 1985), *Skeezer Pleezer* (Select 1986), *Lethal* (Select 1987), *Doin' It* (Select 1989), *Bag It And Bone It* (Jive 1990).

V

Vanilla Ice

Controversial white rapper (b. Robert Van Winkle, 31 October 1968, Miami Lakes, Florida, USA) who borrowed liberally from Hammer's blueprint for commercial success, and scored a UK/US number 1 with 'Ice Ice Baby' (15 million worldwide sales). Just as Hammer utilised easily recongisable rock/pop classics to underpin his rhymes, Ice has used the same technique in re-shaping 'Under Pressure', 'Satisfaction' and 'Play That Funky Music' for his repertoire. Winkle was raised by his mum in a poor area of Miami, and never knew his father. He spent his teenage years hanging out on the street. However, the later claims to the press about being stabbed five times were erroneous - in fact he had merely been slashed across his bottom on a singular occasion. Contrary to his new image he actually sang in church choir until he was 15 and had a step-father who owned a Chevrolet dealership, before he was first discovered playing the City Lights in Dallas, Texas. His debut album covered all bases, the ballad-rap 'I Love You' sitting alongside the gangsta-inclined 'Go III' and dance pop of 'Dancin''. While rap afficinados held up their hands in horror at what they loudly decried as a phoney, Vanilla Ice responded by telling his detractors they could 'Kiss My White Ass' at an MTV Awards ceremony. An obvious reference to contentions that rap was an intrinsically black music, his comments did little to pacify angry factions in the genre. Ironically, Public Enemy had originally encouraged their producer, Hank Shocklee, to sign him to their label, based on his good looks and snappy dance routines. However, following his huge success he fell foul of a management that wished to pigeonhole him within the teen-market. It would take several years before he fully extricated himself from the deal. Whether this, adverse press or a lack of genuine talent called a halt to Vanilla Ice's meteoric rise is a worthy debate. He certainly did little to bring the jury to a favourable verdit with his comeback album. In a desperate attempt to catch up with the gangsta set, *Mindblowing* made frequent references to 'blunts', while the music sampled James Brown and, predictably, George Clinton. It was a blueprint hardcore rap album, but one with fewer convictions, in both senses, than Ice-T or Snoop Doggy Dogg.

Albums *To The Extreme* (SBK 1990), *Extremely Live* (SBK 1991), *Mindblowing* (SBK 1994).

W

Warfield, Justin

Los Angeles, US-based rapper, yet a world away from that region's more typical hip hop fare. Warfield (b. c.1973) dwells over raps which share a common line of descent with the narratives of the beat writers, alongside laid-back beats which borrow heavily from the psychedelic and acid rock traditions (Soft Machine, Moby Grape). There are liberal samples from everything from jazz to Led Zeppelin to keep the grooves fresh. Warfield grew up in the wealthy Laurel Canyon area. Brought up by hippy parents, he can justify lines like: 'Black as a pepper and a lyrical Jew' by his Jewish-Cherokee-Afro-American heritage. Warfield was making demos at the age of 14 and had his first deal three years later, subsequently forming his own band for live work, and coming to prominence via an appearance on QDIII's *Soundlab* compilation. Whether the rap community will swallow lyrics detailing the lives of assorted aliens holed up in aircraft hangars across the USA, or tracks that revel in snatches of ambient noise and rock guitar as part of the menu, remains to be seen. Album: *My Field Trip To Planet Nine* (1993).

Watts Prophets

Treading similarly unchartered waters as the Last

Poets in America's east were hip hop pioneers the Watts Prophets on the west coast. Taking their name from the 1965 Watts Uprising riots, the Prophets comprised Anthony 'Father Amdee' Hamilton, Otis Smith and Richard DeDeaux. Dee Dee MacNeil was also a member. Born out of the Watts Creative Writers' Workshop, together they stalked Los Angeles with their harsh, socio-political commentary, providing the musical jigsaw piece to accompany the rising tide of black consciousness inspired by Malcolm X and the Black Panthers. They would perform largely within their own community, at youth clubs and prisons, spreading the news of emancipation and equality. It was challenging enough to bring them to the attention of the authorities, coming under the scrutiny of the FBI, and they were even infiltrated by undercover agent Darthard Perry. Scary stuff for a posse of poets, but equally an indelible demonstration of white authority's determination to silence black protest. In the mid-70s they largely disappeared from view, though they reamained active individually, and indeed recorded together from time to time. However, it took the intervention of photographer Brian Cross to put them back together on a more permanent footing. Having researched their past he put them in touch with the Dust Brothers production house (Young MC, Tone Loc etc). Together they recorded a demo album to tout around interested parties, which so far has not seen release. Ask about the rise of gangsta rap and their new hip hop contemporaries and the Watts Prophets are less than sparing: 'When we were doing it, the emphasis was on the spoken word and now the emphasis is on the beat. Also, when the emphasis was on the spoken word, the word meant something. Women were considered sisters and queens and now that the emphasis is on the beat more, they are bitches and hoes'.
Albums: *Rapping Black In A White World* (ALA 1971). Solo: Anthony Hamilton aka Father Amde: *Black Voices: On The Streets Of Watts* (ALA 1969).

Wayne And Charlie

One of Sugarhill's more novel acts, Wayne being a ventriloquist's dummy, Charlie his 'right hand'

man. The duo's 'Check It Out' cut in 1981 was a take on Kurtis Blow's 'The Breaks', but a career in the pop world, unsurprisingly, did not beckon.

Wee Papa Girl Rappers

This commercial UK female rap duo's lyrics floated on lively hip hop and house tracks. The two components were sisters TV Tim (b. Timmie Lawrence, London, England) and Total S (b. Sandra Lawrence, London, England). They had been introduced to the world of US hip hop by their club DJ friend 'Junior G'. Finding this new music infectious, they abandoned their previous loves of soul and hard rock to establish themselves as a rap act, taking their name from their father's habit of muttering 'Wee Papa' to himself when he got over-excited. The 'girl rappers' was a natural extension. Snapped up by Jive Records, they debuted with a rap version of George Michael's 'Faith', which just dented the UK Top 60. It was followed by 'Heat It Up', recorded with Cox and Steele (as Two Men And A Drum Machine) of Fine Young Cannibals fame. Reaching number 21 in the charts, it prefaced their most successful single, 'Wee Rule'. Nodding to reggae (and remixed by Aswad), it peaked at number 6 in the UK charts, while the accompanying debut album achieved massive sales in Europe. When they returned after a year and a half away with a second album, it saw them pursue a more commercial-dance direction, with the introduction of producers of the calibre of Cliville and Cole (C+C Music Factory), Coldcut and Danny D (D-Mob). However, their last significant chart position came with 'Blow The House Down'. Innocuous and obvious at best, they amicably dissolved in early 1991. Their most enduring legacy, perhaps, a revamped theme for UK television programme *Jim'll Fix It*.
Albums: *The Beat, The Rhyme, The Noise* (Jive 1988), *Be Aware* (Jive 1990).

West Coast Rap All-Stars

A coalition of prominent West Coast hip hop stars

Whodini

who came together to preach the word of unity, and raise funds for inner-city youth projects. Some of the participants included Hammer, Eazy-E, Above The Law, Def Jef, Digital Underground, Young MC, Tone Loc, NWA, Michel'le, Oaktown's 3-5-7, Ice-T and King Tee. The album's title, which also reached number 35 in the Billboard charts as a single, referred heavily to the gang warfare in areas like South Central and Compton. A touch ironic, perhaps, when so many of the contributors were perceived by 'outsiders' as having exacerbated these problems with their gangsta rap mythology.

Album: *We're All In The Same Gang* (Warners 1990).

Whodini

Brooklyn, New York-based trio of rappers who, from their formation in 1982, pioneered the commercial rap/rock crossover, while many also cite their earliest recordings as precuorsors to the New Jack Swing movement. Whodini are rappers Jalil Hutchins and Ecstasy (b. John Fletcher, c.1964), backed by talented old school DJ, Grandmaster Dee (b. Drew Carter; once described as 'the turntable's Jimi Hendrix). The latter won his reputation for being able to scratch with almost every conceivable part of his anatomy. Prominent in hip hop circles since the earliest days of the movement, he had formerly worked the decks behind The Devastating Two Emcees (a female duo) and the Jazzy Four. More recently he became a convert to Louis Farakhan's Nation Of Islam movement. Generally Whodini's subject matter never wavered too greatly from, reasonably gentlemanly, references to the opposite sex. Their debut release, Magic's Wand' (a tribute to the DJ of the same name on WBLS New York, who gave them a start), was also the first rap single on the Jive imprint, and the first single in hip hop history to have a promotional video filmed. Strangely, it was co-produced by Thomas Dolby, on a rare voyage outside of British techno pop. Following a second single 'The Haunted House Of Rock' they established their name and popularity through the 'Friends' 45, which also crossed over to the soul audience. Other popular tunes included the 'The

Freaks Come Out At Night', 'One Love', and 'Be Yourself', on which they collaborated with soul diva Millie Jackson - having always maintained an R&B flavour to their recordings. They were widely renowned for their innovative stage act, and were the first rap group to perform with their own dancers, Dr. Ice and U.T.F.O.'s Kangol Kid, undertaking two world tours in 1983 and 1984. Later they joined Run DMC, Kurtis Blow, the Fat Boys and Newcleus on a thirty venue 'New York City Fresh Fest' tour, which was so successful it was repeated in 1985. In the autumn of 1986 they released 'Growing Up', an anti-drug video financed by the New York State Division Of Substance Abuse. Although they would again tour in 1987, this time with LL Cool J, the late 80s saw band members sidetracked through marriage and having children, and record company and managerial problems did not help. They made their first comeback in 1990 with an album for MCA, but neither party really understood each other, and the reunion dissolved. They reformed again in 1991 for *Bag A Trix* (which included ballad funk courtesy of Midnight Star) and in 1993 for Terminator X's *The Godfathers Of Threatt* compilation, which included them alongside other old schoolers Kool Herc, Cold Crush Borthers and more. They kicked that set off with 'It All Comes Down To Money', which they were happy to put on record: 'People have a lot of nice things to say about us. They look at us as pioneers and all this but now I want our business to reflect that. We love doing what we do. But we like being taken care of too. And also everybody has kids and this is for them now.' Whatever, it was a welcome return for their langorous narratives, unaffected by the shifts in rap.

Albums: *Whodini* (Jive 1983), *Escape* (Jive 1984), *Back In Black* (Jive 1986), *Open Sesame* (Jive 1987), *Bag-A-Trix* (MCA 1991). Compilations: *The Collection* (Jive 1990).

Whooliganz

Mad Skillz (b. Scott Caan, c.1975; the son of actor James Caan) and Mudfoot (Alan Maman, c.1977) are two white rappers from Beverley Hills (zip code 90210 no less) who have been endorsed by

Whooliganz

one of the hottest names in rap, B-Real (Cypress Hill). This fortunate state of affairs came about when the duo were recording with QDIII in Los Angeles in the early 90s, where B-Real heard their demo. The first results of this match were aired on their 'Put Your Handz Up' 45, which featured Everlast on its b-side cut, 'Hit The Deck'. They moved on to use the production skills of T Ray, the Baka Boys and Lethal (House Of Pain) for the follow-up album, fighting shy of too many comparisons to Cypress Hill or the Soul Assassins enclave.

Albums: *Make Way For The W* (Tommy Boy 1994).

Wild Pitch

New York rap label founded by Stu Fine, which was eventually distributed in England through EMI in 1994. Some of their biggest hits included Gang Starr's 'Manifest', Main Source's 'Fakin' The Funk' and Jamose's 'The Rhythmologist'. Their longstanding artists include Ultramagnetic MCs, while new signings offer Broken English, N-Tyce and The Coup. Their A&R Vice-President is MC Serch (ex-3rd Bass).

Selected albums: Gang Starr: *No More Mr Nice Guys* (Wild Pitch 1990). Main Source: *Breakin' Atoms* (Wild Pitch 1990). Various: *Hi-Phat Diet* (Wild Pitch 1994).

Willie D

b. Willie Dennis, Houston, Texas, USA. Yet another member of the outlandish Geto Boys to hallucinate about having displayed enough talent in his efforts with that band to warrant a solo career. He left the group in 1992: 'It was very rewarding and a good experience for me to have been in the group, working with Bushwick Bill and Scarface. We were always dealing with controversy, and sometimes all we had was each other for support'. His debut solo single arrived with 'Clean Up Man'. It was backed by 'Rodney K', which he used as a platform for an attack on the black community leaders so incensed by the activities of the Geto Boys. Willie subsequently moved to Ichiban to set up his new Wize Up imprint, the first release on which was Sho's *Trouble Man* album. Willie also

featured as a guest rapper on the collection.

Album: *I'm Goin' Out Like A Soldier* (Rap-A-Lot 1992).

Winley, Paul

Winley was a veteran R&B producer and songwriter, running the Paul Winley Jazzland Ballroom on Harlem's 125th Street, before setting up Winley Records in the same location. His musical interests began when his brother was a member of the Clovers in his native Washington, for whom Paul wrote songs. He went on to compose for Ruth Brown and Joe Turner. Together with Dave 'Baby' Cortez he formed a partnership recording doo wop groups like the Duponts, Paragons, Collegians and Jesters. His introduction to rap music came at the behest of his daughters, Tanya (later Sweet Tee) and Paulette. He became famed for a series of compilations entitled *Disco Brakes*, produced by DJ Jolly Roger, which won him his first admirers, combining as it did some of the most popular 'breaks' over which the park rappers would improvise routines. Popular cuts included Dennis Coffey's 'Scorpio' and New Birth's 'Gotta Get Knutt'. *Super Disco Brakes* would add standards like James Brown's 'Funky Drummer' (the so-named pecussionist, Clyde Stubblefield, would later be immortalised on Subsonic 2's 'Unsung Heroes Of Hip Hop') and Incredible Bongo Band's 'Apache' (versions of which would appear on Sugarhill - the first by the Sugarhill Gang and the second by West Street Mob - who featured the Robinson's son, Joey Jnr.), as well as the Meters and Creative Source. Yet until the aforementioned Sugarhill started he never took the opportunity to record anything by the rappers who were buying this product. When 'Rapper's Delight' hit he finally realised its potential, releasing records by, among others, his daughters, who rapped together on 'Rhymin' And Rappin'. Other outstanding releases included Afrika Bambaataa's *Zulu Nation Throwdown Parts 1 And 2*. However, Bambaataa became hugely aggrieved at Winley's business practices, notably the release of one of his live sets as the 'Death Mix', which was of substandard quality and essentially a bootleg. Indeed, Winley would later be arrested for bootlegging activities and copyright infringement.

World Famous Supreme Team Show

One of Malcolm McLaren's many innovative experiments in modern music, this project saw 'Talcy' pull together a team of rappers, singers and DJs from New York and Los Angeles. In their early days the group had hosted their own show on New Jersey station WHBI, alongisde the legendary Mr Magic, before the latter shifted to WBLS. The idea of their partnership with McLaren was to make a modern rap record themed on Shakespearean and Opera models, as demonstrated by the promotional single, 'Opera House'. Main vocalist Mona Lisa Young was saddled, however, by some uninspiring material, co-written between McLaren and MC Hamlet (b. Jason Van Sugars). The album includes a return to the happier times of 'Buffalo Girls'. Indeed, McLaren had formerly employed the Supreme Team on his *Duck Rock* album, where they rapped over T-Ski Valley's 'Catch The Beat'.
Album: *The World Famous Supreme Team* (Charisma 1986), *Round The Outside! Round The Outside!* (Virgin 1992).

Wu Tang Clan

This chess-playing hip hop posse, whose ranks total nine pseudonymous young men - Shallah Raekwon, Method Man, Rebel Ins, Ol' Dirty Bastard, U-God, Ghostface Killer, The Genius, RZA and Prince Rakeem - hail from Staten Island, New York, USA. Each of the team boast keen martial arts prowess. Indeed their debut album was divided into two sides, Shaolin and Wu-Tang Sword, to symbolise the combat-like disciplines they have applied to their rapping. Affiliated group members include Shyheim The Rugged Prince, who has his own, successful solo career. Both Rakeem and The Genius had also released solo records prior to their present duties, for Cold Chillin' and Tommy Boy, which sank without trace. And when the Clan as a whole signed with BMG, provision for each member to work as solo artists was enshrined in the contract. The Genius joined his third record company, Geffen, Method Man linking with Def Jam and Ol' Dirty Bastard

with Elektra. Their producer/DJ, RZA, also works alongside Prince Paul and Fruitkwan (ex-Stetsasonic) as part of the Gravediggaz. Wu Tang Clan's musical armoury centres around old school rhyming and trickery, which with nine contributors offers ample opportunity for quickfire wise-cracking and playing off each other. The musical backing is one of stripped down beats, with samples culled from kung-fu movies. Such appropriation of martial culture is a theme which has occupied rap music from the days of Grandmaster Flash onwards. Their debut album quickly and deservedly notched gold status, setting the underground hip hop scene alight in the process. It was recorded in their own studio, its '36 Chambers' suffix alluding to the number of critical points on the body as disclosed by Shaolin theology. However, all was not well with the Clan in 1994. U-God's two-year old, Dante Hawkins, was hit in a gun battle crossfire as he played outside his babysitter's house on March 13. The bullet destroyed one of his kidneys and damaged his hand. Just a day later a member of the band's inner circle of friends was kiled in a separate incident.
Album: *Enter The Wu Tang (36 Chambers)* (Loud/RCA 1993). The Genius solo: *Words From The Genius* (Cold Chillin' 1991).

X

X Clan

X Clan openly admitted that their recording activities were merely a front to promote the 'Blackwatch' ethos. They held a controversial Cultural Convention at London's Africa Centre in 1989 where they were heckled for their apparent endorsement of separatism and chauvinism. Blackwatch, or that part of it which the group felt able to relate to ousiders, is a movement created by black people, for black people, which invokes a larger brotherhood (specifically between different generations and strata of black society) in order to fight and defeat white oppression, through a variety of means: 'By any means necessary is one of the chief principles we have'. Membership of the rap outlet included rappers/spokesmen Professor X (b. Lumumba Carson; the son of black activist Sonny Carson and former manager of Positive-K), Brother J and DJ Sugar Shaft, plus associate member Lin Que/Isis. On record, as might be expected, they are utterly militant and uncompromising in their advocacy of their chosen lifestyle.

Albums: *To The East, Blackwards* (4th And Broadway 1990), *X Odus* (Polydor 1992).

Y

Yaggfu Front

Despite the unfriendly acronym (Y'All Gonna Get Fucked Up [if you] Front), and their grisly personal tags: D'Ranged & Damaged, Jingle Bel and Spin 4th, this Norfolk, Virginia trio have a lot to offer. They pulled together at university, an educative platform which has provided them with more effective ammunition than the average gun-toting gangsta rappers. There they worked as DJs on North Carolina college radio before uniting as a trio. Using live instruments, including horns and piano, they have perfected a stimulating blend of sharply observed lyrics and clever samples. Their first release was the excellent 'Looking For A Contract', which detailed the lives of starving rap aspirants. Comparisons to A Tribe Called Quest notwithstanding, their debut album was also a splendid, intelligent affair. There were comedic moments too, not least 'My Dick Is So Large', a thinly-veiled parody of stupido ego-rappers. But their style was generally expressive: 'Basically the Yaggful sound is emotional. We want to capture the way someone feels'.

Album: *Action Packed Adventure* (Phonogram/Mercury 1994).

Yo Yo

b. Yolanda Whitaker, 4 August 1971, South Central Los Angeles, USA. A protégé of Ice Cube, Yo Yo is one of the female rappers who likes to play it as rough and dirty as her male gangsta bretherin. Her long playing debut introduced her combatitive attitude, with frequent interjections from Ice-Cube's Lench Mob posse. However, amid the assertive, abrasive lyrics lurked a sophistication which might not have been envisaged by the casual buyer. That album's torch song was 'Sisterland', a rallying call for her fellow female MCs. Titles on her third album included 'The Girl's Got A Gun', and her duet with Ice Cube, 'The Bonnie & Clyde Theme'. Better still, she managed to invert the usual gangsta trappings by acting as a female pimp on 'Macktress'. Yo Yo had previously contributed to Ice's debut album, *AmeriKKKa's Most Wanted*, duetting on 'It's A Man's World', representing her gender in admirable style. An insight that was confirmed by her leading role in the formation of the Intelligent Black Women Coalition.

Albums: *Make Way For The Motherlode* (Atlantic 1991), *Black Pearl* (East West 1992), *You Better Ask Somebody* (1993).

Young Black Teenagers

Toasted as the first to release a 45 on Hank Shocklee and Bill Stephney's Sound Of Urban Listeners label, YBT are in fact three white teenagers, and one Puerto Rican (ATA) from Brooklyn, New York. Their provocative moniker was chosen, they declare, to pay tribute to hip-hop's true originators, to accept that it is primarily an Afro-American format, but that outsiders too are welcome. The group, formed in 1987, comprise ATA, Kameron, Firstborn and DJ Skribble, and their debut release, 'Nobody Knows Kelli', was a tribute to cult American anti-sit-com, *Married With Children*. Although the sleeve of their debut album was a cunning take on the *Beatles For Sale* tableau, the production was haphazard, despite the presence of the Bomb Squad. They switched

from SOUL to MCA for the single, 'Tap The Bootle', which featured a guest appearance from Public Enemy's DJ Terminator X. Ultimately, however, they would fall out with Chuck D and Hank Schocklee, with whom Kamron had previously DJ'd in Roosevelt, Long Island. Not before they had recorded 'To My Donna', an attack on Madonna for using Public Enemy's 'Security Of The First World' beat. Following the wit of their previous releases, YBT fell down heavily on political correctness. When challenged about the predominance of the word 'bitch' in their vernacular, ATA could only muster: 'When I say a girl is a bitch, I'm not saying she's a female dog. We're past that. Let's not take things at face value. Women just tend to be bitches, they tend to be moody....' Elsewhere they were more dextrous. Instead of merely sampling on *Dead End Kidz*, they reinterpreted, to excellent comic effect and with live instruments, ancient nuggets by Diana Ross, the Rolling Stones and even Rush. They are currently managed and produced by ex-Bomb Squad worker Gary G-Wiz.
Albums: *Young Black Teenagers* (SOUL 1993), *Dead End Kidz Doin' Lifetime Bidz* (MCA 1994).

Young MC

b. Marvin Young, 10 May 1967, England, but raised in Queens, New York City. Young went to college in California, earning a degree in economics from the University Of South California, where he also wrote material for Tone Loc (including co-writing credits on his big hits 'Wild Thing' and 'Funky Cold Medina'). His solo work was similarly within the framework of mainstream rap, a highlight being the Top 10 hit, 'Bust A Move' - winner of the Grammy for Best Rap Record. In its wake he started to turn up on television screens advertising Pepsi soft drinks. He cited 'musical and ethical differences' as the reason for his move from Delicious Vinyl in the 90s, though he remained with 4th & Broadway/Island in the UK. By the time he became employed by Capitol, many critics pointed out that his material was becoming both overwrought and overproduced. Unlike many rappers, Young MC brought a post-AIDS conscience to his sexual

boasts, as demonstrated on the second album's 'Keep It In Your Trousers'. He re-emerged in 1993 with the club hit 'Know How', a distillation of the 'Shaft' theme, produced by the Dust Brothers - aka his old friends from Delicious.
Albums: *Stone Cold Rhymin'* (Delicious Vinyl 1989), *Brainstorm* (Capitol 1991).
Video: *Bustin' Moves* (1991).

YZ

New Jersey rapper most famous for his 'Thinkin' Of A Masterplan' cut. Bedecked in paisly shirts and dreads, YZ seemed to offer a neat distillation of Native Tongues philosophy with more street-orientated themes. Despite the good impression this made, it would be four years before a follow-up would be offered, by which time his DJ Tony D had been replaced by the Trackmasterz and God Squad, among others. As a member of the Five Per Cent Nation, a less disciplined than usual Muslim order, he produces a number of 'conscious' rhymes, but his main targets remain opposing MCs, holding Naughty By Nature in particular contempt.
Album: *Sons Of The Father* (Tuff City 1989), *The Ghetto's Been Good To Me* (Livin' Large 1993).

DANCE

A

Aaliyah

b. Detroit, Michigan, USA. Pronounced Ah-Lee-Yah, this female artist is yet another of the growing New Jill swing movement, whose early career was fostered by R. Kelly. Her debut album, *Age Ain't Nothing But A Number* (though it was important enough for her to conceal her own date of birth), included the debut single, 'Back And Forth', which made a strong showing in the national and R&B charts. She travelled to Kelly's home in Chicago for the sessions, while she was still a student at the Detroit High School Of The Performing Arts. She remained a 'straight A's' student throughout the first stage of her recording career, persevering with her education despite commercial success.
Album: *Age Ain't Nothing But A Number* (Jive 1994).

Ace of Base

When Ace Of Base scored a massive worldwide number 1 in 1993 with 'All That She Wants', the comparisons to a fellow Swedish group seemed obvious. Two female vocalists, one blonde, one brunette, and two male musicians, proffering catchy dance pop. Whether Ace Of Base will have the commercial legs to rival Abba is doubtful, but they have certainly scored heavily since their formation in 1990. The group comprise Malin Bergren (vocals), Jenny Bergren (vocals), Jonas Bergren (programming, songwriting) and Ulf Ekberg (programming, songwriting). Before their breakthrough the sisters sang in church choirs in their native Gothenburg, while brother Jonas and Ulf perfected their expertise with new technology. Their disposable, chart-friendly combination of dance/reggae was further revealed on 'Wheel Of Fortune', 'Happy Nation', 'Waiting For Magic' and 'The Sign', while their debut album went to number 1 in six territories. They enjoyed further prolonged stays in worldwide Top 10s when 'Don't Turn Around', a cover of the old Aswad standard, proved another success.
Album: *Happy Nation* (Mega 1993).

Acid House

DJ Pierre was the man, alongside his partner Spanky, who was largely heralded as the figurehead of this musical movement. The sound was developed in a Chicago, Illinois, USA basement in 1986, where the duo had just purchased and installed a bass machine, the Roland TB 303. 'We'd got the 303 and we were trying to figure out what knobs do what. The machine already had acid in it. At first I thought it was some kind of shit we gotta erase out of it before we programme it. Spanky had a 15-minute beat track he'd programmed a couple of days earlier...and I kept turning the knobs to see what kind of effect they had on the bassline'. That session was recorded and passed to DJ Ron Hardy, who mixed it into his sets at Chicago's Warehouse club. Soon this new sound was being much discussed and became known as Hardy's *Acid Tracks* (An alternative theory has been advanced that Marshall Jefferson developed the 'sound' of acid, but Pierre's version has generally been given more credence). Ironically the 303 was a budget bass synthesizer which was designed for use with the 606 drum machine, but flopped commercially. The 'acid' element came about due to the five hand tuned filters which could manipulate and 'squelch' or stress the bass notes, as they were being played back. Originally the 'acid' prefix was bereft of drug connotations. While Pierre released the influential *Acid Trax* series on Phuture, the sound gripped the UK club scene in 1988. Bands like D-Mob emerged to take up the mantle, with a bastardised version (often referred to as 'aciiiied' or versions thereof) taking hold of a nation's youth. Records like 'Acid Man' by Jolly Roger (actually Eddie Richards, later DJ to the Shamen) started to dominate the charts. Ably represented by the 'Smiley' logo and the warehouse party culture, the acid phenomenon of 1988 rivalled the punk scene of just over a decade previous for its notoriety within the establishment and British press. This time the connections between Ecstasy, the scene's drug of choice, and the music were being made more clear cut. Eventually the style went underground again as it was superceded by techno and other dance forms. Notable archivists like Richie Hawtin and Ege Bam Yasi have done much to revive the style, or 'the 303 sound', in the 90s, as have Hardfloor, Laurent Garnier and Cosmic Baby in Europe.

Acid Jazz

Above and beyond a musical movement or record label, to some Acid Jazz is more of a complete lifestyle, complete with Gabbicci clothing and its own secular image. Fighting against the then-

current vogue of jazz as a soundtrack to lounge culture, Acid Jazz reinvented the idea that the music belonged as much to the dancefloor as to smoky cafés. 'Jazz was originally meant for people to dance to, not for boring old people to sit there and applaud everytime there's a nice solo'. Acid Jazz was founded by DJ Giles Peterson and Eddie Piller in April 1988. Piller had worked at indie label Avator, then MCA and Stiff, where he was particularly impressed by Dave Robinson. His first label was Stiff subsidiary Countdown, then Re-elect the President, which found some degree of success via the James Taylor Quartet. The latter band grew out of the Prisoners, who had already served time with Piller on Countdown. The Acid Jazz name was actually a vaguely satirical one, incorporating the then prevalent acid explosion in a tongue in cheek manner. 'We always thought about changing the name, but it stopped being a joke when our international sales started to reach a substantial level'. The first record would be Galliano's 'Frederick Lies Still', followed in short order by *Acid Jazz And Other Illicit Grooves*, packaged with rare-groove and funk material. At least as significant was the huge impact caused by the Brand New Heavies debut. After a few financial setbacks in 1989 Peterson took up an offer from Phonogram, and Piller recruited Polydor A&R manager Kieran Hurley. Together they took the decision to push their jazz dance sounds into a more commercial direction. As part of the deal with Phonogram Peterson was able to fund his own Talkin' Loud label, which maintains a friendly rivalry with Acid Jazz to this day. There are those who argue that the label has lost more than its fair share of quality acts (A Man Called Adam to Big Life, Galliano to Talkin' Loud, and the Sandals and Jamiroquai). However, there are plenty of hotly tipped outfits left behind, including Mother Earth, Emperor's New Clothes, Corduroy, Night Trains and others (the James Taylor Quartet would also return to the label in 1994). The label now boasts offices in London, Milan, Sydney and Dublin, as the 'Acid Jazz' sound, amended to 'Urban Alternative' in the US, has grown. Not bad for a company which started out in a converted stable in Hackney. As Piller reflects: 'To me Acid Jazz is a record label, but I can understand how it has become embodied as a style definition in social culture. Its not something we at Acid Jazz expected when we first started, but it is a term that ourselves, and the artists who are not signed to us but are often referred to as an 'Acid Jazz' act, have to accept'. The label sampler series *Totally Wired* has helped push the label's profile forward, even though tracks are no longer specifically selected from the Acid Jazz roster. Their star certainly remains in the ascendent, as evidenced by the fact that the label helped sponsor Surrey County Cricket Club for their 1994 season.
Selected albums: Various: *Totally Wired 1-7* (Acid Jazz 1988-1993).

Acid Jesus

Acid Jesus are Darmstadt (30 miles from Frankfurt) Germany based Roman Flugal and Jorn Elling-Wuttke, who also record as Rebel Youth, Holy Garage, Playhouse and Primitive Painter. Elling-Wuttke is jointly responsible for running the highly thought-of Delerium record store, also helping out in-house labels like Ongaku, Klangeltronik and Playhouse. 'We're against the whole movement that has developed. In Delerium, we try to show the kids in Frankfurt real techno. Every musician who comes into our shop is offered the chance to come into our studio and be shown how to work the equipment'. Flugal, meanwhile, is a classically trained pianist who sometimes drums for a jazz band. His partner once played in a rock band entitled the Sheets, who toured with the Wedding Present. Among their alter-egos are, strangely enough, Alter Ego, who recorded an album of psychedelia-tinged material, promoted by the 'Nude Restaurant' single, which was remixed by David Holmes and Black Dog. Both would also remix Acid Jesus' 'Move My Body', along with Derrick May. As Primitive Painter, meanwhile, they generally build songs around the 808, providing material influenced by Robert Owens, Fingers Inc and Felix Da Housecat.
Albums: As Alter Ego: *Alter Ego* (Harthouse 1994). As Primitive Painter: *Primitive Painter* (R&S 1994).

Adamski

b. Adam Tinley, c.1968. Adamski's first recordings were cut at the age of eleven as a member of the Stupid Babies, a pre-teen punk duo (with his brother) immortalised on the Fast Products *Earcom 3* sampler. He was also a member of Diskord Kaskord in 1987, who released one single - a cover version of X Ray Spex's 'Identity' (his brother subsequently formed Garden Of Eden). Adamski went on to record as a keyboard player on instrumental dance records after his adolescence. His solo breakthrough came with the release of 'N-R-G', which reached number 12 in the UK charts. Unfortunately, legal action from Lucozade, who claimed the single plagiarised their advertising slogan, forced him to donate £5,000 of his royalties to charity. He replied with the massive dancefloor hit, and UK number 1, 'Killer'. This tautly orchestrated electronic piece was enhanced

by the emotive vocals of guest vocalist Seal (b. Seal Henry Samuel). A follow-up, 'The Space Jungle', derived from 'All Shook Up', was hammered by the critics. While his former vocalist went on to national adoration, Adamski slipped from view somewhat, though he did enjoy a minor hit with 'Flashback Jack' at the end of 1990. An epitaph, of sorts, was offered via *Naughty* album track 'Take The Money And Run': 'I've been chewed up and spat out by the restrictions of dance'. Many critics have judged such petulance as sour grapes following his commercial decline. The same year he joined with Elton John to remix 'Medicine Man' for charity, but was not sighted for some time afterwards. He now forms part of the remix team the Jet Slags with Mr Monday, working on projects like Bump's 'I'm Rushin''.
Albums: *Live And Direct* (MCA 1990), *Doctor Adamski's Musical Pharmacy* (MCA 1990), *Naughty* (MCA 1992).
Video: *Live And Direct* (1990).

Adeva
b. Patterson, New Jersey, USA. The youngest of six children, Adeva joined the church choir at the age of twelve where she remained for ten years, eventually becoming its director and vocal coach. Her mother a misionary and her father a deacon, between stints of teaching (for slow and emotionally disturbed children), she found time to take part regularly in talent contests. She was eventually banned from entering several competitions for winning so often, and turned professional by starting out on the local club scene in the mid-80s. She teamed up with Mike Cameron of the Smack Productions team to record 'In And Out Of My Life' for New York label Easy Street before signing to Cooltempo in 1988. Her success in the singles chart, more so in the UK than the US initially (where, strangely, her first three solo releases all went to number 17), included a cover of Aretha Franklin's 'Respect', 'Treat Me Right', 'Warning', 'Beautiful Love', and the collaboration with New York producer/recording artist Paul Simpson, 'Musical Freedom (Moving On Up)'. Not bad for a young lady whose parents once told her: 'You sing gospel or nothing at all'. However, Adeva never made quite the commercial trasnition which was expected and she was dropped by Cooltempo in August 1992.
Albums: *Adeva* (Cooltempo 1989), *Love Or Lust* (Cooltempo 1991). Compilation: *Hits* (Cooltempo 1992).
Video: *Live At The Town And Country Club* (1991).

A Guy Called Gerald
Heavily influenced by Chicago house and acid, Gerald Simpson's solo career has thus far failed to ignite as many predicted. Simpson, who once sold copies of the *Socialist Worker* on the streets of Manchester departed the 808 State fold after complaining vocally in the press about unpaid royalties. His most notable contribution to the dance scene was 'Voodoo Ray', which scored a number 55 hit in April 1989 before re-entering at number 12 two months later. Those statistics hardly reflect the reverence with which it is regarded in the club scene. He was still working at McDonald's at the beginning of the 90s when he was offerred the chance to remix for Cabaret Voltaire and Turntable Orchestra. CBS allowed him to create his own Subscape label, but it proved impossible to recreate former glories. Simpson did, however, put together a tape to accompany a book from Trevor Miller entitled *Trip City*, and 1992's 'Juicebox' featured old 808 sparring partner MC Tunes on its rap section.
Albums: *Hot Lemonade* (Rham 1988), *Automanikk* (CBS 1990).

A Homeboy, A Hippie And A Funki Dredd
Cross-fertilised dance team who made their name with the club hit, 'Total Confusion', for Tam Tam in 1989, which led to a deal with Polydor. Original 'hippie' Caspar Pound (b. c.1970) soon departed, to find wider fame as The Hypnotist, head of Rising High Records, and sundry other projects. HHFD member Marc Williams would continue to work with Pound's new label under the title Project One. It was with their November 1993 single, 'Here We Go', that the group became firmly etched into the record buying public's minds. This came via the unprecedented coverage of a television advert for British Knights sportswear, using the single as its theme tune. On MTV alone it was shown 277 times in the two months following release, but it was to be their final effort.

Air Liquide
Captivating ambient techno trio who comprise Walker (aka Ingmar Koch), Jammin' Unit and Mary S. Applegate. Koch is a half-German, half-Hungarian graduate of the University of Cologne, where he pursued his music studies, specialising in electronic composition. The strangely named Jammin' Unit is a half-Turkish, half-Finnish musician who had recorded *avant garde* and experimental music for over a decade before the group formed in 1992. He is also a professional sound engineer who runs Air Liquide's own Ocean

Air Liquide

Blue studios, alongside Koch. Finally Applegate, an expatriate American, is the group's lyricist, having previously composed over 20 chart hits including those for Jennifer Rush's 'The Power Of Love'. This unlikely collaboration was informed by mutual tastes in underground exotica and electronica, which was wonderfully captured by the release of 'If There Was No Gravity' (which combined the wide-eyed wonder of Applegate's delivery with a time-sealed ambient production from her partners). The subsequent album, again licensed to Rising High in the UK, was similarly feted, and preceded a collaboration with that label's Caspar Pound on The New London School Of Electronics project. Koch also provided a set for the unrelated but phonetically similar New Electronica series, and records solo as Walker (the best example of which is 'Don't Fuck With Cologne' for DJ.Ungle Fever). Jammin' Unit's solo excursions, meanwhile, include 'Flower Swing' for the same label, which is one of some fourteen labels Koch operates (under the Structure umbrella).
Album: *Nephology* (Blue/Rising High 1994).

Altern 8

Hardcore ravers from Stafford, Altern 8 consisted of Mark Archer and Chris Peat, and were actually an offshoot of their Nexus 21 pure techno act. Of the two, Archer was the house music aficionado, while Peat was a former music technology student with his main interests lying in computers. Former deckchair attendants (or so they claimed), they crashed the chart with 'Infiltrate 202' and 'Activ8', two chaotic slices of overground techno. They were aided in their chart aspirations by the circulation of fictitious press stories concerning their alleged activities. These included; patronage of the decongestant Vicks Vapo Rub, which, it is claimed, can heighten the effects of imbibing the Ecstasy drug; playing shows in a hot air balloon (dispensing Christmas Cakes laced with 'E' to the masses) and standing as candidates for the 1993 General Election. Music journalists lapped it all up, and were roundly beaten in laser combat for their troubles. Their live 'events' were also designed as eye catching, surreal performances where the band donned RAF chemical warfare suits and dust masks: 'Dance music is there to be danced to, not to be looked at like rock music is. But, unfortunately, dance acts have to perform live on occasion, and, when we do, we want to provide something visual'. They were aided by their resident dancers Crez and John Parkes and, in the case of their gig at Stafford Bingley Hall, an actual shaman. His job was to cleanse the venue of its

'rock 'n' roll' past', prior to performance. Their vinyl outings, in addition to the hits, consisted of the *Overload* EP (1990), 'E Vapor 8' (1991) and 'Frequency', 10,000 copies of which were on sale for a single day only. The protagonists long maintained that this was a temporary diversion from their main project, Nexus 21, and confirmed this by releasing a 'final' Altern 8 single, 'Everybody', in June 1993. Mark Archer has gone on to form Slo-Moshun, a duo of Archer and Danny Taurus from Stoke On Trent. They released 'Bells Of New York', one of the biggest dance hits of early 1994, breaking the Top 30 on the back of its house/hip hop undulations. But some of the Altern 8 methodology remained. This time the scam was to trick everyone into thinking it was a US import. Their second single would be summer 1994's 'Help My Friends'.
Album: *Full On...Mask Hysteria* (Network 1992).

A Man Called Adam

Mellow house groovers from North London who started out as a ten piece jazz band. Club-goers got to know them through the vocals of Sally Rogers, the music layered in the best traditions of Chicago House mainstay, Larry Heard (Mr Fingers). Signing to Big Life from their original Acid Jazz home (for whom they released 'APB' and 'Earthly Powers') and Ritmo ('Musica De Amor'), their spatial experiments won through despite an apparent awkwardness with lyrical construction. Easily the best representation of the band would be their minor chart success 'Barefoot In The Head', which remained a highly respected club cut well into the 90s. It was followed-up by 'I Want To Know', which was remixed by Steve Anderson (Brothers In Rhythm) and Graeme Park. Paul Daley, a collaborator alongside prime mover Steve Jones, would go on to join Neil Barnes to become Leftfield. Derek of the Sandals was also a member for a time.
Album: *The Apple* (Big Life 1991).

Anderson, Carleen

Anderson started her professional life as a clerical worker, with very few ambitions to enter the world of showbiz. Her parents, conversely, had been stalwarts of James Brown's touring revue in the 60s and 70s. Her mother, Vicki Anderson, was also a backing vocalist, and her stepfather was Bobby Byrd of the Famous Flames. By her mid-20s Anderson had married, given birth to a son, and started a college scholarship to train to be a music teacher in Los Angeles. However, times were tough, and she eagerly accepted an offer from her parents to travel to London to check out the

emerging soul scene. There she linked with the duo Young Disciples. Though never an official member of the band she did write and sing on most of their best songs, notably 'Apparently Nothin'', written about the Gulf War. However, her tenure with the Young Disciples ended, amicably, with the the the release of *Dusky Sappho*, a limited edition EP. Its title referred to Phyllis Wheatley, an American poet and slave who, like Anderson, had come to Britain, and was a prime mover in the lesbian movement. Enquiries as to Anderson's sexuality followed with predictable speed. Morrissey-like, she advocated celibacy. Anderson's debut single proper came with 'Nervous Breakdown' on Circa records, a seven-minute soul/dance opus.
Album: *True Spirit* (Circa 1994).

Anderson, Jhelisa

American born (Jackson, Mississippi), British-based soul-dance vocalist, and cousin of Carleen Anderson, whose fame initially revolved around her work for the Shamen ('Ebeneezer Goode') and Soul Family Sensation ('I Don't Even Know If I Should Call You Baby') having left her media course and session singing duties in Los Angeles for London in 1988. After guesting on Björk's debut album, she earned herself a solo contract with Dorado Records. The first single to emerge was the self-written 'Sally's Knockin'', followed by 'All I Need', a jazzy hip hop workout which saw her united with Lee Hamblin (famed for his production with Christy Moore, PM Dawn, Sindecut, Maxi Priest etc.). Her muse descends from a childhood love of choir music and blues, her father a prominent gospel DJ.

Angel

b. Brooklyn, New York, USA. A singer, writer, remixer and producer, Angel's talents had largely been honed in her adopted second home of London, before she returned to the west coast of America in 1994. Her lively cocktail of funk and jazz dance: 'I recycle the things I love and give it that 90s edge' - won her a contract with Delicious Vinyl subsidiary, Brass. She first rose to prominence with her first single for them, 'Spirit Of Love', before embarking on a debut album. She has also won a slice of the remix cake, her credits including work with the Pharcyde, Brand New Heavies and Soul Sonics.
Album: *Message From The Angel* (Brass 1994).

Angel, Dave

Clapham, South London-based recording artist, whose father was a professional jazz musician. He consequently grew up listening to Charlie Parker and Miles Davis, and became a jazz session drummer by the age of 14. Yet his background was also one of stifling poverty, his father buying him his first drum kit the day the electricity was cut off. He released his debut single in 1989, just after returning from a nine month prison term for possession of cannabis. He had recorded a bassline on a standard tape deck, before, in a moment of inspiration, he mixed it against a nearby copy of Eurythmics' 'Sweet Dreams'. Once approval had been given from RCA, who signed up the record, it was released as a white label, before Angel moved to Dave Dorrell's Love label for 'Never Leave'. He soon became the name on many people's lips as he began his career in earnest with two strong EPs, *Royal Techno* and *Of The Highest Order*. The critically-acclaimed *Family* followed in 1993, before *Third Voyage* (originally released in April 1991). He has maintained his broad musical vision: 'People always use the word techno to describe what I do, but I prefer to call it 'future jazz''. He continues to DJ at the Orbit club, and remix for various clients. These include Sun Electric's 'En-Trance', Katana for Eastern Bloc and the *Seas Of Tranquility* EP for his own label, Rotation.

Aphex Twin

b Richard James, c.1972, Truro, Cornwall, England. The Aphex Twin began making music in his early teens, before a brief sojourn on an electronics course at Kingston Polytechnic pre-empted his signing to R&S records. His breakthrough release came with 'Didgeridoo' in 1992; 'I wanted to have some tracks to finish the raves I used to play in Cornwall, to really kill everybody off so they couldn't dance any more, and 'Didgeridoo' came out of that'. Since then he has continued to turn out techno/ambient tracks of excellent quality at an astonishing rate. 'I have to try and create an isolated state to exist in - I do that by not sleeping. It's quite mental - you have to get pretty knackered before things start going strange'. However, the Aphex Twin is not his only pseudonym; releases by Polygon Window on Warp (*Surfing On Sine Waves*), Caustic Window ('Joyrex J5', 'Joyrex J4') on Rephlex, a label he co-owns, and other sundry outfits like Blue Calx and PCP all bear his mark. Incidentally, the 'ph' part of the Aphex Twin and any other projects with those letters indicate the music is geared towards 'acid' styled dance. As if that wasn't enough, he is responsible for the manufacture and wiring of all his instruments, and is said to have over 150 hours of recorded music 'in the can' at any given time.

Aphex Twin

As to his inspiration: 'I've thought about analysing where my tunes come from, plotting charts and graphs and so on, but I'm afraid I'll find out something I don't want to know'. By this time he had become highly sought after for his remixing skills, particularly 'progressive' indie bands like Meat Beat Manifesto, Curve, Jesus Jones, St Ettienne, Seefeel and the Cure. The *On* EP in November 1993 saw him signed to Warp on a permanent basis, under a contract which licenses material to Sire in the US. He also engaged in a world tour to promote *Selected Ambient Works 2*, and bought himself an armoured tank to trundle around Truro with. Regarded by many followers as the genre's prime exponent of the 90s, it is possible that his profile has been inflated by those 'outside' the techno world looking in. While he is certainly a major talent, with a superb body of recorded work behind him, the impression sometimes given that all of these are masterworks of the dance world is, contextually and practically, incorrect.

Selected albums: *Selected Ambient Works '85 - '92* (R&S 1992), *Selected Ambient Works Vol. 2* (Warp 1994). As AFX: *Analogue Bubblebath 3* (1993). As Polygon Window: *Surfing On Sine Waves* (Warp 1993).

Apollo 440

Trance-techno combo featuring Trevor Gray (keyboards, vocals), Howard Gray (backing vocals) and Noko (vocals, guitar, keyboards), recording initially for their own Stealth label. Following the release of enterprising early singles 'Blackout', 'Destiny' and club favourite 'Lolita', Apollo 440 soon became more widely known for their remix work, numbering U2, Liz Francis ('Rhythm Of Life'), EMF and Pop Will Eat Itself among their clients. Further notoriety spawned from their sample of Emerson Lake & Palmer on their 1993 single, 'Astral America'. They have also recorded as Fast ('Fast' - Stealth 1992, a pure adrenalin rush at 155bpm).

Astralasia

Pagan house specialists, who record for their own Magick Eye label, and share links to Ultraviolet Explorer (UVX) and Mushroom. As might be expected from such connections, they rejoice in mystical techno/ambience, with song titles like 'Genesis The Spark Of Life' and 'Astral Navigation', while their personnel labour under names like Swordfish, Nosmo, King Os and Moonboot. One ex-member was Jason Relf, whose father was the late Keith Relf - singer with the original Yardbirds. Jason in turn had enjoyed a brief stint as keyboardist in the Magic Mushroom Band before joining Astralasia. When Jason left the band he formed Booma with Scott James (ex-Shave Yer Tongue), who released an eponymous debut single on Leftfield's Hard Hands imprint. The duo had previously released a 12-inch, 'Pleasure', as SYT on Andy Weatherall's Sabres Of Paradise label. Relf has also released solo records as Solar Plexus and Tangled Feet.

Albums: *Pitched Up At The Edge Of Reality* (Magick Eye 1993), *Whatever Happened To Utopia* (Magick Eye 1994).

Atari Teenage Riot

Caustic punk/house terrorists, whose music recoils against the rise of the fascist right in their native Germany with lyrics like 'Put a bullet straight through a Nazi's head'. From Berlin, main man Alec Empire (b. c.1973) grew up with punk and was in bands from the age of 12, but when acid hit in '88, he got hip to club sounds instead. He began DJing in the late 80s and released solo politico techno tunes for the Force Inc label. Slightly bored with the pulpit life of the DJ, he hooked up with Car (b. Switzerland) and Hanin Elias (b. Spain) so he could play live again. Together they signed to Phonogram as Atari Teenage Riot. Though heavily hyped, their records failed to sell in the anticipated quantities, despite an unlikely techno cover of Sham 69's 'If The Kids Are United'.

A13 Productions

The cornerstone in A13's swift rise to prominence in UK dance circles was A&R head/managing director Chris Massey who was 22 years old when he founded the label in October 1993. He had formerly worked as head of promotions for General Production Recordings for two years until 1992. A13 Productions, its title taken from the label's base off the A13 road in Benfleet, Essex, was established after Massey attended a free music industry course for the unemployed, and was aided by cash from the Prince's Trust. The first release arrived in November 1993 with the *Gapar* EP, from former GPR act Repeat (aka Mark Broom, with Ed Handley and Andy Turner from Black Dog). A second release came from highly respected techno/trance producer Simon Berry (Art Of Trance), and the *Northern Lights* EP. A flurry of demo tapes led to a release from aspirants Connective Zone with the *The Holistic Worlds* EP, before a second Mark Broom/Repeat four-track, *Acrux*. With further material issues, including the chilled out techno of Red Union and a compilation album, A13 had quickly established itself in the hearts of the dance populace.

Atkins, Juan

One of the 'Detroit mafia', Juan 'Magic' Atkins, alongside Derrick May and Kevin Saunderson, was responsible for defining techno in the mid to late 80s. Originally fascinated by the concepts of science-fiction, he first pioneered 'techno' music as part of electro act Cybertron (with mysterious Vietnam veteran 30-70), on the Model 500 imprint (his first record having been 'My Cosmic Cause' on Deep Space). An immense influence on everyone from the KLF to the Italian Groove Groove Melody team (behind Black Box), tracks like 'No UFO's', 'Ocean To Ocean', 'The Chase' and 'Electronic' were pivotal period pieces in the development of techno. They were later collected together under the Model 500 banner on a collection entitled *Classics* on the R&S label. However, as the ground he and others had prepared was finally being exploited in the early 90s, he remained aloof, almost invisible apart from occasional DJ stints throughout Europe: 'At the end of the day all of us are in it to sell records. This is all I do. I do it for the love of the music, but I got to survive. I got to eat. So I thought I'd wait a year or two and let people get into the techno thing and get used to being more receptive to what it is, as opposed to what it was in 1986, when nobody knew what the term was and everybody was scared of technology'. Some might consider this a magnificent arrogance, but Atkins' reputation among the cognoscenti argues that it is justified. 1992 also saw him re-open his Metroplex label, which had originally been home to the first releases by many of the aforementioned Detroit mafia (Saunderson, May and Eddie 'Flashin'' Fowlkes). It is now run under the auspices of 'Mad' Mike Banks' (see Underground Resistance) Submerge umbrella organisation. He finally relented in undertaking remix work - notably on Eon's 'Spice', and also collaborated with Altern 8 for Inner City's 'Let It Reign'.

Selected album: As Model 500: *Classics* (R&S 1993).

Atom Heart

The latest in a prestigious list of 'name' producers from Frankfurt, Germany - namely Sven Vath, Peter Namlock and Jam El Mar of Jam & Spoon. He started making music in 1991 and within three years had released over 60 different records on a variety of labels: Pod, Rising High, Delirium, After 6am, US Instinct and Fax. Among his biggest tunes were 'I'm A Secretary' on Fax, 'Mihon' by Ongaku, and 'Elektronikkaa' by Pink Elm and Atom Heart on Rising High. He also works as Atmo Shinzu, Cover Atomique, Datacide,

Autechre

Millenium, I, Lisa Carbon and Resistance D. The name Atom Heart was chosen because he was, and remains, interested in the combination of the emotional and the mechanical/technical.

Aural Assault

An important component of Rising High's roster is Mike Ash, whose home studio recordings have gradually established his reputation on the hardcore techno scene. However, his interest in dance music grew out of the late 80s acid movement, a heavy nod to which occurs on Aural Assault's *Planet 303* EP. His work under this title is characterised by disconcertingly hard rhythms, broken by samples, often taken from film dialogue. As such he has released some of Rising High's most successful tracks ('Pink And Purple Experience', 'Total Techno'). He also records for RH sister label Sappho, under the title Space Cadet (*Don't You Want My Love* and *Third Wave* EPs). He has gone on to form his own record label, Dancing In Complete Apathy, though he maintains links with Rising High.

Autechre

Two Manchester, England, studio-based personnel, Sean Booth (b. 1972, Rochdale, Yorkshire, England) and Rob Brown (b. 1970, Torquay, England), whose debut album was one of the most effective in the evolution of Warp's 'Artificial Intelligence' series. As Booth recounts: 'I just don't rate structured music', a predilection which was obvious from a listen to the set, on which the duo pioneered a free-form dance music which echoed the experimental edge of modern jazz. The band's early demos of 'Crystal' and 'Egg' had first brought them to the attention of Warp who snapped them up and included them on a compilation set.
Album: *Incunabula* (Warp 1993).

Azuli

Record label run by Dave Piccioni through the Black Market dance shop, specialising in quality garage material. Azuli's output began with Chocolate Fudge's 'In A Fantasy' (1991), a collaboration between Miles Morgan, 'Baby' Sean Casey and Larry Dundas, and the *Disco Elements* and *Sensory Elements* EPs. The first two of these were released bedecked with New York telephone numbers and shrinkwrapped to give the impression of being imports. 1992 saw Underground Mass featuring Lisa White's 'Music (Takes Control)' and 'Didn't I'. The label continued to expand, bringing other catalogues like Paramodo from the US and their own Gyroscope under the Black Market/Azuli umbrella. Their 1994 roster included Andrea Mendez's 'Real Love', while they enjoyed a major hit with label stalwart Romanthony's 'In The Mix', a disco/house groover released as a tribute to Tony Humphries, with his name used repeatedly as its hookline. Romanthony had been discovered by Piccioni on one of his frequent trips to the US.

B

B., Lisa

b. Lisa Barbuscia, c.1971. A corporate-groomed garage diva, Barbuscia originally attended the New York School Of Music and The Performing Arts (as featured in the popular *FAME* television series) before being snapped up by a modelling agency at the age of 17. In turn she won a recording contract with London dance subsidiary ffrr, who teamed her up with producers of the calibre of Mike McEvoy (Soul II Soul), Paul Oakenfold and Gianfranco Bortolotti (of Italy's Media team). The resulting material, typified by singles like 1993's 'Fascinated', was very pop-orientated and, it has been suggested, none too authentic. Her record company have had trouble convincing the dance world of the former model's credentials, her relationship with the Marquess Of Cholmondeley (30th in line to the throne) hampering her musical progress.

Baby D

The daughter of a famous Maltese vocalist who has been singing since her childhood, Baby D has become widely recognised as one of the new diva queens of the UK's club scene. Influenced by everything from lover's rock to disco queen Teena Marie, her first experiences in the music business came as part of an all-girl vocal group who sang on backing sessions for several chart acts. She embarked on a solo career by linking with producer Dice, recording the vocals for Jazz And The Brothers Grimm's 'Casanova' in 1989. The first release under her own flag was 1991's 'Daydreaming', her vocals on which were widely sampled on the dance scene thereafter. However, November 1992's 'Let Me Be Your Fantasy' was the real breakthrough, rocketing to the top of the dance charts. A club classic, it was voted the best record of the year by readers of *Ravescene* magazine. She returned in mid-1994 with another version of 'Casanova', originally a hit for Coffee and the song which she had first sung for Jazz And The Brothers Grimm in 1989's Summer Of Love.

Baby Ford

b. Peter Ford, Bolton, Lancashire, England, though he moved to New Zealand at the age of 10. Wigan based Ford is a prolific recording artist. His organic DIY studio sounds have bedecked a plethora of recordings, including the onomatopoeic duo of 'Oochy Koochy (FU Baby Yeh Yeh)', an extreme acid outing, which hit in 1987, and 'Chikki Chikki Ahh Ahh', both housed on the vibrant *Ford Trax* EP. The brace were co-produced with Eon. 'It's not hardcore', he protested, 'I'm about moods and feelings'. Sundry remix projects followed, and he also offered the world live stylophone at venues like the Hacienda during his tours. 1990 saw the release of the limited edition 'Change', then 'In Your Blood' the following year, both of which unveiled a purer techno approach. He has also recorded for Brute Records as Doucen ('White Sands').
Albums: *Ooo The World Of Baby Ford* (Rhythm King 1990), *B Ford 9* (Rhythm King 1992).

Balearic

The most difficult to quantify of all dance genres, at least in terms of musical content. Balearic is a term which documents the sets played in the Balearic islands (notably Ibiza) in the mid-80s. This 'feel good' vibe was imported back to England from venues like Amnesia, Koo and Pacha by Danny Rampling, Paul Oakenfold and Nicky Holloway in the late 80s. Oakenfold even held a 'Ibiza Reunion' party in London. Experienced clubbers still go misty-eyed at the mention of the original Ibiza party scene which the UK partially emulated. As a music balearic can account for records outside of the conventional dance format, as long as the atmosphere, that of uplifting, happy, commercial music is maintained.

Banco De Gaia

The regular dub merchant at Club Dog evenings, Banco De Gaia are the brainchild of Leamington Spa resident, Toby Marks. The band had originally been formed in 1989 with a friend, though he quit before the year was out. Banco De Gaia made its first vinyl outings on three compilations for Beyond (the *Ambient Dub* series) and Planet Dog's *Feed Your Head*. The November 1993 single, 'Desert Wind', was typically described as 'ambient', though it was in actual fact a little tougher than much of his usual material. He had previously released two tape-only affairs: *Medium* and *Freeform Flutes And Fading Tibetans*. The samples utilised were typically wide-ranging, including brass bands. Before Banco De Gaia Marks had played guitar in heavy metal, folk and jazz bands. From there he had moved on to a bhangra collective in London and Glasgow. It was in the Scottish city that he first purchased a sequencer, which would radically alter his musical world-view. Banco De Gaia means, incidentally, world bank. This gives some indication as to the philosophy which supports Banco De Gaia, an impression confirmed by the ethnic flavour of its debut album: 'It's all very well sampling James Brown or Led Zeppelin, but there's a whole world waiting to be used'. Likewise his *Maya* collection, which featured samples culled from his travels in disparate territories such as Israel, Turkey, Jordan and India.

Album: *Maya* (Planet Dog Bark 1994).

Band Of Gypsies

aka 3 Man Island. Band Of Gypsies is the production/writing/recording team of Nigel Swanston and Tim Cox. They met when Cox auditioned as a guitarist for Swanston's band (eventually gaining a job as their keyboardist). They have been working with the Pulse 8 label since joint manager Steve Long found a record they had produced and traced them through their publishing house. As 3 Man Island they had already enjoyed a US Top 10 hit with a 'joke' record, while the original 'Band Of Gypsies' project was actually a track developed over a longer period of time, which eventually emerged as a first single (eponymously credited). They have kept the name going for their productions for Pulse 8 with Sue Chaloner and Rozalla (who described the duo as '*so* talented'). Their own singles include 'Take Me Higher' and 'Stand Up', recorded with the help of ex-September vocalist Juiliette Jaimes.

Bandulu

Trance-dance specialists of some note, who are signed to the Infonet empire (which they had helped Chris Abbott set up), and whose personnel comprise Jamie Bissmire (b. c.1969), John O'Connell (b. c.1970) and Lucien Thompson (b. c.1970). Their HQ is Bissmire's parents' home in Muswell Hill, North London. Influenced by Detroit techno and Chicago house, Bandulu have additionally added tribal percussion and 'real' instruments (guitars, drums). Singles like 'Phaze-In-Version' saw their trancey sounds honed to an intricacy many in the genre could only envy. They had made their debut with 'Better Nation' before 'Internal Ocean' arrived late in 1992. They also recorded as alter-egos ECC (Earth Coincidence Control), Sons Of The Subway, Koh Tao and Thunderground (who include 'fourth member' Lewis Keogh). Thunderground is also the name of the club night they host at London's Bass Clef venue. Bandulu had also remixed the Orb's 'UFOrb' (Keogh, as well as his Thunderground tenure, being the Orb's resident DJ). With a discernible debt to the experimental electronic music of Phillip Glass and Laurie Anderson, Bandulu have nevertheless forged their own identity in the dance world. In the summer of 1994 they released another widely admired single,

'Presence', followed by a second studio album.

Albums: *Guidance* (Infonet 1993), *Antimatters* (Infonet 1994).

Bang The Party

London duo responsible for putting kinky sex on the agenda of the deep house scene. A forerunner of the cybersex virtual reality revolution, Bang the Party, comprising DJ Kid Batchelor (Keith Franklyn) and Bullet, broke through with their 1990 hit, 'Bang Bang You're Dead', which introduced its aural aphrodisiac approach with the memorable line: 'It's basically using music as an everyday stimulant to your heart'. The single was typical of their craft, syncopated, almost hypnotic rhythms aimed firmly at producing a sensual, other-world atmosphere. Keith Franklyn would go on to join Azuli artists KCC.

Albums: *Back To Prison* (Warriors Dance 1990).

Basement Boys

The Basement Boys are a Baltimore production team featuring Tommy Davies (b. c.1958, Jay Steinhour (b. c.1948) and Teddy Douglas (b. c.1963). They won their spurs by propelling a Crystal Waters' track, 'Gypsy Woman (La De Dee)' into the clubs via their 'Stripped To The Bone' remix. It eventually hit number 2 on the mainstream charts. Their first credit arrived in 1986 with a remix of Rose Royce's 'Love Don't Live Here Anymore' for Jump Street. They also produced a track for Profile entitled 'Don't Blame Me', credited to Sublevel featuring Andrea Holdclaw. The big break came with Ultra Nate's 'It's Over Now', which was heavily supported by Tony Humphries. The trio went on to produce an EP for Nu Groove as 331/3, and then 'Tonite' as Those Guys for MCA. Other successes included the succulent Mass Order tune, 'Lift Every Voice (Take Me Away)'. They have continued to remix widely, counting among their core clients Cut N Move ('Get Serious') and Paula Abdul (*Vibeology* EP).

Album: *Blue Notes In The Basement* (Warners 1991).

Bass Bumpers

German-based act whose original line-up, Henning Reith, Caba Kroll (from Bochum's Tarm Center) and vocalist Nana, signed to the Dusseldorf-based Dance Street label in 1990. The resultant 'Can't Stop Dancing' became a huge underground hit throughout Europe and the US that summer, even making the Billboard charts. When the group returned a year later with a new single, 'Get The Big Bass', rapper E-Mello (b. Ian Freeman, England) had stepped in for Nana. However, it was early 1994 before they began to make their presence felt again with 'The Music's Got Me', primarily through its Paul Gotel remix, doing the business.

Bassheads

Birkenhead, Merseyside, England-based duo of Desa and Nick Murphy, who originally came to prominence in 1991 with the release of 'Is There Anybody Out There?'. Although they crashed the UK Top 10, they would find themselves being sued by Afrika Bambaataa, the Osmonds, Pink Floyd and even Talking Heads' representatives for the samples they had employed. Subsequent singles 'Back To The Old School' and 'Who Can Make You Feel Good' refused to compromise on their pulsating house/sample dialogue. However, by the time of their debut long player in 1993, the Bassheads had begun to embrace the ambient house movement spearheaded by the Orb and Aphex Twin. At the core of the album was a 24 minute centrepiece, 'C.O.D.E.', which owed a debt to Brian Eno and, ironically, Talking Heads. Album: *C.O.D.E.S.* (1993).

Bass-O-Matic

A nom de plume for William Orbit (b. William Wainwright), renowned mixer, writer and composer. Bass-O-Matic came to prominence in 1990 with the techno anthem, 'Fascinating Rhythm'. This was included on a debut set which also featured the services of Sharon Musgrave, percussionist Fergus and MC Inna One Step, the title of which was an obvious reference to Pink Floyd's *Set The Controls For The Centre Of The Sun*. In the process, Bass-O-Matic spearheaded a movement in the dance scene which rediscovered elements of music from yesteryear which had something in common with the trance-like state of 90s house. The album actually included a cover version of the Floyd standard, as well as the band's debut single, 'In The Realm Of The Senses'. A year later Orbit unveiled a follow-up, this time utilising vocalist Sindy (ex-Well Red) and rappers Glory and Divine. It proved another competent and intoxicating collection, with Orbit's keen sense of rhythm carrying the album through from deep house to more pop-orientated cuts.
Albums: *Set The Controls For The Heart Of The Bass* (Virgin 1990), *Science And Melody* (Virgin 1991).

Batu

Brighton-based six piece who mingle ethnic drumming with club sounds, topped off by the vocals of Sharon Scott, who had previously worked with Soul II Soul. Formed in 1992, they attracted the powerful advocacy of Kiss-FM DJ Patrick Forge after they handed over a tape at a Talkin' Loud club night in London. He was excited by the authentic Brazilian sounds the band created. Batu's main man, guitarist Chris Franck, after playing samba whilst studying for a degree in France, was tutored by two expatriate Brazilians, Pedro (guitar) and Beberto de Souza (octopusine percussion). Their debut single, 'Seasons Of My Mind'/'Hold It Now', prefaced a samba/house contribution to Island Records' *Rebirth Of Cool* series. Their feel for Latin music was intended as more than imitation however, as the medium they chose to express it within showed: 'What Batu are doing is taking an authentic approach to Brazilian music, but we're 90s people, we come from a club culture. You can't carry on making music now without being aware of hip-hop production'.

Baxter, Blake

From Detroit, former dancer Baxter is a first generation Detroit hero of 'Ride 'Em Boy' and 'Forever And A Day' fame, whose early recordings (with their edgy experimentation) provided a guiding light to the Aphex Twin and others. Closely involved with the *Techno Sound Of Detroit* compilation, releasing his own singles like 'When We Used To Play' and 'Forever And A Day', afterwards he cut his links with the city's 'Big Three' (Atkins, May and Saunderson) and moved on to the Detroit independent Icongnito. He released 'Sexuality' and the *Crimes Of The Heart EP* for the latter, which prefaced a debut album in early 1990. He also provided Jeff Mills/Mad 'Mike Banks' Underground Resistance with a rare outside production in 1991 with 'Prince Of Techno'. Skilled as both a drummer and DJ, he recorded for several European labels in the 90s after relocating to Berlin, including 1992's 'One More Time' and 'Brothers Gonna Work It Out' for Logic.
Album: *The Underground Lives* (Incognito 1990).

Beat Publique

Trio featuring former Soul II Soul vocalist Do'Reen (b. Doreen Parker), plus techno scene mover Lunarci (b. Jim Barnet, c.1973) and Gary Masters. Do'Reen had provided vocals for Soul II Soul's 'Feel Free' and 'Happiness', and also worked on sessions for MC Tunes, the Moody Boyz and Don-E. It was while working for the latter that she met Lunarci (famed for 'Communion' and collaborations with PM Dawn) and Masters (behind Praise's 'Only You'). Together they released 'Realise' for Beat Fantastique in July 1992. Do'Reen went on to work on sessions as a solo artist with Peter Harder (Jocelyn Brown etc.), and also sued Jazzie B for underpayment on her Soul II Soul recordings.

Beatmasters

Writing and production team comprising Richard Walmsley (b. 28 September 1962), Amanda Glanfield and Paul Carter, initially most famous for their work with Betty Boo (b. Alison Clarkson) on tracks like 'Hey DJ, I Can't Dance (To The Music You're Playing)'. Among their other chart coups were the Cookie Crew's breakthrough hit, 'Rok Da House' (number 5), Yazz's 'Stand Up For Your Love Rights' (number 2), and MC Merlin's 'Who's In The House' (number 8). Their fingerprints could also be traced to the PP Arnold comeback hit, 'Burn It Down'. This production line of pop hits won them few critical admirers, but their methodology had been honed when Glanfield and Carter spent time working on television commercial jingles for a production house (Brook Street's 'Get A Job' among them). Although they fell short of the totalitarian commercial knack of Stock Aitken & Waterman, they did manage notable hits under their own steam like 1988's 'Burn It Up'. A second album for Rhythm King saw guest appearances from JC001 and MC Precious. The group enjoyed something of a creative renaissance with 'Boulevard Of Broken Dreams' in 1991, built on Young Holt Unlimited's 'Light My Fire', after lacklustre efforts like 'I Dunno What It Is'.
Albums: *Anywayawanna* (Rhythm King 1989), *Life And Soul* (Rhythm King 1991).

Beats International

This studio team of musicians was formed by Norman Cook (b. Quentin Cook, 31 July 1963; ex-Housemartins) on the advent of the break up of his former employers. Its basic composition was Norman Cook (bass), Linda Layton (b. Belinda Kimberley Layton, 7 December 1970, Chiswick, London, England; vocals), Lester Noel (b. Lester John Noel, 3 September 1962, Paddington, London, England; ex-Grab Grab The Haddock, North Of Cornwallis; vocals), Andy Boucher (keyboards), and MC Wildski (rap). However, to these personnel could be added a gamut of occasional members ranging from Billy Bragg to Definition Of Sound to Captain Sensible. The first Beats International single, 'For Spacious Lies', gathered numerous rave reviews, and was much closer to traditional pop fare than subsequent releases. It included a contribution from Noel, who had met Cook when North Of Cornwallis supported the Housemartins on tour. Beats International shot to prominence in the UK when

'Dub Be Good To Me' hit number 1 in the UK charts in 1990. Controversy followed it shortly afterwards, as the audience placed the bass line as a note for note lift from the Clash album track, 'Guns Of Brixton'. In truth the song also borrowed heavily from the SOS Band's 'Just Be Good To Me'. This 'creative theft' may have diminished royalty cheques, but the interpretation of various styles and even passages of music proved quite a deliberate strategy in Beats International's armoury. Though the subsequent 'Burundi Blues' single, a delicate mix of soul, jazz, and African musics failed to repeat the success, Cook was heavily in demand as a remixer for a variety of projects, ranging from Aztec Camera to the Jungle Brothers. The impossibly diverse debut album charted at number 17, while the follow-up concentrated heavily on ska and reggae rhythms and included a disastrous version of 'In The Ghetto'. Cook would eventually forgo the Beats International banner in order to put together his new band, Freak Power.
Albums: *Let Them Eat Bingo* (Go! Discs 1990), *Excursion On The Version* (Go! Discs 1991).

Beloved

Initially known in 1983 as the Journey Through and comprising Jon Marsh (b. c.1964), Guy Gousden and Tim Havard, the Beloved fell into place a year later when Cambridge University student and ex-postman Steve Waddington (b. c.1959) joined on guitar. It was no straightforward initiation ceremony either. Marsh had placed an advert in the music press which ran thus: 'I am Jon Marsh, founder member of the Beloved. should you too wish to do something gorgeous, meet me in exactly three year's time at exactly 11am in Diana's Diner, or site thereof, Covent Garden, London, WC2'. Tentative stabs at heavy psychedelia evolved into a more pop orientated formula by the mid-80s, with the Beloved's dark, danceable sounds often being compared to New Order and garnering attention throughout Europe. Marsh became a contestant on television quiz show *Countdown* in 1987, featuring on nine programmes before being knocked out in the semi-finals. It was not until 1988, however, that the Beloved started living up to their name: Waddington and Marsh, heavily influenced by the nascent 'rave' scene in London at that time, split from Gousden and Harvard and started forging their own path. Unshackled from the confines of a four-cornered set-up, the revitalised duo dived into the deep end of the exploding dance movement, subsequently breaking into commercial waters with the ambient textures of 'Sun Rising'. The *Happiness* album, backed by Marsh and Waddington's enthusiastic chatter concerning the virtues of floatation tanks and hallucinogenic substances, perfectly embodied the tripped-out vibe of the times and sealed the Beloved's fashionable success in worldwide territories. By 1993's *Conscience*, Marsh had left his former partner Waddington, using his wife Helena as his new creative foil. The resultant album was more whimsical and understated than previous affairs, with a pop rather than club feel.

Albums: *Happiness* (Atlantic 1990), *Blissed Out* (remix of *Happiness*) (East West 1990), *Conscience* (East West 1993).

Beltram, Joey

b. c.1971. Widely considered to be one of the gurus of New York hardcore, Beltram's 1991 cut 'Energy Flash' (R&S) was a milestone in the genre, providing a bass-line that would re-emerge countless time since (not least on Beltram's own recordings). By the age of 16 he was recording for New York labels like Nu Groove as Code 6 and Lost Entity. 'Initially producing records was my way of getting better DJ jobs'. At school he had saved his dinner money in order to buy records at the end of the week to make mix tapes. He certainly boasts eclectic tastes in dance music, at the last count owning over 60,000 records. The follow-up single, 'Mentasm', was credited to Second Phase, a collaboration with Mundo Muzique, and was one of several *nom de plumes* which include Final Exposure ('Vortex', on Plus 8), Disorder ('Panic'/'Groove Attack', on Rhythmatic Rage) and Program 2 ('The Omen', on R&S). He has also recorded in a less frenetic house vein. His work on the Cutting label (Vice Tribe's 'Something Unreal') is a good example of this, while under his own name he has also provided a three-track EP (Beltram Presents...Odyssey Nine - 'Drums Of Orbit') for Visible, which dabbled in trance. However, his best recent work is undoubtedly the *Caliber* EP for Warp, which saw many critics drawing comparisons to the mighty 'Energy Flash'. 'I'm not one of those people that gets too moody and wants to change my style totally all the time. I'm always trying to keep a link between my old records and new records'. His remixes include Orbital's 'Oolaa', and the Smarte's 'Sesame's Treet', for US consumption.

Selected album: *The Re-Releases* (Trax 1994).

Bernard, James

A native New Yorker who programmes synthesizers for Korg as a day job, but releases a gamut of techno odes, under a variety of names, in his spare time. Under his own name he recorded a debut album for Rising High which was a gruelling, slightly moribund ambient affair. However, as Influx he provided the Sappho label (a subsidiary of Rising High) with their first full length album release on a set that reflected Influx's familiar, old school use of electro-drums. It followed three 12-inch releases, 'Influx', 'OD' and 'Disrupticon', for the same stable. Among his other guises is the nom de plume Cybertrax, whose notable credits on the main Rising High imprint included 'Songs For A Rainy Day' and 'Flexor'.

Albums: *Atmospherics* (Rising High 1994). As Influx: *Unique* (Sappho 1994), *The TB Rage* (Sappho 1994).

Better Days

Steve Proctor from Liverpool began DJing in 1979, before moving to London in the mid-80s, guesting at Shoom and Sunrise. He subsequently played at the Promised Land at the London Fitness Centre and Love at the Wag. His 'balearic' reputation revolved around him playing all sorts of tracks at the latter club which had 'love' in the title (including Fleetwood Mac). Better Days was the title Proctor chose as his recording vehicle. Two singles were completed for Virgin before departing for Music For Nations. A club night also titled Better Days came into being at London's Villa Stefano, as did a label of the same title. Releases like Museka's 'Beautiful In Red', Marshall Hains' 'Dancing In The CIty' and John DaSilva's Disco Universe Orchestra's 'Soul On Ice' and 'Sing It' followed. Other artists included the Better Days Project and Santa Esmerelda.

Beyond Records

Birmingham label famed for its ambient dub compilations. Head of the company/collective is Mike Barnet: 'Beyond was originally set up as an outlet for intelligent dance'. They also run the Oscillate club and liaise with the Original Rockers and Higher Intelligence Agency. Many of the acts to be found on the ambient series also play live at Oscillate.

Selected albums: *Ambient Dub Volumes 1-3* (Beyond 1991-1993).

Beyond Religion

A group and record label headed by joint-songwriters Karen Mercer (vocals) and Pete Spence (instrumentalist) based in Enfield, London. They made their debut both as a group and record company with the *Two Worlds* EP, four tracks of synthesized dub and ambient house. The group, formerly known as Chromatic, broke out on their own following problems with major record companies and staked their claim (and an Enterprise Allowance grant) with songs which were just that, rather than merely rhythms. Subsequent releases included 'Planet Of Our Own' (promo only), 'Magic', 'Rescue Me' (remixed by Marc Wilkinson from Flying) and 'Bring On The Goodtimes'.

Big Life

Record label established in 1987 by Jazz Summers, which saw its third release, 'Doctorin' The House' by Coldcut and Yazz, reach number 6 in the UK charts the same year. The follow-up and Big Life's fourth release, Yazz's solo effort 'The Only Way Is Up', reached the top of the UK charts, remaining there for five weeks. It was 1988's biggest selling single. Subsequent hits arrived from indie-dance stalwarts the Soup Dragons, plus dance artists Blue Pearl, the Orb and rappers De La Soul and Naughty By Nature (the latter two via a strong link with US rap base Tommy Boy). There was even room for distinctly non-dance acts like Mega City Four, though their biggest successes came with the Orb, until they departed, acrimoniously, in 1993. Big Life also manages Youth as a producer, and houses his own imprint, Butterfly Recordings.

Biosphere

The creation of former Bleep mainman Geir Jenssen (b. Norway). Jenssen had originally played in Bel Canto, with friends Anneli Decker and Nils Johansen, releasing two albums. Bleep's tally amounted to four 12-inch singles and a solitary album between 1989 and 1990. Three of those singles, 'Sure Be Glad When You're Dead', 'In Your System' and 'A Bite Of AMC' (the video to which was directed by Norwegian film-maker Casper Evenson, who subsequently became responsible for Biosphere's visuals) were all included on Bleep's debut set, *The North Pole By Submarine*, released in 1990. The album was recorded after spending endless nights shuddering in a tent, listening to short wave radio, while taking part in an archaeological expedition to the Arctic Circle. It was followed by 'The Launchpad', bringing Bleep a UK club hit with their final release. The 90s saw Jenssen inaugurate the Biosphere name, releasing the widely-acclaimed *Patashnik* set. However, he also found time to score a soundtrack to the Norwegian film *Evige Stjerner*, produced sounds and images for an exhibition at the Norwegian Ministry of Arts, and collaborated with ambient maestro Peter Namlook on an album, *The Fires Of Ork*. As if that wasn't enough, he also undertook another expedition in 1994, this time as part of an eight-man team scaling mountains in Nepal.

Albums: As Bleep: *The North Pole By Submarine* (SSR 1990). As Biosphere: *Patashnik* (1993). With Peter Namlook: *The Fire Of Ork* (Fax 1993).

Bizarre Inc.

Hardcore disco/fusion activists from Stafford, whose 1991 hit 'Playing With Knives' was a popular staple of many dancefloors (ending up, via a circuitous route, as '(Can You) Feel The Passion' by Blue Pearl). Other singles like 'X-Static', 'Plutonic' and 'Raise Me' followed. The membership included Andrew Meecham (b. c.1968), Dean Meredith (b. c.1969) and Carl Turner (b. c.1969), plus singers Angie Brown and Yvonne Yanni. Mark Archer, of Altern 8 fame, had also been a founding member. Their debut album was primarily a deep house experience, with the reliable remixing input of Todd Terry on 'I'm Gonna Get You' (featuring Angie Brown), which was only available as part of a limited edition CD version.

Album: *Energique* (Vinyl Solution 1992).

Björk

b. Björk Gudmundsdóttir, 21 October 1966, Reykjavic, Iceland. The former Sugarcubes vocalist, armed with a remarkable, keening vocal presence, has crossed over to huge success via her club-orientated material. The success of *Debut* culminated in awards for Best International Newcomer and Best International Artist at the 1994 BRIT Awards. However, she had made her 'debut' proper as far back as 1977, with an album recorded in her native territory as an 11-year old prodigy (including covers of pop standards by the Beatles and others). It was only the start of a prodigious musical legacy. Her next recording outfit were Tappi Takarrass (which apparently translates as 'Cork that bitch's arse'), who recorded two albums between 1981 and 1983. A more high profile role was afforded via work with KUKL, who introduced her to future Sugarcubes Einar Örn and Siggi. The group's two albums were issued in the UK on the Crass imprint. Björk returned to Iceland after the Sugarcubes six year career, partially to pay off debts, recording a first solo album in 1990 backed by a local be-bop group. She re-emerged in 1993 with *Debut* and a welter of more house-orientated material, including four hit singles. These chiefly came to prominence in the dance charts (Björk having placed a first toe in those waters with 808 State on *Ex:El*) via their big name remixers. The most important of these were Underworld and Bassheads

Black Dog

('Human Behaviour'), Black Dog ('Venus As A Boy'), Tim Simenon of Bomb The Bass ('Play Dead', which was also used on the soundtrack to *The Young Americans* cinema release and featured a distinctive Jah Wobble bass hook) and David Morales, Justin Robertson and Fluke ('Big Time Sensuality').

Albums: *Björk* (Fàlkinn 1977), *Debut* (One Little Indian 1993). With Trió Gudmundar: *Gling-Glò* (Smekkylesa 1990).

Black Box

One of the leading exponents of a wave of Italian House music that flourished on the dance floors of the late 80s, Black Box were made up of three Italian studio musos (Daniele Davoli, Mirko Limoni and Valerio Simplici), collectively known as Groove Groove Melody. They were based in the Regio D'Emillia area of Northern Italy, and made frequent use of singer Katrine (b. Catherine Quinol, Paris, France, of Guadelope extract). Simplici was a clarinet teacher and played in the La Scala Classical Music Orchestra in Milan. Davoli was a well known Italian club DJ (known therein as DJ Lelewel), largely at the Marabu Starlight Club, while Limoni was the computer and keyboard whizzkid of the trio and had previously engineered for Italian pop stars, Spagna. The Groove Groove Melody team were quickly established as one of the top two production outfits in Italian dance music, knocking out more than a dozen singles a year in their native country. Katrine was spotted by Spagna's guitarist at a club, and after introductions featured as vocalist on 'Ride On Time'. The single became the first of a series of Italian House records to cross over to the UK charts, staying at number 1 for six weeks in 1989. Controversy reigned when it was realised that the single had sampled the voice of singer Loleatta Holloway from the 'Love Sensation' single she made with Dan Hartman in the late 70s. A deal was eventually worked out with Salsoul (who owned the rights) as both companies benefited from 800,000 UK sales. The Groove Groove Melody team were also behind the production of Starlight's 'Numero Uno' and Mixmaster's 'Grand Piano', another prime example of 'Italo-house', and another crossover hit. Under seven or more pseudonyms, they turned out numerous further records. However, as Black Box their hits included 'I Don't Know Anybody Else', 'Everybody Everybody' (the last of the 'Ride On Time' trilogy), and 'Fantasy', a revamp of the Earth, Wind And Fire hit. They were also responsible for, among other remixes, ABC's 1991 comeback single, 'Say It'.

Album: *Dreamland* (RCA 1990), *Remixed Reboxed Black Box/Mixed Up* (RCA 1991).

Black Dog Productions

Secretive East London techno crew, communicating with the outside world by fax or modem, or their own computer billboard Black Dog Towers, and determinedly obscuring their identities (though these did emerge as the 90s progressed - the group being built around the trio of Ed Handley, Ken Downie and Andy Turner). Black Dog was formed in 1989, releasing their first record, the *Virtual* EP, a year later. The single 'Cost II' preceded their debut album, highlighting their subtle sense of songwriting propriety. Their initial bag was jazz house, later adding those same jazz tones to sets incorporating a leaning towards ambient techno that took viewers and reviewers by surprise, but still won them a legion of admirers. Among their most successful releases have been the *Vanttool* EP, which came out in 1992 on General Productions Recordings. Another alias was Bailil - under which they released the 'Darasight' 12-inch on Rising High. They would go on to tour with the Orb, while Handley released an EP on Carl Craig's Planet E label in Detroit. However, it is their relationship with Warp that has thus far offered the greatest rewards, and best documents their 'theoretical' approach to recorded sound.

Albums: *Temple Of Transparent Balls* (Warp 1993), *Bytes* (Warp 1993).

Blige, Mary J.

b. Bronx, New York, USA. After being promoted by her record company as 'The original queen of hip hop and soul', Mary J. Bilge has gone on to produce an impressive track record, her debut album selling over two million copies (many of the best songs being written for her by P.O.V.). The hip hop quotient was represented by bass-driven rhythms, the soul stylings including her affecting, cool voice. Guest appearances from rappers Grand Puba and Busta Rhymes were merely a bonus on this accomplished piece of work. When she journeyed to England for live shows in 1993 she was widely criticised for overpricing a set that was merely six songs long, but quality rather than quantity remains the keynote to Mary J's career.

Albums: *What's The 411?* (Uptown 1992), *What's The 411? - Remix Album* (Uptown 1993).

Blow

Essentially Gordon Matthewman, who came to prominence in 1988 with the club hit, 'Go' (alongside Adam Routh). Several follow-ups failed to ignite, and it was not until this confirmed rave addict's 1991 hit, 'Cutter', that he really pushed the Blow name back into the limelight again. Its popularity followed the mailing of twelve acetates to selected DJs, with the stock copy eventually emerging on Ten. The track's unusual use of trumpet (an instrument Matthewman had formerly played, alongside his brother, in Sade's backing band) and synthesizer endeared it to many, and it was also remixed by Altern 8. He continued to record into the mid-90s, and by 1994 had moved on to Nutbush/Parlophone for 'You'.

Blue Pearl

Blue Pearl cut themselves an amply proportioned slice of the commercial dance cake in the 90s with their 'Naked In The Rain' hit. Its incisive pop instincts were matched by an album, which featured cameos from Pink Floyd people Dave Gilmour and Rick Wright, alongside mainman Youth of Killing Joke and Brilliant, who wrote, played and produced. Just as the single had been, the set was notable for the attractive voice of Durga McBroom (who had previously toured with Pink Floyd), not least on a version of Kate Bush's 'Running Up That Hill'. Other singles like '(Can You) Feel The Passion' followed, but prompted a legal battle because it was based around a Youth remix of Bizarre Inc's 'Playing With Knives' which that group had rejected. In 1993 McBroom would cease to record exclusively with Blue Pearl, teaming up with German producer Johann Bley, the son of a Bavarian butcher, and British remixer Ben Watkins. Her debut single was 'Fire Of Love' on Logic, based on the Psychick Warriors Ov Gaia standard, 'Jungle High'. On her trial separation, McBroom would comment: 'Being in a group is like a marriage. If you're married to the same person for a long time and you divorce you start dating again. So I've had a lot of good dates recently'.
Album: *Blue Pearl* (WAU! Mr Modo 1991).

Bomb The Bass

Techno dance outfit who are a collective front for Tim Simenon (b. c.1968, Brixton, London, England; of Malay Chinese and Scottish parents). After attending a course in studio engineering he shot to prominence in 1988 with 'Beat Dis', which went Top 5, where the subsequent album followed. Both 'Megablast' and 'Say A Little Prayer' were also Top 10 hits, the latter featuring Maureen Walsh, who would go on to her own solo career, beginning with a cover of Sister Sledge's 'Thinking Of You' for Urban. Simenon then worked with Neneh Cherry (producing her

hits 'Buffalo Stance' and 'Manchild'). After completing work on his new studio he took up production duties for an album by Prince sidekick Cat. Co-production on Adamski's 'Killer' and the Seal single 'Crazy' followed. However, feeling aggrieved at the lack of credit and financial recompense he gained from these ventures, he returned to Bomb The Bass. His timing was less than apt, as the 1991 Gulf War made continued use of the name indelicate. He reverted to his own name instead for the single 'Love So True', co-written with bass player Doug Wimbush (Sugarhill Gang, Tackhead) and vocalist Loretta Heywood. By this time he was also working extensively with guitarist Kenji Suzuki, in addition to a myriad of guest vocalists. Bomb The Bass returned in 1994 with a new album while Simenon unveiled his own label, Stoned Heights, through Island.
Albums: *Into The Dragon* (Rhythm King 1988), *Unknown Territory* (Rhythm King 1991), *Clear* (1994).

Bolland, CJ

Techno maestro Bolland (b. Christian Jay Bolland, Tyneside, England) moved with his family to Antwerp, Belgium at an early age, making his own music as a precocious three year old. Widely respected on the Euro techno circuit, Bolland works principally at the R&S label, specialising in hard edged rave tunes. He has recorded as Sonic Solution ('Music') and provided the *Ravesignals 1, 2 and 3* EPs. However, *The 4th Sign* in 1993 saw him dispense with his other former *nom de plumes* (Pulse, the Project, Space Opera). It included the new dancefloor techno anthem 'Carmague'. His remixes include Human Resource's 'Dominator' and Baby Ford's 'In Your Blood'.
Album: *The 4th Sign* (R&S 1993).

Bones, Frankie

A popular New York DJ (though he was once sacked from a venue for playing Lil Louis's 'French Kissing' against house policy), Bones, a regular visitor to the UK, has completed a number of remix and production projects, several in association with Tommy Musto. His own career has included hits like 1988's 'Just As Long As I Got You'. He also records as Liquid Oxygen, Break Boys ('And The Break Goes On') and Looney Tunes ('Just As Long As I've Got You' and 'Another Place Another Time' for Nu Groove, which also housed his 'Sex 4 Daze' as Lake Errie) and ran the Pyramix label, which housed Mister C's recording, 'Don't Stop', among others. 'I make records to get a job DJing. It's my intention to be one of the best DJs of the 90s' he maintained.

Selected album: *Dance Madness And The Brooklyn Groove* (RCA 1990).

Boogie Beat Records

Record label whose A&R voice is Kid Andy, which has become one of the most popular homes to hardcore/jungle since its inception in February 1992. Andy, a former pirate radio DJ, is joined by George Power, administrative director and engineer/co-producer Ben Wilson as the nucleus of the team. The label's discography kicked off with Order 2 Move's 'Rizla Bass', before following with material by Audio Illusion, Intellect, Dance On Arrival, Ministers Of Dance, Technicians Flingdown, D-Code, Mixmaster Max, Trance 4 Mist, Charl E, Agent 24K, Weekend Rush, Sonic The Dreadlocks and several other, faintly ridiculous *nom de plumes*.

Bortolotti, Gianfranco

One of dance music's most colourful ambassadors, Bortolotti is the name behind many an 'Italo-house' classic through his auspices as manager of Media Records. Bortolotti had originally found himself in the DJ world to supplement his university days. He was initially influenced by DJ Pierre (not the US version), learning his craft from him, and when the latter's career began, actually helped in distributing records. His involvement grew until he too recouped the rewards of a couple of minor hit singles, reinvesting the money in a home-studio and founding the Media label. Since when he has never looked back - indeed he now owns no less than ten studios. His main complex in Brescia, North Italy, is built on the Motown/SAW principle, churning out hits at a rate other factories ship beans. Capella's breakthrough hit, 'Heylom Halib', introduced the formula of insistent rhythm, zany samples, tinkling piano and memorable choruses/catchphrases. This in turn predicted the wave of Italo-house hits (Black Box's 'Ride On Time', Starlight's 'Numero Uno', Mixmaster's 'Grand Piano') that dominated the 1989 dance scene. The rollercoaster has continued unabated ever since. Whatever the names employed: 49ers ('Touch Me'), Fargetta ('The Music Is Movin''), East Side Beat, Clubhouse, Clock, DJ Professor, RAF - the hits have followed with unremitting haste. Just as Berry Gordy might have envisioned had he enjoyed access to the technology, the Media set-up is strictly business-like, with three main producers (DJ Pierre, DJ Professor or RAF) working on their own floor. Each record is mixed between 15 and 20 times to suit individual territories. It is an astoundingly efficient and at times frightening economic approach to making music.

Selected album: Various: *Power Of The Media* (Media 1994).

Botany 5

Botany 500 were formed by ex-Juggernauts (one single, 'Throw Yourself Under The Monstrous Wheels Of The Rock 'n' Roll Industry As It Approaches Destruction') vocalist Gordon Kerr (b. Sterling, Scotland) and David Galbraith. Their early use of ambient textures along with funk and jazz interludes was persuasive and pleasant. A debut single for Supreme, 'Bully Beef', even featured live string accompaniment. Kerr split from Galbraith in 1989, winning a Tennent's Live! talent competition run by Glasgow's Ca Va studio. He signed to Virgin, replacing his partner with Jason Robertson (guitar) and Stevie Christie (keyboards). The name was shortened to Botany 5 when a lawsuit was threatened from the American company Botany 500, responsible for wardrobe on television fare such as *Kojak*. A single, 'Love Bomb', preceded Botany 5's debut album, which was significantly ahead of its time; predicting the chill house tones of the Orb, Aphex Twin etc. It was created as a deliberate antidote to the excess of the Summer Of Love: 'Our album's for when kids come home from raves. No crazy, out of hand stuff. More artistic; slow, mellow, subdued...quiet'. The trio were joined for live extravaganzas by former Orange Juice drummer Zeke Manyika and Paul Weller associate, Carmel, in order to provide more organic backing.

Album: *Into The Night* (Virgin 1991).

Bottom Line Records

Brooklyn, New York label, established in November 1991 with the release of Devastating's 'Givin' It 2 U'. From its base in Coney Island the label is run by expatriate Moscow legend Ed 'The Red' Goltsmann, with his wife Nancy Kay (additional help is often provided by Nelson Roman). Together they are responsible for producing all the tracks on the varied and much admired Bottom Line catalogue. The duo had originally worked as live musicians at parties, clubs and wedding receptions, and first recorded for New Jersey's Vista Sounds (Intro's 'Under Your Spell' and two releases from Red Follies). Even though neither was particularly familiar with the New York club scene, they have gone on to produce a succession of releases which remain highly sought-after on the dance scene. Their biggest successes have included Tammy Banks' 'My Life', and Flow's 'Another Time'. They also record as the aforementioned Devastating ('Givin' It 2 U' and 'Wherever You Are Right Now'), Hearsay ('Move Yo Body, Work Yo Body'), Sample Minded ('Eternity', 'The Sounds Of Redness'), ODC ('My Mind Is Going'), Fast Wheels ('I Never Dreamed It Could Be Like This'), Passion Is Fashion ('You Make Me Want To Love You') and Secret Lovers ('Do Me Right'). They also continued to record as Red Follies ('We Will Survive', 'Sweet Love'), using the vocals of MJ White. More recent productions have been distinguished by material like 'Tonite', a simple jazzy tune credited to Jerzey Boy, or Nelson's 'Paradise'.

Bouncer, Peter

So named because of his previous employment as nightclub security, Peter Bouncer first waved to the nation via Shut Up And Dance's number 2 smash, 'Ravin', I'm Ravin''. He was formerly a devotee of reggae, and a popular dancehall DJ with Unity Sounds. He made his solo debut in a very different vein, that of unrelenting hardcore, on 'So Here I Come'. His forbidding reputation preceded him, but his soulful voice was stretched too thin over the throbbing grooves. Described in the press as the 'Sinatra of hardcore', he has yet to establish a significant audience in this field or any other.

Boy's Own

Once simply an off-the-wall football magazine, Boy's Own has grown to be one of the most prominent and curious of all England's labels. Started by Andy Weatherall, Terry Farley and Steve Mayes in 1986, the magazine picked up on the burgeoning club and fashion scene. At the same time Weatherall began working as a DJ, notably at Shoom during 1988, and was subsequently invited to remix Primal Scream's 'Loaded'. It won him great notoriety, as did Farley's remix of the Farm's 'Stepping Stone'. Both productions were credited to Boy's Own, and a label of the same name was inaugurated with the financial backing of London Records in August 1990. The first release was Bocca Juniors' (Weatherall and Farley's own group) 'Raise (63 Steps To Heaven)' - which maintained their links to the terraces by namechecking the Argentinian football club. The label was managed by Stephen Hall, and boasted the input of several additional club 'names' - Peter Heller (see Farley And Heller), Darren Price (who also records as part of Centuras), Darren Emerson and Rocky & Diesel (X Press 2) among them. Junior Boy's Own was set up after problems with London, to cater for more limited pressings, destined to appeal to genuine dance enthusiasts. However, records like those by Fire Island ('Fire Island', 'There But For The Grace Of God'), X-Press 2 ('Muzik Express', 'London X-Press', 'Say What') Lemon Interrupt ('Big Mouth') and their alter-egos Underworld (the hugely influential 'Mmm...Skyscraper, I Love You') have all contrastingly become popular, often selling out of their original pressings long before demand has been sated. Andy Weatherall had by this time moved over to start his own Sabres Of Paradise projects, as Hall describes: 'We're all very different people and it only takes so long before everyone gets fucked off with each other. Andrew, God bless him, got fucked off first'.

Selected album: Various: *The Junior Boy's Own Collection* (Junior Boy's Own 1994).

Brand New Heavies

Simon Bartholomew and Andy Levy are the central duo behind Ealing, London band the Brand New Heavies, alongside drummer Jan Kincaid and keyboardist Ceri Evans. They had already suffered one aborted deal with Acid Jazz who tried to launch them as a 'rare groove' outfit, before they hooked up with US label Delicous Vinyl. The latter's management put them in touch with N'Dea Davenport (b. Georgia, USA), who had previously provided backing vocals for George Clinton, Bruce Willis and appeared in videos for Young MC and Madonna's former band the Breakfast Club. Word spread throughout the US of their liaison, and soon hip hop teams picked up on the vibe, which was latterly transported back to the UK. They were sampled heavily on a number of early 90s rap records, before inviting members of that community to provide guest raps on their second album, *Heavy Rhyme Experience*. These included Black Sheep, Gang Starr, Grand Puba, Main Source, Kool G. Rap, Ed O.G., Master Ace, Tiger and Pharcyde. Their huge success in the US has managed to compensate more than adequately for any failure to crack the domestic scene. Ceri Evans left the group in January 1992 to undertake production work for Alison Limerick and Galliano, recording solo as Sunship ('Muthafuckin''/'The 13th Key', for Dorado).

Albums: *Brand New Heavies* (Acid Jazz 1990), *Heavy Rhyme Experience* (ffrr 1992), *Brother Sister* (ffrr 1994).

Braxton, Toni

US-born singer from Maryland who, with her four sisters, signed to Arista in 1990 as the Braxtons. It was their 'The Good Life' single which brought them to the attention of producers LA and Babyface, who provided her with solo successes like 'Another Sad Love Song' and 'You Mean The

World To Me'. Though she has been widely described as the 'new Whitney Houston' (a fate which befalls all too many female vocalists), her considerable vocal talent has found an appreciative audience in garage and house circles. Her debut album also shifted more than two million copies. Album: *Toni Braxton* (Arista 1994).

Brothers In Rhythm

Steve Anderson and David Seaman are one of the UK house scene's most adventurous and popular remixing teams, who came to prominence with startling revisions of yesteryear like Heaven 17's 'Temptation', or Frankie Goes To Hollywood's 'Welcome To The Pleasuredome'. Recent work has included engagements with Sabrina Johnson ('Peace'), Pet Shop Boys, Janet Jackson, Secret Life and Judy Cheeks ('Reach'). They also earned the honour of being the first British team to remix Michael Jackson ('Who Is It?'). Their own work has included singles like 'Such A Good Feeling' (remixed by Sasha) and they have also recorded under the alias Brothers Love Dub ('Ming's Incredible Disco Machine'), and as Creative Thieves, for Nasty Rhythm. Seaman is also a leading light behind the DMC/Stress empire, and has signed a publishing deal with MCA.

Brown, Bobby

b. Robert Beresford Brown, 5 February 1969, Boston, Massachusetts, USA. A former member of New Edition, Brown has emerged in the late 80s as the king of New Jack Swing. Like many of the genre's stars, Brown is not gifted with either huge ability or personality, yet he has stamped his authority on the dance scene via a series of immaculately presented crossover singles. On his debut album he was joined by the likes of Larry Blackmon and John Luongo, but it was the follow-up set, and the seamless production technique of Teddy Riley and LA & Babyface, which pushed him high in the charts. Cuts like the US number 1-peaking 'My Perogative' were infectious, irresistible dance workouts, confirming Brown's presence as a commercial hot potato. He would marry Whitney Houston, and has appeared in film roles including a cameo in *Ghostbusters II*. Albums: *King Of Stage* (MCA 1986), *Don't Be Cruel* (MCA 1988), *Dance...Ya Know It!* (MCA 1989), *Bobby* (MCA 1992).

B12

Ilford, Essex-based Michael Golding (a computer expert) and Steven Rutter (who also holds down a bank job), whose singles previous to their album for Warp were credited to alter egos Red Cell and Musicology (and released on their own B12 label). Another pseudonym is C-Metric. When *Electro Soma* arrived as the fourth installment in Warp's Artificial Intelligence series, it did not disappoint. The intention was to try to create the feel of pure, timeless techno: 'Derrick May, Juan Atkins and the rest of the guys started something, that I suppose we feel obliged to continue'. However, as they were keen to point out, this was hardly conventional dance music ('I don't believe anyone's every played it in a club'). Album: *Electro Soma* (Warp 1993).

Bukem, LTJ

His name taken from the famous line in *Hawaii Five-O* ('Book 'em, Danno'), while the LTJ prefix is an Italian version of 'DJ', Bukem was widely credited as giving hardcore/breakbeat music a new lease of life in the 90s. By developing his own rhythm patterns, instead of merely recycling or layering samples, he was able to create a more satisfying and varied palate for his recordings. This was born out of his own frustration at not being able to find enough good records to play out with. The early releases which established his name were 'Demon's Theme' and 'Apollo 2', on his own Looking Good label. He went on to produce for Grooverider, Goldie and Synthetic Records, and worked for the UMR imprint ('Logical Progression', 1992).

Bump

Bump is an umbrella name for the activities of DJ Mark Auerbach and studio boffin and engineer Steve Travell. The two initially met at the 1991 New Music Seminar, where they were overheard congratulating each other on their work. They swapped addresses before returning to their 'day' jobs - Mark DJing with the Slam boys and working with Adamski, while Steve launched his group, the Orange. When that venture ground to a halt he got back in touch with Mark. Under their joint auspices they recorded 'I'm Rushin''. Convinced they had found the perfect meter, they sent out promo copies to prominent DJs, pressed on their own Good Boy Records. Sampling a vocal line from Sir James' 'Special', it saw a stock release on the Strictly Rhythm imprint. In the wake of its success they were invited to provide remixes, notably transforming David D'or's 'Yad Anough', also working with Sue Chaloner, Supereal, Soundsource and the Reese Project. In 1992 they noted: 'We're reaching the threshold where we can be remixers for the rest of our lives if we want to'. However, as Auerbach added, there were drawbacks: 'There's a lot of pressure to turn shit into gems'. Their style has been desribed as progressive house, though this is not a bracket they themselves are happy with.

Bush Records

Label co-owned by Eric Powell and Eric Gooden (aka Sweet Mercy and Temper Temper respectively). Previously they had been behind Manchester's Blip empire (First Offence and their own projects). They were also responsible for discovering Melanie Williams, whose vocals graced Sub Sub's chart foray before going solo. Bush began life as a 'trance-house' label whose style predicted the progressive boom. Releases included Trinity's self-titled debut, and a remix of T-Coy's 'Carino'. The team later collaborated with Felix Da Housecat for 'Thee Lite'. Felix had actually tracked the duo down after hearing their earlier releases, like Rising's 'Lose Yourself' and the Sandman's 'Psychosis' (the label's first release, the b-side to which featured Jean Michel Jarre). 1994 brought fresh material from Dave Clarke ('Red 2').

C

C+C Music Factory

Basically a production team comprising Robert Clivillés (b. c.1960, New York, USA) and David Cole (b. c.1962, Tennessee, USA), who first recorded as 2 Puerto Ricans, A Black Man And A Dominican with 'Do It Properly' on their own label in 1987. As C+C Music Factory they broke through into the singles chart with their number 3-peaking UK hit, 'Gonna Make You Sweat (Everybody Dance Now)', in 1990. Though this was credited to C+C Music Factory featuring Freedom Williams (b. c.1966, a rapper who also appeared on records by New Kids On The Block and Grace Jones), the duo were solely in charge of matters, hiring vocalists and musicians and programming the backbeat. Over the next two years guest singers would include Zelma Davis (b. c.1967, Liberia, whose contribution was lip-synched, the actual vocal provided by Martha Wash of the Weather Girls), Q Unique and Deborah Cooper (ex-Fatback Band, Change). Though they scored six further Top 40 hits during 1991-1992, only 'Things That Make You Go Hmmm', again jointly credited with Williams, would breach the Top 10. It would later be widely aired during a television advertising campaign.

They have also worked as remixers on songs by Seduction, Sandee and Lisa Lisa & Cult Jam, examples of which were contained on their 1992 album, credited under their own names. Their first remix had been Natalie Cole's 'Pink Cadillac', which, in drastically altered form, broke the US Top 5.

Albums: *Gonna Make You Sweat* (Columbia 1991). As Clivillés And Cole: *Greatest Remixes, Vol. 1* (Columbia 1992).

Cake Records

Birmingham label run by DJ Dick (Richard Whittingham), Nigel Blunt and Groove Corporation. The set-up evolved from an 'illegal, irregular, underground little party called Cake'. From there it became a weekly event entitled Breathless, before all the parties involved pooled their resources to form Cake. Each, however, maintains their own individual profiles, with support from the others. DJ Dick's pet project, the Original Rockers, had originally been remixed by Groove Corporation, which led to them joining forces. 'We have a simple manifesto - which is to put out great records, lose no money, and do what comes naturally'. Important releases so far include Original Rocker's 'Push Push', Groove Corporation and Bim Sherman's 'Need More Love (In The Ghetto)' and both parties collaboration, 'Stoned'. Other signings included Bite Time Crime (hip hop) and Sylophonic.

Cajmere

b. Curtis A. Brown. One of Chicago's more memorable efforts of 1993, Cajmere, together with vocalist Dajae (real name Karen), broke through with the club hits 'Brighter Days' and the ragtime-themed 'U Got Me Up'. Cajmere had originally planned to be an engineer, though his degree course took him into chemistry. He soon packed it all in to serve his musical ambitions, hanging around with local house producers and cutting his first tracks, like 'The Percolator'. Influenced by the UK's A Guy Called Gerald as much as the major players in Chicago house, he settled on a successful distillation of diva-vocals and breakdowns. Prior to his work with Dajae, he was best known for his collaborations with Lidell Townsell on 'Get With You', plus the *Underground Goodies* EP for Clubhouse. He also remixed 'Feel It' for Italians Workin' Happily. He runs his own record label, Cajual, along with offshoot Relief, on which he is aiming to develop new talent. He has already released an album by Dajae and 12-inches like 'Preacherman', which owed an obvious debt to one of his idols, Lil' Louis.

Dina Carroll

Capella

Capella scored a major and somewhat unexpected success in 1989 when their 'Heylom Halib' crashed the UK Top 20 (number 11). It was the calling card from one Gianfranco Bortolotti's Media Records empire, which would soon become *the* dominant force in Euro dance/techno. Although their founder would continue to release a slew of records under various umbrella names, he has retained that of Capella as his priority act. Capella's first chart entry had come the year before, when 'Push The Beat' was a minor hit. Bortolotti subsequently employed two Londoners, Rodney Bishop and Kelly Overett, as full-time members of the project. They continued to score hits throughout the 90s, most notable of which was the number 25-peaking 'Take Me Away', licensed to PWL in the UK. This featured the guest vocals of Loretta Holloway - ironic in that Capella's success instigated the Italo-house scene, the biggest commercial hit of which was Black Box's 'Ride On Time' - on which Holloway's vocals were sampled and because of which litigation ensued. Hits through 1993 continued with the typically immediate and anthemic 'U Got 2 Know'. They followed it with the similarly styled but equally successful 'U Got 2 Let The Music' and 'Move On Baby', before the advent of their debut album. Capella are a pop dance duo who specialise in unpretentious, hook-heavy synth pop, and are unlikely to change the winning formula.
Album: *U Got 2 Know* (Internal 1994).

Carroll, Dina

b. Newmarket, Suffolk, England, Dina Carroll's place of birth could actually be a contentious issue bearing in mind it took place in the back of a taxi speeding towards Newmarket Hospital. The daughter of a US serviceman and British mother, Carroll spent a few years in Philadelphia, but was largely brought up in the UK. Her soulful voice (along the lines of Evelyn King) brought her to the attention of Streetsounds, where she auditioned and was rewarded with session work. She released 'People All Around The World' on Jive in 1989 as Deana Carroll. before reverting to the accepted spelling Dina for a cover of 'Walk On By'. 1990 saw her singing Quartz's 'It's Too Late'. Following their split, Carroll nearly gave up on the music business, but A&M heard some of her work and signed her as a solo act, which she helped to establish with the hit singles 'It's Too Late' and 'Ain't No Man'.
Album: *So Close* (A&M 1993).

Carter, Derrick

One of the biggest noises in new Chicago house, Carter was described by Richie Hawtin as 'America's last true underground DJ' in 1994. That seemed likely to change with his debut release, *The Sound Patrol* EP, on the local Organico label (Diatribe etc.), which attracted rave reviews. A second EP, *The Music*, was another slice of pure, unaffected house. It included excellent cuts like 'An Open Secret', which utilised Chaka Khan's 'Ain't Nobody' at its base. Carter continues to work in a 'DJ commune' near the downtown skyscraper precincts of Chicago, equipped with a built-in studio. He had started life as part of the experimental outfit Symbols And Instruments, who scored an underground techno success for Network. He was only 16 at the time, and would go on to a scholarship at engineering college MIT. Following the EPs he embarked on a project for David Holmes' Exploding Plastic Inevitable label.

Chaloner, Sue

In her youth Chaloner was awarded a scholarship by the BBC and attended a school for the performing arts, going on to spend several years in the stage production of *Hair*. In the mid-70s she went on to become half of the Spooky And Sue duo (who scored a novelty hit with 'Swinging On A Star'). By the early 90s she had become a hit with the club cognoscenti via 'Answer My Prayer' and 'I Wanna Thank You', with productions offered by the 3 Man Island/Band Of Gypsies team. 'I Wanna Thank You' namechecked black leaders Nelson Mandella, Marcus Garvey, Martin Luther King and Ghandi. She has been resident in Amsterdam for over twenty years, and appears live backed by her Soul Train team.

Champion Records

The UK's oldest independent dance label, Champion is a North London-based operation headed by Mel Medalie with A&R support from Johnnie Walker. Formed in 1985, a first success arrived with Spanky's 'Oh Baby' from that year. Subsequent hits included Kartoon Krew's 'Inspector Gadget' and Rene And Angela's 'Secret Rendezvous' reissue, before the label really broke big with Whistle's '(Nothin' Serious) Just Buggin'' (over 250,000 sales). As Champion developed they moved away from licensing, which had previously been their main strategy, in to developing some home-grown talent. The most important of these was Sybil, who first recorded for the label in 1986 with 'Falling In Love'. 1987 brought 'Let Yourself Go', *Record Mirror*'s number 1 dance tune of that year (though its commercial performance was somewhat disappointing). As Champion moved into the 90s the best examples of their work included 'Never Give Up' by Todd Terry Project (Terry having had much of his late 80s output housed in Britain via Champion), Kelly Charles' 'Falling In Love' and Dee Dee Brave's 'So Many Roads' and 'There Is So Much' (all 1991). In 1992 they licensed tracks like 'See The Day' (Ann Consuelo), 'Take Me Higher' (Hysteria) and 'Higher Degree' (Blast) from Sweden's Swemix/B-Tech set-up. They opened a New York office the same year, picking up distribution for labels like 111 East and Madhouse Records. In the meantime they continued to license from foreign labels, including Belgium's Dance Opera (picking up Atomizer 2's 'Liberty And Freedom'). Further big garage hits in 1994 arrived with Kristine W (whom Medalie had spotted playing the Las Vegas circuit) with 'Feel What You Want', and Third Nation's 'I Believe'.

Selected albums: Various: *Ultimate Trax Volume 1-3* (Champion 1986-1988, double albums).

Cheeks, Judy

b. Florida, Miami, USA. Of mixed black American and Cherokee ancestry, Cheeks is the daughter of gospel singer Rev. Julius Cheeks, namedropped all the time by James Brown, Otis Redding and others as a pivotal influence in the development of black music. She grew up in Miami where her godfather was Sam Cooke, who once plucked her from the front row of a 6,000 audience and sang the rest of the set to her while cradling her in his arms. Before her solo career began in earnest her voice had been employed by Tina Turner, Jon Bulter, Betty Wright, Leon Ware, Georgio Moroder and Harold Faltermayer, and she has long been a close friend of Stevie Wonder. Indeed, her recording career stretches back to the mid-70s, when she recorded a debut album with Ike and Tina Turner. She subsequently moved to Europe and Ariola records, her first record for whom, 'Mellow Lovin'', was an international success. After she had traversed the language barrier, she became a major German star, appearing in several movies and hosting a television game show with a hamster called Willie. She came to England in 1987, though a singular album for Polydor was never released outside of mainland Europe. Her career lapsed until she finally began recording demos again in the 90s. Their was interest from the PWL stable, but she eventually settled on Positiva, a deal cemented by the release of 'So In Love', written by China Burton. Remixes from Frankie Foncett and Sasha added greatly to the cult status of this minor garage classic. The follow-up, 'Reach',

capitalised on this and her tours of select dance venues, and this time employed the Brothers In Rhythm production team. She subsequently worked with Nigel Lowis (producer of Eternal and Dina Carroll) on tracks for her first Positiva album. Album: *No Outsiders* (Polydor 1988).

Chimes

UK soul/dance trio originating in Edinburgh, Scotland in 1981, when they were initially put together by Mike Pedan (keyboards and bass) and the much-travelled James Locke (ex-Heartbeat, Rhythm Of Life, Bathers, Hipsway, Indian Givers; keyboards and drums). The pair had met when they were backing former Parliament keyboard player Bernie Worell at a local club. Deciding to form their own group they set about writing material and auditioning female singers, eventually settling on Pauline Henry in 1987. With the duo's desperation mounting, her successful audition was held over the telephone, after which she was flown up from London for sessions. After signing to CBS in 1988 they finally released their debut single a year later. '1-2-3' was produced by Jazzie B (from Soul II Soul), a group to whom the Chimes were frequently compared. Their biggest UK breakthrough came in 1990 when they covered U2's 'I Still Haven't Found What I'm Looking For'. Apparently approved of by Bono, the cover was chosen when the band heard Henry singing it in the studio. Aided by an appearance on the mainstream television show *Wogan*, it eventually went Top 5 in both the UK and US. The boys also contributed to old friend Paul Haig's solo LP during 1990, and produced several other artists. Subsequent minor hits included 'True Love' and 'Love Comes To Mind', before Henry left for a solo career midway through sessions for a second album.

Album: *The Chimes* (CBS 1990).

Citybeat Records

Dance label which grew out of brothers Tim and Chris Palmer's Groove Records, Tim forming Citybeat in 1986. Supported by Beggars Banquet, their first release was 'Slap Your Back' by Exception in March 1986 (which went on to feature in the soundtrack to *Mona Lisa*), while the first signed act would be Cairo. Citybeat was also the home to the great rap track 'It Takes Two' by Rob Base and E/Z Rock. Their major personnel in the 90s included Dream Frequency, Awesome 3 ('Dont Go') and Musto & Bones. Citybeat was also the proprietor label to XL, which in some ways eclipsed the mother label in terms of commercial fortune with the advent of techno/rave. However,

Citybeat did beat the rush to license Doop's 'Doop', which bounded all the way to number 1 in the UK.

Clail, Gary, And The On U Sound System

The On U Sound System features a plethora of musicians drawn from Tackhead, Roots Radics, Akabu, Dub Syndicate and others. It was officially launched in 1980 by Adrian Sherwood for a one-off LP by the New Age Steppers, who comprised various members of the Slits, Pop Group and Aswad. The second album was by the Mothmen (who are now the rhythm section for Simply Red), and over the years an impressive roster of collaborative productions took shape. These include works from the likes of Dr Pablo, Prince Far I, Tackhead, Mark Stewart and the Mafia, Dub Syndicate and African Headcharge. Clail's bombastic vocal delivery was honed when he grew up in a predominantly black neighbourhood given rhythm by 'Toasting' Jamaican locals. He is of Irish descent, though his parents moved to Bristol when he was very young. After spells as a scaffolder and runner for the criminal fraternity, he joined Tackhead and became further enmeshed with the On U Sound team. 'Human Nature' was something of a freak hit in 1991. The original intention to sample Billy Graham's 1958 speech of the same name over the beat was rejected by his representatives, forcing Clail to deputise. It also owed a great deal to Paul Oakenfold's production, and his knowledge of the dance clubs. His accommodation from On U Sound's resident misfit in to pop star designate was quite remarkable. He still works mainly as a producer and mixer, and in the long term wants to emulate Sherwood by providing new talent with a forum for exposure. In interviews Clail constantly stressed that he is but one cog in a 32 person music making machine.
Album: *Emotional Hooligan* (On-U-Sound 1991).

Clarke, Loni

b. New York, USA. Clarke originally sang in Harlem church choirs before joining with Luther Vandross in Listen My Brother, eventually striking out solo. She made her recording debut in 1981 for West End Records, scoring a minor dance hit with 'Let's Go Dancing'. She returned to a singing career in the 90s, making the Top 40 in the UK with 'Rushing', and scoring a further success with the Lem Springsteen/John Ciafone written and produced 'U'. Now signed to A&M, the disc saw remixes by hot club acts Mood II Swing and K Klass.

Cleveland City Records

Wolverhampton, Midlands, England-based label, housed in the city's Ruby Red record shop, itself formerly home to the Plan B and Ruby Red imprints. The label was set up to feature local Midlands acts on a first person basis, and has expanded rapidly, helmed by A&R man Lee Arnold. Their debut release was Chubby Chunks' 'Testaments 1, 2 and 3', a big-seller later remixed by Judge Jules and the Jungle Brothers. There is little of the preciousness usually associated with premier dance labels, as the small print on each release indicates: 'DJ warning - Music Is Fun'. Among their best received releases so far have been Direct 2 Disc ('Don't Stop', 'Excuse Me', *The Backstab* EP), Dig The New Breed ('Who's Number 1'), and Herbal Hand ('B Line'/'Come To It', 'Tripped'). Subsidiary labels cropped up early in the label's development, namely Cleveland City Blues (swingbeat and garage) and Cleveland City Imports (Alex Party etc.). Cleveland City Blue brought the empire an immediate success when Italian artist Tony Di Bart's 'The Real Thing' scaled the charts in May 1994. It will be interesting to see what part such widespread exposure will play in the development of this young label.

Coco Steel And Lovebomb

Brighton-based combo who scored in 1992 with the house/techno crossover hit, 'Feel It'. It was inspired by the Zap club's smouldering Saturday nights, a venue run by Chris 'Coco' Miller. It was followed by the 12-minute 'You Can't Stop The Groove', compiled so that it could be played as a whole or segmented by DJs, which included a sample of Hamilton Bohannon from 'Let's Start The Dance'. The rest of the band numbered Craig Woodrow (Lovebomb) and Lene (Steel). 1993's 'Work It Tough Bitch' was championed by Junior Vasquez at the Sound Factory in New York, as the trio's reputaton grew. Mellor maintains that CS&A is 'more of an idea than a fixed project', and continues to edit a specialist DJ magazine. 'I was writing about music and rapidly becoming one of those music journo bores that listen to a record and gripes 'I can do that', or 'I'd edit that there'. So I thought rather than moaning about it I'd get on with it'. Mellor also went on to remix for Underworld, Wild Planet and others.
Album: *It!* (Warp 1994).

Cola Boy

aka Peterborough artist Andrew Naughtie. Cola Boy's '7 Ways To Love' was mailed out as a white label with a press release saying the record had been financed by a Hong Kong teenager who had sold his collection of rare Coke bottles to subsidise the project - one Jesse Chin, who was acknowledged on the sleeve of the stock release. Some people continue to give credence to the story to this day. Naughtie had previously worked with Bob Stanley and Peter Wiggs in the early days of St Ettienne, who remixed the track. '7 Ways To Love' would become a big crossover hit, after being widely bootlegged, with its subtle vocal contribution from Janey Lee Grace. The follow-up was 'He Is Cola', which featured Burundi drumming.

Coldcut

Once innovative but recently largely discarded by dance cognoscenti, Coldcut represents the work of UK DJ/producers Jonathan Moore and Matt Black. Influenced by US stars Double D and Steinski, they made their first recording in 1987, 'Say Kids What Time Is It?', improvised in their kitchen with a box of records and a four-track cassette recorder. A sample of the track would later be used on MARRS' 'Pump Up The Volume'. Coldcut continued on their way as an acid house remix team, bringing their eclectic taste, and widely varied record collections, to the genre. Their breakthrough came with a remix of Eric B and Rakim's 'Paid In Full', and they also gave Yazz her debut hit with 'Doctorin' The House', a UK number 6 hit in 1988. Further success followed with another reggae singer, Junior Reid, when 'Stop This Crazy Thing' made number 21 the same year. Coldcut's debut album featured a then unknown Lisa Stansfield on 'People Hold On', and ever more unlikely, the nasal sneer of the Fall's Mark E. Smith on '(I'm) In Deep'. The duo founded their own labels, Ahead Of Our Time/Ninja Tunes, which initially operated through Big Life, though it was then switched to Arista. That label dropped them from their roster in 1994. Nowadays the group partially sustains itself via the process of dubbing rave videos, having already produced video games in association with the Hardwire software house. They also joined with computer programmers Rob Pepperall and Miles Visman as Hex, a multi-media trance-techno collaboration for the CD-Rom generation.
Albums: *What's That Noise?* (AOOT/Big Life 1989), *Some Like It Cold* (AOOT/Big Life 1990), *Philosophy* (Arista 1993).

Cook, Norman

b. Quentin Cook, 31 July 1963. A former member of the Housemartins, following their split Cook returned to Brighton and his old job as a DJ, and released 'Blame It On The Bassline' under his own name. Vocals on the a-side were provided by future Beats International member MC Wildski, while another future collaborator, Billy Bragg, wrote the b-side, 'Won't Talk About It'. A second single, 'For Spacious Lies', followed. Beats International shot to prominence in the UK when 'Dub Be Good To Me' hit number 1 in the UK charts in 1990. Cook was already heavily in demand as a remixer for a variety of projects, ranging from Aztec Camera, James Brown, Nitro Deluxe and Eric B. And Rakim to the Jungle Brothers, often using the title The Mighty Dub Cats. Another nom de plume was Pizzaman, under which he propelled Jon Pleased Wimmin's 'Passion' and helmed several other productions. By this time Cook had long foregone the Beats International banner in order to put together a new band, Freak Power. However, the single 'most likely to' in 1994 was Pizzaman's 'Tripping On Sunshine'.

Cooltempo

One of the most prolific and identifiable dance music labels in the UK, Cooltempo is backed by the muscle of Chrysalis records. The label was formed by Pete Edge in 1984. 'We started off with Change, and BB&Q, then Doug E. Fresh ('The Show'). Then we went on and did a lot of rap music, Eric B, UTFO. Then we got involved with house music'. Among their many notable late 80s/early 90s acts have been Shara Nelson, Guru/Gang Starr, Arrested Development and Brand New Heavies. By the early 90s they had become a fixture of the dance music charts with hits like 'Always' (Urban Soul), 'Everybody Jump' (DJ Power) and 'Don't Let It Show On Your Face' (Adeva). They also helped set up Paul Oakenfold's Perfecto subsidiary in its original incarnation.
Selected album: Various: *Quality Produce* (Cooltempo 1994).

Corridor

Techno outfit comprising the surname-less Ashley and Chris. Corridor's origins lay in Tunbridge Wells, Kent, where in 1982 Chris bought his first synthesizer after seeing a Tangerine Dream gig. Both were originally in an indie band the Merkins (the name taken from a pubic wig used by prostitutes who had been shorn following lice infestation). The name Corridor was taken from the Sam Fuller film about a mental asylum (*Shock Corridor*). Together with friends Nat and Grant they recorded a demo which was sent to Andy Weatherall at his Sabres Of Paradise enclave. The latter released Corridor's debut, 'Element',

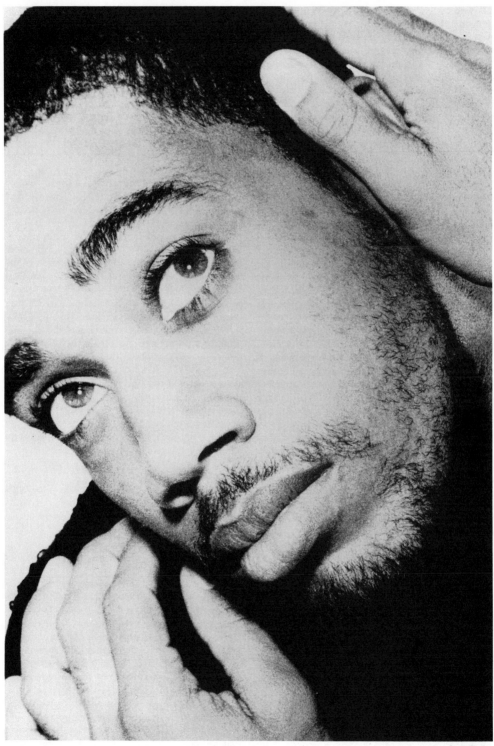

Carl Craig

followed by 'X'. The first was dreamy, soundscape techno, the second a much harder regime. Afterwards Nat and Grant took off to join Conemelt, who released their debut EP on Ashley's New Ground label. Chris and Ashley continued as a duo, their 'Two Days' cut, also on New Ground, providing them with a big club hit in late 1993. Their hard techno is informed by their love of the industrial genre - it was the Sabres remix of Throbbing Gristle's 'United' that originally encouraged them to contact Weatherall.

Cosmic Baby

b. c.1966, Germany. Ambient sound sculptor whose methodology reflects his erudite philosophy on music - 'Trance isn't purely mind music. It's body and soul music and therefore cannot be represented simply by sounds of the sea and mystical flutes. My own music is far too complex to be reduced to a label like trance. My music has nothing to do with creating a functional dance or ambient track.'. His music conversely, has led to him being widely regarded as 'The Star Of Trance', or worse, 'The Modular Mozart' or 'Sir Trancealot'. He had actually been perfecting his technique since the late 80s, and even resisted approaches to sign him from Rhythm King in 1990. Claiming to have been making music since the age of four, Cosmic Baby is actually a trained musician, who studied at the Nuremberg Conservatory at the age of seven. As well as classical music (notably Erik Satie) he was also heavily influenced by his native forebears such as Kraftwerk, or Tangerine Dream. He has recorded widely in his own country since 1991, under the Energy 52 and Futurhythm monikers. Eventually he signed with the Berlin-based MFS label in 1992. He first graced the British club scene, and charts, with a collaboration with Paul Van Dyck, under the name Visions Of Shiva, scoring with 'Perfect Day'. An appearance at the Eissenporthall in Cologne brought him many plaudits as a live entertainer, as did another PA at Club UK in London. On record he became widely noted for his 'Loops Of Infinity' cut, which prefaced a stylistically varied second album. Alongside the conventional trance of 'Cosmic Greets Florida' lay such splendours as a re-writing of Debussy's 'L'apres-Midi D'une Faune'.
Album: *Stellar Supreme* (MFS 1992), *Thinking About Myself* (Arista/Logic 1994).

Cowboy Records

Record label founded by Dean Thatcher and Charlie Chester in mid-1992, as a complementary operation to London's Flying Records. The turning point came when Thatcher grew tired of not being able to sign artists to Flying when tapes were brought into the shop for him, and Cowboy was used as a more 'street' label with the ability to release smaller-scale runs that would have been impossible on a bigger label. Chester and Thatcher had originally run Volante Records, through a licensing deal with Cooltempo (Audio Deluxe, Tyrrel Corporation etc.). Chester is also manager of Secret Life and the Aloof, both of whom enjoyed early success for the label with 'As Always (Farley/Heller mixes)' and 'On A Mission (Fabio Paras mixes)' respectively. Cowboy went on to establish a strong reputation in their year of inception with releases like Sona Lakota's 'Ice And Acid', Faith Department (Phil Perry)'s 'Initiation' or Well Hung Parliament's 'We Can Be'. In 1993 Pulse 8 bought a substantial share in the operation, bringing over artists like Deja Vu (who had scored big club hits with 'Why Why Why', a cover of the balearic classic by the Woodentops, of whom Deja Vu mainman Rollo was a member, and 'Never Knew The Devil') and Talisman, providing distribution through Pulse 8's deal with Sony/3MV in return. It was originally anticipated that the deal would be struck with Sony's Licensed Repertoire Division, through whom they had worked Secret Life's 'Love So Strong'. Chester made his own vinyl debut as Perks Of Living Society, which was the name he gave to his own club, which he runs alongside Back To Basics' Dave Beer. The track was a cover of 'Too Damn Free', previously a test pressing only by YB Experience. New vocals were added by Val Chalmers.

Cox, Carl

b. Sutton, Surrey, England. Cox is one of the UK's best loved DJ's, his reputaton for playing up to 14 sets a week and being a permanent fixture on the rave circuit enshrined in dance legend. Cox left school to attend an electrical engineering course at Carshalton College, which he would never complete. Instead he chanced his arm as a painter and decorator. After serving an apprenticeship as host to a thousand house parties, he eventually graduated to weddings and finally clubs. He helped pioneer the house scene in Brighton in the late 80s, and was highly involved in the development of acid. He played at the first night of the Shoom club as well as other famous nurseries like Spectrum and Land Of Oz. He was then the first to introduce a 'third' deck into a set at the 1989 Sunrise show. Cox remains a great advocate of European techno and house, which forms the basis of most of his live sets. As his popularity grew, so it became inevitable that he too would step into the recording arena.

Following his 1991 hit single, 'I Want You (Forever)' (number 23), he attempted to woo the airwaves with 'Does It Feel Good To You'. He even received an invitation to join a Radio 1 show live on tour, but saw it backfire. All ready to dance and sway, the sound system cut in instead with the Smarte's 'Sesame's Treet', which he was forced to mime, before returning to give the scheduled 'Does It Feel...' a hearing.

Craig, Carl

A prolific techno third columnist from Detroit, Michigan, Craig rose to prominence on Derrick May's Transmat imprint, releasing material under names like Psyche (famed for the pre-trance 'Crackdown' epic) and BFC (notably 'Static Friendly'). Originally he had been inspired by Kraftwerk and early Human League, but after supporting Derrick May as a component of Rhythim Is Rhythim his tastes broadened, taking a more ethno-centric view of his surroundings. Following recording sessions for 'Strings Of Life '89' with May he set up his own label, Planet E, before a six month sabbatical to England in 1990 (at which time Fragile released his 'Galaxy'). Increasingly welcomed across two continents as a prime mover in the Detroit techno sound, Craig has issued a plethora of subsequent material. Most notable among these are his collaboration with Maurizio ('Mind') and his work as Paperclip People ('Remake Uno'), which were licensed from Planet E to Ministry Of Sound's Open label in the UK. He signed his 69 moniker to R&S in 1994. That name had first been employed for his epic 1991 12-inch, 'Ladies And Gentleman', which latterly found favour as a Sound On Sound reissue with DJs like DJ Pierre, Andy Weatherall and Amsterdam's Dimitri. He also announced plans to set up a new label in conjunction with the latter. In the meantime the duo remixed 'Le Funk Mob' for Planet E, while Craig offerred a new version of 'Throw' for Open.

Crammed Records

Brussels, Belgium-based label distinguished by releases such as Avalon (aka Tim Handel)'s *Earth Water Air Fire*. They also released Geir Jenssen (of Biosphere)'s *North Pole By Submarine* collection of late 80s ambient house cuts. On the single front 1991 was typified by material which included YBU featuring Jonell's 'Soul Music', which would be licensed to Mark Moore of S'Express' Splish label

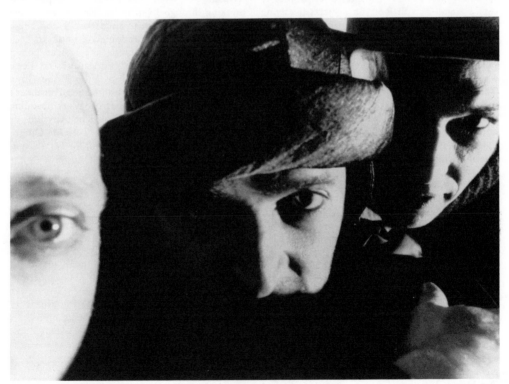

Cranium HF

in the UK and Flying in Italy. Follow-up releases by YBU (essentially Hans Gottheim, b. Tromso, Norway) included 'Apache', which again found its way on to Splish. Otherwise Crammed's main artists were Modulate, Bobuan and Solar Quest. Later material included Hector Zazov's remarkable 1993 set, *Sahara Blue*, which featured Bill Laswell, Tim Simenon (Bomb The Bass), Khaled, John Cale, Ryuichi Sakamoto and Gerard Depardieu. An Algerian/French composer, Zazov used this personnel and others to set the backdrop to a selection of Rimbaud's poetry, in six different langauges. A finger in the eye to those who suggest dance music is intellectually/artistically limited. Selected album: Hecktor Zazov: *Sahara Blue* (Crammed Discs 1993).

Cranium HF

Hardcore industrial dance trio featuring the talents of Fisheye (vocals), Kev and Ross. The initials at the end of their name stand for 'Head Fuck'. Fisheye was living on an abandoned fire engine on a waste disposal dump when he hooked up with his compatriots. The mutual connection was formed when they roadied for Daisy Chainsaw. On the tour Fisheye and Kev devised an impromptu supporting rap act. Kev had previously worked as sound engineer with Ross on projects involving Meat Beat Manifesto and Sheep On Drugs. The trio decided to give it a go as a professional act and settled in London for the release of *Nation Of Pinheads* (1992). They followed up a year later with a second EP for Hydrogen Dukebox, *The Deal*. The music is a mixture of old style house, rap and industrial music. 'Who says you can't be into club tunes and rock groups? There's too much snobbery and not enough risk-taking.' Afterwards they moved on Sappho for the *Summer Rain* EP, then parent label, Rising High Records.

Culture Beat

Euro-dance sensations who were created by Torsten Fenslau (b. c.1964, Germany, d. November 1993, Darmstadt, Germany) in 1989 by putting together the more visual duo of Jay Supreme and Tania Evans. Fenslau had begun his career DJing at the Dorian Gray club at Frankfurt Airport, also working on Hessen State radio presenting the Club Night and Maxi-Mix shows. He subsequently moved into production, scoring a solo hit under the banner Out Of The Ordinary with 'Los Ninos Mix', although it did not find success outside of his native Germany. The same could hardly be said for Culture Beat, who quickly racked up huge overground dancefloor hits with 'No Deeper Meaning', 'Mr Vain' and 'Got To Get

It'. In its wake Fenslau remixed for the Shamen ('Coming On Strong') and released a solo progressive trance single, 'Come Into My Heart', as Abfahrt, and was behind Cheery Lips' 'Das Erdbbermund'. 'Mr Vain' sold over two million copies, but sadly Fenslau didn't live long enough to see his endeavours bear fruit. He was involved in a car crash in November 1993, dying from internal injuries when he reached hospital. The Culture Beat members informed the press of their intention to carry on in his absence, scoring another Top 10 hit with 'Anything' in 1994. Alex Abraham became Fenslau's replacement as musical guru to Culture Beat, alongside long-term collaborators Peter Zweier and Nosie Katzman.
Albums: *Horizon* (Epic 1991), *Serenity* (Epic 1993).

Cutting

US label formed in 1984, originally as a side venture for record store owners Aldo and Amado Marin. Cutting has displayed a tremendous variety in its first decade of operation, having moved from hip hop related matters to the overground house movement. Huge commercial success arrived with Corina's 'Temptation' and Two In A Room's 'Wiggle It'. Other classics like Hashim's 'Alnaaflysh' were well regarded despite not breaking through to quite the same extent. Label boss Aldo Marin maintained that 'I don't like music labels, I just look for good music to keep people dancing'. This propensity to span genres from techno to house and garage has been continued by releases like Vibe Tribe (Joey Beltram)'s 'Something Unreal', Pamela Frenandez's 'Kickin' In The Beat', Masters At Work (featuring Jocelyn Brown)'s 'Can't Stop The Rhythm' or Praxis (featuring Kathy Brown)'s 'Turn Me Out'.
Selected album: Various: *Cutting It To The X:Treme Volume 1* (Cutting 1994).

D

D*Note

Expert peddars of jazz, rap and rare groove, whose strings (sometimes literally) are pulled by musician and film-maker Matt Wienevski, together with scratcher Charlie Lexton and occasional keyboard player Matt Cooper (who records for Dorado in his own right as Outside). D*Note's debut album was intended to reflect narrative structure by establishing each song as a stand-alone but complementary chapter. It housed the singles 'Now Is The Time', 'Bronx Bull', 'Scheme Of Things' and 'The More I See', each of which had brought good reviews in their original formats. Wienevski's first film, a ten minute short entitled *Round the Block*, was given a viewing on Channel 4.
Album: *Babel* (Dorado 1993).

Dakeyne, Paul

A DJ since 1980, Windsor-based Dakeyne went on to become in-house prodcuer to the DMC organisation in 1986. Having remixed for Bass-O-matic, Erasure, James Brown and C+C Colour Factory, Dakeyne became one of the resident DJs at U2's Kitchen club. He went on to establish the Zone club night in North London, and launched Zone Ranger, alongside Terri Heywood (vocals), Matt Eld (keyboards) and Suzanne (dancer). They made their debut with the double a-side '2 Be Reel'/'Kaleidoscope Girl', the latter remixed by 808 State's Eric Powell. '2 Be Reel' included a sample drawn from Echo & The Bunnymen's 'The Cutter'. However, for the stock release on Omen, Dakeyne was forced to recreate the keyboard section when he failed to gain clearance for the sample. It would not be the last time Dakeyne's career has suffered at the hands of the copyrighters. A side project, at first veiled in secrecy, saw Dakeyne introduce Tinman. Tinman became instantly famous for '18 Strings', inspired by Nirvana, which had a devastating effect when it was released as a white label at the end of 1993. His intention was to re-record the 'Smells Like Teen Spirit' riff, rather than sample it, *ala* Abigail's 'Teen Spirit' on Klone Records, thereby simplyfying sample clearance. The move backfired horribly. Though the 20 white labels mailed to DJs were hugely successful (with Jon Pleased Wimmin etc), changing hands at some £150 a throw, Dakeyne was unable to get full permission on the track from Nirvana manager John Silva - which ironically would not have been required had it been merely 'sampled'. To make matters worse, Cobain died, ensuring the track, though still hugely popular, was held in limbo and ineligible for its projected stock release on London. It finally emerged on 14 August 1994, by which time the Abigail version had already charted.

Dale, Colin

Dale is the techno guru of London's Kiss FM radio station, where he took up a post in 1986 after packing in his day job at the bank. He played a selection of music drawn from house, funk and garage, until visiting Detroit DJs Derrick May, Blake Baxter and Juan Atkins, who turned him on to techno. His first move into recording came in 1994 when he put together the *Outer Limits* compilation on Kickin' Records, featuring Luke Slater, Carl Craig and Peter Namlook. He also started his own Abstract Dance imprint (named after his show), with the intention of becoming 'the UK's Strictly Rhythm', a statement which was rapidly approaching cliche status among new label entrepreneurs. He also collaborated with Dave Angel on recording projects, and runs the Deep Space club with Colin Faver, and Knowledge with Jane Howard.

Davis Jnr, Roy

Old school Chicago DJ and producer, who grew up with disco, purchasing his own turntables at age 15, before he started hanging around local celebrity DJ Pierre. He eventually progressed to a position as part of Pierre's Phuture production team, alongside first lieutenant Spanky, who also provided vocals, and Felix Da Housecat. His first solo recording was 'Twenty Below' for Jack Traxx, but it was again credited to the better known Pierre. Unimpressed but undaunted, he continued to record under various guises, including an update of Phuture's 'Rise From Your Grave' (at Pierre's suggestion), before switching to New York and Strictly Rhythm, where he recorded the floor-filler 'Mental Behaviour'. A liaison with the UK's Ministry Of Sound saw the 1994 release of 'Who Dares Believe In Me' (credited to the Believers), which at last looked like bringing him out of the shadows of his mentor.

Da Yeene

Female Swedish sisters duo who made it to the UK clubs with two celebrated tracks; 'Alright' and 'Body Action'. Da Yeene is composed of Dianne and Jeanette Söderholm, who are in turn half-sisters to Rita Marley and Ranking Miss P. They combine sweet, harmonious garage vocals over the traditional backing of their label Swemix, notable for their deep house releases. However, so far their muse has earned them little respect in their native country: 'House is not that big here. Tempos are very slow. We're making music for other countries'. Their debut album brought them their greatest domestic success, in 'Big Bad World'. A follow-up set was produced by Stonebridge, the man credited with revitalising the career of Robin S. More recently they have been working with Martin White, Denniz Pop and Douglas Carr - the latter two famous for work with fellow Swedish exports Dr Alban and Leila K.

Albums: *United Soul Power* (Swemix 1990), *Primetime* (Swemix 1992).

Dead Dead Good

Based in Whitton Walk Cheshire (not to be confused with Yorkshire label Dead Good), and founded by owner and managing director Seve Harrison. Dead Dead Good was the home of 1991's biggest dance single, Oceanic's 'Insanity'. It was a record that cost less than £1,000 to make yet netted some 365,000 sales. Their other acts included Bowa, Joy Salinas, Digital Orgasm ('Moog Eruption'), N Trance, Rig and That Uncertain Feeling. They enjoyed a further crossover hit with Italian-based, Los Angeles-born singer Katherine E's 'I'm Alright', and continued to release northern rave with tunes like Rhythm Device's 'Pink Champagne'. However, they returned to total independence in 1992 after Warners Music pulled out when the label failed to replicate its 1991 success.

Death Of Vinyl

Toronto, Canada based record label run by Jerry Belanger, who describes himself as 'more of a scientist than a businessman'. Death Of Vinyl specialises in trance, hard house, acid, and various other sonic anomalies, and began in 1990. Three years later they picked up a distribution deal in the UK with the aid of Ninja Tunes (Matt Black and Jonathon Moore of Coldcut fame). The back catalogue includes over a dozen collections of ambient, industrial, techno and mystic music. Among the artist titles on offer are 'Chaosphere' by Automata and DIN's 'Watersports'. Other groups include Digital Poodle, Infor/Mental and the Tape Beetles (who have apeared on material from the Orb and Positiva). The label also distributes albums from countries as far apart as Brazil and Croatia as part of an international networking exercise in weirdness.

DeConstruction

Mainstream dance label which has been responsible for some of the late 80s/early 90s most important club releases. Co-founded by Keith Blackhurst and Mike Pickering (see M People), later joined by a third partner Pete Hadfield, they released the compilation album *North* in 1988 (which has been cited as the first UK house compilation, though it was primarily the work of Pickering). It was followed a year later with *Italia* and *Decoded And Danced Up* in 1991. The sound of DeConstruction has been compared to that of modern disco, modern soul, and several less flattering classifications. However, their roster tends to encompass too many groups to make any single category effective. Notable artists include the aforementioned M-People, Guru Josh, whose early success was vital, N-Joi, Ben Chapman, Wendell Williams, the Grid, Sasha, Millionaire Hippies and Lionrock. In 1994 they added the services of Liverpool DJ James Barton, who had originally put them in touch with another of their successful acts, K-Klass. DeConstruction continues to offer tunes a little less brash and demanding than much of the parallel crop of rave and techno, but maintains its own energy and profile.

Selected albums: Various: *North - The Sound Of The Dance Underground* (DeConstruction 1988), *Italia* (DeConstruction 1989), *Decoded And Danced Up* (DeConstruction 1991).

Deee-Lite

Formed by American Lady Miss Kirby (b. Youngstown, Ohio; vocals) and Russian Super DJ Dmitry Brill (b. Kiev) after they met in a New York park in 1982, Deee-Lite are a house/pop dance band who cracked the UK charts with the groundbreaking 'Groove Is In The Heart'. The couple, who later married, had by this time added Japanese computer expert Jungle DJ Towa Towa (b. Towa Tei, Tokyo) to make them a truly cosmopolitan proposition. 'Groove Is In The Heart' featured additional guest artists Bootsy Collins and Q-Tip (A Tribe Called Quest), though the follow-up, 'Power Of Love', and subsequent efforts have failed to replicate their impact. 1992's *Infinity Within* saw a band toned down in sound as well as visual garb. It included tracks like the half-minute 'Vote, Baby, Vote', which served as something of an antidote to the aesthetics of the 'Second Summer Of Love' to which 'Groove Is In The Heart' had proved so pivotal. By the advent of their third set they had been joined by new member On-e. Kier has gone on to earn herself a niche market in computer graphics, designing covers for Deee-Lite and others.

Albums: *World Clique* (Elektra 1990), *Infinity Within* (Elektra 1992), *Dew Drops In The Garden* (Elektra 1994).

Deee-Lite

Deep Forest

Ambient techno group whose 'Sweet Lullaby' track was one of the most popular of 1993, with its rich, warm tones and ethnic instrumentation. It was based on the sampled voices of Pygmies drawn directly from the African rain forest. The duo in charge of proceedings were Eric Mouquet and film composer Michael Sanchez. Based in Paris and Lille, their collaboration was the result of Sanchez returning from Africa with boxes of records from all over that continent. However, most of the actual sounds used on the track were taken from record libraries. 'Sweet Lullaby' is the story of a young girl who tries to get her brother to stop crying by insisting that if he doesn't his parents will never come back. Remixes of the track were offered by both Apollo 440 and Jam And Spoon (Deep Forest would return the compliment by providing Apollo 440's 1994 single, 'Liquid Cool', with their first ever remix). Deep Forest themselves have found themselves hugely popular, their album going platinum in Australia and being nominated for a Grammy in America.

Album: *Deep Forest* (Columbia 1993).

Degrees Of Motion

New York band (Kit West, Balle Legend, Mariposa) which enjoyed both underground cult status and overground success with singles like the club classic 'Do You Want It Right Now' (number 31), featuring the vocals of Biti in 1992. It had originally been released on the Esquire imprint in the US, before transferring to ffrr. The song itself had first appeared on Taylor Deane's *Tell It To My Heart* album in 1989. It was produced by Richie Jones with keyboards from Eric Kupper, and topped the *Record Mirror* Club Chart for no less than four weeks. Other hits included 'Shine On' (number 43, remixed by Farley & Heller, again originally on Esquire) and 'Soul Freedom - Free Your Soul' (number 64), on the ffrr imprint, while Jones remixed Sheer Bronze's 'I'm Walkin''.

Delorme

Chris Day, who is also a DJ at Club For Life, Martin Tyrell and Jason Hayward comprise the nucleus of Delorme, who first recorded for the MFF label with 'Guitar Dance' and 'Physical Energy', before they broke through in 1993 with 'Beatniks'. The latter saw them signed to north London's Zoom enclave, though it was also licensed to European operation ZYX. Bouyed by their success, Delorme were invited to pick up remixing duties, initially on Lost Tribe's 'Gimme A Smile'. They were also transported to the US for live dates alongside Mindwarp's Jon Debo, and

recorded the *Spanish Fly* EP, which saw the introduction of vocalist Hayley Kay.

Dennis, Cathy

b. 1969, Norwich, Norfolk, England. Dennis displayed early vocal poise and by the age of 13 she was singing in her father's Alan Dennis Band at Butlins' holiday resorts. Cathy started her career proper in the mid-80s singing in a covers band where she was spotted by Dancin' Danny D's manager, Simon Fuller; at the time looking for a female singer to work with the producer and remixer. She subsequently signed to Polydor and started writing her own songs and recording solo. She put this parallel career on hold to work with Danny D's D-Mob, between them achieving a chart hit with 'C'Mon Get My Love'. While other D-Mob tracks employed a variety of backing vocalists, Dennis was also featured on 'That's The Way Of The World'. By the end of 1989 she was able to resume her solo career with 'Just Another Dream' and her debut album. Her first significant success came in the US, with three Top 10 hits including 'Touch Me (All Night Long)', after which recognition in her native country followed. She was, infact, the most successful UK singles artist in the US charts in 1991. *Into The Skyline* saw her team with Madonna's favoured producer, Shep Pettibone. She also reunited with Danny D for the 1993 D-Mob single, 'Why'.

Albums: *Move To This* (Polydor 1991), *Into The Skyline* (Polydor 1992).

Depth Charge

Basically a home to former DJ Jonathon Saul Kane's bizarre thematic house singles. The most memorable of these was undoubtedly 'Goal', which sampled an excitable Brazilian football commentator holding the 'Goooooaaaall' crow throughout its recording. Released at the height of World Cup '90 fever, it caught the imagination of the terraces after they had retired to the clubs of a Saturday evening. Other such releases included 'Depth Charge (Han Do Jin)' (sampling U-Boats from hoary old B&W films), 'Bounty Killers' (which did the same with cowboy films) and 'Dead By Dawn (horror movies). All were released on the Vinyl Solution imprint.

Digi Dub

Digi Dub is a label, a studio, an occasional recording act and a Camberwell squat collective, which provides its personnel. Spin-off bands include Mk3, RIP and LS Diesel & Launch Dat. Their manifesto is collected together on *South East Of The Thames*, a collection of tracks by those artists passing through the Digi Dub studios. An intriguing combination, they are a collective which crosses the dialectics of the Crass generation - they refuse interviews and personality profiles, with the aesthetics of the club scene. In 1994 they also managed to pen a song about the joys of drinking Special Brew.

Selected album: *South East Of The Thames* (Digi Dub 1993).

Dimitri

Publicity-shy DJ (b. Amsterdam, Holland), who regularly hosts the Hi-Tech Soul Movement nights at the Roxy, and also plays the Richter club, both in his hometown. He began his DJ career on the radio in the early 80s, before graduating to clubs. Famed for his mix tapes and CDs, he has latterly hooked up with Carl Craig and Rhythim Is Rhythim (Derrick May) to set up a new record label. He is the part owner of the Outland shop and label, and has founded two further labels, Spiritual and BeST. Some of this roster's better known releases include Super Jazz's 'Hi-Tech Soul Anthem' and MDMA's 'Cerebral Asendence'. He has also worked with fellow-Amsterdam talent Eric Nouhan ('Tecnobility' etc) and released his own material in conjunction with Jaimy ('Don't Be A Prisoner Of Your Own Style', which neatly encapsulates his own DJing principles). In 1994 he established the Outland imprint in the UK, commemorating the occasion with the release of a compilation, *The Best Of Outland And Spiritual*. He also licensed recordings like Two Men Will Love You's 'Goodbye Thing' and remixed for Chanelle ('Work That Body').

Selected album: Various: *The Best Of Outland And Spiritual* (Outland 1994).

Disco Evangelists

The Disco Evangelists comprised Ashley Beadle (b. London, England), David Holmes (b. Belfast, Northern Ireland) and Lyndsay Edwards (b. London, England; ex-If?). Originally released on Beadle's Black Sunshine label before Positiva picked it up, their 'De Niro' hit referred to the eponymous actor's movie, *Once Upon A Time In America*. The follow-up, 'A New Dawn', also found a home on Positiva's release schedule. Beadle worked alongside the Stereo MCs' Nick and Rob as Axis ('Rollin' With Rai'), and as part of Workshy, Xpress 2, Black Science Orchestra and Marden Hill. In 1994 he unveiled a new outfit, Delta House Of Blues, which signed to Go! Discs. He has also worked remixed for Jodeci and East 17 ('Deep'). Similarly Holmes is one of the most interesting and prolfic of England's DJ fraternity, working as part of Scubadevils (with ex-members of Dub Federation) and running the Sugarsweet/Exploding Plastic Inevitable club/label empire in Belfast.

Disco Magic Records

Italian label Disco Magic was the original home to Black Box's groundbreaking 'Ride On Time'. They also introduced artists like rapper Tony Carrasco, who released a cover version of Adamski's 'NRG' on the label. Disco Magic's popularity continued with Pierre Feroldi's 'Moving Now', Hoomba Hoomba's "Voice Of Africa' and, later, Rhythm Orchestra's 'Such A Good Feeling', a revision of David Seaman and Steve Anderson's Brothers In Rhythm original, orchestrated by DJ Oliver. Other artists like Marmalade (obviously not the 60s version) contributed 'Mi Piace' from 1992.

DIY

Nottingham based party collective, populated by numerous contributors the best known of which are Harry, Damien, Digs and Woosh. 'Our main intention from the start was really to be able to do our own thing...rather than havng to pander to club owners, record labels, managers or whoever'. Their releases include the *Duster* EP, and the acclaimed 'Shock Disco Invasion'. Their debut album numbered some 14 assorted DJs, remixers and musicians working in a spirit of collective adventure. *Strictly 4 Groovers*, its title also doubling as the name of their record company. In 1994 the group recorded a split single with Chumbawamba to protest at the Criminal Justice Bill, and launched a second imprint, Spacehopper, for hip hop/funk projects.

Album: *Strictly 4 Groovers* (Warp 1993).

DJ Dag

Frankfurt, Germany-based DJ/producer, with many classic releases like 'Sun Down' (released on the Eye Q label and credited to the Volunteer) to his name. One of the pre-eminent forces in the development of trance, he was originally based at the Dorian Gray club in Frankfurt before moving to Sven Vath's Omen club in 1993. Dag was behind the chart success of Dance 2 Trance, a collaboration with Jam El Mar (of Jam & Spoon) and vocalist Tony Clark, breaking the Top 40 with 'Power Of American Natives' and 'Take A Free Fall'. He worked with Jam El Mar on Peyote's 'Alcatraz' for R&S, and in 1994 was purporetedly purchasing land in Dakota in order to give it back to the indigenous population.

DJ Duke

An underground DJ talent (though he rarely plays his native New York clubs these days) who exploded as a crossover proposition in the early 90s when 'Blow Your Whistle' became a chart fixture. Duke had served a long apprenticeship, however. He made his first record in 1990 on a white label, selling out of its first five hundred records shortly after. Faced with rejection from every record company he approached, he set up his own label. These have eventually expanded to include four separate imprints: Power Music Records (vocal tracks), Power Music Trax (harder techno), Sex Mania (sexually inspired trance themes, like Erotic Moments' 'Touch Me') and DJ Exclusive (for other artists) - housed under the collective Power Music umbrella. Group names exercised have included Inner Soul, Club People, The Music Choir, Tribal Liberation and The Pleasure Dome. As DJ Duke the follow-up to 'Blow Your Whistle' was 'Turn It Up', which again followed the route from club to chart. He also talked of his plans to move into film work.

DJ International

Alongside Trax, DJ International was the pivotal label in documenting the rise of Chicago house music (priding itself on never releasing anything in a different musical category). The imprint was founded by DJ Rocky Jones, and picked up on DJ artists like Mr Fingers ('Mystery Of Love', 'You're Mine') Tyree ('Tyree's Got A Brand New House' and, with Kool Rock Steady, 'Turn Up The Bass'), Joe Smooth ('Promised Land'), Sterling Void ('It's Alright'), Pete Black ('How Far I Go') and Fast Eddie ('Hip House', 'Get On Up', 'Let's Go', 'Yo Yo Get Funky'). On the ground floor of the label's premises the Chicago Music Pool was located, where promotional releases were distributed to DJs, thereby ensuring that the label kept its ear to the ground for new talent. The backroom stalwarts included Frankie 'Hollywood' Rodriguez, who produced much of the label's output as well as his own solo projects (including the jokey Lincoln Boys). He also mixed for house radio show B96. Other prominent names were Julian Perez and Martin 'Boogieman' Luna, who recorded 'House Express'/'Pump It Up Homeboy', the latter forming the backbone of D Mob's 'Come And Get My Love'. Like many of the label's releases, it became sample-fodder to the European masses.

Selected album: Fast Eddie: *Most Wanted* (DJ International 1990).

DJ Pierre

Beginning his DJing career in 1983, Pierre was his second choice of name after hosting a disastrous set under his original title. He would play at several early Lil' Louis parties, before he was credited with developing acid house, alongside his collaborator Spanky, in a Chicago basement in 1986. The duo had just purchased a bass machine, the Roland TB 303. Through a process of experimentation the 'acid squelch' sound came forth, which was recorded and passed on to DJ Ron Hardy to play at his Warehouse club. These quickly became known as Hardy's 'Acid Tracks' and the term stuck. Pierre went on to form Phuture Records, started in 1987, which consolidated on his invention with the hugely influential *Acid Trax* series. From there his name became synonymous with first the Acid House movement, before tiring of Chicago and moving to New York to help establish the Strictly Rhythm empire. His work there in the capacity of A&R head, producer and artist was pivotal. Pierre's discography is a varied and prolific one, beginning with singles like 'Annihilating Rhythm' (as Darkman), 'Masterblaster', 'Rise From Your Grave', 'Musik' and 'Generate Power'. In New York he perfected the 'Wyld Pitch' musical style (where the groove builds a hypnotic, trance-like effect through repetition), and in more recent years operated more as a free agent (releasing material like 'More Than Just A Chance' on the UK's Vinyl Solution, and 'I Might Be Leaving U' for Moving, which featured a vocal from LaVette). However, he maintains links with Strictly Rhythm. He has also remixed widely, his clients including Yo You Honey, Midi Rain and DIY. Not to be confused with the similarly titled DJ Pierre (Pierre Fieroldi) from Italy, who, along with Gianfranco Bortolotti has been responsible for Euro hits by the 49ers, Cappella and others, plus his own cuts like 'We Gonna Funk'. Various heated letters were exchanged between the two as confusion increased, and so far the matter remains unresolved.

Djaimin

b. Dario Mancini. Swiss DJ whose 'Give You' cut was discovered by Tony Humphries, who unveiled it at 1992's New Music Seminar. It was quickly picked up by Strictly Rhythm, and then licensed to Cooltempo in the UK. 'Give You' featured singers Mike Anthony and Alessandra. Djaimin himself had been a DJ since the age of 16. Born of mixed Italian and English parentage, he is based in Lusanne, the French speaking region of Switzerland. He moved there in 1986, hooking up with Anthony, best known for his 1983 cover version of Timmy Thomas' 'Why Can't We Live

Together'. Together they run a national Swiss radio show. The follow-up to 'Give You' would be 'She's Ga Ga', again for Strictly Rhythm.

Djax Up Beats

House label esteemed by the critics and run by the similarly garlanded Dutch DJ, Miss Djax (aka Saskia Slegers). Voted Best DJ by German magazine *Frontpage* in 1992, she started DJing in her native Eindhoven in the mid-80s, establishing the record label in 1989. Djax Up has released records by the likes of Trance Induction, Terrace (aka Stefan Robbers, *The Turning Point* EP), Mike Dearborn (*Unbalanced Frequency* EP), Planet Gong (Dylan Hermeljin), Edge Of Motion, Acid Junkies and Random XS, just a few of the better examples of a very strong discography. However, the one thing which singles out Djax Up among other UK and European labels is its profligate release schedule (Paul Johnson's 'Psycho Kong' being its 200th release). Despite the extensive catalogue (and the fact that over 90% of sales originate from outside of Holland) there have been relatively few lapses of taste. For example, they conquered the rise of ambient house with releases from Optic Crux, a group from Utrecht whose output was engineered by Random XS.

D-Mob

The creative vehicle of 'Dancin'' Danny D (b. Daniel Kojo Poku), an ex-McDonald's employee, rising as high as the floor-sweeping position there. He found solace by DJing for three or four years in the evenings, at one point working with journalist James Hamilton at Gullivers in Park Lane, London. He subsequently started club promotions for Loose Ends (for whom he contributed his first remix), Total Contrast and Full Force, before taking up an A&R post at Chrysalis. This brought a number of further remixing opportunities, including Nitro Deluxe, Kid N Play, Adeva and Eric B & Rakim's 'I Know You Got Soul' in tandem with Norman Cook. By the time he had invoked the D-Mob name he had already released two records, as the Taurus Boys, which were minor hits in the US. Then came 'Warrior Groove', about the tribe his Ghanese parents came from, the Ashantis. The first D-Mob release was 1989's crossover hit, 'We Call It Acieed', which featured Gary Haisman on vocals. It was a stirring acid house tune, bringing the underground scene a good deal of notoriety when politicians and papers determined its subject matter was drugs-related. The BBC, in its wisdom, banned it from *Top Of The Pops*. However, as Poku confirmed to the press: 'I don't take any form of drugs. I don't even go the doctor to get

something for my cold'. Follow-up hits included 'It Is Time To Get Funky' (with London Rhyme Syndicate), 'C'mon And Get My Love' and 'That's The Way Of The World' (with Cathy Dennis) and 'Put Your Hands Together' (with Nuff Juice). He also produced/remixed records for Adeva, Juliet Roberts ('Another Place, Another Day, Another Time'), Monie Love, Diana Ross ('Working Overtime'), Chaka Khan ('I'm Every Woman') and the Cookie Crew ('Love Will Bring Us Together'), plus literally dozens more. In 1993 he brought back Dennis (who had enjoyed huge subsequent solo success) for vocals on 'Why', his 'comeback' single as D-Mob. As an in-demand producer and remixer he had never been away.
Album: *A Little Bit Of This, A Little Bit Of That* (ffrr 1989).

D.O.P.

West London artists Kevin Hurry and Kevin Swain, who met at Shoom in the late 80s, are the men behind the D.O.P. banner, an acronym for Dance Only Productions. Their first chance to DJ came at Gary Haisman's infamous Raid club. They have interspersed their regular sets at venues like Flying, Love Ranch and Sign Of The Times with their recordings as D.O.P. throughout the 90s (their first vinyl outing was credited to Bliss on the *Live At The Brain* compilation set). D.O.P.'s first single, 'Future Le Funk', sampled Visage, and was picked up by Guerilla in the summer of 1991. The second, 'Get Out On The Dancefloor', used strings borrowed from a Japan record, while they also remixed stablemates React 2 Rhythm's 'Whatever You Dream'. They eventually dissolved in 1994, stating they had 'taken the band as far as we possibly can'. As further evidence of this they pointed out the way in which D.O.P.'s music had cropped up on compilations spanning garage, hardcore, progressive house and techno. However, they will be fondly remembered for singles like 'Oh Yeah' and 'Groovy Beat'.
Albums: *Musicians Of The Mind* (Guerilla 1992, double album).

Dorado Records

Eclectic London imprint, easily recognisable from its gold and blue sleeve designs, which has had fingers in many musical pies since its inception. Primarily, though, it has been identified as the UK's number one jazz fusion outpost, with a predilection for the club sounds of that spectrum. The label was established by Ollie Buckwell in 1992, and quickly became pre-eminent in its field, particularly in mainland Europe where much of Dorado's output is revered. It debuted with

Monkey Business' 'Ain't No Fun'. The main artists on the label include Matt Cooper, a hugely talented young artist who writes, composes and arranges his own material as Outside, and Matt Wienevski's ambitious D*Note (whom Buckwell managed). Other releases have included material by Jhelisa Anderson (ex-Soul Family Sensation and Shamen), Ceri Evans (former Brand New Heavies' keyboard player), Mesh Of Mind ('Learn The Words'), Origin ('Music Man', which featured Jah Shaka), Ute ('Soul Thing'), and even hip hoppers like Dana Bryant or Brooklyn Funk Essentials ('The Revolution Was Postponed Because Of Rain'). 'I like to think of Dorado as more progressive' summarised Buckwell, 'It's almost the second wave. Talkin' Loud and Acid Jazz kind of broke the market, and we're trying to develop it - push it forward'.

Selected albums: Various: *A Compilation Volumes 1 - 3* (Dorado 1992 - 1994).

Dr Alban

b. Alban Nwapa, Nigeria. Swedish-based euro rapper who rose to prominence with his curious *pot pourri* of styles, christened 'jungle reggae hip hop' by some commentators. Of all the artists to employ the title Doctor in their names, Alban is one of the few to do so with legitimacy. He originally came to Stockholm in Sweden to train as a dentist, and qualified too. He started the Alphabet Club in the city, which eventually spawned a record and clothes shop of the same name. His attempts to 'toast' over the records he played at the venue attracted the attention of the Swemix label. The result of this first view of the studio was the 1990 single, 'Hello Afrika', which immediately launched him in the national and international charts. With the anti-drug 'No Coke' and pro-unity 'U & Mi', Dr Alban continued to cut himself a large slice of credibility in the European mainstream dance market. The musical style combined techno, with club vocals and Arican rhythms. Among the most notable traits are the Nigerian percussive effects and dancehall chanting. His unique, Afro-Swedish patois has also earned praise from a variety of quarters; and emphasised the fact that rap has now become a universal currency. The man behind the good doctor's production on the big hits was Denniz Pop, who also provided Ace Of Base's number 1, 'All That She Wants'. Dr Alban has started his own Dr. label, whose first release was the 'Alrabaiye Take Me Up' single by Amadin.

Albums: *Hello Africa - The Album* (Swemix 1990), *One Love* (Swemix 1992).

Dread Zone

Trance-dub club duo who comprise Greg Roberts (ex-BAD, Screaming Target) and Tim Bran. Roberts is responsible for rhythms and sampling, Bran for programming and other feats of technology. Part of Dread Zone's distinctive charm is drawn from Roberts' appetite for cult films, many of his samples being taken from this field. Dialogue from b-movies (often to avoid the problems of copyright clearance) being a particular favourite. However, their dub credentials were ensured by the arrival of the single, 'House Of Dread'. This came complete with a 'Howard Marks' remix - the latter being among the world's most famous cannabis traffikers.

Album: *360°* (1993).

D:Ream

London pop-dance artists who have crossed over from clubs to daytime radio, and won themselves impressive chart placings in the process. D:Ream originally comprised Al Mackenzie (b. Alan Mackenzie, 31 October 1968, Edinburgh, Scotland) and Peter Cunnah (b. 30 August 1966, Derry, Northern Ireland; ex-Tie The Boy, Baby June). Their first outing came at the JFK Bar in Great Portland Street, London, in February 1992. Four months later Rhythm King released their debut 45, 'UR The Best Thing' (the Prince-like spellings would become a regular feature of their titles). Although they failed to score many credibility points amongst their dance music peers (when asked in one survey which were their favourite DJs, Mackenzie had the temerity to include Steve Wright), they nevertheless became a sought-after remix team among mainstream pop artists (Deborah Harry, EMF, Duran Duran). Both 'UR The Best Thing' and, later, 'Things Can Only Get Better' were reissued in the wake of their higher profile and initial chart appearances. Their debut album, released in August 1993, was roundly rubbished by the press. MacKenzie too appeared less than happy with its new pop direction, and announced his decision to leave the band in October 1993 and return to DJ work. Shortly afterwards the revitalised 'Things Can Only Get Better' enjoyed a long stay at the top of the UK pop charts. At which time there was some note of derision among the puritan dance community from whence they came, Pressure Of Speech lambasting the track for its potential to be: 'the next Tory Conference song'. MacKenzie, meanwhile, was embarking on a solo career as (among other things) Kitsch In Sync ('Jazz Ma Ass' for Global Grooves in 1994).

Album: *D:Ream On 1* (Rhythm King 1993).

Dream Frequency

On the back of popular club tunes like 'Feel So Real' and 'Take Me', Debbie Sharp and Ian Bland have conquered a niche market, especially in being among the few dance acts to avail themselves of the live arena. They generated several column inches when they were originally sought out by Madonna's Maverick label (whose interest, they claim, dropped when it was realised that Sharp was pregnant). Further success, however, arrived with the stylish 'So Sweet', which became another club favourite. Bland has also worked with Martin Lever as Museka (The *M-Series* EP).

Drizabone

Club trio (named after an item of riding apparel) who made a big splash in 1991 with the 'Real Love' cut. In its aftermath many record companies sought to wave chequebooks at the group - 'Real Love' having first emerged on a white label 12-inch - but they held out until they received an album offer from Island Records. The success of 'Real Love' had taken Drizabone too by suprise, and it would not be until 1994 that their debut album arrived. At the time of the single Drizabone were mainstays Vincent Garcia and Billy April plus vocalist Sophie Jones. She had performed the original demo versions of the song but was not really interested in a musical career. Dee Heron (b. Jamaica, West Indies) gave up her secretary's job to take over her role. However, she became the group's second casualty after a follow-up single, 'Catch The Fire'. Having decided that the latter's vocal range was too limited, the backroom duo spent several months auditioning for more suitable replacements, also filling their time by performing remix duties for Linda Layton ('Without You (One On One))', Alison Limerick, Lisa Stansfield ('Change') and Shanice. They eventually met Atlanta, Georgia-based singer Kymberley Peer (b. Detroit, Michigan, USA), who had formerly worked with Howard Hewitt, Freddie Jackson and other soul artists. She was also a partly-established actress, having appeared alongside Marvin Winans and Vanessa Bell Armstrong in the musical *Don't Get Got Started*. She was on hand to record Drizabone's first single in three years, 'Pressure', which prefaced their long-awaited debut album.

Drug Free America

Atmospheric Leeds, Yorkshire-based techno group who originally worked in a more funk-orientated vein for Blind Eye ('Throw A Crazy Shape', 'Day-Glo Pussycat', 'Heaven Ain't High Enough') and Concrete Productions ('Just Like Daddy's Gun') between 1988 and 1990. Afterwards the group:

Brian Moss and Steve Dixon, split to travel around the globe. They reunited in 1991, along with female vocalist Goochie, and signed to York's Cybersound label, releasing 'Can You Feel' and 'Loud Everybody'. Moss had formerly worked with Soft Cell on their debut album and was also a member of the heavily experimental Vicious Pink.

Drum Club

The Drum Club, named after a Sunderland nightspot that imported balearic beat in 1983, and more recently Charlie Hall's own club night, comprise the duo of Lol Hammond (b. 7 January 1960, Stoke Newington, London, England) and Hall (b. 25 October 1959, Whitstable, Kent, England). The latter, self-effacing both on stage and off, and a former book reviewer for the *Catholic Herald*, is nevertheless perceived as the group's creative lynchpin. Before the Drum Club he was already a well-known London club DJ, and had also played in the Apaches and London Cowboys. Hammond, meanwhile, had been part of the many and varied line-ups of Spizz (Spizz Oil, Athletico Spizz etc). The Drum Club's first recording arrived via the Sprial Tribe label in March 1992. 'U Make Me Feel So Good' was an instant club classic, and would be re-released a few months later on the Guerilla imprint. A follow-up, 'Alchemy', was similarly well-received. In the meantime the Drum Club were becoming a favoured remixing stable, a variety of musicians seeking out their talents. These included Jah Wobble's Invaders Of The Heart, Meat Beat Manifesto, Psychick Warriors Of Gaia and would-be progressive outfits Curve and Chapterhouse. Most notable, however, was their work on Killing Joke's alternative dancefloor staple, 'Change'. In addition to their studio wizardry, the duo were also keen to 'play out', making their debut at the Ministry Of Sound, London, in October 1992. Steve Hillage and Emma Anderson from Lush would later guest on their live dates. Anderson would also contribute guitar to *Everything Is Now*, and record a 1993 single, 'Stray', with the Drum Club, under the name Never Never. It was Hall who came up with the idea of the MIDI circus (to rival rock's Lollapalooza touring phenomenon), which also featured Orbital, Aphex Twin, Underworld etc. By the time of their debut album they had moved on to Big Life, signifying the very real commercial status open to their mesmeric, shimmering music. The venue named after them, which had long been a popular attraction in the club world, closed its doors on June 30 1994, with farewell appearances from Fabio Paris, Justin Robertson, Billy Nasty (Zoom) and others.

Albums: *Everything Is Now* (Butterfly 1993), *Drums Are Dangerous* (Butterfly 1994).

Dub Federation

MERC recording artists whose career with that label saw the release of 'Space Funk' and 'Love Inferno'. The group, which split at the beginning of 1994, comprised Andy Ellison, Pete Latham and the surname-less Elton. After the band's demise Ellison and Latham would go on to work alongside David Holmes as part of the Scubadevils (who recorded a track for the *Trance Europe Express* compilation), while Elton relocated to Scotland, before guesting alongside the Grid on their *Top Of The Pops* appearances for 'Swamp Thing'.

Dub Syndicate

An On U Sound offshoot which Adrian Sherwood has used as a flag of convenience for various collaborations. The debut Dub Syndicate cassette, for example, saw contributions from Aswad, Roots Radics and Creation Rebel, while their 1993 LP, *Echomania*, included credits for U Roy, Lee Scratch Perry, Akabu and Michael Franti (Disposable Heroes Of Hiphoprisy). The group had previously made their name as dancefloor dub reggae/bass heavy tunesmiths, fostered under Sherwood's watchful eye. Personnel were recruited as the need arose: their *Vol. 2* selection was given focus by the voice of Andy Fairley, who also appeared on the 'Lack Of Education' 45. More recent material has included ethnic chants and mantras, a nod to the global ambient school of club music.
Albums: *One Way System* (ROIR 1983; cassette only), *Tunes From The Missing Channel* (On-U-Sound 1985), *Pounding System* (On-U-Sound 1988), *Classic Selection Vol. 1* (On-U-Sound 1989), *Strike The Balance* (On-U-Sound 1990), *Classic Selection Vol. 2* (On-U-Sound 1991), *Echomania* (On-U-Sound 1993).

Dust Brothers

Tom Rowlands (b. Hanley-On-Thames, England) and Edward Simons (b. Dulwich, London, England) first met in 1989 at Manchester University. Inspired by the Hacienda venue, they decided to launch their own club, Naked Under The Leather. The trajectory continued to a point at which musical recording was the next obvious step, and in 1991 they released 'Song To The Siren'. This conceptual performance - all breakbeats, airhorns and diva vocals - was a powerful statement on their love of club and hip hop culture. Rowlands was still a member of indie-dance band Ariel, who enjoyed a minor hit in 1993 with 'Let It Slide', but this career was soon jettisoned in favour of the expanding sound of the Dust Brothers. They were invited to remix for locals Lionrock, as well as the Leftfield/Lydon opus 'Open Up' and Saint Ettienne. Maintaining their own recording track record, they issued the *14th Century Sky* EP on Junior Boy's Own and a follow-up 45, 'Kling To Me And I'll Klong To You'. Both revealed their craft, that of crushing hip hop beats with a sheen lifted directly from the rave/acid scene of the late 80s. The *My Mercury Mouth* EP which followed secured another batch of Single Of The Week Awards. Further remixes for the Charlatans and Prodigy followed. Huge fans of the Beastie Boys, they are not the popular rap production crew of the same name who worked on their *Paul's Boutique* opus.

D-Zone Records

The man behind this Essex-based record label is DJ Andre Jacobs. Jacobs started DJing in Romford at the age of 15 and has since been lumped in with the 'Essex techno scene' which also comprises Codeine and Ray Keith. D-Zone has thus far given the world Tekno Too (Jacobs' own recordings, such as 'Jet Star'), Turntable Symphony (Jazzy Jason and Aston Harvey of the Blaaps! Posse, responsible for 'Instructions Of Life' and other tunes), Is That It (again Jacobs), Toxic (*Toxic* EP), Easymo (*Cut And Run* EP), Artful Dodgers ('Pure Love - Pure Energy') and Greed (DJs Mike Gray and John Pearn - 'Love' etc.).

East End

Remix team who have closely protected their anonymity. Their client list includes artists such as Dina Carroll, Judy Cheeks, Eternal and Pauline Henry. The four members include a 'UK record company boss', 'an engineer who's worked on Eric Clapton and Phil Collins albums', while the other two are 'A&R Men'. East End was set up to remix dance music in a commercial manner, with the participants tired of the esoteric and wholly unmarketable remixes offered to their clients by 'name' producers.

Eastern Bloc

Famed as the North of England's premier record shop, Eastern Bloc's in-house Creed imprint launched 808 State, K-Klass, Ariel and Justin Robertson, The latter and Mike E-Bloc (see E-Lustrious) worked together on the counter before pursuing their own musical careers. Creed was brought under the generic MOS label banner in 1991 (MOS standing for More O' Same - to be pronounced in a thick Mancunian accent). Eastern Bloc inaugurated its own brand label in 1993. Peter Waterman (of SAW fame) was the unlikely purchaser of the establishment when it ran into financial difficulties. He then placed DJ and club owner Peter Taylor in charge of proceedings, with a brief to record strong, commercial dance music. Taylor had formerly worked with Waterman as part of the PWL set-up, notably remixing Kylie Minogue's 'Keep It Pumping'. He also runs the Angels club in Burnley, Lancashire. The label's first release was a licensed track, 'Waterfall', by Atlantic Ocean, the second 'She' by Ideal - Manchester DJs Jon Dasilva and A.G. Scott. However, it was the 'Loveland saga' which earned their biggest headlines. A band of that title, affiliated to Eastern Bloc, released their version of Darlene Lewis' 'Let The Music (Lift You Up)' without obtaining sample clearance. A legal tussle ensued, until both parties agreed to release a joint version, performing together on *Top Of The Pops*.

Eat Static

Prime exponents of the nouveau hippy trance/rave culture, allied to the Planet Dog emporium and an offshoot of Ozric Tentacles, Eat Static are essentially Merv Peopler and Joie Hinton of that band. Much of this Somerset duo's recorded material concerns their mutual obsessions with UFO's. 'We can't take techno as seriously as some purists do so we've coated it in this sci-fi motif. And we're mad for all that anyway'. 'Gulf Breeze', for example, was actually written about the area near Penascola, Florida, where Ed Walters was purportedly kidnapped by aliens in 1987. That track was also remixed by Junior Vasquez after he heard the song in his hotel room. Earlier singles had also been well-received, despite frequent disparaging references to their crusty origins. For example, 'Lost In Time' was a *Melody Maker* single of the week late in 1993. Their *Implant* album continued with previous fixations. 'Cydonia' was titled after an area on Mars where pyramids have been 'sighted', while 'Dzhopa Dream' concerned an ancient Tibetan tribe allegedly descended from alien visitors.
Albums: *Abduction* (Planet Dog 1993), *Implant* (Planet Dog 1994).

Edwards, Scott

Bristol, England-based electronic musician who, though he has never DJ'd, has become a name on the dance circuit through his experimental craft. Recording for Out Of Orbit, a subsidiary of Italian label ACV (Annibaldi, Armani etc.), his work reveals a stylistic debt to the Detroit techno godfathers: 'There's nothing pretentious about what I do, it's just that I have ideas which are a little different to most other people. I'm not making music which says 'take ecstasy all the time'. I'm trying to think beyond that'. It is a discourse which his electronics courses and wider reading (notably Alvin Toffler) have stood him in good stead for.
Album: *Distant Horizons* (Out Of Orbit 1994).

EFX and Digit

A pair of complementary West Coast DJs, EFX (b. Raul Recinos) began his career overseeing the decks at funk and hip hop parties, also playing hi-NRG in gay clubs by night. His partner, Digit (b. Jeremy Cowan), took an active role in a succession of funk and ska bands, and was a DJ at Powerplant in Chicago when that city underwent its famous house revolution. After meeting at a record shop they steadily built a reputation with their releases, which kicked off on Strictly Rhythm with two records as Politix Of Dancing. These were followed with a solo EFX record, 'Is It Like My Dil-Doe', before they reunited as Killa Green Buds. They were gradually invited in to the lucrative world of remixing (although EFX complains of several unpaid invoices), often under the name Third Floor Productions. After a breakthrough rebuilding Rozalla's 'Everybody's Free', further big names followed, including Sting ('Demolition Man'), Deep Forest ('Sweet Lullaby') and even Beavis & Butthead, the MTV cartoon drop-outs. They also produced a welter of productions for the N-Fusion label, before that was succeeded by their own operation, Freshly Squeezed. Credited with being the harbingers of musical movements like San Trancedisco or San Frandisko, their style remains relentlessly buoyant, happy house.

Ege Bam Yasi

b. c.1958, Edinburgh, Scotland. Mr Egg is a thoroughly bald Scot and former plumber who took the name for his techno operation from a Can album. The group began as a band proper back in the mid-80s, touring a tacky cabaret show with on stage S&M and a paper mache penis which squirted shaving foam. Despite such antics, he built his reputation with a slew of increasingly successful acid tracks. These include the *Indigestion* EP (1991) and 'Highblow' (Groove Kissing 1991), though the then-group's career had first begun way back in 1986 with 'Circumstances' on Survival. His philosophy is simple and unrelenting: 'I'm not into techno or dub or airy-fairy ambient music. My stuff is pure fucking acid. Full stop'. His mini-album, *Ex Ovo Omnia* (meaning 'Everything Comes From The Egg' in Latin) was released on Finitribe's Finiflex imprint, and included such gastronomic delights as 'The Good, The Bad And The Acid'. It was distinguished by the fact that all the effects were played live, without the use of either a sampler or DAT machine. He uses his new-found fortunes to invest in vast quantities of his chosen passion; eggs. Big, small, battery, free range, ornamental, decorative or edible, Mr Egg has an appetite for the eponymous foodstuff which knows no bounds. He has continued to develop his talents as a remixer for such as the Fugues ('Sensityzed').

Album: *Ex Ovo Omnia* (Finiflex 1994, mini album).

808 State

Manchester's finest dance combo of the late 80s, comprising Martin Price (b. 26 March 1955), owner of the influential Eastern Bloc record shop, Graham Massey (b. 4 August 1960, Manchester, Lancashire, England; ex-Beach Surgeon, Danny & The Dressmakers, Biting Tongues), Darren Partington (b. 1 November 1969, Manchester, Lancashire, England) and Andy Barker (b. 2 November 1969, Manchester, Lancashire, England). The final two had already worked together as DJ double act the Spin Masters. Massey had previously worked in a cafe opposite the Eastern Bloc shop, while Partington and Barker had been regular visitors to the premises, proffering a variety of tapes in the hope of getting a deal with Price's Creed label. Together with Gerald Simpson, they began recording together as a loose electro house collective, and rose to prominence at the end of 1989 when their single, 'Pacific State', became a massive underground hit. It proved to be a mixed blessing for the band, however, as they were lumped in with the pervading Manchester indie dance boom (a term they despised). *Newbuild* and *Quadrastate* helped to establish them as premier exponents of UK techno dance, leading to a lucrative deal with ZTT Records. However, Simpson had left to form his own A Guy Called Gerald vehicle, and launched a series of attacks on the band concerning unpaid royalties in the press. *Ex:El* featured the vocals of New Order's Bernard Sumner on 'Spanish Heart', and then-Sugarcube

Bjork Gudmundsdottir on 'Oops' (also a single) and 'Qmart'. They also worked with Mancunian rapper MC Tunes on the LP *North At Its Heights* and several singles. In October 1991 Price declined to tour the US with the band electing to work on solo projects instead, including managing Rochdale rappers the Kaliphz, and his own musical project, Switzerland. 808 State persevered with another fine album in 1993, which again saw a new rash of collaborations. Featured this time were Ian McCulloch (ex-Echo And The Bunnymen) adding vocals to 'Moses', and samples from the Jam's 'Start', UB40's 'One In Ten' and even *Star Wars*' Darth Vader.

Albums: *Newbuild* (Creed 1988), *Quadrastate* (Creed 1989), *808:90* (Creed 1989), *Ex:El* (ZTT 1991), *Gorgeous* (WEA 1993). With MC Tunes: *North At Its Heights* (ZTT 1990).

Eight Records

Liverpool record label formed by the trio of Ian Wright, Peter Coyle and Steve Cummerson. They first started working together in 1989, originally envisioning licensing their work to the majors. Their debut, Morina Van Rooy's 'Sly One', was consequently placed on Deconstruction, but in short order the trio decided to set up their own company. Since its inception Eight Records has specialised in matching strong house tunes with unusual vocalists. Among the best examples of this have been Connie Lush, a local pub blues singer ('Shame'), Van Rooy ('Sly One') and G Love (DJ John Kelly) featuring Jayne Casey's 'You Keep The The Love', in 1991. Jayne Casey being, of course, the former Pink Military/Pink Industry chanteuse. G Love is also the name of the club the trio run in association with Liverpool's other leading label, 3 Beat. Coyne, formerly of Lotus Easters, also records on the label as Coloursex (*Deep And Devastating* EP).

Selected album: Various: *Give Love* (Eight 1991).

8 Ball Records

New York, USA record label famous for its mellow approach to house music, with offices on the 12th floor of a building in the Chelsea district of Manhattan. The imprint was established in 1991 by Alex Kaplan, then a video-maker, who still leads the company in association with A&R head Kevin Williams, a veteran of the New York club scene. It was Kaplan who recorded the label's debut single, Napoleon-Soul O's 'Come On Girl', a jazzy, funky house tune which set out 8 Ball's stall. Artists and producers were subsequently recruited and acquired by word of mouth. As well as stalwarts like Williams' sister Joie Cardwell

('Goodbye', 'If We Try', 'Trouble') and Lectroluv (Fred Jorio) the label is just as famous for its T-shirt and merchandising, its enblem being among the most popular in the UK. Other prominent recordings arrived from African Dream, Groove Thing, Wall Of Sound, Screamin' Rachael, and Mack Vibe's 'I Can't Let You Go' (Al Mack, who had previously recorded as the Al Mack Project for Strictly Rhythm). 8 Ball also runs the Empire State deep house subsidiary label, and has its own record store in Greenwich Village. Kaplan would return to video-making by launching his own compilation video series.

Electribe 101

Electro-dance band centred around the voice of female vocalist Billie Ray Martin (b. Hamburg, Germany). When she moved to Berlin it was in the hope of setting up a R&B band with 60s influences, especially the Motown sound. However, numerous musicians later, the single-minded Martin set sail for England in 1985, in search of a more sympathetic hearing than she was receiving from the German music industry. Based in South London, it was 1987 before the ball started rolling, after she placed an advert stating: 'Soul Rebel seeks genius'. This brought her to the attention of the rest of Electribe 101; Joe Stevens, Les Fleming, Rob Cimarosti and Brian Nordhoff ('...we don't have defined instruments, they don't belong to us anymore. They belong to the fictitious greed between the speakers'). Their initial meeting was not portentous, though they remained in touch while the Birmingham born quartet constructed their own studio in their native city. They recorded eventually however, and their first two singles 'Talking With Myself' and 'Tell Me When The Fever Ended' were instant hits with the acid generation. The debut *Electribal Memories* confirmed their arrival, with the press slavering over the band's ability to combine sustenance for the mind with impulse for the body. In particular, they welcomed the arrival of a voice which drew comparisons to Marlene Dietrich and Aretha Franklin. Despite the acclaim, Electribe 101 ceased to be shortly afterwards, with Martin setting out on a solo career. As Brian Nordhoff explained: 'It became more to do with being celebrities, or with a certain female member of Electribe being a celebrity, than about music. The whole thing became nonsense. The music side got stunted as a result'. The males in the team would go on to form their own group, Groove Corporation.
Albums: *Electribal Memories* (Mercury 1990).

E-Lustrious

Comprising Manchester duo Mike 'E-Bloc' Kirwin (nicknamed after the famed Eastern Bloc record shop he works at) and Danny 'Hybrid' Bennett. Mike is among the North of England's most popular DJs, though his profile is lessened by his refusal to attend events in the nation's capital. After learning the tuba at school he progressed to sundry hopeful punk bands like Bastard Antelopes. Danny, meanwhile, grew up on breakdancing and breakbeats, and was an early scratch DJ. They began working together at the end of the 80s, when Mike and then fellow Eastern Bloc co-worker Justin Robertson planned to record a single. Danny was hauled in due to his having access to rudimentary recording equipment. Though the track was never completed, Danny and Mike continued as a duo. Their first major success came as the men behind the Direkt single, 'I Got The Feeling', which enjoyed a curious germination. *Mixmag Update* magazine invented a white label record entitled 'I Got Ya' by Direckt, giving it a magnicent review in order to guage the reaction. As thousands assailed their local dance counters in the hope of finding this invisible disc, few noticed that Direckt was an anagram of 'Tricked'. When the scam was revealed the enterprising E-Lustrious made the most of the furore by hijacking the name for 'I Got The Feeling', enjoying instant record sales and notoriety. They have gone on to establish their own record label, UFG, which has subsequently housed tunes from the Luvdup Twins ('Good Time') and material from DJ EFX and Digit and DJ Tandoori. Under their principal name, E-Lustrious, they have established themselves with the success of 'Dance No More'. Just as notable was their second single as Direkt, 'Two Fatt Guitars', a fabulous piece of digifunk which became a party standard in 1993. They also record as Rolling Gear ('I've Got It').

Emerson, Darren

Also half of Underworld and Lemon Interrupt, Emerson is a very active and highly visible DJ, who became a fan of electro as a 14-year old at which time he also bought his first decks. He was in place for the rise of acid house, spinning at a Southend club, before emerging as a real talent at venues like the Limelight and Milky Bar. However, his attitude to his craft is refreshingly ego-free: 'At the end of the day all a DJ does is put pieces of plastic on turntables'. Stylistically his modern tastes favour trance and European hard house. His remixes include Simply Red's 'Thrill Me', Gat Decors' 'Passion',. Björk's 'Human Behaviour' and

Shakespeare's Sister's 'Hey You (Turn Up Your Radio)' and 'Black Sky'.

Emotive Records

New York dance label founded in January 1990 when their debut release was licensed from an Italian label. Emotive is one of the new breed of hip US imprints which have emerged in the 90s. Generally the label creed has been to promote new names and talent on their schedule, while the style encompasses garage and house in its myriad forms. The first release 'proper' came from Toronto artist Matt Di Mario (M1's 'Feel The Drums', the same artist going on to release 'Dynamite' and the *Then And Now* EP for the label). He was joined by Smoke Signals ('I Want Your Love'), B-Town ('Weekend'), Insomnia ('I'll Be There'), Deep Expressions (*Deep Expressions* EP), Michael Lavel ('Do Me This Way') and Michael Ayres ('Share My Love'). Jame's Howard's 'We Can Do It (Wake Up)' was arguably the biggest Emotive tune in its early stages, though Valerie Johhson's 'Step Into My Life' and 'Inside', and Jovonn's 'Out All Nite' were also key releases. The latter was the first 'established' artist on the roster, and ran his own Goldtone imprint through the parent label. The second James Howard release would be 'Feeling Good', again created by label mainstay Charles Dockins (who also contributed to Bobby Konders Jus' Friends project (for 'As One'). Other 1992 releases included Producers On Wax (DJ Romain Gowe and Matt 'Keys' Echols El) with 'Feel The Piano' and Karen Pollack ('You Can't Touch Me'). 1994 brought material from Project 4007 ('It's Our Turn') as Emotive continued its ascendency.

En Vogue

Vocal dance/R&B outfit consisting of Dawn Robinson (b. c.1965, Connecticut, USA), Terry Ellis (b. c.1966, Texas, USA), Cindy Herron (b. c.1963, San Francisco, California, USA) and Maxine Jones (b. c.1962, Patterson, New Jersey, USA). They formed in Oakland, California, where they were auditioned by Denzil 'Denny' Foster and Thomas McElroy. The duo had worked together in both the Timex Social Club and Club Noveau (who enjoyed big hits with 'Rumours' in 1986 and 'Lean On Me', a hip hop version of Bill Withers' 70s classic, and a Grammy winner, in 1987). Afterwards they decided to write and produce under their own steam: 'When Tommy and I bumped into each other in the early 80s, we had the same notion. Everyone was saying R&B was tired and worn out. The new era was hip hop and rap. But we thought: why not combine the two eras? Put good songs – and the 70s were loaded with good songs – over the new grooves'. En Vogue were formed in October 1988 after the duo auditioned to establish their own 'girl group'. Of the four selected, only Cindy Herron had previous 'showbiz' experience, winning Miss San Francisco and Miss Black California pageants, and also working as an actress. The groups remained primarily responsible for their own image and songs, but they were groomed for success by joining Hammer's 1990 tour, and that of Freddie Jackson a year later. They would go on to score singles success with 'Hold On' and 'Lies' in 1990. The latter introduced female rapper Debbie T, and added a new, post-feminist outlook to traditional R&B concerns. Their second album, meanwhile, would incorporate two Curtis Mayfield covers, and produce further hits in 'Free Your Mind' and 'Give It Up, Turn It Loose'. Heavily influenced by Chaka Khan, En Vogue have in turn helped kickstart the New Jill Swing movement, which has so far thrown up the likes of SWV, Jade and TLC. They were approached by Roseanne Cash and then-husband Tom Arnold to appear in their own sitcom.
Albums: *Born To Sing* (Atlantic 1990), *Remix To Sing* (Atlantic 1991), *Funky Divas* (East West 1992).

Eon

aka Ian Loveday, whose first interest in electronica and music was inspired by the *Dr Who* television theme, alongside Jonathan Saul Kane (aka Depth Charge). Eon released a sequence of impressive singles: 'Light, Colour, Sound', 'Infinity' 'Inner Mind' (featured in the film *Buffy The Vampire Slayer*) and 'Spice'. The latter was remixed by Loveday's longstanding hero, Juan Atkins, and featured samples taken from sci-fi epic *Dune*. They continued their association with Vinyl Solution for singles like 1992's horror film-inspired 'Basket Case'.
Album: *Void Dweller* (Vinyl Solution 1992).

Eskimos & Egypt

One of the few legitimate 'bands' involved in the modern dance industry, E&E are a highly regarded mellow groove coalition. Their name was originally invoked as a gesture in support of the Inuit people's struggle for their own homeland. The four-piece, Salford, Manchester-based band is populated by: Paul Cundall (b. 5 April 1963, Manchester, Lancashire, England; keyboards, sequencer), Christopher O'Hare (b. 13 October 1966, Manchester, Lancashire, England; vocals, keyboards), Mark Compton (b. 14 October 1963, Salford, Manchester, England) and David Pryde (b.

David Cameron Pryde, 1967, Dublin, Eire). They made their vinyl debut in December 1987 with 'The Cold' on Village Records, shortly after appearing live for the first time at Manchester's Cloud Nine venue. After a succession of singles that built their dancefloor credentials, including the Axl Rose-slamming 'The Power Of G N'R', their breakthrough release came with the gangland inspired 'US:UK' single. Typically it was awash with sweet female harmonies, furious raps and a slice of rock guitar. Other singles like 'Fall From Grace' followed, with remixes from Moby and the Beatmasters. However, by 1994 they had been dropped by One Little Indian (though the band itself insisted that they had walked).
Album: *Perfect Disease* (One Little Indian 1993).

ESP

Leading Amsterdam techno label with a release schedule featuring Nico, Ken Ishii (Rising Sun), Black Scorpion and Blake Baxter. The label was started in 1991 as the underground rave offshoot of Go Bang!, who had in turn scored hits with D-Shake, GTO and Turntable Hype. The ESP boss is Fred Berkhout, who describes the label's orientation as 'experimental'. Other artists on ESP include Orlando Voorn, who records as Format, the Nighttripper and the Ghetto Brothers (with Blake Baxter), Dr No No ('Paradise 3001') and Jeff Mills.

Espiritu

Latin-flavoured dance duo from Brighton who comprise the contrasting physical properties of Vanessa Quinnones and Chris Taplin (ex-Frazier Chorus). Quinnones, half-Peruvian and half-French, grew up in an affluent suburb of Paris under the care of a South American nanny. Her name, 'Francisca', was subsequently employed as the title of Espiritu's debut single in 1992. It was a paean to her treatment at the hands of Quinnones' mother. The group's second single, 'Conquistador', was another slice of classy Latin dance. Its Andy Weatherall remix had originally taken the club scene by storm, with copies reaching extravagant prices of over £100, before the stock release arrived. Signed to Heavenly Records, the single was a continuation of their thoughtful approach to lyrics demonstrated by their debut. This time the subject was the exploitation of South American Indians in the name of civilisation. A third single, 'Bonita Monana', continued the club/chart crossover in 1994.

Eternal

Pop dance quartet made up of lead singer Esther Bennett, Vernie Bennett, Louise Nordling and Kelle Bryan, who met in a Croydon Baptist church. Coming to the attention of manager and soul svengali Dennis Ingoldsby, they made an immediate impact on the charts with 'Stay' and 'Save Our Love'. However, much more strident and demanding of the listener was the third volley, 'Just A Step From Heaven', whose video depicted a gang of youths populating scenes of urban desolation, before switching to a female rendering a lecture of self-awareness beneath the symbol of the Black Panther movement. It was perhaps a little disappointing, then, to learn that Eternal's songs were wholly crafted and written by back-room staff.
Album: *Always And Forever* (EMI 1994).

Exist Dance

Los Angeles trance/techno label run by Tom Chasteen and Mike Kandel, covering artists like Merge (whose 'You Move Me' was their debut release), Tranquility Bass ('They Came In Peace'), High Lonesome Sound System ('Love Night', 'Were Go', 'Waiting For The Lights'), Eden Transmission ('I'm So High'), Odyssey 2000 ('The Odyssey'), Voodoo Transmission ('Voodoo Fire'), Up Above The World ('Up Above The World') and Freaky Chakra ('Freaky Chakra'). The latter was the first outside production to emerge on the label, but like the rest of their catalogue it was distinguished by an approach that cross-fertilised dance rhythms with tribal chants and environmental effects. Chasteen and Kandel met at art school, and began recording *avant garde* electronica, heavy with loops and repetition, which is again visible in their modern output.

Experimental

US label based in Broadway, New York, noted for its deep house, trance and acid releases. The roster included the dark, Euro-flavoured house of Big Dreams, the hard house of The Rising Sons, and the effusive deep groove of Symphony Of Love. The operation was masterminded by Damon Wild, who distinguished each of his releases via a catalogue number. Hence 'EX17' by Bio Dreams, 'EX19' by the Lazer Worshippers and 'EX22' by Diffusions. 'Basically we're finding American producers who need a home for their records' is Wild's statement of intent. He started DJing in the mid-80s, and was once half of the team behind Toxic Two's 'Rave Generator'. Experimental is part of New York's Northcott stable (run by Tommy Musto), which also includes the Sub-Urban imprint. However, Wild departed from Experimental, amicably, in March 1994, setting up the Synewave label with Tim Taylor, releasing material like Equinox's 'Pollox'.

F

Family Foundation

Manchester based jungle techno crew, made famous by their 'Express Yourself' white label single, which was selling for upwards of £100 to hip DJs in 1992. The head honcho is producer Johnny Jay, and the track was eventually given an official release a year later on Mancunian label 380. However, it was never originally intended to be a Family Foundation number. Jay had produced the track for an artist called Franschene Allea, but when BMG dropped Omen Records the title never saw the light of day. Instead he covered it when FF were doing demos, utilising the services of Rachel (vocals) and Shine (ragga vocals). It proved a hugely winning formula. A debut album included picks like 'Gunchester', a comment on Manchester's rising gang problems, and 'Red Hot'. This saw a guest appearance from ex-Smiths' guitarist Craig Gannon, while over the top of the record Terry Christian and Johnny Rogan discussed accusations of racism directed at Morrissey.

Album: *One Blood* (380 1992).

Farley & Heller

London-based DJ's Terry Farley and Pete Heller first came to light, alongside the likes of Andy Weatherall, as part of the Boy's Own collective. Farley, an ex-gas fitter, was initially playing dub and reggae upstairs at Paul Oakenfold's Spectrum club when acid house arrived and changed everything. Afterwards he would join with Heller to become the simply-titled Farley & Heller, a production/remix team. The Farm in the mid-80s had seemed an unlikely target for dancefloor adulation, but that was what they became when the duo took hold of their 'Groovy Train' single (going on to remix 'Altogether Now' later). It was a landmark almost as important as Weatherall's work on 'Loaded'. Their more indigenous dance projects included work with Espiritu ('Francisca'), K Klass ('Don't Stop'), Sunscreem ('Perfect Motion') and Secret Life ('As Always'). They additionally operate as Fire Island, whose releases on Boy's Own have become hugely popular. As for their status as remixers to the stars: 'Remixing's what we have to do to make a living'.

Farley Jackmaster Funk

The resident DJ at Chicago's Playground between 1981 and 1987 (often combining live drum machine with his selection of Philly soul and R&B), Farley was also one of the earliest house producers, with 'Yellow House' being the first record on Dance Mania Records. He was also a key component of the Hot Mix 5, the DJ group which provided Chicago's WBMX radio station with its groundbreaking mix shows. As Chicago backroom boy Mike 'Hitman' Wilson once stated: 'To me Farley started house. Because while Frankie (Knuckles) had an audience of 600, Farley reached 150,000 listeners'. He scored a hit in 1986 with a cover of 'Love Can't Turn Around', with a vocal from Greater Tabernacle Baptist Choir's Daryl Pandy (although this actually hijacked a Steve 'Silk' Hurley song). Other notable releases include 'Aw Shucks', 'As Always' (with Ricky Dillard) and 'Free At Last' (with the Hip House Syndicate).When WBMX went off air his career ground to a halt, an intermission he occupied by exploring rap and R&B. He returned to DJing in England in the 1990s, where his reputation had not diminished, and started a new Chill-London imprint.

Fehlmann, Thomas

b. Switzerland. An elder statesman of the German techno/house scene, with an intriguing history. Fehlmann originally met guitar wizard Robert Fripp in Hamburg in 1979, where he was studying art, and it was Fripp who inspired him to learn the synthesiser. Later he would make the acquaintance of the Orb's Alex Paterson while working on Teutonic Beats, a mid-80s dance project. Paterson tried to sign him to management company EG, but the deal fell through. Undeterred, the two remained firm friends. Before joining the Orb as an ambient DJ and electronics consultant, he recorded as Readymade and produced the *Sun Electric* LP, joining with the Juan Atkins for the release of 'Jazz Is The Teacher' on Belgian imprint, Tresor (licensed to Novamute in the UK). This was recorded under the group name 3MB, with Morris Von Oswald, an old friend whom he had known from the time they liaised on Palais Schaumburg's third album from a decade previously. They have worked together intermittently since. His contributions to the Orb also include 'Towers Of Dub' on the latter's live double, Orb Live 93. Following touring commitments, he teamed up once more with old guru Fripp to put together the *ad hoc* project, FFWD (Fripp, Fehlmann, Weston and Dr Alex Paterson). According to the latter, Fehlmann had also been 'the first person to put a house record out in Britain in 1986' - as Ready Made on Rhythm King.

Felix

UK house artist Felix represents something of an enigma – never talking to the press or appearing in his videos. He even took the stage at the DMC awards sporting a lion suit. However, his anonymity hasn't been helped by the massive success of singles like 'Don't You Want Me' and 'It Will Make Me Crazy', which sold nearly two million copies between them worldwide. Both predicted the rise of trance and hard house.
Album: *One* (DeConstruction 1992, mini album).

Felix Da Housecat

b. Felix Stallings, Chicago, Illinois, USA. The childhood friend of house legend DJ Pierre, Stallings' youth was spent experimenting in musical electronica, on equipment afforded him by indulgent parents. He had taught himself keyboards by the age of 14, and a year later stepped into a studio for the first time. An early tape had been passed on to the elder Pierre by a mutual playground acquaintance. Intrigued, he decided to record it properly, and from those sessions 'Phantasy Girl' would finally emerge. Based on the original keyboard motif from the demo tape, it became one of house music's biggest early cult smashes. Felix would go on to release a steady stream of dance vinyl, establishing his name alongside that of Pierre, who remained his mentor. Unfortunately, as school ended so did his parents' tolerance of his extra-curricular pursuits, and he was ordered to attend college in Alabama. Three years later he returned to Chicago, taking up the house mantle once again. Numerous releases ensued on all the major 'name' imprints; Strictly Rhythm, Gurerilla ('Thee Dawn'), Nervous, D-Jax Up, Chicago Underground and Freetown. Under the title Thee Madkatt Courtship he also provided a long player for Deep Distraxion, while as Afrohead he preferred 'In The Garden', a classic cut, much revered by DJ's like Darren Emerson.
Selected album: *Thee Madkatt Courtship* (Deep Distraxion 1994).

ffrr

London records' dance arm headed by Andy Thompson, though Radio 1 DJ Pete Tong provides A&R support. Tong joined London in 1983 after leaving his job as advertising manager for *Blues & Soul* magazine. He became the label's club promotions manager, and was the first to import the sound of the Chicago house explosion via Farley Jackmaster Funk and Steve 'Silk' Hurley. Tong 'began' ffrr in 1986. It had originally been a label launched as a subsidiary of Decca in 1946 to celebrate the advent of high fidelity recordings, and

had been dormant for several decades. The original intention was to use the imprint to develop acts on a long-term basis. Hence the signing of major acts like Brand New Heavies, Salt N Pepa, L'il Louis and Degrees Of Motion. A second outlet, ffreedom, was launched in 1991 by Thompson, who, like Tong, had progressed through the ranks as club promotions director, with former Hooj Choons employee Phil Howells as his partner. The idea was to specialise in rave culture, and be flexible enough to pick up on tunes as they broke in the club scene. They even took a bite out of the toytown techno cake by providing the nation with Shaft's ridiculous 'Roobarb & Custard' in 1992. A second subsidiary, Internal, was launched in late 1992 for album-based techno projects. The main label ffrr played things a little safer. As Thompson admitted during the recession of 1992: 'The doctrine of our company is that caution pays and we only believe in spending money where we think there is a reason to'. Nevertheless, ffrr's strict sense of discipline has not prevented it from being both prolific and successful. In the late 80s they boasted some of the cream of the acid house generation's music with artists like D-Mob, also picking up on commercial hip hop with the Cookie Crew (since dropped). They also lost Orbital, who had given them a major hit in 1992 with the *Mutations* EP, but maintained relationships with a series of female house vocalists including Lisa B. Among the major hits of recent times have been DJ Duke's 'Blow Your Whistle', Good Men's 'Give It Up', Joe Roberts' 'Back In My Life' and the omnipresent Brand New Heavies' 'Back To Love' alongside sundry quality releases from Frankie Knuckles. ffrr has gone on to become the most credible and successful dance division of a major label.

Finitribe

Scottish dance outfit, who shared the same One Little Indian label as their fellow countrymen the Shamen, but failed to replicate their success. It was not through want of effort, or, for that matter, talent. The band took their name from 'Finny Tribe', a name given to the fish species by Irish religious sect the Rosicrucians, as well as the common people of that country. Originally a six-piece formed in Edinburgh in 1984, they founded their own label, striking out with a debut EP, *Curling And Stretching* in October. One month later they played their first gig together supporting Danielle Dax at London ULU. By 1986 they had acquired their first sampler, and released 'DeTestimony', an influential cut in both the balearic and, later, house movements. The

Finitribe

following year they begun an ill-fated liaison with Chicago's Wax Trax Records, releasing a version of Can's 'I Want More'. Following problems with the label vocalist Chris Connelly eventually elected to remain, ostensibly as part of Ministry and Revolting Cocks, also recording solo. Finitribe re-emerged in 1989 with the curtailed line-up of Mr Samples (b. John William Vick, 6 November 1965, Edinburgh, Scotland), Philip Pinsky (b. Philip David Pinsky, 23 March 1965, Appleton, Wisconsin, USA) and David Miller (b. David Francis Ashbride Miller, 20 July 1962, Moffat, Dunfrewshire, Scotland). Vick and Pinsky had previously been colleagues in Rigor Mortis, Miller having served in Explode Your Heart. Their influences remained both traditional rock and indie giants (Dog Faced Hermans, Magazine) and a myriad of new and old dance innovators (Jah Wobble, Tackhead, Sparks, Sub Sub, Orbital). A succession of well-regarded releases on One Little Indian failed to deliver them much in the way of commercial reward. The first and most notable of these was the acidic 'Animal Farm', which sampled the 'Old McDonald' nursery rhyme and laid torrents of abuse at the door of the McDonald's hamburger chain. The ensuing fuss, hardly deflated by a 'Fuck Off McDonald's' poster campaign, brought the band significant media exposure for the first time. Entering the 90s they looked as

though they might expand beyond cult tastes with a new, kitsch image (white boiler suits peppered with stars) and more pop-dance-orientated material. As critics pointed out, they resembled an underground version of the Pet Shop Boys. By 1992 they had resurrected the Finiflex label and opened their own studio complex in Leith.
Albums: *Noise Lust And Fun* (Finiflex 1988), *Grossing 10K* (One Little Indian 1990), *An Unexpected Groovy Treat* (One Little Indian 1992).

Finn, Mickey
b. Michael Hearne. One of the more publicity shy name DJ's, Finn's ambitions stretch to writing film soundtracks rather than desiring pin-up pieces in the popular music press. His musical inclinations were established at blues parties before he got hooked by Eric B & Rakim. He purchased his own decks and starting mixing, getting his first paid engagement at the Tunnel Club, near Blackwall Tunnel (run by his sister Nancy, who first invoked the 'Finn' nickname). From such humble beginnings in 1988 he progressed to the Genesis and Biology nights. He recorded a solo track, 'She's Breaking Up', for US label Focus in January 1991, before going on to remix for a multitude of labels including Suburban Base, ffrr, Champion and PWL (Mandy Smith's 'I Just Can't Wait', of all things). A more representative example of his work

would be his contribution to Urban Shakedown with friends Gavin King and Claudio Guissani on 'Some Justice', which enabled it to become a real chart contender (despite problems obtaining clearance for the sample of Ce Ce Rogers' 'Someday'). He remains a huge name on the DJ circuit.

First Choice

New York label and studio in Greenwich Village founded by DJ/remixer Andrew Komis in conjunction with Network. His intent to return dance music to the late 80s when the dramatic garage divas like Adeva and Kym Mazelle held sway, was first attempted at the Big Shot label in Canada (see Hi-Bias). His roster of acts at First Choice offered similar prospects. Among those involved are Pandella, the well-regarded house diva veteran and Dyone, a highly-touted disco diva whose upfront personality and sexuality have endeared her to many, including actor Robert De Niro, which sent rumour mills into a frenzy of activity. A former beauty queen, dancer and college graduate, Dyone has been heralded as a sussed Teena Marie of the 90s. Komis himself records under the nom de plume Komix And Co. Of the opinion that the 90s US dance scene is dead, he formed First Choice primarily to reach English and European markets, linking up with Network after they had opened up a New York office in 1990.

Flash Faction

UK techno outfit comprising Matt Nelmes, Richard Johnstone and Jake Davies. The three worked as engineers at Soho's Berwick Street Studios, before deciding to give it a go themselves with the help of DJ Sean Johnstone in late 1993. They began 1994 with two hard trance releases, 'Robot Criminal' on Labello Trax, and 'Repoman' on Andy Weatherall's Sabres Of Paradise label. The latter was envisioned as an 'alternative soundtrack' to Alex Cox's film of the same name. It was followed up with the release of 'Mad Moog Rising' for Third Mind.

Floorjam

The creation of one Nick Newell, a man whose dance records show a clear line of descent from Kraftwerk's computerised pop. His 'Stone Age' has become a widely venerated track, but it was not always a life of boundless techno experimentalism. In 1993 he returned to his former occupation, that of session musician, picking up contracts for Gary Glitter and Take That tours to pay the bills.

Fluke

Purveyors of charismatic, electronic dance music, Fluke are both a stand-alone musical project and a mixing house for others. The band consists of Mike Bryant (b. Michael James Bryant, 1 May 1960, High Wycombe, Buckinghamshire, England), Michael Tournier (b. Michael James Tournier, 24 May 1963, High Wycombe, Buckinghamshire, England) and Jonathan Fugler (b. 13 October 1962, St Austell, Cornwall, England). Fulger and Bryant were both formerly in third-rate teenage punk bands, titled the Leaky Radiators and Lay Figures respectively. Tournier and Fugler had more prominently been part of Skin. Together they emerged as Fluke in August 1989 with the white label 12-inch, 'Thumper!'. Other early singles included 'Joni' (complete with a sample from the eponymous Joni Mitchell) and 'Philly', their debut non-white label outing on Creation. Their first live gig was on the lawn of a Kent country house at a Boy's Own party - a set which subsequently became their second album release, Out, in November 1991. This arrived as part of a new deal with Virgin subsidiary Circa, with whom they released their third album, Six Wheels On My Wagon, in 1993. This included a limited edition vinyl freebie of their long deleted Techno Rose Of Blighty debut. Six Wheels also included the club hit, 'Groovy Feeling'. The band have their own West London studio, and remain somewhat aloof from the dance music community. This has not stopped them from earning an enviable crust as remixers: World Of Twist, JC001, Opik, Tears For Fears and Talk Talk numbering among their clients. More recently their 'Slid' single came close to breaking the UK Top 40, signposting their potential as a commercial as well as club act

Albums: Techno Rose Of Blighty (Creation 1991), Out (Circa 1991), Six Wheels On My Wagon (Circa 1993).

Flying Records

Italian label, and that country's biggest independent dance distributor, who also have a London arm which distributes its own product and that from Media, Ummm and other labels. The UK operation was set up by Dean Thatcher in association with Charlie Chester and Cooltempo. Their debut release was a Thatcher remix of 'Hit Me With Your Rhythm Stick' by Ian Dury And The Blockheads. The idea was taken from Glen Turner who played the original at the end of one of his 1990 sets at Ibiza. It had previously been remixed in 1985 by Paul Hardcastle, but it was the Flying version that got the chief Blockhead's

Andrew Komis of First Choice

blessing. Since its inception Flying has offered a consistent diet of quality dance for their many advocates in the media and the nation's club scene. Their signings include End ('Rebel Song'), Joy Salinas ('The Mystery Of Love'), Korda ('Move Your Body'), Ferrante & Co featuring Kay Bianco ('Breakin' Away'), Kwanzaa Posse ('Wicked Funk'), Digital Boy ('This Is Muthafucker', '1-2-3 Acid'), Nexy Lanton ('I Am'), Jamie Dee ('Memories, Memories'), Latin Blood ('Deseo') and Lamott Atkins ('Communicate'). A series of background personnel, affiliates and colleagues were routinely involved, sometimes English, often Italian. For instance, Daybreak's 'Tomorrow' was created by Gino 'Woody' Bianchi and Corrardo Rizza and Dom Scuteri, and sung by Karen Jones. The label's other major successes include Gat Decor's 'Passion', remixed for the label by Darren Emmerson, and Ami Stewart's 'Friends '91'.

Force Inc

German label run by Achim Szepanski whose ethos is not timid: 'The philosophy is to play really energetic music, like punk where everything you say is squeezed into one moment'. Force Inc made its name with Exit 100's harsh 'Liquid', before Szepanski pulled the label away from the acid/trance direction with which it had become associated. Later releases invoked what the label termed 'Rauschen', or 'white noise', with a fusion of breakbeats and jungle techno. The best example of which was undoubtedly Biochip C's *Hell's Bells* EP. The label's catalogue also features artists like Alec Empire, Jamin' Unit Vs Walker (whose *Egglayer* EP in 1992 was popular) and Space Cube. Force Inc set up an English office in 1993.

Formation Records

Record label specialising in hardcore/darkside techno, inaugurated by Leroy Small (aka DJ SS) and Eidris Hassam in 1992. They grew up as part of a breakdancing crew before joining a DJ clique entitled Formation 5 in their native Leicester. Formation was formed as an arm of their 5HQ shop in the city, to fill a gap for the region's underground dance punters. The records were distributed by their own F Project operation, which also released records just as frequently in its own right. This in addition to their own house and rap labels. 'Our music's made underground to appeal to a commercial crowd. We've survived because we've stayed versatile. The whole feel and vibe of the scene has gone so we've had to change with the times'. In just over a year, via their various networking operations, Formation had dropped over 40 dance tunes on their enthusiastic

record-buying public, the best of which including several items from DJ SS (including his collaborations with EQ and Tango, who record in their own right), Oaysis, Mastersafe, Darkman, Bizz and Mickey Finn.

Fowlkes, Eddie 'Flashin''

One of the less celebrated techno expatriates from Detroit, though releases like 'Turn Me Out', produced by Graeme Park, are certainly not lacking in quality. Fowlkes was a friend and co-conspirator with all the Detroit giants, DJing alongside Derrick May and Juan Atkins in the early 80s and recorded his debut, 'Goodbye Kiss', on Atkins' Metroplex imprint. His nickname, incidentally, comes from his early prowess as a scratch and mix DJ. In the 90s he was still attending the decks at Detroit's The Alley, and in 1991 released *Serious Techno Vol. 1*, another tough but soulful encounter. As he reasoned, 'most Euro techno has no feeling because the makers haven't got the history'. He would also provide Detroit label 430 West with 'Inequality'.

FPI Project

Principally Damon Rochefort (b. c.1965, Cardiff, Wales), a former law student, and Sharon Dee Clarke (b. c.1965), a part-time actor with bit parts in several television soap operas. They scored an instant hit in late 1989/early 1990 when 'Going Back To My Roots' gatecrashed the UK Top 10. It was available in two formats, the first with a Paulo Dini vocal, the second version by Clarke. Following further singles 'Risky' and 'Everybody (All Over The World)', the two protagonists would go on to enjoy further chart success as Nomad. However, Rochefort continued to use the FPI banner on occasion, such as the 1992 *Paradise* EP.

Freaky Realistic

Peckham, London outfit founded by Justin Anderson, whose cockney leer is the focal point for much of their press. He is joined by Texan rapper Michael Lord and female Japanese vocalist, Aki Omori. Three singles, 'Something New'/'Cosmic Love Vibes', 'Leonard Nimoy' and 'Koochie Ryder' all featured on their debut album, before Lord quit the band in the summer of 1993.
Album: *Frealism* (Polydor 1993).

Freedom Of Speech

Comprising Luke Losey, Mickey Mann and Stika, Freedom Of Speech are proponents of what has come to be known in dance clubs as 'darkside', a style of techno which attacks the conscious and

Eddie Flashin' Fowlkes

Friends, Lovers & Family

subconscious with images culled from horror books, nursery rhymes and Kafka-esque noises. The trio met on the Shamen's Synergy tour in 1987, and each member has subsequently made a sizeable contribution to the evolution of dance music. Losey prepared lights for stage shows from the KLF and Curve, Mann co-produced an album with Orbital, and continued to organise warehouse parties, often in conjunction with the Mutoid Waste Company. The trio came together as part of the Midi Circus tour, and made their debut with 'Surveillance', which appeared on Planet Dog's *Feed Your Head* compilation. There was a big brother theme to back it up, the single built on samples of surveillance workers. They also released 'X-Beats', which preceded their debut album. 'We're into the kind of paranoia and bleakness of emotions which Joy Division used to put across' they noted. The 'negative vibes for the future of the world' syndrome was informed in part by a visit to Russia when supporting the Shamen on tour.

Albums: *Art Of The State* (1994).

Friends, Lovers & Family

Formed in South London in 1991, Friends Lovers & Family is a trio of Lawrence Elliot-Potter (b. c.1968), Nicky Howes (b. c.1972) and Wilf Frost (b. c.1970). They were quickly picked up by Rising High soon after the release of their debut single, 'Children's Stories', for Beatfreak Records. Immediately they were distinguished by their strong use of visuals, with Frost providing their distinctive artwork (he had formerly worked at various warehouse parties offering his skills). Elliot-Potter had served his apprenticeship engineering, going on to work with Rising High stalwarts like Mixmaster Morris, as well as other prominent techno/house labels like R&S, Hooj Choons and Pulse 8. Howes, meanwhile, was a prominent DJ in his own right. As Friends, Lovers & Family, their most prominent early foray for their new label was the *Focus* EP, its quasi-Gothic feel endearing it to many. It was followed by 'Signals Of Decay'/'Signs Of Rebirth', which previewed a debut mini-album in the progressive ambient mode. Elliot-Parker also worked with Epiphany and alongside Rising High supremo Caspar Pound on the New London School Of Electronics project.

Album: *At Home With Friends, Lovers & Family* (Rising High 1994; min-album).

Fresh Fruit Records

After ESP/Go Bang!, Amsterdam's most important, slightly more underground dance label. The location of the enterprise, run by Rene 'DJ Zki' and Gaston Dobre, is a bedroom in Gaston's mother's house. From this impromptu studio emerged records by the Goodmen (the debut 'Give It Up', which brought them mainstream chart success), Klatsch ('God Save The Queer') or Rene Et Gaston ('Contes De Fees'), which are the three names the duo employ. They also use these monikers for their remixing activities, i.e. the Goodmen's work on Ricky Rouge's 'Strange Love'. The label was inaugurated in November 1991, before which they had both aleady been active in the dance scene. Rene's string of Euro house credits included SiL and World Series Of Life ('Spread Love'), while Gaston operated as Trancesetters, Virtual Reality, Jark Prongo, Con-Am, Jamshed and 41 Days. Working together Gaston adopts responsibility for keyboards and computers, while Rene, with 15 years DJing work behind him, furnishes ideas. Their mode of operation involves a week-long bedroom routine, with sampling a key, but invisible component: 'We use records for sampling...we build a song around the sample, then we take the sample away'. 'Father In The Bathroom', the title-track to the Goodmen's debut album, was in fact a sample of exactly that; Gaston's father cleaning the bathroom. Other names used by the duo include South Street Player.
Album: As the Goodmen: *Father In The Bathroom* (Fresh Fruit 1994).

Fun-Da-Mental

An Asian 'world dance' band, the original Fun-Da-Mental had formed in Bradford, Yorkshire, in August 1991, specifically to play the Notting Hill Carnival of that year. Though all of the initial four-piece were born in Pakistan or India, they had each grown up in Northern English cities. The initial line-up was Propa-Ghandi (b. Aki Nawaz: aka Prince Haq), DJ Obeyo, Bad-Sha Lallaman and Man Tharoo Goldfinger (b. Inder Matharu; also of Trans-Global Underground). Their debut single was 'Janaam - The Message', which immediately brought them to the attention of the national music press, particularly the dance magazines. After a cassette-only release, they followed up with 'Gandhi's Revenge', before 'Sister India', initially recorded for a live John Peel Radio 1 session. On the back of such exposure they looked certain to be on the verge of a significant break through - when they themselves broke in two in late 1993, during a video shoot in Pakistan. Industry conjecture suggested rows over royalty payments and allocations, as rappers Goldfinger and Bad-Sha Lallaman left to team up with DJ Obeyo, and attempted to take the name with them. Eventually they became Det-ri-Mental. Fun-Da-Mental carried on, their first release since the departures was 'Countryman', in November 1993. Fun-Da-Mental's leadership remained Propa-Ghandi, formerly a member of gothic bands Southern Death Cult and Getting The Fear, who is also responsible for Nation Records, and DJ Blacka D. They joined with Pop Will Eat Itself for the 'Ich Bin Ein Auslander' anti-racism tirade. Another controversial single followed in 1994, 'Dog Tribe', which began with a recorded answerphone message left at the offices of Youth Against Racism by a member of sinister far-right group, Combat 18. Fun-Da-Mental themselves have been targeted by the likes of the British National Party - who were forced to apologise after printing their picture in one of their magazines with the caption 'a gang of Asian thugs'. They also became one of the first bands to visit the post-apartheid South Africa, which left a lasting impression on them, prior to the release of their debut album. This, the title adapted from Black Panther Bobby Seale, included remixes of 'Wrath Of The Black Man' and 'Countryman', guest appearances by Neil Sparkes of Trans-Global Underground, poet Subi Shah and ex-Collapsed Lung singer Nihal.
Album: *Seize The Time* (Beggars Banquet 1994).

Future Sound Of London

Offered to dance punters as the 'intelligent way out of blind-alley hardcore', Future Sound Of London emerged in the 90s, the brainchild of Gary Cobain (b. Bedford, England) and Brian Dougan. They had met in 1985 in Manchester, when Cobain embarked on an electronics degree, while Dougan studied the allied science of sound engineering. Cobain soon jilted college, and by 1987 had enrolled on an Enterprise Allowance Course in order to set up his own studio. The duo continued to record discordant electronic pieces together, but it wasn't until the house explosion of 1988 that they discovered like minds and a new musical structure. Both would go on to earn their spurs in the Manchester house scene, Dougan completing a ground-breaking Top 10 hit (as Stakker) with 'Humanoid'. Their other projects together spawned Semi Real ('People Livin' Today'), Yage, Metropolis (*Metropolis* EP), Art Science Technology, Mental Cube ('So This Is Love'), Candese, Intelligent Communication and Smart Systems. However, under the title Future Sound Of London they scored a major crossover success

with 'Papua New Guinea', an enticing, beautifully orchestrated piece which was also recorded in session version for the John Peel programme in 1992; one of the few dance bands to achieve (or cherish) this status. Still under the FSOL banner the duo released the single 'Cascade' in October 1993, which clocked in at 30 minutes and 50 seconds. Originally recorded in five separate segments, it was pieced together specially for the release, combining breakbeats with rumbling bass and heavy atmospherics. Utilising their Amorphous Androgynous *nom de plume* they also recorded the *Tales Of Ephidrina* long player, one of many concurrent pseudonymous excursions. Virgin were allegedly so desperate to sign the band from their own Jumpin' And Pumpin' that they were allowed freedom to record elsewhere, as long as the label had access to all releases under the Future Sound Of London moniker. They have also earned their way as a remix team, rejigging Inner City's 'Praise' among others. They now own their own studio, Earthbeat, in Dollis Hill, London, and talk vividly of their desire to expand into multi-media, including the production of books, videos and radio shows. The most famous of these was a stint at Kiss-FM which produced an incredible response from listeners who were quite unaccustomed to anything like it. Rather than tour in a conventional manner, which they see as a concession to a redundant musical lifestyle, they have organised 'radio tours', intermittently broadcast on various BBC stations. The event which caused most reaction came in May 1994 when they played a set from their North London studio which was sent via modem to be aired on Pete Tong's *Essential Mix* show on Radio 1. A telephone number was given over the air, which allowed listeners to view video graphics on their home computers as a soundrack.
Albums: *Accelerator* (Debut 1992), *Lifeforms* (Virgin 1994). As Amorphous Androgynous: *Tales Of Ephidrina* (Virgin 1993).

Gabrielle

The corporate record industry's new garage diva of the 90s, Gabrielle has earned a high profile in commercial dance via a series of perfectly realised, expertly pitched releases. Visually distinguished by a black eye patch, she tore up the charts with her debut single, 'Dreams', in 1993. Equally accessible was a follow-up, 'Going Nowhere' The album that followed was assembled by seven different producers, including the Boilerhouse (Cox and Steele of the Fine Young Cannibals) and Steve Jervier (famed for his work with Take That). She was feted in various awards ceremonies, and became such a celebrity that she was invited to appear at the Armani fashion show in Milan.
Album: *Find Your Way* (Go! Beat 1994).

Gage, Mark

b. c.1961, USA. From Rochester, New York, Gage can genuinely point to a life-long committment to his art. 'I've been possessed by music ever since I was a very little kid. I was collecting 45s when I was four or five years old. I had boxes for them, and I would go off to my Grandma's house and just play records the whole time I was there. So, in a sense, even at that age I was a DJ'. However, until the early 90s he subsisted entirely on wages from waiting tables. Two cult 12-inch successes, the *Cusp* EP and Vapourspace's 'Gravitational Arch Of 10', both for Plus 8, changed that. 'Gravitational Arch Of 10', was, infact, a misprint. The title was meant to have read 'Arch of Lo', but a mix up at the pressing plant ensured that it passed into techno folklore under a slightly different title. He went on to tour as Vapourspace, which is also the name of his studio, and was quickly signed up to a mult-album deal with ffrr/Internal, gaining rave reviews from a US tour with the Aphex Twin, Moby and Orbital.
Album: As Vapourspace: *Themes From Vapourspace* (Internal 1994).

Galliano

b. Rob Gallagher. New age rapper and jazz poet who was originally inspired by a school visit to see Linton Kwesi Johnson, and subsequently retraced rap's origins to the Last Poets. When he left school Galliano began broadcasting on pirate radio and made appearances on the underground poetry circuit. The most important of these dates was at

Giles Peterson's 'Babylon' club in Charing Cross. There he enthusiastically partook of the resident rare groove/jazz sounds, and incorporated these as his musical backing. He released his first record, 'Frederick Lies Still', a tribute to Curtis Mayfield and Last Poet Jalal Mansur Nuriddin, with Peterson, but his first vinyl as Galliano was to be 'Welcome To The Story'. Galliano became an intrinsic component in the early rise of Acid Jazz, building a fruitful relationship with producer Chris Bangs. When Peterson was headhunted by Phonogram Records to set up the similarly-inclined Talkin' Loud label, Galliano was his first signing. Although his solo work had thus far been successful, he elected now to extend his live and studio performances by adding musicians and collaborators. Thus vocalist Constantine Weir (who sang on S-Express' two major hits, and managed the 70s funk club, the Shack) and drummer Bro.Spry (b. Crispin Robinson, formerly a professional skateboarder and a session contributor to Soul II Soul, Yazz, Bananarama, Young Disciples etc.) became official members of Galliano, as well as occasional appearances from Jalal Nuriddin. Aided by former Style Council member Mick Talbot, this line-up completed Galliano's debut album. By the advent of the group's third album, the line-up boasted singer Valerie Ettienne, Ernie McKone, Talbot, Spry and Mark Vandergucht (guitar). This formation's May 1994 single, 'Long Time Gone', a cover of the David Crosby song, was their first release in over two years. It took them to the *Top Of The Pops* stage and the verge of commercial breakthrough.
Albums: *In Pursuit Of The 13th Note* (Talkin' Loud 1991), *A Joyful Noise Unto The Creator* (Talkin' Loud 1992), *The Plot Thickens* (Talkin' Loud 1994).

Garage

A musical term which, in the dance world, is generally taken to indicate smooth house music with female diva vocals, rather than the ragged guitar bands it represented in the late 60s and 70s. It took the name from the success of its principal early venue, Larry Levan's Paradise Garage, in New York. Levan (b. c.1954, d. 8 November 1992) was the producer behind 'electro' standards from the Peach Boys ('Don't Make Me Wait'), and produced Taana Gardner's 'Heartbeat', Instant Funk's 'I Got My Mind Made Up' and Skyy's 'First Time Around'. Best of all, arguably, was his remix of Gwen Guthrie's 'Ain't Nothing Goin' On But The Rent'. This lent him obvious 'disco' credentials, which proliferate in the garage music of the 90s. Levan ran the Paradise Garage from opening to closure (1976 to 1987), but died in the early 90s after a heart attack brought on by cocaine addiction. Others had already accepted the torch, with Junior Vasquez (an early attendee at Paradise Garage) launching the hugely popular Sound Factory night, and producers like David Morales perfecting the formula. Much generic garage music has come and gone, its origins in disco ensuring that it is the staple output of many mainstream pop dance acts. At its best (Crystal Waters, the aforementioned Morales) it can be an elegiac, uplifting art form, at its worst it is all too often predicatable, formulaic and stiflingly unadventourous.

Garnier, Laurent

Regarded as France's finest techno DJ, Garnier, who started behind the decks in 1987, insists that his musical spectrum is much wider. Although he has been a powerful advocate of all things Detroit for some time, he has also had a hand in the establishment of the European hard trance movement. His reputation was built on a punishing schedule, performing five nights a week at up to four different countries within Europe. He also runs a club in Paris called Wake Up, whose free-ranging music policy was reflected on the 'Wake Up' remix of Moby's 'Hymn'. The latter was just one such remixing project, which has brought him to the forefront of the dance world. So too his label, FNAC, which, jointly helmed with Eric Morand (his PR) pioneered French dance music. It has been superseded by a new imprint, F. However, before they bowed out of their involvement with FNAC, they put together a compilation, *La Collection*, which was extraordinarily well-received by dance critics and pundits. Many of the acts featured followed Garnier and Morand to their new label.

Gee Street Records

Gee Street (aka Gee St) was established at the end of 1987 by managing director Jon Baker, who had lived in New York in the early 80s, gaining his roots in black music, hip hop and electro. He returned to London but tired quickly of music industry machinations within the majors and elected to set up a separate entity. He enrolled his co-conspirator DJ Richie Rich as his partner and Gee Street was born. The label began with 'Scam 1 & 2', but soon built up an eclectic dance/rap roster, gaining a distribution deal through Rough Trade. They immediately set up a sister office in New York to allow them to guage and exploit both markets, their first US signing being the Jungle Brothers. The label also licensed material from US labels like Warlock and Idlers. However,

Galliano

the most succesful act would prove to be the Stereo MC's and their Ultimatum remix arm (Birch and 'The Head' having played a prominent role in establishing Gee Street studio). Other early acts included Outlaw Posse and Boonsquawk. Rich, who also recorded for the label, went on to found Happy Family Records in 1992 and become a video jockey for MTV. He split with Baker when Island bought out Gee Street, but agreed to still offer their artists his remix skills. Simon Quance took over as label manager, while the label also grew an extra tentacle with the Gee-Zone subsidiary (Doi-ing etc).

Gipsy

Among Limbo's most prestigious recordings acts, Gipsy is the Glasgow-born musician Graham Drinnan (also referred to by some as 'the hardest working man in house music'). His recordings include the wonderful 'I Trance You', released when he was just 18 in 1992, which has remained a standby in many DJs playlists ever since. 1994 material included 'Funk De Fino', while he also mixed the 17 track *Transend* compilation for Rumour. He formed Sublime in 1992 with Circa DJ Matt Brown, who have also gone on to release a slew of hugely impressive dance cuts for Limbo: 'Fight The Feeling', 'Theme', 'Trans American' (one of 1993's most popular club cuts) and 'TGV'.

Gloworm

Group fronted by Sedric Johnson (b. Alabama), currently resident in California, USA. The leader of the 100-strong Long Beach Choir, he was spotted at a soul revue by Englishman Will Mount, who was on the lookout for a singer. After an impromptu performance Mount, who together with producer/remixer Rollo forms the musician team behind Gloworm, was won over. They anchored Johnson's gospel inspired vocals to a club beat to produce memorable records like 'I Lift My Cup' and 'Carry Me Home', both based on traditional songs. The result was reviewed as 'spiritual hard house', and widely admired. 'I Lift My Cup' was unveiled on Hooj Tunes at the end of 1992, before the group switched to Go! Beat.

Good Boy Records

Mark Auerbach and Steve Travell's London-based operation. The company was formed in December 1992. Auerbach and Travell were already well-known in dance circles for their work as Bump (whose 'I'm Rushin'' graced the label). They have their own studio, and elected to start Good Boy because they were giving away too many of their own ideas on remixes for other people. A 'Classy New York style' is the intention, based on their admiration for the Strictly Rhythm empire. Distributed through the Network umbrella, they started well with releases like Wax Factor's 'Only Love'.

Grid

Another of techno's many duos, the Grid comprise Dave Ball (b. 3 May 1959, Salford, Greater Manchester, England) and Richard Norris (b. 23 June 1965, London, England). Ball's name was familiar to many through his work as part of another highly successful pair, Soft Cell. Having split from Marc Almond, Ball would work with Psychic TV and Jack The Tab where he first linked with Norris, a veteran of several outfits including the Fruitbats, Innocent Vicars, East Of Eden and Mr Suit. He was also well known through his writing in *Boy's Own* magazine, *New Musical Express* and the b-movie and 60s-fixated periodical *Strange Things*. Jack The Tab recorded one album of early British acid house, ostensibly as a compilation of 11 artists but actually just the duo. Like many of techno's new breed, the Grid have not limited themselves to their own releases, clocking up an impressive array of remixes for other artists as well. These have included several major names, Brian Eno, Happy Mondays, Pet Shop Boys, the Art Of Noise and Ball's old friends, Soft Cell. Even Vic Reeves ('Abide With Me') came in for the Grid treatment. Their own recording career has attracted plenty of praise in both the mainstream and specialist dance press, who have even tolerated the band playing live behind screens, *ala* PiL. However, since their debut, 'On The Grid', in June 1989, their CV has been chequered by short tenures with their record labels. Following four singles and an album for East West, the group joined Rhythm King for a one-off single ('Timothy Leary Meets The Grid'), before departing for Virgin. Their eclectic *456* set for the latter included collaborations with Robert Fripp, Yello and Sun Ra. Singles like 'Crystal Clear', however, revealed a return to the stripped down, meaner techno sound. They split for DeConstruction in late 1993, their debut single for the label being 'Texas Cowboys'. However, it was 'Swamp Thing' that provided the real fanfare, predicting the hoedown sound that was creeping in to house with its use of banjos, and catapulting them to the UK Top 10. Norris subsequently set up his own label, Candy Records.
Albums: *Electric Head* (East West 1990), *456* (Virgin 1992).

Groove Corporation

Groove Corporation

Essentially the remainder of Electribe 101 minus original vocalist Billie Ray Martin. After they had buried their former incarnation, Joe Stevens, Les Fleming, Robert Cimarosti and Brian Nordhoff retreated to their Birmingham studio complex to regroup. They re-emerged in 1993 with a new, reggae-influenced club sound. They also hooked up with Birmingham independent label Cake, joining DJ Dick and Nigel Blunt (aka the Original Rockers) on a 'dub-clash' 12-inch, 'Stoned'. They also worked with local reggae movers such as Captain Animal and Bim Sherman, as well as the more conventional techno sounds of Kevin Saunderson's Reese Project. Their own accounts were opened with the *Passion* EP and the club hit, 'Summer Of Dub'. Their debut album was the result of sessions with local rappers and singers working as a collective, in a manner which echoed Massive Attack's Bristol operation.
Album: *Co-Operation* (Network 1994).

GTO

One of the many outfits which feature the talents of London-based former video artist Lee Newman, among the few women involved in the evolution of techno. Influences primarily came from the industrial sector, and groups like Test Department and the output of the Wax Trax label. She has spent several years DJing, remixing and programming, and contributes a column to *DJ* magazine under the title Technohead. Together with her partner, Michael Wells, GTO was an acronym for Greater Than One, the original title of their band in the mid-80s who released a string of experimental albums. Together they have contributed some of the essential modern techno cuts ('Pure' for Go! Bang, 'Listen To The Rhythm Flow' for Belgium label Jumping Man), the best of which were compiled on their debut album. Yet instead of the anticipated rigid, hard beat techno experience, it circumvented expectations by partially adopting the innovations of the trance movement. It was preceded by another excellent single, 'Love Is Everywhere'. Later came 'Dub Killer', which went further still and slowed down the pace to a crawl. As Tricky Disco they released two singles, 'Tricky Disco' (1990) and 'Housefly' (1991) for the Warp empire, and recorded as John & Julie (hardcore) and Church Of Ecstasy (for Rising High). There have also been collaborations with Germany's DJ Tanith and the US' Underground Resistance.

Guerilla

Record label formed by William Orbit and Dick O'Dell (previously owner of Y Records) in London in 1990, in furtherance of their mutual devotion to house music. Guerilla was originally set up as an outlet for Orbit's Bass-O-Matic project, who gave the label their debut release, 'In The Realm Of The Senses'. In the wake of that track's success several offers came from major record labels, and Guerilla eventually signed to Virgin. The label managed to maintain its own image and identity, however, not least through their now-famous 'camouflage' sleeves. The most successful of Guerilla's artists include Spooky, Moody Boyz, Outermind, D.O.P., React 2 Rhythm, Trance Induction and others. The sound of the label has most frequently been described as 'progressive' house, though this hardly pleases the protagonists: 'What we do have ben hijacked and turned into this thing called progressive house, which I absolutely loathe. It's possible that people might say we're following a trend that we started!'. Guerilla has successfully built its own audience with its generic cover designs and fully-realised, polished recordings, which are just as suitable for home listening as the club scene. As O'Dell notes: 'Unlike the majors we don't have to keep releasing records at a breakneck speed. If we don't feel we have any material ready to release in any particular month then so be it'. The label signed a US deal with IRS to licence their (increasingly popular) product in that territory.
Selected albums: Various: *Dub House Disco* (Guerilla 1992), *Dub House Disco 2000* (Guerilla 1993). React 2 Rhythm: *Whatever You Dream* (Guerilla 1992). Spooky: *Gargantuan* (Guerilla 1993). Moody Boyz: *Product Of The Environment* (Geurilla 1994).

Guru Josh

Noted for his goatee beard, flailing live performances and three word songs, Guru Josh (b. Paul Walden, c.1964) nevertheless helped kickstart the DeConstruction success story. He had originally run a club night in Putney entitled the Happy House, and sang in a rock band, Joshua Cries Wolf. Of his singles at least 'Infinity' was propelled by a great saxophone sequence, and 'Whose Law (Is It Anyway?)' also had its fans. The title might have given the impression that this was some sort of rave 'mission statement', but typically the 'lyrics' made absolutely no sense whatsoever. If Guru Josh was, as *Smash Hits* magazine delcared, 'spokesman for the warehouse generation', he was an embarassingly inarticulate role model. When critics spotted a cover of 'Louie Louie' on his debut album the game was definitely up.
Album: *Infinity* (DeConstruction 1990).

Guy

Widely applauded as the originators of swingbeat, a fusion of hip hop beats with gospel/soul vocals, Guy comprised Teddy Riley (ex-R&B group Kids At Work) and brothers Aaron and Albert Damion Hall. At the close of the 80s the New York trio broke big by combining Aaron's talented larynx with the studio know-how of producer Riley. The sound and image was much copied both by artists and consumers. Riley went on to become a multi-millionaire for his sins, though his acrimonious split from former business partner Gene Griffin helped sour a couple of the more rap-based tracks on the band's follow-up album. However, as with many of Riley's projects, the group have yet to replicate their US success in Britain. Aaron Hall's first solo album, *The Truth*, was released in 1993, including the swing classic 'Don't Be Afraid'. Riley would go on to produce, among several other projects, Michael Jackson's *Dangerous* in 1991.

Albums: *Guy* (Uptown 1989), *The Future* (Uptown 1990).

Gyrlz

The first genuine New Jill Swing act, the Gyrlz were formed in 1987 by Terri, Monica and Tara. Their initial demo tapes were produced by the omnipresent Teddy Riley and Kyle West. 'When we recorded our demos with Teddy he was still living in the St. Nicholas Projects in Harlem. Those were the good old days' remembers Terri. They thence met up with Uptown Records' mainman Andre Harrell, who asked them, via the intervention of Heavy D, to record an album. They enjoyed minor success with 'Wishing You Were Here', before joining Al. B. Sure as backing singers on his *Heartbreak* tour. From there they became the opening act for Bobby Brown and New Edition, but split at the end of the tour. 'We were lost rebels without much of a cause and with nowhere to go' is how Monica painfully records the experience. Terri returned to New York, briefly singing for Key West, another Uptown band who never released an album, before moving back to Philadelphia. There she decided to reunite with Monica, as Terri And Monica, with Tara becoming their manager.

H

Haddaway

b. Nester Alexander Haddaway, c.1966. A lightweight, chart-friendly techno pop artist from the Arista stable. Haddaway scored a huge crossover hit throughout Europe with the anthemic 'What Is Love', followed by the equally strident 'Life'. Born in Chicago, his album was little more than a roster of fillers sandwiching the two hits. However, those two hits are as good as commercial hip house comes. Haddaway himself, though often compared to the Euro fare of 2 Unlimited and Cappela, is a far more sophisticated proposition. He has a college degree in marketing, his own business career, his own fashion company (Energy) and until 1994 was completely self-managed. Prior to his chart residency he was also a professional US footballer for the Cologne Crocodiles.

Album: *Haddaway - The Album* (Arista 1993).

Hannant, Beaumont

York, England-based Hannant (b. c.1970) boasts Austrian, English and Yugoslavian ancestors. Working during the day at the Depth Charge record shop in York, he also DJs at local techno and jazz/hip hop clubs. He began recording for the first time in 1992, releasing one EP before a mini-album, *Basic Data Manipulation,* was unveiled on General Productions Recordings. He principally came to prominence via the compilation, *Positiva Ambient Collection*, with 'Awakening The Soul'. Predicted by no lesser a tipster than Andy Weatherall as techno's great white hope, his first full album in 1994 arrived in two completely separate versions: one intended for CD consumption, the other a vinyl variant. It was a clear indication of the different requirements of dance fans in the 90s. Hannant also talked widely about future projects mixing his current Detroit-derived techno flair with the music of prominent 'indie' bands like Madder Rose and Screaming Trees, his own personal listening favourites.

Albums: *Basic Data Manipulation: Tastes And Textures Vol. 2* (General Production 1993, mini-album), *Texturology* (General Production 1994).

Hardcastle, Paul

b. 10 December 1957, London, England. Hardcastle is a producer, mixer, composer and

keyboard wizard specialising in dance orientated product. He worked in a hi-fi shop and developed an interest in electronics in his teens. His first group was First Light, alongside Derek Green, whose output included a deplorable 'Horse With No Name'. After four solo minor hits in 1984, '19', a record about the Vietnam conflict utilising spoken news reports, went straight to number 1 in the UK in 1985. The follow up, 'Just For The Money', was based on the Great Train Robbery and boasted the voices of Bob Hoskins and Sir Laurence Olivier. Further singles were progressively less successful before he scored with 'Papa's Got A Brand New Pigbag' under the pseudonym Silent Underdog. He also wrote the *Top Of The Pops* theme, 'The Wizard', in 1986, before switching to production for young funk band LW5, providing remixes for anyone from Third World to Ian Dury. Another production credit was the last ever Phil Lynott single, coincidentally called 'Nineteen'. Other engagements came with Carol Kenyon (previously vocalist on Heaven 17's 'Temptation') most notably on her 1986 Top 10 hit 'Don't Waste My Time'. Recently Hardcastle has 'retired' to his Essex home studio and releases records under such pseudonyms as the Def Boys, Beeps International, Jazzmasters and Kiss The Sky (the last of which is Hardcastle and Jaki Graham). Most sell in reasonable quantities. He is also founder of his own label, Fast Forward, and has recently written the theme music to two BBC nature series, *Supersense* and its sequel, *Lifesense*
Albums: *Zero One* (Blue Bird 1985), *Paul Hardcastle* (Chrysalis 1985), *No Winners* (Chrysalis 1988). Compilation: *Soul Syndicate* (K-Tel 1988).

Hardbag
A collaborative project launched by Red Marc, a resident DJ with the Drum Club, and Matt Early, formerly of Bumble, who once enjoyed a club hit via a celebrated Andy Weatherall remix of 'West In Motion'. Their debut release together, 'Ceasefire', was recorded with sampled sounds from the war in the former Yugoslavia, to raise money for the Serious Road Trip charity. This was no idle conscience-appeasing effort, but an attempt to ship food and medical supplies directly to Sarajevo. The samples were collected personally by Early on a visit in 1993, and as well as the sounds of conflict embraced library recordings of many years of native Yugoslavian music. The project was designed to portray ravers and dance music fans as something more than mere hedonists and consumers. Early has also lectured to the British Council on the positive, unifying nature of club

music. 'Ceasefire' was released on the Drum Club's Midi Circus Projects imprint, only their second release.

Hardfloor
Oliver Bandzio and Ramon Zenker are the duo behind these Dusseldorf-based acid house revivalists. Typically, Bandzio's life was changed by 1988's flourishing acid scene. Unlike many, however, he was determined to recreate the excitement of those heady days, and spent no less than three years attempting to track down his own Roland 303, responsible for much of the sound of that period. After having finally traced one he made the acquaintance of studio wizard Zenkler, and together they debuted with 'Hardtrance Acperience', on Sven Vath's Harthouse label late in 1992. Some critics questioned whether the track contained the longest snare roll ever committed to vinyl, while its stylings were inextricably those of the summer of 1988 (it became arguably the most important post-acid house acid house record ever). The follow-up 12-inch sampled hunting horns, hence its name 'Into The Nature', on which production was orchestrated by 303 guru Richie Hawtin.
Album: *Funalogue* (Harthouse 1994, mini-album).

Hardkiss
Scott Hardkiss grew up in San Francisco's house sub-culture, although he was originally inspired by hip hop. He DJ'd at Tenerife in 1989 and Glastonbury in 1990, where he was fondly remembered for his determination to incorporate a live 303, usually played by Space Time Continuum's Jonah. He had formed the Hardkiss trio with DJs Robbie Hardkiss and label manager Gavin Hardkiss after meeting them at college - they were later joined by John Williams. They travelled from the East (where they were at college) to the West Coast, and made their name on the warehouse scene there. Things were going swimmingly until a rival promoter contacted the police, the subsequent raid scuppered them to the tune of $10,000. Though they continued the high profile Sunny Side Up nights, they also moved into label management, the *Magic Sounds Of San Francisco* EP being their debut release. A major cult item, it boasted samples drawn from both the Beatles and Shamen, to a hip hop backdrop. Under the title Hawke their third release, '3 Nudes In A Purple Garden', was similarly inventive. 'Raincry' and 'Phoenix' by God Within (aka Scott Hardkiss) arrived in typically glossy packaging and psychedelic artwork. Meanwhile their highly personalised, off-centre live sets continued, with

Robbie typically dropping 'Radio Clash' into a set at the Ministry Of Sound. Scott remixed One Dove's 'White Love' in an acid version, and turned the Drum Club's 'Drums Are Dangerous' into 'Shrubs Are Dangerous' for US consumption.

Harthouse

German label overseen by Heinz Roth and Sven Vath, which began its account with the latter's 'My Name Is Barbarella'. Harthouse is also the umbrella organisation for sister labels Eye Q and Recycle Or Die. 'The music is the main thing. We're all crazy about music and we're like a big family'. The stable is home to prolific artists like Arpeggiators (who release material as Microbots, Phuture Wax etc.), Marco Zaffarono and Jurgen Kreschel ('MZ 5', 'Minimalism' etc.) and PCP (Planet Core Productions - who released over 50 records in 1992 alone). Other successful releases included Spicelab's eponymous EP and, most impressive of all, Hardfloor's 'Hardtrance Acperience', which revisited the acid scene with its nostalgic but fearsome delivery. As Harthouse's popularity grew they signed some of their Eye Q/Recycle Or Die product compilations through Warners for superior distribution, having also worked alongside the UK's Rising High.
Selected album: Various: *The Point Of No Return Chapter 1* (Harthouse 1993).

Hawtin, Richie

b. 1973, Windsor, Ontario, Canada. The 303-renaissance man, better known for operations under two separate guises. As Plastikman he debuted with the 'Spastik' 12-inch, an unreservedly harsh and abrasive cut, followed by an album on his own Plus 8 records. The tail-end of 1993 saw the release of 'Krakpot' on Novamute, another intense house workout. The Plastikman moniker allows Hawtin to indulge his love of the 'acid' house sound of the 303: 'I find that many people are bastardising the 303 so all the tracks sound the same. It's OK to use it, but use it differently, that's my stance'. The FUSE moniker tends to encompass Hawtin's more disparate solo projects. As such the recording trail began in 1991 with 'F.U.', which launched the Plus 8 offshoot Probe Records. Other allied imprints include Definitive and Telepathic, all run in conjunction with John Acquaviva. The FUSE acronym stands for Further Underground Subsonic Experiments, and the releases are usually limited to between 500 and 800 copies, thereby ensuring that they are quickly circulated and collected by DJ's. Hawtin was also 'Richard Michaels', the man behind the deep house remix of The Blunted Dummies' 'House For

All'. Despite this busy schdule, he still hosts his Hard, Harder and Hardest warehouse parties in Detroit.
Album: As Plastikman: *Sheet One* (Plus 8 1993), *Recycled Plastik* (Plus 8/Novamute 1994). As FUSE: *Dimension Intrusion* (Warp 1993).

Heckmann, Thomas

b. Mainz, Frankfurt, Germany. Acid/techno DJ who first became interested in music through his father's collection of electronica; Jean Michel Jarre, Kraftwerk, Tangerine Dream and Pink Floyd via the early innovations of bands like the Human League and Throbbing Gristle in the late 70s. Afterwards he listened to more guitar orientated bands until the acid scene of 1988 and the work of 808 State returned him to his first love. Although he himself had recorded as early as 1980, buying his first synthesizer four years later, it wasn't until 1991 that he began to record acid cuts, the first of which was 'Liquid' (recorded under the name Exit 100). Since then, as well as his regular club spots throughout Europe, Heckmann has collaborated on a number of projects. His pseudonyms include Age, Skydiver, Spectral Emotions, Parot Torture, and he has also worked with Hoschi of Labworks as Purple Plejade. Having previously temped with D-Jax Up Beats, Sony and Edge, in 1993 he set up his own label, Trope Recordings, which became famed for a series of recordings under the Drax banner: 'Interior', 'Section 2' and 'Phosphene'. Other projects on the label include tracks from Christian Vogel and Mono Junk. Exit 100 separated from Sony in mid-1994, just before his first album proper on Trope as Drax.
Album: *Age* (Sony 1994). As Drax: *Drax Red* (Trope 1994).

Hedningara

Swedish dance crew signed to China Records in the UK, whose musical motifs generally encompass a feel for traditional folk music as much as new technology. Hedningara translates as 'the Heathens', and embraces five people: Anders Stake (string, wind instruments), Björn Tollin (string and percussion, programming), Hallbus Totte Mattsson (string), Sanna Kurki-Suoni (vocals), and Tellu Paulasto (vocals). They formed in 1987 when the three male members became disillusioned with the traditional folk world and travelled round museums searching for newer means of expression. Based on historical documents, they constructed their own instruments with which to conduct their experiments. They were joined by their two vocalists after a trip to Finland, who themselves were conducting research into the musical properties of the former Finnish (now Russian) state of Karelia. The two strands of music sat together well, yet instead of regaling folk audiences with it, a more natural market was found within the world of dance - the energy of their performances reflecting communal club culture more than any personality-led, secular music.

Albums: *Hedningarna* (MNW 1989), *Kaksi!* (Xource 1992, Silence 1994).

Heidi Of Switzerland

Also known simply as HOS, this is a Swiss operation which relocated to London in January 1993. Headed by owner/producer Hilary, the label has quickly become popular for its underground dance records, generally located in the fields of techno or trance. Other styles of music are diverted through HOS' sister labels, Budgie (Euro techno), Flash Your Tits (progressive) and De'Crust (ambient and dub). The label's most famous advocate is probably German artist Kinky Roland, whose material permeates through the label via several different pseudonyms. A good example being Dinge Queen In The Mist's 'Let Me Be Your Tupperwear' for the FYT subsidiary. Other artists include Trance Uber Alles, who work techno in a dramatic Teutonic style (notably 'Ich Shalte'), Innersystem (mainstream dance) and

Tranceparents (a highly-regarded soulful techno team). HOS also operates its own distribution, exporting under the title Wasp.

Selected album: *Erotic Tracks Vol. 2* (HOS 1994).

Henry, Pauline

The former Chimes' vocalist whose solo work brought about a reassessment of her career: 'After the Chimes, I took a while to think about what I really wanted to do with my career. I got my head down writing and had 25 songs. I learned my craft live, as opposed to being 'created' in the studio. I didn't know much about studios until I joined the Chimes'. As she idolises Tina Turner, it was doubtless no accident that her debut album included compositions such as 'Can't Take Your Love', co-written with Terry Britten, who had penned many of Turner's biggest hits. There was also a cover of Bad Company's 'Feel Like Making Love', revealing her R&B roots.

Album: *The Harder They Come* (Sony 1993).

Hermeljin, Dylan

Dutchman Hermeljin was still studying business economics part-time when his first brace of 2000 And One records were released on Fierce Ruling Diva's Lower East Side label in 1989 preceding 1992's 'Focus', which arrived on fellow

Richie Hawton

countryman Stefan Robber's Eevolute imprint. It was a typical slice of passionate techno. Much of his output remains mysterious, though 100% Pure is him and Sandy, his partner at the Black Beat record store. The tribal techno opus 'My Life In The Bush' arrived on their own 100% Pure label. Other monikers include Planet Gong ('Planet Gong', a Djax Up Beats dose of Detroit techno, actually recorded two years before release in 1994), Babies From Gong and Edge Of Motion. After just four releases 100% Pure were rewarded with an installment on Beechwood's *New Electronica* series, an album entitled *The Lowlands* emerging. Hermeljin decribed his music as 'from the heart and soul. It's designed to give you goose pimples'.
Album: *New Electronica Presents: The Lowlands* (Beechwood 1994).

Higher Intelligence Agency

Higher Intelligence Agency are Dave Wheels and Bobby Bird, part of the Birmingham Oscillate Collective, who first set up their own ambient/dub club in the back of a local pub in 1992. Next to London's Megadog, the Oscillate night soon emerged as one of the leading such establishments, with a strong reputation built on HIA's 'non-DJing' live sets plus appearances from Autechre, Biosphere, Orbital, Banco De Gaia, Drum Club and others, plus DJ sets from Mixmaster Morris and the Orb's Alex Paterson. They released their debut album in 1993 on the local Beyond imprint, and a remix EP, *Re-Form*, the following year. This featured the imprints of Autechre, The Irresistable Force, Pentatonik and label-mates, A Positive Life. However, playing live remained their forte, using an improvised set and state of the art equipment to produce a powerful fusion of dub and club music.
Album: *Colourform* (Beyond 1993).

Hi-Bias Records

Canadian dance imprint based in Toronto, and widely proclaimed as 'the DJ's label'. Hi-Bias grew out of the collapse of Big Shot Records (Index, Dionne, Amy Jackson, Dream Warriors etc.) in 1990, with producer and founder Nick Anthony Fiorucci then describing his new label as 'the next progression to the Big Shot sound'. In the fallout Ron Allen went on to form Strobe, and principal producer and co-founder Andrew Komis would create First Choice (the term Hi-Bias was first invoked as an artist title on Big Shot for the single, 'Wanna Take You Home'). High profile releases on the new label included Z Formation's *Brutal* EP in 1991, a typically collaborative project which featured remixes from Michael Ova, Fiorucci, Jason 'Deko' Steele and Nicky Holder. Another

outing for the 'Rhythm Formula Team' which forms the production basis of the label was Red Light's *Rhythm Formula* EP. Oval Emotion's 'Do It' from 1991 (sung by Cissy Goodridge and created by her producer brother Kenny Moran and Fiorucci) was another distinctive cut. Fiorucci's influence was recognised in the 90s when he was invited over to the UK to play sets at the Ministry Of Sound. 1992 saw material like Syndicate 305's 'I Promise' and Groove Sector's 'The Love I Lost'.

Higher State Records

London based record company formed in 1992 and run by Mark Dillon and Patrick Dickens, whose backgrounds were resolutely in the funk and soul traditions. As such they played out live as DJs in these genres, before the upsurge of house finally swept them up. However, the twenty-odd releases in their first two years revealed a strong residual flare for digifunk aesthetics. They soon cut out a niche with releases by Disco Biscuit, Spacebase and Sound Environment. There was also evidence of wider listening tastes, including dub reggae, new wave experimentalism (early Simple Minds) and proto hip hop (Mantronix): 'I could never listen to one particular kind of music all night in a club - it'd get too monotonous'. By 1994 they were still going strong with releases like 'My Geetar Hertz' by Roller Coaster and Lafferty's 'Thinkin' Bout'.

Hithouse

Label and studio, a subsidiary of ARS, founded by Dutch DJ and producer Peter Slaghuis, whose surname literally translated as Hithouse (hit as in 'strike' rather than in the pop chart sense). He used the same name to score in 1988 with 'Jack To The Sound Of The Underground', one of a rash of such records utilising the 'jack' word following the breakthrough success of Steve 'Silk' Hurley. Hithouse would host a slew of Dutch and Belgian techno acts, including Global Insert Project, Problem House, Holy Noise and Meng Syndicate ('Artificial Fantasy' etc.). Sadly Slaghuis died in a car crash on 5 September 1991.

Holmes, David

Holmes is a former member of the Disco Evangelists. After the latter's successes for Positiva ('De Niro', 'A New Dawn'), he recorded the solo effort, 'Johnny Favourite', for Warp. An enormously popular DJ, Holmes also found time to collaborate with former Dub Federation personnel Andy Ellison and Pete Latham as one third of the Scubadevils. The latter two met him while performing at the Sugarsweet nightclub. Together they recorded 'Celestial Symphony' for the *Trance*

Europe Express compilation, which was also remixed for a Novamute 12-inch release. This was backed by Holmes solo on 'Ministry' (credited to Death Before Disco). He has also recorded as the Well Charged Latinos ('Latin Prayer') and 4 Boy 1 Girl Action ('The Hawaian Death Stomp'). Holmes' remixing projects include stints for the Sandals ('We Want To Live'), Robotman ('Do Da Doo' for Novamute), Fortran 5 ('Persian Blues', 'Time To Dream'), Freaky Realistic ('Koochie Ryder'), Secret Knowledge ('Sugar Daddy'), Abfahrt ('Come Into My Life'), Bahia Black ('Capitao Do Asfolto') and Sabres Of Paradise ('Smokebelch'). He was also partially behind Sugarsweet, the Belfast dance label, run with Ian McCready and Jim McDonald. As Holmes explained at the time: 'It's more of a front to feed our obsession with music, to put out what we like when we like'. Releases included Wah Wah Warrior (essentially Ian McCready)'s Arabic house excursions, plus Holmes' Death Before Disco. The label staff also collaborated with DJ Ashley Beadle's Black Sunshine and MERC's Dub Federation. However, when it was clear that Sugarsweet was not going to take off it was replaced by the Exploding Plastic Inevitable imprint. In 1994 Holmes signed with Sabres Of Paradise as a solo artist.

Holy Ghost Inc

One of a number of groups picked up from the underground and hoisted on to a major in the early 90s, in this case Island subsidiary Blunted. Holy Ghost Inc were formed in 1989 and produced two EPS, *The Word*, and the widely praised *Mad Monks On Zinc*, prior to the move. *The Megawatt Messiah* EP, a slower techno piece continuing their religous themes, was their first release for Blunted in January 1994. Other associated projects run in conjunction with the group exist, under the titles Saucer Crew ('Andromeda' etc) and Ouija Board, though the participants continue to shroud their identities in mystery.

Hooj Toons

One of the more upfront house labels, whose *esprit de corps* seems to rise from knowing how to spot a breaking tune - rather than veiling themselves in clique mystique. Among their many notable releases were Simon Sed's 'Wigged Criminal', Felix's 'Don't You Want Me' (which made the UK Top 10), Hyper Go Go's 'High', Dis-Cuss' 'Pissed Apache' (a gay anthem from DJ Malcolm Duffy, Jonothan Blanks and DJ Kenny Clarke), Gloworm's 'I Lift My Cup', Andronicus' (Blanks again) 'Make You Whole' and DCO2's 'Do What

You Feel', all of which were included on the listed sampler album. They were also the first to release JX's 'Son Of A Gun', before licensing it to the London-affiliated Internal Dance imprint. The label originally grew out of Greedy Beat Records, which was set up by an accountant, before A&R man Jerry Dickens joined after leaving college. Dissatisfied with the small returns on his imput, Dickens spent most of 1993 trying to disentangle himself from the relationship, eventually setting up his own studio and gaining his own publishing deal. With slightly more solid financial footing, 1994 saw Dickens sign his first act for more than a one-off deal, JX (Jake Williams and vocalist Billie Godfrey). He also set up a subsidiary operation, Prolekult.

Selected album: Various: *Some Of These Were Hooj* (Hooj Toons 1994).

House

Chicago was the kindergarten of the warm, feel-good music that came to be known as house, though its actual birthplace was New York, and the Loft. House was built on the innovations of disco but with less of the 'flash' and even less of a reliance on lyrics. 'House isn't just derived from disco. It *is* disco', noted Nile Rodgers of Chic. In 1983/1984 dance music was, indeed, essentially disco, though hybrids like electro, go go and rare groove also existed. The term was invoked due to the warehouse parties it was to be heard at during its infancy. The music arrived in Chicago when DJ Frankie Knuckles relocated to the region and inaugurated the original Warehouse club. The scene was confined to the gay clubs until Farley Jackmaster Funk began to play it on the radio. As the house scene evolved its early were stages chronicled by records like Colonel Abram's 'Music Is The Answer' (the first to press a record was Jesse Saunders). The trickle became a river as Chicago releases like J.M. Silk's 'Music Is The Key' (an answer record to the aforementioned Colonel Abrams' release), Jack Master Funk's 'Aw Shucks' and Jamie Principle's 'Waiting On My Angel' piled up. Many of these were housed on imprints like Trax and DJ International, which ably documented the era. Following Farley important early mixers and movers on Chicago radio included Julian Peruse, Frankie Rodriguez, Mike 'Hitman' Wilson, Bad Boy Bill, Tim Shomer and Brian Middleton. It would be Steve 'Silk' Hurley's 'Jack Your Body' which finally took the new music to commercial recogntion and the number 1 slot in the UK charts. Variants like acid house were also given birth in Chicago via DJ Pierre, while Detroit took the electronic elements to forge techno.

Frankie Rodriguez arguably has the best answer to a rigid definition of house: 'If I go out the country, the first thing anyone asks is 'What Is House?'. Who cares? Put the record on, enjoy it'.

Hubba Hubba Records

Falkirk, Scotland label, formed in late 1992, whose eclectic release schedule quickly established the name. Among their earliest releases were Ohm's 'Tribal Zone' and Sheffield-based techno crew the Forgemasters' *Quababa* EP. The latter outfit were picked up after spells at Warp and Network. Other signings included Scotland's Dub Commission ('Lost In House'), and Bamboo ('Coney Island'). Their product was lincensed to Murk subsidiary, Vibe, while Hubba Hubba also housed material from US label MegaTrend (run by Photon Inc's Roy Davies Jr). The label is run by Utah Saints' manager John MacLennan.

Humphries, Tony

Legendary for his shows on New York's Kiss FM, New Jersey-born Humphries was a hugely influential figure in the development of the East Coast dance scene. His support for Adeva's 'Respect', for instance, was the essential ingredient in her winning a record contract. Humphries gained access to the radio after meeting Shep Pettibone in 1981, who approved of his demo cassette. His break as a live DJ was offered in the same year by Larry Patterson. Previously he had been a mobile jock and worked for the *New York Daily* newspaper. Patterson gave him his opportunity at the Zanzibar club which became New Jersey's premier nightspot. Humphries has gone on to produce and remix for a huge variety of clients, just a smattering of which include Mass Order ('Lift Every Voice'), Alison Limerick ('Make It On My Own', 'Hear My Call'), Bananarama ('Movin' On'), KLF ('3AM Eternal'), Cure ('Love Cats'), Jungle Brothers ('What Are You Waiting For'), Steel Pulse ('Rollerskates') and Evelyn King ('Shakedown') - which represents a mere fraction of his client list. He moved to the UK in 1992 to start a residency at the Ministry Of Sound, while in 1994 Romanthony's 'In The Mix' (on Azuli) celebrated his status by building a song out of the repetition of Tony Humphries' name.

Hurley, Steve 'Silk'

Formerly a DJ at Chicago station WBMX, Hurley's first recordings, like many of his peers, were originally cut specifically to augment his DJ repertoire. One such track, 'Music Is The Key', got a particularly warm reception, and Hurley borrowed money from his father and placed it on his friend Rocky Jones' DJ International label. It made number 9 in the US dance charts, though no royalties were forthcoming. He was similarly dismayed when his 'I Can't Turn Around' was hijacked by Farley Jackmaster Funk, and turned into 'Love Can't Turn Around', with new vocals by Daryl Pandy. It became a hit in 1985 without any of the credit being extended to Hurley. Even worse, Pandy was Hurley's former flatmate. However, his reward was just around the corner. After recording the mighty 'Baby Wants To Ride' with Jamie Principle he scored the first house number 1 with 'Jack Your Body' on January 24, 1987. He subsequently liaised with Keith Nunnally as J.M. Silk for 'Let The Music Take You' and an album (Nunnally had previously sung on 'Music Is The Key', but would depart for a solo career). Later Hurley would create Kym Sim's 'Too Blind To See', and was invited to remix Roberta Flack's 'Uh Uh Ooh Ooh Look Out' - which he saw as a great personal achievement. Other remix projects came thick and fast, including Paula Abdul (*Vibeology* EP), Yasmin ('Sacrifice'), Simply Red ('Something Got Me Started'), Ce Ce Peniston ('We Got A Love Thang') and Rodeo Jones ('Get Wise'). At one time in the 90s it seemed that a dozen such remixes were appearing on the market at the same time, and in truth they were all relatively similar, albeit polished and accomplished. Hurley had few complaints, raking in the money at a reported $20,000 per throw, and working with heroes like Stevie Wonder. In addition he established his own production company ID (signed to Sony in the UK and Europe, its remix roster including Chicago DJ Ralphi Rosario and Juan Atkins).

Selected album: *Work It Out* (Atlantic 1989). With J.M. Silk: *Hold On To Your Dreams* (1987).

Hustlers Convention

A duo of Mike Gray and John Pearn. Mike had been a DJ for 14 years, spinning old school disco from labels like Prelude and Salsoul etc., playing various gigs around Croydon. He met Pearn when he was operating the lights at a local pub. They started to collaborate together, bringing samplers in for live mixes with drum machines and records. Although John did not at that time possess Mike's experience, he quickly became a self-taught engineer, and offered megamixes and remixes for DMC. Hustlers Convention is essentially 'Mike's baby', and is disco based, with samples culled from old disco records from Chic to more obscure Prelude 12-inches. A good example was the well-received *Groover's Delight* EP for Stress in 1992. They also record as Greed. for Virgin, as a more vocal orientated group. In addition to their own output the Hustlers have also remixed for mainstream star Kenny Thomas ('Trippin' On Your Love').

Hyper Go-Go

Never regarded as strikingly original, Hyper Go-Go are nevertheless one of the most commercially prominent UK house acts, a fact confirmed when their early singles, including 'High' (UK number 30) and 'Never Let Go' (number 45), both crossed over into the UK charts. The team, James Diplock and Alex Ball, have been working together since they left school in the mid-80s. They have their own studio, a converted warehouse in the middle of a disused airfield, in the heart of the Essex countryside. 'High' was originally released on Hooj Tunes before being picked up by DeConsruction. For 'Never Let Go', a typical 'storming piano house tune', they switched to the Positiva label on a more permanent footing. 'Raise' used the familiar 'Raise Your Hands' vocal line as its core, with guest vocals from Brian Chambers. Other contributors have included Sally Anne Marsh, currently of Hysterix. Bell and Diplock are also one half of techno/rave sideline Electroset (whose 'How Does It Feel?' was their 'rave thing') and experimental electronic outfit Compufonic ('Ecstacy 0376' for Ocean Records in 1992, now signed to Mute for whom they debuted with the *Make It Move* EP).

Hypnotist, The

Comprising Rising High Records' owner Caspar Pound (b. c.1970; once the 'hippie' in A Homeboy, A Hippie And A Funki Dred), and in the early stages Pete Smith. Pound rejoiced in statements like: 'I wanna scare people on the dancefloor. I wanna use sounds that are disturbing to the mind and really freak people out when they're tripping'. He seemed determined to prove his mettle with cuts like debut 12-inch 'Rainbows In The Sky' and 'This House Is Mine', the latter a Top 75 hit single in September 1991. More notorious was the December release, *The Hardcore* EP, which included the neo-legendary 'Hardcore U Know The Score'. Follow-ups included 'Live In Berlin' (The Hypnotist was celebrated as a pop star in Germany) and 'Pioneers Of The Universe'. Pound also works as part of Rising High Collective with former Shamen vocalist Plavka, and records under the name New London School Of Electronics (with Laurence Elliott-Potter of Friends, Lovers & Family) and several more. He is, finally, also a distant relative of American poet Ezra Pound.

Album: *The Complete Hypnotist* (Rising High 1992).

Hypnotone

Hypnotone revolves around Tony Martin, who had previously worked with Creation Records as a one-man band with the addition of vocals by Denise Johnson on releases like 'Dream Beam' (remixed by Danny Rampling and Ben Champion) and 'Keeping The Faith'. The modern Hypnotone includes vocalist Cordelia Ruddock, discovered by Martin at a fashion show, Lee Royle, whom he met through a computer bulletin board (they rarely talk face to face, preferring to saw MIDI files down the modem) and Cormac Fultan, a pianist and organist, who met Martin in the more conventional environment of a bar. Hypnotone thus switched to Manchester house label First Love in an attempt to make commercial as well as critical progress with material like 'Be Good To Me' and 'Deeper In My Mind'.

Hysterix

Formed when the principal members met up on the Tokyo scene, where Tony Quinn was DJing at the Gold club for Yohji Yahamoto, Hysterix are not yet the most renowned of DeConstruction's acts. However, they have not been absent through want of trying. A typical act of anarchy came in 1993 when, via a live pirate broadcast, they illegally interrupted terrestrial television to transmit the slogan 'You've been Hysterixed!'. Dance magazine columns regularly overflowed with tales of their clubland ligging. They blew their record advance on tequila during an all-expenses trip to Mexico to shoot a video, which never materialised. Another five day jaunt to Florida was arranged when they pretended to be a completely different band. They joined Technotronic on their Eastern European tour, demanding payment in champagne and caviar, and persuaded Jean Michel Jarre to let them mix his work, staying at a hotel drinking Dom Perignon at his expense and completely forgetting to deliver the tape. They have also kidnapped their manager and booking agent and left them tied up at Skegness railway station, among many other pranks. Influenced by the original disco sounds of T Connection and Earth Wind And Fire as much as late 80s house, they were signed to their label for a full three years before a debut single, 'Must Be The Magic', emerged. DeConstruction had originally been impressed by the 'Talk To Me' 12-inch, which later saw a tremendously popular, but elusive Sasha remix. The nucleus of the group is 'Tokyo' Tony Quinn, Darren Black and Richard Belgrave. Their numerous female vocalists have included ex-KLF singer Maxine, though from October 1993 the band settled on Marie Harper and Sally Anne Marsh (who was persuaded to join after a barrage of free drinks in Blakes Hotel, which they charged to their friends). Marsh had originally been part of Tom Watkins (manager of Bros, East 17 etc) pop act Faith Hope And Charity when she was 14, alongside television 'presenter' Danni Behr. She also sang on Xpansions Top 10 hit, 'Move Your Body', in 1991, and has worked with Hyper Go Go and Aerial. Harper, meanwhile, formerly operated on the jazz circuit. Hysterix finally looked as though they were getting their house in order for 1994, supporting D:Ream on their UK tour and garnering good press for the single.

I

If?

If? emerged in 1990's Summer Of Love, graduating from the back rooms of the Brain Club, which was co-managed by the group's Sean McLusky. They hit the rave scene in turn, before organising a London Calling tour with Airstream, Natural Life and others. With vocals from Paul Wells, If? peddled a straightforward balearic model of 90s dance culture. Member Lyndsay Edwards would go on to join the Disco Evangelists.
Album: *English Boys On The Love Ranch* (MCA 1992).

Infinite Wheel

North London-based ambient techno duo who consist of former Pigbag percussionist/guitarist James Johnstone and Mark Smith. Their first recording, 'Segun International', was unveiled on cult New York label Nu Groove in 1991 after the duo simply sent them a tape in the post. They folowed it with the *Dharma Sunburst* EP in 1992 for Braniak. They described the latter thus: 'We wanted to use sounds that had some sort of depth to them, rather than pure bleeps. So it's a mixture of deep and shallow'. They made an appearance on Positiva's Ambient Collection ('Digi Out'), as well as releasing 'Gravity Attack' on R&S. Their other releases have graced imprints like Tomato, marking an effective sweep of the very best in international record labels..

Infonet

The dance label subsidiary of Creation Records, managed by Chris Abbot who enjoys total creative freedom in his selection of artists. This has resulted in a refreshing lack of 'house style' (in both senses), with Infonet regaling its followers with a variety of shades of electronic music. Their premier acts include Bandulu and Reload, while among their most significant releases were the *Thunderground* EP (Thunderground), 'Better Nation' and 'Guidance' (Bandulu), 'Terminus' (Syzygy), 'Liquid Poetry' (Subterfuge), 'Phase 4' (Reload) and 'I'm A Winner, Not A Loser' (Eddie 'Flashin'' Fowlkes). New signings in 1994 included Sons Of The Subway, Indika and Kohtao.
Selected albums: Various: *Beyond The Machines* (Infonet 1993). Bandulu: *Antimatters* (Infonet 1994).

Inky Blacknuss

A highly regarded new techno duo comprising Alex Knight, a DJ and proprietor of London's Fat Cat record store, fellow DJ Andrea Parker and engineer Ian Tregonim. The latter, who handles production, was for many years responsible for Yello's engineering. Parker takes charge of mixing, while Knight looks after percussion. Together they made a strong impression on their debut 1993 release, 'Blacknuss', on the Sabrettes imprint, which was awarded the *New Musical Express*' hastily improvised 'Filthy, Dirty, Techno Thing Of The Week' award. Dark and foreboding, its menacing ambience was recreated by a follow-up release, 'Drumulator'. Utilising backwards synthesiser sounds and 'natural noises', Parker described her interests as being 'anything that blows the speaker up'.

Inner City

Dance team built around the prolific genius of Kevin Saunderson (b. Kevin Maurice Saunderson, 9 May 1964, Brooklyn, New York, USA; programming), and the vocals of Paris Grey (b. Shanna Jackson, 5 November 1965, Glencove, Illinois, USA). Kevin, who is also widely revered for his remix and recorded work under the title Reese Project, is brother to a member of Brass Connection, and his mother was a member of the Marvelettes. He went on to study telecommunications at university, firing an interest in technology that would quickly become obvious in his musical leanings. Saunderson is the creative powerhouse of the unit, a studio denizen who writes all the songs and plays all the instruments. Grey is responsible for writing her own melodies. Their first single together, 'Big Fun', was lying around unissued in Saunderson's home base of Detroit until a friend discovered it while looking for tracks for a compilation LP. The record-buying public homed in on the strength of the tune (arguably one of dance music's all-time top five anthems), and with its follow-up, 'Good Life', Inner City had discovered a commercial career, with their debut album going on to worldwide sales of six million. Further singles have included 'That Man (He's Mine)', while the album which housed it, *Fire*, even boasted a token effort at rap. Other notable singles included 'Back Together Again', a stylish 1993 cover of Roberta Flack and Donnie Hathaway's standard. Saunderson runs his own label, KMS, through Network, whose Neil Rushton is his manager. This led to Network also picking up the Inner City name when Virgin allowed the group to run out of contract in the 90s.

Albums: *Paradise* (Ten 1989), *Paradise Remixed* (Ten 1990), *Fire* (Ten 1990).
Video: *Paradise Live* (1990).

Innocence

Comprising brother/sister combination Mark and Anna Jolley (guitar and vocals respectively), plus Brian Harris (percussion), Mattie (synthesizer) and Phil Dane (production) - though former Donny Osmond and Pet Shop Boys session singer Gee Morris (b. Camberwell, London) also featured heavily on their debut album. Innocence scored a Top 20 hit in 1990 with 'Natural Thing', a good part of the notoriety surrounding the release caused by one of the mixes featuring a sample of Pink Floyd's 'Shine On You Crazy Diamond'. Since then they have gone on to a run of minor achievements: 'Silent Voice', Let's Push It' and 'A Matter Of Fact' (all 1990), 'Remember The Day' (1991), 'I'll Be There', 'One Love In My Lifetime' and 'Build' (1992) all charting but none breaching the Top 20.
Album: *Belief* (Cooltempo 1990), *Build* (Cooltempo 1992).

Inoue, Tetsuo

b. Japan, but based in New York, USA, where he emigrated because of the greater opportunities for techno artists. Inoue has recorded for New York's Mik Mak and, more prolifically, Germany's Fax label. In 1993 he released two LPs for the latter, and has also collaborated with German producer Atom Heart on the acid-inspired 'Datacide' project.
Albums: *Shades Of Orion* (Fax 1993), *2351 Broadway* (Fax 1993), *Ambient Otaku* (Fax 1994).

Internal Records

A connoisseurs' dance label formed in 1992 by Christian Tattersfield, the former Marketing Manager of London Records, with whom the label is financially linked. They struck immediately; their first signings were Orbital, whose second album having moved over from sister label ffrr would sell over a million copies. Zero B's *Reconnections* EP followed, before an album of Yellow Magic Orchestra remixes which featured the work of the Orb, 808 State, Shamen and Altern 8 among others. Vapourspace also recorded for the label, before the unexpected, runaway success of Capella on the Internal Dance subsidiary. On the same imprint JX's 'Son Of A Gun' also hit, though the Outthere Brothers' 'Fuk U In The Ass' was probably a little risque even for underground dance punters. More recent signings include Cisco Ferreira and Salt Tank.
Selected album: Orbital: *Untitled 2* (Internal 1993).

Ishii, Ken

b. c.1970, Tokyo, Japan. Ishii's early infatuation with music arrived via the electonica of Yellow Magic Orchestra, Kraftwerk and DAF. It was a fixation he would follow until it led him to the work of Derrick May. Impressed and inspired, he subsequently immersed himself in what little dance culture and recordings made it over to Japan. His modern tastes include the Black Dog and D-Jax Up Beats empires, whose experimental edge is reflected in his own works. These began with 'Rising Sun' for Dutch label ESP, before a double-pack R&S release, 'Garden On The Palm', and the *Utu* EP for Richie Hawtin's Plus 8 label. Nominally a day-time office worker, Ishii's wild and bracing material, often reflecting the keyboard undulations of his earliest influences, have made him Japan's biggest techno export.
Album: *Innerelements* (R&S 1994).

Isotonik

Isotonik is essentially Chris Paul, helped out by the likes of DJ Hype and Grooverider, who claims to have remixed everyone from 'Mozart to Yazz'. He is also an efficient multi-instrument musician, especially adept at keyboards and saxophone. As well as working widely as a session musician he has DJ'd at venues like Camden Palace, and ran the Orange Club in North London. His first record came out in 1986 - 'Expansions '86'. However, there was a long gap before his next major success with 'Different Strokes', on ffrr in 1992, which sampled the Ten City song of the same name. This had been picked up following release on his own label, again titled Orange Records, in 1991. It was

Inner City

succeeded by an eponymous EP the following year.

Izit

Rare groove revivalists whose name stemmed from a technological mishap; when they were sampling the word music their sequencer messed up and looped 'Izit' instead. They enjoyed breakthrough success with 'Stories', on their own Pig & Trumpet label in 1989, a version of the rare groove staple originally recorded by Chakachas. The group, who comprise former Tarzan-a-gram Tony Colman (guitar, keyboards; ex-Pulse, who once appeared on *Wogan*), Peter Shrubshall (flute, tenor saxophone) and sister Catherine Shrubshall (soprano, alto and baritone saxophone) were originally a studio-based enterprise. However, they added drummer Andrew Messingham and a bass player to the line-up for their first live shows. A huge hit in 1989, Messingham had actually scratched 'Acid Free Zone' on to 'Stories'' run-out grooves. Despite their avowed wish to slow the pace of the summer's soundtrack, the single was widely adored by the acid crowd after the track was initially bought on import (Izit having licensed its release in Italy). Eventually it transferred to Paul Oakenfold's Perfecto label where he produced a popular remix, before the group joined Maze on a tour of the UK and Europe. They eventually followed up with 'Make Way For The Originals', again on Pig & Trumpet, before electing to sign with the independent Optimism. However, when the latter neglected to pay the studio bill for Izit's debut album the tapes were retained, though the set did emerge under the name Main Street People in late 1993. Disillusioned, original members of the band drifted away, though Colman beavered away in the background, setting up a new Tongue & Groove imprint, which eventually saw Izit return on 'Don't Give Up Now' and 'One By One' featuring vocalist Sam Edwards. Later material introduced Nicola Bright, who co-wrote much of *The Whole Affair*. Other guests/semi-permanent members include Byron Wallen (trumpet), Andy Gangadeen (drums), Steven Lewinson (bass) and Haji Mike and MC Mell 'O' (rappers).
Album: *The Whole Affair* (Tongue & Groove 1993).

J

J., Ollie

b. Oliver Jacobs, c.1975, London, England. One of techno's new breed of studio operators, who first locked horns with a control panel at the age of 13. After which his education went to the cleaners, as he spent every waking hour at the consoles, using school as a dormitory. The end would, however, justify the means. By the age of 19 he had remixed for Adamski, Frankie Goes To Hollywood, D:Ream and Take That, and provided full production for Rozalla, East 17 and Deja Vu. As well as engineering for Leftfield and Delta Lady, he would help on sessions at Rollover Studios in Kilburn, owned by his father Phil Jacobs. The studio has seen notable works recorded by Sure Is Pure, Paul Gotel, Qui 3, the Sandals and the Leftfield/Lydon collaboration ('Open Up'). Jacobs has a big future ahead of him; judged on the terms of an age to output matrix there is nobody to touch him.

Jackson, Chad

Larger-than-life cult DJ who in 1987 won the World DJ Championships. Like so many others behind the decks in the house boom, Jackson's origins were in hip hop, though his other interests included reggae and punk. He scored a surprise number 3 in the UK charts with 'Hear The Drummer (Get WIcked)', before going on to remix for numerous clients including Gang Of Four ('Money Talks'), De La Soul ('Magic Number'), Beats International ('Dub Be Good To Me'), Public Enemy ('Bring The Noise'), Prince ('Sign Of The Times') and Kraftwerk ('Tour De France').

Jam & Spoon

Duo credited by some as the originators of the 'trance' style. Based in Frankfurt, Germany, the faces behind the team are producer Jam El Mar and DJ Mark Spoon. Their groundbreaking work on a remix of Alex Lee's 'The Age Of Love' was the first track to set the ball rolling, followed in quick succession by work with Moby, Cosmic Baby and Frankie Goes To Hollywood. The latter was a difficult but rewarding project, as it had been this band and the production work of Trevor Horn in general which had originally inspired Jam El Mar into music. Another key reference point are the soundtrack recordings of Tangerine Dream. Only one single under their own name, 'Stella', preceded the release of their debut double album in the early months of 1994. This time they had moved away from the fast, pumping backbeat and acid tones which had flavoured their remixes, opting instead for a much more commercial slant. A sleevenote written for R&S label boss Renaat wryly declares: 'I hope this is not too commercial for your uncommercial label". Perhaps not, but it did see them crossover into the pop charts proper. Other 45s like 'Follow Me' were considered to be *bona fide* trance classics. Mark Spoon was also head of A&R for Logic and is boss of Frankfurt's XS Club. Album: *Tripomatic Fairytales 2001/2002* (R&S 1994).

Jaydee

b. Robin Alders, c.1958, Holland. Alders is a regular DJ at Utrecht, Holland's Vlanen venue. His beautiful trance cut 'Plastic Dreams' crossed over massively on the Belgian R&S label in 1993, with its distinctive Hammond B3 organ signature. It was his first release, previously he had been three times winner of the Dutch arm-wrestling championship, and a member of the national baseball team. Since the early 80s he had worked on Dutch radio, proffering a critically-lauded selection of house music. He turned to recording when his radio show was axed. After 'Plastic Dreams', the first release on the reactivated UK arm of R&S, he also released the 'Acceleration By Trance' 12-inch as Graylock on Logic's Save The Vinyl imprint. Far from usual rave convention, this contained the ominous 'Everybody Feel Free' warning on the flip-side. This boasted a spoken word narrative on the dangers of Ecstasy, which also plotted Alders' semi-autobiographical downfall through the drug. A second Graylock release, 'The Movement', emerged on Belgium's Mental Radio Records, before he returned as Jaydee for 'The Hunter' for Dutch label Clubstitute.

Jazzy Jason

Artist who first emerged with Epitome Of Hype's 'Ladies With An Attitude', which sampled Madonna, and was first released on his own Pure Bonhomie label before being licensed to Big Life. Further funky rave tunes, dominated by breakbeats, followed. As part of Blapps Posse! he was also behind 'Bus It'/'Don't Hold Back', which sold some 10,000 copies on white label before being picked up by Rebel MC's Trible Bass label. He moved over to Essex's rave central HQ - D-Zone Records, for Turntable Symphony's 'Instructions Of Life', created with fellow Blaaps Posse! member Aston Harvey.

Jazzy M.

DJ who started out on that career's familiar route to stardom by working at a record shop counter, before appearing on the LWR pirate radio station, playing early Detroit techno and Chicago house on his *Jackin' Zone* shows. After DJing at his own Mania nights and varous club appearance he joined with Pete Tong to compile ffrr's *The House Sound Of London Vol. 4*, which featured his first recording, 'Living In A World Of Fantasy', a collaboration with Fingers Inc. He ran his own shop, Vinyl Zone, and launched his first label, Oh Zone Records. The first release on which was Orbital's 'Chime', lincensed to ffrr. It sold 66,000 copies after being passed to Jazzy M on a TDK cassette. His second label was Delphinus Delphis which dealt with more garage-house themes. It saw the release of the well-received 'Hold On' by Cuddles, before a third label was mooted, Spankin'. This produced several notable cuts, like the *Rubberneck* EPs and Dub Nation's 'I Can't Help Myself', produced with partner Doug Martin. Jazzy continued to play out all the time, feeding back the results into his recordings and *vice versa*. Not surprising then that the Spankin' releases were held in high regard by the DJ fraternity, like Tony Humphries and C+C Colour Factory. He continues to play regular sets at Release The Pressure.

Jefferson, Marshall

b. c.1960. One of the legends of acid house, Jefferson claims to have invented the familiar 'squelch' of the Roland TR 303 (a claim hotly countered by DJ Pierre). Jefferson's reputation rests more squarely on records like Reggie Hall's 'Music', Richard Rogers' mighty 'Can't Stop Loving You', and Ce Ce Rogers' epic 'Someday'. Afterwards he would move on to helm production for Ten City, but was criticised at the time of their arrival for what some critics observed to be a fixation with nostalgia in the latter's soulful house grooves. Jefferson preferred the description deep house, and was quick to proclaim the death knell for acid. Nevertheless, Ten City hit with singles like 'That's The Way Love Is' and 'Right Back To You', with Byron Stingily's distinctive vocals providing an excellent outlet for Jefferson's studio craft. He has also worked with Tyrrel Corporation and Kym Mazelle ('I'm A Lover') amongst many others, and recorded as Jungle Wonz ('Time Marches One') and Truth ('Open Your Eyes'). Selected album: Ten City: *Foundation* (East West 1988).

Johnny Vicious

Jellybean

John 'Jellybean' Benitez, a native of the Bronx and renowned Manhattan club DJ, made his mark in the early 80s as one of the post-disco dance scene's most favoured remixers/producers. Eventually he would earn his own record contract, though his *modus operandi* did not change; maintaining instead a largely supervisory role on his output. His debut release under his own name was the 1984 EP, *Wotupski!?!*, which carried two minor dance classics, 'The Mexican' and 'Sidewalk Talk', the latter penned by Madonna (he had significantly enhanced his own personal reputation by working on tracks for her earlier, including her breakthrough hit 'Holiday'). It wouldn't be until *Spillin' The Beans*, however, that Jellybean would actually record his own voice, alongside guest vocalists like Nikki Harris, who, ironically, had last been seen on Madonna's tour.

Selected albums: *Just Visiting This Planet* (Chrysalis 1987), *Jellybean Rocks The House* (Chrysalis 1988), *Spillin' The Beans* (Atlantic 1991).

Jodeci

New Jack Swingers with considerable attitude, Jodeci consist of two pairs of brothers (Joel 'JoJo' and Gedric 'K-Ci' Hailey, and Dalvin and Donald 'Devante Swing' DeGrate Jr) who began their musical career by harmonising in their local Tiny Grove, North Carolina church services. They signed to prominent swingbeat emporium Uptown in 1991, and the initial results were impressive. Their silky soul vocals were stretched over sparse hip hop beats to produce a debut album that was at once tough and elegant. It sold two million copies and in the process earned Jodeci accolades as one of the greatest incarnations of the hip hop/R&B crossover.

Albums: *Forever My Lady* (Uptown 1991), *Diary Of A Mad Band* (Uptown 1993).

Joe

b. Joe Lewis Thomas, c.1972, Cuthbert, Georgia, USA, and raised to sing gospel by his minister father, Joe is another at the cutting edge of the commercial hip-hop/R&B crossover. As a youth he decided to move away from vocal, guitar and piano chores at his father's church and relocated to New Jersey, picking up a whole slew of new jazz, soul, R&B and hip hop influences in the process. He was eventually discovered singing in a Newark church by R&B producer Vincent Henry. He was employed regularly in local studios to add his various musical abilities to records cut in New York studios for swingbeat acts like SWV and Hi-Five. Others who used his services included Toni Braxton, TLC and Vanessa Bell Armstrong. The success of his debut album, and the Top 30 UK single 'I'm In Love', encouraged his new label Mercury to employ him as staff producer for their black acts.

Albums: *Everything* (Mercury 1993).

Joey Negro

b. David Lee, Essex, England. A remixer, producer and artist, and champion of the garage/disco revival, Negro's work on cuts from Adeva and Kim Sims is among the most representative of his style. The media-labelled 'England's David Morales' can trace his heritage back to M-D-Eemm (the chemical formula for acid) in the late 80s. He is a fanatical record collector who often works alongside DJ Andrew 'Doc' Livingstone. Together they have worked on remixes for Brand New Heavies, the Reese Project and Negro's own album. Negro's career began at the Republic label, where he was taught the art of remixing by a friend. Together with Mark Ryder, he produced a number of cuts for the same label, using production team names ranging from Quest For Excellence to Masters Of The Universe. Republic was responsible for classics like Phaze II's 'Reachin'' and Turntable Orchestra's 'You're Gonna Miss Me'. However, Negro ran into trouble when he created the persona Kid Valdez of Mystique. Under that name they mixed the club hit 'Together' for Raven Maize. The track was licensed to an American label, but when the single topped the dance charts journalists tried to hunt down Mr Maize. He was of course, totally fictional, the figure on the cover having been scanned in and adapted from an old rap record. Negro also licensed tracks to Republic, including several house classics, and compiled the *Garage Sound Of New York/Chicago* series. From this point on he picked up the Negro moniker and began to establish an identity as a talented disco remixer. Negro's own material reflects the tastes of his record collection; a penchant for US labels like Prelude and West End, 70s funk (Brass Construction, Cameo), jazz fusion and disco (notably the latter's 'syn drums'). His debut album additionally includes a version of the Gibson Brothers' 'Oooh What A Life', featuring Gwen Guthrie. Recent mixing work has included Hue & Cry, Sister Sledge, Fortran 5 ('Look To The Future'), Soul II Soul ('Move Me No Mountain') and Take That ('Relight My Fire'). In 1994 he became half of the Hedboys, again partnering Livingstone.

Album: *Universe Of Love* (Virgin 1993).

Johnny Vicious

The proprietor of New York's Vicious Muzik label, Johnny Vicious is one of the most exciting up and coming producer/remixers on the circuit. A rock 'n' roller who got bored of rock music after he heard Tony Humphries on Kiss FM, he was championed by Junior Vasquez in his early days. His career proper began with tunes like 'Liquid Bass' and 'Frozen Bass', before reworking the Loletta Holloway standard 'Dreaming' as 'Stand Up' (released in the UK by Six By Six, the label being licensed to the Network umbrella organisation). This demonstrated his technique, which was essentially slicing up old classics in an arlarmingly cavalier fashion and producing a punk disco hybrid. 1994 records like JV verus MFSB's 'TSOP' (another disco chestnut) continued his ascendency and cult status.

Johnson, Denise

b. 31 August 1966, Manchester, Lancashire, England. Former backing vocalist on some of Primal Scream's finest moments, Johnson has also worked with A Certain Ratio, Electronic and sundry other more minor local projects like the Jam MCs' 'Ironweed'. She had initially been discovered by Maze's Frankie Beverley singing in Fifth Heaven, who supported Maze on their Wembley dates in the UK. She was subsequently enlisted as backing vocalist for Maze. Johnson's solo career began in 1994 with the marvellous 'Rays Of The Rising Sun'. Produced by David Tolan of the Joy (for whom she was also a vocalist), it was due for release a year previously, but saw delays caused by major label manoeuvring. Eventually she settled on East West/Magnet, who invited K Klass to remix the song. It gave her a sizeable club hit, though this time the version somewhat diminished Johnson's vocal imput. A radio mix also featured Johnny Marr (Smiths) on guitar, presumably through his pervious liaisons with K Klass.

Jomanda

New Jersey trio who enjoyed chart action in the late 80s and early 90s with sweet vocals embodying what those in dance circles affectionately term 'girlie house', or New Jill Swing. Cheri Williams, who started singing from the age of 14, met Joanne Thomas in 7th grade at college, though they lost contact when each went to high school. They reunited in 1987, when they were joined by Renee Washington, whose youth was spent singing in Baptist church choirs. She had also attended the Newark School Of Performing Arts. Their recording career began in 1988, when they enjoyed hits with 'Make My Body Rock'.and 'Gotta Love For You'. The combination of swing and house with soulful hip hop vocals was instantly popular. 'Make My Body Rock' would also provide the sample around which Felix's huge hit, 'Don't You Want My Love' was built. Nubia Soul, referring to the skin pigmentation of 'blackness', was more R&B-based, as Washington explained: 'The reason why we're heading for an R&B market is that we feel club music is very limited and I personally fell we've done all that we could as a group as far as club music is concerned'. That did not stop them from employing Sasha for a very well-received remix of 'Never', however. On the album they worked with Buff Love (ex-Fat Boys), Dave Hall and Kenny Kornegay of the Untouchables, and the Band Of Gypsies.
Albums: Nubia Soul (East West 1993).

Jon Pleased Wimmin

b. c.1969, London, England. Transvestite DJ who has built his reputation on the dexterity of his deck technique and record selection, rather than his dress sense: 'I get so annoyed by all these bedroom DJ's who say I've done well because I have a gimmick. But my dress doesn't play records'. He began his adult life attending a four-year course in fashion design, eventually running his own shop in Kensington Market. He started out as a DJ at clubs like Glam, Kinky Gerlinky and Camp in the capital, before opening up his own nightspot, Pleased, in Sutton Row, London, in October 1993. The Pleased Wimmin transvestite posse was first sighted as live backing on Linda Layton PA's. Their leader's first major appearance on record came with the dancefloor hit 'Passion', released on Southern Fried in 1990. A cover of Bobby Orlando's Hi-NRG classic from 1980, it was produced by Norman Cook. He went on to record further ambivalent gender/genre classics like 'Hammer House Of Handbag'.

Joy

Built around the production duo of David Tolan (b. 3 May 1967, Dublin, Eire; programming, percussion) and Ali Fletcher (b. Alistair Fletcher, 27 May 1968, Newcastle, England; drums, programming), the Joy additionally number Gavin O'Neill (b. 20 September 1965, Worcester, England; vocals) Denise Johnson (b. 31 August 1966, Manchester, Lancashire, England; vocals) and Andy Tracey (b. 11 September 1965, Harehills, Leeds, Yorkshire, England; guitar). Johnson is best known to club-goers for her contributions to Primal Scream's epoch-making Screamadelica, but Tolan also produced her debut solo single. He and

O'Neill had initially worked together in Perspex Spangles, while Fletcher had been part of the Canoe Club and Tall Americans. The Joy took their name as a revolt against the rejection offered to them by record companies in their early days. They played their first gig at the Buzz Club in Manchester in September 1992, and kicked off their new contract with Compulsion Records in 1994 with a re-release of 'Shine', previously a minor club hit in April 1993 for Playground Records. As Joy Productions Tolan and Fletcher have also contributed remixes, most notably for the Dub Disciples' 'Hyperphoria Parts One And Two'.

Joy, Ruth

London-born Joy came to prominence as the writer and singer of Sheffield-based Krush's 'House Arrest' crossover success from 1987, at which point she was widely touted as the 'new Neneh Cherry'. However, it would take three years of work, and several dumped producers, before her debut solo album finally saw the light of day. Among those involved were Mantronix (who produced her debut solo single, 'Don't Push It'), Loose Ends' Carl McIntosh and Aswad. Singles culled from the set included 'Feel' and 'Pride And Joy'.
Album: *Pride And Joy* (MCA 1992).

Juan Trip

Versailles-based French team built around mainman Basil, who mortified several commentators with their 1994 *Masterpiece Trilogy* EP. The controversy centred on main track, 'Louis' Cry'. This used a sample of a particularly unhappy one year old of the author's acquaintence who died shortly after the record was made. One of his screams was used, alongside a loop of organist Jimmy Smith, to puncuate the track. When the newshounds rang round to confirm the existence of the 'dead baby track' Basil, who had formerly promoted the hugely successful Fantom nights in France, confirmed its origins (though it was conceived more as a tribute to the child's life than anything more exploitative). Released on F Communications in France, many DJ's refused to play it because of the unsettling nature of the scream, including Darren Emerson, who even asked permission to re-record the masterful backing track without it.

Judge Jules

b. Julius O'Rearden. Together with partner Michael Skins, Jules has become one of the UK's leading remixers. He was originally bedecked with the Judge prefix from Norman Jay during the mid-80s house/rare groove scene, at which time he was

studying law. Apparently he proved exceedingly useful when police raided parties, tying the officers up in legal jargon while his friends extinguished their herbal cigarettes. Together with Jay (nicknamed Shake And Finger Pop, while Jules was Family Function) they performed at about thirty warehouse parties between the years 1984 and 1987. He earned a living from buying up rare house records on trips to America and bringing them back to England to sell at exhorbitant prices. As house turned to acid he remained a prominent figure in the rave scene, playing at many of the larger events like Evolution, Sunrise and World Dance, after which he earned his first remixing credits. The clients included Soft House Company, Fat Men, Big Audio Dynamite and, bizarrely, the Stranglers. In 1991 he re-aquainted himself with an old school-friend, Rolo. They set up a studio together, and learned how to produce and engineer properly, an aspect they'd previously bluffed their way through. A studio was slowly established in the basement of his house, before he teamed up with ex-reggae drummer Michael Skins. By remixing a devastating version of M People's 'Excited' in 1992 the team was established, with guesting musicians like guitarist Miles Kayne adding to the musical melting pot. Having set up Tomahawk Records Jules has gone on record his own work. These have included Datman (licensed to ffrr), the All Stars ('Wanna Get Funky', which sampled from Andrew Lloyd Webber's *Jesus Christ Superstar*) and 290 North ('Footsteps'), as well as guest appearances from ex-KLF singer Maxine Hardy (Icon's 'I Can Make You Feel So Good') and ex-O'Jays singer Ronnie Canada ('Heading For Self-Destruction'). More recent remixes have included T-Empo's handbag house classic 'Saturday Night, Sunday Morning' , Melanie Williams ('Everyday Thing'), BT Express ('Express'), Jeanie Tracy ('Is This Love'), Our Tribe ('Love Come Home'), plus the big money-spinners Doop ('Doop') and Reel 2 Real ('I Like To Move It'). Which has ensured he can practically write his own cheque for remixing engagements now, of which he is offered at least ten a week. He also records two radio shows a week for Radio One.

Jungle

The evolution of jungle is hard to pin down in exactitude. However, the term 'junglist' is Jamaican patois for a native of Trenchtown, the ghetto area of Kingston from whence came Bob Marley. Despite this, controversy persists over the use of the name, with some commentators insisting it is a derogatory term. Musically jungle rides on a combination of breakbeats and samples, with

Juno Reactor

ragga's staccato rhythms, and subsonic bass. The tempo is roughly double that of ragga, clocking in at around 160bpm. The use of the hardcore breakbeats neatly completes a circle - they were originally a derivation of hip hop, which in turn leaned heavily on the reggae culture. It is a music widely perceived to be created by and for black people who are disaffected with the sound of 'white techno' (another anomaly considering that all of techno's originators were themselves black). The sound was pioneered in clubs by DJ Ron, Randall, Bobby Konders and on radio by Jumping Jack Frost (on Kiss FM) and pirates like Kool FM, Transmission One and Don FM. The earliest sighting of it outside of the underground came when SL2's 'On A Ragga Tip' broke through in 1993. There had been antecedents, however. Singles like Genaside II's 'Narra Mine', material by Shut Up And Dance and even Rebel MC's Comin' On Strong', built on a riot of breakbeats, all predicted the jungle sound. Recent innovations in the style have arrived from more traditional reggae acts like General Levy ('Incredible' on Renk Records) who have begun 'voicing' words over the rhythms, where previously sampled chants sufficed. Amongst the better modern proponents, who tend to be anonymous even by dance music's standards, are Blame and Bubbles.

Juno Reactor

Helmed by Ben Watkins, alongside DJs Stephane Holwick (of Total Eclipse), Jans Waldenback and Mike MacGuire, the Juno Reactor's musical territory spans ambient, house and techno. Their name was inspired by a piece of art from Norma Fletcher - of which the group were so impressed that they also wrote an ambient soundtrack for its display. Watkins was formerly a member of Empty Quarter (with Youth of Killing Joke) and the Flowerpot Men. For the Juno Reactor he travelled the globe from North Africa to India, collecting environmental oddities and sounds on a portable DAT. These are the final ingredient in Juno Reactor's distinctive recordings. Wakins also has several concurrent projects including Electrotete, Psychoslaphead and Jungle High. Their most effective record in the early part of their career was 1994's 'High Energy Protons', with its engaging intro and ominous 'Everything's going extremely well' dialogue snatch. Wakins' also became famous by default for becoming the second techno wizard, after the Aphex Twin, to have links with the armoured car industry. His girlfriend, a sculptor, purchased a Saracen tank, painted it white and gutted it for an appearance at the Royal Albert Hall exhibition. Afterwards the plan was to install DAT equipment and arrive at gigs, ready to play (or so the story goes..).
Albums: *Transmissions* (Mute 1993), *Luciano* (Inter Modo 1994).

K

Kelly, R.

b. Robert Kelly, c.1969, Chicago, Illinois, USA. Dance/R&B artist who made his first impact with the release of a debut album in 1991, with his band, Public Announcement. Kelly grew up in the housing projects of Chicago's South Side, but channelled his energies away from fast money-making schemes and into long-term musicianship. He had a natural flair for most instruments, eventually becoming, more by accident than design, a useful busking act. It earned the young Kelly a living, until constant police disruptions forced him to reconsider his employment. He put together the R&B group MGM, and went on to win a national talent contest on the *Big Break* television show, hosted by Natalie Cole. Unfortunately, that group's energy dissipated, and his next major break came when manager Barry Hankerson spotted him while auditioning for a play at the Regal Theatre in Chicago. He soon had Kelly acting as musical co-ordinator/producer for a slew of acts, including Gladys Knight, David Peaston, Aaliyah and the Hi-Five (who scored a number 1 single, 'Quality Time', with Kelly at the controls). His diversity was confirmed by his work with the Winans gospel family, notably a duet with Ronald Winans on 'That Extra Mile'. However, all this would be surpassed by the success of his second album, which stayed on top of the R&B charts for all of nine weeks. Two huge singles were included on the set, the tearaway hits 'She's Got That Vibe' and 'Bump 'N Grind'. As if from nowhere, despite a long apprenticeship, Kelly had acquired the Midas touch.
Album: *Born Into The '90s* (Jive 1991), *12 Play* (Jive 1994).

Kickin' Records

Record label originally established in 1988, at that time under the name GTI Music (the Great Techno Institution), based in Notting Hill Gate in West London (still its current home). At first the label supplied a demand for tough street soul, with

April 1988's 'Good Living' from Dave Collins their first release. However, there was an immediate musical shift afterwards, with label boss Peter Harris signing Shut Up And Dance after hearing a demo track (eventually releasing '5678'). The Kickin' Records name was first invoked in 1990 when the Scientist's 'The Exorcist' arrived. This, claimed to be the first record with a BPM above 130, became a *de rigeur* accessory among followers of the burgeoning rave scene. The follow-up, 'The Bee', also sold strongly, and the Scientist would go on to join Kickin' at 1991's 'first ever Russian rave'. 1991 saw the label signing a second, hugely successful rave act, Messiah. Two years later the label began its popular *Hard Leaders* compilation series, which has become a favourite among hardcore fans. In the meantime a new roster of artists had been assembled, including Wishdokta, Xenophobia (a front for former members of Rubella Ballet), PMA, Kicksquad (Scientist with DJ Hype), Flat 47, Noodles & Wonder, Giro Kid and Green Budha. Kickin' also set up two subsidiary operations, Slip 'n' Slide (house/garage) and Pandemonium (indie guitar), as well as liaising with Colin Dale for his *The Outer Limits* series.
Selected albums: Various: *Hard Leaders 1-4* (Kickin' 1993-1994).

Kinchen, Mark

In 1988, together with Terrence Parker, Mark 'MK' Kinchen was part of Separate Minds for the techno/soul cut, 'We Need Somebody'. He went on to engineer on many of the early Inner City Records, and most of Kevin Saunderson's associated KMS label product, having been adopted as 'studio mascot' by Saunderson from the age of 17 onwards. He began to make records on his own as MK - like 'Mirror Mirror', 'Somebody New' and 'Get It Right'. However, he was still eclipsed by his boss, and elected to relocate to Brooklyn, New York, recording songs like 'Play The World'. This was somewhat removed from the Detroit sound, confounding expectations: 'Everybody thought I made Detroit techno', he conceded, but he certainly wasn't anymore. 'Techno needs more humanity, more groove'. A good example was the 'Burnin'' single (featuring vocal support from Alana Simon), given a UK release after success as an import on Kinchen's own Area 10 label in 1992. He also returned to the Separate Minds name for '2nd Bass', a full three and a half years since recording '1st Bass'. Among other *nom de plumes* he also records as 4th Measure Men, and has remixed for Bobby Brown ('Get Away'), Shamen ('Phorever People'), Masters At Work ('Can't Stop The Rhythm'), B-52's ('Tell It Like It Is') and

Chez Damier ('Never Knew Love'), as well as much of Saunderson's work as Inner City/Reese Project.

King, Morgan

Alongside Nick E, the London-based King was responsible for over 90% of Sweden's B-Tech label output. Some of his flags of convenience include Clubland (soulful garage), Soundsource ('Take Me Up' and other balearic moments), Al Hambra ('Al Hambra'), Maniac Tackle ('Bass FU'), Technoir ('Logic And Knowledge'), Control E ('The Power Of Freedom'), Bassrace ('Futurama'), Full On Sound ('Mayhem') - all housed on B-Tech. King also remixed Moodswings' 'Spiritual High' for Arista, and played a large part in establishing London label, Om.

Kirk, Roland H.

Founding member of Cabaret Voltaire whose releases under his own name in the 90s have seen him increasingly accommodated by the rave generation. Kirk released his first solo set in 1981, following it with the double album, *Time High Fiction* two years later. His taste for dance music was probably most obviously previewed by the release of Cabaret Voltaire's 'James Brown', before further solo work in 1986 with *Black Jesus Voice*, a mini-album, and *Ugly Spirit*. This was followed a year later by a collaborative project, *Hoodoo Talk*, with the Box's Peter Hope. Further expansions in Cabaret Voltaire's dance sound were refined by the 1989 single 'Hypnotised', after the duo had visited Chicago. A year later Kirk released 'Test One', an excellent example of the acid house style, under the guise of Sweet Exorcist. It launched what became known as the 'bleep' sound, which was widely imitated and dominated clubs for almost a year. A second hugely popular 12-inch arrived with 'Clonk'. Kirk currently enjoys his own Western Works studio in Sheffield, and is one of the true survivors of the late 70s industrial scene centred in that town.
Albums: *Disposable Half Truths* (Rough Trade 1981), *Time High Fiction* (Rough Trade 1983, double album), *Black Jesus Voice* (Rough Trade 1986), *Ugly Spirit* (Rough Trade 1986), *Virtual State* (Warp 1994). As Sweet Exorcist: *Clonk's Coming* (Warp 1991). With Peter Hope: *Hoodoo Talk* (Native 1987).

Kiss Of Life

Kiss Of Life comprise Mike Benn (b. c.1963, keyboards) and Victoria Maxwell (b. 1970, vocals). Formed in 1991, their jazz, soul and R&B mix, with soothing female vocals and a leaning towards the club scene, soon attracted the attention of Virgin Records. The duo had met in Hamburg, where Victoria, classically trained, was a dancer, while Benn was working on session tracks. Back in London, Benn hooked up with Acid Jazz man Chris Bangs, for whom Benn had co-written one track on the *Totally Wired 9* album. It was through Bangs that Paul Weller got involved with Kiss Of Life, guesting on the track 'Fiction In My Mind'. Singles so far have included 'Love Has Put A Spell On Me' and 'Holding On To A Dream'. The name comes from an incident witnessed by Benn when a friend tried to save a drowning man by artificial resuscitation. The man died. Presumably Virgin records had higher hopes for their investment, but there has been little evidence of a breakthrough so far.

Album: *Reaching For The Sun* (Circa 1993).

K Klass

Four piece dance troupe from Wrexham, Wales, who formed in late 1988 when Andy Williams (technical supervisor) and Carl Thomas (various instruments) packed in their former outfit, Interstate. They had supported 808 State in their early days, forging links that would prove pivotal to their future. The duo recruited locals Paul Roberts (ideas and lyrics) and Russ Morgan (various instruments), more recently acquiring talented female vocalist Bobbi Depasois. Funded in part by an Enterprise Allowance grant and Roberts' British Telecom redundancy money, their debut *Wildlife* EP topped all sorts of dance charts in 1990. Its extensive samples of Tony Soper's *Wildlife On One* television theme tune framing a strong subconscious hook with UK residents. After further supports with 808 State and hard gigging around the country, Martin Price of the aforementioned Manchester combo released 'Rhythm Is A Mystery' on his Eastern Bloc shop's Creed label. Although it sold an impressive 13,000 copies, it took six months and a new label to launch it in to the UK Top 10 at the tail end of 1991. Immediately they were heralded as one of the few house outfits with more than one song and two rhythm tracks: 'Anyone can learn how to use a synthesizer, anyone can make a dance record. But it's all about making good ones'. They continued in the same vein with 'Don't Stop' (1992) and 'Let Me Show' (1993), the latter prefacing their long-prepared debut album. This included, of all things, a guitar contribution from Johnny Marr (the Smiths) on 'Cassa' (he had obviously travelled a long way from that band's previous rallying call, 'Hang The DJ'). They have remixed for Oceanic' ('Wicked Love'), New Order, Seven Grand

Mark Gamble of Krush

Housing Authority (Terrence Parker) and Denise Johnson.

Album: *Universal* (DeConstruction 1993).

KLF

Since 1987 the KLF have operated under a series of guises, only gradually revealing their true nature to the public at large. The band's principal spokesman is one Bill Drummond (b. William Butterworth, 29 April 1953, South Africa), who had already enjoyed a chequered music industry career. As co-founder of the influential Zoo label in the late 70s, he introduced and later managed Echo & The Bunnymen and Teardrop Explodes. Later he joined forces with Jimmy Cauty (b. 1954), an artist of various persuasions and a member of Brilliant in the mid-80s. Their first project was undertaken under the title JAMS (Justified Ancients Of Mu Mu - a title lifted from Robert Shea and Robert Anton Wilson's conspiracy novels dealing with the *Illuminati*). An early version of 'All You Need Is Love' caused little reaction compared to the provocatively-titled LP which followed - *1987 - What The Fuck Is Going On?* Released under the KLF moniker (standing for Kopyright Liberation Front), it liberally disposed of the works of the Beatles, Led Zeppelin *et al* with the careless abandon the duo had picked up from the heyday of punk. One of the disfigured super groups, Abba, promptly took action to ensure the offending article was withdrawn. In the wake of the emerging house scene the next move was to compromise the theme tune to well-loved British television show *Dr Who*, adding a strong disco beat and Gary Glitter yelps to secure an instant number 1 with 'Doctorin' The Tardis'. Working under the title Timelords, this one-off coup was achieved with such simplicity that its originators took the step of writing a book; *How To Have A Number One The Easy Way*. Returning as the KLF, they scored a big hit with the more legitimate cult dance hit 'What Time Is Love'. After the throwaway send-up of Australian pop, 'Kylie Said To Jason', they hit big again with the soulful techno of '3 A.M. Eternal'. There would be further releases from the myriad of names employed by the duo (JAMS; 'Down Town', 'Its Grim Up North', Space; *Space*, Disco 2000; 'Uptight') while Cauty, alongside Alex Peterson, played a significant part in creating the Orb. Of the band's more recent work, perhaps the most startling was their luxurious video for the KLF's 'Justified And Ancient', featuring the unmistakable voice of Tammy Wynette. The song revealed the KLF at the top of their creative powers, selling millions of records worldwide while effectively taking the michael. They were subsequently voted the Top British Group by the BPI. Instead of lapping up the acclaim, the KLF, typically, rejected the comfort of music biz grandstanding, and deliberately imploded at the BRITS award ceremony. There they performed an 'upbeat' version of '3AM Eternal', backed by breakneck speed punk band Extreme Noise Terror, amid press speculation that they would be bathing the ceremony's assembled masses with pig's blood. They contented themselves instead with (allegedly) dumping the carcass of a dead sheep in the foyer of the hotel staging the post-ceremony party, and Drummond mock machine-gunning the assembled dignitaries. They then announced that the proud tradition of musical anarchy they had brought to a nation was at a close: the KLF were no more. Their only 'release' in 1992 came with a version of 'Que Sera Sera' (naturally rechristened 'K Sera Sera', and recorded with the Soviet Army Chorale), which, they insisted, would only see the light of day on the advent of world peace. The KLF returned to their rightful throne, that of England's foremost musical pranksters, with a stinging art terrorist racket staged under the K Foundation banner. In late 1993, a series of advertisements began to appear in the quality press concerning the Turner Prize art awards. While that body was responsible for granting £20,000 to a piece of non-mainstream art, the K Foundation (a new vehicle for messrs Drummond and Cauty) promised double that for the worst piece of art displayed. The Turner shortlist was identical to that of the KLF's. More bizarre still, exactly £1,000,000 was withdrawn from the National Westminster bank (the biggest cash withdrawal in the institution's history), nailed to a board, and paraded in front of a select gathering of press and art luminaries. The money was eventually returned to their bank accounts (although members of the press pocketed a substantial portion), while the £40,000 was awarded to one Rachel Whiteread, who also won the 'proper' prize. Urban guerrillas specialising in highly original shock tactics, the KLF offer the prospect of a brighter decade should their various disguises continue to prosper.

Albums: *Towards The Trance* (KLF 1988), *The What Time Is Love Story* (KLF 1989), *The White Room* (KLF 1989), *Chill Out* (KLF 1989). As JAMS: *1987 - What The Fuck Is Going On?* (KLF 1987), *Who Killed The JAMS?* (KLF 1988), *Shag Times* (KLF 1989).

Video: *Stadium House* (1991).

KMS Records

One of the original Detroit techno stables, and

home to Kevin Saunderson's Inner City/Reese Project family, with its title taken from the proprietor's full name (Kevin Maurice Saunderson). Its important releases during the late 80s included Inner City's 'Big Fun' and Reese & Santonio's 'Truth Of Self Evidence'. However, by the 90s, in tandem with the Reese Project's more soulful approach to techno/house, Saunderson was using the label for more vocal-based tracks. A new subsidiary imprint, Transfusion, was planned to house any idiosyncratic excursions into techno. Just to confirm what he has always said: 'If its dance music, I do it all'. The label was also home to Saunderson projects like E-Dancer's 'Pump The Move', which was remixed by Joey Beltram and Tronik House ('Straight Outta Hell') while guest artists included Chez Damier ('Can You Feel It', which also featured Mark 'MK' Kinchen). In 1994 the label unveiled a triple compilation set featuring tracks from Inner City, Esser'ay, Members Of The House, Chez Damier and Ron Trent. KMS product is licensed in the UK through Network.

Knights Of The Occasional Table

South-east London multi-racial dance band, comprising Steve, Nygell, Moose, Andrew and vocalist Aquamanda. Their debut album was initially released on their own label before being picked up by Club Dog. Its title - *Knees Up Mother Earth* - offered a big clue to their sound, wherein modern technological means (programmes, drum machines, samplers) were employed to deliver a primal beat with varied ethnic stylings. The Knights have not been as immediately successful as stylistic counterparts Fun-Da-Mental or Trans-Global Underground, ensuring Steve and Andy continue their day-time jobs as psychiatric nurse and journalist for *Stage And Television Today* respectively.
Album: *Knees Up Mother Earth* (Club Dog 1993).

Knuckles, Frankie

b. c.1955, New York, USA. Knuckles is often credited with 'creating' house music while a Chicago DJ at venues like the Warehouse and Powerplant. As a child he was inspired by his sister's jazz records, and took up the double bass. He attended the Dwyer School Of Art in the Bronx and F.I.T. in Manhattan to study textile design. However, he was soon lured into DJing at $50 a night at the Better Days emporium. Eventually Larry Levan of the Paradise Garage asked him to work at the Continental Baths club, and he was subsequently invited to travel to Chicago for the opening of the Warehouse. At the time he played mainly Philadelphia soul and R&B,

bringing back hot records from New York for his shows. According to Knuckles, the term 'house' had not yet been coined. 'One day I was driving in the South Side and passed a club that had a sign outside that read 'We Play House Music'. I asked them what it meant and he told me that they played the same music as I did'. Into the 90s he was still to be found orchestrating the dancefloor until 10am at New York's Sound Factory on a Saturday night. The Powerplant, which he set up after the Warehouse, lasted for three years before outbreaks of violence and the criminal fraternity appeared on the fringes. Knuckles moved into production and recording work with DJ International, recording 'Tears' with the help of Robert Owens and also producing 'Baby Wants To Ride' for Jamie Principle on Trax. About which DJ International's Rocky Jones was singularly unimpressed, obtaining a tape of the record and pressing it up in competition, though Knuckles reasoned he was only signed to DJI as an artist. He had first started to remix records for his own DJing purposes, but later would do so for everyone from Chaka Khan to the Pet Shop Boys and Kenny Thomas following his unofficial peerage by dance cognoscenti. He even remixed Nu Colours version of his own classic, 'Tears'. Knuckles became the partner of David Morales in Def-Mix Productions, one of the most high profile remix and production teams ever. Morales was present on Knuckles' 1991 album, along with frequent co-conspirators Satoshi Tomiie, Ed Kupper (who wrote the hit single, 'The Whistle Song') and Danny Madden. Brave attempts to tackle ballads proved misguided, though back in the familiar territory of house Knuckles can usually be relied upon to at least pull muster, and at best pull the foundations down.
Albums: *Frankie Knuckles Presents: The Album* (Westside 1990), *Beyond The Mix* (Ten 1991).

Konders, Bobby

b. c.1962. New York DJ whose mixture of dancehall reggae with house and hip hop breakbeats is widely acknowledged as a harbinger of the nascent jungle scene. Konders is a white boy from Philadelphia who ended up mixing it up for WBLS and living in the Bronx. He started DJing at the age of 15 at house parties, playing funk and reggae back to back. By 1986 he had started the Saturday Lunch Mix for WBLS. With singles like 'Mack Daddy' he successfully combined the new rap language with dance stylings. Konders also worked on mixes for Maxi Priest, Shabba Ranks, Papa Dee and Shinehead and used dancehall vocalists like Mikey Jarrett on his own recordings.

KWS

His *Massive Sounds* set saw him teamed with artists like Connie Harvey, Monyaka's Raphael and soulstress Lisa Makeda.

Selected album: *Cool Calm And Collective* (Desire 1990), *Massive Sounds* (Mercury 1992).

Krush

Commercial house artists from Sheffield who scored a big breakthrough hit with 'House Arrest', which rose to UK number 3 in 1988, featuring the vocals of later Definition Of Sound member Kevwon (Kevin Clark). The band comprise Mark Gamble and Cassius Campbell, who lace their standard house/disco rhythms with a quicksilver backbeat which was actually less obtrusive than many similar outfits. The unobscured vocals belonged to Ruth Joy, the veteran house diva. The follow-up material was less effective largely because it lacked the hypnotic, catchy tone of 'House Arrest'. Following record company problems Gamble would go on to work with Rhythmatic. The Krush name was revived in 1992 with a cover of Rockers Revenge's 'Walking On Sunshine', by which time they had moved from Fon to Network records.

KWS

Dance team from Nottingham, England, featuring Chris King and Winnie Williams with a series of guest vocalists. Their big hit arrived with the anthemic 'Please Don't Go', a cover of the KC And The Sunshine Band standard which followed the European success of a dance version by Double You? (on ZYX). KWS had originally been part of the Network roster as B-Line, but knocked their version out in a couple of hours in their bedroom, at a total cost of £242. The record, which featured Delroy Joseph on vocals (ex-T Cut F) stayed at number 1 for five weeks. The follow-up, 'Rock Your Baby', was a second KC composition, and was actually recorded in part at the same session as 'Please Don't Go'. Once again it jumped in front of a proposed ZYX label release - who were at that time trying to license Baby Roots' mistitled 'Rock You Baby'. But this time Network could point to the fact that the seeds of 'Rock Your Baby' had been sewn well in advance. The members of KWS left Network amicably in 1994 to form X-Clusive.

Album: *Please Don't Go (The Album)* (Network 1992).

L.A. & Babyface

US songwriters and producers who have become the Chinn and Chapman of black pop/dance in the 90s. Sharing a knack for knowing what can be tolerated by both radio and clubland, L.A. Reid (also of the Deele) and Babyface (b. Kenneth Edmonds, ex-Manchild and the Deele, originally nicknamed Babyface by Bootsy Collins) began a glittering career when helming Pebbles instant smash, 'Girlfriend', in 1988. Reid would later marry the San Franciscan diva, while Babyface can boast kinship with Kevon and Melvin Edmonds of After 7. Their output is typified by hard, fast rhythms, an uptempo approach enhanced by the strong melodic abilities of their chosen vocalists. These have included such prestigious names as Bobby Brown, Paula Abdul, the Boys, Midnight Star, Toni Braxton and the Jacksons. Babyface, meanwhile, has also released a succession of smooth, lovers' rock albums. His 1991 set included duets recorded for albums by Pebbles and Karyn White.

Albums: Babyface: *Lovers* (Solar 1989), *Tender Lover* (Solar 1989), *A Closer Look* (1991), *For The Cool In You* (Epic 1994).

L.A. Mix

Despite the title this is a British concern, L.A. stading for main man Les Adams, a long-term disco mixer and club DJ, and his production partner and wife, Emma Freilich. Adams has earned a weighty crust in the late 80s/early 90s releasing pop-house singles like 'Check This Out' (UK number 6) and 'Get Loose', a success after the team had been diagnosed by Stock Aitken And Waterman as being 'unlikely to score another hit'. They were not without their detractors but, as Adams insisted: 'We never said we set out to break new ground or deliver a message. We just want to make dance records that people will enjoy and buy'. He had already taken Maurice Joshua's 'This Is Acid' to the top of the US club charts in 1988. However, chart placings for subsequent singles, 'Love Together', 'Coming Back For More', 'Mysteries' etc. were comparitively poor. His 1991 album for A&M was a familiar blend of old school British soul dance, including Juliet Roberts on 'All Mine' and Beverley Brown on 'Mysteries Of Love'. Another of his vocalists, Jazzie P, would embark on a solo career for the same label. Adams concentrated on production work, including 'Baby Love' for Dannii Minogue.

Albums: *On The Side* (A&M 1989), *Coming Back For More* (A&M 1991).

Larkin, Kenny

b. c.1968, USA. A popular DJ through his European travels, Larkin began his musical career in 1989 after having served two years in the US Airforce. Returning home to his native Detroit, he discovered the underground techno scene by attending the Magic Institute and Shelter clubs. He subsequently met Plus 8 proprietors Richie Hawtin and John Aquiviva, for whose label he recorded his debut 12-inch, 'We Shall Overcome', in 1990. A year later he returned with the *Integration* EP. He formed his own label, Art Of Dance, in June 1992, going on to record 'War Of The Worlds', as Dark Comedy, on Transmat/Art Of Dance in the US, and on Belgium label Buzz Records in Europe. He also provided the latter with the *Serena* EP, under the guise of Yennek, and the *Vanguard* EP, as Pod.

Layton, Linda

b. Belinda Kimberley Layton, 7 December 1970, Chiswick, London, England. Renowned for her vocal contribution to Beats International's 'Dub Be Good To Me', Layton's mother was a professional dancer, responsible for choreographing West End productions of *The King And I* and *The Sound Of Music*. Layton's solo album was a disappointment, with a limp cover of Janet Kay's 'Silly Game' notwithstanding. An MOR club sound was engaged which did little to bolster the flimsy song structures, even though Norman Cook from her old band and Jolly Harris Jolly were still on hand as part of the backroom set-up.

Album: *Pressure* (Arista 1991).

Leftfield

Leftfield originally comprised just Neil Barnes, formerly of Elephant Stampede and, bizarrely, the London School Of Samba. He released a solo track, 'Not Forgotten', on Outer Rhythm, before Leftfield were expanded to a duo with the addition of former A Man Called Adam contributor Paul Daley. Barnes first met him through a poetry group who wanted live backing. However, as 'Not Forgotten', a deeply resonant song, broke big, disputes with Outer Rhythm followed. Unable to record due to contractual restraints, they embarked instead on a career as remixers to the stars. This first batch included React 2 Rhythm, Ultra Nate and Inner City. They were profligate in order to keep the Leftfield name prominent in the absence of their own brand material. Later remixes for

David Bowie, Renegade Soundwave and Yothu Yindi would follow, but by now the duo had already established their Hard Hands imprint. This debuted with the reggae-tinted 'Release The Pressure' (featuring Earl Sixteen), then the more trance-based 'Song Of Life', which gave them a minor chart success in 1992. Other artists housed on Hard Hands included Dee Patten ('Who's The Badman?'). They subsequently teamed up with John Lydon (Sex Pistols/PiL) for what Q magazine described as the unofficial single of 1993, 'Open Up'. Remixed in turn by Andy Weatherall and the Dust Brothers, it was an enormous cross-party success - especially for Barnes, whose primary musical influence had always been PiL. It might have risen higher in the charts had it not been pulled from ITV's *The Chart Show* at the last minute because of the line 'Burn Hollywood, burn' embedded in its fade, as parts of Los Angeles were by coincidence affected by fire. They also produced a soundtrack for Channel 4 film, *Shallow Grave*, and recorded as Herbal Infusion ('The Hunter'), alongside Zoom Records boss Dave Wesson.

Album: *Backlog* (Outer Rhythm 1992).

Leiner, Robert

b. c.1966, Gothenburg, Sweden. One of the first techno artists to actually appear, in soft focus, on his album sleeves, robbing the genre of its usual anonymity. Leiner was formerly the in-house engineer for the Belgian-based R&S Label. He himself has relocated to Ghent after establishing himself as a DJ in Gothenburg. His own output reflects his prolific nature: 'I have ideas all the time, it never ends. I just wish I could put something into my head and record direct from there'. He started making music at the age of 14, and keeps a stock of old tapes, sounds or sequences that he constantly returns to in the way of samples. Hence his second album was titled *Visions Of The Past*, as it included snapshots from several eras of his life. His first dancefloor manoeuvres were conducted under the name the Source, and included two double-pack 12-inches, 'Organised Noise' and 'Source Experience'. Both showcased Leiner's trippy, engaging work, redolent in tribal, spacey rhythms which have also characterised his work under his own name.

Albums: *Organised Noise* (R&S 1993), *Visions Of The Past* (Apollo 1994).

Lewis, Darlene

Garage diva whose original 'Let The Music (Lift You Up)', licensed in England through Network, started a strange, and influential chain of events in

Darlene Lewis

dance music. Manchester band Loveland (affiliated to the Eastern Bloc record shop/label) released their own version of the record without obtaining sample clearance. A major war of legal attrition looked sure to ensue, until both parties agreed to release a joint version, performing together on *Top Of The Pops*. The case was hailed in turn as a perfect example of inter-artist co-operation and goodwill. Lewis herself is a former music student who was spotted as a waitress 'humming' by producer Hassan Watkins. Asking her to put words to the tune, a few mintues later she received a standing ovation from the clients at her restaurant. Not surprising, perhaps, as she was already engaged in the process of winning some 40 odd awards for her opera singing. Although she also loves country, rock and opera, she has an instinct for club music which was honed in the Chicago house party scene. Following the success of 'Let The Music (Lift You Up)', she was signed to Kevin Saunderson's KMS label.

LFO

Among the most unrelenting and popular exponents of hardcore techno, LFO's output on Warp represents everything an outsider might fear of the music. Harsh, crashing, thumping 'bleep' music. Steve Wright, when forced to play their debut single 'LFO' on Radio 1, was ungracious enough to describe it as the worst record in the world. There is nevertheless more guile employed than may at first be apparent. Jez Varley and Mark Bell were the mainstays, though extra keyboard players Simon Hartley and Richie Brook (from Wakefield band Wild Planet) were drafted in for occasional live outings. Jez and Mark (both b. c.1972) met at college in Leeds, where they discovered mutual interests in music and technology. As well as being students they also became teenage ravers at the city's clubs, where local production team Nightmares On Wax held sway. The duo gave the DJ's a demo of a track they had recorded on a tiny Casio SKI keyboard. When it was played at the club the crowd loved it. Among the audience were the fledgeling Warp team, who decided to put it out. The single, 'LFO', crashed them straight into the Top 20 in 1990. While everybody in the techno world was busy namechecking Kraftwerk, the Germans were namechecking LFO, with Bartos, Schult and Flür working alongside LFO for their *Elektrik Music* recordings. LFO also remixed 'Planet Rock' for Afrika Bambaataa, after having been signed up to Tommy Boy in the US. Mark Bell would eventually join up with Simon Hartley of Wild Planet to form Feedback, who released the *I'm For*

Real techno-acid EP.
Album: *Frequencies* (Warp 1991).

Lieb, Oliver

b. c.1970, Frankfurt, West Germany. A well-known and highly-regarded member of Sven Vath's Eye Q/Harthouse stable, Lieb's most popular work thus far came out under the Spicelab moniker, which varied between hard house, acid and trance cuts. Contrastingly he utilised the name Mirage for the more spacey, transcendental theme of 'Airborn'. Other *nom de plumes* employed include Ambush, whose debut album was an enchanting collection of 'world techno' tracks, dominated by a thorough exploration of drums and rhythm: 'I programmed it in the way that I would lay the drums, the way I would feel them, and then I took vocals from CDs and old records'. Lieb also works as Superspy, Infinite Aura, LSG, Psilocybin and Azid Force. He is half of Paragliders with Torsten Stenzl ('Paragliders (The Remixes)'), and has remixed for Sven Vath, Vapourspace and Messiah among others. Together with Dr Atmo he recorded *Music For Films*, for Peter Namlook's Fax label, an alternative score to Philip Glass' ambient documentary *Koyaanisquatsi*.
Selected albums: As Ambush: *The Ambush* (Harthouse 1994). With Dr Atmo: *Music For Films* (Fax 1994).

Lil' Louis

b. Louis Jordan. Lil' Louis is the son of Bobby Sims, one of Chicago's premier blues guitarists who has played with BB King and Bobby 'Blue' Bland. The most notable moment in his son's career came with 'French Kiss' in 1989, peaking at number 2 in the UK charts, reportedly having been licensed from Diamond Records to ffrr for a figure in the region of £30,000. It was banned by the BBC because of its female 'vocal' (heavy breathing) being too near the knuckle. The censorship was not merely a British invention, however. New York DJ Frankie Bones was sacked for playing it at his club night in breach of prior warnings. Previous singles had included 'War Games', 'Video Clash' and 'Seven Days'. Other hits in the piano-house mould followed 'French Kiss', notably 'I Called U But You Weren't There'. Again this was no ephemeral dance tune, concerning instead a disastrous relationship with an ex-girlfriend which got so out of hand he was forced to take out a restraining order. His debut album was a surprisingly pleasing and varied selection, with tracks spanning soul and jazz (and including contributions from his father). Louis was responsible for singing, producing and much of the instrumentation. He returned after a long break in 1992 with 'The Club Lonely' and 'Saved My Life', having relocated from Chicago to New York, and taken time out to update his keyboard skills and reacquaint himself with the jazz records of his youth.

Albums: *From The Mind Of Lil' Louis* (London 1989), *Journey With The Lonely* (London 1992).

Limbo

Emergent record label based in Bath Street, Glasgow, Scotland. Since the release of Havanna's 'Schtoom' in August 1992 Limbo has built an enviable profile as a home to underground house. The label was inaugurated by Billy Kiltie (b. c.1973) and Davey Mackenzie through the auspices of their 23rd Precinct shop. Both had been involved in DJing and running clubs in the area over several years. Originally titled 23rd Precinct, the label was launched in early 1992 at which point dozens of demo tapes flooded in through the doors (not least due to the fact that a dance newsletter was distributed to Scotland from the premises). One was passed to Kiltie by local act Q-Tex, and their *Equator* EP consequently became the first release. By the time of Q-Tex's second, *Natural High* EP, they had national distribution through Revolver. Soon Limbo emerged, with most of the tracks released in its short history centering on funky, accessible house with distinctive breakbeats. Their success is founded, according to the label's proprietors, on the fact that every record features the involvement of DJ's: so that each is geared to ensuring a strong club reaction. Other staples in its schedule have included Gipsy ('I Trance You'), Mukkaa, Deep Piece (Kiltie himself with releases like 'Bup, Bup, Birri, Birri' and 'Torwart', in association with Stuart Crichton) and Sublime ('Sublime'). They have also added the experimental Out On A Limb subsidiary for material like Space Buggy's eponymous debut (a side project from one of the Havanna team).

Selected albums: Various: *House Of Limbo Vol. 1 & 2* (Limbo 1993-1994).

Limerick, Alison

b. c.1959, London. The first part of Limerick's entertainment career was spent on roller skates in the stage production of *Starlight Express* in London's West End. Her recording work, predictably, kicked off with sumptuous garage tunes, notably 'Where Love Lives (Come On In)', which showcased a simplistic but well executed musical approach, and was voted dance record of 1991 by *Billboard* magazine. This despite the fact that it was never released in the US. Alongside fellow Top 20 singles, 'Make It On My Own' (co-written and produced by Steve Anderson of Brothers In Rhythm, and featuring Limerick's boyfriend jazzman Roger Beaujolais) and 'Come Back (For Real Love)', it was housed on an impressive debut album. The presence of David Morales and Frankie Knuckles on her second album, *With A Twist*, added further spice to the formula.

Albums: *And Still I Rise* (Arista 1992), *With A Twist* (Arista 1994).

Liquid

Group who originally comprised Eamon Downes and Shane Honegan, until the latter party left. They had become one of the first progressive house acts in the Top 20, with 1992's 'Sweet Harmony', recorded while they were still a duo, as a reaction to the 'louder faster' rules of hardcore techno. It cost only £200 to record yet saw them grace the *Top Of The Pops* stage. Downes re-emerged in 1993 on the XL roster, after a period in the shadows with the *Time To Get Up* EP. He maintains that he calls himself Liquid because he 'likes the odd drink'. Early influences were dub maestros like Barrington Levy and Scientist.

Little Louie Vega

A New York-based DJ, Vega's career began at high school at the age of 18, after watching his friends spin records. He played high school parties before eventually establishing his own label. He went on to DJ at the Devil's Nest (regarded as the birthplace of the New York 'freestyle' approach, alongside TKA and Sa-Fire), then Hearthrob and 1018. By the time he had reached the 4,000 capacity Studio 54 Todd Terry would pass Vega his new mixes to try out on the crowd. His first remix job was 'Running' by Information Society, then Noel's 'Silent Morning'. He even worked Debbie Gibson's first record. He began his own-name productions with the instrumental 'Don't Tell Me' for SBK in 1989 and 'Keep On Pumpin' It Up' (as Freestyle Orchestra), before signing to CBS subsidiary WTG Records with singer Mark Anthony. He had previously been commissioned to write songs for the movie *East Side Story*, where he first met the singer. Together they hooked up for a Latin R&B flavoured album and single, 'Ride On The Rhythm'. He also worked with his girlfriend, 'India', and Todd Terry for the latter's 'Todd's Message'. Together with Barbara Tucker, Vega runs the Underground Network Club in New York, and he has also produced 'Beautiful People' for that artist. Despite this background as an established house star, he is probably best known now for his work alongside Kenny 'Dope' Gonzalez as half of the Masters At Work remix team. He is not to be confused with Chicago house veteran Lil' Louis, or, for that matter, with the Louie Vega who remixed for Lakim Shabazz, despite the fact that both shared the same management. Vega's most recent remix clients include Juliet Roberts and Urban Species.

Loaded Records

Record label which is also the home of the Brighton-based remix team of JC Reid and Tim Jeffreys (also a *Record Mirror* journalist), who operate under the name Play Boys. Their first production work together was for the London Community Gospel Choir in 1992 with 'I'll Take You There' and 'Ball Of Confusion', before they set up the Loaded imprint. Titles like 'Ransom' and 'Suggestive', co-produced with Pizzaman, aka Norman Cook, emerged. Their next work was on a hot re-activated version of 'Love So Strong' by Secret Life which proved more than merely a remix, with re-recorded Paul Bryant vocals. Other projects included Brother Love Dub's 'Ming's Incredible Disco Machine', PM Dawn's 'When Midnight Says' and Talizman. As the Play Boys they also released in their own right, including 'Mindgames' from 1992, and they also returned the compliment to Norman Cook by remixing his Freak Power track, 'Turn On, Tune In, Cop Out'. The Loaded release schedule continued apace too, with records like those from Key Largo (Eddie Richards) and the garage house of Wildchild Experience (the *Wildtrax* EP, which ran to several volumes, created by Southampton-born DJ Roger McKenzie). Other artists included Jason Nevins ('The Upper Room').

Locust

In the accelerating flurry of ambient dance releases following the Orb's breakthrough, at least the work of Mark Van Hoen contains a snatch of humour. The track 'Xenophobia', for example: 'I started with this Japanese vocal sample, and began thinking I'd have to surround it with five-note Japanese pentatonik scales. Then I gave up and called myself xenophobic'. Elsewhere the musical territory on his debut album was mapped out in traditional genre style, eerie mood pieces with more than a passing nod to composers like Steve Reich. Diverting enough, but hardly a substantial listening experience. He originally came to prominence through the heavily-imported *Skyline* EP, before a deal with R&S subsidiary Apollo for six albums. Unlike many similar artists, however, Van Hoen has no ambitions to remix other people's music, preferring instead to concentrate on his own wares (though he does plan to produce other artists, from outside the house/techno sphere).
Album: *Weathered Well* (R&S 1994).

Logic Records

Founded in Frankfurt, Germany by Luca Anzilotti and Michael Munzig, Logic was the original home to their mega-techno creations like Snap!'s 'Exterminate'. The label was set up because: 'With Logic we have total creative control over every aspect of a record: the mixes, the artwork, the promotion, everything'. This is in addition/complementary to the duo's interests in the Omen club in Frankfurt. The label has also released high profile techno from Blake Baxter ('One More Time') and Rapination featuring Kym Mazelle ('Love Me The Right Way'). Others included Pressure Drop's 'Release Me' and Durga McBroom (ex-Blue Pearl)'s solo debut. Mark Spoon of Jam & Spoon fame held the A&R post for a number of years. Logic is just as well known for its impressive compilations like *Logic Trance 1 & 2*. There is also a successful subsidiary imprint, Save The Vinyl, which produces work on vinyl only.

Loop Guru

The listening tastes of spokesman Jal Muud (South American pipe music, Morrocan indigenous sounds) has informed the career of Nation Records' Loop Guru. Together with Salman Gita he forms the core of the band, aided by up to ten guest musicians for various events (who include former Pigabag drummer Chip Carpenter and percussionist Mad Jym). The duo have been involved in music since 1980 when they were early members of the Megadog enclave, meeting through mutual friend Alex Kasiek (Trans-Global Underground). It was at this time that Jamuud: '...stopped listening to Western music altogether. I foudn that the wealth of sound and mood in Asian and African music was vastly more alive than its Western counterparts.' Offering their listeners 'total enlightenment through music', Loop Guru have perfected a package of chants, laments, tablas, Eastern religion and ethnic samples, which was first brought to the public's attention via their *Sus-San-Tics* EP, which featured the guest vocals of Sussan Deheim (b. Iran). A debut album was recorded, its title, *Duniya*, translating from Urdu as 'The World'. Part of the methodology evolved from Brian Eno's 'Choice Cards' ethos, wherein different instructions on musical structure are carried out via the turn of a set of cards. It placed them at the forefront of the 'world dance'

movement. Arguably their most effective and popular single to date has proved to be 'Paradigm Shuffle', which included at its core Martin Luther King's 'I Have A Dream' speech.
Album: *Duniya* (Nation 1994).

Love To Infinity

Garage production duo comprising the brothers Andrew and Peter Lee, who have been working together since the late 80s. Both were trained in classical music, while their modern work recalls the heyday of disco, with strings, diva vocals and uptempo rhythms. Peter is responsible for programming, while Andrew acts as engineer. In addition to remixing for the Other Two, Melanie Williams, D:Ream and Grace Jones, they have also worked as a band in their own right, notably with Bruce Forest in 1990. They co-wrote with Boy George, and released their own album in Japan. They also released a solitary 12-inch for Big Life, before eeking out a living with engineering work for Sub Sub and the Mock Turtles. They returned to their own recording profile in the early-90s, alongside vocalist Louise Bailey, on singles like 'Somethin' Outta Nothin'' for Pigeon Pie.

Lucky People Center

Swedish dance terrorists whose samples on their debut album built on the best traditions of Test Department by using speeches from world leaders, in this case marrying George Bush and Saddam Hussein to a backbeat on 'It's Still Cloudy In Saudi Arabia'. The group were formed in 1992 by Johan Söderburg (percussion), Lars Åkerlund (samples) and Sebastian Öberg (electric cello). The relentless barrage of samples (Rodney King, Bishop Desmond Tutu, the lawyer of massacre-priest Jim Jones) were adopted in a vein more prevalent within hip-hop than the dance scene, though Lucky People Center are firmly placed in the latter tradition by their dominant rhythms.
Album: *Welcome To Lucky People* (MNW 1993).

Luvdup Twins

Twins Mark and Adrian Luvdup, who won numerous Single Of The Week plaudits with their debut 12-inch, 'Good Times'. This was released on Manchester's UFG label (set up by E-Lustrious), and featured mixes from Jon Dasilva and John McCready. The duo play out at the Jolly Roger night in their native Manchester's Paradise Factory venue, review for *Mixmag Update* (having formerly run the well-regarded Luvdup fanzine), and have remixed for Awesome 3 among others.

M

M People

The key component of M People is Mike Pickering (b. March 1958, Manchester, England; keyboards, programming), a man of many talents and former DJ at the Factory owned Hacienda club in Manchester. *The Face* magazine went as far as to describe Pickering as 'England's most revered DJ'. After school Pickering worked in a fish factory and engineering warehouse, becoming a major Northern Soul fan. He played saxophone for mid-80s indie dance forerunners Quando Quango and had various connections with New Order, including sharing a flat with their manager, Rob Gretton. Among several weighty notches on his bedpost was the distinction of having booked the Smiths for their first Manchester gigs. He had also signed James and Happy Mondays in his role as Factory's A&R man. After Factory he became a junior director at the DeConstruction label, where he brought Black Box and Guru Josh, the label's two most important early successes. He provided DeConstruction with *North - The Sound Of The Dance Underground*, arguably the first UK house compilation, though it was Pickering and his band T-Coy behind seven of the eight cuts. He is also the founder member and songwriter for M People - the M standing for his Christian name - who also record for DeConstruction. The band includes ex-Hot House vocalist Heather Small (b. Heather Marguerita Small, 20 January 1965, London, England) and Paul Heard (b. 5 October 1960, Hammersmith, London, England; keyboards, programming), formerly of Orange Juice and Working Week. They debuted in May 1991 with 'Colour My Life', scoring with the club hit 'How Can I Love You More' at the end of the year. These singles promoted a first album which took its name from Pickering's early musical leanings, *Northern Soul*. 1993 was M People's breakthrough year. On the back of colossal UK hits like 'Movin' On Up', they were afforded a BRIT Award for Best UK Dance Act. The album which housed the hits, *Elegant Slumming* (whose title was taken from a Tom Woolfe book), included a cover of Dennis Edwards' 'Don't Look Any Further', and vocal support from Nu Colours.
Albums: *Northern Soul* (DeConstruction 1992), *Northern Soul Extended* (DeConstruction 1992), *Elegant Slumming* (DeConstruction 1993).

Mackintosh, C.J.

One of the UK's most widely revered DJs and remixers, to whom major record companies regularly indulge their A&R budgets. Chris 'C.J' Mackintosh's standard approach, that of radio-friendly, lush garage arrangements, is too MOR for many of the nation's more underground clubbers, but his technique has become the epitome of taste in the mainstream. Clients have included Whitney Houston, Lisa Stansfield and Janet Jackson. Mackintosh actually started out as a rap DJ, going on to win the 1987 finals of the DMC mixing championships. After this initial success he would provide hip hop megamixes for labels like Champion. His first venture into remixing proved even more rewarding. Together with Dave Dorrell, he mixed MARRS' 'Pump Up The Volume', one of dance music's most portentious moments. Mackintosh happily continues his day time job, that of club DJ, and on this basis is one of the first of the UK's 'names' to play in the States. However, it is as a remixer he has won fame and fortune, although he also sees the dangers inherent in a DJ-led music scene: 'With remixing, everyone's doing it and it's wrong, but I think it'll go on because there's nothing to stop it...All sorts of bands are depending on it, they all want a dance mix... remixing's easy because you're using someone else's ideas. Production, and writing, is a totally different thing'. A list of his credits could fill a small book, but some of the most important include Inner City ('Good Life'), Dina Carroll ('Ain't No Man'), PM Dawn ('Reality'), A Tribe Called Quest ('Bonita Applebum'), De La Soul ('Ring, Ring, Ring'), Digital Underground ('Packet Man'), Simple Minds ('Sign Of The Times'), Gang Starr ('Take A Rest'), Whitney Houston ('Queen Of The Night') and Luther Vandross and Janet Jackson ('The Best Things In Life Are Free').

Main

Minimalist ambient dance band formed by Robert Hampson of Loop. Taking the repetitive motifs from that band, Main refined the formula to accentuate the aesthetics of post-rave dance 'chill'. They draw heavily on environmental sounds (ie a road at night) on which they dub synths and electronically generated effects as well as guitars. Their first EP, *Hydra*, was dedicated to the German composer Karlheinz Stockhausen. Follow-up EPs included *Dry Stone Feed* and *Firmament*.

Mantra, Michael

A California-based musician/experimentalist who has sought to advance on the ambient ethic of

Brian Eno and more recent 'chill-out' arists such as the Orb. Mantra describes his methods as 'Brain Hemisphere Harmonic Healing', which spells out his intention to create sound structures that 'induce a meditative state that synchronises brain wave frequencies'. After synchronising the mind and the body, Mantra's work claims to release endorphines (part of the human body's natural pharmacy which work at the level of opiates). To achieve this electronics are combined with field recordings of the Pacific sea, seagulls, and natural instruments such as the didgeridoo. Such experiments in the neural affects of sound could well represent a previously unchartered future for music.

Album: *Sonic Alter* (Silent Records 1994).

MARRS

A collaboration between two 4AD bands, Colourbox and AR Kane which, though a one off, was enough to set both the independent, dance and national charts alight during Autumn 1987. 'Pump Up The Volume' was augmented on the a-side by UK champion scratch mixer Chris 'C.J' Mackintosh and London DJ/journalist Dave Dorrell. The record was originally mailed to the 500 most influential regional club and dance DJs on an anonymous white label, in order that it received exposure six weeks prior to its stock version. On official release it entered the charts at number 35, a figure attained on 12-inch sales only. Daytime radio play ensured the single was the next weeks' highest climber, rising 24 places to number 11. The following two weeks it stayed at number 2 before reaching the number 1 spot on 28th September 1987. Originally the idea of 4AD supremo Ivo, the single featured samples of James Brown, a practice already common in hip hop which would soon come into vogue for an avalanche of dance tracks: 'We've used a lot of rhythms and time signatures from old records, classic soul records, but mixed that with modern electronic instruments and AR Kane's guitar sound', was how the single was described. 'Pump Up The Volume' was never followed-up, apparently due to acrimony between the involved personnel over finance, which was a great shame. As such the MARRS discography is a brief but blemishless one.

Mass Order

A Baltimore-based duo of Mark Valentine and Eugene Hayes, who grew up listening to the O'Jays and soul standards. Mass Order scored a huge Autumn 1991 'hit' with their gospel house cracker, 'Take Me Away', a popular but elusive disc. It was actually a bootleg which had been

pirated from a DAT tape at New York's New Music Seminar. It was eventually given a proper release (under its full title, 'Lift Every Voice (Take Me Away)') with remixes from the Basement Boys and Tony Humphries. As a footnote the bootlegging incident went to court, but the miscreants, David Cooper and William Lynch, still escaped justice. They were acquitted because they 'did not know they were breaking the law'.
Album: *Maybe One Day* (Columbia 1992).

Massive Attack

This loose Bristol collective have grown to become one of the premier UK dance/rap outfits. The group features the talents of rapper '3D' Del Najo (b. c.1966), and his cohorts Daddy G (b. c.1959) and Mushroom (aka Tricky Kid, b. c.1968, Knowle West, Bristol, England). They began in 1988 having spent several years working on various mobile sound systems, as well as releasing records under The Wild Bunch moniker ('Fucking Me Up', 'Tearing Down The Avenue'). Nellee Hooper, a former member of the Wild Bunch, left to work with Soul II Soul, while Milo Johnson began work in Japan. 3D is also a well respected graffiti artist, having his work featured in art galleries and a television survey on Channel 4. Liaisons with Neneh Cherry, for whom 3D provided the lyrics to 'Manchild', eventually led the remaining three to a meeting with Cameron McVey, who produced Massive Attack's debut LP. The resultant *Blue Lines* boasted three hit singles; 'Daydreaming', 'Unfinished Sympathy' (which also featured an orchestral score) and 'Safe From Harm'. The blend of rap, deep reggae and soul was provocative and rich in texture. It featured the aforementioned Cherry and Shara Nelson with effective vocal contributions. An outstanding achievement, it had taken eight months to create 'with breaks for Christmas and the World Cup'. 'Unfinished Symphony' was particularly well received. *Melody Maker* magazine ranked it as the best single of 1991, and it remains a perennial club favourite. One minor hiccup arrived when they were forced, somewhat hysterically, to change their name during the Gulf War in order to maintain airplay. It was duly shortened to Massive. Their philosophy singled them out as dance music's new sophisticates; 'We don't ever make direct dance music. You've got to be able to listen and then dance'. That status was franked when U2 asked them to provide a remix for their 'Mysterious Ways' single. Despite *Blue Lines* being widely celebrated, the band would disappear from view shortly afterwards. Shara Nelson would go on to a solo career. As would rapper Tricky Kid, who took the abbreviated title of Tricky, releasing 'Aftermath' in 1993. According to the latter, Massive Attack remains on permanent hold, with the possibility of the trio reuniting at some point in the future.
Album: *Blue Lines* (Wild Bunch/EMI 1991).

Mastercuts Series

A Beechwood subsidiary masterminded by former Northern Soul DJ Ian Dewhirst, Mastercuts was launched in June 1990 to document some of dance music's most essential moments, in all its myriad forms. Initial releases like *Jazz Funk 1* sold 25,000 copies, while *New Jack Swing* climbed as high as number 8 in the *Music Week* compilation chart, showing well against much better-funded, television-advertised albums. The first record in the series had been Classic Mix, but other formats were explored in the following order: Jazz-Funk, Mellow, New Jack Swing, Funk, Salsoul, Rare Groove, P-Funk, 80s Groove, Electro and House. Each came complete with insightful sleevenotes and anecdotes, in a manner which suggested that at last dance music might be taking its history as seriously as other forms of music: 'What we're striving for is that every time people see that embossed Mastercuts logo we want that to be the sign of quality'. In 1994 the label also relaunched the legendary Streetsounds label, while Beechwood was also behind the *New Electronica* series of experimental albums.

Masters At Work

aka Little Louie Vega and Kenny 'Dope' Gonzalez, who marked the inception of their partnership by releasing 'Ride On The Rhythm' in 1991. On the back of that and their well established personal reputations (appearances as extras in Spaghetti Westerns notwithstanding), they subsequently undertook a vast array of remix projects. These began with St Ettienne ('Only Love Can Break Your Heart'), plus Chic, Debbie Gibson, Melissa Morgan, BG The Prince Of Rap ('Take Control Of The Party'), Lisa Stansfield, Deee-Lite ('Bittersweet Loving') plus legendary Latin jazz player Tito Puente's 'Ran Kan Kan'. In turn Puente contributed three times to Vega's 1992 album with singer Marc Anthony. They also recorded, in their own right, material like 'Can't Stop The Rhythm (with Jocelyn Brown) for US label Cutting. Widely regarded as the cream of the profession, not everybody was clamouring for their wares - Jamiroquai's 'Emergency On Planet Earth' remix was rumoured to be hated by the artist concerned. His was a very rare dissenting voice, however.

May, Derrick

If one name crops up again and again in discussions of techno, it is that of Derrick 'Mayday' May (b. c.1964, USA). Alongside Juan Atkins, Carl Craig and Kevin Saunderson, with whom he ran the Music Institute club and attended high school, May is the king of the Detroit sound. His work in the late 80s has provided literally thousands with inspiration, cuts like 'The Dance', 'It Is What It Is' and particularly 'Strings Of Life' defining a moment in time in dance music. In his youth he was inspired by Yello and Kraftwerk, and he began to make electronic music with Atkins and Saunderson while studying at Belleville High, Detroit. Recording as Mayday or Rhythim Is Rhythim, generally on his own Transmat label, he went on to carve out a new vein in dance music, which synthesised the advances of the electro movement with the more challenging end of the house movement. A music that was christened 'techno', though May conceded in 1992 that 'I don't even use the word techno anymore'. He has never proved prolific in his recordings, and aside from occasional European jaunts has proved an elusive spokesperson. To such an extent that when Chris Peat of Altern 8 stood for parliament, he made a manifesto commitment to use MI5 to track May down. A self-evident example of May's belief in Kraftwerk's 'less is more' mystique. After the success of 'Strings Of Life' he largely fled the dance scene, aside from a remix of Yello's 'The Race'. His chief notoriety ath the time rose from an argument at the 1990 New Music Seminar in New York when Factory personnel, Tony Wilson in particular, attempted to lecture the Americans on dance music (specifically that they did not know what they had created). Rhythim Is Rhythim did not follow up 'Strings Of Life' until 1990, when 'The Beginning' was released. May went on to cut three tracks on System 7's debut album, before, in 1991, Network released *Innovator: Soundtrack For The Tenth Planet*, an EP which comprised some of May's definitive moments to date. It was followed in 1992 by *Transmat Relics*, a double album of the label's finest moments, heavily featuring Rhythim Is Rhythim. The Transmat logo had been reactivated via a deal with Belgium label Buzz. 'Strings Of Life' was also re-released in the same year after being heavily sampled on Altern 8's 'Evapor 8' - this time in a new, drumless version. May, meanwhile, could not be found, having relocated to Amsterdam to play a leading role in that city's 'Hi-Tech Soul' movement in 1993.

Selected albums: *Relics: A Transmat Compilation* (Buzz 1992). As Rhythim Is Rhythim: *The Beginning* (Big Life 1990).

Media Records

See Bortolotti, Gianfranco

Me'Shell

b. Me'Shell NdegéOcello, Berlin, West Germany. Introduced by her PR machine as a female equivalent to Prince, Me'Shell has embarked on a solo career which embraces both the hip hop and R&B markets. Like Prince, she is a multi-instrumentalist, and writes, produces and plays on all her songs. Her given name was Swahili, indicating 'Free Like A Bird'. After a nomadic life as the child of a US forces man, her first love was art rather than the jazz skills of her father and brother. She was, however, inexorably drawn to music as she grew, and much of her youth was spent in Washington's 'go-go' scene, where at one point she was actually shot at whilst on stage with Little Bennie and the Masters, at the Cherry Atlantic Skating Rink. Her interest in music had blossomed when her brother played guitar in a local band, whose bass player left his instrument lying around after rehearsal. She was a quick convert. At the age of 19, she uprooted for New York 'with my baby and my bass'. There she joined Living Colour's Black Rock Coalition, and recorded sessions for artists of the calibre of Caron Wheeler and Steve Coleman. She was the musical director for Arrested Development's *Saturday Night Live* show, though her own demos were receiving little response. Until, that is, Madonna stepped in, inviting her to become one of the first artists signed to her Maverick empire. A palpable maturity was at work on her debut, with a combination of acid jazz and R&B rhythms backing her beat poetry. She scored a breakthrough hit with 'If That's Your Boyfriend (He Wasn't Last Night)', a provocative post-feminist statement. Despite the sexual overtones of her packaging, she was not averse to strong political statements; material like 'Step Into The Projects' retaining a cutting edge. Or the line 'The white man shall forever sleep with one eye open' (from 'Shoot'n Up And Gett'n High'), which had an almost Public Enemy-like ring to it. The album was produced by A Tribe Called Quest's Bob Power, alongside guests including DJ Premier and Geri Allen (Blue Note). Though she attracted some criticism for espousing the corporate rebellion angle, her connections with Maverick hardly passing unobserved, there was substance and fire in the best of her work.

Albums: *Plantation Lullabies* (Maverick/WEA 1993).

Metalheads

Purveyors of hardcore techno whose *Angel* EP

Derrick May

Mixmaster Morris

invoked the rather over-employed 'intelligent hardcore' term. Whether or not it was correct for sections of the cognoscenti to herald it as a great leap forward for the genre remains to be seen. The main man behind the record was Goldie, an ex-grafitti artist of some note, who has spent time in New York, Miami and Birmingham. Possibly his most famous illustration was his 'Change The World' mural at Queens Park Rangers football ground, Loftus Road. Before Metalheads he had recorded a solo white label EP under the name Ajaz Project, then 'Killer Muffin' on Reinforced, with whom he is now employed. His compatriots in the project are experienced DJs Fabio and Grooverider, both of whom have strong cult followings on their own terms.

Messiah

Ali Ghani and Mark Davies, from Hounslow and Barnet respectively, met while students at the University Of East Anglia. They represent the talent behind the Messiah name, which moved from the independent Kickin' Records to WEA in 1993. Their debut album was completed with the aid of Def American's Rick Rubin, who saw the group as the perfect embodiment of dance with which to convert an American audience. Old habits died hard however, and he hooked them up with Ian Astbury of the Cult to produce one of their debut album's tracks. He had picked the band up from their previous American base, Moby's Instinct label. Their debut for WEA arrived with the aid of Precious Wilson's vocals, and included re-runs of their previous club favourites '20,000 Hardcore Members', 'Temple Of Dreams' (based on This Mortal Coil's 'Song To The Siren'), 'I Feel Love' and 'There Is No Law'. The middle two of that quartet had given the band Top 20 crossover hits too. In addition they unveiled the impressive 'Thunderdome', with remixes from Spicelab, Secret Knowledge and Gods Underwater. Album: *Beyond Good And Evil* (Kickin' 1991), *21st Century Jesus* (WEA 1993).

Metroplex

Juan Atkins' Detroit record label, which housed several of his greatest moments as Model 500 ('No UFO's', 'The Chase', 'Off To Battle', 'Interference'). In the 90s it has gone on to be operated under the aegis of 'Mad' Mike Banks' Submerge umbrella organisation. Atkins also devoted a lot of his time, through the auspices of Metroplex, in to developing new talent. 'A lot of people keep everything for themselves, I guess that's the greed element, the less you have the more there is for you which is very limiting. I

think people who have that attitude don't see the bigger picture. They will only go so far'.

Miller, Duncan

The studio boffin behind such dance chart regulars as Esoterix (whose product includes 'Void', the first release on Positiva, and 'Come Satisfy My Love' for Union) and Monica De Luxe ('The Temperature's Rising' and 'Don't Let This Feeling Stop'). This is only the tip of the Miller iceberg, however. He garnered an *Echoes* Single Of The Week award for 'South By South West', from his jazz-based project, As One, on Wow Records, and another creation, Feelgood Factor's 'Jump Up In The Air' also showed strongly in several club listings. Miller operates out of his own West London studio, working alongside various DJs and musicians. In this role he produced 'U Don't Have To Say You Love Me' for React Records, and 'Bonour M. Basie' for Wow. He has also produced a track for Robert Owens and provided keyboard services for remixer Frankie Foncett. His own remixing projects included working with Paul Gotel on the Well Hung Parliament takes of Nu Colours' 'The Power', McKoy's 'Fight' and Monie Love's 'Never Give Up'.

Ministry Of Sound

London club whose unique atmosphere has led to a series of highly successful releases. The first of these was a compilation mixed by Tony Humphries in August 1993. Heralded by promotions man Jason Hill as 'a natural progression', it was among the fastest-selling items in dance shops throughout the UK in 1993, moving over 35,000 copies. This first set compiled a series of club classics, such as Mother's 'All Funked Up', X-Press 2's 'London X-Press' and Gabrielle's 'Dreams', the latter a staple at the club long before it scaled the national charts. A second, similarly successful set, followed in 1994. This time there were remixes from Paul Oakenfold, who helmed a live touring version of the club through 1994. The club also rose to prominence by projecting their logo onto the Houses Of Parliament as part of their second birthday celebrations, despite police objections. Albums: Various: *The Ministry - Vol 1* (MOS 1993), *The Ministry - Vol 2* (MOS 1994).

Mix Tapes

An attempt to recreate the 'buzz' of live DJ performances, mix tapes are a musical format whose ancestry can be traced back to reggae's yard tapes. Often of similar dubious origins and quality, very few are cleared through copyright, bearing in mind the number of samples and tracks involved in a single one or two hour set. However, the official lines, such as those promoted by *Mixmag*, have undergone this process. It is a noble but inherently flawed medium, but also the closest recorded approximation of a night clubbing or raving.

Mixmaster Morris

House guru, who arrived in the early 90s at the height of hardcore techno's domination (he titled his own music weirdcore), and whose name is subsequently graced dozens of releases, both as a producer and remixer. Morris' first live performances were at the ICA Rock Week in 1980, before he began to work with samplers in 1983. He has since claimed the honour of being 'the first to play a house set in the UK', at the Fridge in London in 1987 at his Madhouse nights. He also prepared pirate radio tapes for his 'Mongolian Hip Hop Show', and worked with experimental pirate television. He met Colin Angus of the Shamen via mutual Psychic TV acquaintances, and began DJing on their Synergy tours. His musical style was certainly unique, often building a set to the centrepiece section, which would as likely be a This Heat track as anything more conventional. He also stressed the importance of providing DJ's with label information, not just bpm's but also the key a track was played in. In addition to his sampling and rhythmic wizardry, he has gone on to record in his own right. The first such release was 'Space Is The Place' on the Rising High label, a relationship with whom prospers to this day. Following late 80s singles 'Freestyle' and 'I Want You', his debut album arrived, also credited to The Irresistable Force, in 1992. It boasted a splendid holographic label, and was filled with samples taken from obscure and obtuse sources. A more detached, ambient based project, after a brief Kraftwerk parody on the intro it branched out into seamless 'chill-out' territory. This was the man, after all, who invented the phrase 'I think, therefore I ambient'. He has gone on to record with the new king of chill, Peter Namlook, as part of the latter's Dreamfish project, and remixed for Spiritualized among others.
Albums: As The Irresistable Force: *Flying High* (Rising High 1992, double album). With Peter Namlook: *Dreamfish* (Rising High 1993).

MLO

A collaboration between Jon Tye and Pete Smith through the Rising High imprint, MLO's debut album was also the soundtrack to a film of the same name - shown as live accompaniment to Pink Floyd gigs in 1994. The project was put together in an intensive two week period inside one of the world's most advanced multi-media studios. The term ambient was almost inevitably invoked, though the duo opted to disassociate themselves from the bulk of the artists working within that genre. The album was titled after the seventh moon of Jupiter, the only entity in the solar system, aside from the earth, known to be volcanically active. As well as recording a film for use alongside their debut album, and producing videos for other artists, Tye has also recorded solo as Flutter ('Flutter').
Album: *Io* (Rising High 1994).

Mo Wax

An indepedent label run from Oxford, England, whose musical predilictions cover a territory which takes in Acid Jazz and the ambient strains of new dance gurus like the Aphex Twin. The label was formed by James Lavelle (b. c.1973, Oxford, England), who started compiling his own electro tapes at the age of 10. Three years later he developed his interest in hip hop, going on to work experience at Bluebird Records in London, and DJing in his native Oxford. The eclecticism of his early musical tastes broadened through exposure to acid house then techno and jazz, as he worked in a record shop by day and wrote a column for *Straight No Chaser* in the evenings. By the age of 20 he had established his record company, Mo Wax, bringing his diverse musical tastes to bear on its catalogue. The label's inventry kicked off with Repercussions' 'Promise' and Stylus' 'Many Ways'. Within a year of operation its discography boasted vital cuts like those by RPM ('2000'), DJ Krush ('Krush'), DJ Shadow (the superb 'In Flux'), and Lavelle's own Men From Uncle project. There was even a hip hop record remixed by techno ambassador Carl Craig, while the Federation (the Bristol based team of Alex Swift, St. John, Julie Lockhart and Stepchild) returned to a more conventional jazz groove. The boundaries were stretched further by invoking a second label, Smoke Filled Thoughts, through London.
Selected albums: Various: *Royalties Overdue* (Mo Wax 1994). The Federation: *Flower To The Sun* (Mo Wax 1994).

Moby

A New York DJ, recording artist, Christian, vegan and Philosophy Graduate. Moby (b. Richard Melville Hall, c.1966, New York, USA) is so nicknamed because of the fact that he can trace his ancestry to the author of the famous Captain Ahab whaling tale. This is by no means the only interesting aspect of his idiosyncratic artistic life. He refuses to travel anywhere by car because of the environmental considerations, and generally displays little of the public anonymity that is the creed of the underground DJ. In 1991 he took the *Twin Peaks* theme, under the guise of 'Go', into the Top 10. Although that appealed to the more perverse natures of both mainstream and club audiences, the release of 'I Feel It'/'Thousand' in 1993 was yet more bizarre. The latter track was classified by the *Guinness Book Of Records* as the fastest single ever, climaxing at 1015 bpm. It was typical of Moby's playful, irreverent attitude to his work. In his youth he was a member of hardcore punk outfit the Vatican Commandos, and even substituted as singer for Flipper while their vocalist was in prison. He has brought these rock 'n' roll inclinations to bear on the world of dance: at the 1992 DMC/Mixmag Awards ceremony he symbolically trashed his keyboards at the end of his set. His introduction to dance music began in the mid-80s: 'I was drawn to it, I started reading about it, started hanging out in clubs. For me house music was the synthesis of the punk era'. He collected cheap, second hand recording equipment, basing himself in an old factory/converted prison in New York's Little Italy. He signed to leading independent Mute in 1993. *Ambient* was a collection of unissued cuts from 1988 to 1991, composed of barely audible atmospheric interludes. *Story So Far* gathered together a series of tracks he cut for Instinct Records. The following year Moby released 'Hymn', a transcendental religious techno odyssey, distinguished by a 35-minute ambient mix and a Laurent Garner remix. His own remix catalogue includes Brian Eno, LFO ('Tan Ta Ra'), Pet Shop Boys, Erasure ('Chorus'), Orbital ('Speed Freak'), Depeche Mode and even Michael Jackson. Albums: *Ambient* (Mute 1993), *The Story So Far* (Mute 1993).

Moody Boyz

Tony Thorpe's incarnation of the dub-house ethic, his most high-profile banner since 80s experimentalists 400 Blows. After the demise of that tempestuous outfit he formed Warrior Records, which would be superceded by his BPM label, which won its spurs releasing compilations like *Acid Beats* (1988), the musical tastes determined by Thorpe's immersion in the club scene (the legendary Spectrum nights in particular). Later he became in-house remixer for the KLF, before the Moody Boyz' name was first employed on a series of acid-inspired 12-inch releases such as 'Boogie Woogie Music', 'King Of The Funky Zulus' and the *Journey Into Dubland* EP. His debut long playing set combined his traditional love of reggae bass with a strong philosophy of black emancipation, particularly on 'Fight Back (27-4-94)', dedicated to the democracy movement's victory in South Africa. There were also intriguing collaborations with Black Dog on 'Elite Doodz Presents Snooze', and the Italian Vibraphone set-up. Thorpe has also recorded as Voyager, House Addicts and Urban Jungle, and remixed for Joi, Bocca Juniors and Fun-Da-Mental. He also provides Channel 4 with much of its incidental music.
Albums: *Product Of The Environment* (Guerilla 1994). As Voyager: *Transmission* (Underworld/Virgin 1993).

Morales, David

b. c.1961, Brooklyn, New York, USA. Born and bred in the capital of Puerto Rican parents, David Morales is the leader of the pack in terms of his country's leading remixers. His style, melodic garage house with a strong disco influence, belies his personal physique and presence, that of a pencil-bearded, tattooed body-builder. Married with a son, he works out for two hours every day, though he also employs a bodyguard for his regular evening shows (he was shot in his youth). As a young man he attended both the Loft and Paradise Garage, before being invited to play at the latter through Judy Weinstein's For The Record organisation. His other stomping grounds included all the major New York clubs, such as the Ozone Layer, Inferno and Better Days. The Morales style has graced literally hundreds of records, his first remix being Insync's 'Sometimes Love'. He possibly works best in tandem with a strong garage vocalist (Alison Limerick, Ce Ce Peniston, Yazz, Jocelyn Brown, Chimes etc.). A good selection of his greatest work might be permed from the following: Robert Owens' 'I'll Be Your Friend', Clive Griffin's 'I'll Be Waiting', Black Sheep's 'Strobelite Honey', Pet Shop Boys' 'So Hard', Thompson Twins' 'The Saint' or Limerick's 'Where Love Lives'. Many other remixes have been completed with longstanding friend Frankie Knuckles (as Def-Mix), who he also met through For The Record (Weinstein going on to manage both artists). His productivity is made possible by the fact that he is happy to churn out up to two remixes a week under his own auspices. His live sets, however, are often less glossy than the productions he is best known for: 'When I DJ I'm not as pretty as a lot of the records I make'. He has had trouble in constructing solo hits on his own account, though his debut album included guest appearances from Sly Dunbar and Ce Ce Rogers. Album: *The Programme* (1993).

Morillo, Erick 'More'

b. c.1971. Morillo started DJing at the age of 11, playing sets in his local New Jersey that matched ragga with techno (a precursor to the sound of Reel 2 Real). As a student at New York's Centre For The Media Arts, he started collecting studio equipment, and became a self-taught maestro. He graduated to recording his own material by sampling Jamaican toasters on to DAT. One night a gentleman came forward from the crowd to enquire as to the source of a particular sampled voice. It transpired that the questioner, known as General, was the owner of said layrnx. Together they went on to record 'The Funky Buddha' and *Move It* album for RCA. Influenced by old school Chicago house like Lil' Louis, Todd Terry and Kenny 'Dope' Gonzalez, Morillo has gone on to build his own studio, Double Platinum, where Little Louie Vega's *Hardrive* EP and Barbara Tucker's 'Deep Inside' were recorded. His own productions included Deep Soul's 'Rhythms' (which featured future Smooth Touch collaborator Althea McQueen). He tried to get work at Nervous but was continually turned down by A&R head Gladys Pizarro. On the day he tried Strictly Rhythm instead Pizarro had just been installed in their offices, and this time she relented. He has gone on to be one of the leading lights of the Strictly Rhythm empire, for whom he released over 25 records, under nearly as many pseudonyms, within 1993 alone (his first release on the label having been Reel 2 Real's debut). Among his productions were Deep Soul's 'Rhythm', RAW's 'Unbe', Smooth Touch's 'Come And Take A Trip' and Club Ultimate's 'Carnival 93'. He was also represented by albums in 1994 by Deep Soul and Reel 2 Real (whose 'I Like To Move It' and 'Go On Move' were both massive worldwide hits), and recorded his own *More* EP. Part of the secret of Morillo's success may lie in his refusal to simply sample current rhythms and beats, preferring instead to write his own drum patterns and arrangements. He is nicknamed 'More' due to everybody connected being astonished at the number of different mixes he would put on to each of his releases.

Mother Earth

East London jazz funkers who existed for some time as a studio only outfit, before Acid Jazz label founder Eddie Piller asked them to play at the label's fifth birthday party. Neil Corcoran (bass) and Matt Deighton (vocals, guitar; ex-Wolfhounds) are the main creative engine behind the band, which they formed in 1991. The other members included Byrn Barclam (keyboards),

Chris White (drums; ex-mod band the Kick) and Bunny (percussion), but by 1993 they had dispensed with their photogenic vocalist, Shauna Greene. After appearing on the *Totally Wired* series, notably with the Spinal Tap-inspired 'The Warlocks Of Pendragon' on volume nine, singles like 'Illusions' stamped them as more politicised than typical members of the 'goatee beard' crowd, by criticising foreign policy decisions in Bosnia.

Albums: *Stoned Woman* (Acid Jazz 1992), *The People Tree* (Acid Jazz 1993).

Movin' Melodies

Label founded in March 1993 by DJ's Rob Boskamp and Patrick Prins. Boskamp had started as a mobile DJ at the age of 14 in his native Amsterdam, joining DMC Holland in 1986. He worked with Go! Bang and ESP before releasing his own material on MTMT Records. Boskamp's other labels include Urban Sound Of Amsterdam, Gyrate, Weekend, Dutch Volume, Looneyville, Ces, Dutch Club Culture, Mulatto, Fast Food and Red Skins. Prins started DJing in Vegas, learning drums and keyboards before taking a course in production/engineering, building up his own studio. The two partners were introduced in January 1993 by a Dutch dance magazine. The Movin' Melodies name was first invoked for an EP on Urban Sound Of Amsterdam in March 1993. The label was inaugurated properly by July's *French Connection* EP, then 'Bailando Guitarra' a month later. 1994 brought Peppermint Lounge ('Lemon Project') and Artemsia ('Bits & Pieces').

Moving Shadow Records

Rob Playford's hardcore label, founded in Stevenage in 1990 ('Hardcore is totally different from the rest of the music industry, cos its not showbiz. There's no band loyalty and nothing to read about in teeny mags'). Playford comes from a hip hop DJ background, and records on the label with various guest personnel as 2 Bad Mice (including 'Waremouse' and 'Bombscare', both of which featured the label's distinctive, heavy snare sound which was widely imitated/sampled subsequently). The label found its stride in 1992 with major releases from 2 Bad Mice ('Hold It Down'), Cosmo & Dibs ('Sonic Rush' - Playford and 'Little' Stevie 'T' Thrower's follow-up to 'Oh So Nice' and 'Star Eyes') and Blame ('Music Takes You'), which went to the top of the dance lists. By 1993 the roster included 'intelligent techno/ambient tunes like Omni Trio's 'Mystic Stepper' and 'Renegade Snares', Four Play's 'Open Your Mind' and Hyper-On-Experience's 'Lords Of The Null Lines'. The label also started the *Two*

On One series of EPs, where two artists were encouraged to experiment on either side of one record. The label's biggest record in the first half of 1994 would be Deep Blue's 'The Helicopter Tune'. Playford also promotes parties and raves (Voodoo Magic etc), runs a record shop (Section 5) and the compilation label Reanimate.
Selected album: Various: *Renegade Selector Issue 1* (Reanimate/Moving Shadow 1994).

Mr Fingers

b. Larry Heard. Fingers was given his nickname by his younger brothers, alluding to his long fingers which he would employ when spinning records. Before his career in house music Heard had been a percussionist in more conventional bands (notably Infinity), until he became fascinated by electronica and its possibilities. 'There wasn't a lot happening at that time apart from Jamie Principle and Steve 'Silk' Hurley stuff, and that wasn't even on vinyl'. He made his recording debut in 1985 with Fingers Inc's 'Mystery Of Love' (the originaly copies credited it solely to Mr Fingers) on Chicago's DJ International, following it a year later with 'You're Mind'/'A Path'. He also put together the It with Harry Dennis, releasing two further important singles, 'Donnie' and 'Gallimaufry Gallery', named after a Chicago club (a companion album saw further Gil Scott-Heron styled interludes from Dennis). It has been said by some commentators that Fingers 'invented' acid house in 1986 via 'Washing Machine', included on a three-track single headed by 'Can You Feel It?' (on Trax), though both DJ Pierre and Marshall Jefferson probably have prior claim on the accolade. However, there was no arguing with the strength of his mid-80s releases like 'Slam Dance', or his production of Robert Owens' 'Bring Down The Walls' and 'I'm Strong'. Owens, who had also sung on 'Washing Machine' and other Fingers Inc projects (together with third contributor Ron Wilson), would go on to a solo career. After label problems in Chicago he set up his own Alleviated, though this too was ill-fated. 1988 brought the House Factors' 'Play It Loud', and a first album as Fingers Inc. The following year found him in the engine room of projects with Kym Mazelle ('Treat Me Right'), Lil' Louis ('Touch Me'), Blakk Society ('Just Another Lonely Day') and Trio Zero ('Twilight'). His own contribution as Mr Fingers arrived with 'What About This Love?', which placed him on the ffrr roster for the first time. Inbetween times he would remix/produce sundry other artists including Adamski, Electribe 101 and Massive Attack. A second long player attributed to Mr Fingers arrived in 1992, and included singles like 'Closer' and 'On A Corner Called Jazz'. Though promoted as his debut, that had arrived in 1989 on Trax as a double instrumental set.
Albums: *Amnesia* (Trax 1989, double album), *Introduction* (MCA 1992). As Fingers Inc: *Fingers Inc* (Jack Trax 1988). As The It: *On Top Of The World* (1990).

Mr Lee

b. Lee Haggard, c.1968, Chicago, Illinois, USA. Haggard's introduction to music came via his elder brother, who taught him bass, drums and keyboards in the tradition of James Brown, Parliament and Funkadelic. By the time he was 18 he was to be caught DJing at local clubs and recording demo tapes at home, perfecting his own sound. Confident of his newfound abilities, he approached a friend, who brought him to the attention of Mitchball Records. A few singles emerged from the deal, but failed to sell. More success was to be found with the Trax label, for whom he recorded the hip house cut 'Shoot Your Best Shot'. Popular in his native Chicago, it paved the way for the follow-up, 'I Can't Forget', on which he sang for the first time, to become an international hit. However, from then on he changed his vocal delivery to that of a rapper, releasing singles like 'Pump Up Chicago' and 'Pump Up England'. While promoting these in the latter territory he was the subject of intense bidding by the majors, finally signing with Jive. Following singles like 'Do It To Me' (which featured an all-star cast, being produced by Mr Fingers, part-penned by Stevie Wonder and featuring samples of Quincy Jones' 'Betcha'), his debut album would sell over one million copies worldwide, the title-track reaching number 1 on the Billboard dance chart when released as a single. By the time of his second collection he was experimenting with the New Jack Swing sound, a new way of maintaining the blend of R&B/house and rap which had served him so well perviously. His adoption of the style was made explicit on album cuts like 'New House Swing'. The first single taken from it, 'Hey Love', featured labelmate R. Kelly, though there was a return to hip hop roots with the samples of Chuck D (Public Enemy)'s 'Bring The Noise' chant on 'Time To Party'.
Albums: *Get Busy* (Jive 1990), *I Wanna Rock Right Now* (Jive 1992).

Murk

US record label, based in Miami, who are best known for club hits like the Funky Green Dogs From Outer Space's 'Reach For Me' (voted third best dance song of 1992 by the *New Musical*

Express) and Coral Way Chiefs' 'Release Myself'. Label heads Ralph Falcon (previously behind DSR with Aldo Hernandez) and Oscar Gaetan also remixed D.O.P.'s 'Oh Yeah' for Guerilla, and Karen Pollack's 'You Can't Touch Me' for Emotive, and provided Warp with their *Miami* sampler EP. In 1992 they bowed to consumer demand and released a three-track DJ sampler which combined the hard-to-find trio of Funky Green Dogs From Outer Space ('Reach For Me'), Liberty City ('Some Lovin'') and Interceptor ('Together'). In the wake of their cult success the label's product was licensed to Network in the UK.

Musto And Bones

A highly successful, albeit brief, liaison between Tommy Musto and Frankie Bones, which resulted in success with singles like 'Dangerous On The Dance Floor' and 'All I Want Is To Get Away'. In retrospect 'Dangerous' might well have achieved more significant crossover success had it been more fully backed by the duo's record company, with a long time delay between its UK and domestic release. The partnership eventually dissolved after a solitary album as Bones spent more of his time DJing, while Musto remained in New York to oversee their company and studio projects: 'Basically, we also grew apart musically' is how Musto remembers this period. He would go on to become a hugely successful remixer to the stars, while his former partner persevered on the live circuit. The duo were still contracted to Beggars Banquet for another album, however, and subtle, but amicable, litigation proceeded until Bones could be removed from the contract, Musto offering instead his collaboration with Victor Simonelli, Colourblind.
Album: *The Future Is Ours* (Citybeat 1990).

Musto, Tommy

b. c.1963, New York, USA. Formerly recognised for his hit singles as part of Musto And Bones, under his own steam Musto has grown to become one of dance music's prime remixing talents, with close to half a century of projects under his belt. These include many major artists attempting to dip a toe into the world of dance (Michael Jackson, Gloria Estefan, Cyndi Lauper, Erasure). Musto grew up on a diet of Philly soul, before going on to present his own mix show on WAKT alongside the then-underground talents of Shep Pettibone and Tony Humphries on Kiss FM. He began remixing for other artists, the first example of which was Junior Byron's 'Woman' for Vanguard Records, and also taught himself keyboard skills.

His first major label commission was S'Express' 'Nothing To Lose' in the early 90s. His biggest commercial break, however, was the opportunity to remix Michael Jackson's 'In The Closet', which went gold. In 1994 he formed Colourblind with Victor Simonelli, partially to satisfy a contract that was still extant between his former Musto And Bones partnership and Beggars Banquet. After removing Bones from the contract, he teamed with Simonelli and added first Barbara Tucker then Dina Roche. They initially provided a single, written and produced by Musto, 'He's So Fine', before an album scheduled for late 1994. He also runs the Northcott Productions empire, home to Experimental Records.

N

N-Joi

Essex-based 'brothers of hardness', N-Joi comprise Mark Franklin and Nigel Champion, plus singer Saffron. Their five minutes of fame arrived with 'Malfunction' (DeConstruction 1991), a completely over-wrought affair much admired by their near-neighbour, Liam Howlett (Prodigy). They released a recording of their stage set, *Live In Manchester*, for the same label in February 1992, which lasted over 28 minutes and included over a dozen separate tunes in the mix. They followed up with a more conventional EP, which included a Moby remix of their 'Mindflux' single for RCA in the US. Saffron attempted to launch herself solo with garage singles like 'One Love' for WEA in 1992.

Namlook, Peter

Namlook is comfortably the most prolific and arguably the best of the new wave of ambient/house artists. Before his immersion in the world of dance, he had experimented with the sitar and new age jazz. His early solo EPs were shrouded in mystery, the labels distinguished solely by the contact number Fax +49-69/454064 - which later transpired to be the title of the label. Since then his ouput has been fantastic, in both the literal and accepted senses of the word. From his base in Frankfurt, Germany, two or three collaborations emerge every week on 12-inch, via a stable of co-conspirators who include Dr Atmo, Craig Peck, DJ Hubee, DJ Brainwave, DJ Criss,

Pascal FEOS and Mixmaster Morris (the latter also recording with Namlook as Dreamfish on the Faxworld subsidiary). Releases are colour-coded to differentiate between the types of music - yellow for trance, black for hardcore, green for house and blue for ambient - the most popular genre in terms of sales reaction. Each is also recorded in a cycle of eight - one with each collaborator, always beginning with DJ Criss (as Deltraxx). Only five or six hundred of any given release ever emerges, quickly selling out, before the 'cycle' is reissued on a compilation CD. As if that were not enough, Namlook also records ambient 'solo' records as Air, Sin or Silence (with Dr Atmo). These recordings are symptomatic of the 'chill-out' factor which hit European clubs in the early 90s. On several of the tracks it can take up to ten mintues for a distinctive beat or rhythm to appear, spending time building its atmospheric, neo-filmic musical soundscapes. Namlook has also found time for the Sequential project. Released in the UK via Rising High, this allows him to work with any of his roster, ironically, out of sequence. Namlook is also perceived to be at the forefront of what has been termed the 'ethno-trance' movement. Rather than riding the ambient bandwagon, he has an overview of this new music's place and purpose: 'I think it's very important to enhance the notion of a global ambient movement, and to realise that a lot of music which we didn't expect to be ambient is in fact very, very ambient. When you examine other cultures you discover that what we recognise as a very new movement is in fact incredibly ancient'. Selected albums: *Air 2* (Fax 1994). With Dr Atmo: *Silence* (Rising High 1993). With Bill Laswell: *Psychonavigation* (Fax 1994).

Naturists

Seven-piece nude techno group (yes, really), led by Wilmott Doonican, who claims to be a relative of Val Doonican, and Sid Raven. Following the release of a mini-album (which despite the 'gimmick' was well-received in the press), they released an appropriate cover version in Blue Pearl's 'Naked In The Rain', in mid-1994. 'We were all into naturism before we started making records', they claim, 'in fact we all met at a small naturist reserve near Reading'. Their lack of clothing attire apparently acts as a key ingredient in the recording process too. 'When we went into the studio and recorded naked we found that the sound was much better because the top end frequencies weren't absorbed by out clothes'. Album: *Friendly Islands* (1993, mini-album).

Navarre, Ludovic

b. c.1967, Saint-Germaine-En-Laye, France. French techno/ambient artist who records as Modus Vivendi, Deepside, Hexagone, Soofle, LN's, Deep Contest, DS and Saint-Germaine-En-Laye (titled after his hometown). A mainstay of Laurent Garnier's FNAC and F imprints, Navarre has contributed to over 90% of both label's output as a musician/technician. Each of the names he has employed for his own recordings has seen him adapt a different house style, from techno to electronic jazz. Among his more impressive outings have been his work as Saint-Germaine-En-Laye ('Alabama Blues', 'My Momma Said', 'Walk So Lonely'), Modus Vivendi ('Modus Vivendi') and DS (*Volume 1, Volume 2*).

Nelson, Shara

Former Massive Attack singer who kicked off her solo career with 'Down That Road' on Cooltempo in July 1993. Both Paul Oakenfold and Steve Osbourne were involved in remixing the single, which marketed her as the new Aretha Franklin. She had always admitted to her Motown influences, and the arrangements on her debut album were sumptuous affairs, with heaped strings and gushing choruses. Not that she had deserted her dance/hip hop roots entirely, with co-writing credits for Prince B of PM Dawn ('Down That Road'), Adrian Sherwood (title-track) and St Ettienne ('One Goodbye In Ten') offering a nice balance. The latter was the second single to be lifted from the album, bringing her a first major hit. Album: *What Silence Knows* (Cooltempo 1993).

Nervous

New York based label almost as familiar to its adherents via a range of clothing merchandise emblazoned with its distinctive cartoon logo, as it is for its bouncing house tunes. Nervous came into being in the summer of 1990, through the efforts of Michael Weiss and Gladys Pizarro (who would subsequently split to return to Strictly Rhythm). The label was launched on to New York's club underground via three specially selected releases - Niceguy Soulman's 'Feel It' (Roger 'S' Sanchez), Swing Kids' 'Good Feeling' (Kenny 'Dope' Gonzalez) and Latin Kings' 'I Want To Know (Quiero Saber)' (Todd Terry). Since then the label, and its merchandising arm, has been run on the basis of continuous throughput. New music is recorded and released week on week, and clothes lines are changed on a similar timescale. The philosophy is that this is the one way in which the label can maintain its link to the street, although it doubtless also increases profit margins too. Some of

Shara Nelson

the label's better known later cuts include Nu Yorican Soul's output and Loni Clarke's 'Rushin'' and 'You'. However, Nervous' ambitions do not end at merely providing quality dance material from established stars. There are already four subsidiary labels, Wreck, Sorted, Weeded and Strapped. Wreck covers hip hop, scoring immediately with the signing of Black Moon (whose 'Who Got The Props' single moved over 200,000 units). Sorted documents more trance and ambient focused material, while Weeded hosts underground reggae and dub artists. The newest offshoot is Strapped, which is more funk-orientated. Despite a number of instant successes, the Nervous empire continues to maintain its commitment to its original vision: 'When we put out a record, it's from the street level, if it crosses over, that's just a plus, we don't tailor a record to become a crossover hit. We want to keep our roots in the street'.

Network

London-based duo of Tim Laws and Ryan Lee, who were friends from the age of 12, and formed their first band at the age of 13. Two years passed before they became Two Extremes, playing the London rock circuit. Afterwards Laws set up a fully equipped 16-track studio in his parent's garden shed. He is also an accomplished guitarist, having contributed to five of the songs on the debut Undercover album. Lee, meanwhile, concentrated on his vocals, seeking guidance from Elton John/Annie Lennox coach Glynn Jones. The duo formed Network while playing together in a covers band, the Max Wall Experience. Immediately they broke the charts with 'Broken Wings', following up with the 1993 release, 'Get Real'.

Network Records

Brimingham dance label which originally grew out of the underground success of Kool Kat Records. Kool Kat was formed in 1988 by the partnership of Neil Rushton and Dave Barker. Rushton was a well known northern soul DJ in the 70s and a journalist for Echoes and other periodicals, and in the 80s managed the Inferno record label which re-released northern soul records and material by psychedelic soul group Dream Factory. He stumbled on Detroit techno through his connections in the US, and met leading lights Derrick May then Kevin Saunderson, in time becoming the latter's manager. He subsequently compiled an album of Detroit techno for Virgin (the first in the UK, later packaging similar collections like the Retro Techno/Detroit Definitive sets for Network). His partner Dave Barker's background was as a jazz-funk DJ in the Midlands. Kool Kat began with a number of underground records (experimental techno, psychedelic techno and Chicago house). The policy from the outset was to combine the cream of US releases with plenty of upfront British material. They consequently took on board several local groups, the best known early example of which were Nexus 21/Altern 8. Proclaimed as one of the hip record labels of the day, funds still remained in short supply and the label was on the verge of collapse. The team had a rethink and formed a new label, Network. From the start Network has employed its own, hard imagery and defined, generic sleeves. The musical range, however, was much broader than had been the case with Kool Kat. The first record to be released was Neal Howard's 'Indulge', while the honour of first chart appearance came with Altern 8's 'Infiltrate'. 'Activ8', by the same group, would do even better, reaching number 3. Network's money problems were easing, and with the advent of KWS and 'Please Don't Go' they disappeared altogether. Neil Rushton had heard the track in a Birmingham club and saw the potential in making a pop record out of it. He approached ZYX who held the rights to the Double You? version of the KC & The Sunshine Band song, only available in Europe, but was turned down unceremoniously. So Rushton arranged for KWS, then recording for Network as B-Line, to re-record it. It stayed at number 1 for five weeks. The follow-up, another KC cover, 'Rock Your Baby', was also hugely successful, though a lawsuit from ZYX, still unresolved years later, was underway. After KWS the label delivered Altern 8's debut, which effectively summarised the high watermark of the rave generation, with Network personnel taking a full hand in the various pranks and schemes which became synonymous with the group. However, they ran into trouble in June 1992 over Manchester rave band Rhythm Quest's The Dreams EP, which used expletives to criticise police procedures in closing down raves. The police expressed their fears to Network that the record, which featured ex-boxer Mark Hadfield, could incite violence, and it was subsequently reissued in a 'cleaned up version', just missing the Top 40. By the end of 1992 the label had grown unhappy with their distribution set-up with Pinnacle, and at great expense bought themselves out with two years of the contract to run. They initially contacted Sony with a view to distribution only, but in the end the notion of a bigger tie-in was mooted. After eight months of negotiations Sony bought 49% of the shares in the company in August 1993, and Network officially became (on the headed notepaper rather than record labels) Best Beat Dance Limited. It immediately allowed the company far greater freedom. Disenchanted with the reputation given to Network by KWS, they launched SiX6 (most commonly referred to as Six By Six) for street level house. Again a strong generic look was invoked with different colours to distinguish releases. The first product for the imprint was 'Hell's Party' by Glam, an immediate success, which secured the more underground vibe and credibility which Six By Six had been searching for. The Sony deal had also given the company the power to distribute records themselves, and thus help out younger labels by offering them the same service (as long as they pass the Network taste barometer). Some of these 'third party' distributed labels include Bostin' (which is owned by a band called Mother, whose main man is DJ Lee Fisher), Other Records, the 'Journeys By DJ' series, Good Boy, DiY/Strictly 4 Groovers, Sure Is Pure's Gem, the Ritmo Rival's Planet Four, Hott Records from London and Manchester's UFG and Silver City. In addition there are several labels that Network actually owns. In 1990 the company opened an office in New York, and the First Choice garage/disco label (also a recording studio based in Greenwich Village) grew out of that set-up. Baseroom Productions is similar to First Choice in that it evolved out of a recording studio, based in Stoke On Trent. Artists like Sure Is Pure, BIzarre Inc, Altern 8 and MC Lethal had been recording there, and with the name cropping up so frequently Network investigated. They eventually bought out the Baseroom as part of their deal with Sony, and launched a label around the studio, specialising in techno and experimental ambient/non-vocal material. The label's principal artists include Aquarel and the System, and Laurent Garnier has also collaborated on projects emanating from there. As if that were not enough, there are additionally three or four labels with whom deals have been signed where Network handle all the rights for releases in the UK. KMS UK was inaugurated via Rushton's management of Saunderson, which made the move inevitable. The label specialises in strong vocal house while spin-off label Eclipse offers the non-vocal techno for which Saunderson is famous. Another Detroit label is Serious Grooves, an underground techno/disco imprint pioneered by Terrence Parker. It is overseen by DJ Tone, a well-known underground DJ and the keyboard player in Inner City's live band. Vicious Muzik in New York is a label owned and run by Johnny Vicious, one of the most exciting new arrivals on the dance scene of the 90s. Other labels under the Network umbrella include Vinyl Addiction (underground house, and the outlet for the highly-regarded Stereogen), Stafford South (called from the motorway junction, where Mark Archer, who A&Rs the label, lives - the label logo being a photograph of that sign), Stafford North (a more hardcore sister label), Eu4ea (for trance releases), Hidden Agenda and One After D. Not bad for a company with a staff team of seven. Intriguingly, bearing in mind the label's early sponsorship of modern techno, the team work in Birmingham's oldest building (a 'haunted Elizabethan house').

Selected albums: Various: *Retro Techno/Detroit Definitive* (Network 1991). Altern 8: *Full On...Mask Hysteria* (Network 1992).

Neuro Project
Simon Sprince, Dave Nicoll and Stewart Quinn originally introduced themselves on R&S Records with the sublime techno hit, 'Mama'. Their 90-minute long playing debut arrived shortly afterwards on 3 Beat, but retained the promise of their first release, offering a wide array of styles and structures.

Album: *The Electric Mothers Of Invention* (3 Beat 1994, double album).

Neuropolitique
Detroit-influenced mannah often credited as 'organic techno'. This, the work of Matt Cogger, was first premiered by two limited edition EPs for London label Irdial. By the time a full-length album emerged its creator was still engaged in the ceaseless exporation of percussion patterns, though never to the detriment of a strong tune. His work was widely compared to that of Carl Craig.

Album: *Menage A Trois* (Irdial 1994).

Neutron 9000
aka Dominic Woosey. Globetrotting techno star who began his career as an engineer based at Sonet studios in London. He was soon working on masters for dance stars like Adonis, Mark Moore (S'Express) and even George Michael. Afterwards he turned to DJing, appearing at several prime European dates (including Germany's Mayday festival, and all of the Berlin Love Parade dates), as well as Tokyo and New York. When Woosey entered the recording world it was under the Neutron 9000 shroud, earning respect via his 'Sentinel' (Profile) and 'Tranceplant' (MFS) singles, with two albums, *The Greenhouse Effect* and *Walrus* also released on Profile. He simultaneously emerged as a remixer of some distinction, working with Sven Vath ('Ritual Of Life'), Talk Talk ('It's

Neutron 9000

My Life'), Test Department ('New World Order'), West Bam ('Liberation'), Shriekback ('Black Light Trap') and Nina Hagen ('Farbfilm'). Moving to Berlin in 1991, he worked closely with Cosmic Baby as a component of the country's burgeoning trance/techno scene, before setting up his own label, United Frequencies Of Communications. The artist roster saw Woosey working with other luminaries such as Dr Motte, while his Bassic Instinct club saw a subsidiary of the same name. He has continued to record for other labels, including Recycle Or Die and, in 1994, joined Rising High. Selected albums: As Dominic Woosey: *Straylight* (Recyle Or Die 1991). As Neutron 9000: *The Greenhouse Effect* (Profile 1991), *Walrus* (Profile 1992).

Nevins, Jason

A top New York producer/remixer, whose first involvement with music was at his college radio station at Arizona State University, where his sets were primarily composed of techno. He went on to release product as Plastick Project, Crazee Tunes, the Experience and Jason Nevins Movement. 'The Viper Rooms', licensed to Brighton label Loaded, was typical of his output, being completely unabashed in its use of samples. He has gone on to record with Nervous, Logic, Strictly Rhythm and Tribal. He has also remixed Ann Consuelo for Champion, and is also signed to MCA as Analogue.

Nexus 21

Namely Mark Archer and Chris Peat, more famous (in some quarters) for their work as Altern 8. They began their career as Nexus 21 - their 'core' project - with the 'Still Life' 12-inch for Blue Cat in September 1989, following it a few months later with 'Rhythm Of Life', this time for Blue Chip. After a 12-inch promo, 'Self-Hypnosis', they delivered *Logical Progression* in October 1990 on R&S, a second EP, *Progressive Logic*, following two months later. The duo have also released two singles ('Another Night' and 'Flutes') under the name C&M Connection. Archer has also recorded solo for the Stafford North Imprint as DJ Nex (The *DJ Nex* and *Poundstretcher* EPs) and Xen Mantra (The *Midas* EP). In 1994 he formed Slo-Moshun with Danny Taurus, scoring immediately with the Top 30 'Bells Of New York' cut.

Nicolette

b. Nicolette Okoh, c.1964, Glasgow, Scotland. Shut Up And Dance's first female signing, whose approach to her vocal craft was more blues-based and less shrill than many garage divas. She also

wrote her own songs, demonstrating a keen talent on singles like 'Wicked Mathematics'. However, she was quick to affirm that 'I really do see myself as a dance act', despite her debut album featuring more political material like 'No Government'. Though born in Glasgow she was brought up in Nigeria, Paris, Geneva and Cardiff.

Nightmares On Wax

Nightmares On Wax are a duo of George 'E.A.S.E.' Evelyn and Kevin 'Boy Wonder' Harper. After the bombast of the *Dextrous* EP and 'Aftermath' for Warp, the club hits continued with 'A Case Of Funk'. Sampling funk rhythms and soca drumming to work up a strong was a distinctive and endearing trait, while subsequent issues like 'Set Me Free' and 'Happiness' continued to gain critical applause. 'Set Me Free' saw the band using the vocals of Desoto, who had formerly appeared on *Junior Showtime* with a spring-heeled Bonny Langford (who said techno wasn't a broad church?).
Album: *A Word Of Science* (Warp 1991).

Ninjatune

Coldcut's record label, distributed by Revolver, and founded in 1991 as a protest against the way that group had been dealt with by major record companies. The label has gone on to sell well, especially in Japan where Ninjatune CD's have become an essential consumer product among that nation's dance fans. Staples of the imprint include the DJ Food breakbeat series of albums, Bogus Order (*Da Sound Of Zen* EP and 'The Return Of The Brother Zen'), Euphoreal's jungle-based *The Ride* EP, and Coldcut's own 'Autumn Leaves'/'Fat Bloke'. As might be envisaged from such a wide discourse, the label's philosophy is not restrained by musical genre: 'We don't have any kind of real agenda in terms of what we're releasing'.
Selected albums: DJ Food: *Jazz Brakes Vols. 1-4* (Ninjatune 1991-1993). Bogus Order: *Zen Brakes Vol. 1* (Ninjatune 1992).

Nitzer Ebb

The driving force behind this electronic based band are Douglas McCarthy (b. 1 September 1966, Chelmsford, England; vocals), and Bon Harris (b. 12 August 1965, Chelmsford, England; percussion, vocals). Frustrated by their environment at school in Chelmsford, and inspired by bands like DAF, Bauhaus and the Birthday Party, they began their first experiments with synthesizers and drum machines in 1983. They were joined in their strictly amateur pursuits by school-mate David Gooday. They had summoned enough experience and confidence to release their first single the next year, 'Isn't It Funny How Your Body Works', on Power Of Voice Communications. They were nothing if not prolific, releasing a further five singles over the next twelve months, which led to a deal with the premier UK independent stable Mute, and Geffen in the US. 1987 saw their first album on the shelves, *That Total Age*, home to a seam of minimalist aggression, and the beginning of a long-term relationship with producer Flood, who would remix the single 'Join In The Chant'. On Gooday's departure Julian Beeston was enrolled. After a lengthy European trek with Depeche Mode, the band recorded *Belief*, and in 1989 followed up their own world tour with *Showtime*. Their third album revealed a swing in attitude, with music that was less confrontational and more consumer friendly. This was particularly true in the US, where the single 'Fun To Be Had' peaked at Number 2 in the US dance charts. Their most recent album has confirmed their popularity with fans and a previously reluctant press. As McCarthy puts it: 'With the advent of *Ebbhead*, I think we've managed to twist listenability around to our way of thinking'.

Albums: *That Total Age* (Mute 1987), *Belief* (Mute 1988), *Showtime* (Mute 1989), *Ebbhead* (Mute 1991).

Nomad

Band whose press largely revolved around two facts. First their vocalist, Sharon Dee Clarke (b. c.1965), was formerly the black nurse in *The Singing Detective* television programme. She was also filmed in the bed next to Michelle when the latter was giving birth in *Eastenders*. Secondly, their single, 'Devotion', comprised samples from the British Poll Tax Riots and even transferred one of Thatcher's more rabid outbursts onto tape. It was also a huge hit, reaching number 2 in the charts and becoming the biggest dance single of 1991 in the process. It was co-written and produced by future Undercover producer Steve Mac. The other personnel in the band were rapper MC Mikee Freedom (b. c.1969, Bristol, England) and Damon Rochefort (b. c.1965, Cardiff, Wales). Freedom was discovered by former law student Rochefort while rapping on a song entitled 'Love Don't Live Here Anymore' by Fresh Connection. Rochefort himself had worked with Clarke on the FPI Project's 1990 hit, 'Going Back To My Roots'. Unfortunately their debut album was thin on original songs, comprising three versions of 'Devotion', while elsewhere formulaic Euro dance pop held sway. Though the follow-up single, 'Just A Groove', made the Top 20, subsequent efforts

('Something Special' - originally recorded by Clarke solo for a compilation album, 'Your Love Is Lifting Me' and '24 Hours A Day') failed to replicate their original success. Rochefort also embarked on a side project, Serious Rope, again featuring Clarke, who scored a 1993 hit with 'Happiness', recorded as a tribute to the Flesh club in Manchester. Freedom would go on to a solo career with TEK, beginning with 'Set You Free' for Dave Pearce's Reachin' label.

Album: *Changing Cabins* (Rumour 1991), *Different Drum* (Rumour 1992).

Novamute

The dance/techno arm of Mute Records independent empire, launched in January 1992 with Mick Paterson (promotions, subsequently departed), Pepe Jansz (A&R) and Seth Hodder (production). Unlike many other established record companies trawling the backwaters of club music angling for financial reward, Mute had established its own tradition in commercial dance with Depeche Mode and Erasure, or more particularly Renegade Soundwave and Nitzer Ebb. They had also supported the fledgeling Rhythm King for several years, before that label branched out on its own in the 90s. The step to the burgeoning house/techno scenes was a natural one, particularly as the parent label had already released Exit 100's 1991 12-inch 'Liquid', the Underground Resistance mini-album *X101*, and licensed a Black Market compilation set. The original plan for Novamute then, was to license 12-inch white labels and imports and give them a proper release. In the US this was achieved via a distribution deal with independent rap label, Tommy Boy. Three compilations were crucial in establishing Novamute: *Tresor 1 (The Techno Sound Of Berlin* and *Tresor II (Berlin-Detroit: A Techno Alliance)* - from the Berlin based Tresor label, and *Probe Mission USA* - drawn from Canada's Plus 8 Records. Their roster of artists has grown to include Moby, Richie Hawtin/Plastikman, 3Phase, Juno Reactor, Spirit Feel ('Forbidden Chant'), 3MB ('Jazz Is The Teacher'), Compufonic (aka Hyper Go-Go: 'Make It Move') and Doof ('Disposable Hymns To The Infinite').

Selected album: Various: *Version 1.1* (Novamute 1993).

Nu Groove Records

Revered New York-based record label owned by Frank and Judy Russell but established in the public's mind and ears by house producers and twins Rheji and Ronnie Burrell, who had formerly recorded for Virgin subsidiary Ten as Burrell. It

Doof of Novamute

was originally created for them as 'an alternative outlet... because we had a lot of material that we were doing and we couldn't put it all out on Virgin', but went on to become their priority operation. The first record on the label was Tech Trax Inc's 'Feel The Luv' in August 1988, created by Rheji. Further early material arrived from Ronnie's Bas Noir project and Rheji's 'You Can't Run From My Love'. The original plan was to release a record by each brother every two weeks, and they have not fallen far short of that blistering schedule. Among their more successful vinyl expeditions have been 1989's 'It's Power House Brooklyn Style' - created by Powerhouse, aka Masters At Work, 1990's 'The Poem' and 'Rydims' (Bobby Konders) and Transphonic's 'Tune In Light Up' and 'Bug Out'. Most featured the keyboard talents of Peter Daou (formerly, and incredibly, a member of the Beirut Jazz Trio, where he grew up). Together with wife Vanessa he released 'Law Of Chants' and 'Part Two' (as Vandal). Rheji was also behind the *New York House N Authority* album (SBK 1990), a softer, more reflective affair. Another significant record from this time was 'Major Problem', an anti-drugs parody from Lennie Dee and Ralphie, which utilised samples from Yello and others. 1991 brought the *Metro* EP, a weighty, bass-driven house cut from Rheji, and Lost Entity's 'Bring That Back On'/'The Verge', which boasted the label's familiar deep soul feel. Other examples were Howie How and Little Carlos' 'Cause I Need You' (as the Divine Masters), the Vision's 'Laidback And Groovy', created by Eddie 'Satin' Maduro, and Transphonic ('Club Tools (Professional Use Only)'). 1992 brought Ize 2's 'House Trix' (an Isaac Santiago production). This was also the label which housed Joey Negro's Mr Maize scam, when his club hit 'Together' was licensed to the US. When the single topped the dance charts journalists tried to hunt down the entirely fictional Mr Maize. Other notable appearances included Victor Simonelli (under the guise of Groove Committee) with 'Dirty Games', and the Houz Negroz 'How Do You Love A Black Woman', produced once more by the Burrell brothers. Tracing the Nu Groove discography remains an arduous but rewarding task for fans of class house music.

Oakenfold, Paul

Renowned DJ and remixer Oakenfold was first active in club promotions during dance music's underground days. Having formerly trained as a chef he was introduced to the decks by his friend Trevor Fung at a Covent Garden bar in 1981. He eventually moved to New York and worked for Arista, before returning to England as Profile's UK agent. He spent 1987 DJing at Ibiza clubs like Amnesia, and when he returned to England in November of that year he staged a near-legendary, invite-only 'Ibiza Reunion Party' at his Project Club in Streatham. During his various residencies he was of pivotal importance in the emergence of the hip hop, balearic and house movements. Famed for his sets at the Future Club (which he launched), Spectrum, Theatre Of Madness, Land Of Oz, Shoom (alongside Andy Weatherall) and Hacienda, he would go on to become synonymous with the Ministry Of Sound venue, playing a major role in preparing tracks for 'in-house' compilations. However, he had long since established his name as a remixer. Together with Steve Osbourne he gave the Happy Mondays' 'Wrote For Luck' a new club edge in 1989. It won them the plaudit 'Dance Record Of The Year' from the *New Musical Express*. Other remix clients tumbled quickly after, including the Shamen, Massive Attack, M People, New Order, Arrested Development and U2 (mostly under the Perfecto *nom de plume*, indicating Oakenfold/Osbourne). Perfecto also operated as a label, initially through RCA. Oakenfold would later tour with U2, spinning diverse selections including sections of the *Blade Runner* film (the soundtrack album being among his favourite musical mediums). However, Oakenfold also made the rarer transition to full-blown producer on projects by the aforementioned Happy Mondays, Solid Gold Easy Action ('Enjoy' in 1990) and Deacon Blue. In 1991 he was nominated, alongside Osbourne, for a BRIT award for best producer. He maintained his sense of propriety on singles like Movement 98 featuring Carroll Thompson's 'Joy And Heartbreak' - part of his intention to pull down the bpm of dance records to 98 following the hardcore explosion. It predicted the rise of ambient house by including a snatch of Erik Satie's 'Trois Gymnopee'. Just like Weatherall, he was signed up by a major in 1994 (in this case as A&R consultant for East West), and launched his own career with the single, 'Rise'. His more interesting recent remixing projects have included Stones Roses and Snoopy Doggy Dogg.

Album: *Journeys By DJ* (Music Unites 1994).

Olympic Records

Record company formed in Liverpool by James Barton and Andy Carroll, named after their respected club night. Barton was a DJ who served his apprenticeship on the Northern club scene, going on to launch one of the best known venues, Cream. He was then instrumental in setting up Olympic Records in 1992 with Carroll, who was also a DJ. The label earned its biggest success with Seven Grand Housing Authority (Terrence Parker)'s 'The Question'. Barton also furnished K-Klass, who remixed the record, with management services, and introduced them to their, and his, future employers, DeConstruction. He joined the latter label in early 1994 to take a hand in their A&R operation, though he retained his interests in Olympic and Cream.

Om Records

'The idea of Om is to cover the spectrum of house music and to do absolutely the best stuff that house can offer', explained DJ Nick Hook, who founded Om together with *New Musical Express* dance correspondent Sherman and Morgan King. The label was thus inaugurated with three double-pack EP's which displayed just that: a *pot pourri* of modern house, labelled *Absolute Om*, *1 - 3*. Other bands on the label included mainstays Soundsource (essentially Morgan King, whose recordings, such as 'Take Me Up' and 'One High', also appear on Sweden's B-Tech imprint), ex-Geurilla act Euphoria, Bump and Marine Boy (who are one-time Ruts member Segz and engineer Steve Dub's deep house/ambient project, disinguished by releases of the calibre of 'Fluid'). 1994 releases included 108 Grand featuring Roy Galloway's 'Love U All Over'.

Omar

b. Omar Lye Fook, c.1968. Omar was born the son of a Chinese Jamaican father and an Indian Jamaican mother. A former principle percussionist of the Kent Youth Orchestra, he would later graduate from the Guildhall School Of Music. His debut singles were 'Mr Postman' and 'You And Me' (featuring backing vocals from Caron Wheeler), before his first album was released, via Harlesden's Black Music Association's Kongo Dance imprint, on a slender budget. Nevertheless, it made the Top 60. In its wake Omar's name suddenly started cropping up everywhere, be it as a singer, writer or producer. Following a high profile Hammersmith Odeon concert in December 1990 Giles Peterson of Talkin' Loud persuaded financial backers Phonogram to open their wallets. The debut album was slightly remixed and re-released, the title-track having already earned its stripes as a club favourite. Although by definition a soul artist, Omar's use of reggae, ragga and particularly hip hop has endeared him to a wide cross-section of the dance community. RCA won the scramble to sign Omar after departing from Talkin' Loud in January 1993. Since then Omar has continued to collaborate with a number of premier R&B artists: songwriter Lamont Dozier, keyboard player David Frank (famed for his contribution to Chaka Khan's 'I Feel For You'), bass player Derek Bramble (ex-Heatwave), Leon Ware (arranger for Marvin Gaye) and no less than Stevie Wonder himself, who contacted Omar after hearing his 'Music' cut.

Albums: *There's Nothing Like This* (Kongo Dance 1990, remixed and re-released Talkin' Loud 1991), *For Pleasure* (RCA 1994).

One Dove

Glasgow, Scotland trio, who caught the nation's imagination in 1993 with their mellow musical depths. The group comprise Ian Carmichael (b. 1 June 1960, Glasgow, Scotland), Jim McKinven (b. David James McKinven, c.1959, Glasgow, Scotland) and former chemical engineering student Dot Allison (b. Dorothy Elliot Allison, 17 August 1969, Edinburgh, Scotland). McKinven had been in an early incarnation of the Bluebells (rehearsal only), but was best known for his stint in Altered Images. Carmichael owns Toad Hall Studios, and has engineered or produced for many Glaswegian acts (Orchids, Bachelor Pad etc.). The group made their first public appearance at the Rock Garden, Queens Street, Glasgow, in August 1991. They would soon break into the rave scene's elite with the single 'Fallen', released on Soma, before the band had changed their name from their original selection, Dove. However, litigation followed from representatives of Supertramp (the band had, inadvertently, used a sample from an Italian house record which in turn had sampled the prog-rockers). They met Andy Weatherall in Rimini in 1991. After he agreed to work with them there was some discussion in the press that One Dove's debut album would signal another landmark episode, ala Primal Scream's *Screamadelica*, but this was perhaps over-optimistic. It was at least a solid, musically enthralling collection conveying One Dove's biggest influence: King Tubby and Jamaican dub music.

Album: *Morning Dove White* (Boy's Own 1993).

Omar

One Records

Record label run by Eddie Colon (pronounced 'Cologne'), a former Kiss FM DJ, ex-proprietor of Renegade Records and a recording artist in his own right (scoring a US hit with 'Upfront') and the celebrated Roger Sanchez. They first met in 1991 when Colon was still a struggling DJ. The first One record was 'No Way' by Countdown, produced by Toddy Terry/Kenny 'Dope' Gonzalez. The release schedule continued apace with material by Murk's Oscar G, more Kenny 'Dope' Gonzalez ('Axis Project' etc.) and Victor Simonelli ('I Know A Place') - almost a who's who of US house producers. The label was invoked: 'to bring quality records out of New York... a soulful, house type of sound. We want to start developing artists. I'm an old song guy and I don't like this whole track thing'. One would sign Farley and Heller as their remix team, as well as UK singer J.B. Braithwaite ('Love Me Tonite'). In January 1994 the operation unveiled Sanchez's first ever long playing release.
Selected album: Roger Sanchez: *Secret Weapons Vol. 1* (One 1994). Various: *The Sound Of One* (One 1994).

Opus III

Vocalist Kirsty Hawkshaw (b. c.1969), attired with boots and mohican haircut coupled with dayglo beads, led this pop house outfit on their breakthrough single, 'It's A Fine Day'. An update of Jane & Barton's faint ballad, mixing poetry with sweet, harranguing vocals, it added a generic backbeat and little else. Hawkshaw had led a gypsy lifestyle since leaving school (her father composes theme music for television programmes, including *News At Ten*, *Grange Hill* and *Countdown*). As a child she recorded cover versions of the hits of the day for cheap compilation albums, before travelling around the free festival circuit selling home-made jewellery (and MCing for Spiral Tribe). She met Opus III's boiler room staff; Ian Dodds, Kevin Walters and Nigel Munro, at a rave. They form part of the Ashebrooke Allstars, and also recorded as A.S.K. ('Freedom We Cry' for MCA). The follow-up to 'It's A Fine Day' would be a cover of King Crimson's 'I Talk To The Wind'. Nurtured by her record company and band as chanteuse straddling the pop/rave market, Kirsty has yet to provide adequate substance to sustain her strong visual image. However, the band did eventually return in 1994 with 'When You Made The Mountain', and a new, 'spiritual' album.
Album: *Mind Fruit* (PWL 1992), *Guru Mother* (PWL 1994).

Orb

Basically the Orb is one man, Dr Alex Paterson (b. Duncan Robert Alex Paterson, hence the appropriation of the Dr title), whose specialist field is the creation of ambient house music. A former Killing Joke roadie, member of Bloodsport, and A&R man at EG Records, he formed the original Orb in 1988 with Jimmy Cauty of Brilliant fame (for whom he had also roadied). The name was taken from a line in Woody Allen's *Sleeper*. The band first appeared on WAU! Mr Modo's showcase set *Eternity Project One* (released via Gee Street), with the unrepresentative 'Tripping On Sunshine'. However, their first release proper came with 1989's *Kiss* EP, again on WAU! Mr Modo (which had been set up by Paterson with Orb manager Adam Morris). It was completely overshadowed by the success of the band's subsequent offering, 'A Huge Ever-Growing Pulsating Brain Which Rules From The Centre Of The Ultraworld'. It was an extraordinary marriage of progressive rock trippiness and ambience, founded on a centrepoint sample of Minnie Riperton's 'Loving You' (at least on initial copies, being voiced by a soundalike due to clearance worries later). The group signed with Big Life, but Cauty departed in April 1990. He had wished to take Paterson and the Orb on board in his new KLF Communications set-up. There was no little acrimony at the time and Cauty re-recorded an album, which was to have been the Orb's debut, deleting Paterson's contributions, and naming it *Space* (also the artist title). In the event the ethereal 'Little Fluffy Clouds', with co-writer Youth, was the next Orb release, though that too ran into difficulties when the sample of Rickie Lee Jones' attracted the artist's displeasure. Paterson did at least meet future co-conspirator Thrash (b. Kristian Weston) during these sessions, who joined in late 1991 from a punk/metal background, hence his name (though he had also been a member of Fortran 5). Their debut album (and the remix set of similar title) was based on a journey to dimensions beyond known levels of consciousness, according to the participants. It soared, or perhaps sleepwalked, to the top of the UK album charts, and led to a plunge of remixes for other artists (including Front 242 and Primal Scream). The album was fully in tune with, and in many ways anticipating of, the blissed out rave subculture of the early 90s, mingled with dashes of early 70s progressive rock (Pink Floyd were an obvious reference point). There was also an LP's worth of the band's recordings for John Peel's Radio 1 show. This included a 20 minute version of 'Huge Ever-Growing...' which prompted fellow DJ Andy

Orb

Kershaw to ring the BBC to complain, mockingly, about the return of hippy indulgence on a gross scale polluting the nation's airwaves. The Orb signed to Island in 1993 following a departure from Big Life that took seven months and eventually the high court to settle. The deal with Island allowed Paterson to continue to work on collaborative projects, through his own label Inter-Modo, outside of the Orb name. Other projects included a remix album for Yellow Magic Orchestra, though a previous request by Jean Michel Jarre for them to do the same for his *Oxygene* opus was declined. They also took the opportunity to play live at unlikely venues like the Danish Island of Trekroner, and generally appeared to be having a hugely enjoyable time of their unlikely celebrity, Paterson even being awarded the status of honorary president of Strathclyde University's Student Union. However, their first studio set for Island, *Pomme Fritz*, saw them witness the first signs of a critical backlash.

Albums: *The Orbs Adventures Beyond The Ultraworld* (WAU! Mr Modo/Big Life 1991), *Peel Sessions* (Strange Fruit 1991), *Aubrey Mixes, The Ultraworld Excursion* (WAU! Mr Modo/Big Life 1992), UFOrb (WAU! Mr Modo/Big Life 1992, double album, available as a triple in limited edition), *Live 93* (Island 1993), *Pomme Fritz* (Island 1994, mini album).

Orbit, William

b. William Wainwright. Techno's renaissance man, formerly a bass player for Torch, who in addition to heading up the Bass-O-Matic group, has also remixed for the likes of Prince, Madonna ('Justify Your Love'), Belinda Carlisle, S'Express, Les Negress Vertes, the Cure ('Inbetween Days') and Shakespeare's Sister. From the beginning he would recruit musicians and vocalists in line with the needs of the moment, rather than evolve any permanent line-up. Orbit had originally started cutting songs as part of Torch Song, releasing two albums (*Wild Thing* 1984, *Exhibit A* 1987) with Laurie Mayer. He then took the Orbit moniker and brought in vocalist Peta Nikolich for an eponymous album, retaining Mayer as his co-writer. This included bizarre covers of the Psychedelic Furs' 'Love My Way' and Jackie Mittoo's 'Feel Like Jumping'. It was the club favourite, 'Fire And Mercy', which brought him to the attention of dance pundits, however. This was housed on the intensely moody *Strange Cargo*, a collection of soundscapes recorded between 1984 and 1987. *Strange Cargo II* also steered away from the electronic house textures which had marked Orbit's work with Bass-O-Matic, resembling instead the experimental pieces of Brian Eno or Holger Czukay.

Albums: *Orbit* (MCA 1987), *Strange Cargo* (MCA 1988), *Strange Cargo II* (IRS 1990), *Strange Caro III* (IRS 1993).

Orbital

Ambient techno outfit who have done much to bring about the possibilities of improvisation to live electronic music. Unlike many other groups, their stage performances do not depend on DAT or backing tapes. They also have a more varied scrapbook of samples, using the Butthole Surfers on 'Satan', then Crass on 'Choice'. Comprising brothers Paul (b. 19 May 1968, Dartford, Kent, England) and Phillip Hartnoll (b. 9 January 1964, Dartford, Kent, England), the Orbital moniker was first suggested by their friend Chris Daly of the Tufty Club. With all the M25 dance parties happening so close to their homes in Dunton Green they named themselves after the UK's least adored stretch of road. It also helped convey the idea of tape loops which are so central to their craft. Before the band began its active life in 1987, Paul had played with an outfit by the name of Noddy & The Satellites and done some labouring odd jobs, while his brother had been a bricklayer and barman. They made their live debut in the summer of 1989 at the Grasshopper, Westerham, Kent, hooking up with the ffrr imprint shortly afterwards. They opened their account for the label with 'Chime' in March 1990, setting a pattern for a sequence of dramatic, one-word titles ('Omen', 'Satan', 'Choice', 'Mutations'). They moved to Internal for 'Raddiccio' in October 1992, while work continued apace on their remixing chores. These included work on releases by artists as diverse as the Shamen, Queen Latifah, Meat Beat Manifesto and EMF. In 1994 they appeared at the Glastonbury Festival and contributed to the *Shopping* film soundtrack.

Albums: *Untitled 1* (ffrr 1991), *Untitled 2* (Internal 1993), *Snivilisation* (Internal 1994).

Original Rockers

Midlands based dance outfit, led by DJ Dick (b. Richard Whittingham) and musician Glynn Bush, who have been compared to the On-U Sound troupe via their ambient dub/deep trance techniques. They made their debut in February 1992 with a single, 'Breathless', dedicated to DJ Dick's club of the same name. Their 1993 single 'Rockers To Rockers' was originally issued a year before as the b-side to limited edition promos of 'Push Push' (previously titled 'Come Again'). As is usual, it was based on deep dub grooves, with

adventurous drum and bass patterns. Other singles include the self-descriptive 'Stoned', recorded in collaboration with fellow-Brummie outfit Groove Corporation.
Album: *Rockers To Rockers* (Different Drummer 1993).

Other Two
The most pure dance-orientated of the three major New Order spin-offs, the Other Two features arguably the least attention-seeking of the Manchester quartet: Stephen Morris (b. 28 October 1957, Macclesfield, Cheshire, England) and Gillian Gilbert (b. 27 January 1961, Manchester, England). Recording at their own studio in rural Macclesfield, they debuted on the charts with the number 41-peaking 'Tasty Fish' in 1991. The follow-up, 'Selfish', came two years later, but featured fashionable remixes by both Moby and Farley & Heller.
Album: *The Other Two & You* (Lonon 1993).

Oui 3
Qui 3 are Blair Booth (b. California, USA, vocals, programming), Phillip Erb (b. Switzerland, keyboards) and Trevor Miles (lyrics, rapping). In addition their debut album featured the formidable rhythmic skills of Youth (Killing Joke, Brilliant etc), Jah Wobble, Galliano and the Brand New Heavies. It revealed an obvious debt to PM Dawn, with a flat, distinctively English rapping style. Booth was once a sidekick of Terry Hall of the Specials/Fun Boy 3 (as part of Terry, Blair and Anouschka), while Erb worked alongside Billy MacKenzie (ex-Associates). Together they met unknown rapper Miles, who shared their interest in George Clinton and Lee Scratch Perry. Their speciality then, was a witty mix of vocals and raps, with clever observations on a series of tightly wound scenarios. 'Break From The Old Routine', for example, depicted a collapsing relationship: 'We ain't gelling these days - we're congealing'. They returned to their reggae roots with the 45 'Arms Of Solitude', which featured of all things, an Augustus Pablo mix.
Album: *Oui Love You* (MCA 1993).

Our Tribe
Our Tribe is essentially Rob Dougan and Rollo Armstrong. They first met when Rollo travelled to Australia with his friend Will Mount (later to become Gloworm) after finishing university, where he studied gynaecology. He met Rob, who was then training to be an actor in Australia, signing a deal together for the RooArt label (nothing was released). On his return to England Rollo became a successful producer in his own right, and when Rob emigrated they teamed up again. Their debut release for ffrr, 'I Believe In You', became a number 1 in the dance lists. Mel Medalie of Champion soon came along with the offer of both recording opportunities and their own subsidiary label (Cheeky). It was this which housed the duo's 'Understand This Groove' (as Franke), Gloworm's 'I Lift My Cup' and the OT Quartet's 'Hold That Sucker Down', a Top 10 hit. Our Tribe went on to remix for U2 ('Numb'), Pet Shop Boys ('Can You Forgive Her', 'Absolutely Fabulous'), M People ('How Can I Love U More?'), Wonderstuff ('Full Of Life'), Shola ('Love, Respect & Happiness'), 3rd Nation ('I Believe'), Raze ('Break 4 Love') and Gabrielle ('Dreams'). The duo were also behind the writing and production of Kristine W's 'Feel What You Want' and Our Tribe featuring Sabrina Johnston's 'What Hope Have I?'

Outer Rhythm Records
A subsidiary of Rhythm King Records, established in 1989 in order to license hot 'outside' product. Early releases on the label included Leftfield's 1990 single, 'Not Forgotten', released before that band had become a duo. They also scored with Digital Excitation (Frank De Wulf)'s 1992 trance hit, 'Pure Pleasure', plus other material under license from R&S. They imported heavily from Detroit, notably Random Noise Generation's 'Falling In Dub' in early 1992, which had originally been housed on the 430 West imprint, and Germany's Hithouse stable. The label closed in June 1992 due to 'changing forces in the market place'.

Outside
Namely one Matt Cooper (b. c.1973), who is widely recognised among club and genre cognoscenti as the most talented arrival on the jazz/funk scene in the last decade. Classically trained on the piano, he went on to a deal with Dorado Records that allowed him to install a new digital recording studio in his own North London abode. Their relationship began with the singles 'No Time For Change' and 'Big City', whose featured vocalists included Cleveland Watkiss, with a bass line from Gary Crosby, before collaborating with fellow Dorado interns D*Note and jazzmen like Steve Williamson and Ronnie Laws. A third single, ''Movin' On', was completed as a typically strong and energetic debut album was assembled in late 1993. Outside also comprise Patrice Blanchard (bass) and Byron Wallen (trumpet), plus various session musicians as the occasion demands.
Album: *Almost In* (Dorado 1993).

Owens, Robert

A long time collaborator with Mr Fingers in Fingers Inc, Owens provided the vocal for early house classics like 'Washing Machine' and 'Music Takes Me Up'. He also sang on classics like Frankie Knuckles' 'Tears' and (uncredited) on the Bobby Konders' production, Jus' Friends' 'As One'. Owens grew up, inspired by Stevie Wonder, Patti Labelle and others, with a church choir background, going on to sing in several bands. As a youth he travelled between his Los Angeles-based mother and Chicago-stabled father, where he was first introduced to house music. Ironically his first experience of a warehouse party left him overpowered, and he left after fifteen minutes. He would later watch the assembled masses through a window, and decided to begin DJing himself, combining deck skills with his own vocals. It was at this point that he was introduced to Larry Heard, aka Mr Fingers. Owens would select from the tunes presented to him by Fingers and choose the ones he wished to write lyrics for. This paved the ground for Owens' breakthrough performance on Fingers Inc's 'Can You Feel It?'. When his songwriting partnership with Fingers broke up due to financial pressures, he recreated the method with Frankie Knuckles and David Morales (hardly a step down in quality) for his debut solo album. He was eventually dropped from his contract with Island in 1992 despite US success with 'I'll Be Your Friend' (which came out on Paul Oakenfold's Perfecto, and was remixed by Morales and Satoshi Tomiie) and the self-produced 'You Gotta Work'. Owens remains one of house music's great showmen, offering uplifting live sets with his Freetown posse (which was also the name of the label he helped establish, before he defected to Musical Directions in 1994). Earlier he had been the star turn on the first house package tour to London which arrived on English shores in February 1987.
Album: *Rhythms In Me* (4th & Broadway 1990).

Pal Joey

Pal Joey is merely the best known of New Yorker Joey Longo (b. c.1964)'s inumerable aliases. He earned his spurs with early house recordings on pivotal New York deep house imprint Apexton, also playing out regularly in Manhattan. Like so many others he began life working in a record shop, Vinyl Mania, before becoming an apprentice at a local studio. His more recent recordings, which have steadily built an audience in clubs, generally consist of loose, happy house textures, often released on his own label, Loop D' Loop. Examples include 'Flight 801' from 1991, or Espresso's 'Ping Pong' for Maxi Records from earlier the same year. Other names he hides behind include Earth People, Soho (not the UK outfit - scoring a big hit with 'Hot Music'), House Conductor, Espresso and Dream House. As Pal Joey his productions include 'Jump And Prance', arguably the first ska/house tune, for Republic. He has produced widely, notably for Boogie Down Productions.(half of *Sex And Violence*, also appearing alongside KRS-1 on REM's 'Radio Song'). Other clients include Deee-Lite (remixing their 'What Is Love' and 'ESP'). More recently he is often to be found working under the CFM Band moniker (Crazy French Man).

Paras, Fabio

London-based DJ renowned for his sets at Boy's Own parties, and equally admired for his 'bongo mixes' and eclectic record collection (ie playing the Clash to bemused but still receptive punters). His remixes inlcude React 2 Rhythm's 'I Know You Like It', Aloof's 'On A Mission', Deja Vu's 'Never Knew The Devil' and Outrage's 'Drives Me Crazy' (which sampled the Fine Young Cannibals song of the same name) and 'Tall 'n' Handsome'. The last named cut was issued on his own label, Junk, which he set up to house percussion-based material. He has also released records for Cowboy as Charas. However, he is not one of the DJ fraternity to push his own name with any vigour: 'I'm happy doing my own stuff. I'm just a mellow geezer minding my own business'.

Paris, Mica

b. Michelle Wallen, 27 April 1969, London, England. Having written, recorded and produced with the aid of heavyweights like Nile Rodgers

(Chic), Prince and Rakim (Eric B And Rakim), Paris remains one of the UK's biggest talents to never make the great leap forward. It has not been for want of effort or ability, yet somehow no-one has yet found a way of getting the most out of one of the world's most delightful soul-dance performers. Stronger material would certainly help. There are examples from her debut album when she hits a perfect beat, as when she matches the tenor sax of Courtney Pine for its dexterity on 'Like Dreamers Do'. Her second album chose new, hot producers as a remedy (Charles Mantronik of Mantronix, and Dancin' Danny D of D-Mob). A sense of frustration still pervades her career, however.

Albums: *So Good* (4th & Broadway 1989), *Contribution* (4th & Broadway 1990).

Video: *Mica Paris* (1991).

Park, Graeme

b. c.1963. Classically trained saxophonist and clarinetist turned DJ, famed for his sets at such venues as Manchester's Hacienda and London's Ministry Of Sound. He began his career in the music industry by working behind the counter (buying in second hand stock) at Nottingham's Select-A-Disc Records. His boss, Brian Selby, purchased a reggae club entitled Ad-Lib, but on opening night didn't have a DJ and hence asked his first lieutenant Park to take the job. Park carried on DJing there for several years, but as his listening tastes broadened (especially with the advent of hip hop and electro) he eventually began to incorporate more adenturous music into his sets. He went on to play at Sheffield's Leadmill, Nottingham's Kool Kat and the Hacidenda, alongside Mike Pickering (M People). His style could be categorised as deep house and garage, though as he prefers to state: 'If you look at my playlists over the past eight years, you'll find a common thread - songs'. His most famous remix was probably for New Order and the England World Cup Squad's 'World In Motion'. Other credits include D-Influence's 'Good Lover' and work with Temper Temper and Eddie 'Flashin'' Fowlkes. He was voted *Mixmag* DJ of the year in 1992, but he remains a good-humoured and approachable representative of his craft: 'It's nice to be important, but it's more important to be nice'.

Parker, Terrence

Parker burst into the UK public's imagination when 'The Question', by his *nom de plume* Seven Grand Housing Authority, was played by Tony Humphries at Cream in Liverpool. The track was taken from the *Soul Beats* EP, built over a sample of Kenny 'Dope' Gonzales' 'Axis Project'. Among those who were astonished by the track were James Barton of Olympic Records (who subsequently joined deConstruction), and he and others walked over to inspect the record's label. The track was soon licensed from Detroit's Simply Soul label to Olympic, arriving with a K-Klass remix. Parker had been making house music since 1988, at which point he joined Mark Kinchen to become Separate Minds for the techno soul track, 'We Need Somebody'. He also remixed and produced in Detroit under the aliases Express, Trancefusion, Transsonic and Simply Soul. His earlier releases included the 'Call My Name' cut for Detroit label 430 West. He was additionally responsible for running Intangible Records - at all stages defying the musical bent of his geographical home by remaining faithful to his love of Chicago house rather than techno. In confirmation of this, 1994 saw the release of the *Disco Disciple* EP.

Peniston, Ce Ce

b. Cecelia Peniston, c.1971, Phoenix, Arizona, USA. Ce Ce started acting at school when in her early teens. She went on to appear in numerous talent contests and also won the beauty pageants Miss Black Arizona and Miss Galaxy. She worked as a backing singer and whilst still at school wrote 'Finally', which would become her fist solo single. Fresh out of college, and with only the faintest hopes of a music career, she nevertheless sprang in to the Top 10 lists of both the UK and US on the back of a speculative demo. The music which backed 'Finally' had more than a passing resemblance to the Ce Ce Rogers (no relation) underground hit, 'Someday'. A singer and dancer slightly reminiscent of late 70s soul, most of her compositions are piano based with strong similarities to Aretha Franklin and Whitney Houston. While her modelling career has been put on the backburner, her attitude to singing remains refreshingly uncomplicated; 'What I know best is singing my lil' old heart out'. 'We Got A Love Thang' became a second hit early in 1992, as did the re-released 'Finally', before her debut album which was somewhat disjointed. She has also sung backing vocals on Kym Sims' 'Too Blind To See'. Her second album included contributions from David Morales and Steve 'Silk' Hurley, but was generally more R&B-focused.

Albums: *Finally* (A&M 1992), *Thought Ya Knew* (A&M 1994).

Pettibone, Shep

Famed for his late 80s/early 90s remix and production work for Bros, Madonna and other major league pop stars, Pettibone's early origins actually lie in hip hop. Together with Arthur Baker he was behind the Jazzy 5's groundbreaking 'Jazzy Sensation' release. He also pioneered the 'mastermixes' of Kiss FM Radio, introducing a new methodology by segueing records to build 'sequences', almost like movements in classical music. It was a parallel development to hip hop's scratching and DJ innovations, which were undoubtedly an ongoing influence. Afterwards he moved into a musical area which is probably best described as disco, reviving the sounds of Loletta Holloway to great success, ensuring his status as an in-demand mixer for large budget studio sessions.

Pigeon Pie Records

London record label headed by Joe Borgia which in its first few years of operation has earned itself a healthy reputation with its dozen or so releases. The catalogue began with two La Comoora records, 'Oki-Dokey' and 'Te Quiero'/'What Is Love'. Subsequent material included Rhythm Eclipse ('Feel It In The Air'/'Thru The Night'), Marco Polo ('Zuazuzua'), Cecer ('Skyline', 'I Need Your Love'), Delphine ('Baby Don't You Go'), Mind The Gap ('Mind The Gap'), FOD ('All It Takes), Jupiter ('Destiny') and Love To Infinity ('Somethin' Outta Nothin''). The latter, a garage cut from brothers Andrew and Peter Lee, was typically well-received by the dance music press.

Planet Dog Records

A band/label/multi-tentacled collective founded in Wood Green, London in 1985, who abhor their media definition of 'crusty techno'. They started running weekly nights at the Robey in Finsbury Park (Club Dog), as well as monthly all-night parties at the Rocket in Holloway (Megadog). Regular contributors to these performances included Banco De Gaia, Suns Of Arqa and the Ullulators. Other early associates were Ozric Tentacles, from whence came the more progressive (in the purest sense) Eat Static. Regular DJs included Quark and Phidget from underground sound system Zero Gravity, Michael Dog and *New Musical Express* journalist Sherman. They quickly acquired a reputation as an attractive alternative to conventional club culture: 'When we first started the Dog, we used to go to other people's clubs and feel terribly self-conscious'. Their Megadog bashes were distinguished by an open-door and open-minded policy. The central figures are the publicity shy Bob and Michael Dog. The enclave have additionally set up their own label, Planet Dog records, which focuses on ambient and psychedelic dance tracks. The label's first release came from Eat

Static with 'Abduction'. They also run the Wolf Distribution network, catering for Astralasia, Alpha And Omega, the Magic Mushroom Band, Zion Train, Psychedelic Psauna and even Hawkwind. Planet Dog label signings, meanwhile, include techno act Timeshard, from Liverpool.

Plus 8

Record label based in Detroit, Michigan, run by Richie Hawtin (b. 1973, Canada) and John Acquaviva (b. c.1963, London, Canada). Plus 8 has become one of the most influential outlets for new techno and acid, and hybrids thereof. The idea started when Hawtin lived near a club in Detroit called the Shelter. This ensured that he was in the same vicinity as techno innovators Derrick May, Juan Atkins and Kevin Saunderson. It was in this club scene that he first met partner Acquaviva and fellow Canadian Dan Bell. The latter helped instruct them in translating theiir ambitions of making music from theory in to practice. Plus 8 was set up in May 1990, taking its name from the familiar Detroit practice of spinning discs at increased volume. Their breakthrough release was Cybersonic's 'Technarchy', which featured old pal Dan Bell alongside Hawtin and Acquaviva. Afterwards Bell would move on to his own label Accelerate. Plus 8 'signings' include Speedy J ('De-Orbit', and, as Public Energy, *Binaural Signal Generator* EP), Circuit Breaker (*Circuit Breaker* EP), Vapourspace (Mark Gage) and Sysex (*City Points* EP). In 1991 they launched the sister label Probe, which introduced itself with FUSE's 'FU'. Probe is intended to be the more steadfast hard techno label, allowing Plus 8 to dabble in ambience and other realms. Recently the label has hooked up with Mute Records dance empire, Novamute, to license material in the UK. However, Hawtin and Acquaviva continue to oversee quality control, from inception to finished artwork. Other merchandise includes a comic book and Plus 8 condoms. The future seems to hold a shift towards ambient sounds, though Hawtin will continue to be revered as the man who brought the 303 back into vogue.

Selected album: Various: *From Our Minds To Yours* (Plus 8 1991).

Polo, Jimmy

b. c.1966, Alabama, but raised in Chicago, Illinois. Polo sang in gospel choirs as a boy, before becoming a musician in his teens around the local circuit. His first recorded outing was 'Libra Libra' in 1985 on Chicago Collection. His breakthrough hit, 'Shake Your Body', also emerged on that label, but the artist later complained bitterly that no

Terrence Parker

royalties were forthcoming. Consequently Polo moved to the UK to join Champion, but this led to the break up of Polo's original Libra Libra group. 1989 brought another genre classic in 'Free Yourself'/'Better Days', released on Urban Records in the UK, and played keyboards for Soul II Soul. He also immersed himself in the UK's nascent acid/rave scene, alongside flatmate Adamski, who dedicated his 1990 hit album to Polo (they also recorded together on the 1992 single, 'Never Goin' Down'). The same year he signed to Perfecto for the soul-influenced 'Express Yourself' single, and released his first album.
Album: *Moods* (Perfecto 1992).

Porky's Productions

'Hull's only record label' - which sprang to prominence when they unveiled Opik (Murray, Dean Dawson, Rob Everall and Chris Devril) and their 'Feel Yourself' monster, which big boys DeConstruction would go on to licence. By the time Opik broke the label had already established itself with cuts such as Fila Brazilia's 'Mermaids' and Heights Of Abraham's *Tides* EP. Heights Of Abraham comprised ex-Chakk members Jake Harries and Sim Lister, the latter co-writer of Cath Carroll's *England Made Me* album), plus Ashley & Jackson guitarist Steve Cobby.

Portishead

Yet another dance discovery from Bristol, home of Massive Attack, Tricky et al, Portishead, named after the sleepy West Coast port, made their indelible mark with the release of 'Dummy'. The man behind the song was the reserved Geoff Barrows (b. c.1971) - 'I just wanted to make interesting music, proper songs with a proper lifespan and a decent place in people's record collections' - and Beth Gibbons (b. c.1965). Geoff started out as a tape operator, working in a minor capacity with Massive Attack and Neneh Cherry, writing songs for the latter. With the aid of an Enterprise Allowance grant he recruited jazzman and musical director Adrian, drummer/programmer Dave and vocalist Beth, who he encountered rendering Janis Joplin covers in a local pub. Together they recorded a soundtrack and film, *To Kill A Dead Man*, with themselves as actors because 'we couldn't find anyone else to do the parts'. They followed the feted 'Dummy' with a second out-take from their debut album, 'Numb', then 'Sour Times'.
Album: *Dummy* (Go! Beat 1994).

Positiva

EMI's dance subsidiary headed by Nick Halkes (b.

c.1967, Portishead, Bristol, England), who was headhunted after taking XL recordings to the forefront of the dance market with releases by the Prodigy SL2, Liquid and House Of Pain. He also crunched into the Top 10 alongside one-time partner Richard Russell with 'The Bouncer', recorded under the name Kicks Like A Mule. He had also worked as Life Like (on the Depeche Mode-sampling 'Like Life'), again with Russell. Halkes' attended Goldsmiths University in London before kidding his way into a DJ slot on WRLS, the New York black music station. While in the third year of his degree he had become the UK representative of Easy Street Records, before DJing in Ibiza in 1988. He also worked part-time for Secret Promotions (Rebel MC, Massive Attack), then Citybeat, eventually A&Ring his own 'underground' dance label, XL. The success of which made his name a hot property in the UK dance market, with EMI eventually offering him adequate terms and conditions to set up Positiva at the beginning of 1993. His second-in-command was to be DJ and journalist Dave Lambert. Positiva's first release was Exoterix's 'Void'. However, it was the Disco Evangelists' 'De Niro' which was the first significant record, before the ongoing success of Hyper Go-Go ('Raise'), Judy Cheeks ('So In Love' etc.), Barbara Tucker ('Beautiful People'), Critical ('Wall Of Sound') and Reel To Real (house-ragga crossover 'I Like To Move It') began to really pay back EMI's investment. All the hits were collected on the *Phase One* compilation, while the label was also responsible for July 1993's *Ambient Collection* - one of the best introductions to this music yet compiled (Orb, Visions Of Shiva, Black Dog, Orbital, Aphex Twin, Irresistible Force, Moby, Beaumont Hannant etc.). Halkes has indicated that the next objective of the label will be to take club acts and break them as album artists. Recent signings include rappers the Whooliganz.
Albums: Various: *The Positiva Ambient Collection* (Positiva 1993), *Phase One* (Positiva 1994).

Praga Khan

Comprising Jade 4U (b. Nikki Danlierop) and Maurice Engelen (b. c.1974), the latter an 80s DJ and 'New Beat' pioneer. By 1993 Praga Khan had sold over half a million records together under various guises, such as Lords Of Acid, Channel X, Digital Orgasm and Jade 4U solo. Danlierop was certainly a vivacious character, she had apparently been 'sacked' from the band at one stage for 'biting' her partner on stage, due to over-excitement. As Praga Khan they had enjoyed a 1991 rave hit with 'Injected With A Poison', which cased a furore when it entered the Top 20 due to perceived drug connotations. It would go all the way to number 1 in Japan. In the US they were signed to Rick Rubin's Def Jam on a five album contract, where Rubin hoped to market them as his 'next big thing'. On the commercial breakthrough of their music they commented: 'We have to see techno/rave for what it is, as the rock 'n' roll of the 90s'.

Album: As Digital Orgasm: *Come Dancin'* (Dead Dead Good 1992). *Spoon Full Of Miracle* (Profile 1993).

Pressure Drop

Originally Justin Langford (percussion), Mike Puxley (keyboards) and Gareth Tasker (guitar), Pressure Drop made their debut with 'Feeling Good - Touch 1 2 3' for Big World in March 1990. The group met at the Heavy Duty Club where Justin was DJing. It was he who obtained the bank loan in order to set up an eight-track studio in his front room. Afterwards Pressure Drop re-emerged as a duo of Langlands and Dave Henley (a hairdresser at Kensington Market, and Langford's partner in Blood Brothers, who had remixed Pressure Drop's first record). Their four-track *Sampler* EP in 1991 made waves, featuring Joanna Law, Galliano and Mark Cornell, as well as live Hammond organ, Indian tabla and African drums. The most notable track was 'You're Mine', an adaptation of 'Transfusion', by the Blood Brothers. However, despite selling over 30,000 copies on German independent label Boombastic, their debut album would not receive a UK release.

Album: *Upset* (Boombastic 1992).

Pressure Of Speech

Taking their name from a condition of manic depressives, a stage at which victims are unable to express the multitude of ideas and words engulfing their minds, it should come as no surprise that Mickie Mann was once a pyschiatric nurse in Aberdeen, Scotland. After a spell in the army he joined Orbital, the Shamen, Meat Beat Manifesto and Ultramarine, among others, as live sound engineer. Pressure Of Speech were formed with lighting expert Luke Losey and DJ Stika, formerly of Fun-Da-Mental and Spiral Tribe. They made their debut with the track 'Surveillance' on Planet Dog's *Feed Your Head* compilation, before stepping out on their own with 'X-Beats' on the North South label. Their debut album proved to be one of the most specific and obvious assaults on the UK's Conservative government within the previously largely apolitical techno/dance movement. They also proved keen to take their

music out to a live audience, touring as part of a Megadog-styled collective.

Album: *Art Of The State* (North South 1994).

Principle, Jamie

Famed for his breathy, Smokey Robinson-styled delivery, Principle's classic early house recordings were 'Waiting On My Angel' and 'Baby Wants To Ride'. The latter gave this Chicago house master and innovator a hit after a long time in the shadows (although a more or less identical version appeared at the same time from Frankie Knuckles). Following 'Rebels' there was a long absence from the nation's dancefloors punctuated only by US tracks 'Cold World' (during a brief liaison with Atlantic Records) and 'Date With The Rain' on a Steve 'Silk' Hurley compilation. He re-emerged with a US smash in 1991 with 'You're All I've Waited 4', self-written and co-produced with Hurley again.

Prodigy

The Prodigy represent the vanguard of the UK's hard dance scene, and are one of the few collectives operating in these waters not to be cloaked in anonymity. The band, based in Essex, comprise MC Maxim Reality, dancers Keith Flint and Leeroy Thornhill, plus mastermind Liam Howlett (b. c.1971). Howlett, a former breakdancer and DJ with Cut To Kill, handles the compositions and governs the band's style. They began their career with the *What Evil Lurks* EP, which showcased their speeded up hip hop breakbeats (the band are all rap fans). The big time beckoned when they scored a UK number 3 with 'Charly', a children's public information film sample overlaying a pulsating backbeat. It would start a huge trend of rave singles incorporating signature tunes to popular kids television programmes. More importantly it signified the crossover of rave music from the clubs to the chart. They followed up with the equally impressive *Everybody In The Place* EP. Originally a track on the *What Evil Lurks* EP, it would go all the way to number 2 in the charts, giving the Prodigy their biggest hit. The single, 'Fire' also won many fans, the topside utilising the famous opening of Crazy World Of Arthur Brown's 'I am the god of hell fire'. In 1992 they became, as one magazine put it: 'The only techno outfit with the legs to be able to put together a whole album', though perhaps that comment was a little prejudicial against the genre. By 1993 Howlett had built his own home studio in his native Braintree, Essex. He also occupied himself with remixes for Front 242, Dream Frequency, Art Of Noise and Jesus Jones, amongst others. Acknowledging his weighty and sometimes unwarranted reputation, he then released 'One Love', putting it out initially on white label only, so that underground DJs, who had foresworn the Prodigy once they had become a chart act, might give it needle time (which they did). 1994 saw the release of an accomplished double set which confirmed the group's ability to operate outside of club waters as a standalone musical project, and also put on record their response to their numerous critics. The set opened with the words 'So I've decided to take my work back underground, To stop it falling into the wrong hands'. 'Their Law' (which featured a guest appearance from Pop Will Eat Itself), maintained links to the rave scene which broke the Prodigy by attacking the Criminal Justice Bill which sought to legislate against such events. It included the number 4-peaking taster single, 'No Good (Start The Dance)'.

Album: *The Prodigy Experience* (XL 1992, double album), *Music For The Jilted Generation* (XL 1994, double album).

Production House

London label set up in 1987 by Phil Fearon, formerly of Brit-funk act Galaxy, with help from Laurie Jago. Primarily orientated towards hardcore and rave music, the self-distributed imprint rose to prominence in 1992 via the success of Acen ('Trip II The Moon') and Baby D ('Let Me Be Your Fanstasy'), both of which reached the top of the national dance charts and also broke the mainstream listings. Solo artist Acen (b. c.1972, Tottenham, London, England) had been unlucky not to do so previously with 'Close Your Eyes', which sold 25,000 copies without ever entering the charts. In the event 'Trip II To The Moon', Production House's 42nd release, would be the one to bring them their first hit. Other notable signings include the House Crew ('Keep The Fire Burning' and 'We Are Hardcore'), Nino ('Future Of Latin', from Terry 'The Chocolate Prince' Jones), Brothers Grimm's ('Field Of Dreams' and 'Exodus' - which sampled Mike Oldfield's 'Tubular Bells') and X Static ('Ready To Go'). A subsidiary outlet, Special Reserve, was also founded to house swingbeat and soul material, beginning with MC Juice's 'Freak In Me'.

Psychick Warriors Ov Gaia

Ethnic trance team from the low countries, often featuring 'organic' live percussion, whose main man is Bobby Reiner. They started out as an industrial music project before picking up on the house music scene, with their debut single, 'Exit 23', appearing in 1991, followed by 'Maenad', both

on Belgian label KK. Their most widely-renowned release, however, was 'Obsidian'. They also joined the throngs in the Midi Circus tour. As for their musical ethos, Reiner would note: 'One of our main ideas about making dance music is the deconstruction of old values, deconstruction of what music is about and re-establishing ritual and trance states'. Former member Robert Heyman would go on to form Exquisite Corpse.

Album: *Ov Biospheres And Sacred Grooves (A Document Ov New Edge Folk Classics)* (KK 1993).

Pulse 8 Records

Pulse 8 is, by accident or design, the British home of the female vocalist, with label personnel seemingly unable to resist signing or licensing a belting diva performance on garage or house discs. As A&R director Steve Long pointed out: 'We are quite keen to sign male vocalists. But there don't seem to be many about'. Managed by Frank Sansom, the duo behind the label had originally promoted artists like New Kids On The Block, Foster & Allen and even Max Bygraves. They moved to dance because they believed 'the real artists, the future artists, album artists, are going to come from the dance area'. The label's most prominent artist was arguably Rozalla, whose 1991 cut 'Faith (In The Power Of Love)' brought them chart success. Other releases included 4T Thieves' 'Etnotechno' in 1991, licensed from Italy's Calypso imprint and Friends Of Matthew's 'The Calling' from the same year, a follow-up to 'Out There'. Other pivotal artists were Sue Chaloner ('Answer My Prayer' and 'I Wanna Thank You'), Rave Nation ('Stand Up') and Clubland (introducing Zemya Hamilton) ('Hold On (Tighter To Love)'). Their major hits of 1992 included Reckless ('Reckless Karnage'), Debbie Malone ('Rescue Me (Crazy About Your Love)') and Rozalla ('Are You Ready To Fly?'). Rage (Pierson Grange, Angela Lupino, Tony Jackson, Jeffrey Sayadian and Toby Sadler) would take them into the Top 10 with, of all things, a Bryan Adams song - 'Run To You'. It was produced by Barry Lang and Duncan Hannant. Lang had previously overseen Amii Stewart's 'Light My Fire', Hannant having worked with Bomb The Bass and Betty Boo. However, the lynchpin producers behind the label's output are Band Of Gypsies. They recorded cuts like 'Take Me Higher' in their own right, as well as providing Australian singer Juliette Jaimes with hits in 'Stand Up' and 'Summer Breeze' (also working with Chaloner and Rozalla). Other material arrived from Lee Rogers (formerly of Temper and her own group, Suspect, and also a Hollywood actor, with 'Love Is The Most'). Sadly the label fell out with Rozalla when she attempted to release her debut album, recorded at Pulse 8's expense, on Epic. Pulse 8 won the subsequent court case in February 1992, despite Rozalla having at no time signed a contract. Their quest for a talented male vocalist alighted on Keith Nunnally (ex-JM Silk with Steve 'Silk' Hurley), who, fronting Intuition, provided 'Greed (When Will The World Be Free)', a revision of the same artist's DJ International oldie. 1993's major advances included the tearaway success of Urban Cookie Collective's 'The Key, The Secret'. Pulse 8 is also the mother label to the Faze 2 subsidiary, famed for its contribution to the world of toytown techno with Urban Hype (Bobby D and Mark Lewis) and 'A Trip To Trumpton'. That group had previously scored with the more sober 'Teknologi'. Faze 2 also provided a home for Visions Of Shiva and others.

PWL

Hardly the coolest record label on the dance scene, owned as it is by the Stock Aitken & Waterman triad, PWL has nevertheless made a massive contribution to the subculture by licensing mainstream successes (on PWL Continental) from Europe, including DJ Professor, 2 Unlimited, Capella and RAF, while PWL International has offered the world Toxic Two ('Rave Generator'), Opus III ('It's A Fine Day'), Vision Masters ('Keep On Pumpin' It') and Undercover ('Never Let Her Slip Away', 'Baker Street' etc.). In addition there was a rave offshoot/promo label Black Diamond which originally housed tunes like 'Rave Generator' and 2 Unlimited's 'Workaholic', until they crossed over. However, Black Diamond disappeared in 1992 to be replaced by 380, headed by John Barratt, and named after its address at a converted church on Manchester's Deansgate. Its career began with Family Foundation's 'Xpress Yourself', then Ultracynic's 'Nothing Is Forever'.

R&S Records

Ghent, Belgium techno label/talent pool founded by Renaat Vanderpapeliere and Sabine Maes in the early 80s. R&S's high profile has been earned on the back of some of the dance scene's most innovative aritsts: Kevin Saunderson/Derrick May,

Dave Angel ('Planet Function', 'Stairway To Heaven'), Joey Beltram (*Vol 1-2* etc.), CJ Bolland (*Ravesignal 1-3*), Jam & Spoon ('Stella', etc.) and the Aphex Twin ('Didgeridoo') - a who's who of techno in itself, have all seen their vinyl bedecked by the familiar R&S enblem of a reering steed. In 1987 Code 61 provided the label with 'Drop The Deal', which became an early balearic hit and established R&S' credentials. From their roots in the much-maligned 'Belgian new beat' scene, the label picked up the Detroit sound and nurtured it into a hard house style best recalled on tracks like Spectrum's 'Brazil'. Subsequent records like Human Resource's 'Dominator' and Beltram's 'Mentasm' proved hugely important to the UK's rave generation. However, it is far more than a one horse stable, as can be discerned by its subsidiary operations. These include Apollo (ambient), Global Cuts (uplifting club house), Outrage (experimental) and Diatomyc (acid). Notable also have been two series of compilations, *TZ* (Test Zone) and *In Order To Dance*. The latter gathers highlights from the R&S roster at more or less regular intervals, providing DJs and clubbers with the most important cuts. The label set up a UK outlet in the beginning of 1993, which co-ordinates releases and promotion in tandem with the six person team in Ghent. Among the label's most satisfying current projects have been Jaydee ('Plastic Dreams'), Biosphere ('Microgravity'), CJ Bolland ('The 4th Sign'), Source ('Organized Noise') and Locust, whose album project for Apollo was produced in association with a documentary. R&S planned to delve further into multi-media projects with a MTV tie-up party and the inclusion of a computer game, film and subliminal artwork as part of *In Order To Dance 5*. Plans for a 'helicopter shuttle service' for staff members between Ghent and London were probably an exaggeration, but it would be unwise to rule anything out bearing in mind R&S' formidable former achievements and appetite for dance music.

Selected albums: Various: *In Order To Dance Volumes 1-5* (R&S 1990 - 1994).

Rampling, Danny

Rampling is a staple of the Manchester DeConstruction label, a member of the Kiss FM team, and a hugely popular DJ the world over. DJing since the age of 18, he was pre-eminent in the balearic movement in the late 80s, and has successfully negotiated dozens of shifts in dance music's climate since. He was pivotal in importing the acid sound, after playing legendary sets at Ibiza clubs like Koo and Pacha. His nights at South London's legendary Shoom Club, which he opened with his wife Jenny in 1988, are now legendary. Shoom introduced many of the 'Phuture' tracks imported from Chicago, though Rampling also mixed this up with other dance sounds, he himself having come from a soul background. He waited some time before releasing his first record, Sound Of Shoom's 'I Hate Hate' in 1990, a cover of an obscure soul cut from Razzy Bailey sung by Stephen Eusebe. In the meantime he had remixed for the B-52's, Beloved, Erasure and James Taylor Quartet, among many others. He went on to form the Millionaire Hippies, who have released strong singles like 'I Am The Music, Hear Me!', featuring the vocals of Das Strachen and Gwen Dupree, with remixes from Farley And Heller.

Rave

Specifically a one-off gathering for late night consumption of pre-recorded dance music, a musical definition of rave is more problematic. Descending from the acid house sound and ethos, the main fare tends to be fast techno and hardcore records, pitched between 125 and 140 bpm and often released on tiny independent labels with little background information. Some of rave's established anthems include Toxic Two's 'Rave Generator' and Human Resource's 'Dominator'. Like other forms of dance music, rave has its favoured DJs and remixers. The most recognisable and popular of the 'rave' acts are Liam Howlett's Prodigy. Other venerated artists include Altern 8, Bizarre Inc, Bassheads and early K Klass material.

Raze

US house group from Washington D.C. whose mainman was Vaughn Mason, aided by singer Keith Thompson (b. Bronx, New York, USA). Raze perfected the house formula with club classics (and crossover hits) 'Jack The Groove', originally released in 1986, which re-entered and broke the UK Top 20 in January the following year. 'Let The Music Move U', and particulary 'Break 4 Luv' (a US dance number 1) also became house standards. Controversy followed the latter when Thompson alleged that Mason had wrongly appropriated all the writing and publishing credits. 'During that time', Thompson recounts, "Break 4 Love' sold one million copies worldwide and it was tough when people didn't believe I was the vocalist or had anything to do with it'. A settlement was finally reached and Thompson starting releasing solo product and founded his own Level 10 label. Happily for him, when the record was restored via the Mastercuts series Classic House compilation, this

time his name featured. Raze persevered with tracks like 1991's 'Bass Power' (Champion), with vocals by Pamela Frazier and rapper Doug Lazy.

React Records

Label established by former Rhythm King director James Horrocks with new partner Thomas Foley. After Rhythm King had gone overground in a big way, Horrocks bailed out, and kicked around for a couple of years before taking up an A&R job for Really Useful's short-lived dance label (also called React). Afterwards he moved on to his own project, initially packaging compilations like Deep Heat, Thin Ice and Megabass. The first single proper came about via ex-bootlegger John Truelove, who, as the Source featuring Candi Station, recorded 'You Got The Love'. It would sell over 200,000 copies in the UK. It was at this point that Horrocks made the acquaintence of Foley, who introduced him to the house scene (establishing the React-backed Garage night at Heaven). He has gone on to be the prime mover behind the label's highly successful Reactivate compilation series. On the single front React maintains an enviable reputation. Their biggest releases include Age Of Love's classy 'Age Of Love', arguably the perfect example of trance house, remixed by Jam And Spoon. In 1991 React were joined by scene stalwarts Fierce Ruling Diva, a duo of Amsterdam DJ's Jeroen Flamman and Jeffrey 'DJ Abraxas' Porter (famous for hosting the Planet E club in Amsterdam and an after hours barge club, Subtopia). In 1991 they released 'Rubb It In' for the label, then 'You Gotta Believe' a year later. The label also signed Italian producer Alex Lee, releasing his 'Take It' in June. Unfortunately the latter artist would be drafted for national service in Italy for two years just as his career was beginning to take off. They also provided a home to GTO (who recorded two of the earliest singles on the React catalogue in 'Listen To The Rhythm Flow' and 'Elevation'), Ether Real ('Zap'), Elevator ('Shinny') and MASH ('U Don't Have To Say U Love Me').

Reckless

aka Vivian Ulson, b. c.1968, London. Reckless is widely known for his mixing and DJing skills, having won the European DMC championships in 1990 and 1991. However, he shunned hip hop for the 1992 house release, 'Karnage'. His interest in dance music heightened in 1987, and a year later he found himself DJing at raves. His first recording was Genaside II's 'The Motiv', which brought his keyboard skills to the fore. 'Karnage' was built around Four For Money's 'A Moment In Time' bassline, with samples from Crystal Waters'

'Making Happy'. The follow-up was 'Time To Make The Floor Burn'. He also remixed Kariya's 'Let Me Love You For Tonight' in 1992.

Recycle Or Die

Frankfurt, Germany-based record label associated with the Harthouse/Eye Q group, whose managing director is Heinz Roth. They had the sum total of their product, six albums, released in the UK for the first time in 1994. Each CD arrived in a cover painted by a cult German arist, packaged in recyclable cardboard. The albums were: *Straylight* (Dominic Woosey), *Looking Beyond* (Ralf Hildenbeutel), *Constellation* (Oliver Lieb), *Baked Beans* (Helmut Zerlett), *Archaic Modulation* (Stevie Be Zet) and *Rhythm & Irrelevance* (#9 Dream). Roth: 'It's very much like a community project...Recycle Or Die is not an ambient label. It's more experimental. It's not like putting together a couple of sounds and smoking a joint'. To prove his point Recycle Or Die took a stage in the 1994 Montreaux Jazz Festival, where Ralph Hildenbeutel, Sven Vath's engineer, played.

Reel 2 Real

Featuring the antics of The Mad Stuntman (b. c.1969, Trinidad, West Indies), whose vocals towered over the house ragga breakthrough 'I Like To Move It'. A resident of Brooklyn, New York, since the age of nine, Stuntman took his name from the Lee Majors' television series *The Fall Guy*. He met prolific producer Erick 'More' Morillo through a friend and the two combined on tracks for Strictly Rhythm which they never envisioned to be crossover material. They were proved emphatically wrong by the sustained sales of 'I Like To Move It', when it was licensed to Positiva in the UK. Its chart life was an erratic one, running a sequence of weekly positions which read 10, 12, 12, 10, 9, 7, 5, 8, 7, 7, boosted by a 40-date club tour, though at no stage was it playlisted by Radio 1 DJs. They followed up with 'Go On Move', which began a second chart tenure.

Reese Project

Along with Inner City, the Reese Project is the other regular home to Detroit techno guru Kevin Saunderson (b. Kevin Maurice Saunderson, 9 May 1964, Brooklyn, New York, the second syllable of his middle name providing the term Reese). He had relocated to Detroit at the age of 15, and was a proficient running back in college football until he became a DJ. His musical inspirations were his mother, a former member of the Marvelettes, and his brother, a road manager for rock bands. His first release would be 'Triangle Of Love' on Juan

Atkins' Metroplex imprint, before breaking through with 'The Sound'. With techno in its infancy, Reese's 'Rock To The Beat' (1987) was a hugely influential, hypnotic marvel. His other early releases came as either Reese or Reese Santonio (Saunderson with DJ Tone aka Antonio Eccles). The Reese Project was incorporated in 1991 to allow a venue for his more soul-inspired techno outings. It was specifically geared towards productions of around 120bpm (making it 'in tune' with the human heartbeat, and also, apparently, the abilities of his vocalists). However, as Saunderson recounts: 'The Reese Project is not about me, myself and I. It's not about indulging myself musically. It's my chance to take a back seat, and give the platform up to talented people who only need a break, but give back as much as they get'. The three main vocalists on the album - Raechel Kapp, LaTrece and Terence FM - who featured on the single 'I Believe' (Kapp taking the honours on 'Direct Me', LaTrece on 'So Deep'), are part of a family environment overseen by Saunderson's wife Ann, who also writes the words and melodies. They met after Saunderson recorded his first remix for Wee Girl Papa Rappers' 'Heat It Up' for Jive, where she formerly worked. 'I Believe' was one of two minor UK hits in 1992 (number 74), the other being 'The Colour Of Love' (with Kapp on vocals, number 52). A further single, 'Miracle Of Life', featured Kapp alongside Byron Stingily of Ten City. In furtherance of his ambitions to give Detroit musicians a chance, Saunderson also reactivated the KMS label to expose undiscovered talent. A new line-up of guest artists was recruited for the Reese Project's 1994 tour, though Kapp was retained after returning from having her child. Album: *Faith Hope And Clarity* (Network 1992, also issued as a double remix set in 1993).

Reinforced Records

Premier hardcore label begun in 1990 by Gus Lawrence, Mark, Dego, and Ian, who collectively record as 4 Hero. It was their debut, 'Mr Kirk's Nightmare', which opened the label's catalogue. After consistently innovative releases from Nebula II ('Seance'/'Atheama'), Manix ('Oblivion (Head In The Crowds)') and others from One II One and Basic Rhythm, the quartet were joined by a fifth member, former New York-based grafitti artist Goldie, who took on the A&R, graphic design and spokesperson roles. He had previously recorded as the Ajaz Project before his first outings on Reinforced as Rufige Cru. He is also behind the Metalheads project. Other early releases on the label included material by Doc Scott (as Nasty Habits - 'As Nasty As I Wanna Be'), Internal

Affairs and Primary Sources. As with that other mainstay of hardcore music, Suburban Base, Reinforced recognise the contribution hip hop and breakbeats have made to the foundation of the music. The label closely observed the shifts in techno during the 90s, being a staple source of 'darkside' hardcore in 1992. So too the arrival of ambient techno, or what they preferred to describe as 'a blues for the 90s kind of ambient', previewed on their continuing *Enforcers* series of experimental EPs. These used newer signings AK47, Covert Operations, Peshay (Coventry's Neil Trix), Open Skies (Norwegian techno crew Bjorn Torske, Ole J Mjos and Rune Hindback) and Myserson, a Philadelphian import.

Selected albums: 4 Hero: *Parallel Universe* (Reinforced 1994). Various: *The Definition Of Hardcore* (Reinforced 1994).

Reload

Yeovil band based around former DJ Mark Pritchard and one-time Aphex Twin collaborator Tony Middleton (the 'other' twin, who shares the same date of birth as Richard James). The duo also record under several different monikers including Global Communications, Link, E621 and Rebos. They have their own label, Evolution, though their debut album came via the Infonet imprint. Their work blends dark hardcore with ambient strains, augmented by multi-media presentations drawing in environmental sounds like the ticking of clocks. *A Collection Of Short Stories* arrived with a book of accompanying essays written by their friend Dominic Fripp. Some of the text was designed to be read in-sync with the music. Both Pritchard and Middleton actually draw on a strong musical devotion to the likes of Peter Gabriel, Jean-Michel Jarre and even the Smiths, as well as the more anticipated Detroit techno and Eurobeat. Their *Auto Reload* EP late in 1993 continued to cement their profile with the more demanding club-goers. In 1993 they signed with indie label Dedicated, for whom they had previously remixed the Cranes and Chapterhouse.

Albums: *A Collection Of Short Stories (Soundtracks Without Films)* (Infonet 1993). As Global Communications: *76:14* (Dedicated 1994).

Renegade Soundwave

London born and bred esoteric dance trio whose recordings have been variously described as 'Dance-Noise-Terror' and 'Chas 'n' Dave with a beatbox'. The group originally consisted of three multi-faceted instrumentalists, Danny Briotett (ex-Mass), Carl Bonnie and Gary Asquith (ex-Rema Rema, Mass). 'We're a by-product of punk. It forged the way we think, though the sound is nothing to do with it.' Their first single 'Kray Twins' emerged on Rhythm King Records, the sound of a television documentary set to a throbbing bass undertow. After the equally notorious 'Cocaine Sex' they switched to Mute because of the greater eclecticism of their catalogue. A series of dancefloor singles like 'Biting My Nails' and 'Probably A Robbery' prefaced a debut album which included an unlikely cover of the Beat's 'Can't Get Used To Losing You'. Their aggressive dancefloor attack was continued the same year with *In Dub*, on which 'Holgertron' made use of the theme music to television's *Doctor Who*. The group re-emerged in 1994 with another fine album, one of the tracks, 'Last Freedom Fighter', announcing that 'We've all been asleep for a very long time'. It was a welcome return, though Bonnie had long since left for a solo career. Briotett also worked alongside his wife, Linda X, as half of Planet X (who recorded the *James Bond* tribute, 'I Won't Dance', and 'Once Upon A Dancefloor').

Albums: *Soundclash* (Mute 1990), *In Dub* (Mute 1990), *How You Doin?* (Mute 1994).

Rephlex

Record label set up by the Aphex Twin and Grant Wilson-Claridge, a friend from school. The idea was to offer local Cornish DJs some new material to play, and the first releases were all the Aphex Twin under various guises; Caustic WIndow, Blue Calx etc. New signings, however, include the intriguing u-Ziq. Other artists signed for one-off or longer deals included Seefeel, Kosmic Kommando (eponymous debut EP) and Kinesthesia.

Selected album: Various: *The Philosophy Of Sound And Machine* (Rephlex 1992).

Republic Records

Record label founded by Ian 'Tommy' Tomlinson in association with Dave Lee (aka Joey Negro), both of whom formerly worked for Rough Trade Records. Together they approached Geoff Travis of that label in February 1989 to suggest the instigation of a dance subsidiary, and by May of the same year Republic had released its first record (by M-D-Emm). Lee was given the A&R say, as the label follwed up with material by Blaze, Phaze II and Turntable Orchestra (many of which were Lee in disguise). As well as the occasional licensing deal (notably Kym Mazelle), they pressed on with a catalogue of material distinguished by releases from the aforementioned M-D-Emm ('Can't Win For Losing') and Phaze II ('I Wanna Do It' and 'Burning To The Boogie'). The label split from

Renegade Soundwave

Rough Trade following the latter's financial problems in the early 90s, but in any case Lee has gone on to concentrate on his many other projects.

Rhythm Invention

Rhythm Invention are Nick Simpson and Richard Brown. Together they offered one of the better examples of the trance formula, or deep house without the sexuality, or rave without the front running electronics. Their early singles 'Crunch' and 'I Can't Take It' caught the media's attention with their simple but irresistable percussion effects. Typically their 1993 effort, 'Ad Infinitum', was fairly uneventful, but produced a tangible hypnotic effect.

Album: *Inventures In Wonderland* (Warp 1993).

Rhythm King

One of the UK's largest and most successful mainstream dance labels, Rhythm King was an idea originally mooted in 1976 by two friends, Martin Heath and James Horrocks, who shared a love of Motown and soul music. An initial parent deal with a major was abandoned when that label refused to pay a minimal advance to licence an American track, 'Love Can't Turn Around'. They hooked up instead with Daniel Miller's highly successful independent label, Mute, who granted

them the necessary artistic freedom and budget. One of their first signings was 3 Wise Men, arguably the first ever British rap group. Another notable early rapper, Schooly D, was licensed from the US to their Flame subsidiary. Other signings included Chuck Brown and Gwen McCrae. The other subsidiary, Transglobal - was a disco-styled operation, which delivered a hit with Taffy's 'I Love My Radio'. It had been popular in clubs for several months before Transglobal gave it a stock release, their reward coming with a number 6 national chart success. 1987 was a quiet year for the label, though King Sun/D Moet's 'Hey Love!' picked up lots of airplay (but few sales), and Shawnie G's 'Mission Impossible' and Denise Motto's 'Tell Jack', licensed from the *Chicago Jackbeat* compilations, kept things ticking over. It was 1988 before Rhythm King re-established itself with the Beatmasters' featuring the Cookie Crew's 'Rok Da House', which had ironically been a flop when released in its original version a year previously. It was at this point that Horrocks' growing dissatisfaction with the label's direction forced him to leave, going on to establish React Records. Undeterred, Adele Nozedar stepped in and new commercial heights were achieved with Bomb The Bass hitting number 5 in the charts, and S'Express (Mark Moore having originally brought

Taffy, the Cookie Crew and Beatmasters to RK's attention) bringing them a first number 1 with 'Theme From S'Express' in the summer of 1988. This triumvirate of bands (S'Express, Bomb The Bass and the Beatmasters) continued their ascent throughout the year, both in albums and singles sales. The 1989 signings were a less viable crop, however. Rapper Merlin, who had originally appeared on Bomb The Bass's 'Megaton', proved a disappointment, as did Hotline, a house duo from Huddersfield. The saving grace was Baby Ford, who provided a run of hits, while the label expanded in opening the Outer Rhythm subsidiary, ostensibly to license tracks. Their major success of the 90s would prove to be D:Ream, though other artists included bhangra house duo Joi, industrial dance groups KMFDM and Sheep On Drugs, and indie pop outfit Sultans Of Ping.
Selected albums: Bomb The Bass: *Into The Dragon* (Rhythm King 1988). S'Express: *Original Soundtrack* (Rhythm King 1989). Beatmasters: *Anywayawanna* (Rhythm King 1989). Baby Ford: *Ooo The World Of Baby Ford* (Rhythm King 1990). D:Ream: *Dream On Vol. 1* (Rhythm King 1993).

Riley, Teddy

Widely regarded as not only the originator, but the whole motivating force behind New Jack Swing, Riley remains arguably the most successful and revered producer in commercial dance music. His writing, remixing and production credits include numerous Bobby Brown records, and work with Keith Sweat, Jazzy Jeff And The Fresh Prince, Wreckx-N-Effect, James Ingram and Michael Jackson (*Dangerous*). Despite this profusion, he maintains that 'I don't work with anyone who isn't a real singer. I've turned down a lot of artists who are big but who I reckon don't have the ability.' His 'swing' groups included the originals, Guy, on which he sang vocals, as well as Jodeci, Mary J. Blige and soundtrack work on *New Jack City* and *Do The Right Thing*. His origins were in the R&B group, Kids At Work, and his step-father was Gene Griffin, who released one of the earliest rap tracks in Trickeration's 'Rap, Bounce, Rollerskate'. Riley's own rap connections included an uncredited appearance on Doug E. Fresh's 'The Show', but by the turn of the decade he would be a multi-millionaire. He returned to the group format in 1994 as vocalist for his latest project Blackstreet, who also boasted Chauncey 'Black' Hannibal (an original member of Jodeci), Levi Little (bass, guitar, keyboards) and David Hollister (formerly backing vocalist for Mary J. Blige, Al B. Sure, Patti LaBelle and 2Pac).
Selected albums: Guy: *Guy* (Uptown 1989). Blackstreet: *Blackstreet* (East West 1994).

Rising High Collective

Rising High Collective

Namely one Caspar Pound (b. c.1970), of The Hypnotist fame, and also the man who formed Rising High Records, and vocalist Plavka (b. Los Angeles, California, USA). Pound's ancestry extends to spells in A Homeboy, A Hippie, And A Funki Dred, before he found Top 75 success no less than seven times in his own right, and also navigated three Top 40 remixes into the charts, including the Shamen's number 1, 'Progen'. Plavka came to fame via the former group, gracing their first Top 30 cut, 'Hyperreal'. She came to London in 1989, immersing herself in the rave scene and passing herself off as a journalist in order to make the acquaintance of the Shamen. But ater they broke through together she quit the group to concentrate on projects where she could have more input into the songwriting, in addition to her much-admired operatic soprano range. She met Pound in 1991, the duo releasing their first single, 'Fever Called Love', in December of that year, for R&S. It was a stunning cut, above and beyond the novelty value of hearing a genuine techno track with genuine vocals. It was not until the summer of 1993 and a Hardfloor remix that the song really took off, however. After slightly misfiring with 'Reach', which was nevertheless a minor hit, 'There's No Deeper Love' (whose lyrics quietly provided a text on astrology and the formation of the universe) proved another club hit, this time with the progressive house faction. They made an acclaimed appearance at the 1993 Reading Festival, as well as many PA's at venues like the Ministry Of Sound, Heaven and Camden Palace. 1994's *Liquid Thoughts* EP provided further well-received slices of deep trance. They additionally recorded togetether as Dominatrix (two EPs, *Possession* and *Discipline*) while Plavka released a solo single, 'Maximum Motion' (all on Rising High or their Ascension/Sappho subsidiaries), and guested for Jam And Spoon ('Right In The Middle').

Rising High Records

Record label founded in London, England, in February 1991 by Caspar Pound, initially as an outlet for his own material, having recently disengaged from chart act A Homeboy, A Hippie And A Funki Dred. Having spent time living in Italy he returned to England bluffing his way into studio work with reggae producer Mad Professor and hi-NRG man Ian Levine. Soon he had learned enough to give his own operation a shot. Since its inception (the honour of first release going to Pound as The Hypnotist, with 'Rainbows In The Sky'), the label has grown to be much more than an inventive young man's hobby. Rising High has

been at the forefront, if not beyond it, in all of the major developments of dance music in the 90s. Pound has developed a second sense in recognising or anticipating trends such as jungle/breakbeat, trance and finally ambient. Their early hardcore techno is best sampled on Aural Assault, Earth Leakage Trip and Project One releases. As Pound asserted, unrepentently, at the time: 'I like nosebleed techno, the more nosebleedy the better'. A good example was Earth Leakage Trip's techno rave anthems on the *Neopolitan* EP, which featured the improbably bombastic 'The Ice Cream Van From Hell' - a furious rhythm track anchored by coy samples. A regular feature of the label has been the artistic growth of Mixmaster Morris (aka the Irresistable Force). After making his debut for the label with 'Space Is The Place' his recordings have continued to be a prominent fixture of Rising High's release schedule. As Rising High has grown it has spawned its own subsidiary imprints. Sappho (specialising in the harder, experimental end of the techno spectrum, set up in conjunction with RH A&R scout Pypee) and Ascension. They also brought the exciting sounds being developed in Germany at Harthouse/Eye Q via a link-up as Harthouse UK (earning significant kudos for giving the British public Hardfloor's 'Hardtrance Acperience'). Yet Rising High has also retained an endearing self-mockery and unfettered approach to dance music. Their slogans: 'You're going home in a fuckin' ambience', or Mixmaster Morris' 'I Think Therefore I Ambient' notwithstanding. Most of 1993/1994's innovations were in the latter sector, flooding the market with a noble array of compilations such as *Chill Out Or Die* and *Definitive Ambient Collection* - the former specially packaged by Mixmaster Morris, the latter by German ambient meister Peter Namlock. That duo also recorded together for the label under the title Dreamfish.

Selected albums: Various: *Techno Anthems Vol. 1 & 2* (Rising High 1991), *Chill Out Or Die 1 & 2* (Rising High 1993), *Secret Life Of Trance 1, 2 & 3* (Rising High 1993 - 1994). The Hypnotist: *The Complete Hypnotist* (Rising High 1992). Peter Namlook & Mixmaster Morris: *Dreamfish* (Rising High 1993).

Roberts, Joe

Manchester-based soul-dance vocalist, and an ex-mod who was brought up in a commune (when his parents moved from London to Karling in Norfolk, his father switching jobs from economist to carpenter). This can be guaged in his lyrics, which come heavily laden with peace 'n' luv metaphors, but also reflect the early influence of

Sly Stone, Al Green and Marvin Gaye, who were introduced to him by later collaborator Eric Gooden. He had been been learning the piano from the age of eight, and this experience is reflected in the musicianship of his club music. After moving to Manchester in 1981 he became a member of local covers band the Risk, who eventually used Roberts' own songs. He hit sprightly single form on cuts like 'Love Is Energy' - recorded with the aforementioned Eric Gooden, whom he had met at college, and is his current songwriting partner - and 'Back In My Life'.
Album: *Looking For The Here And Now* (London 1994).

Roberts Juliet

The term house diva does not fully cover the career or capabilities of Juliet Roberts, who is in addition a proficient singer/songwriter, and a veteran of the early days of British soul. Unlike many in the field, she did not learn her craft at the church choir, having instead been brought up in the more restrained Catholic faith. However, music was still in her blood. Her father was formerly a member of the calypso band the Nightingales, and took her to various concerts. Her first performances came as a member of reggae band Black Jade, before she signed solo to Bluebird Records in 1980, a label set up by her local record shop in Paddington, North London. Two tracks, a cover of the Police's 'The Bed's Too Big Without You' and 'Fool For You' emerged, while she was still engaged in her day job as a sports' tutor. They were enough to attract the attention of fellow Londoners the Funk Masters. She appeared as lead singer on their Top 10 hit, 'It's Over', in 1983. After a year's sabbatical in the US she embarked on her music career proper, and, within a week of returning to British shores, was enlisted as singer for Latin jazz band Working Week. When that group floundered (after several noble releases) she finally signed to Cooltempo as a solo artist.
Album: *Natural Thing* (Cooltempo 1994).

Robertson, Justin

Robertson (b. c.1968) is a songwriter, producer and remixer who has worked on tracks by the likes of Talk Talk ('Dum Dum Girl'), Yargo ('Love Revolution'), Finitribe ('Forevergreen'), Erasure ('Snappy'), React 2 Rhythm ('Intoxication'), Inspiral Carpets ('Caravan And Skidoo'), Shamen ('Boss Drum'), Coco Steel & Lovebomb ('Feel It'), Gary Clail ('These Things Are Worth Fighting For'), Sugarcubes ('Birthday' and 'Motorcrash'), Happy Mondays ('Sunshine And Love') and the rather less-celebrated Candy Flip ('Red Hills Road'). He was even asked to do his thing for the Fall. On his remixing ethos: 'With me its always a case of to butcher or not to butcher. Usually its the former'. His first remix was actually housed on Eastern Bloc's Creed operation (Mad Jacks' 'Feel The Hit'), and he is one of a number of famous people to have staffed that record shop's counters. He started DJing while at Manchester University, playing parties because, more or less, he had the best record collection. It was through his purchases at Eastern Bloc that he eventually landed a job there (establishing the Spice club with fellow internee, Greg Fenton). Robertson is now the motivating force behind hip Manchester outfit Lionrock, who specialise in warm, uplifting house. The group's singles include 'Packet Of Peace' (which cracked the charts and featured a rap from MC Buzz B) and 'Carnival' in 1993, which again collared numerous Single Of The Week awards. The band's full line-up boasts Justin Robertson (keyboards) and Mark Stagg (keyboards). Robertson was also behind the label which housed Lionrock's first record, MERC. This was formed with Ross McKenzie, and stood for Most Excellent Record Company. Other releases included Life Eternal's 'Come Into The Light' and Dub Federation's 'Space Funk' and 'Love Inferno' releases, prior to that group splitting in 1994. Robertson later abdicated much of his responsibility for the imprint, signing to DeConstruction as a solo artist. The mid-90s saw him raise his profile outside of dance music by touring with Primal Scream.

Rogers, Ce Ce

b. Kenny Rogers. The gentle giant from Cleveland, Ohio, Rogers is not actually a house artist *per se*, but certainly his records for Atlantic made him a hallowed name in those circles. 'Someday' sold over 100,000 copies on import before his record company finally had the good sense to release it in England as the b-side to 'Forever'. 'Someday' formed the basis for rave anthems like Liquid's 'Sweet Harmony' and Urban Shakedown's 'Some Justice', among many others. Ironically, when Marshall Jefferson first brought him the track the artist himself had little faith in it. Rogers was born the son of a music teacher, alongside three brothers and sisters, and was raised on a diet of gospel and soul. It was certainly a musical family. His rapping brother Marcski signed to CBS, while his sister Sonia is a backing vocalist (for Intense among others). Before Rogers left school he toured with the Jazz Messengers, before meeting up with the likes of Branford Marsalis at Berkeley. From there he moved to New York,

RuPaul

where Marshall Jefferson spotted him in a club leading Ce Ce And Company (who included subsequent solo artist Sybil). It was Jefferson who introduced him to Atlantic Records at the age of 25. Following 'Someday' his other great moment came with 'All Join Hands', again later re-released, this time on East West. It came with a David Morales remix, and was a second all-consuming, passionate, pure house affair.

Album: *Ce Ce Rogers* (Atlantic 1989).

Ronin

Taking its name from an ancient term for a Samurai warrior who has elected to go 'solo', Ronin Records is configured of various members of the musical tribe which used to travel under the name 23 Skidoo. In the early 90s the line-up included Alex Baby, Sketch, Johnny 2 Bad, Fritz C, Agzi and the DJing team of Force & K-Zee. The latter, as well as running their own clubs and recording music for adverts and jingles, are also well known for their contributions to the UK hip hop culture (including the *X Amount* EP for Ronin). Based in London, Ronin have their own studio complex cum living quarters. The participants have produced an admirable body of work on their own imprint, which began with Ronin Inc's 'Soul Feels Free'. The same name was behind 'On Tha Mix', while other artists include Paradox ('Jailbreak'), Bahal And Nal Street Gang ('Summer Breeze'), International Stussy Tribe Force ('Pure Power') and Normski ('Rockin' On The Dancefloor').

Rozalla

Zambian born rave queen, whose singles like 'Are You Ready To Fly?' were surefire dancefloor meteorites. She began life singing over records at fashion shows and nightclubs at age 13. She then performed with a band in Zimbabwe, going on to become that nation's most famous famale singer. At the age of 18 she appeared as an extra (a prostitute) in Richard Chamberlain's *King Solomon's Mines*. Despite parental misgivings, she subsequently launched a recording career in England. Singles like 'Everybody's Free To Feel Good' (created by 3 Man Island/Band Of Gypsies duo Nigel Swanston and Tim Cox) duly apeared on Pulse 8, who released her debut ablum. This came after something of a legal squabble, with Rozalla attempting to take the studio tapes to Epic. Pulse 8 objected and won their day in court.

Album: *Everybody's Free* (Pulse 8 1992).

RuPaul

A seven foot tall, trans-sexual American diva package. Raised in San Diego, at age 15 RuPaul took himself (as he then was) off to Atlanta, where he hung out with the B-52's and appeared on cable television. Moving to New York, he would become part of the Wigstock counter-culture that also gave birth to Deee-Lite. He subsequently became a figurehead for the US gay movement when his debut album crossed over to the mainstream, and was a chat show favourite. He has been keen to tackle the role of spokesperson, leading a demonstration against the Ku Klux Klan in full drag. He landed his own television series, and helped to present the 1994 BRIT Awards alongside a dwarfed Elton John.

Albums: *Supermodel Of The World* (Tommy Boy 1993).

S

S-1000

The moniker of Spencer Williams, who had previously remixed for the Sugarcubes and the Art Of Noise, and, alongside Paul Gotel, is half of Well Hung Parliament. 'I'm Not Gonna Do It' was a typical bouncing dub 45, while he scored further club hits with 'Flatliner' and 'Look Inside'. Williams also has the distinction of having been 'on the ground', literally, when the Los Angeles earthquake struck. He was actually in the middle of a set at the Sketch Pad in Hollywood when the earth started moving. S-1000 has now moved from Guerilla to Deep Distraxion.

Sabres Of Paradise

Andy Weatherall's favoured dance emporium, whose releases include 'Smokebelch' - arguably *the* UK techno tune of the early 90s. In addition to Weatherall, Nina Walsh helms the ship, aided by Jagz Kooner and Gary Burns. Walsh was a regular at Weatherall's Shoom evenings during the heady days of 1988's acid scene. She in turn worked for the Boy's Own stable and Youth. The duo set up their own label under the Sabres name, and released work from the likes of SYT, Blue, Secret Knowledge, Musical Science, Waxworth Industries, Jack O' Swords and the Corridor. The label operation eventually became known as Sabrettes. There was also a studio and club (based in a brick-dust cellar under London Bridge) both titled Sabresonic, as was the group's debut long

player. This seamless collection of post-Orb, dreamscape dance, with a vaguely industrial edge, increased the avalanche of plaudits which usually accompany Weatherall's best work. Together with assistants Gary and Jagz, Weatherall has turned the Sabres into one of the UK's premier remix teams. Their portfolio includes work with everyone worth noting in the dance scene, right through to hardcore rockers Therapy? Two other accomplices, Mick and Phil, help out with live work. The group have contributed one track, 'Sabres Them', to the film *Shopping*, and it seems likely that more soundtrack work will follow. Typically, despite the otherworldly grandeur of this music, the Sabres studio remains located above a Tandoori house in West Houndslow.
Album: *Sabresonic* (Sabrettes 1993).

Sabrettes

Originally titled Sabres Of Paradise, after Andy Weatherall and Nina Walsh's band of the same name, this emergent label has so far released Voodoo People's *Altitude* EP, the Cause's 'Through The Floor And Charged' (aka DJs Scott Braithwaite and Craig Walsh, Nina's brother), and two 12-inch techno opuses from Inky Blacknuss (DJ's Alex Knight and Andrea Parker). Future plans include a collaboration between Les from Holy Ghost and Anna Haigh (ex-Bocca Juniors). The label is stated to be based on Nina Walsh's personal taste. It gives her an outlet to escape the perennial 'DJ's girlfriend' tag she has found herself lumbered with, following her relationship with the much in demand Weatherall.
Album: Various: *Pink Me Up* (Sabrettes 1994).

Salt Tank

Internal Records' signings who, under the 'intelligent techo' mantle, have broken several musical barriers, notably supporting Hawkwind on live dates. Their sequence of releases runs chronilogically *ST1*, *ST2* and *ST3*, the latter EP comprising seven different 'stereotypical' approaches to modern techno, all of which are carried off with aplomb. They are a duo comprising Malcolm Stanners, who had worked with Derrick May and Kevin Saunderson in the late 80s, and partner David. They made their debut with 'Ease The Pressure'/'Charged Up'', which sold well in mainland Europe, then 1993's 'Sweli'/'Meltdown' - a record packaged to resemble a Djax-Up Beats disc, with David's phone number on the label. The first person to ring up was Andy Weatherall. *ST3* also featured samples of Simple Minds and David Byrne (Talking Heads).

Sanchez, Roger

Widely regarded as one of the hottest US remixers, New York-based Sanchez made his name with a series of devastating releases for Strictly Rhythm, such as Logic's 'One Step Beyond'. He finally made his solo long-playing bow with an album in January 1994. As might have been expected from the man who provided Juliet Roberts' with hits like 'Free Love' and 'Caught In The Middle', it preferred a blend of sweet soul and house. It was released under the acronym, Roger S, already familiar through his remixes for Michael Jackson and others. Graced by the deep house vocals of Jay Williams, it reinstated his integrity in the underground dance scene at a time when he was handling more and more major league clients. It was released on One Records, which he jointly owns with Eddie Colon. He also set up a management company with UK partner Marts Andrups (who also represents Benji Candelario and Danny Tenaglia in Europe), titled Indeep, signing artists like vocalist Melodie Washington. Sanchez was also partly behind the Sound Of One hit, 'As I Am', for Cooltempo, and Logic's 'One Step Beyond'. He also produced an album for Kathy Sledge, among sundry other projects.
Album: *Secret Weapons Vol. 1* (One Records 1994).

Sandals

Nouveau hippies the Sandals consist of Derek (vocals; ex-Espresso 7, A Man Called Adam), John Harris (flute, vocals), Ian and Wild Cat Will. Signed to Acid Jazz, they confessed to being conceptual recording artists rather than musicians, specialising in a Latin-tinged trance-funk, and operating in the manner of a 60s collective. They came together initially in a seedy Soho bar in the summer of 1987, organising a 60s style 'happening' night, with poetry readings, party games and jazz spots. Since then they have opened a shop, Rich And Strange, which sells their art and second-hand fashion. After which they also started their own club night, Tongue Kung Fu, which was exported to Los Angeles, Tokyo and Istanbul. They run their own label too, the appropriately titled Open Toe stable. Their third single, 'Profound Gas', was remixed by old friends Leftfield (Derek having been a one-time member of A Man Called Adam with Leftfield's Paul Daley), while 'We Wanna Live' was produced as a 'live remix' by the Disco Evangelists and Sabres Of Paradise - with all three parties present on the studio take, working together.

Sasha

Wales-born Manchester-based 'top DJ pin-up' whose regular nights include Renaissance

(Manchester) and La Cotta (Birmingham). A former fish-farm worker and grade eight pianist, after pioneering Italian house in 1989 and 1990 he made his name with a jazzy, garage style as a remixer on projects like Mr Fingers' 'Closer' and Urban Soul's 'He's Always' and 'Alright'. Sasha moved to DeConstruction in 1993 in a three album deal. Most had expected him to sign with Virgin following the success of his BM:Ex (Barry Manilow Experience) cut, 'Appolonia', a double-pack 12-inch with a running time of over an hour, on their Union City Recordings subsidiary. 'Appolonia' originally emerged as an obscure Italian white label promo, and was a record Sasha played regularly at the end of his sets at Shelley's in Stoke without ever being able to discover the identity of its originators. As nobody could find out any further details he decided to re-record it himself. The first result of the liaison with DeConstruction was 'Higher Ground', constructed with production partner Tom Frederikse and vocalist Sam Mollison. He also provided a single, 'Quat', for Cowboy, who were originally set to release 'Feel The Drop', which ended up as the b-side to 'Appolonia'. Sasha was also signed up to PolyGram Music in 1993 for publishing, indicating that at last dance songwriters were beginning to be taken seriously by the music industry, rather than as short-term recording artists. As Sasha himself expounded: 'I've plans for bigger things. I don't want to be restricted by the dancefloor. That's where my inspiration is, but I want to do something with a little more longevity than the latest number 1 on the Buzz chart'. He has thus far turned down interview opportunities with the *Daily Mirror* and *Sun*. Among his many other remix/production clients have been Ce Ce Rogers, Unique 3 and soundtrack composer Barrington Pheloung.

Scanner

Named after the hand-held device which can intercept telephone and radio calls, Scanner comprise the duo of Robin Rimbaud (b. c.1964) and Steve Williams - who are regularly on patrol to pick up conversations on mobile phones, replaying them alongside their own studio sounds. In turn their recordings were adorned with some of the more memorable/bizarre findings they had tuned in to with their own scanner, from aural pornography to static and more everyday conversation. These delights had graced two albums for Ash International by 1994. The equipment was originally purchased from a group of fellow hunt sabateurs who were using it to monitor police movements. Rimbaud also runs the Electronic Lounge, a monthly 'event' in the ICA bar, and lectured on the art of 'scanning' at London University. The duo have remixed for Autechre and Reload.

Schutze, Paul

b. Australia. With a background in industrial/*avant garde* music, notably the Melbourne jazz artists Laughing Hands and film scores, Schutze was quick to see the possibilities in the artistic marketplace opened up by techno. Although *More Beautiful Human Life* was his first recording for R&S subsidiary Apollo, it was in fact his sixth album in total. This was a collage of sounds and noises melded into a cinematic narrative, underpinned by his studies of Indian percussion and tabla music. Schutze has also undertaken remixing chores for guitar bands like Main and Bark Psychosis, in an attempt to broaden both his and their musical palates.
Selected albums: *New Maps Of Hell* (Extreme 1994). As Uzect Plaush: *More Beautiful Human Life* (Apollo 1994).

Secret Knowledge

Dance collective featuring singer Wonder (b. West Virginia, USA) and Kris Needs, a man with a long and shady history. His chequered past includes stints in greaseball pub rockers the Vice Creems, and a part-time position as John Otway's bongo player. He began writing for *ZigZag* magazine in 1975 going on to take over the editorship in 1977. In the 80s and 90s he concentrated on writing dance reviews for *Echoes* and other magazines. Wonder meanwhile had formerly fronted a Munich, Germany-based jazz/blues band titled Strange Fruit. Unlike many of the predominantly soul-based female vocalists who regularly add their voices to house/trance cuts, Wonder is responsible for writing lyrics as well as the occasional melody (including 'Sugar Daddy'). The duo met together in the late 80s in New York, recording a one-off rap single together, 'Rap Too Tight'. Once they had returned to the UK, and Needs had discovered the burgeoning acid house movement, they cut their first track under the Secret Knowledge flag: 'Your Worst Nightmare'. Influenced by the deep house of New York's Strictly Rhythm label, they followed their debut with 'Ooh Baby', one of the first releases on Andy Weatherall's Sabres Of Paradise label. Next up came one of the biggest club hits of 1993, 'Sugar Daddy'. It has been reported that this 'orgasmic' track was used widely to help stimulate sexual relief in prisons and detention centres throughout Britain. In its wake Secret Knowledge were elevated to the status of

Kevin Saunderson see Inner City/Reese Project

hot producers/remixers. Among their other collaborative monikers are Delta Lady (Secret Knowledge under a different name reflecting a more urbane, funk-based side to their nature), 4 Boy 1 Girl Action (whose 'Hawaiian Death Stomp' combined Needs with David Holmes and members of the Sabres enclave), the Rabettes (featuring Weatherall's girlfriend Nina's assorted rabbits and guinea pigs), Hutchbern, The Pecking Order (featuring various impersonations of chickens) and Codpeace (with Alex Peterson of the Orb). Needs has also stepped out as a remix artist, converting artists from many fields incuding the Boo Radleys. They clashed with the compilers of the excellent Trance Europe Express 2 in mid-1994 over their contribution, 'Afterworld'. The lyrics addressed Wonder's cousin, an AIDS sufferer, but the track was deemed to be out of context on an otherwise instrumental set. While compromises were still being discussed a vocal-less version was 'inadvertently' included instead, as Needs discovered after returning from touring with Primal Scream. They issued the 'correct' version on Kris' Stolen Karots label instead.

Secret Life

Band whose principals include Charton Antenbring (DJ and club reporter for The Big Issue), Andy Throup (classically trained pianist and studio owner) and Paul Bryant (vocals). However, Secret Life is officially an umbrella organisation with a number of producers and musicians (notably Throup's fellow studio co-owner Jim Di Salvo) also contributing. They made headlines together with 1992's 'As Always' cut for Cowboy (whose Charlie Chester manages the band), which was among that label's biggest successes. It was based on Stevie Wonder's 'Songs In The Key Of Life' (which had previously been issued in a 'house' version by Chicago-based Ricky Dillard of Nightwriters' fame).

Seefeel

An intriguing combination of introspective ambient (though they abhor the term) textures and propulsive guitars have distinguished Seefeel's nascent career. Guitarist and songwriter Mark Clifford answered an advert which Justin Fletcher (drums) had placed on a noticeboard at Goldsmith's College, London. They added Darren 'Delores Throb' Seymour (bass) and set about auditioning over 70 hopefuls for the singer's job. In the end Clifford responded to another ad, 'Wanting to join or form band into My Bloody Vlanetine and Sonic Youth', and called ex-animation student Sarah Peacock, who had placed it. As her tastes reflected

Seefeel's personal creed, a distillation of MBV's guitar abuse with ambient's drone, she was immediately taken on board. The made their recording debut with the More Like Space EP - which confused BBC Radio 1 DJ John Peel as to whether to play it at 33rpm or 45rpm. Two EPs and an album for Too Pure quickly followed, 'Pure, Impure' featuring a spectral Aphex Twin remix. They also collaborated and toured with heroes the Cocteau Twins (the question Clifford asked Sarah when he rang her up was whether or not she liked them). Another EP in 1994, Starethrough, was their first for Warp, and again provoked interest, coinciding with and reflecting a move from indie to dance coverage in the UK music weeklies.
Album: Quique (Too Pure 1993).

7669

Four New York New Jill Swingers (they prefer the term new ghetto revolutionary music) with rap's hardcore attitude, 7669 arrived on the scene in 1994 amid a swirl of deliberately provocative press shots, notably topless poses astride large motorcycles, which also graced the album cover. Less readily apparent was the fact that the backdrop of shrubbery was in fact a 'field of pot'. Their name was taken from the year of US indepedence (1776) crossed with the 'date' of the sexual revolution (1969). The members; Shorti-1-Forti, Big Angel, El Boog-E and Thickness, preferred songs with dubious titles like '69 Ways To Love A Black Man' and 'Cloud 69', the duplicity of lascivious titles being an obvious clue to the lack of imagination inherent in the project. However, the production, helmed by Kangol, Ali Dee and Forceful, was enough to make proceedings listenable.
Album: East From A Bad Block (Motown/Polydor 1994).

S'Express

Home to Mark Moore (b. 12 January 1965, London, England), who was aruably the best British interpretor of the late 80s Italo-house phenomenon. Moore is half-Korean, though his early claims that he had a twin brother in that nation's army were spurious. More factual were the revelations that he was put into care at the age of nine, when his mother had a breakdown. As a youth he ligged outside Siouxsie & The Banshees gigs begging 10 pence pieces to get in. After the punk explosion, the first time he felt he belonged to anything, he made his name on the domestic DJ circuit, notably the Mud Club. At one point his record collection was so large he was forced to have his flat strengthened. He broke through with

a series of singles which combined Euro-pop stylings with a hard funk spine: 'Theme From S'Express', 'Superfly Guy', 'Hey Music Lover' and 'Mantra For A State Of Mind' among them. After which the chart action dissipated somewhat. 'Nothing To Lose', ironically one of his strongest singles, stalled at number 32, as dance music upped a gear and discovered hardcore. Moore set up the Splish label, through Rhythm King, in the early 90s, opening with Canadian-born singer Tiziana's 'Seduce Me' and Yolanda's 'Living For The Nite', licensed from Underground Resistance. Former S'Express vocalist Linda Love would go on to record with Word Of Mouth ('What It Is (Ain't Losing Control)'). A delayed second album *Intercourse* failed to revive S'Express fortunes, despite the gifted vocal presence of Sonique. A sample of John Waters ('Bad taste is what entertainment is all about') preceded a demonstrably shabby, tongue in cheek rendition of 'Brazil' on the album's best track. Moore would continue to earn a crust as a remixer however, notably on Malcolm McLaren's 'Something's Jumpin' In Your Shirt' (with William Orbit) and Saffron's 'Fluffy Toy' (with Peter Lorimer).
Albums: *Original Soundtrack* (Rhythm King 1989), *Intercourse* (Rhythm King 1992).

Shamen

From the ashes of the moderately successful Alone Again Or (named after the track from Love's *Forever Changes*) in 1986, the Shamen had a profound effect upon contemporary pop music over the next half decade. Formed in Aberdeen by Colin Angus (b. 24 August 1961, Aberdeen, Scotland; bass), Peter Stephenson (b. 1 March 1962, Ayrshire, Scotland), Keith McKenzie (b. 30 August 1961, Aberdeen, Scotland) and Derek McKenzie (b. 27 February 1964, Aberdeen, Scotland; guitar), the Shamen's formative stage relied heavily on crushing, psychedelic rock played by a relatively orthodox line-up. Their debut album, *Drop*, captured a sense of their colourful live shows and sealed the first chapter of the band's career. Soon after, Colin Angus became fascinated by the nascent underground hip hop movement. Derek McKenzie was rather less enamoured with the hardcore dance explosion and departed, allowing William Sinnott (b. 23 December 1960, Glasgow, Scotland, d. 23 May 1991; bass) to join the ranks and further encourage the Shamen's move towards the dancefloor. In 1988, their hard-edged blend of rhythms, guitars, samples, sexually explicit slideshows and furious rhetoric drew anger from feminists, politicians and - after the scathing 'Jesus Loves Amerika' single - religious groups.

That same year the band relocated to London, slimmed down to the duo of Angus and Sinnott who concentrated on exploring the areas of altered states with mind-expanding psychedelics. By 1990 the Shamen's influence - albeit unwitting - was vividly realised as the much-touted indie-dance crossover saw bands fuse musical cultures with the likes of Jesus Jones openly confessing to the Shamen's groundbreaking lead. By this time the Shamen themselves had taken to touring with the 'Synergy' show, a unique four hour extravaganza designed to take the band even further away from their rock roots. After four years of such imaginative adventures into sound, 1991 promised a huge breakthrough for the Shamen and their fluctuating creative entourage. Unfortunately, just as the group inexorably toppled towards commercial riches, Will Sinnott drowned off the coast of Gomera, one of the Canary Islands, on the 23rd of May. With the support of Sinnott's family, the Shamen persevered with a remix of 'Move Any Mountain (Pro Gen '91)' which climbed into the Top 10 of the UK chart, a fitting farewell to the loss of such a creative force. Mr C (b. Richard West), a cockney rapper, DJ and head of the Plink Plonk record label, had joined the band for a section of 'Move Any Mountain (Pro Gen '91)'. Although many found his patois ill-fitting, his rhymes founded the springboard for UK chart success 'LSI', followed by the number 1 'Ebeneezer Goode' - which was accused in many quarters for extolling the virtues of the Ecstasy drug ('E's Are Good, E's Are Good, E's Are Ebeneezer Goode'). The Shamen denied all, and moved on with the release of *Boss Drum*. Its title track provided a deeply affecting dance single, complete with lyrics returning the band to their original, shamanic ethos of universal rhythms. Placed next to the teen-pop of 'LSI' and 'Ebeneezer Goode', such innovative work reinforced the Shamen's position as the wild cards of the UK dance scene.
Albums: *Drop* (Moshka 1987), *In Gorbachev We Trust* (Demon 1989), *Phorward* (Moshka 1989), *En-Tact* (One Little Indian 1990), *En-Tek* (One Little Indian 1990), *Progeny* (One Little Indian 1991), *Boss Drum* (One Little Indian 1992), *Different Drum* (One Little Indian 1992), *The Shamen On Air* (Band Of Joy 1993).

Sharp, Jonah

Ambient artist lcoated in San Francisco who records as Space Time Continuum on his own Reflective Records. In 1993 he undertook an album with Peter Namlock for Fax, and a second collection with Californian hippy mystic Terrence

McKenna for Caroline. Originally a jazz and session drummer in the UK, he played at several London parties as a DJ before relocating to the US. He has since set up a new studio in San Francisco. As well as his own *Flourescence* EP, other Reflective releases have included a Namlock remix CD and a techno-flavoured 12-inch by emiT ecapS.

Shut Up And Dance

Hip hop/house artists PJ and Smiley (both b. c.1969) comprise this duo, who are also producers and owners of the Shut Up And Dance Rerord label (run from a bedroom in Stoke Newington). The group formed in Spring 1988, the record label coming a year later. This has seen releases by the Ragga Twins ('Spliffhead'), Nicolette and Rum & Black. Shut Up And Dance all began with the intoxicating club cut '5678', which eventually moved over 14,000 copies. This helped fund Shut Up And Dance as a full-scale label enterprise, with a penchant for the absurd. Their own '£10 To Get In' and 'Derek Went Mad' being good examples. One 12-inch, 'Lamborghini', stitched together Prince and Annie Lennox (Eurythmics), and though it made the UK Top 60 radio stations refused to play it fearing punitive writs. The duo had originally recorded a novelty single under the name Private Party which featured various characters from the *Thunderbirds* and *Muppets* television programmes. Their anonymity was enhanced by the lack of detail which usually accompanied their releases, helping them become leaders in the UK's underground dance scene. Musically they spliced their recordings with samples drawn from a myriad of sources; running the gamut from dub reggae through to techno beats. However, it was the number 2 chart smash 'Ravin' I'm Ravin'' (sung by Peter Bouncer) which brought them real commercial attention, more than they either envisaged or welcomed. It also sent copyright lawyers into apopletic overdrive. They spent almost two years struggling in court following action taken by the MCPS on behalf of six major record companies for uncleared use of samples. Although they returned with an EP in 1994, the appropriately titled *Phuck The Biz*, their legal problems were far from over, their business having long since been declared bankrupt. It would be a shame if their brushes with the law overshadowed classic records like 1992's 'Autobiography Of A Crack Head'.
Albums: *Dance Before The Police Come* (Shut Up And Dance 1990), *Death Is Not The End* (Shut Up And Dance 1992).

Silent Records

San Francisco label headed by managing director Kim Cascone, who had previously been in charge of sound on two David Lynch movies, *Twin Peaks* and *Wild At Heart*. Formed in 1989 (the first release being PGR's 'Silent', which gave the label a name), the company is the ultimate ambient/subsconscious operation, based on a desire to experiment with the dynamics and properties of sound. Cascone's own Heavenly Music Corporation is but one of the names on the catalogue, whose discography included over 50 records by 1994. Others include Cosmic Trigger, Michael Mantra, Spice Barons and Thessolonians. The label is best sampled on the popular compilation series, *From Here To Eternity*. 'What we're about is open systems, an inclusive kind of nurturing of ideas, and of using people who have some kind of a different spin on the genre'.

Simonelli, Victor

b. c.1967, USA. Brooklyn-based producer who learnt his craft at the knee of Arthur Baker, working in his Shakedown Studio. After editing work on tracks by Al Jarreau and David Bowie, he joined Lenny Dee to establish Brooklyn Street Essentials, a remix team. He has worked widely in this territory ever since. His own *nom de plumes* included Groove Committee (cutting 'Dirty Games' for Nu Groove), Solution, Ebony Soul and the Street Players. Throughout he has maintained his belief in working with fully-fledged songs rather than simply strong rhythmic tracks. He has recently recorded with Tommy Musto as part of Colourblind.

Slam

Like so many techno operations, Glasgow-based Slam are a duo, comprising Orde Meikle and Stuart McMillan. And, again like others in the field, they do not limit themselves to one activity. They DJ regularly at the Arches and Sub Sub clubs in Glasgow, and are also responsible for running the pre-eminent Soma label, as well as remixing for A Man Called Adam, Sunscreem ('Love You More'), Perception, Mark Bell, Botany 5, DSK ('What Could We Do'), Joey Negro and Kym Sims ('Too Blind To See'). Slam took clubland by storm in 1992 with 'Eterna', repeating the feat in 1994 via their no-holds-barred revision of Jean Michel Jarre's 'Chronologie 6'. After attending outdoor raves in Berlin, Holland, and Belgium, Jarre confessed he rather liked what they had done to his opus. Slam were less charitable: 'I read an interview with Jarre which gave me the impression that he's very excited about the European dance scene, but doesn't quite understand it and doesn't have the right contacts. So we had no qualms about ripping his track to pieces'.

Slater, Luke

b. c.1968, St Albans, Hertfordshire, England. Techno guru Slater mixes hair-raising darkside nuances with somnambulist ambient doodlings, occasionally revisiting the 303 sound with releases like 'Sea Serpent'. Of half-American, half-Korean descent, he is now based in Crawley, Sussex. Slater has recorded under a multitude of pseudonyms (Marganistic, Clementine, Planetary Assault System, Offset) for a variety of labels (D-Jax Up Beats, Spacehopper, Loaded, his own Jelly Jam). He has been heralded in some quarters as the UK torch bearer for the Detroit sound, particularly through his work with Planetary Sound Assault. However, as 7th Plain his music has mined a deeper shaft, and is in many ways divorced from dance music in any previous convention, alluding instead to classical textures. The presence of a strong strings quotient on the *Four Cornered Room* set prefigured the rise of the classical ambient movement that was beginning to take hold in the mid-90s.
Album: *X-Tront - Volume 2* (1993). As 7th Plain: *Four Cornered Room* (General Productions 1994).

Slip 'n' Slide Records

Slip 'n' Slide was launched as a subsidiary of Kickin' Records for less hardcore tastes in 1993. The first record to cause a major ripple was Adonte's house track 'Dreams', mixed by Pete Lorimer. In the year of their inception they continued to plough a bold furrow with hits by Diggers ('Soweto', produced by Lyndsay Edwards of Disco Evangelists fame), the trance house of H.A.L.F. ('I Don't Need You Any More') and Soundscape ('Amoxa'), while club hits were provided by Boomshanka ('Gonna Make You Move', though the duo also record for their own Can Can imprint as Avarice) and Rock & Kato ('Jungle Kisses'). The label also licensed a compilation from German imprint Suck Me Plasma! (Dance 2 Trance, Norman etc.), and scored with Vivian Lee's 'Music Is So Wonderful' (remixed by Fire Island). Other artists include 3 Man Jury ('Digital Autopsy'), Decoy ('Open Your Mind'), John Bullock (whose 'Hendrix' sampled one of the great man's riffs), Men Of Faith ('Dance') and more.
Selected album: *Dance & Trance* (Slip 'N' Slide 1993).

SL2

SL2 consist of two Essex-based DJs, Slipmatt (b. Matthew Nelson, c.1967) and Lime (b. John Fernandez, c.1968), joined by video 'stars' Jo and Kelly for live appearances. Already well established as DJs on the rave circuit, they introduced themselves to a wider audience with debut single 'Do That Dance', a more acid-influenced cut, and 'The Noise'. The impact proved to be small beer against that of the subsequent 'DJ's Take Control', which disappeared from its original 1,000 pressing on Awesome within two hours, before being picked up by XL. The song was built around a keyboard line from the Nightwriter's 1987 underground house cut, 'Let The Music Use You'. The b-side, 'Way In My Brain', hoisted one of reggae's most profligate bass lines, 'Under Me Sleng Ten'. It predicted the chart breakthrough of their next single, 'On A Ragga Tip', which brought the jungle style into the charts for the first time, and gave SL2 a Top 10 placing in their own right. This time it was built over a rhythm based on Jah Screechie's 'Walk And Skank'.

Sly And Lovechild

Curious duo who debuted with the singles 'The World According To' and 'Rainbow', whose stormy relationship led to them being described as the Ike & Tina Turner of the dance scene (on-stage bitings notwithstanding). People were allegedly so desperate to get into their 1992 gig at Manchester's Most Excellent night that disgruntled punters ram-raided the doors, an experience described as 'exciting' by vocalist Elliot Lovechild. Together with 'Sly' Simon, their stated intention was to bring glamour back to faceless dance music. They broke through with 'Spirit Of Destiny'. 'We're quite ahead of our time because the dance scene hasn't really thrown up any strong songwriters or people with longevity' was their claim.
Album: *The World According To* (Citybeat 1993).

Smith And Mighty

Bristol duo comprising Rob Smith and Ray Mighty who broke through in 1988 with two memorable cover versions of Bacharach/David songs, 'Anyone' and 'Walk On By'. Both were effortless, breezy interpretations of the originals, tuned up via dub house and hip hop stylings, garnished with the sensitive addition of female vocals. London Records were first off the mark in signing them up, having previously worked on their own Three Stripe imprint (which also issued records like Tru Funk's '4AM (The Lucid Phase)'). However, the momentum was lost when the debut

LP for Bristolian artist Carlton bombed. Smith and Mighty's reputation for the Midas touch went down with that album, and in the fast-changing world of dance music they became yesterday's men. However, they persevered in relative silence (as well as fathering six children between them), re-emerging in 1994 with a new album and single, a cover of Diana Ross's 'Remember Me', featuring their new vocal discovery, Marilyn. Their highly individual breakbeat style, which remained with them over the years, was to be sampled on the U2 cover, 'Drowning Man', while elsewhere the album contained denser material akin to the 'jungle' movement. Underpinning it all, however, was the seismic bass which had characterised their early recordings, their philosophy on low frequency incorporated into the album' title.
Album: *Bass Is Maternal - When It's Loud, I Feel Safer* (London 1994).

Smooth, Joe

b. Joseph Welbon, USA. One of early house music's most distinctive vocalists, recording material like 'Time To Jack' and working with Fingers Inc. He actually started out as a DJ in 1983 at the Smart Bar in Chicago. There the staff were so impressed by his mixing that they dubbed him Joe Smooth for the first time. A genuine musician, he insisted on bringing his keyboards and drum machine on stage with him for his live shows. He went on to produce two house classics in 'You Can't Hide' (with Frankie Knuckles) and 'Promised Land' (later covered by the Style Council). His debut album featured guest vocals rather than his own as he concentrated on his musicianship. The singers included Anthony Thomas, former backing vocalist to the Ohio Players. The set included both 'Promised Land' and an unlikely Jimi Hendrix cover in 'Purple Haze'.

Snap!

Durron Butler (b. Maurice Durron Butler, 30 April 1967, Pittsburgh, Pennsylvania, USA) was initally a drummer with a heavy metal band in his hometown. Later he joined the army and was posted to Germany where he became a bomb disposal expert. Whilst there he teamed up with Rico Sparx and Moses P. for several musical projects. After his discharge he returned to the States but went back to Germany to tour with the Fat Boys. German based producers Benito Benites (b. Michael Munzing) and John Garrett Virgo III (b. Luca Anzilotti), operating under pseudonyms, had put together a project they would call Snap!, after a function on a sequencing programme. Previously the producers had recorded widely in

their Frankfurt studio, for their own label, Logic Records (whose former A&R man, Mark Spoon, is now part of Jam And Spoon). They also ran their own club, Omen. Notable successes prior to Snap! included the 16-Bit Project ('Where Are You' and 'High Score') and Off's 'Electric Salsa', which featured Sven Vath as frontman and singer. They then recorded a song called 'The Power' which was built from samples of New York rapper Chill Rob G's 'Let The Rhythm Flow'. They added the powerful female backing vocals of Penny Ford, who had previously worked with George Clinton, Chaka Khan and Mica Paris, amongst others. Jackie Harris (b. Jaqueline Arlissa Harris, Pittsburgh, USA) was also credited for providing 'guide' vocals, and appeared in press interviews. The record was first released on the Wild Pitch label in America with the credit 'Snap featuring Chill Rob G'. However, after the first 30,000 sales problems with Chill Rob G (b. Robert Frazier) began to manifest themselves and they sought a replacement. They chose Butler, who was now rechristened Turbo G. He had already recorded for Logic as back-up rapper for Moses P. Chill Rob G was allowed to release his own version of 'The Power' in America. Around the rest of the world a new cut, featuring Turbo G, topped the charts. To promote the record he and Ford toured widely, before the latter embarked on a solo career. She was replaced by Thea Austin. Throughout Benites and Garrett utilised Turbo G as the public face of Snap!, remaining shadowy figures back in their Frankfurt studio, which was now a hugely impressive complex. Though they continued to score colossal hits with 'Oops Upside Your Head' and 'Mary Had A Little Boy', dissent had set in within their ranks. Turbo wanted more artistic imput, and hated 'Rhythm Is A Dancer' the projected lead-off single for the band's second album. When a substitute, 'The Colour Of Love', crashed, the duo went ahead without his agreement. Their judgement was proved correct when 'Rhythm Is A Dancer' became another international smash (the biggest selling UK single of the year). But by now the rift between the parties was irreconcilable. Turbo G had signed up for a solo career (debuting with 'I'm Not Dead' on Polydor) while the Snap! single was still climbing in several territories. Austin too found herself a solo contract. The producers proved that they could survive without a front man when 'Exterminate', the first record not to feature Turbo G, became another million-seller.
Album: *World Power* (Arista 1990), *The Madman's Return* (Arista 1992).
Video: *World Power* (1990).

Soho

Identical twin sisters Jackie (Jacquie Juanita Cuff) and Pauline (Pauline Osberga Cuff) were both born on 25 November 1962 in Wolverhampton, England. Together with guitarist Tim London (b. Timothy Brinkhurst, 20 November 1960) they comprise the briefly successful dance band Soho. They started singing in the early 80s as student nurses in St Albans. After meeting London they became Tim London's Orgasm, and Tim London and the Soho sisters before settling on Soho. London had left school in 1977 and played in several small punk bands. Another early member was Nigel Dukey 'D' who left in 1989. They signed to Virgin for early singles 'You Won't Hold Me Down' (1988), and 'Message From My Baby' (1989). However, these and their first LP proved flops. Despite garnering lots of press, their brand of dance was a little less frenetic than the burgeoning acid house scene and they were dropped from the label in 1989. They spent the next year singing covers in an Italian disco, before signing a new deal with Savage Tam Records. Their breakthrough came with their second single for the label, 'Hippychick', which sampled Johhny Marr's guitar effervescence from the Smiths 'How Soon Is Now'. Lyrically, it challenged the prevailing new age ethos of blissful hegemony ('Got no flowers for your gun'). However, Soho proved unable to capitalise on the Transatlantic success of the single. Tim and Jacqueline had a daughter in 1993, Charlie, and they were encouraged back into the studio for a new album to celebrate his arrival.
Albums: *Noise* (Virgin 1989), *Goddess* (Savage 1991), *The View* (1994).

Soma Records

Scottish record label based in Otago Street, Glasgow, opened in August 1992 and championed by Orde Meikle and Stuart McMillan, better known as the duo behind Slam. Other members of the team are Dave Clark, Nigel Hurst, Jim Muotone and Glen Gibbons. The latter two are Slam's studio engineers, played the major role in starting the Soma imprint, and also record for the label as Rejuvenation (*Work In Progress* 1992, 'Requiem' 1993, 'Sychophantasy' 1994). Slam had originally been an all-night party convention which evolved into an umbrella remix-production team. A record label was the obvious next step: 'Soma was set up to fill a void in Scottish music', noted Meikle. 'No one was paying attention to dance music here, so the label is a medium or catalyst for some of these people who are very talented, but don't have the confidence to approach a major record company down south'.

Early signings included Rejuvenation, Dove and G7. Dove released 'Fallen' for them, before becoming One Dove and moving to Boy's Own. Amongst other triumphs, the label housed Otaku's 'Percussion Obsession', the first vinyl outing for Back To Basic's Ralph Lawson, Sharkimaxx's 'Clashback' (aka Felix Da Housecat) and Piece & Jammin's *One For The Road* EP.

Soul II Soul

Highly succesful rap, soul and R&B group primarily consisting of Jazzie B (b. Beresford Romeo, January 26 1963, London, England; rapper), Nellee Hooper (musical arrangement) and Philip 'Daddae' Harvey (multi instrumentalist). The name Soul II Soul originally described Jazzie B and Harvey's company supplying DJs and PA systems to dance acts. They also held a number of warehouse raves, particularly at Paddington Dome, near Kings Cross, before setting up their own venue. There they met Hooper, formerly of the Wild Bunch and currently a member of Massive Attack. Joining forces, they took up a residency at Covent Garden's African Centre before signing to Virgin subsidiary Ten. Following the release of two singles, 'Fairplay' and 'Feel Free', the band's profile grew with the aid of fashion T-shirts, two shops and Jazzie B's slot on the then pirate Kiss-FM radio station. However, their next release would break not only them but vocalist Caron Wheeler (b. 19 January 1963) as 'Keep On Movin' reached number 5 in the UK charts. The follow-up, 'Back To Life (However Do You Want Me)' once more featured Wheeler, and was taken from their debut *Club Classics Volume One*. The ranks of the Soul II Soul collective had swelled to incorporate a myriad of musicians, whose input was evident in the variety of styles employed. Wheeler soon left to take up a solo career, but the band's momentum was kept intact by 'Keep On Movin' penetrating the US clubs and the album scaling the top of the UK charts. 'Get A Life' was a further expansion on the influential stuttering rhythms which the band had previously employed on singles, but Jazzie B and Hooper's arrangement of Sinead O'Conners UK number 1 'Nothing Compares To You' was a poignant contrast. Other artists who sought their services included Fine Young Cannibals and Neneh Cherry. The early part of 1990 was spent in what amounted to business expansion, with a film company, a talent agency and an embryonic record label all branching out from the Soul II Soul organisation. The band's second album duly arrived half way through the year, incorporating Courtney Pine and Kym Mazelle amongst a star studded cast. However, despite entering the charts at number 1 it was given a frosty reception by some critics who saw it as comparitively conservative. Mazelle would also feature on the single 'Missing You', as Jazzie B unveiled the (ill-fated) new label Funki Dred, backed by Motown. As for a definition of what Soul II Soul are, Jazzie B is uncomplicated: 'Its a sound system...an organisation (which) came together to build upon making careers for people who had been less fortunate within the musical and artistic realms'.

Albums: *Club Classics Volume I* (Ten 1989), *Volume II: 1990 A New Decade* (Ten 1990), *Just Right Volume III* (Ten 1992). Compilation: *Volume IV - The Classic Singles 88-93* (Virgin 1993).

Soulsonics

Seen as a West Coast answer to the Brand New Heavies, Soulsonics are one of the first native American flowerings of what that continent terms 'urban alternative' (more specifically Acid Jazz in UK parlance). The group were formed by Willie McNeil (b. Kansas, Misouri, USA; drums, ex-Animal Dance, formerly a cohort of Joe Strummer) and Jez Colin (b. England; bass). Primarily a live attraction, the band were inaugurated after Colin had returned home to London and caught the energy of the Talkin' Loud movement at Dingwalls nightclub. Determined to export that culture to Los Angeles, he formed the King King club with McNeil. The Soulsonics grew out of the club, initially as a quartet, with regular jamming sessions slowly extending the band's roster. Rather than a direct copy of UK groups like Galliano, Soulsonics tempered their fusion with a more specifically Latin flavour of Jazz, a style that has always been popular within California.

Album: *Jazz In The Present Tense* (Chrysalis 1993).

Sounds Of Blackness

Led by bodybuilder Gary Hines, a former Mr Minnesota, Sounds Of Blackness are a gospel/soul 40-piece choir whose work has also torn up the dance charts. Stranger still, perhaps, was the fact that they broke though so late in their career. They were 20 years old as an outfit when they came to prominence in 1991. Hines took them over from their original incarnation as the Malcalaster College Black Choir in January 1971, running the group on a strict code of ethics and professional practices. The rulebook is sustained by the long waiting list of aspiring members, and Hines' self-appointed role as 'benevolent dictator'. They first made the charts under the aegis of Jimmy Jam and Terry Lewis, who had spotted the band and used them for backing vocals on their productions for Alexander O'Neal. In turn they used the choir to launch their new record label, Perspective, scoring almost immediately with 'Optimistic'. Released in 1991, it single-handedly sparked off a revival in the fortunes of gospel music. The album which housed it went on to win a Grammy award, as 'The Pressure' and 'Testify' also charted. Recent singles have again, via remixes from the likes of Sasha, and hugely emotive vocals from Ann Bennett-Nesby, proved extremely popular in the thoroughly secular arena of the club scene. Hines is ecstatic rather than hesitant about this, insisting that their message can seep through despite the environment. Sounds Of Blackness also sang 'Gloryland', alongside Daryl Hall, as the official theme to the 1994 World Cup.

Albums: *The Evolution Of Gospel* (Perspective/A&M 1991), *The Night Before Christmas - A Musical Fantasy* (Perspective/A&M 1992), *Africa To America* (Perspective/A&M 1994).

Speedy J

Speedy J (b. Jochem Paap, c.1969, Rotterdam, Holland) is a successful solo artist who started DJing in the early 80s and earned his nickname through his fast mixing and scratching technique. After picking up the house bug from America, he began to extend his musical set-up with drum machines and synthesizers and made the evolutionary leap to recording artist. His first efforts, 'Lift Off' and 'Take Me There', were released on a 12-inch compilation on Hithouse Records. Afterwards he hooked up with Detroit label Plus 8 for the *Intercontinental* EP. Between this and a second EP for the label, *Evolution*, he also recorded a 12-inch for R&S (as Tune), and worked with Holland label Stealth. A track on the Plus 8 compilation *From Our Minds To Yours Volume 1*, 'Pullover', might have proved just another footnote had it not been picked up in the clubs and given subsequent release by Music Man. It eventually went Top 40 in several territories. A third Plus 8 EP, *Rise*, featured another big club hit in the live track, 'Something For Your Mind'. However, he was beginning to become stereotyped as a conventional, basic house operator, where his vision was originally broader. Consequently he developed the Public Energy pseudonym for such hard house material, from thence forward recording more divergent, experimental work as Speedy J. He was largely quiet during recording sessions for his debut album, aside from remixes for the Shamen and Bjork. When 'Pepper', the album's promotional single emerged it was housed on Warp, except for Benelux territories where Paap invoked his own Beam Me Up! label in association with Gijs Vroom (Vroom and Beyond) and Rene Van Der Weyde (TFX, Atlantic Ocean's

'Waterfall', etc.), and on Plus 8 in the US and Canada. Other releases on Beam Me Up! include Resonant Interval's 'Memory'. Paap also records as Country And Western. This moniker was utilised to house the first 'Positive Energy' release, which was originally a dancefloor hit for Speedy J on the Canadian techno label, Plus 8. It was remixed under this title with the aid of Effective's Simon Hannon and Lawrence Nelson. Paap went on to remix for Killing Joke in continuance of his hectic career.
Album: *Intrusion* (Warp 1993).

Spiral Tribe

At the forefront of alternative culture and its attempts to embrace the new sounds of the 90s, Spiral Tribe will probably never leave their crusty-techno reputation far behind. Not that it would seem to unduly worry them. As part of the free festival movement, members have personal injunctions against them in most parts of England. Indeed, they headed to Europe in mid-1993 where legislation against travelling musicians is much more relaxed. They see music as a fluid, evolving medium, going to the extent of sampling the sound of their parties and feeding it back into the mix - thereby giving the audience an active role in proceedings. They came to the attention of the populace at large, *Sun* readers notwithstanding, by staging two huge outdoor raves: the first at Castlemorton, the second at Canary Wharf. Their first single, 'Breach Of The Peace', arrived in August 1992, followed by 'Forward The Revolution' in November. They were helped in no small part by the financial assistance of Jazz Summers, former manager of Wham! and Yazz. A debut album, *Tecno Terra*, was recorded during commital proceedings at Malvern Magistrates Court concerning the Castlemorton affair - one of the most notorious live music events of recent years, and one which saw any number of media reports bearing false witness to what really happened. Via draconian legal rulings Spiral Tribe were forced to stay within 10 miles of the court, and managed to squat a deserted farmhouse where they could record. The resulting album was perhaps a less worthy cause than the plight of travelling sound systems themselves, especially where it embodied the cod-mysticism of 'chaos theory' (ie references to the number 23). Elsewhere Spiral Tribe's philosophy is well worth investigating: 'If industrialisation had to happen in order for us to get Technics desks and Akai samplers, so be it - in the same way that the blues grew out of the pain and suffering of the slaves that built the American railways'. Their membership is

fluid, numbering about 15 DJ's and musicians at any given time.
Album: *Tecno-Terra* (1993).

Spooky

London-based progressive/ambient dance duo comprising Charlie May (b. 7 March 1969, Gillingham, Kent, England) and Duncan Forbes (b. 29 January 1969, Yeovil, Somerset, England). They signed to Guerilla for their first release, 'Don't Panic', in May 1992. The name came about as a 'last minute decision, which just seemed to fit in with the sound of our music'. May had previously worked as a sound engineer and caffeine research analyst, seeing service in Psi'Jamma and as keyboardist for Ultramarine. His partner Forbes had played in a variety of indie bands, including Red Ten, and enjoyed temporary positions as a school chef, van driver and bar tender. Influenced by a variety of musical media (Cocteau Twins, Detroit techno, Underworld etc), Spooky have won their spurs as much for their remixing talents as their own product (which includes the well received singles 'Land Of Oz', 'Schmoo' and 'Little Bullet'). Recent clients include Ultramarine, William Orbit, Sven Vath and Billie Ray Martin (ex-Electribe 101). As with work recorded under their own name, these remixes offer a textured, tranquil shimmer to proceedings.
Album: *Gargantuan* (Guerilla 1993).

Stereolab

From South London, Stereolab wear their John Cage and John Cale influences on their sleeves, but within a short time span have amassed an impressive body of work. The principal mover is Tim Gane (ex-McCarthy), who was at first joined by his girlfriend Laetitia Sadier (b. 1968, Paris, France), Martin Kean (ex-New Zealand band the Chills), and Th' Faith Healers' drummer Joe Dilworth, also a *Melody Maker* photographer. Tim gave the band their name; after an obscure offshoot of 60s folk label, Vanguard (it has also been stated that the title was taken from a hi-fi testing label). At their early gigs they were joined by Russell Yates (Moose) on guitar and Gina Morris (*New Musical Express* journalist) on vocals. Too Pure signed them, allowing them to keep the Duophonic imprint. By the time of the release of the 'Low-Fi' 10-inch in September 1992, Mary Hansen had arrived to lend keyboard and vocal support, and Andy Ramsay replaced Dilworth on drums. 'John Cage Bubblegum', which some critics have noted as an adequate description of their sound, was released in the US only, on Slumberland, via a limited edition version containing a stick of gum. By the time *The Groop Played Space Age Bachelor Pad Music* was released in March 1993, further line-up changes had occurred, with Duncan Brown joining on bass and ex-Microdisney guitarist Sean O'Hagan also joining. This set was the closest to ambient soundscapes, ala Martin Denny or Arthur Lyman, that they had yet come. The group left Too Pure for Elektra at the end of 1993, once again retaining the Duophonic Ultra High Frequency Disks imprint for their domestic releases. Duophonic would also issue material by Arcwelder and Herzfeld, the latter featuring another former McCarthy member, Malcolm Eden. The double LP, *Transient Random Noise-Bursts With Announcements*, straddled both indie and dance markets. This was more minimalist than ambient, and maintained their reputation not only as a competent rock outfit, but also a fixture of the club scene.

Albums: *Peng!* (Too Pure 1992), *The Groop Played Space Age Bachelor Pad Music* (Too Pure 1993), *Transient Random Noise-Bursts With Announcements* (Duophonic 1993, double album).

Stereo MC's

This UK rap/dance outfit's commercial breakthrough has been the result of both sustained hard work and an original talent. The band comprise three women and three men; Rob Birch (b. Robert Charles Birch, 11 June 1961, Ruddington, Nottinghamshire, England; vocals), Nick 'The Head' Hallam (b. 11 June 1962, Nottingham, England; synthesizers, computers, scratching), and Owen If (b. Ian Frederick Rossiter, 20 March 1959, Newport, Wales; percussion; ex-Bourbonese Qualk), plus Cath Coffey (b. Catherine Muthomi Coffey, c.1965, Kenya - 'I can't tell you my real age because I act and tell different casting directions various different ages'), Andrea Bedassie (b. 7 November 1957, London, England), and Verona Davis (b. 18 February 1952, London, England) on backing vocals. Hallam and Birch had been friends in Nottingham since the age of six. There they formed a rock duo titled Dogman And Head, before moving to London in 1985 when they were 17 years old. Together they started recording rap music, though keeping intact their original love of soul, and set up their own label Gee Street with John Baker and DJ Richie Rich, from their base in Clapham. They were given a cash windfall when they were each handed £7,000 by a property developer to move out of their adjacent flats. This allowed them to establish the Gee St studio in a basement on the London street of the same name. The Stereo MC's first recording was 'Move It', released before the duo recruited Italian-British DJ Cesare, and formed their alter-ego remix team, Ultimatum. In the meantime, Island Records signed up Gee St for distribution, re-releasing 'Move It' in March 1988. Their first remix as Ultimatum arrived shortly afterwards (Jungle Brothers' 'Black Is Black'). Cesare left after a tour supporting Jesus Jones, stating that he was unhappy with the band's direction and financial arrangements. He would go on to produce in his own right. Hallam and Birch pressed on, recording a debut album, *Supernatural*, with Baby Bam of the Jungle Brothers. They also recruited Owen If, originally for live percussion, who had previously been employed at Pinewood Studios as a special effects trainee, working on films like *Batman* and *Full Metal Jacket*. A support tour with Living Colour turned out to be a disaster, however. 1991 brought their first crossover hit with 'Lost In Music', based on the Ultimatum remix of the Jungle Brothers' 'Doin' Your Own Dang'. Their remixes have since encompassed artists like Aswad ('Warrior Re-Charge'), Definition Of Sound ('Wear Your Love Like Heaven'), Disposable Heroes Of Hiphoprisy ('Television - The Drug Of The Nation', 'Language Of Violence'), Dreams Warriors ('Follow Me Not'), Electronic ('Idiot Country Two'), Mica Paris ('Stand Up', 'Contribution'), Monie Love ('It's A Shame', 'Monie In The Middle'), PM Dawn ('Reality Used To Be A Friend Of Mine'), Queen Latifah ('Dance 4 Me') and U2 ('Mysterious Ways'). Coffey was added to the line-up for 'Elevate My Mind', her two female compatriots joining shortly after. She enjoys a concurrent career as an actor and dancer, mainly in black theatre productions. She was even in the famed Broadway flop version of *Carrie*. 'Elevate Your Mind' actually gave the group a Top 40 hit in the US - a first for UK hip hop. Bedassie arrived as a qualified fashion designer, while Davis had formerly worked in a hip hop act with Owen If, titled Giant. The powerful *Connected* was released in September 1992 to mounting acclaim; previous albums had all been well received, but this was comfortably their most rounded and spirited effort. However, it was not until the title track and the exquisite rhythms of 'Step It Up' hit the UK charts that it was brought to the wider audience it richly deserved. In its wake the Stereo MC's collared the Best Group category at the 1994 BRIT Awards ceremony, part of a growing volume of evidence that locates the band within the commercial dance field rather than their roots in hip hop.

Albums: *33, 45, 78* (4th & Broadway 1989), *Supernatural* (4th & Broadway 1990), *Connected* (4th & Broadway 1992).

Video: *Connected* (1993).

Stereo MC's

Stress Records

An arm of DMC Ltd, who are also responsible for
Mixmag and *Mixmag Update* magazines, and artist
management. DMC was originally set up as a DJ
club, providing exclusive megamix albums in the
80s for DJs. It was an operation that evolved into
releasing remix albums every month. In the process
DMC gave a lot of young producers a break as
these reached the ears of A&R staff. They thus
discovered the likes of Sasha, who like many artists
made his first recordings on DMC. Stress grew out
of a younger element, like Dave Seaman (half of
Brothers In Rhythm), getting involved in DMC.
After entering the DMC chamionships he was
invited over to New York to play at the New
Music Seminar and was offerred a job in the late
80s. Rather than merely 'passing on' their trained-
up production discoveries to the major labels and
talent scouts, Stress was inaugurated to provide
DMC with an in-house outlet, should they prefer
it. Nick Gordon Brown and Seaman remain the
prime movers behind Stress, which exists as a
separate, independent entity within the DMC
umbrella, having the final say on A&R decisions.
Records like Rusty (David Syon and Andrea
Gemelotto)'s 'Everything's Gonna Change',
Hustlers Convention's *Groovers Delight* EP and Last
Rhythm's 'Last Rhythm (Sure Is Pure '92 remix)'
established the label. Some of their bigger hits over
the 1993/1994 period included Chris & James'
'Club For Life', Reefa's 'Inner Fantasy',
Bubbleman's 'Theme' and Brothers In Rhythm's
'Forever And A Day'. The same duo also remixed
Voices Of 6th Avenue's 'Call Him Up' for the
label. In 1994 Reefa! contributed 'Inner
Fantasy'/'Get Up Stand Up', while other releases
included Masi's 'Apache', Mindwarp's 'Too' (the
Boston, USA-based crew's follow-up to 'One')
and Coyote's 'Jekyll & Hyde'.
Selected albums: Various: *DJ Culture* (Stress 1993),
Club Culture (Stress 1994).

Strictly Rhythm

Manhattan, New York house stable which, whilst
still remaining a cult taste in their native country,
has become the most popular of all foreign labels in
the UK. The Strictly Rhythm boss is one Mark
Finklestein, who established the company in 1989:
'Everybody's heard of the label but few can name
three acts on it. If you ask me if I'm happy with
that then I'd have to say yes, because at the end of
it the philosophy and vision are mine. But I'd be
equally happy if one act came along and blew that
away'. Finklestein originally entered the music
business by taking over Spring Records for three
years (home to various earlier dance artists like Isis

– or Todd Terry in disguise). He recruited Gladys
Pizarro from the latter as his A&R right hand. The
label went on to score enormous cult success with
records like Logic's 'The Warning', Underground
Solution's 'Luv Dancing', Slam Jam's 'Tech Nine'
(Todd Terry), the Untouchables' debut EP (Kenny
'Dope' Gonzalez) and others. Pizarro left in 1991,
joining Nervous, her role taken by DJ Pierre and
George Morel (ex-2 In A Room). However, when
Pierre elected to return to his own recording
projects, Pizarro switched back. The change had
not interrupted the flow of hits, with Photon Inc's
'Generate Power', Simone's 'My Family Depends
On Me' and New Jersey duo William Jennings and
Eddie Lee Lewis' Aly-Us project (whose 'Follow
Me' became a massive club staple) among them. It
is important not to underestimate the role DJ
Pierre played in Strictly Rhythm's development.
As an artist and musician Pierre offered
'Annihilating Rhythm' by Darkman, the
aforementioned 'Generate Power' by Photon Inc.
(with Roy Davis Jnr), 'Love And Happiness' by
Joint Venture alongside Morel, and dozens more.
Gonzalez continued his ascendancy by providing
material like Total Ka-Os' 'My Love'. Erick
'More' Morillo, too, was just as prolific – claiming
to have released over 25 records on Strictly
Rhythm during 1993 alone (the best of which
included the Smooth Touch sequence). Morillo
was also behind 'I Like To Move It (Reel To
Real), which, like Barbara Tucker's 'Beautiful
People', was licensed to Positiva in the UK.
Widely revered, and often imitated, Strictly
Rhythm has enjoyed a longevity in musical fashion
which defies the short shelf-life usually afforded
house styles. One of the few UK-based acts invited
on board was Caucasian Boy ('Northern Lights'),
but otherwise it was generally a one-way import
business for British dance fans. In 1994 Hardheads'
'New York Express' broke big for the label, with
its escalating BPM count once again sucking the
dance fraternity in. Others from more recent times
include 2 Direct (Anthony Acid and 'Brutal' Bill
Marquez)'s 'Get Down'/'Free' and Morel's
Grooves Part 5, with 'I Feel It' (Morel with
vocalist Zhana Saunders). But this is just the tip of
the iceberg. It would be possible to justify spending
an entire book merely documenting the Strictly
Rhythm discography. They remain the
connoisseur's house label, with its name as close to
a guarantee of quality as the music comes.

Structure

Structure is an umbrella organisation for a series of
labels which includes Monotone, Trance Atlantic,
DJ.ungle and Digitrax Int. After an initial flurry of

acid tracks in 1988, Trance Atlantic was the first of these associated labels to make a name for itself in 1991, by reinstating the 303 sound. Structure itself was formed early the next year, releasing just over a dozen records in its first two years with pressings limited to 2,500 copies. Artists included the aforementioned Bionaut and Mike Inc, alongside Air Liquide (umbrella label-boss Ingmar Koch and Jammin' Unit, both solo stars, alongside lyricist Mary Applegate). The labels in the group are organised to represent differing musical approaches: for instance: Structure (acid), Blue (ambient), Digitrax (ambient/techno) and Monotone (hardcore).

Sub Sub

Pop dance crew from Manchester, England who have been together since 1989, originally comprising Melanie Williams (vocals), Jimi Goodwin, Jezz Williams and Andy Williams. Their earliest releases were based more in the DIY-bedroom techno mode than that which would bring them to *Top Of The Pops* and the Top 10. 'Space Face' was a white-label release hawked via the boot of their cars, followed by the instrumental *Coast* EP. This was the only result of a deal they inked with Virgin Records, before transferring to New Order manager Rob Gretton's Rob's Records, who reissued it in August 1992. Their breakthrough hit arrived with the stirring 'Ain't No Love (Ain't No Use)', with a particularly virulent mix from DJ Graeme Park. In its wake they were invited to produce remixes for a range of artists (including Take That and, insult of insults, Sinitta). They have thus far kept their credits to more credible productions. Their 1994 album was preceded by a single, 'Respect', which introduced their new vocalist, Nina Henchion.
Album: *Full Fathom Five* (Robsrecords 1994).

Subterfuge

An alias for Thomas Barnett (b. c.1967), who once held down a day job alongside Chez Damier, a friend of Juan Atkins and Derrick May, who had recorded for the former's KMS label. Through these connections Barnett met May and recorded 'Nude Photo' with him for Transmat (as Rhythim Is Rhythim). The duo fell out when Barnett received no monies for the track and his name disappeared from the credits. After dropping out and working in his own home-studio he re-emerged on Infonet with the *Liquid Poetry* EP. He also worked for the Dutch label Prime, putting out a set of 'Nude Photo' remixes. A series of EPs then the *Synthetic Dream* album followed, a set overshadowed by the poverty he was experiencing

while recording it, which is evident throughout its tough, remorseless grooves.
Album: *Synthetic Dream* (Prime 1993).

Suburban Base

The home of 'ardkore' techno and breakbeats, established by Dan Donnelly in Romford in 1990 as an offshoot of his record shop, Boogie Times (which was also the title of a subsidiary label). What may seem strange to fans of techno is that Suburban Base's ethos was evolved from hip hop: 'It was the breakbeats that really got me into hardcore. I'd never really been into acid and techno, I was a hip hop fan. What a lot of people miss is that hardcore comes more from rap than from rave. Like early rap, with the breakdancing and graffiti, hardcore is a whole culture, not just a style of music, it's a way of life, an attitude and a look'. Good examples of the Suburban Base creed came in the shape of Sonz Of A Loop Da Loop Era's 'Far Out', which transferred from the Boogie Times subsidiary, or Aston And DJ Rap, who also worked on a production basis under the alias Rhythm for Perfecto records. They released the 'Vertigo' 45 in May 1993. Earlier worthy samples of the label's produce came with Q Bass's 'Hardcore Will Never Die', typical of 1992's 'faster, louder' aesthetics. Danny Breaks (with the rave anthem 'Far Out'), Timebase (aka DJ Krome and Mr Time), M&M, Austin Reynolds (an in-house studio operative who recorded 'I Got High' under his own name and as the Phuture Assassins with the *Future Sound* EP) filled out the artist roster. The homegrown talent also included E Type (studio engineer Mike James) and Run Tings (shop worker Winston Meikle). Rachel Wallace (once a star of a *South Bank Show* talent contest), who featured on the remix of M&M's 'I Feel This Way', was given full billing on her own single, 'Tell Me Why'. However, their biggest hit came with the 'kiddie techno' novelty, 'Sesame's Treet', by the Smarte's (Chris Powell, Tom Orton and Nick Arnold). Suburban Base set up an offshoot, Fruit Tree, for house productions, hiring Luke Coke as its A&R man. This was because they were so pleased with his work on their material via his job at Phuture Trax Promotions. That imprint's life began with Vibe Tribe's 'Rock It', which again was Austin Reynolds, who also remixed for Andronicus and East 17 A further subsidiary was launched as an outlet for compilations, Breakdown Records. This does not involve exclusively Suburban Base tracks, but also scans the shelves for important hardcore tunes which may have escaped the net. In 1992 the label had signed a US deal with Atlantic worth a reported $500,000.

Selected albums: Various: *Base For Your Face* (Suburban Base 1992), *Drum & Bass* (Breakdown 1994).

Suns Of Arqa

Exceedingly pleasant, sitar-soaked, cross-cultural house music, often to be caught live at Planet Dog events. The main man behind Suns Of Arqa is Lancashire-based Mick Ward, whose fusion of flute, violin, keyboards and sitar sounded highly original in the dance music sphere. Previous to their celebrity in that scene, Suns Of Arqa had already recorded a set for ROIR in association with Prince Far I. In 1994 they had 'Govinda's Dream' remixed by A Guy Called Gerald.
Albums: *Cradle* (Earthsounds 1992), *Kokoromochi* (Arqa 1993).

Sunscreem

Lucia Holmes, from Maidstone, Kent, but of half-Swedish parentage, is the vocalist and programmer with this band, who developed an affinity for the nether regions of the UK pop charts in the 90s. They have their own Essex based studio, and were touted as the first live band playing rave music, scoring with singles like 'Luv U More' and 'Perfect Motion' (which went Top 20). Their version of Marianne Faithfull's 'Broken English', performed live on television show *The Word*, also won them admirers. The other main mover behind the band is technical guru Paul Carnell, along with Darren Woodford, Rob Fricker and Sean Wright. However, that self-same studio he had played a major role in building brought them grief in 1993 when they left some of their friends in charge while they went on holiday, returning to discover that they had made use of their time by recording an album, *Panarama*, for the Big Fish label.
Album: *03* (Sony 1993).

Supereal

A London-based duo of Peter Morris and Paul Freegard who branched out to cult dancefloor status following their origins in Meat Beat Manifesto. Their music incorporated the more forboding elements which were always associated with their former employers, as well as rich breakbeats and informed treatments of house styles. Tracks such as 'Terminal High RIP' seem to have been provoked by a restless, playful spirit, which was somewhat lacking in MBM. Their career had begun in 1990 with 'Body Medusa', before 'United State Of Love' for Guerilla in 1992. The first of these was remixed by Leftfield, the second by Slam.
Album: *Elixir* (Guerilla 1992).

Sure Is Pure

Remix team probably best known for their work with the Doobie Brothers, an unlikely teaming which saw the soft rockers back in the charts after several years absence. Based in Stoke On Trent, Sure Is Pure are built around lynchpins DJ Kelvin Andrews (also of indie band the Stems) and Danny Spencer (ex-Candy Flip). The team started off by providing mixes for the DMC organisation, which would not see general release. Afterwards came remixing chores for Yothu Yindi ('Treaty'), Degrees Of Motion ('Do You Want It Right Now'), Cookie Crew ('Like Brother Like Sister'), Showbiz & AG ('Soul Clap'), Bizarre Inc ('Took My Love'), Club 69 ('Let Me Be Your Underwear') and other major league outfits like INXS. They have recorded in their own right, including the 1991 EP *Proper Tunes* for their own imprint Gem. The same label would also be the first home to their 'Is This Love Really Real?' single, featuring vocalist Aphrique, before it transferred to Union City in 1992. Again for Gem they picked up and remixed Unique featuring Kim Cooper's 'Danube Dance'. In 1994 Andrews formed another indie rock band called Camp Carnival, who recorded a version of Sure Is Pure's 'Grind Zone Blues' (from the *Out To Lunch* EP), and signed to Vinyl Solution.

Swemix Records

Swedish dance label which was inaugurated in 1989 by a group of local DJ's headed by Jackmaster Fax (Rene Hedemyr) and JJ (Johan Jarpsten). The latter pairing also recorded for the label as Dynamic Duo. Once described as the Nordic equivalent to the UK's DMC enclave, each month Swemix released a Remixed Records double album package of the hottest club hits. Other staples of the Swemix catalogue included the Stonebridge remix team (who recorded as Mr Magic) and artists like Frankie LaMotte and Terry Leigh, on the Basement Division subsidiary. The idea for the label was first mooted because the collective thought they could remix better and more suitable cuts than they were being handed by the major record companies. Thus their roster grew to accomodate major clients like Milli Vanilli, Neneh Cherry, Pasadenas and Gloria Estefan. In so doing they revolutionised the Swedish, and to some extent, mainland Europe, dance music scene. Among their higher profile signings were Da Yeene (who hit in the 90s with cuts like 'Alright' and 'Good Thing') and Dr Alban, whom they had watched setting up the Alphabet Street club in Gothenburg, a frequent haunt of many of the Swemix principals. It was this artist more than any other which established both the label and a new style of Eurodance in the 90s, signing to Arista via Germany's Logic. There were also two further subsidiary operations, B-Tech and Energy (who released Clubland's 'Hold On' and Paradise Orchestra's 'Colour Me', later licensed to Pulse 8). Swemix has subsequently metamorphosised into Cheiron, and no longer deals exclusively in dance.

Swingbeat

A musical format often titled New Jack Swing (or indeed New Jill Swing when it concerns female performers). Swingbeat's origins lay in the 80s and Teddy Riley, who remains the music's most important figurehead to this day. As a Harlem based hip hop DJ, Riley began to experiment with rap's beats, adding soul vocals to produce a more upfront, demanding blend of R&B. The hybrid quickly picked up the title swingbeat, the derivation of which is obviously onomatopaeic. Although it was initially accepted by neither hip hop nor soul purists, the music found a keen, and predominatly young audience, with early supergroups including Today and Guy. In the 90s, by now rechristened New Jack Swing by the American media, the format continued its commercial ascendency. The first of the New Jill Swing groups were Gyrlz, another of Teddy Riley's protégés. After which would come the highly succesful TLC, Jade and SWV. Prime swingbeat movers now include Jodeci, Wreckx-N-Effect, Mary J. Blige and Bobby Brown (plus other former members of New Edition). English outfits like Rhythm Within, and, on the female front, TCW (Twentieth Century Women), have also picked up the trail.

SWV

Standing for Sisters With Voices, these 'ghetto sisters' from Brooklyn and the Bronx comprise the talents of Coko (b. Cheryl Gamble, c.1974) Taj (b. Tamara Johnson, c.1974) and Lelee (b. Leanne Lyons, c. 1976). Shaped by producer Teddy Riley to reflect streetwise dress and attitude, the band's sound is somewhat harder than that which might be expected of New Jill Swingers. On tracks like 'Downtown' they revealed themselves as happy to engage in intimate details of the sex wars. Their debut album also encompassed both rap and a capella, and included the hit single 'I'm So Into You', which crossed over into the Billboard Top 20.
Album: *It's About Time* (RCA 1993).

System 7

Ambient dance duo featuring Miquette Giraudy (b. 9 February 1953, Nice, France; synthesizers, samples) and the more celebrated Steve Hillage (b. Stephen Simpson Hillage, 2 August 1951, Walthamstow, London, England; guitars, samplers, synthesizers). Giraudy is a former film-maker from the south of France, where she met up with Hillage's band, the cult synth prog rockers Gong. Her films had included *More* and *La Vallee*, both of which featured Pink Floyd on their soundtracks. Fascinated by synthesisers, she became a self-taught musician and in the current format writes most of the material before Hillage adds a layer of guitar work. Hillage enjoys his own cult following through his work with Kevin Ayers, Gong and the Steve Hillage Group, and had become enveloped in the ambient house explosion via the work of Spooky, the Drum Club, Orbital, Black Dog and Fluke, before collaborating with another listening favourite, the Orb. In turn System 7 have been joined on vinyl by a host of rock, pop and dance stars; Alex Paterson (Orb), Youth (Killing Joke/Brilliant), Mick McNeil (Simple Minds), Paul Oakenfold and Derrick May. Their recording career started in August 1991 with 'Miracle' on Ten Records, after which they moved to Big Life but sought their own Weird & Unconventional imprint. Singles of the quality of 'Freedom Fighters' and 'Sinbad' have helped them garner a considerable reputation among both their peers and late-night ravers searching for the perfect chill-out tune.
Albums: *System 7* (Ten 1991), *777* (Weird And Unconventional/Big Life 1993).

Syzygy

Dominic Glynn and Justin McKay first met at the end of the 80s, when the former was working part-time providing BBC Television's *Doctor Who* series with incidental music. Mutually inspired by Detroit techno, their first recordings emerged on Infonet, before adopting the names Mind Control and Zendik, subsequently signing to Rising High as Syzygy. Two EPs, *Discovery* and *Can I Dream* began to push their profile in the 'intelligent techno' scene. A debut album, meanwhile, drew its title from 'the collective consciousness of the planet, a phenomenon for which there is no easy explanation'. This was a concept ambient album, taking as its theme a musical fable of the earth, and stretched over four sides of vinyl.
Album: *The Morphic Resonance* (Rising High 1994, double album).

T

Tackhead

A dub/hip hop/dance outfit who formed in 1987 and released a remarkable first single, 'The Game', with a Brian Moore (football commentator) sample and backbeat which comprised metal guitar and electro 'Hi-NRG' attack, together with football chants. The band comprised Keith LeBlanc (previously behind the groundbreaking 'Malcom X' single; percussion, keyboards), plus Doug Wimbush (bass) and Skip MacDonald (guitar). Together they had previously operated as the Sugarhill Gang house band, in their home town of Bristol, Connecticut, USA, performing on the likes of 'Rapper's Delight', 'The Message' and 'White Lines'. Before which they had also been major contributors, as Wood Brass & Steel, to many of the recordings which emerged from another Sylvia Robinson label, All Platinum. Migrating to London in 1984, they became a central component in Adrian Sherwood's On U Sound label. Sherwood became the mixmaster who would take the trio's basic tracks and add a little club magic. Although they all appeared on LeBlanc's solo work, their first recording as Tackhead came with Gary Clail as vocalist in 1987 - *Tackhead Tape Time* - which was jointly credited. They subsequently recruited Bernard Fowler, who appeared on their best album, *Friendly As A Hand Grenade*. Its follow-up set, *Strange Things*, was an unfortunate shot at crossover success, following the band's relocation to the US. Guest contributions from Melle Mel, Lisa Fancher and even Mick Jagger on harmonica did little to elevate a dour reading of dance-rock. In 1991 Leblanc joined with Tim Simenon (Bomb The Bass) in a new project titled Interference.
Albums: As Gary Clail's Tackhead Sound System: *Tackhead Tape Time* (Nettwerk/Capitol 1987). As Tackhead: *Friendly As A Hand Grenade* (TVT 1989), *Strange Things* (SBK 1990).

Talkin' Loud

Giles Peterson's extension of the original Acid Jazz empire, which has, if anything, gone on to outshine that imprint. Peterson originally ran a jazz funk pirate station from his own garden shed. He subsequently gained his own show on the leading Invicta pirate in exchange for lending them his transmitter. Taking a residency in the jazz room of the Electric Ballroom in Camden, he was invigorated by the legendary atmosphere and freeform dancing that occurred there. The formula was relocated to Soho's Wag Club, then Dingwalls. The first Talkin' Loud nights began at the Fridge. He had returned to piracy after his *Mad On Jazz* show had been axed after encouraging people to join the anti-Gulf War marches, and he eventually settled at Kiss-FM. In the meantime he was also working alongside Eddie Piller at Acid Jazz, before splitting to form his own label, named after his Talkin' Loud nights, when the finance was put forward by Phonogram. Signings included Galliano, Young Disciples, Omar (before he departed for RCA), Urban Species (probably the label's biggest hopes for the future) and others. Talkin' Loud's greatest moments so far have included the triology of Galliano releases which culminated in 1994's *The Plot Thickens*, which at last saw the band doing the business for the label, the Young Disciples' 'Apparently Nothin' 45 with Carleen Anderson's unmistakable vocal, and Omar's 'There's Nothing Like This' cut. The Urban Species debut album was also widely applauded. New signings include hip hop/jazz fusioners the Roots, from Philadelphia, as Talkin' Loud continues to explore a number of new musical horizons. Peterson has also started a new club, The Way It Is, with James Lavelle of Mo Wax.
Selected albums: Young Disciples: *Road To Freedom* (Talkin' Loud 1991). Urban Species: *Listen* (Talkin' Loud 1994). Galliano: *The Plot Thickens* (Talkin' Loud 1994).

Techno

An easy definition of techno would be percussion based electronic dance music, characterised by stripped down drum beats and basslines. However, the real roots of techno can be traced back to the experimental musicologists like Karl Heinz Stockhausen. In terms of equipment there was no greater precedent than that set by Dr Robert Moog, who invented the synthesizer in California, and provoked the first fears of the 'death of real music' which have shadowed electronic recordings ever since. If Chicory Tip's 'Son Of My Father' was the first to employ the Moog in 1972, then Kraftwerk were certainly the first to harness and harvest the possibilities of the synthesizer and other electronic instruments. Kraftwerk served as godfathers to UK electro pop outfits like the Human League (in their early experimental phase) and Depeche Mode. It is hard to imagine now but groups like these and even Gary Numan proved a huge influence on the US hip hop scene and the development of New York 'electro' in the early 80s (particularly Afrika Bambaataa's 'Planet Rock'). But techno as we now know it descended from the

Detroit region, which specialised in a stripped down, abrasive sound, maintaining some of the soulful elements of the Motown palate, over the innovations that hip hop's electro period had engendered. Techno also reflected the city's decline, as well as the advent of technology, and this tension was crucial to the dynamics of the sound. As Kevin Saunderson recounts: 'When we first started doing this music we were ahead. But Detroit is still a very behind city when it comes to anything cultural'. Techno as an umbrella term for this sound was first invoked by an article in *The Face* in May 1988, when it was used to describe the work of Saunderson (particularly 'Big Fun'), Derrick May (who recorded techno's greatest anthem, 'Strings Of Life') and Juan Atkins ('No UFO's'). The Detroit labels of note included May's Transmat, Juan Atkins' Metroplex, Saunderson's KMS, Underground Resistance, Planet E, Red Planet, Submerge and Accelerate. Much like house, the audience for techno proved to be a predominantly British/European one. Labels like Rising High and Warp in the UK, and R&S in Belgium helped build on the innovations of May, Atkins and Carl Craig. UK artists like the Prodigy and LFO took the sound to a new, less artful but more direct level. According to Saunderson, the difference between most Detroit techno and its English re-interpreters was that it lacked the 'spirituality' of the original. Had he wished to produce more controversy, he might have substituted 'blackness' - all of the main Detroit pioneers were black. Most UK techno, conversely, at least until the advent of jungle, were white. Techno utilises the establishment of a groove or movement by repetition, building a framework which does not translate easily into more conventional musical terms. Some obviously find this adjustment difficult, but the variations in texture and tempo are at least as subtle as those in rock music - often more so, due to the absence of a lyrical focus.

Technotronic

Belgian techno/house outfit created by producer Jo 'Thomas DeQuincey' Bogaert. He was looking for a female rapper to sing over a backing track he had produced, before stumbling upon Ya Kid K in the Antwerp rap group, Fresh Beat. Born Manuela Kamosi in Zaire, she moved to Belgium when she was 11. At 15 she spent some time in Chicago and was introduced to rap and Deep House, then currently in vogue. She returned to Belgium where she hooked up with Bogaert. Together they created 'Pump Up The Jam', though the cover shot actually featured a model named Felly and the record was credited to Technotronic featuring Felly. Ya Kid K was righteously indignant and by the time the first album was recorded care was taken that the act was rebilled Technotronic featuring Ya Kid K. Her rapping partner was MC Eric, whose most notable contribution would be the chant sequence from 'This Beat Is Technotronik'. 'Pump Up The Jam' eventually reached the UK's number 2 spot in 1989. Follow-ups would include 'Get Up (Before The Night Is Over)' with Ya Kid K, 'This Beat Is Technotronik', 'Rockin' Over The Beat', 'Megamix' (Bogaert on his own) and 'Turn It Up' (Technotronic featuring Melissa and Einstein). Ya Kid K would go on to perform on Hi Tek's 'Spin That Wheel' in 1990 (a version of which is also included on Technotronic's *Trip On This* remix album), and enjoy her own solo career, as would her partner MC Eric. By the time of *Body To Body* Technotronic had recruited Reggie/Rejana Magloire (of Indeep fame, but not the singer on 'Last Night A DJ Saved My Life', who was Rose Marie Ramsey) as their female frontperson. Jo Bogaert would go on to record a solo album, *Different Voices*, for Guerilla.

Albums: *Pump Up The Jam* (Epic 1990), *Trip On This - The Remixes* (Epic 1990), *Body To Body* (Epic 1991). Jo Bogaert solo: *Different Voices* (Guerilla 1994).

Video: *Pump Up The Hits* (1990).

Technova

David Harrow was previously a London musician best known for his work with the On-U-Sound team on material by Gary Clail, Lee Perry, Bim Sherman and, under his own auspices, for Jah Wobble's *Without Judgement* album. As Pulse 8 (not the record label) he also issued 'Radio Morocco', the first ever single on Nation Records in October 1989. His first UK release as Technova was 'Tantra', a 25-minute trance/ambient affair with a strong reggae undertow, released on the Sabres Of Paradise imprint. He had impressed the latter's Andy Weatherall with an appearance at the Sabres Christmas party, accompanied by naked (except for luminous paint) tattooed and pierced dancers. The single was actually taken from an album released in Australia on the Shock label in 1993, though Weatherfield quickly announced plans to re-release it on the Sabres imprint. 'The basic idea of the album is to simulate a long journey. It's totally seamless and it took a lot of preparation to get it to flow the way that I wanted'. The project made plentiful use of DAT-recorded environmental sounds picked up on Harrow's own journey through Australasia.

Album: *Trantic Shadows* (Shock 1993).

T-Empo

One of the major proponents of what has been fetchingly described as 'handbag house' is Tim Lennox (b. c.1966, Birmingham, Midlands, England). Lennox, like many before him, has stepped out from behind the decks to switch from being DJ to producer. He had been DJing for ten years, starting at a gay club called Heroes, in Manchester, before helping set up the notorious Flesh events at the Hacienda in 1991, settling on current home Paradise Factory shortly afterwards. His first recorded effort, featuring a typically striking vocal from Sharon Dee Clarke and help from producer Aron Friedman and Damon Rochefort (of Nomad fame along with Clarke), was a cover of Cuba Gooding's 'Happiness', released under the title Serious Rope. A second cover, this time of Barbara Mason's 'Another Man', also sustained critical approval. This diarama of a Brooklyn housewife dumped by her man for another lover, also male, had the camp, heightened sense of drama intrinsic to the Lennox style. This was released as Shy One, after which he switched to the T-Empo name in order to engender a more structured approach to making music. Hence his band evolved, featuring Adam Clough, session singer Loretta and engineer Simon Bradshaw. After the huge success of 'Another Man' several record companies were fighting to sign Lennox, and he eventually opted for ffrr, based on their good record with gay/hi-NRG/house acts. However, a third release, 'Saturday Night Sunday Morning', the first to use the pseudonym T-Empo, arrived jointly with the exclusively gay record label Out On Vinyl, on which Lennox holds a director's chair. His remixing skills also rose in popularity, and, again under the name T-Empo, included the Brand New Heavies ('Dream On Dreamer'), RuPaul ('House Of Love'), Grace Jones ('Slave To The Rhythm'), Joe Roberts ('Lover') and K Klass ('Rhythm Is A Mystery'). The Joe Roberts mix was a particular triumph, when ffrr promoted it to a-side status over a version from Lennox's long-time hero, David Morales.

Ten City

Consistent, sometimes spectacular Chicago house group, with philosophy graduate Byron Stingily's falsetto always the focus. The other members are Byron Burke and Herb Lawson. They met in a rehearsal studio in Chicago in 1985, Herb being drawn from R&B band Rise, while Stingily was then fronting B Rude Inc. The trio recorded two singles as Ragtyme, 'I Can't Stay Away' and 'Fix It Man'. In 1986 they signed to Atlantic and made the name change. The debut single, 'Devotion', was an instant hit (it would later be revamped by Nomad for their '(I Wanna Give You) Devotion' hit). Their production was helmed by Marshall Jefferson, who was responsible for shaping much of their early character and sound. The band began making steady progress in the late 80s, going chartbound in the UK the following year with 'That's The Way Love Is'. Ten City, aside from the Jefferson connections (their union ended by the advent of their third album), are good writers in their own right, having provided for Adeva and Ultra Nate among others. Their sound is also distinguished by live musicianship, and they claim to the 'the first true musicians to play house'. If plagiarism amounts to tribute, then their basslines, rhythms and melodies have re-appeared on enough occasions to suggest a lasting influence on dance music.
Albums: *Foundation* (East West 1988), *State Of Mind* (East West 1990), *No House Big Enough* (East West 1992), *Love In A Day* (Columbia 1994).

Tenaglia, Danny

Italian-American Tenaglia has, together with keyboard player Peter Dauo, played host to an impressive slew of garage/house cuts emanating from New York in the 90s. He first turned to dance music when hearing a mix tape for the first time, subsequently selling them for the artist concerned. He was a keen enthusiast in the early disco boom, and played his first gig at a local club in Bayside, Queens, New York, when he was still 14. From there he picked up on musical trends as they occurred, being particularly influenced by the early innovations of David Morales and Kevin Saunderson. His productions of cuts like 'Glammer Girl' by the Look (a Jon Waters tribute), and the tehcno-jazz innovations of his partner Dauo, built an enviable reputation, as his profile grew alongside that of fellow New Yorkers DJ Duke and Junior Vasquez. Naturally this helped bring in the remix projects, including Right Said Fred and Yothu Yindi. Despite his obvious musical merits Tenaglia has yet to crack the US scene, which contrasts alarmingly with his popularity in Euorpe and even the Orient. In the UK his reputation has been franked by performances at the musically-sympathetic Ministry Of Sound club nights.

Terry, Todd

Terry is a house production innovator and expert with a reputation second to none (in fact, some UK journalists have taken to nicknaming him 'God' for easy reference). An established producer and DJ, he learned his trade playing early house and hip hop at parties in New York. 'Bongo (To The Batmobile)', a major signpost in the development of acid house, and further singles were credited to the Todd Terry Project. In addition to an album and singles licensed to Champion (including the mighty 'Put Your Hands Together'). His early aliases masked a wide variety of hugely innovative work. Namely Giggles' 'Love Letter' (Cutting), Fascination's 'Why You Wanna Go' and 'Don't You Think It's Time' (Vinyl Mania), LA Girls' 'No More No More' (Easy Street), Isis' 'Let Me Hold You' (Spring), Royal House's 'Party People' and 'Can You Party?' (Idlers), Black Riot's 'A Day In The Life Of' and Orange Lemon's 'The Texcian' (Idlers). More recently he has cut records for Strictly Rhythm, Nervous and Freeze (SAX's 'This Will Be Mine'). His distinctive use of samples underpins all his production and remix work: "What I try to do is to make an art out of the samples'. This often involves multi-layers of creative theft without allowing a given example to offer its 'signature' to the listener. His remix clients have included Bizarre Inc ('I'm Gonna Get You') and Snap!, and he also collaborated with old friend Tony Humphries to remix Alison Limerick's 'Make It On My Own'. 'Whenever I do a remix I strip the vocal right down and use just a little bit. That's why I don't do many remixes, they are a long way from the original'. A good example was the magic he worked on PM Dawn's 'From A Watcher's Point Of View'. He partially became involved because members of that band had previously worked for him at Warlock Records. He owns his own home-studio, the Loudhouse, in his native Brooklyn, and remains unjustifiably humble. 'A low profile does you good. I'm not into being an artist. I'm just a producer who makes records.'

Selected albums: As Royal House: *Royal House* (Idlers 1986). As Todd Terry Project: *To The Batmobile* (Sleeping Bag 1986), *This Is The New Todd Terry Project Album* (Champion 1992). As Black Riot: *Kamikaze* (Fourth Floor 1987). As Todd Terry: *Bonus Acid Tracks* (Warlock 1988).

Three Beat Records

Liverpool dance label, headed by Hywel Williams, a local rave organiser, alongside Dave Nicoll, Jonathan Barlow and Phillip Southall. Like many dance imprints Three Beat grew out of a successful record store operation, at first releasing vinyl on a 50:50 basis with local acts who brought in their own demo tapes. They also responsible for assisting in running a series of club nights in and around Merseyside, including G-Love, Grin and

Heaven. One of the label's first releases was Oceanic's 'Insanity', before it was picked up by Dead Dead Good and sent into the Top 3. Other notable early volleys included Zenana's 'Just Dance', Dub Federation's 'Keep Giving', 1st Team's 'Feel It', the World Upstair's 'The Deep' and New Atlantic's 'Take Off Some Time'. Their early-90s roster also included Cordial, Neuro Project, Jeaney Tracey, Bong Devils, Supernature, Bandito and Vicki Shepherd. Having thus built their reputation Three Beat signed a licensing deal with London/ffrr in 1994. Although the label remained indepedent ffrr were to be given the option of picking up any of their product. The first release under the new arrangement was 2 Cowboy's 'Everybody's Gonfi-Gon', a huge hit. Selected album: Neuro Project: *The Electric Mothers Of Invention* (3 Beat 1994, double album).

3Phase

Signed to Novamute, 3Phase is essentially Sven Roehrig (b. Berlin, Germany) plus his various associates and technological aides. He in turn is part of the Berlin-based Tresor club and label, which has achieved lots of good press (not least via the patronage of the Orb's Alex Paterson). His debut album (*Schlangenfarm* translates as 'Snake Farm') revealed Roehrig's debt to his industrial music past - he had formerly been a member of Justice League, Tox Movement and Boom Factory, and his earliest major influence was Throbbing Gristle. The 3Phase banner had first been invoked as his interests in techno grew, and also reflected the post-Wall Berlin spirit which gave birth to a regenerated club scene. In 1992 he collaborated with DJ Dr. Mottke for 'Der Klang Der Familie', which became the theme song to Berlin's third annual Techno festival - the Love Parade. It also provided the title of Tresor's first compilation album, and proved a massive European-wide hit in its own right.

Album: *Schlangenfarm* (Novamute 1993), *Rota* (Novamute 1993).

Time Records

Nottingham label run by Dave Thompson and Chris Allen, based around the Squaredance Recording Studio and Venus club nights. Via a monthly mail-order release schedule they built up an admirable catalogue, pushing out double pack EP's which matched established acts like Moodswings and Deja Vu with new, up and coming outfits. A good example was April 1993's *Back In Time* EP, wherein four 'classics' (DIY's 'Excommunicate', Association's 'Ciao', Mad's 'India Kinda' and IDG's 'Family') were remixed by

the God Squad, Back To Basics, Sure Is Pure and Huggy. This process threw up a series of techno and house gems, some of which were licensed to R&S and Flying. In 1993 they launched the Emit imprint for collections of ambient music. 'Ambient music is taking what house was supposed to be about quite a bit further. Its more of an international language'. Not to be confused with the Brescia based Italian dance label (famed for work with Carol Bailey, Deadly Sins, Usura and Silvia Coleman).
Selected album: Various: *EMIT 0094* (emiT/Time 1994).

T99

This group, whose roots were in Belgian new beat, produced one of 1991's biggest rave tunes with 'Anasthasia', after which they moved from XL to Columbia. The followed it up with 'Nocturne', sung by Perla Den Boer with a rap from Zenon Zevenbergen. Their debut album saw them add a second rapper for several of the cuts, but they were still some way short of the artistic mark set by the Detroit stalwarts, which they were desperately trying to emulate. However, the resonant 'Anasthasia' was later sampled by both 2 Unlimited and even Kylie Minogue. T99 is a duo of Patrick De Meyer and Oliver Abeloos.
Album: *Children Of Chaos* (Columbia 1992).

Tomato Records

Record label established by Ross Nedderman and Tim Reeves (formerly of Virgin) in Lillie Road, London. Reeves had previously been best known for dropping an 'E' in the middle of a seminar at Manchester's In The City conference. Tomato's first release was Pascal's 'Bongo Massive' - a first taste of the percussive conga sound which rapidly became fashionable for a few months thereafter. It led to descriptions in some quarters as 'the bongo label', which was something of a simplification. Nedderman and Reeves pressed on regardless, releasing the *2 Clouds Above 9* set, an album sponsored by Sega which gave new producers and musicians access to vinyl. The Tomato backroom boys also recorded, as Two Shiny Heads, a track for Geurilla ('Dub House Disco'). Other releases like Infinite Wheel's 'Lake Of Dreams' (which used everything from kettle drums to xylophone in execution of its percussion) and Nature Boy's eponymous EP and 'Ruff Disco' 12-inch maintained their credentials in the world of underground dance, and the boys intend to keep things 'red, round and light-hearted' for the forseeable future.
Selected album: Various: *Cream Of Tomato* (Tomato 1993).

Tony! Toni! Tone!

R&B/hip hop crossover band from Oakland, California, comprising the brothers Dwayne (guitar) and Raphael Wiggins (vocals), and their cousin Timothy Christian Riley (drums). They arrived with 'Little Walter' in 1988, combining the best traditions of soul with new age rap. They are at their most successful when moving, unceremoniously, from tight, gospel-tinged harmonics to assured, laconic hip hop, as on the ballad hit, 'It Never Rains (In Southern California)'. Despite their high profile (notably as support to Janet Jackson's 1993 US tour), they retain a sense of propriety and musical history. Tim still plays for his church when at home, while Raphael made his public debut at age seven playing bass with his father's semi-pro blues band. Their name (pronounced Tony throughout its three incarnations) was taken from a character they invented when they went out shopping to buy vintage clothing. They have also appeared in the *House Part 2* film.
Albums: *Who?* (Wing 1988), *The Revival* (Wing/Mercury 1990), *Sons Of Soul* (Wing/Mercury 1993).

Toop, David, And Max Eastley

Ambient sculptors based in North London, whose albums have brought many admiring glances via their organic use of animal and wildlife sounds, interfacing with experimental technology. Contrary to what might have been expected of the dance scene in the 90s, Toop is a well known writer for *The Times* and *The Face*, as well as being one of hip hop's most poweful advocates and chroniclers. He first performed with Eastley as far back as 1971, after meeting at Alexandra Palace Art College in the mid-60s. They have been working on atmosphere-music ever since - Toop releasing several solo albums for Brian Eno's label, as well as taking a role in experimental pop band the Flying Lizards. The cliché 'ahead of their time' does not seem out of place.
Selected album: *Buried Dreams* (1994).

Tournesol

Techno duo comprising Danish pair Tommy Dee and Thomas 'Tutor' Lange. Their first recording bout came via a track on *Secrets*, a 1991 compilation album prepared by the Danish government to showcase new artists. They went on to work alongside Kenneth Baker, before a remix of Cut N Move's 'Give It Up', which sold especially well in Germany and mainland Europe. Their debut album, *Kokotsu*, was named after the Japanese term 'trance', while their own name is derived from the professor of Herge's comic

stories.
Album: *Kokotsu* (Apollo 1994).

Toytown Techno
A sub-sub-genre of dance music, 'Toytown Techno' was the term invoked to describe the strange phenomenon of records which emerged from 1991 to 1992 which were essentially themed on children's television and other signature tunes. A precedent had been set with the KLF alter-egos Justified Ancients Of Mu Mu's 'Doctorin' The Tardis', but in reality it all started off with the Prodigy's 'Charly'. This used the infamous UK children's information film character dialogue. It broke the Top 10 but was quickly considered an embarassment by Liam Howlett, as accusations of 'cheapening', even 'killing' rave music followed. However, so did a legion of impersonators. The Smarte's 'Sesame's Treet' (Suburban Base) was probably the best known and most successful, despite the fact that it came from a stable previously known as the antithesis of commercial music. There was soon no let-up in the avalanche. Urban Hype provided 'A Trip To Trumpton' (Faze 2), Mike Summer the *Magic Roundabout* tribute 'Summer Magic', Shaft offered 'Roobarb And Custard' (ffrr), while the *Blue Peter* theme was mugged for Monster Rush's 'The Hypnotizer' (G-Spot). Horsepower trotted up with the *Black Beauty*-themed 'Bolt', while DJ Excell's 'Just When You Thought It Was Safe' brought in the film world by sampling the famous bass-line from *Jaws*. The various shady individuals behind this surfeit soon realised the resonance of computer signature tunes, paving the way for Ambassadors Of Funk's 'Super Mario Land' and Power Pill's 'Pac Man'. Toytown Techno was an early example of post-rave, multi-media entertainment in its most insidious form. Hardly any of these tunes are worthy of more than a single play, but each managed to raise a smile on first hearing. At least among non-puritans.

Trance Induction
Holland trance/ambient outfit led by one Tjeerd Verbeek, who broke through with the amazing 'New Age Heartcore'. This looped guitar distortion over a melange of techno to quite startling effect. An eclectic debut album saw him fuse Detroit rhythms with all manner of musical subcultures, from house to bhangra.
Album: *Electrickery* (Guerilla 1994).

Transcendental Love Machine
South London team who made their bow with 'Unity', then *The Silver Atomic* EP, which saw them shift towards trance/dub aesthetics. Following *The Dragonflymania* EP came *The Love Machine Remixes*, part of which was shortlisted by the BBC as the theme to their Winter Olympics coverage. Following a further EP, *Machine Mania*, the group unveiled a debut album for Hydrogen Dukebox, which had also housed the earlier releases.
Album: *Orgasmatronic* (Hyrdrogen Dukebox 1994).

Trans-Global Underground
A band who rose to fame by fusing house and hip hop with Indian stylings, to the live accompaniment of a Turkish belly dancer. They were described in the press (somewhat patronisingly) as an Asian Public Enemy, or forerunners of 'World House'. Their first single, 1991's 'Templehead', was a masterful example of their craft, including upfront keyboards and chanting Napalese monks. The group is certainly liberal in the way it sources its music - anything goes, as long as it can be pinned together by breakbeats or upheld by a steady tempo. The band's major participants were originally Alex Kasiek (keyboards), DJ Man Tu (b. Hamid Mantu) and Donald Dubwee (bass), the line-up eventually expanded to include Belgian/English singer Natacha Atlas, Indian tabla player Inder Matharu (aka Goldfinger from Fun-Da-Mental) and Guyanan story teller/percussionist Tuup. Spokesman Mantu was keen to remind those who admired the selection of music cultures that all the sounds used could be found in ethnic traditions now native to Britain, be they Turkish, Hindu or Arabic. In 1994 Atlas struck out to record a solo single, 'Yalla Chant'/'Dub Yalil', though Trans-global were still involved in backing her, while she was also aided and abetted by Kevin Haskins of Love And Rockets.
Album: *Dream Of 100 Nations* (Nation 1993).

Transmat Records
US dance label run by Derrick May, releasing most of that artists best work as Rhythim Is Rhythim in the late 80s, i.e. 'The Dance', 'Strings Of Life' and 'It Is What It Is'. Other artists included X-Ray ('Let's Go'), Psyche/Carl Craig ('Elements' and 'Crackdown'), K. Alexi Shelby ('All For Lee Sah'), BFC ('Static Friendly' - again Craig) and Suburban Knight ('The Art Of Stalking'). It is impossible to overestimate the importance these records had on the evolution of techno. The label was reactivated in 1992 with Dark Comedy's *War Of The Worlds* EP.

Trax Records

Legendary record label, the home to much of the early Chicago house sound, headed by Larry Sherman. Among the hugely influential artist roster were Mr Fingers' seminal 3-track single, 'Beyond The Clouds' (which housed 'Washing Machine'), Jamie Principle's 'Baby Wants To Ride' and Mr Lee, with 'Pump Up Chicago' and 'Shoot Your Best Shot'. Less celebrated artists included Grant & Dezz's 'You're Too Good' and Virgo Four's 'Do You Know Who You Are?' from 1989. As Trax's influence grew as the revered home to 'jack tracks' alongside DJ International, few would have envisaged its home in a disused, run-down warehouse, boasting an in-house pressing plant.

Tucker, Barbara

Tucker's induction into the world of music came at the hands of Tommy Musto and Victor Simonelli, who used her vocals on a range of their products. Her delivery and visual presence soon established her as an icon of New York's gay/Hi-NRG scene. In the UK it was the uplifting soul/house cut, 'Beautiful People', which utilised the 'Deep Deep Inside' hook from Hardrive's track of the same name, remixed by CJ Mackintosh, which gave her an audience. The song was produced by Little Louie Vega, with whom Tucker runs the Underground Network Club in New York. The cast of backing singers reflected the esteem she is held in within that community, numbering Michael Watford, India and Ten City's Byron Stingily within their ranks.

2 Unlimited

Cod-house act from Holland who enjoyed two weeks at the top of the UK charts with 'No Limits', featuring Anita Dels' diva vocals and Ray Slijngaard's hilarity-inducing chorus of 'Techno! Techno! Techno!'. It was mangificently parodied in an episode of television series Spitting Image, where the puppet Anita recited 'No lyrics, no no no no, no no there's no lyrics'. An album of the same name contained further variations on the formula, though arguably of an even lower quality threshold. Slijngaard rejoices in the distinction of having previously been a chef at Amsterdam airport - affording snide journalists the opportunity of comparing 2 Unlimited's brand of Euro-pop with greasy fast-food. Dels previously worked as a secretary, singing part-time with the Trouble Girls. The men behind the group are Jean-Paul De Coster and Phil Wilde, of Byte Records (who previously tasted success with Bizz Nizz's 'Don't Miss The Party Line'). Their philosophy is redolent of the Euro-techno axis, but anathema to traditional British views of artistic imput: '2 Unlimited is trendy music that appeals to the youths, it's not aggressive so the kids kids can enjoy it. There's also a strong melody that stays in the head, and the visuals are good too'. They readily admit to creating music to satiate a market rather than attempting to build a fan base around any creative vision. The statistics, whilst not exonerating them, did prove them to be entirely correct in their suppostion - in 1993 2 Unlimited sold over a million singles in Britain alone. 'No Limits' was also the biggest selling European record of the year, while their second album sold nearly three million copies. Earlier success had included the arguably more interesting 'Workaholic'.
Album: Get Ready (PWL 1992), No Limits (PWL 1992), Real Things (PWL 1994).

Tyree

b. Tyree Cooper. Cooper first got involved with music at the age of 15, gatecrashing parties led by Farley Jackmaster Funk and Jesse Saunders. Together with friend Mike Dunn he hung out with the likes of Saunders and eventually met Marshall Jefferson, borrowing his 808 to record his first demos. His first release was 'I Fear The Night', sung by his sister 'Chic', then 'Acid Video Crash', 'Acid Over' and 'Turn Up The Bass' (with Kool Rock Steady). His debut album, meanwhile, included the anti-Todd Terry message, 'T's Revenge'. Tyree also worked with Martin 'Boogieman' Luna as Cool House ('Rock This Party Right') and other members of the DJ International inner sanctum.
Selected album: Tyree's Got A Brand New House (DJ International 1989).

Tyrrel Corporation

Named after the economic monolith depicted in cult sci-fi film Blade Runner, this Redcar, England-based pop house duo's North East Of Eden set was one of the genre's most striking pieces in 1992. Joe Watson's smooth tones helped create a unique hybrid of house and Philly soul, with accessible lyrics tackling the personal and the political (as in 'Ballad Of British Justice'). The other pricipal of the band is lyricist and synthesizer player Tony Barry (though Watson also provides keyboard expertise). He had left Redcar for London in 1984, ending up as a pub manager. Watson, after working as a bingo caller, followed him down from the North East six years later, and stayed on his couch. They embarked on their musical adventures, with various day jobs enlisted to fund night recordings. Tyrrel Corporation made their debut in 1990 with the release of '6 O'Clock' on

tiny independent About Time Two Records. Straight away it showcased their strengths. While the song was undoubtedly in tune with the modern house sound, they imposed their songwriting skills rather than simply working a groove. 'A lot of the stuff around at the moment, you could never sit down and play it in a bar, but everything we do is a song and can be played that way' attested Watson. Signing to Cooltempo (originally through Charlie Chester's Volante subsidiary) follow-up singles 'The Bottle' and 'Going Home' were equally effective, with critics drooling at what one described as the lyricism of the Smiths combined with the funk of Mr Fingers. While '6 O'Clock' took British licensing laws to task, the time in question being the legal opening hour, 'The Bottle' continued their drink associations with the mighty hookline 'the bottle is mightier than the pen'. The subject matter of 'Going Home' was much more downbeat, reflecting the sharp decline of the industrial North East and the death of its culture. This was a theme more fully explored in their debut album.
Album: *North East Of Eden* (Cooltempo 1992).

U

Ubik

North London-based duo of Dave Campbell and Viv Beeton who formed to release their own material after offering remix and production work for Michael Rose and Kym Mazelle. They debuted with 'Techno Prisoners', a Detroit-derived mantra which featured the hook from Rochelle Fleming's 'Love Itch'. It cost just £70 to record (the hire of the DAT machine), but introduced them and their local Zoom label to many new admirers.
Album: *Just Add People* (Zoom 1992).

Ultra Naté

b. c.1968, Baltimore, Maryland, USA. Soul/disco/garage diva, who first rose to fame via the club hit, 'It's Over Now'. Ultra Naté (which is her real name) is a former trainee pyschotherapist. She was originally spotted by the Basement Boys in 1989, going on to sing backing vocals on Monie Love's debut album. The Basement Boys then persuaded her to step into the spotlight: 'Every now and then I'd go in the studio and do some stuff. We just wrote 'It's Over Now' one night, by

chance. They started circulating the demo and it created a really big buzz and they gave it to Cynthia Cherry who'd worked for WEA years ago. She originally started at Jump Street Records and signed the Basement Boys as artists. She brought my tape to Peter Edge at WEA, they signed me and the rest is history'. Reminiscent of a souped up Philly soul singer, or Donna Summer, Ultra Naté has all the correct stylings down to a tee, measuring jazz, funk and gospel within her compass. All are made distinctive by her slightly unconventional, and highly arresting, vocal phrasing. And for once, a garage vocalist with lyrics which, taken in isolation, aren't an embarassment. Her second, wildly diffuse, album for WEA, *One Woman's Insanity*, broke her internationally, and included duets with childhood hero Boy George (who wrote the song, 'I Specialize In Loneliness' for her), as well as D-Influence, Nellee Hooper (Soul II Soul), Ten City and the omnipresent Basement Boys.
Albums: *Blue Notes In The Basement* (WEA 1991), *One Woman's Insanity* (WEA 1993).

Ultramarine

London based progressive dance crew comprising Paul John Hammond (b. 12 December 1965, Chelmsford, Essex, England; bass, keyboards) and Ian Harvey Cooper (b. 15 August 1966, Derby, England; programming, guitars). They took their name from the A Primary Industry LP of similar title, who in turn had lifted it from a Mexican brand of Mescal. Both members of Ultramarine are veterans of the latter band, Hammond having also played with God And The Rest. Previous to this both had earned their crust in a variety of professions, Paul as an orchard worker and in publishing, Ian as a furniture salesman and insurance clerk. Influenced by the Canterbury Scene (Kevin Ayers, Robert Wyatt etc) and modern dance music (Massive Attack, Orbital, Spooky, Digable Planets), Ultramarine made their recording debut in 1989 with 'Wyndham Lewis', on Belgian label Les Disques Du Crepescule. After a further single, 'Folk', in 1990, Ultramarine moved on to Brainiak, then Rough Trade, before their current home, Blanco Y Negro. They introduced themselves more fully with their debut set, *Every Man And Woman Is A Star*, which was based on an imaginary canoe journey across America. The warm song structure was embossed by a dub-heavy backbeat and strong, resonant melodies. By the time of its follow-up, *United Kingdoms*, their Canterbury influences were beginning to show, and Robert Wyatt was invited to join them in a rendition of a hundred-year old weaver's folk song, 'Kingdom', and 'Happy Land'. Among their more notable single successes have been 'Stella', 'Weird Gear', 'Saratoga' and 'Nightfall In Sweetleaf', while their double EP *Hymn* was written by Kevin Ayers.

Albums: *Every Man And Woman Is A Star* (Rough Trade 1992), *Every Man And Woman Is A Star - Expanded* (Rough Trade 1992), *United Kingdoms* (Blanco Y Negro 1993).

Uncanny Alliance

This dance duo comprised Yvette and Brinsley from Queens, New York, who scored a club hit with their debut single, 'I Got My Education', in 1992. Both were long-term friends, regularly attending the Paradise Garage club, where New York's garage ethic was first perfected. Together they formed Deep Inc. in 1990, transfiguring into Uncanny Alliance shortly thereafter. Despite the pervading liberal tolerance vibe of dance music, 'I Got My Education' was actually an attack on fake beggars - chastising them for feigning injuries ala Brecht's *Threepenny Opera*. It was also extremely immediate and very funny, though the pair have failed to ignite commercially since.

Undercover

One of Stock Aitken & Watermen's less blessed creations, Undercover seemed to have been unveiled for the sole and ignominious purpose of releasing cover versions of golden oldies revamped for the 90s. Their idea of revamping being to insert a sickly backbeat underneath. Most notable was the breezy chart smash 'Baker Street', which was symptomatic of their cod house efforts. It was pieced together in just half an hour so that the participants could catch the FA Cup Final kick-off that afternooon. 'I can't understand why some bands take so long to produce records' was a deeply incriminating statement in the circumstances. The guilty trio comprised John Matthews, John Jules and producer Steve 'Mac' McCutcheon (who had previously co-written and produced Nomad's 'Devotion', 1991's biggest selling dance single, and also helmed Linda Layton's '(I'll Be A) Freak For You'). The two Johns had previously been club and pirate radio DJs together, working for a month as part of WLR Radio's failed franchise trial. Their 1992 album consisted entirely of cover versions written to the same irritating formula, albeit with the occasional sprinkling of Italian piano. Their nomination for a BRIT award in 1992 was one of the most singularly revealing indictments on the state of the UK music industry.

Album: *Check Out The Groove* (PWL 1992).

Underground Resistance

Detorit techno label/act, founded by Jeff Mills and 'Mad' Mike Banks in November 1990, currently overseen by the latter. It was formed to promote the techno sound when that music was at a low-point in its evolution. Via crucial releases like 'Eliminator' and 'The Punisher' (credited simply to Underground Resistance), Mills and Banks did much to revitalise a flagging scene. These were hard-nosed, insistent salvos which re-estalbished the music's fan base, particularly in Europe (Underground Resistance's following in its native national territory, like so much of the vital music which Detroit and Chicago have unveiled, would pass largely undiagnosed). Only Blake Baxter ('Prince Of Techno') would be welcomed as an outside producer in the label's early stages. Mills would go on to establish Axis while Banks continues to record as Underground Resistance, but also utilises nom de plumes like Acid Rain for their eponymous debut EP (a plea against local environmental carnage). He has also established Submerge as an umbrella administrative core - overseeing labels like Night Groove (house), Happy (garage), Metroplex (run by Juan Atkins), Red Planet and Shockwave.

Album: Various: *Revolution For Change* (Underground Resistance 1992).

Underworld

Based in Romford, London, England, Underworld were formed from the ashes of Freur in the late 80s, featuring former members of that band Karl Hayde (vocals), Alfie Thomas and Rick Smith, alongside Baz Allen (bass) and video-maker John Warwicker. Smith had also performed on sessions for Bob Geldof, while Hyde worked with Debbie Harry. After their debut album as Underworld, a funk-rock affair produced by Tom Bailey of the Thompson Twins, Burrows was replaced by Pascal Consolli (ex-Boys Wonder). By 1990 Thomas too had departed. Hyde (who had by now taken part in sessions for Prince at his Paisley Park studio complex) and Smith continued with the addition of DJ Darren Emerson - a journeyman of clubs like the Limelight and Milky Bar. Allen and Consolli went on to become the rhythm section of D-Influence, Burrows eventually joining Worldwide Electric. Mark II of the band debuted as Lemon Interrupt with the harmonica-drenched 'Big Mouth'. Underworld's breakthrough single, though, was the wonderful 'MMM...Skyscraper I Love You', released on Junior Boy's Own, encapsulating the chilled-out house movement perfectly. It was hailed as influential to the likes of Fluke, One Dove and Orbital, but many others have taken it as a signpost in the emergence of dance music in the 90s. Underworld mix live instruments with their studio wizardry, expanded by an eclectic, often plain odd collection of samples. They confounded expectations by playing live on the MIDI Circus roadshow and are one of the few techno outfits to actually relish such activity, mixing live on the decks for a unique experience at each date. Accordingly they were applauded for a stunning, improvised set at Glastonbury in 1992. They are also part of the Tomato collective, a multi-media enclave which produces art, film and graphics for the band's record sleeves, as well as advertising campaigns for prestigious accounts like Red Mountain, Nike and Adidas - all of which feature Underworld's soundtracks. The follow-up single to 'Skyscraper' was 'Rez', but it was the attendant album, *Dub No Bass With My Head Man*, that engendered further excitement. Among the more modest critical responses, the album was described as a 'fantastic synthesis of dance, techno, ambient, dub, rave, trance and rock...the most important album since the Stone Roses and the best since *Screamadelica*'. More than any other artefact, it was the one single record that saw audiences and critics switch allegiances from guitar bands to more 'progressive' outfits. Some even suggested it was the soundtrack to the death of rock 'n' roll, which was, perhaps, overstating the case.

Albums: *Underneath The Radar* (Sire 1988), *Change The Weather* (Sire 1989), *Dub No Bass With My Head Man* (Junior Boy's Own 1994).

U96

aka Hamburg, Germany DJ Alex Christensen (b. c.1967, Hamburg, Germany), whose single, 'Das Boot', went Top 20 in 1992. A revision of a ten year old Klaus Doldinger film/televison theme, this might have been unexpected had it not been for the fact that it had spent nearly three months on top of the German charts. In the UK it was originally released on Dave Dorrell's Love label in January, before being remixed by Mickey Finn and licensed to the M&G label in August. The album which followed was full of techno stompers and commercial electronica.

Album: *Das Boot* (M&G 1992).

Union City Recordings

UCR was launched as a subsidiary of Virgin's Circa label by Rob Manley, Circa's A&R manager, and Simon Gavin in the early weeks of 1992, 'to take advantage of the one-off, 12-inch market that's so vibrant in Britain'. The label was operated as a 'part-time' concern, with both principal movers staying on Virgin's payroll. Union City

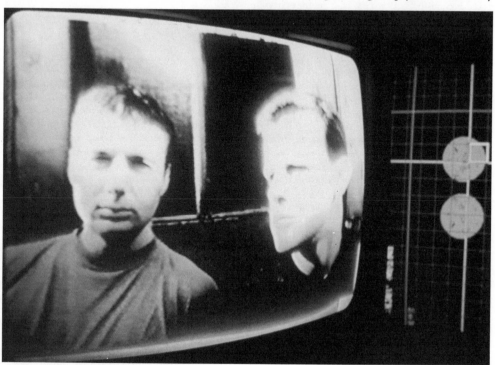

Union Jack

Recordings licensed brightly during the 90s, picking up Mark Kinchen's 'Burnin'', and TC1992's Top 40 hit 'Funky Guitar'. More home-grown product included the gospel-tinged 4 Love song, 'Hold Your Head Up High'. 'We wanted to build a faster response little number that always covered its costs. The majors are guilty of saying that there are no faces in dance music, thus pressurising people into giving them faces, so you get two keyboards and a couple of girl dancers miming to a DAT. Why try to maufacture an image that doesn't exist?' They were also represented by the ethnic dance of Mombassa and the techno of Metropolis and Earthbeat (two of Future Sound Of London's many guises). They signed M.A.N.I.C. (Lee Hudson and Keiron Jolliffe, who met on a YTS scheme) in 1992, after the success of their 'I'm Comin' Hardcore' white label, which they re-released. A second Mark Kinchen tune, 'Always', followed, as did Sasha's first solo record (as BM:Ex). By 1994 UCR was Virgin's last dance/club offshoot, having jettisoned both More Protein and Ronin.

Album: Various: *Colours: A Compilation* (UCR 1993).

Union Jack

Simon Berry and Claudio Guissani are the creative force behind the Union Jack banner, though each enjoys his own profile in dance music due to previous exploits. From 1990 to 1993 Guissani was one half of Urban Shakedown, who broke the Top 40 with tunes like 'Some Justice' and 'Bass Shake', augmented by their sponsorship from Amiga computers. They were also behind their own Urban Shakedown imprint (through Black Diamond), and remixed for Carl Cox and Eon among others. Berry, meanwhile, was involved in a project titled Conscious, before becoming ensnared by the growing techno scene and forming his own Platypus label in 1993. This housed his own releases as Art Of Trance ('Cambodia'), while he also remixed for Berlin's Kid Paul. The duo teamed up as Union Jack in the summer of 1993, choosing the name in rejection of the commonly held tenet that good techno was always non-UK in origin. Their debut record, 'Two Full Moons And A Trout', emerged on Platypus before being re-released on the Rising High roster, to mounting acclaim.

United Future Organization

A trio of former DJs, numbering French-born Raphael Sebbag and Japanese personnel Tadashi Yabe and Toshio Matsuura, based in Japan, whose mix of dance-jazz, Latin and club sounds has endeared them to a British audience. Talkin' Loud boss Giles Peterson heard their singles 'I Love My Baby' and 'Loud Minority' and chose the band (aka UFO) to launch a new label, Brownswood. The idea was to contrast natural elements in urban settings, though the label was actually named after his 'local'. There is a warm, breezy feel to their material, and a genuine conflagration of styles. Their debut album featured contributions from Galliano and MC Solaar, plus jazz luminaries Jon Hendricks and Japanese talent like singer Monday Michiru. As part of their Brownswood/Phonogram deal, they were invited to supervise a Japanese jazz compilation.

Album: *United Future Organization* (Brownswood 1993).

Urban Cookie Collective

Urban Cookie Collective scored a major breakthrough in 1993 with 'The Key: The Secret', one of the most riveting dance tracks of the season. The band comprises Rohan Heath (keyboards), Diane Charlemagne (ex-Nomad Soul; vocals), Marty (MC) and DJ Pete (DJ). The project is masterminded by Heath, who had formerly worked with Yargo and A Guy Called Gerald. He had learned classical piano as a child, going electric in time to perform with the latter two outfits. He had decided on music after abandoning a PHD at Vermont University. After a tour of Japan supporting the Happy Mondays, he left A Guy Called Gerald to release 'Hardcore Uproar' as Together, which made number 12 in the UK charts in August 1990. A brief stint with Eek A Mouse later, he elected to concentrate squarely on solo work, and inaugurated Urban Cookie Collective. 'The Key: The Secret' was originally a track written at home by Heath, in a soul/hip hop vein, produced by Chapter And The Verse on the tiny Unheard Records imprint. However, after a remix provoked a massive club response it was picked up by Pulse 8, who also issued a debut double album the same year.

Album: *High On A Happy Vibe* (Pulse 8 1993, double album).

Urban Dance Squad

Dutch rock/rap troupe, whose debut album included the tearaway hit single, 'Deeper Shade Of Soul' (US number 21 and a Top 40 entry in most other countries). Their association with the charts looked to be temporary one, until they re-emerged in 1994 with an accomplished collection for the Virgin-backed Hut imprint. The group, based in Amsterdam, comprise Rude Boy (b. Patrick Remington; raps) plus Magic Stick, DNA, Silly Sil

Utah Saints

and Tres Manos.
Albums: *Mental Floss For The Globe* (Arista 1990), *Persona Non Grata* (Hut 1994).

Utah Saints

Leeds, Yorkshire, England-based duo of Jez Willis (b. 14 August 1963, Brampton, Cumbria, England; ex-Surfin' Dove, Cassandra Complex) and Tim Garbutt (b. 6 January 1969, London, England; also a DJ at Bliss in Leeds). Both were formerly members of MDMA, who practised an unlikely and somewhat unappetising hybrid of electro-gothic dance. They released five 12-inch singles on their own Ecstatic Product label, the band name taken from the chemical label for the 'Ecstasy' drug, though neither have actually ever used it. However, both were more than familiar with developments in the club scene. After MDMA Willis drifted into DJing, specialising in 70s disco evenings, while Garbutt had already served time behind the decks from the late 80s onwards. Together they established their name at their own Mile High Club nights at Leeds venue the Gallery. These were such a success that corresponding events also transferred to York and then London. They soon returned to recording, however, using the Utah Saints' moniker salvaged from Nicholas Cage film *Raising Arizona* (it had previously been employed on a MDMA b-side). The duo's move in to dance, resplendent in samples and a driving backbeat, proved much more successful than the efforts of their former incarnation. After acclimatising to the charts with 'What Can You Do For Me' (with a Eurythmics sample), they moved on to 'Something Good'. This was built around a Kate Bush sample from 'Cloudbursting', but it had other strengths too. 'We're trying to get a bit of rock 'n' roll into rave' they commented. They later backed Neneh Cherry on a version of the Rolling Stones' 'Gimme Shelter' for the *Putting Our House In Order* campaign for the homeless in 1993, one of several acts to release the song. Their own follow-up was 'Believe In Me', this time featuring a sample of Philip Oakey of the Human League on 'Love Action'. Other steals are less obvious, and include the likes of arch Satanists Slayer. Their playful instincts offer an accesible bridge between rock audiences and more adroit techno/dance units.
Album: *Utah Saints* (ffrr 993).

u-Ziq

U-ziq are North Londoners Mike Paradinas and, occasionally, Francis Naughton. Both were students when they first met the Aphex Twin, who invited them to join his new Rephlex imprint.

Unlike the aforementioned ambient guru, however, neither are technocrats. Their debut double album was recorded using only synthesizers, a beatbox, and a four-track mixer. Within a few months of studio time u-Ziq claimed to have over 300 tracks, ready to go, sitting on the shelf. Though an unarguably productive operation, they manage to retain an organic sound that much of the genre has lost.
Album: *Tango N' Vectif* (Rephlex 1994, double album).

V

Vasquez, Junior

Junior Vasquez (not his real name, he is in fact a German-American from Philadelphia, but declines to provide further details) found his induction into the world of dance music as a (reluctant) dancer at Larry Levan's Paradise Garage. He soon decided the life of a DJ was the one for him. He applied himself to his apprenticeship, working his way up the ladder via shops (working at Downstairs Records in the early 80s where he first met friends like Shep Pettibone), clubs and house parties (notably the Kiss FM bashes), until he had built his own following. This allowed him to put together his own clubs - starting with the Hearthrob nights at the Funhouse, then the Bass Line club, and finally the Sound Factory (owned by Christian Visca). One of New York's premier nights, it quickly saw Vasquez's reputation as a firecely hot turntable operator soar. Innovating live by playing backwards and forwards, alternating rhythms and throwing in live samples, he offered a total aural experience. There was a visual dimension too; with Vasquez stepping out from behind the desks to present his adoring public with flowers. His reputation spread to the point at which Madonna was spotted at the Sound Factory on several occasions (he also DJ'd at her party to celebrate the launch of *Sex*). As a recording artist Vasquez provides Tribal Records, named after his favourite form of house music, with the majority of his labours, including cuts like 'X', 'Get Your Hands Off My Man' and 'Nervaas'. Previously he had recorded as the cult gay persona Ellis Dee. He has also written for artists like Lisa Lisa and Cindi Lauper and remixed for many others, ranging from Eat Static ('Gulf Breeze') to Ce Ce Penniston ('I'm

In The Mood'). Vasquez's technique is described by the man himself thus: 'I seem my style rooted in house/club music. I like a harder modern sound. I'm not interested in anything fluffy'.

Vath, Sven

Frankfurt, Germany-based Vath first DJ'd at his father's bar, the Queens Pub, playing old disco and Barry White records. He started his recording career as frontman for the Off, whose 'Electic Salsa' was a big Euro hit, and one of the first for Michael Munzing and Luca Anzilotti, the backroom boys behind Snap! He had grown up listening to varied electronica by Tangerine Dream, Ryuichi Sakamoto, Holger Czukay and Jean Michel Jarre, but was equally inspired by the house explosion of the 80s. He went on to become synonymous with ambient house, with some critics accusing him of hanging on to the coat-tails of the Orb. However, tracks like 'Barbarella' (which included samples of Jane Fonda's dialogue from the film of the same name) had a great deal more than novelty value. He runs his own record labels, Harthouse, Eye Q and the enivoronmentally-pleasing Recyle Or Die Records (whose CD-only issues each arrived in bio-degradable cardboard packaging). *Accident In Paradise* involved reworked rhythms he discovered on his regular travels in India. The record was a collage of sounds and mental footnotes tapered over refracting rhythms.
Selected album: *Accident In Paradise* (Eye Q 1993).

W

Wagon Christ

Wagon Christ is Falmouth-based Our Price employee Luke Vibert (b. c.1972), a star of the Rising High roster. Like his friend the Aphex Twin, with whom Vibert is a near-neighbour, this is another artist interested in pushing the possibilities of electronica, despite his musical origins as a drummer in a punk band: 'Where I live no-one pays attention to music's different categories. We just listen to whatever we can get our hands on'. He was also a classically trained musician before he entered the twilight bedroom world of avant garde music, marking his vinyl debut with the *Sunset Boulevard* EP. The continuation of his reckless musical adventures on an album did little to avert further comparisons to the Aphex Twin.
Album: *Phat Lab Nightmare* (Rising High 1994).

WAU! Mr Modo Records

Headed by Adam Morris and Youth, but popularly conceived to be 'the Orb's record label' (Dr Paterson part-owning the company), after housing their debut single, 'A Huge Ever-Growing Pulsating Brain That Rules From The Centre Of The Ultraworld'. It cost only £20 to record, but led the label to a licensing deal with Big Life. WAU! Mr Modo is an acronym for What About Us!, the Mr Modo part referring to Orb manager Adam Morris' pseudonym. Future Orb member Thrash (aka Kristian Weston) engineered much of the label's product, including Jam On The Mutha's 'Hotel California'. Outside of Orb activities the label also picked up releases like German import Maurizio's 'Play' at the end of 1992. The latter release added a 'Battersea Was An Island Of Mud' Orb remix, as well as another by Underground Resistance. Other releases included Shola's 'Hold On (Goa Mixes)' in 1991, Shola Phillips being the vocalist on the Orb's 'Perpetual Dawn'. The same year saw Zoe's 'Sunshine On A Rainy Day', a reissue of the September 1990 club 'grower', backed by remixes from the Orb, and produced by Youth. The latter split from WAU! Mr Modo in 1992 to establish Butterfly Records. while his former label continued with releases like Suzuki's 'Satelliete Serenade'. However, WAU! Mr Modo could do little to escape their Orb connections when the band terminated their contract with Big Life, with that record company serving an injunction on the label to prevent it releasing any records just in case they were by the Orb under a pseudonym.
Selected albums: Various: *Dancebusters* (WAU! Mr Modo 1990). The Orb: The Orb's *Adventures Beyond The Ultraworld* (WAU! Mr Modo/Big Life 1991).

Warp

Sheffield, Yorkshire-based dance label, headed by Rob Mitchell and Steve Beckett, which rose from the ashes of the FON record store in the city (Warp itself is also a retail outlet). The two partners had formerly been playing in an indie band together, but on opening Warp they found themselves inadvertently cast into the maelstrom of acid house and rave music in the late 80s. They were also inundated with demo recordings handed in by aspiring artists who perused their racks. The first release on the label came from the Forgemasters (producer Rob Gordon, Shaun Maher and DJ Parrot, the latter also of Sweet

Exorcist fame). 'Track With No Name' was cut on a limited 500 copy pressing (via an Enterprise Allowance grant) and was followed as 1990 dawned with Nightmare On Wax's 'Dextrous', which had the financial backing of Rhythm King. By the advent of Warp 6 (LFO's 'LFO') the label had broken the Top 20, while Tricky Disco's similarly eponymous debut made number 14. Both were examples of Warp railing against the prevailing acid ethos with deeply experimental electronic music (with a nod, at least in Nightmare On Wax's case, to Sheffield's traditional *avant garde* fare of early Human League and Cabaret Voltaire). 1991 saw successful albums from both LFO and Nightmares On Wax. It was a move into viewing dance music as an unexplored medium for home listening that would be crystalised by 1992's *Artificial Intelligence* compilation. Featuring the Diceman (Aphex Twin), Autechre, Alex Paterson (Orb) and others, it was a more reflective, cerebral approach that had historical links to Brian Eno (though the protagonists are generally wary of the 'ambient' tag). 'The idea was to re-educate people who bought dance records to sit down and pay attention'. The series was extended with individual albums from several of the participants, with Polygon Window (Aphex Twin), Black Dog, B12, FUSE (Richie Hawtin) and Speedy J all participating. These, bedecked in lavish gatefold sleeves with limited edition coloured vinyl, were released alongside a 40-minute animated film of the same title by Warp's sleeve designer Phil Wolstenholme. Among Warp's other notable acts are Sweet Exorcist (Roland H. Kirk of Cabaret Voltaire fame), Rhythm Invention, Joey Beltram and Coco Steel & Lovebomb. They have also signed Aphex Twin, the techno scene's most high profile artist, on a more permanent footing, and set up their own indie guitar subsidiary, Gift (Various Vegetables, Pulp etc).

Selected albums: Sweet Exorcist: *Clonk's Coming* (Warp 1991). Fuse: *Dimension Intrusion* (Warp 1993). Nightmares On Wax: *A Word Of Science* (Warp 1991). Various: *Artificial Intelligence* (Warp 1991). Polygon Window: *Surfing On Sine Waves* (Warp 1993). Black Dog: *Bytes* (Warp 1993). B12: *Electro Soma* (Warp 1993). Speedy J: *Intrusion* (Warp 1993).

Was (Not Was)

An unlikely recording and production duo, childhood friends David Weiss (saxophone, flute, keyboards, vocals) and Don Fagenson (bass, keyboards, guitar) have used a variety of singers to front their records, including Sweat Pea Atkinson, Leonard Cohen, Harry Bowens and Donny Ray

Mitchell. Their debut album sought to imbue dance music with an intellectual credibility which it had previously lacked. While musicians were plucked from sources as varied as P-Funk and MC5, 'Tell Me That I'm Dreaming' incorporated a mutilated sample of a Ronald Reagan speech. 1983's *Born To Laugh At Tornadoes* included, bizarrely, Ozzy Osbourne rapping, and a snatch of Frank Sinatra. Geffen rewarded their eclecticism by dropping them. They moved on to Phonogram, managing to focus much more clearly on their prospective dance market in the process. Their biggest hit was the anthemic 'Walk The Dinosaur', which topped the US singles chart for six weeks, while 'Spy In The House Of Love' had similar crossover appeal. However, the music industry knows them better for their numerous production credits. These include the B-52's, Iggy Pop, Bonnie Raitt and Bob Dylan. The latter fulfilled an ambition for Weiss, who had long held Dylan as his personal idol. 1990's *Are You Okay?* was critically lauded, and they remain an enigmatic attraction on the periphery of the dance scene.

Albums: *Was (Not Was)* (ZE-Island 1981), *Born To Laugh At Tornadoes* (Ze-Island 1983), *What Up, Dog?* (Chrysalis 1988), *Are You Okay?* (Chrysalis 1990).

Waters, Crystal

Waters' enjoys one of the more colourful backgrounds among dance music's modern female exponents. Born in South New Jersey, she majored in Computer Science at Howard University. Her father was jazz musician Jr. Waters, and her great-aunt Ethel Waters. Indeed everyone in her family played an instrument, though some of her own initial forays were as the youngest member of the American Poets Society. Her entry into the music scene could hardly have been more dramatic. 'Gypsy Woman' was the song that did it for her, propelled by an unforgetable 'La Dee Dee, La Dee Da' refrain, and the production know-how of the Basement Boys, it became the summer anthem of 1991 in many clubs throughout Britain and Europe. At the time she was still employed as a computer technician issuing the FBI with warrants at the Washington DC parole board. The song eventually rose to number 3 in the UK charts, and brought her success over in America too, though her first album received mixed reviews. She returned in 1994 with '100% Pure Love', a first recording in over three years, and a second album. This time her songwriting was significantly stronger, representing a more satisfying, less rushed collection.

Albums: *Surprise* (Mercury 1991), *Storyteller* (1994).

Wagon Christ

Watford, Michael

A classy garage artist hailing from New Jersey, though born and raised in Virginia, Watford's distinctive, soulful baritone has graced a number of successful records since his debut, 'Holdin' On', for East West. He grew up performing song and dance routines for his parents with his brothers and sisters, before joining gospel group The Disciples Of Truth at the age of five. From there he joined Smack Music (Michael and Debbie Cameron), the New Jersey production team from whose services Adeva has also benefitted, in 1987. It took some time for Watford to progress to centrestage but this is typical of his retiring, almost reticent nature. It was 'Holdin' On' which provided the push. Originally housed on a 1992 Atlantic Records' compilation (*Underground Dance Volume 1*), it was soon picked out by club DJs. The Smack team also worked on his debut long playing set, assisted by producer John Robinson. This housed successful singles 'Luv 4-2' and 'So Into You' which authenticated his appeal to club audiences and soul fans alike, though he maintains his deep religious beliefs.

Album: *Michael Watford* (East West 1993).

Weatherall, Andy

Dance magnate Weatherall (b. 6 April 1963) began the 80s working on building sites and film sets before picking up DJ work. His career proper began with residencies at the Shoom and Spectrum clubs in the acid house boom of 1988. Afterwards he founded the Boy's Own fanzine with Terry Farley and Steve Mayes, which concentrated on club music, fashion and football. When Boy's Own became a record label, he also appeared, as a guest vocalist, on a Bocca Juniors track. He made his name, however, by remixing Primal Scream's 'Loaded'. The likes of James, Happy Mondays, That Petrol Emotion, St Ettienne, Grid, Meat Beat Manifesto, Big Hard Excellent Fish, S'Express, Orb, Finitribe, A Man Called Adam, Jah Wobble, Future Sound Of London, Moody Boyz, One Dove, Throbbing Gristle, Galliano, Flowered Up, Björk, Espiritu, Yello, Stereo MC's and New Order followed. His landmark achievement, however, remains his supervising role on old friend's Primal Scream's *Screamadelica* - the album which effectively forged a new musical genre. He also enjoyed a stint as DJ on Kiss FM, before his eclectic, anarchic tastes proved too much for programmers. 'My background is rock 'n' roll. The Clash are still the best band in the world'. His recording methodology has been compared to that of Joe Meek: sampling strange sounds such as answerphones and dustbin lids for percussion. Or

'Techno's Phil Spector' quoth Q magazine. He has subsequently set up a further label, recording and remix operation under the title Sabres Of Paradise, which has also proved hugely successful. Weatherall continued to play out regularly at Sabresonic club nights, and in 1993 signed a major publishing deal with MCA Music.

Well Hung Parliament

Essentially record plugger turned remixer Paul Gotel and Spencer Williams, of S-1000 fame. Gotel had taken over Power Promotions from Paul Oakenfold in 1989, after having managed an advertising agency during the 'city boom' years of the late 80s. Well Hung Parliament's recording career began with 'We Can Be' for Cowboy Records, but they also functioned highly productively as a remix team - earning commissions for Nu Colour's 'The Power', Erire's 'I Just Can't Give You Up', the Shamen's 'LSI', Synergy's 'One Way Only', Chosen Few's 'Positivity', Madness' 'Night Boat To Cairo' and Conrad's 'Doesn't Time Fly'. Many of these artists were also clients of Gotel through Power Promotions.

West Bam

The king of the balearic beat, West Bam was a prime mover in the early days of acid house. DJing since 1983, he had indulged in industrial/experimental music before he was led to Detroit techno via house (he had, in fact, organised Berlin's first 'House Party'). He established his own Low Spirit label in the late 80s (having released his first record in 1985), titled after his club night, which housed cuts like Grace Darling's 'Dreams'. His own classics include 'Alarm Clock', from which Andy Weatherall sampled the bells for his remix of My Bloody Valentine's 'Glider', and 'Monkey Say, Monkey Do' from 1989. By 1994 he claimed to have over 100 productions to his name. The West Bam remix schedule was equally hectic, and included Deskee's 'Let There Be House' and Flower Ltd's 'Swinging Thing', before further classic cuts like 'The Roof Is On Fire' (for Swanyard in 1990). His 1994 single 'Celebration Generation' (which included a Justin Robertson remix) was more pure techno. His philosophy on the importance of this music is crystal clear: 'Nothing reflects our time so exactly as electronic dance music. It's the first real international music'. He is currently signed, via Low Spirit, to Polydor.

Wheeler, Caron

b. c.1962, England, but raised in Jamaica. Her father a bass player, her mother a singer with a

Jamaican drama company, Wheeler's interest in music began at the age of 12, singing lovers rock with female reggae trio Brown Sugar, who had four number 1 singles in the specialist charts by the time she was 16. She moved on to form backing trio Afrodiziak, whose vocals were utilised live or on sessions with artists like the Jam. Other backing duties for Elvis Costello, Phil Collins, Neneh Cherry and Aswad followed, earning a gold record for her liaison with Erasure in 1988. However, she became frustrated with the record business and effectively retired that year, taking a job in a library. The break refuelled her creative instincts, and when she returned as part of Soul II Soul in 1990 it was to her greatest success so far. Though never part of the group proper, she would win a Grammy for Best Vocal Performance on 'Back To Life', one of the two platinum singles she sang on (the other being 'Keep On Movin''). She subsequently embarked on her solo career by signing with Orange Tree Productions, eventually securing a contract with RCA. Her distinctive voice was soon utilised not only for the blend of pop, soul and hip hop which shadowed the music of her former employers, but also for blasting the white domination of the UK record industry. Her alienation was revealed in the title-track of her debut album: 'Many moons ago, We were told the streets were paved with gold, So our people came by air and sea, To earn a money they could keep, Then fly back home, Sadly this never came to be, When we learned that we had just been invited, To clean up after the war'. Afterwards her frustration with Britain saw her move Stateside for a second collection. This diverse set included a collaboration with Jam and Lewis on 'I Adore You', the production of former Soul II Soul man Jazzie B on 'Wonder', and a cover of Jimi Hendrix' 'And The Wind Cries Mary'.
Albums: *UK Blak* (RCA 1990), *Blue (Is The Colour Of Pain)* (RCA 1991), *Beach Of The War Goddess* (1993).

Whycliffe

b. Donovan Whycliffe. Born into a music-loving family of twelve, his parents encouraged him to sing in the Pentacostal choirs in his youth. Whycliffe's name was first mooted when he handed over a demo tape to Tim Andrews Of Nottingham's Submission Records. The ensuing buzz ensured that the A&R men flocked to his door, and he eventually signed to MCA. He scored an almost immediate hit in 1991 with 'Roughside', backed by an album, which saw the press lodge comparisons to Terence Trent D'Arby. He returned in 1993 with the single, 'Heaven', and a new long playing set the following year. Remix guidance was offered by Tim Simenon (Bomb The Bass) and CJ Mackintosh. The producers on his second album, *Journeys Of The Mind*, were Chris Porter (famed for his work with George Michael) and Simenon.
Albums: *Roughside* (MCA 1991), *Journeys Of The Mind* (MCA 1994).

Wikman, Eric

b. New Jersey, New York State, USA. Wikman was a former rock fanatic until his friend's dance mix tapes caught his attention. He was a quick and enthusiastic convert, particularly to the compilations of Mathias Hoffman (Mosaic and Harthouse). Wikman soon got involved in the creative process too, remixing techno cuts for San Francisco's Megatone label with DJ Mark Lewis. On his own terms he cut 'Body Baby' on Champion Records, under the mantle Global Groove. The follow-up was 'Cry Of Freedom', before he began remix work for D:Ream and Michael Watford.

Wreckx-N-Effect

With their Teddy Riley-produced single of the same name in 1988, Wreckx-N-Effect announced the arrival of New Jack Swing. The intervening period has not been especially kind in terms of commercial fortunes, with others capitalising on their style. However, they did score a minor hit in 1992 with 'Rump Shaker' for MCA. The band is made up of vocalists Markell Riley (Teddy's brother) and Aquell Davidson. They were joined by a rap from Apache Indian on their 1994 single, 'Wreckz Shop'.
Album: *Hard Or Smooth* (MCA 1992).

X

XL Recordings

The brainchild of Tim Palmer, managing director of Citybeat, who installed Nick Halkes as A&R chief. It was while working for Citybeat that he picked up Starlight's 'Numero Uno' as his second signing, giving the label an instant Top 10 hit. On the strength of which Palmer employed him to A&R a subsidiary imprint for 'underground' dance records (though the impression given that Halkes was solely responsible for the label's success is very misleading). XL's most notable hits included the Prodigy's rich vein of form (beginning with 'Charly'), SL2 ('On A Ragga Tip' etc.), Liquid ('Sweet Harmony'), T99 ('Anasthasia') and House Of Pain ('Jump Around'). The latter was released on Ruffness, an in-house subsidiary. Other artists on XL included Nu-Matic (*Hard Times* EP), Cubic 22 ('Night In Motion'), who also recorded under the guise of Set Up System ('Fairy Dust'). XL continued to prosper through the efforts of the Prodigy, Liquid, Johnny L, House Of Pain and others, despite its limited budget and independence, relying instead on the dedication of the staff working in close co-operation with the artists.

Selected album: The Prodigy: *Music For The Jilted Generation* (XL 1994, double album).

X Press 2

Aggressive acid house revisionists Rocky, Diesel and Daddy Ash (Ashley Beadle, of Disco Evangelists/Black Sunshine fame), who have run up an impressive sequence of club cuts ('Muzik Express', 'London X-Press', 'Say What', 'Rock 2 House' - remixed by Richie Hawtin and Felix Da Housecat) on Junior Boys Own. In addition to becoming one one of that popular label's most talked-about acts, Rocky and Diesel are also well known DJs in their own right, as is Beadle.

Yazz

b. Yasmin Evans, 19 May 1960, London, England. Pop house singer who began her career in the music business as part of a quickly forgotten act , the Biz. After becoming a catwalk model and working as George Michael's stylist, she laid plans for a return to recording work. When she did she found rewards immediately, joining with Coldcut on 'Doctorin' The House'. In its wake 'The Only Way Is Up' soared to the number 1 spot in 1988, followed shortly after by 'Stand Up For Your Love Rights'. Both of the latter were credited to Yazz And The Plastic Population. After a couple of further hits and tours she took time out to have her first baby. She returned alongside Aswad in 1993 for 'How Long', but this failed to break the Top 30. A new solo single, 'Have Mercy', was the first evidence of her attempts to re-establish herself via a

contract with Polydor.
Albums: *Wanted* (Big Life 1988), *The Wanted Remixes* (Big Life 1989), *One On One* (Polydor 1994).
Videos: *The Compilation* (1989), *Live At The Hammersmith Odeon* (1989).

Yello

A Swiss dance duo led by Dieter Meier, a millionaire business man, professional gambler, and member of the Switzerland national golf team. Meier provides the concepts whilst his partner Boris Blank writes the music. Previously Meier had released two solo singles and been a member of Periphery Perfume band Fresh Colour. Their first recording contract was with Ralph Records in San Francisco, a label supported by the enigmatic Residents. They opened their accounts there with 'Bimbo' and the album *Solid Pleasure*. In the UK they signed to the Do It label, launching their career with 'Bostisch', previously their second single for Ralph. They quickly proved popular with the Futurist and New Romantic crowds. Chart success in the UK began after a move to Stiff in 1983 where they released two singles and an LP. A brief sojourn with Elektra preceded a move to Mercury where they saw major success with 'The Race'. Accompanied by a stunning video - Meier saw visual entertainment as crucial to their work - 'The Race' easily transgressed the pop and dance markets in the wake of the acid house phenomenon. On the LP *One Second*, they worked closely with Shirley Bassey and Billy McKenzie, and have recently become more and more embroiled in cinema. Recent soundtracks include *Nuns On The Run*, and the Polish filmed *Snowball*, a fairytale whose creative impetus is entirely down to Yello. Meier and Blank also run Solid Pleasure, the innovative Swiss dance label.
Albums: *Solid Pleasure* (Ralph 1980), *Claro Que Si* (Ralph 1981), *You Gotta Say Yes To Another Excess* (Elektra 1983), *Stella* (Elektra 1985), *1980-1985 The New Mix In One Go* (Mercury 1986), *One Second* (Mercury 1987), *Flag* (Mercury 1988), *Baby* (Mercury 1991).
Videos: *Video Race* (1988), *Live At The Roxy* (1991).

Yothu Yindi

Aboriginal group fronted by spokesman Mandaway Yunipingu, based in the remote, crocodile-infested region of Arnhem Land in the Northern Territories. They became a big force in both Australia and the rest of the world via their serene, indigenous sounds. 'Treaty' also crossed over to the UK dance charts. Licensed from the Australian

Mushroom label to Hollywood, it appeared in a remix from Melbourne DJ's Gavin Campbell and Paul Main and programmer/musician Robert Goodge. Resplendent in digeridoo, clap sticks and tribal chants, it quickly became a hot DJ item.

Young Disciples

Although their roots were in the rave scene, the Young Disciples' debut single, 'Get Yourself Together', combined hip hop with jazz inflections, and featured the voice of Carleen Anderson and MC Mell 'O' on either side. The group, who comprised the duo of Mark 'O' and Femi, would win much of their notoriety through Anderson's vocal attributes. It was her that wrote and sang on many of their best recordings, including 'Apparently Nothin''. Her final release with the Young Disciples was *Dusky Sappho*, a limited edition EP, after which she concentrated on her solo career. Femi and Mark continued to use the Young Disciples banner, though the former would also undertake remix work for Xscape ('Just Kickin'') and others.
Album: *Road To Freedom* (Talkin' Loud 1991).

Z

Zhane

An East Coast R&B/dance duo consisting of Renee Neufville and Jean Norris, who started signing together whily studying at Philadelphia Temple University, and were discovered at a talent show by DJ Jazzy Jeff And The Fresh Prince. They went on to contribute backing vocals to the latter's 1991 single, 'Ring My Bell', before linking with another prominent rapper, Queen Latifah, as part of her Flavor Unit collective. Their debut, 'Hey Mr DJ', was first featured on the compilation album, *Roll Wit Tha Flava*, before subsequent release as a single saw it go Top 5 in the US. Like Latifah, they would sign on the dotted line with Motown, enjoying further success with follow-up single 'Groove Thang'. Both hits were produced in association with DJ Kay Gee, of Naughty By Nature fame, and prefaced a similarly successful debut album, the title of which offered instruction as to the pronounciation of Zhane's name. As to their musical bent: 'Our music is R&B with a jazzy attitude and hip hop flavour'.

Album: *Prounounced Jah-Nay* (Illtown/Motown 1994).

Zion Train

North London collective headed by Colin C (who once had connections with Spiral Tribe), alongside three team-mates, whose dub/roots dance equation was unveiled first on sequential singles 'Power One' and 'Power Two'. However, their most effective and highly-regarded work so far was the 'Follow Like Wolves' single, a fertile cross between dub and house music, with samples drawn from the Specials' back-catalogue. This was no idle reinvention of King Tubby rhythms, the Zion Train dub rattling along at a 125bpm rating. Its popularity was enshrined by remixes from the Drum Club, Mike 'Club Dog', and David Shakra. Further collaborations on their debut album and elsewhere followed, including Consolidated, as well as Indian tabla players and Brazilian drummers. The group even turned its hand to writing soundtracks for Terrence McKenna lectures. 1993 brought the 'Getafix In Dub' collaboration, followed in 1994 by 'Conscious Sounds'.
Album: *Passage To India* (1993).

Zoom Records

Camden, North London operation run by popular DJ Billy Nasty and Dave Wesson, whose clients include Delorme and 3:6 Philly. The label came to prominence in 1989 with the release of two singles by Brit hip-hoppers Red Ninja. Later their attention turned to the dance scene, releasing a particularly harsh techno album by Ubik in 1992. Nasty's reputation as a DJ was franked by being the first to appear on the Music Unites' *Journeys By DJ* series, with a set composed of modern house standards (Havanna/Leftfield/Gipsy). He also recorded alongside Morgan King as VFN Experience. Wesson similarly colluded with Leftfield to record 'The Hunter (The Returns)' (as Herbal Infusion). The duo have also remixed for Acorn Arts, St Ettienne and Nush. Other members of the Zoom staff include the Sensory Productions team of three DJ's - Robert R. Mellow, Zaki Dee and Adam Holden, who released the double a-side 'Keep It Open'/'Jumping' for the label in 1992. Mellow works behind the counter at the Zoom shop, while Dee provided a similar service at the Black Market emporium.

ZYX Records

Widely venerated as 'the balearic label', ZYX is a German distributor and dance specialist which set up a UK operation in 1990, attempting to profit through 'cheaper imports and exclusive foreign product'. Their 1991 releases included De Melero featuring Monica Green's 'Night Moves' - a house standby brought up to date by Spanish brothers Cesar and Chito de Melero, DJs at Ibiza's Ku and Barcelona's The Club respectively. 1992 brought Renee Thomas' 'I'm So In Love With You', from Fred Jorio and Sean Tucker. However, much of the label and A&R manager Alex Gold's notoriety during the 90s revolved around its public bust-ups with Network Records. The latter's overtures to obtain the license for Double You?'s version of KC & The Sunshine Band's 'Please Don't Go' were rejected. Network got KWS to record a version instead, earning a five week number 1 in the process. The same thing happened with a second KC cover, 'Rock Your Body'. Originally a number 1 hit for Gwen McRae in 1974, once again it jumped in front of a proposed ZYX label release - who were at that time trying to license Baby Roots' mistitled 'Rock You Baby'. When Double You?'s manager Roberton Zanetti collapsed of nervous exhaustion it could have taken few people by surprise. ZYX did at least enjoy success by licensing two contrasting Euro hits in 1992, the hard German techno of Misteria's 'Who Killed JFK?', and the clean Italian house of Jennifer Lucas' 'Take On Higher'. Other notable hits included Interactive's 'Who Killed Elvis?', LA Style's 'James Brown Is Dead' and Area 51's 'Let It Move You', a piano-rave classic. Gold would go on to establish a new record label in 1994, Escapade.